صَحِيحُ مُسْلِم

SAHIH
MUSLIM
ABRIDGED

Translated & Edited by
AFTAB SHAHRYAR

SAHIH MUSLIM (Abridged)

Translated & Edited by Aftab Shahryar

ISBN: 81-7231-592-9

First Edition: 2004

Published by *Abdul Naeem* for

Islamic Book Service

2241, Kucha Chelan, Darya Ganj, New Delhi-110 002 (INDIA)
Tel.: 23253514, 23265380, 23286551, Fax: 23277913
E-mail: islamic@eth.net & ibsdelhi@del2.vsnl.net.in
website: www.islamic-india.com

Printed at: *Noida Printing Press,* C-31, Sector-7, Noida (Ghaziabad) U.P.

CONTENTS

SAHIH MUSLIM

Preface

The Sahih of Imam Muslim is a pure work of traditions written for the purpose of enabling Muslims to find their way with its aid in all crucial issues and problems of *Fiqh*. Across the Muslim world the Sahih of Imam Muslim and Imam Bukhari are considered as authentic recording of Hadith. The *Hadith* sayings are a panorama of daily life in the seventh century.

Hadith is the recording in writing of everything that the prophet is supposed to have said or done. His opinion, his reaction to events, the way in which he justified his decisions, were recorded in writing during the lifetime of the Apostle of Allah (peace & blessings of Allah be with him) and in the post-Prophetic period, so that they could be drawn upon and referred to later, in order to distinguish what is right from what is wrong.

This volume purports to be a translation of the Traditions of the sayings and doings of the holy Prophet Muhammad (peace & blessings of Allah be with him) as narrated by his companions and compiled under the title of *Al-Jami as-Sahih* by Imam Muslim. The venerable Imam collected about 300,000 Traditions and after a thorough examination accepted only 4000 *Hadith*, that he considered to be genuine.

Translation from one language to another is always a difficult task specially when the time span between the original language and the target language is more than a millennium and the difference in the genius of the two languages is enormous. Arabic is a rich, colorful, vigorous language with the ability to express ideas and concepts in concise manner due to the extraordinary flexibility of its verbs and nouns. English too is a pulsating, vibrating language but is considered to be a language of understatement. More importantly it may not be possible to translate cultural signifiers from one culture to another. A translator needs to have some command not only of the target language culture but also of original language culture. And there is always a risk of sacrificing fidelity of the text in the interest of making translation comprehensible. Above all, the task of translating the divinely inspired words and actions of the Apostle of Allah, who was blessed with an extraordinary chaste mode of expression, may be too daunting a task for an ordinary mortal like the translator.

Under these very obvious limitations the translator has tried his very best to be literally accurate and faithful to the original text. Voluminous literature exists on Sahih Muslim in many languages that many would find too intimidating to read. The Abridged Sahih Muslim has been written in simplified language to make it easy for the readers to comprehend the language and meaning of the text. The text is sometimes shortened without losing the essential message and meaning of the original. An attempt has also been made to avoid repetitions wherever possible and to incorporate the most important Hadith reported by Imam Muslim in one comprehensive single volume. In spite of best efforts the translator accepts all responsibility for all acts of omission and commission, if any.

Aftab Shahryar
New Delhi

Introduction

Next in importance to the holy Qur'an as a source for Islamic faith and practice is the corpus of Tradition. The holy Book as the word from Allah offers a primary rule of life, but there are many matters where guidance for practical living is found in the custom or the Sunna of the holy Prophet. The holy Qur'an has been declared as a light and guide for humanity by Allah and the life of the holy Prophet (peace & blessings of Allah be with him) is considered as a beautiful model for the believers:

Indeed, there has come to you from Allah a Light and a Book Luminous (Q.5: 15) and *verily in the Apostle of Allah you have the best example for everyone who believes in Allah and* the Day of Reckoning (Q. 33: 21).

Again the holy Prophet (peace & blessings of Allah be with him) is guided by Allah to proclaim:

Say: O mankind, surely I am the Messenger of Allah to you all; of Him Whose is the Kingdom of the Heaven and the Earth. There is no god but He; so believe in Allah and His Messenger, the Ummi Prophet, who believes in Allah and His words, and follow him so that you may be rightly guided. (Q.V11: 158).

During his farewell sermon, on mount Rahmah at Arafat on the ninth day of the month of Dhul Hijjah (AD 632) the holy prophet (peace & blessings of Allah be with him) is reported to have remarked: O people, reflect on my words. I leave behind me two things — the Qur'an and my *Sunna* (*Hadith*), and if you follow these, you shall not fail. To show the believers through the *Hadith* and the commentaries on the Qur'ân, the right way (al-tariq al-mustaqim) followed by the holy Prophet (peace & blessings of Allah be with him) is to map out for them the path that leads to a worthy life on earth and to paradise after death.

Abdullah ibn Mas'ud is reported to have said: The most beautiful

Hadith is the Book of Allah, and the best guidance is that of Muhammad (peace & blessings of Allah be with him). This statement was ascribed to the holy prophet who was reported as saying, in an exhortation to the community: The most beautiful Hadith is the Book of Allah, blessed is he whose heart is adorned therewith by Allah (literally: into whose heart Allah has put it as an ornament), he whom He has permitted to be converted to Islam from unbelief, and he who prefers it to all other hadiths of men. Verily; it is the most beautiful and perfect *Hadith*, (quoted in Ibn Hisham p.340). In later days it was found objectionable that the Qur'an be called *Hadith* and in this sentence Hadith was altered to *'kalam,'* meaning speech (Ibn Maja p.8).

The term *Hadith* is restricted to the sayings of the holy Prophet (peace & blessings of Allah be with him) made either on his own initiative or in response to a question. The followers of the holy prophet have reverently repeated the illuminating sayings of the Great Teacher and have endeavored to preserve for the edification and instruction of the community everything that he said, both in public and private, regarding the practice of religious obligations prescribed by him, the conduct of life in general, and social behavior.

Hadith, therefore, refers to the oral communication derived from the Prophet whereas *Sunna* refers to religious or legal point. A norm contained in a *Hadith* is regarded as *Sunna*; but it is not necessary that the *Sunna* should have a corresponding *Hadith* that gives it sanction. The power attested to the *Sunna*, as the normative principle in the life of a Muslim, is as old as Islam.

Hadith is the recording in writing of everything that the prophet is supposed to have said or done. His opinion, his reaction to events, the way in which he justified his decisions, had to be put in writing so that they could be drawn upon and referred to later, in order to distinguish what is right from what is wrong.

The *Hadith* sayings are a panorama of dally life in the seventh century, a vivid panorama, extremely varied because there are different versions of the same event.

Medina was the first Muslim community and constituted for generations to come the model to be followed and the experiment to be imitated for it was led by the prophet as the political and military chief, the arbiter (*Hakam*), and the legislator inspired by

God himself. It was Allah who answered, through the medium of the *ayat* (verses), the questions of the converts about the way to be Muslim.

The problem of Hadith came up after the Holy Prophet left for his heavenly abode, During the Medinese period, the community lived out the Muslim ideal in which Allah and his prophet could be consulted at any moment the former through the intermediary of the latter. The problem of succession to the holy Prophet was resolved by developing the theory of the Caliphate. And to resolve the problem of the *Sharia*, the sacred law, the experts elaborated a body of religious knowledge, the *Fiqh*. This consisted, on the one hand, controlling the interpretation of the Qur'ân, the text revealed by Allah, and on the other hand, establishing the *Sunna* of the prophet putting into writing *Hadith*, everything that the Prophet said in order to illuminate the way of Islam.

Each generation of experts had to personally collect the testimony of those who had heard the *Hadith* directly spoken by the prophet (that is from the companions of the prophet) to collect the indirect testimony of those who followed the companions, or the second generation after the companions. Not only the *Hadith* had to be recorded as faithfully as possible, but also its *isnad*, that is the chain of people who transmitted it from its source, had to be established. The immediate entourage of the prophet — his wives, secretaries, relatives, and companions form an important source of *Hadith*.

Yet thousand of fabricated or spurious Hadith were floated largely due to the fact the Muslims world was torn by dissension in the post-Prophetic period. In the winds of discord, the fierce hatreds, the struggles for power, the sacred text was used as a political weapon and was manipulated by all sides.

The body of traditions circulated orally for some time and the demand for it naturally created a supply which put into circulation a vast number of spurious traditions. Moreover, once it was recognized that tradition was coming to have a place of authority as a supplement to the Qur'an every group, every party, every movement, developing within the community, supplied itself with a selection of traditions that would give prophetic authority for its particular point of view. Such a situation led the great collector of prophetic tradition Sayeed al-Qattan sadly remarking: In nothing will you find pious men greater lairs than in *Hadith*.

It was thus inevitable that sooner or later an attempt would have to be made to form some sort of authoritative collection of such traditions as could be reasonably considered genuine, and which were of a nature to give guidance to the community in matters where no sufficient rule of life could be found in the holy Qur'an. In this way the *Sunna* or practice and sayings of the prophet came to take its place next to the Qur'an as normative for Muslim teaching and practice.

Frightened by this misuse of religious knowledge some men of religion tried to correct this state of affairs by writing down the *Hadith* that were known, certain, and authentic. Two contradictory trends were at odds with each other in the elaboration of *Hadith*. On the one hand, the desire of each interest group to seek legitimacy in and through the sacred text. On the other hand, fierce determination of the scholars to oppose such manipulation of the sacred text through elaboration of the *Fiqh* (a veritable science of religion) with its concepts and methods of verification and counter verification.

Although Malik's Muwatta is considered as the first great collection of tradition in Islam it is not in the proper sense a collection of tradition. It is a *corpus juris*, not a corpus traditionum. Malik is not a mere collector of traditions but is first and foremost an interpreter of them from the point of view of praxis.

Historically, the recording of the Hadith had begun during the lifetime of the holy Prophet (peace & blessings of Allah be with him). Some of his companions wrote down the incidents and sayings of the Great Seer in *Sahifahs*. The companions left behind large number of *Sahifahs*, for example the *Sahifah Sadiqah* compiled by Hadrat Abdullah ibn Amr ibn Al-A'as, *Sahifah* of Hadrat Ali, *Hadith* collection of Hadrat Rafi ibn Hadij, Hadrat Jabir ibn Abdullah, Hadrat Samurah ibn Jundab, Hadrat Abu Hurayra, Hadrat Abd Allah ibn Abbas, Hadrat Abd Allah ibn Mas'ud, and *Sahifahs* of Hammam ibn Munabbih (may Allah be pleased with them). The *Hadith* collection continued with greater urgency after the holy Prophet (peace & blessings of Allah be with him) left for his heavenly abode and the Muslim *Umma* got embroiled in the struggle of power.

Sprenger, who was the first European scholar to submit the sources of the life of the holy Prophet (peace & blessings of Allah be with him) to a critical scrutiny, writes:

It is generally believed that the Traditions were preserved during the first century of the Islamic calendar solely by memory. European scholars think that none of the Traditions contained in the collections of al- Bukhari (and Imam Muslim) had been written down before their times. This appears to be an error. Ibn Amr and other companions of Muhammad (peace & blessings of Allah be with him) committed his sayings to writing and their example was followed by many of the *Tabiun* (followers of the companions of the holy Prophet). Side by side with the collection of *Hadith* was initiated their critical scrutiny so that genuine Traditions may be sifted from the concocted ones. The fact that there are numerous spurious *Ahadith* did not in the least escape the attention of the *Hadith* Scholars, as European scholars naively seem to suppose. On the contrary, the critical science of Hadith was initiated by the necessity of discerning between authentic and spurious, and the very *Imams*, Bukhari and Muslim, not to mention the lesser Traditionists, are direct product of this critical attitude. The existence, therefore of false Hadith as a whole is no more than a fanciful tale from the *Arabian Nights* and therefore it cannot be regarded as an argument against the authenticity of any historical report of the corresponding period.

However, there was never any formal canonization in Islam of a corpus of Tradition, comparable to Hadrat Uthman's canonization of the Medinan text of the Qur'an. Nevertheless, gradually six collections, made in the latter part of the third Islamic century, succeeded in gaining such general approved that later generations tacitly accepted them as six canonical collection.

These are the Sahih of al-Bukhari (d. 256 A. H. — 870 AD), the Sahih of Muslim (d. 261 A. H. —875 AD), the Sunan of Ibn Maja (d 273 A.H. — 887 AD), the Sunan of Abu Da'ud (d. 275 A.H. — 888 AD), the Jami of at-Tirmidhi (d. 279 AH — 892 AD) and the Sunan of an-Nasa'i (d. 303 AH — 915 AD).

The earlier formal collection of traditions was generally in the form known as *Musnad*. In these each *Hadith*, or statement which related the saying or described the action of the prophet, was preceded by an *isnad*, or chain of transmitters taking it back to the companion of the holy Prophet who had himself heard the statement or witnessed the event given in the text of the *Hadith*, as authority for the *Sunna* of the Prophet. These were then listed under the name of the final link in the *isnad*.

A more practical arrangement, however, was by subject matter, and as at an early period the working jurists needed collections of traditions which they might use in rendering decisions on practical cases, there grew up the practice of arrangement collections under the rubrics suggested by the needs of the jurists— marriage, inheritance, debts, etc.

In making their collection these Traditionists obviously used a critical technique of selection to decide what they would include and what they would reject. Bukhari, for example, is said to have examined some six hundred thousand traditions of which he accepted only 7, 397. Their purpose was to assemble a body of traditions which would serve as a rule of life for practicing Muslims, so their primary interest was in selecting such traditions as gave clear guidance concerning what Muslim belief and practice should be, what things were permissible and approved, and what were not permissible and disapproved. At the same time the presence of so much spurious material in circulation made them anxious to set up tests of authenticity that would exclude unauthentic material.

Al-Bukhari is a good representative of these tensions. As an intellectual he isolated himself from power in order to concentrate on research necessary for an objective editing of the *Hadith*, and at the same time he was the object of political pressures that threatened him to put his knowledge in the service of politics—which he refused to do.

Al-Bukhari was born in Bukhara, in Central Asia in 194 of Hijra (AD. 808) and died in year 256 of Hijra (AD. 870). Like other scholars of his time, he traveled throughout the Islamic lands, seeking better teachers and universities. After pausing in Syria and Iraq and visiting Hijaz, he settled for a time in Egypt. He made the rounds of all the known scholars who were expert in the area in which he was to specialize — the *Hadith*. Once these were recorded in a collection, the *Hadith* constituted the *Sunna*, the teachings of Prophet Muhammad (peace & blessing Allah be with him). Al- Bukhari through his methodical and systematic way was able to interview 1,080 persons and collect 600,000 Hadith. Once the contents of a Hadith were recorded, the work consisted, above all, assuring its authenticity. Al-Bukhari's problem was a methodical one. How is the truth or falsity of a *Hadith* to be verified? For him, writing the history of the Prophet was a serious undertaking: I wrote only after hearing the testimony of 1080 persons and I entered *Hadith* in the book before having carried out the ritual purification and praying twice.Al-Bukhari purified himself through prayers, thereby expressing the transcendent dimension of the function that he was performing and the distance that should exist between the scholar and the material he was handling. For the scholars of the first centuries of Islam, religion was definitely a scientific endeavor. It was necessary to avoid, as much as possible, letting subjectivity intrude, all the while humbly recognizing that it could not be wholly mastered. The way to do this was to see that the maximum number of versions were reported, to include repetitions in order not to neglect any point of view, and above all, to distrust the witness and transmitters:

When Al-Bukhari's scientific method had attained its fullest development, he began to distinguish authentic (*Sahih*) *Hadith* from the others. After having developed a very advanced knowledge of the various kinds of *Hadith*, he mastered the techniques for uncovering their faults. No one could equal his ability in this matter. (Asqalani, Fath Al-Bari Vol.I).Once his method of verification was perfected, al-Bukhari retained as authentic only 7,257 *Hadith*, if the repetitions, numbering 4,000, are eliminated. In his commentary on Al-Bukhari, Fath al-Bari, al-Asqalani eliminates still more repetitions and reduces the number of *Hadith* in Sahih al-Bukhari to less then 2000. During his time almost 596, 725 false Hadith were in circulation.

Al-Bukhari was not content with verifying what he recorded, but in order to show his veneration for the sacred text, he wrote an important study on the life of the transmitters of *Hadith*, Al-Tarikh al-Kabir (The Great History). The study of the transmitters became a scientific endeavor during the second century of the *Hijra*, with the triumph of traditionalists.

Al-Bukhari became a celebrity, and the politically powerful were not slow in taking an interest in him. When the Amir of Bukhara requested al-Bukhari to read to him in private some excerpts from his work Bukhari told the Amir's emissary: Tell your master that I hold knowledge in high esteem, and I refuse to drag it into the ante- chambers of sultans. (Asqalani, Fath al-Bari Vol. I, p.265).

Not all the scholars had the same pride in their work as al-Bukhari. And it is the lasting contribution of al-Bukhari and Muslim that Islamic tradition contains an authentic body of material.

Bukhari's work was to be recognized a century and half later as the definitive collection of unquestionably authentic sayings of the holy Prophet. However in his lifetime it was subjected to severe attacks. When he settled in Nisabur he was so severely oppressed on that account by the orthodox leader Dhuhli (d.258AH); and very well known for his *Zuhriyat*, collection of all the traditions going back to Zuhri, that he finally left the city and moved to Bukhara. He was expelled from the city of his birth because he refused to bend to the wishes of the Amir of Bukhara and spent the last year of his life in the village of khartank in Samarqand where he died in 256 A.H., not quite 62 years of age.

In al-Bukhari's times and largely through his influence, the rules for preserving traditions began to assume strict forms. As a conscientious collector, al-Bukhari never deviated an inch from the strictest discipline. Literal accuracy, with which scholars were not concerned before, became the watchword in reproducing what had been heard. If there were any doubts about the smallest details, these doubts had to be faithfully registered subjective judgment in such questions of textual criticism must never influence the text, even if there was an obvious mistake. The collector had to write down everything according to the words of an equally conscientious informant.

Although Imam al-Bukhari shows conscientious fidelity in reproducing his text several scholars who directly heard Sahih from al-Bukhari have handed down this work and a dozen different Bukhari texts appeared with substantial variations in their contents. The text now commonly used is due to Muhammad al Yunini (d.658) who took as his base a copy preserved in the madarsa of Aqbogha in Cairo that was itself based on good early texts.

Imam Muslim al-Hajjaj of Nisabur (d.261) was a younger contemporary of al-Bukhari who made a collection of Traditions. These are famous in the Islamic world under the name of al-Sahih.

Abul Hussain Asakir ud Din Muslim ibn Hajjaj al-Qushayri al-Nisaburi, famously known as Imam Muslim belonged to the Qushayr tribe of the Arabs, an offshoot of the great tribe of Rabia, was born in Nisabur or Nishapur towards the close of the second decade of ninth century AD. Coming from a family of religious scholars Imam Muslim had the good fortune of finding great teachers of Tradition such as Ishaq ibn Rahwaih, Ahmed Ibn Hanbal, Ubaydallah al-Qawariri, Qutayba ibn Sayeed, Abdullah ibn Muslama, Harmalah ibn Yahya among others. He also traveled widely in the Arabian Peninsula, Egypt, Syria and Iraq to collect traditions. In Nishapur where he finally settled, Imam Muslim came into contact with Imam Bukhari who was a great collector and teacher of Traditions and Imam Muslim remained his disciple until the great master passed away.

During the major part of the fifty-five years of his life the major passion of Imam Muslim remained learning the Traditions, compilation of the *Hadith*, its teaching and transmission. He wrote many books and treatises on *Hadith* such as Kitab al-Musnad al-Kabir, Jami Kabir, Kitab al- Asma wa al- Kuna, Kitab al-Ilal, Kitab al-Wajdan; but his magnum opus is the collection (Jami) or his Sahih that is considered in some respects the best and the most authentic work on the subject.

In importance Sahih Muslim is considered next only to the holy Qur'an and Sahih al-Bukhari. Imam Bukhari's Sahih is considered the most authentic book of Islamic Shari'ah. However in certain respects the Sahih of Imam Muslim is considered better than Sahih of al-Bukhari. Imam Muslim strictly observed many principles of the science of *Hadith* that had been at times ignored by his great teacher the venerable Imam Bukhari. Imam Muslim considered only such Traditions to be genuine and authentic as had been transmitted by an unbroken chain of reliable sources and were in perfect harmony with that had been related by other narrators whose trustworthiness was unanimously accepted and who were considered free of all defects. Moreover Imam Muslim takes particular care in recording the exact words of the narrators and points out even the minutest difference in the wording of their reports. He is believed to have recorded only that *Hadith* which, at least, two reliable *Tabiun* had heard from two companions and this principle is observed throughout the subsequent chain of narrators.

Unlike Imam Bukhari, Imam Muslim recorded Traditions in their integrated form that makes it easier to understand to those who do not have great knowledge of the *Hadith* literature. The Sahih of Imam Bukhari is considered a difficult work because in it the different portions of *Ahadith* are fragmented into parts, and these are mentioned under different headings according to their importance from the point of view of *Fiqh* (Islamic jurisprudence). Without sound religious knowledge the readers are unlikely to grasp and appreciate the compilation of Imam Bukhari. When compared to al-Bukhari, with which it has most of the contents in common from different oral sources, a formal difference is most obvious. Muslim's work in also a *Musannaf*. *Musnad* and *Musannaf* are two chief forms of collecting Traditions. Musnad is a more of a theoretical statement of traditions used as a repertory. Musannaf is written to facilitate the practical use of the accumulated Traditions. They provide relevant material for any given question together in critically sifted form.

Muslim's work is also a *Musannaf* and like al-Bukhari, parallel work is arranged according the chapters of the *Fiqh*, but the various paragraphs (*abwab*) in the original edition of Muslim himself have no headings. Thus Muslim also like his contemporary, intended to serve the *Fiqh* through his work but he left it to the reader to draw from the collected *Hadith* material the conclusion that seem to him to correspond most closely to the truth.

Bukhari and Muslim made it their business to give the same *Hadith* according to various *turuq* (that is, according to different informants with different *isnads*), since a *Hadith* is the more authenticated the more parallel versions it has. Whereas however, al-Bukhari often quotes the different parallel versions of the same Tradition under different chapters, Muslim always quotes related versions together without repeating material that has already been dealt with. His purpose, unlike Bukhari, was not a priori to equip the whole scheme of Fiqh with Hadith material.

Muslim was primarily concerned, as he says in his preface, to purify the existing Hadith material of all dross: the unreliable and untrustworthy element that had attached to this material during the course of time.

The Sahih of Bukhari and of Muslim represent, for the first time in the literature, a more rigorous criticism of the *isnad* than was customary in the preceding period. Previously it was considered sufficient if the *isnad* chain was entirely made up of names of informants known as reliable; only now the inner coherence of the *isnad*, begins to be tested and the admission of Traditions as legal sources is now made contingent upon correct *isnads*.

The Sahih of al-Bukhari and of Muslim occupy an exceptional place in the literature of Tradition. When they first appeared the two works had to compete for the first place in public preference, and in different provinces and circles of Islam, some times the one and some times the other were preferred.

Muslim was praised for his better arrangement of Hadith, al-Bukhari for his greater care over his *shurut* and perhaps also for greater usefulness of his work for practical purposes. Public opinion eventually accepted the pre-eminence of Sahih al-Bukhari.

With the passage of time the veneration for al-Bukhari increased to such an extent that al-Bukhari became almost a hallowed person in Islam. Pilgrimage was made to his grave and his Sahih became a privileged book on which—especially in North African Islam—people swore as other Muslims do only on the Qur'an.

Though Muslim's book was never thus honored and no superstitions regarding special privilege became attached to it, both books are considered equal as sources of Islamic law and are collectedly referred to as al-Sahihan, or al-Shaykhan par excellence.

However it would be wrong to think that the canonical authority of the two Sahi's is due to undisputed correctness of their contents and is the results of scholarly investigations. The authority of these books has a popular basis and holds good in spite of the free scrutiny of individual paragraphs. Nor does it refer to an indisputable correctness of the contents, the details of which have been the subject of some criticism. The contents of the Sahih al-Bukhari and Sahih Muslim are considered authoritative in religious praxis. The popular basis for this authority is the *ijma-al-umma*, the unanimous collective consciousness of the Islamic community that elevated these works to the heights, which they have attained.

Despite this general recognition of these works the veneration never went so for as to cause free criticism of the sayings. Veneration is directed to these works as a whole but not to individual lines and paragraphs. Nevertheless Sahih al-Bukhari and Sahih al-Muslim remain highly esteemed works in the eyes of the Muslim public across the world.

Bukhari and Muslim and the authors the four *Sunan*, were only fellow disputant in the minds of their contemporaries, not leaders in the battle against heresy. Their Judgments in no way were regarded as binding; nevertheless traditionalism had performed its task. From the traditions of the first two centuries it made a selection of traditions that formed the image of the holy prophet for all time and provided believers with an exemplary model after which they called pattern their lives.

On the other hand, it was impossible to transmit the traditions of a Bukhari or a Muslim unchanged down through the centuries. Slowly it succumbed to all those forces that had grown to independence and had come to express themselves in canonical law, Qur'ânic exegesis, scholasticism, and, above all, in Sufism.

Yet through the centuries tradition held fast unrelentingly to the *Sunna* and prevented foreign influences from destroying the distinctive character of Islam.

It is for the reason that the uniformity of Islamic culture is one of the most fascinating features of the vast Islamic civilization. In spite of all geographical and temporal variations a homogeneous Islamic culture succeeded in establishing itself across the globe. The credit for this uniformity goes to the example of the prophet, the Sunna that, with its constant impact on the life of the believers over the centuries, was the primary factor responsible for the unity of Islamic culture. It stamped itself upon the face of Islam and gave it those features that are apparent today through out the Muslim world.

The exemplary character the Prophet (peace & blessings of Allah be with him) is rooted in the very essence of Islam. The holy prophet did not claim to bring a new revelation. His message was the same as that of the preceding prophets. The essential kinship of his teachings with that of the older revealed religions was in fact so great that its continued existence as a separate religion must astonish those who focus attention only on doctrinal content of Islam. The unprecedented success of Islam can be explained only if one takes into account the uniqueness of the personality of the holy Prophet (peace & blessings of Allah be with him), whose power derived not from doctrine but from the new life to which he summoned humankind.

The distinctive character of the original community of Medina resided not so much in the new word of from Allah in which they believed as in the person of the Prophet (peace & blessings of Allah be with him). According to the holy Qur'ân they had in him "a good example (Surah 33:21). From the beginning there stood, beside the word of Allah, the living example of Prophet Muhammad (peace & blessings of Allah be with him). So great was the spell cast by his personality that it has continued to the very present to exercise power over the community of believers.

1

Book of Faith

1. It is reported on the authority of **Abu Hurayra** that one day the Apostle of Allah (Peace & blessings of Allah be with him) was sitting with some people when a man appeared and asked: "O Messenger of Allah! What is faith?" The holy Prophet (Peace & blessings of Allah be with him) replied: Faith is to believe in Allah, His angels, His Book, His messengers and the Day of Judgment. Then he asked: O, Messenger of Allah! What is Islam? The Great Teacher (Peace & blessings of Allah be with him) replied: Islam is to worship Allah alone and no one else, to establish prescribed prayers, to pay Zakat (poor due) and to observe the fast during the month of Ramadan. Again the holy Prophet was asked: what are good deeds (al-Ihsan)? The Messenger of Allah (Peace & blessings of Allah be with him) replied: Good deed is to worship Allah as if you can see Him, and if you cannot attain this then to worship Him as if He is seeing you. Asked about the final Hour, the Great Seer (Peace & blessings of Allah be with him) replied: The one who answers has no better knowledge of that than the one who asks, but I will tell you of its signs; the mother will give birth to her mistress, this is one of its signs, and the contemptible will become the chiefs of the people, this is one of its signs, and the camel herders will boast and compete with others in constructing lofty buildings, this is one of its signs. And the (final) Hour is one of five things in the knowledge of Allah alone. The holy Prophet (Peace & blessings of Allah be with him) then recited the following lines from the Qur'an: Certainly the knowledge of the Hour is with Allah alone, and He sends down rain, and He knows what is in the wombs. No soul knows what it shall earn tomorrow, nor does any soul know in which land it shall die, indeed Allah is All-Knowing, All-Aware. (Q. 31: 34) Then the man left and the Messenger of Allah (Peace & blessings of Allah be with him) asked his companions to call him back. They looked for him but could not find him. The Great Seer (Peace & blessings of Allah be with him) then said that it was Gabriel, who appeared in order to instruct you in religion.

2. *Saeed ibn al- Musayyib* reported on the authority of his father that when Abu Talib was about to die the Apostle of Allah (Peace & blessings of Allah be with him) visited his ailing uncle and found Abu Jahl and Abd Allah ibn Abi Umayya ibn al-Mughira by his side. The holy Prophet (Peace & blessings of Allah be with him) spoke to Abu Talib: 'O my uncle! Say: 'There is no deity but Allah', and I shall bear witness to this before God.' Abu Jahl and Abd Allah ibn Abi Umayya said: 'O Abu Talib! Would you abandon the creed of Abd al Muttalib?' The holy Prophet (Peace & blessings of Allah be with him) repeatedly urged Abu Talib to affirm the oneness of Allah until Abu Talib spoke his last words saying that he would hold to the creed of Abd al-Muttalib. Then The Apostle of Allah (Peace & blessings of Allah be with him) said: I will continue to seek Allah's forgiveness for you unless I am forbidden. Thereafter the verse concerning him was revealed: 'It is not befitting for the Prophet (Peace & blessings of Allah be with him) and the believers to ask for forgiveness for the unbe-lievers, even though they be close relatives, after it had been made known to them that they were the denizens Hell'. (Q. 9:113). And it was also revealed to the holy Prophet regarding Abu Talib: Surely you cannot guide to the right path whom you love, but Allah guides whom He pleases, and He knows best those who would be guided. (Q. 28:56).

3. *Abu Hurayra* is reported to have said: When the Messenger of Allah (Peace & blessings of Allah be with him) died and Abu Bakr became Caliph, some of the Arabs reneged on the payment of Zakat and the Caliph contemplated war against them. Umar ibn al-khattab asked Abu Bakr: 'How can you fight those people when the Messenger of Allah (Peace & blessings of Allah be with him) said: 'I have been commanded to fight the people until they affirm: 'There is no deity but Allah', and whoever affirms that will have his life and property spared by me except if he breaks the law, and his reckoning will be with God'.' Abu Bakr responded: By God! I will fight those who sever the prayer from the Zakat; the Zakat is the obligatory right to be taken from their property. By God! If they refuse to give as much as a cord that they used to do during the lifetime of the Messenger of Allah (Peace & blessings of Allah be with him), I will fight them for their refusal.' Then Umar bin al- Khattab said: 'By God, it was none, but Allah Who guided Abu Bakr to fight, and I later realized that he was correct'.

4. *Abd Allah ibn Umar* reported that the Messenger of Allah (prayers & peace be upon him) said: I have been comman-ded to fight the people until they testify that no one has the right to be worshipped but Allah and that Muhammad is His

Messenger, and to establish prayers and give obligatory charity (*Zakat*). If they perform all this, then their lives and property are safe except what is due in law, and their affairs rest with Allah.

5. *Miqdad ibn al Aswas* reported that he asked the Messenger of Allah (Peace & blessings of Allah be with him): If I encounter one of the unbelievers and we fight and he strikes me with his sword and cuts my hand off and then took refuge under a tree and said: 'I submit to God,' should I kill him, O Messenger of Allah, after his having said that?' The holy Prophet (Peace & blessings of Allah be with him) replied: You should not kill him. Al-Aswas said: O Messenger of Allah! But he had cut off my hand and then said the words?' The holy Prophet (Peace & blessings of Allah be with him) replied: You should not kill him, for if you did than he would be in the position you had been before killing him and you would be in the position he was in before he said those words.

6. *Usama ibn Zayed* is reported to have narrated that: The Messenger of Allah (Peace & blessings of Allah be with him) sent us out in a battalion to Al- Huruqa, a tribe of Juhaina, and the next morning we launched an attack on them. A man from the Ansars and myself pursued one of their men and when we caught up with him he said: 'There is no god but Allah.' But I killed him and then felt uneasy about it. So I mentioned it to the holy Prophet (Peace & blessings of Allah be with him) and the Apostle of Allah enquired: Did you kill him after he had said: 'There is no god but Allah?' I said: O Messenger of Allah! He only said it to save himself from the sword. The holy Prophet (Peace & blessings of Allah be with him) then said: Did you open his heart to know whether he said it in truth or not? And he repeated these words so many times that I wished I had not become Muslim before that day.

7. *Safwan ibn Muhriz* reported that Jundab ibn Abd Allah Al Bajalli sent a messenger to As'as ibn Salama saying: Assemble a group of your brethren so that I may speak to them." So when they gathered, Jundab said: I have come only to talk to you about your Prophet, The Messenger of Allah (peace & blessings of Allah be with him) sent a squad of the Muslims to a tribe of unbelievers. When the two armies encountered each other, a man from the unbelievers was killing the Muslims at will, so one of the Muslims sought an opportunity and killed him. When Usama ibn Zayed raised his sword to kill the unbeliever, that man said: There is no deity but Allah.' But Usama killed him. When the news of it reached the Prophet, he asked him what he had done, so he told the Prophet exactly what happened. The Prophet asked why had he killed him then. He said: O Messenger of Allah! he was killing many of the Muslims. And he

named many of those he had killed. So I had to overcome him. But when he saw the sword he said There is no deity but Allah. The Apostle of Allah (peace & blessings of Allah be with him) said: And then you killed him? He said: Yes. He said: And what will you do with 'There is no deity but Allah' when he comes before you on the Day of Judg-ment? He said: O Messenger of Allah! Seek forgiveness for me. And he continued to say nothing but: And what will you do with 'There is no deity but Allah' when he confronts you on the Day of Judg-ment?

8. It is reported that **Uthman** heard the Apostle of Allah (peace & blessings of Allah be with him) as having said: Whoever dies belie-ving that there is no deity but Allah will enter Paradise.

9. It is reported from **Abu Sayeed** or **Abu Hurayra** that during the campaign of Tabuk foodstuff became short and the army was famished. They asked per-mission of the holy Prophet to slaughter their camels to eat and use their fat. The Apostle of Allah (peace &blessings of Allah bc with him) agreed. However Umar arrived and said: O Messenger of Allah! if you permit them to do that there will be insuf-ficient mounts. So let them bring you whatever food they have left and invoke Allah's blessings over them, that maybe Allah will bless them. The holy Prophet (peace & blessings of Allah be with him) agreed. He called for a mat to be laid out, and then asked the people to gather leftovers of their food. When the food was gathered upon the mat then the holy Prophet (peace & blessings of Allah be with him) invoked blessings upon them and said: Fill up your containers with this food. They (about thirty thousand troops) filled up their containers ate to their fill and yet some food remained. Upon this the Apostle of Allah (peace & blessings of Allah be with him) remarked: I bear witness that there is no deity but Allah, and I am The Messenger of Allah. Whoever encounters God without having the slightest doubt about these two verities will never be kept away from Paradise.

10. **Sunabihi** reported that he visited Ubada ibn Samit as he was on his death-bed. As "I cried" Ubada said to me: 'Wait, why are you weeping? By God, if I should be asked to bear witness, I would surely testify for you. If I should be asked to inter-cede, I would surely intercede for you, and if I am able, I would surely do good for you.' Then lie said: 'By God, I never heard any-thing from The Messen-ger of Allah (peace & blessings of Allah be with him) which could have been of benefit to you without conveying it to you with the exception of this one Hadith, which I shall relate to you today as I am soon to die. I heard the Mes-senger of Allah (peace & blessings of Allah be with him) say: Whoever bears witness that there is no deity but Allah and that Muhammad is the Messenger of

Allah (peace & blessings of Allah be with him), God will prohibit the Fire (of Hell) from touching him.

11. It is reported on the authority of *Abu Hurayra*: We were seated around the Messenger of Allah (peace & blessings of Allah be with him), and Abu Bakr and Umar were among those present. The holy Prophet (peace & blessings of Allah be with him) rose up and left us, he did not return and we feared that an enemy might attack him in our absence, so we rose up in apprehension. I was the first to be concerned, so I went to search for the Apostle of Allah (peace & blessings of Allah be with him) and I reached a garden that belonged to Bani An-Najjar, a family of the Ansars. I walked around the garden looking for its gateway but could not find one. Then I spotted a stream flowing into the garden from outside, so I slid myself inside, where I found the Messenger of Allah (peace & blessings of Allah be with him). He said: 'Is that you Abu Hurayra?' I said: 'Yes, O Messenger of Allah.' He said: 'What is the matter with you?' I said: 'You were with us and then you left and did not return, so we feared that an enemy might attack you in our absence, so we came looking for you. The holy Prophet (peace & blessings of Allah be with him) said: O Abu Hurayra, take my sandals and when you meet anyone outside the garden who bears witness that there is no god but Allah, being certain of that in his heart, then, give him the glad tidings that he shall enter Paradise. The first one I met was Umar, who asked: 'whose sandals are these' Abu Hurayra?' I said: They belong to The Messenger of Allah (peace & blessings of Allah be with him) and he has sent me with them to give the glad tidings to anyone I meet who bears witness that there is no god but Allah, being certain of that in his heart, that he shall enter Paradise. At that Umar struck me upon my chest and I fell upon my back. Then he said: O Abu Hurayra, return. So I returned to the Messenger of Allah (peace & blessings of Allah be with him) and I was almost in tears. Umar was following me close behind. The Apostle of Allah (peace & blessings of Allah be with him) asked: 'What is the matter, Abu Hurayra?' I said: I happened to meet with Umar and I gave him your message but he struck me upon my chest and caused me to fall on my back and told me to return. At this the holy Prophet (peace & blessings of Allah be with him) said: What made you do that, Umar? He replied: O Messenger of Allah! May my father and mother be redeemed for you, did you send Abu Hurayra with your sandals to proclaim to anyone he meets who bears witness that there is no god but Allah, being certain of that in his heart, to give him the glad tidings that he shall enter Paradise? The holy Prophet replied in the affirmative and Umar said: Do not do so, I fear the people will trust in it solely, let them continue doing good deeds. The Apostle of

Allah (peace & blessings of Allah be with him) agreed and said: Let them do so.

12. It is reported on the authority of *Anas ibn Malik* that Muaz ibn Jabal was riding behind the holy Prophet (peace & blessings of Allah be with him) and the Messenger of Allah (peace & blessings of Allah be with him) told him: O Muaz 'Do you know what is due to God from His servants?' I said: Allah and His Messenger know best.' He said: 'What is due to Allah from His servants is that they worship Him alone and do not associate partners with Him.' Then we went on for another hour and then he (peace & blessings of Allah be with him) said: 'O Muaz ibn Jabal!' I replied: 'Here I am, at your beck and call, O Messenger of Allah!' He said: 'Do you know what is due from Allah to His servants if they do that?' I said: Allah and His Messenger know best.' He said: 'He will not punish them.'

13. It is reported from *Mahmoud ibn al Rabi'a* on the authority of Itban ibn Malik that Itban arrived in Medina and sent a request to the holy Prophet (peace & blessings of Allah be with him) saying: 'It is my greatest wish to invite you to grace my house with your presence and to pray in it so that I might take it as a place of prayer.' He said: 'The Prophet came with those of his Companions whom God pleased, he entered and offered prayer in my house and his companions talked to

each other, then they spoke concerning the hypocrites, and in particular about Malik ibn Dukhshum. They said that they wished the Prophet would invoke the curse of Allah upon him so that he would perish or suffer some misfortune. Meantime the Prophet finished praying and then said: 'Does not Malik ibn Dukhshum bear witness that there is no deity but Allah and that I am indeed The Messenger of Allah (peace & blessings of Allah be upon him)?' They replied: 'Yes indeed he does so all the time, but not with sincerity.' The holy Prophet asserted: 'Whoever bears witness that there is no deity but Allah and that I am The Messenger of Allah will not enter the Fire nor will its flames consume him.' Anas relates that he was so moved by this Hadith that he asked his son to record it in writing and he did so.

2

Book of
Definition of Faith

1. *Abu Hurayra* is reported to have narrated that the Apostle of Allah (peace & blessings of Allah be with him) said: All Prophets were given miracles and human kind believed in them. But I have been given the Revelation that Allah revealed to me; and I hope to have the greatest number of devotees on the Day of Reckoning.

2. *Sufyan ibn Abd Allah al-Thaqafi* reported that he said: O Messenger of Allah! Teach me something of Islam that I would not have to ask anyone after you (or other than you). The holy Prophet (peace & blessings of Allah be with him) replied: 'Say 'I believe in Allah' and thereafter be constant in doing good deeds.

3. *Abu Hurayra* narrated that the holy Prophet (peace & blessings of Allah be with him) said: By Him in Whose Hands is the soul of Muhammad, anyone of this nation, Jews or Christians, who hear me and do not believe in the message revealed to me and then die disbelieving, shall be the dwellers of the Fire (of Hell).

4. *Abu Zarr* reported that he asked the Messenger of Allah (peace & blessings of Allah be upon him): 'Which are the best deeds?' He said: 'To believe in Allah and to strive in His cause.' I asked: 'Which is the best slave to free?' He said: 'The most valuable and highly priced to his master.' I asked: 'If I cannot do that?' He said: 'Help a craftsman or make something for someone who cannot do anything for himself.' I said: 'O Messenger of Allah! I am old and unable to do these things.' The holy Prophet replied: Avoid wrongdoing to the people, that will be a charity from you to yourself.

5. *Abu Hurayra* reported that the holy Prophet (peace & blessings of Allah be with him) said: People will continue to question you about knowledge to the point that they will say: Allah created us, so who created Allah? He said thus while holding the hand of a man, and that man said: Allah and His Messenger are truthful, two people have just asked me that question and thus have the third. And it was also reported that Abu Hurayra said that the Apostle of Allah (peace & blessings of Allah be with him) asserted: People will continue to question you, O Abu Hurayra, to the point that they will say: 'So there is Allah, but who created Allah? he said: 'While I was in the mosque some bedouin came to me saying: 'O Abu Hurayra, Allah created us, so who created Allah?' He said: 'I picked up some pebbles in my hand and threw at them and said: 'Get out, my friend is truthful.'

6. It is reported that **Saleh ibn Saleh al- Hamadani** said that Sha'bi was asked by a man of Khurasan: O Abu Amr! some of the people of Khurasan among us say that a man who frees his slave girl and then marries her is as one who has ridden over a sacrificial animal. Sha'bi said: Abu Barda ibn Musa related to me that his father said that the Messenger of Allah (peace & blessings of Allah be with him) had said: There are three who will be given a double reward, for the one from the People of the Book who believed in his Messenger and lived to witness the era of the Prophet (Muhammad-peace & blessings of Allah be with him) and who believed in him and followed him and bore witness to his truth, for such there is a double reward, and for the slave who fulfills his obligations towards Allah Almighty and fulfills his obligations to his master, for such there is a double reward, and for the one who has a slave girl and feeds her well and taught her good manners and did

that well and then freed her and then married her, for such there is a double reward. Then Sha'bi said to al Khurasani: 'Take this Hadith freely, you should know that a man used to travel to Medina for a lesser Hadith than this.

7. *Anas* reported that the holy Prophet (peace & blessings of Allah be with him) said: Whoever possesses the following three traits will have the sweetness of faith:

That Allah and His Messenger are dearer to him above all else. When he loves someone he does so only for Allah's sake. That he despises to revert to atheism - after Allah has saved him from it - as much as he despises to be cast into the Fire (of Hell).

8. *Anas* reported that the holy Prophet (peace & blessings of Allah be with him) said: None of you will have attained faith until he loves me more than his father, his children and all mankind.

9. It is reported from *Anas* that the holy Prophet (peace & blessings of Allah be with him) said: By Him in Whose hands is my soul, no servant will have attained faith until he loves his neighbour. And it was also related that he said: Until he loves for his brother what he loves for himself.

10. **Al Abbas ibn Abd Al Muttalib** reported that he heard the Messenger of Allah (peace & blessings of Allah be with him) say: The one who is satisfied with Allah as

his Lord and Islam as his Religion, and Muhammad as the Messenger of Allah, will taste the sweetness of faith.

11. It is reported from **Abd Allah ibn Amr** that the Messenger of Allah (peace & blessings of Allah be with him) said: There are four traits, whoever has them all is an utter hypocrite and whoever has one has that trait of hypocrisy until he gives it up. If he speaks he lies, if he is trusted he betrays, if he promises he breaks it and if he is an adversary he is vulgar. And it was also related that Abu Sufyan said: If one has one of those traits he has the trait of hypocrisy.

12. According to a tradition related by **Abu Hurayra** the Messenger of Allah (peace & blessings of Allah be with him) said: There are three traits in a hypocrite; when he speaks, he lies. When he promises, he fails. When he is trusted, he betrays.

13. It is reported from **Ka'b ibn Malik** that the Apostle of Allah (peace & blessings of Allah be with him) said that the believer is like a young plant, the wind flexes it, once it bends it and then it straightens it, until it grows. But the unbeliever is like the pine tree that is solid to its roots; nothing can bend it until it is broken once and for all. It was also related, "Once it straightens until its destiny is fulfilled. And the similitude of the hypocrite is as the pine tree solid to its roots, nothing affects it.

14. **Abd Allah ibn Umar** is reported to have said: We were with the Messenger of Allah (peace & blessings of Allah be with him) when he said: 'Tell me the name of the tree which is like the Muslim, whose leaves do not fall and which gives fruit all the time.' Ibn Amr said: 'I thought of the palm but I saw that Abu Bakr and Umar did not speak so I felt disinclined to answer, when Umar came to know he said: 'Had you answered, it would have been better for me than so and so.

15. It is reported from **Abu Hurayra** that the holy Prophet (peace & blessings of Allah be with him) said: Faith consists of a little over seventy - or a little over sixty elements, the best of them is 'There as no god but Allah' and the least of them is removing harm from the way, and shyness is a part of faith.

16. **Abu Qatada** is reported to have said: We were in a group sitting with Imran ibn Hussain and Bushair ibn Ka'ab was with us. That day Imran related that the Messenger of Allah (peace & blessings of Allah be with him) said: Shyness is the best virtue, or he said: 'Shyness is the best of virtues.'

17. **Abu Shuraib al-Khuza'i** reported that the holy Prophet (peace & blessings of Allah be with him) said: Whoever believes in Allah and the Last Day, let him be good to his neighbor, and whoever believes in Allah and the Last Day, let him honour his guest, and whoever

believes in Allah and the Last Day, should either utter good words or better remain silent.

18. It is reported from *Abu Hurayra* that the Messenger of Allah (peace & blessings of Allah be with him) said: He will not enter paradise whose neighbour is not secure from his wrongful conduct.

19. It is narrated on the authority of *Taqiq ibn Shihab* that the one who initiated the practice of delivering the khutba (sermon) before the prayer on Eid day was Marwan. A man rose up and told him: 'The prayer should precede the sermon.' Marwan replied that this practice had been abandoned.' Then Abu Sayeed remarked: 'That man has fulfilled has responsibility, I have heard the Messenger of Allah (Peace & blessings of Allah be with him), say: 'If any of you see something wrong he must try to correct it with his hand, and if he is unable to do so then with his tongue, and if he does not have the strength to do so then (he should abhor it) with his heart, and that is the weakest of faith.

20. It is reported that from *Abd Allah ibn Mas'ud* said that the Messenger of Allah (Peace & blessings of Allah be with him), said: Faith will find its refuge in Medina, as the snake finds refuge in its hole.

21. *Jabir ibn Abd Allah* reported that the Messenger of Allah (Peace & blessings of Allah be with him) said: Hardness of heart and severity are in the East and faith is in the people of Hijaz.

22. It is reported on the authority of *Hadrat Ayesha* that she asked the holy Prophet: O Messenger of Allah! Ibn Judan used to keep his womb relations and feed the poor during the times of ignorance. Will that benefit him? The Apostle of Allah (Peace & blessings of Allah be with him), said: That will not benefit him because he did not ever say: My Lord forgive me my sins on the Day of Judgment.

23. It is reported from *Abu Hurayra* that the Messenger of Allah (Peace & blessings of Allah be with him), said: You will not enter Paradise until you believe, and you will not believe until you love one another, shall I tell you of something which if you do it, you will love each other? Spread peace among yourselves.

24. *Abu Hurayra* reported that the Apostle of Allah (Peace & blessings of Allah be with him), said: The fornicator does not commit fornication while he is a believer, and the thief does not steal while he is a believer, and the drunkard does not intoxicate himself while he is a believer. Abu Hurayra added to that: No well-respected man who is admired by the people forcibly snatches the property of others without right while he is a believer.

25. *Abu Hurayra* reported that the holy Prophet (Peace & blessings of Allah be with him) said: A believer is never harmed twice by the same thing.

26. *Abd al-Rahman ibn Abi Bakra* reported that his father said: We were seated among a group with the Messenger of Allah (Peace & blessings of Allah be with him), when he said: Shall I tell you what are the greatest sins? He repeated the question three times. 'Associating anything with Allah, disobedience to parents, bearing false witness.'

27. *Abu Hurayra* reported that the Messenger of Allah (Peace & blessings of Allah be with him), said: Abstain from the seven most destructive things. It was said: O Messenger of Allah! What are they? He said: Associating anyone with Allah, magic, killing the soul which Allah has forbidden except by right, devouring usury, devouring the wealth of orphans, desertion on the battlefield, slandering of an innocent believing woman.

28. *Abd Allah ibn Umar* reported that the holy Prophet (Peace & blessings of Allah be with him), said on his farewell pilgrimage: Woe to you! Do not return to unbelief after me, striking at one another's necks.

29. *Abu Zarr* reportedly said that he heard the Messenger of Allah (Peace & blessings of Allah be with him), say: Anyone who claims a father other than his true father knowingly is an unbeliever. And whoever deliberately claims anything that is not his, is not one of us. Let him await his place in the Fire (of Hell). And anyone who calls another an unbeliever or says he is

the enemy of Allah, while he is not, he has oppressed him.

30. *Abd Allah ibn Mas'ud* reported that a man asked the Messenger of Allah (Peace & blessings of Allah be with him): Which is the most grievous sin? He said: To associate an equal to Allah Who is The One who created you. The man again asked: And what is the next most grievous sin after that? The holy Prophet replied: To kill your child from fear of poverty. The man asked: And what is the next most grievous sin after that? The Apostle of Allah said: To commit adultery with your neighbor's wife. Then Allah revealed: And they do not invoke with Allah any other god, nor kill any soul Allah has forbidden, except by right, nor commit adultery, and whoever does 'this shall meet the price of sin." (Q. 25: 68).

31. *Jabir ibn Abd Allah* reported that a man visited the holy Prophet (Peace & blessings of Allah be with him), and said: O Messenger of Allah! what are the two determi-ning characteristics (for entering paradise and Hell)? The Apostle of Allah (Peace & blessings of Allah be with him), remarked: Anyone who dies without attributing any partner with Allah shall enter Paradise and anyone who dies while attributing any partner with Allah will enter the Fire (of Hell).

32. *Abu Zarr* is reported to have said: I visited the holy Prophet (Peace & blessings of Allah be with him), when he was sleeping wearing white garments. Then I went to him again and he was still sleeping, then I visited him when he had woken up and I sat beside him. He said: Anyone who says: 'There is no deity but Allah,' and then dies believing in that will be admitted to Paradise.' I said: Even if he has committed adultery and theft? He said: Even if he committed adultery and theft. I said: Even if he had committed adultery and theft? He said: Even if he had committed adultery and theft. I said: Even if he had committed adultery and theft? Upon the fourth time the holy Prophet (Peace & blessings of Allah be with him), said: Even so despite Abu Zarr's dislike of it.

33. *Abd Allah ibn Mas'ud* reported that the holy Prophet (Peace & blessings of Allah be with him), said: Whoever has as much as the weight of an atom of pride in his heart will not be admitted into Paradise. A man said: People like to dress well and to wear fine shoes? He said: God is beauty and He loves beauty, and pride is rejection of rights (of others) and oppression of the people.

34. It is reported from *Abu Hurayra* that the Messenger of Allah (Peace & blessings of Allah be with him), said: There are two traits in people which are equal to disbelief: To deny one's lineage and to wail over the deceased.

35. It is reported from *Zayed ibn Khalid al Juhni* that the Messenger of Allah (Peace & blessings of Allah be with

him), led the dawn prayer at Hudaybiyah. There were signs of rain having fallen during the night. After the prayers the Apostle of Allah (Peace & blessings of Allah be with him), turned to the people and said: Do you know what your Lord has said? They said: Allah and His Messenger know best. The holy Prophet said: Allah has said: 'Some of My servants came as believers this morning and some as unbelievers, those who said 'It has rained as a mercy from Allah' were believers in Me and disbelievers in the stars. Those who said 'It has rained because of the ascent of a certain star' disbelieved in Me and believed in the stars.

36. *Amr ibn al- A'as* reported that he heard the Messenger of Allah (Peace & blessings of Allah be with him), saying out aloud: Indeed! The relatives of my father - meaning so and so - are not my friends, but indeed Allah and the righteous believers are my friends.

37. *Anas ibn Malik* reported that the Messenger of Allah (Peace & blessings of Allah be with him), said: Allah does not deny a believer the reward for any good deed, He rewards him for it in the life and in the Hereafter, but Allah rewards the unbeliever for whatever charity he does for Allah's sake in this world until he dies. Thereafter there is no reward for him in the Hereafter.

38. It is reported from *Talha ibn Ubaydallah* that a man from Najd

approached the Messenger of Allah (Peace & blessings of Allah be with him), and enquired about the essential duties to be performed in Islam. The holy Prophet (Peace & blessings of Allah be with him), replied: You have to establish prayer five times over the course of a day and night. The man asked: Are there any other prayers due? The Great Teacher (Peace & blessings of Allah be with him), replied: No, but you may offer voluntary prayers, and you have to fast during the month of Ramadan. The man asked: Is there any other fasting due? The Messenger of Allah (Peace & blessings of Allah be with him), replied: No, but you may offer voluntary fasting. The Apostle of Allah (Peace & blessings of Allah be with him) then said to him: You have to give Zakat (the obligatory poor-due). The man asked: Is there any other charity due? The Great Seer (Peace & blessings of Allah be with him), observed: No, but you may offer voluntary charity. As the man was leaving the man said: By God! I will do neither more nor less than that! The holy Prophet (Peace & blessings of Allah be with him), said: If he does as he says, then he will be successful.

39. *Abdullah ibn Umar* reported that the holy Prophet (Peace & blessings of Allah be with him), said: Islam was established upon five pillars, the Oneness of Allah, the establishment of prayer, the payment of Zakat, the fasting of Ramadan and the Pilgrimage. A man asked: The Pilgrimage and the fasting of Ramadan? He said: No, fasting during Ramadan and Pilgrimage.

40. *Abd Allah ibn Umar* is reported to have said that a man asked the Messenger of Allah (Peace & blessings of Allah be with him),: Whose Islam is best? The Great Master (Peace & blessings of Allah be with him), replied: The one who feeds others and greets those who he knows and those who he does not know.

41. *Abd Allah ibn Mas'ud* reported that the Apostle of Allah (Peace & blessings of Allah be with him), said: To abuse a Muslim is evil and to kill one is disbelief.

42. It is reported from *Abd Allah ibn Mas'ud* that some people asked the holy Prophet (Peace & blessings of Allah be with him): O Messenger of Allah! Will we be punished for our deeds of the days of ignorance before Islam? The Great Seer (Peace & blessings of Allah be with him), remarked: Whoever becomes a devout Muslim will not be questioned about them, but whoever is an evildoer will be punished for his deeds of the days of ignorance and of Islam.

43. *Abu Hurayra* reported that the Messenger of Allah (Peace & blessings of Allah be with him) said that Allah has ordained: When My servant intends to do a good deed but does not do it, I will record a reward for him. But if he does it, I will record ten rewards for him.

And if he intends to commit a sin I will forgive him as long as he does not do it. But if he commits it I will record the like of it for him. The Messenger of Allah (Peace & blessings of Allah be with him), said: The good deed of a devout Muslim will be recorded as ten times the like of it in reward. It even will be multiplied to seven hundred times in reward. And every sin he commits will be recorded as the like of it until he returns to Lord Almighty.

44. It is reported from *Abu Hurayra* that the Messenger of Allah (Peace & blessings of Allah be with him) said: God forgives my people for the sins they intend to do as long as they do not speak of them nor commit them.

45. *Abd Allah ibn Amr ibn al A 'as* has reported that a man asked the Messenger of Allah (Peace & blessings of Allah be with him): Whose Islam is the best? He replied: The one who avoids harming other Muslims with his hands or his tongue.

46. It is narrated by *Urwa ibn al Zubair* that Hakim ibn Hizam said that he asked The Messenger of Allah (Peace & blessings of Allah be with him): Before I became Muslim I used to perform charitable deeds, free the slaves and preserve good relations with my blood relatives, will I be rewarded for these deeds?" The holy Prophet (Peace & blessings of Allah be with him), replied: When you became a Muslim all your good deeds remained with you.

47. *Hudhaifa* is reported to have narrated: We were with the holy Prophet (Peace & blessings of Allah be with him), when he said: 'Count how many people have embraced Islam.' 'We said: 'O Messenger of Allah, do you worry about us while we number about six to seven hundred?' The Apostle of Allah (Peace & blessings of Allah be with him) said: 'You do not know, you may be put to test.' The narrator said: 'so we were put to test to the point that none of us dared to pray except in secret.

48. *Urwa ibn al-Zubair* has narrated that Hadrat Ayesha, the wife of the holy Prophet said: The Messenger of Allah (Peace & blessings of Allah be with him), at first began to receive Revelations in the form of true visions in sleep which came like bright gleam of dawn. Thereafter solitude became dear to him. He used to go into seclusion in the cave of Hira where he would meditate (engage in *tahannuth*) continuously for many nights before returning to his family; until suddenly the Truth descended upon him while he was in the cave of Hira. The angel came to him and asked him to read. The holy Prophet (Peace & blessings of Allah be with him), replied: 'I do not know how to read. ' The holy Prophet (Peace & blessings of Allah be with him), added: 'The angel then held me and pressed me so hard that I could bear it no longer, he then released me and again asked me to read and I replied: 'I do not know how to read.' At which he held me again and pressed me a second time until I could bear it no more. He then released me and asked me again to read but again I replied: 'I do not know how to read.' At which he held me for a third time and pressed me and then released me and said: 'Read in the Name of your Lord Who created- Created mankind from a clinging entity. Read! And your Lord is the Most Noble- Who taught by the pen- taught man what he did not know' (Q. 96:1-5) Then The Messenger of Allah (Peace & blessings of Allah be with him), hurried home with his whole body shaking and his heart beating rapidly until he reached Khadija and said: 'Cover me! Cover me!' She covered him until his fear subsided and then he told her everything that had happened and said: 'I fear that something may happen to me.' Khadija replied: Never! By God, God will never disgrace you. You keep good relations with your kin, you are truthful, you help the poor and the destitute, you serve your guests generously and you assist the deserving who are beset by adversity'. Khadija then accompanied him to her cousin Waraqa ibn Naufal, who had converted to Christianity and was knowledgeable in Christian and Jewish holy Books. He was an old man and had lost his eyesight. Khadija said to Waraqa: Listen to the account of your nephew, O my cousin. Waraqa ibn Naufal asked: O my nephew! what have you seen? The Messenger of Allah (Peace & bles-sings of Allah be with him), described all that he had seen, and Waraqa said: This is the same *Namus* (angel) who keeps the secrets, whom God sent to Moses, I wish I were young and could live until the time when your people will drive you out. The Messenger of Allah (Peace & blessings of Allah be with him), asked: Will they drive me out? Waraqa replied in the affirmative and said: Anyone who ever brought such as you now bring was treated with hostility, and if I live until the day when you will be driven out then I will give you my fullest support.

49. Yahya reported that he asked *Abu Salama* which verse was revealed first from the Qur'an. He said: 'O the shrouded one.' I said: Or 'Recite.' Jabir said: I am relating to you what the Messenger of Allah (Peace & blessings of Allah be with him), related to us. He said: I spent one month in the cave of Hira then I descended from there into the valley where I heard my name being called out. I looked around but saw no one at all. Again my name was called out and I looked around but saw nothing. Then I was called again and then I looked up and saw Gabriel seated upon a throne covering the horizon. I started shaking with fear, I reached Khadija and said: 'cover me, so she covered me and poured water over me. Then Allah Exalted and Glorious revealed: 'O you who are shrou-ded! Arise and warn and magnify your Lord and purify your garments.' (Q. 74:1-4)

50. *Anas ibn Malik is* reported to have said that: Allah Almighty bestowed the revelation upon the Messenger of Allah until the end of his earthly life. And the Messenger of Allah (Peace & blessings of Allah be with him), received more revelations on the day he left for his heavenly abode than on any other day.

51. It is reported from *Anas ibn Malik* on the authority of Abu Zarr that the Messenger of Allah (Peace & blessings of Allah be with him) said: I rode upon Al Buraq - which is a long white mount larger than donkey and smaller than a mule, whose stride was equal to the length of its vision." He said: "I rode it until I reached Al Aqsa Mosque in Jerusalem and tethered it where the prophets used to tether their mounts. Then I entered the Mosque and I prayed two Rak'at and went out. Gabriel came to me with two vessels, one of wine and one of milk. I chose the milk and Gabriel (peace be upon him) said: 'You have chosen instinctively.' Then he ascended with me to the nearest heaven, and Gabriel said to the gatekeeper of the heaven: 'Open.' The gatekeeper asked: 'Who is it?' Gabriel answered: 'Gabriel." He asked: 'Is there anyone with you?' Gabriel replied: 'Yes, Muhammad is with me.' He asked: 'Has he been summoned?' Gabriel said: 'Yes.' Then the gate was opened and we saw Adam. He welcomed me and prayed for me. Then he ascended with me until he reached the second heaven and he said to its gate-keeper: 'Open.' The gatekeeper asked: 'Who is it?' Gabriel answered: 'Gabriel." He asked: 'Is there anyone with you?' Gabriel replied: 'Yes, Muhammad is with me.' He asked: 'Has he been summoned?' Gabriel said: 'Yes.' Then the gate was opened and I found the two maternal cousins Jesus, son of Mary, and Yahya (John the Baptist), son of Zakaria. They both welcomed me and prayed for me. Then he ascended with me until he reached the third heaven and said to its gatekeeper: 'Open.' The gatekeeper asked: 'Who is it?' Gabriel answered: 'Gabriel." He asked: 'Is there anyone with you?' Gabriel replied: 'Yes, Muhammad is with me.' He asked: 'Has he been summoned?' Gabriel said: 'Yes.' Then the gate was opened and I found Yusef (Joseph) who had been blessed with half of all beauty. He welcomed me and prayed for me. Then he ascended with me until he reached the fourth heaven and said to its gatekeeper: 'Open.' The gatekeeper asked: 'Who is it?' Gabriel answered: 'Gabriel." He asked: 'Is there anyone with you?' Gabriel replied: 'Yes, Muhammad is with me.' He asked: 'Has he been summoned?' Gabriel said: 'Yes.' Then the gate was opened and I found Idris. He welcomed me and prayed for me, God Almighty has said: "And We elevated him (Idris) high in Heaven." (Q. 19:57). Then he ascended with me until he reached the fifth heaven and said to its gatekeeper: 'Open.' The gatekeeper asked: 'Who is it?' Gabriel answered: 'Gabriel." He asked: 'Is there anyone with you?' Gabriel replied: 'Yes, Muhammad is with me.' He asked: 'Has he been summoned?' Gabriel said: 'Yes.' Then the gate was opened and I found Aaron. He welcomed me and prayed for me. Then he ascended with me until he reached the sixth heaven and said to its gatekeeper: 'Open.' The gatekeeper asked: 'Who is it?' Gabriel answered: 'Gabriel." He asked: 'Is there anyone with you?' Gabriel replied: 'Yes, Muhammad is with me.' He asked: 'Has he been summoned?' Gabriel said: 'Yes.' Then the gate was opened and I found Moses. He welcomed me and prayed for me. Then he ascended with me until he reached the seventh heaven and said to its gatekeeper: 'Open.' The gatekeeper asked: 'Who is it?' Gabriel answered: 'Gabriel." He asked: 'Is there anyone with you?' Gabriel replied: 'Yes, Muhammad is with me.' He asked: 'Has he been summoned?' Gabriel said: 'Yes.' Then the gate was opened and I found Abraham reclining against the wall of the Sacred House in Heaven (Al Bait Al Ma'mur) into which seventy thousand angels enter every day never to return to it again. Then I was taken to *Sidratul Muntaha* (the remotest Lote Tree), whose leaves were as large as elephant ears and whose fruits were as large as pottery jars. And the Command of Allah covered the Tree with such beauty that cannot be described by a mere mortal. And Allah revealed to me what He willed and then

Allah enjoined fifty prayers on my followers over every day and night. When I returned with this order from Allah, I passed by Moses who asked me: 'What has God enjoined upon your followers?' I replied: 'Fifty prayers.' Moses said: 'Go back to your Lord and seek a reduction (in the number of prayers) for your followers will not be able to bear it. I tried the Children of Israel likewise and they failed.' So I returned to my Lord and I said: O my Lord! Reduce it for my followers. Allah reduced it by five. Then I returned to Moses and told him about it, he said: 'Go back to your Lord and seek a reduction for your followers will not be able to bear it.' So I continued to return to my Lord and then back to Moses until Allah said: 'O Muhammad! These are five prayers for every day and night and each prayer is equal to ten, and so they are all equal to fifty in rewards. Whoever intends to do a good deed but does not do it, I reward him the equal of it. But if he does it, I will record it for him as ten. And whoever intends to commit a sin, but does not do it, nothing will be recorded for him, but if he commits it then it will be recorded as one sin.' I descended until I reached Moses and I told him, so he said: 'Go back to your Lord and ask Him for another reduction. The Messenger of Allah (Peace & blessings of Allah be with him), said: 'I replied, I have been to my Lord (many times) and I feel shy now of asking my Lord again.

52. *Abu Hurayra* reported that the

Messenger of Allah (Peace & blessings of Allah be with him), said: When I ascended (the heavens) I saw Moses- then the Prophet described him as a slim man whose combed hair was neither too straight nor too curly, he resembled those of the tribe of Shanu's- then I looked behind and saw Jesus. Then the Prophet described him as red-complexioned man as if he had emerged from a steamy place- meaning bath. He said: I saw Abraham and I look most like him from (among) those of his descendants. He said: Two vessels were placed before me, one of milk and one of wine. It was said to me 'choose whichever you wish'. So I chose the milk and drank it. Then he said: 'I was guided to choose instinctively. But if you had chosen the wine your followers would have gone astray.

53. It is reported from *Abd Allah ibn Umar* that: One day the Messenger of Allah (Peace & blessings of Allah be with him) told the people about the Antichrist. He said: 'God Almighty is not one eyed, but the Antichrist has a sole eye on the right, his eye is like a floating grape.' He also said that 'I saw a vision in which I saw myself close to the Ka'ba and there was a man there whose complexion was brown, a most handsome man. His locks of hair were falling on his shoulders with water dripping from his head. His hands were placed upon the shoulders of two men, and leaning over their shoulders he was going around the Ka'ba. I asked:

'Who is he?' They said: 'He is Jesus the son of Mary.' Then I saw a man behind him with very curly hair who was blind in his right eye, he resembled Ibn Qatan, the Antichrist. He was circumambulating the Ka'ba with his hands placed upon the shoulders of two men. I asked: 'Who is he?' They said: 'He is the Antichrist.'

54. *Abu Hurayra* reported that the Messenger of Allah (Peace & blessings of Allah be with him), said: I found myself in Hijr, standing in the rocky tract and the Quraysh were questioning me concerning my Ascension to Heaven. They asked me about Bait ul Muqaddas which I was unable to recollect, I was perturbed as never before. Then Allah raised the Grand Mosque before my eyes and I was able to answer their questions. I also saw myself amid a group of Prophets, Moses (peace be upon him) was standing in prayer and he was a robust looking man like the men of the tribe of Shanu'a. I saw Jesus the son of Mary (peace be upon him) standing in prayer, he closely resembled Urwa ibn Mas'ud al Thaqafi and Abraham (peace be upon him) standing in prayer. And the closest to him in resemblance is your companion –(Muhammad). Then the time for prayer was due and I led them, upon completing the prayer a man said: O Muhammad, this is Malik, the Keeper of Hellfire, so greet him.' I turned towards him but he greeted me first.

55. *Abd Allah ibn Mas'ud* is reported to

have said that when the Messenger of Allah (Peace & blessings of Allah be with him), was taken on the Night Journey (ascension to Heaven) his journey terminated at *Sidrat ul Muntaha* (the Farthest Lote Tree) in the sixth Heaven. Everything that ascends from earth is held there and everything that descends from above it is held there. He said: "And the Tree was covered by that which cannot be described." (Q.53: 16) He said: It was golden moths. There the holy Prophet (Peace & blessings of Allah be with him) was given three things: Five prayers, the concluding verses of Surah Al-Baqarah, remission of serious sins for those believers who do not associate Allah with any partners.

56. It is related that *Ibn Abbas* (may Allah be pleased with them) said regarding the revelation: 'The heart (of Muhammad) belied not what he saw ... And certainly he saw him at another time.' (Q.53: 11,13) implies that the holy Prophet saw Gabriel twice in his heart and he had six hundred wings.

57. *Masruq* is reported to have said that: I was reclining in the house of Ayesha (may Allah be pleased with her) when she said: O Abu Ayesha, there are three things which if anyone speaks of, any one of them, he would be fabricating a great slander against Allah.' I asked: 'What are they?' She said: whoever asserts that Muhammad saw his Lord has fabricated a great lie against Allah. He said: I was recli-

ning and so I sat to attention and said: O Mother of the Believers! allow me to take my time, did not God Almighty say: 'And he saw him on the clear horizon.' (Q. 81:23) and 'And certainly he saw him at another time.' (Q.53:13) She replied: I was the first one of this commu-nity to question the Messenger of Allah (Peace & blessings of Allah be with him), about that and he said: That was Gabriel (peace be upon him) and I never saw him fully except on those two occasions, I saw him descending from the heavens and his form filled the space between the earth and the sky.' She also said: 'Have you not heard that Allah said: 'Nor sight can reach Him, but He can reach all sight, He is the Subtle, the All Aware.' (Q.6: 103.) And have you not heard that Allah said: 'And it is not for any mortal that Allah should speak to him, except by revelation, or from behind a veil, or by the sending of a Messenger, to reveal whatever He pleases by His Command, surely He is the Most High, the All Wise.' (Q.42: 51) and she said: Whoever asserts that the Messenger of Allah (Peace & blessings of Allah be with him), has concealed anything from the Book of Allah has invented the greatest lie against Allah Almighty.' Lord has said: O Messenger, convey that which has been revealed to you from your Lord, and if you do not, then you would not have conveyed His Message. And Allah will protect you from the people, and Allah does not guide the unbelieving people.' (Q.5: 67) She said: And whoever asserts that he can tell what will happen tomorrow has invented the greatest calumny against God Almighty. And Allah Almighty has said: 'say, thou (Muhammad) no one knows the Unseen in the heavens and the earth except Allah, and they do not know when they will be raised." (Q.27: 65).

58. It is related that *Abu Musa* said that the Messenger of Allah (Peace & blessings of Allah be with him), was standing amidst us when he mentioned five things to us saying: God Almighty does not sleep, it does not befit Him to sleep, He is the One Who lowers and raises the scales; at night all the days deeds are raised to Him and during the day all the deeds of the night are raised to Him. The Light is His veil, if He were to lift it, the magnificence of His countenance would obliterate His creation to the extent of His vision.

59. *Abu Hurayra* has reported to have said: The people said: 'O Messenger of Allah! Will we see our Lord on the Day of Judgment?' He replied: 'Do You doubt that you will see the full moon on a clear night in the middle of the month?' They replied: 'No, O Messenger of Allah!' Thereafter he said: 'Do you doubt that you will see the sun when there are no clouds?' They replied: 'No.' The holy Prophet (Peace & blessings of Allah be with him), said: 'You will see Him likewise. On the Day of Judgment Allah will gather the people and He will order them to follow what they used to worship.

Thus will some follow the sun, and some will follow the moon, and some will follow those who misled them, and only this community will be left with its hypocrites. God will turn to them in a form they will not recognize and say: 'I am your Lord.' They will say: 'We seek refuge in Allah from you and we shall stay here until our Lord comes to us and when our Lord comes to us we will recognize Him.' Then Allah will turn to them in the form that they will recognize and say: 'I am your Lord.' They will say: 'Yes indeed, You are our Lord.' And they will follow Him. Then Allah will call them and a bridge will be laid across Hell and I shall be the first to cross it with my followers. No one except the messengers will then be able to speak and on that Day they will say: 'O God! Save us, O God! Save us.' There will be hooks like the thorns of Sa'dan in Hell, have you seen the thorns of Sa'dan? The people said: 'Yes, O Messenger of Allah! He said: 'These hooks will be like the hooks of Sa'dan but no one knows how big they are except Allah and they will entangle the people according to their deeds; some of them will fall and stay in Hell forever; others will receive punishment and then get out of Hell, until when God completes His Judgment over His servants and intends mercy on whoever He pleases from the people of Hell, He will order the angels to remove those who worshipped Him alone from the Fire. The angels will recognize them from the traces of their prostration and take them out, as God has not permitted the Hell Fire to consume such traces. Thus will they be removed from the Fire, it will consume their entire bodies except for the traces of their prostrations. They will emerge as mere skeletons, then the Water of Life will be poured upon them and they will bloom like seedlings on the bank on a flowing river. Then when God has completed the Judgment of His servants, a man will remain between Hell and Paradise, he will be the last man from the people of Hell to enter Paradise, as he emerges from the Fire he will say: 'O my Lord! Turn the Fire away from my face as its wind has dried me and its steam has burnt me.' God will ask him: 'If I grant you this favour will you ask for anything else?' Then he will say: 'No by Your Glory! And he will make many promises to God that he will not ask for anything else. God will then turn the Fire away from his face. Then he will be taken towards Paradise and he will see its delights and he will be awed and speechless as God pleases. Then he will say: 'My Lord, let me approach the gates of Paradise.' God will ask him: 'Did you not promise that you would not ask for anything else? Woe to you, son of Adam, how you break your promises!' He will say: 'My Lord! I do not wish to be the most wretched of Your servants.' God will say: 'If I grant you this favour will you ask for anything else?' He will say: "No, by Your Glory! I shall not ask for anything else.' And he will make many promises to God that he will not ask for anything else. God will then allow him to approach the gates of Paradise. When he reaches them and he sees its delights and pleasures he will be awed and speechless as God pleases. Then he will say: 'My Lord, let me enter Paradise.' God will say: 'May God be merciful to you, O son of Adam! How treacherous you are! Did you not make many promises that you would not ask for anything else?' He will say: 'My Lord, I do not wish to be the most wretched of Your servants.' And he will beseech God Almighty until God Almighty laughs at his persistence. Then God will allow him to enter Paradise and will tell him to ask for as much as he wishes. He will do so until he fulfills all his desires. Then God will say: 'Ask for more of anything." And when he fulfills all his desires God will say: 'All this is granted to you and the like of it besides."' It was also related that At'a ibn Yazid said that Abu Said Al Khudri and Abu Hurayra said that God would not refuse him anything he asks. Abu Hurayra said that the Messenger of Allah (Peace & blessings of Allah be with him) said that God Almighty told that man: 'This is for you and the like of it.' Abu Saeed said to Abu Hurayra: 'O Abu Hurayra, God said: 'This is for you and ten times the like of it.' Abu Hurayra said: 'I do not recall the Messenger of Allah (Peace & blessings of Allah be with him) saying other than: 'All this is granted to you and the like of it besides.' Abu Saeed said: 'I bear witness that I recall that I heard the holy Prophet (Peace & blessings of Allah be with him) say: 'This is for you and ten times the like of it'. Abu Hurayra said: That man will be the last man to enter Paradise.

60. It is reported from *Abu Saeed al-Khudri* that the Apostle of Allah (Peace & blessings of Allah be with him) said: The inhabitants of the Fire (of Hell) are those who shall abide in it and indeed they shall neither die nor live. But those who will be punished therein for their sins will be condemned to perish until they will be reduced to ashes, then intercession will be granted them and they will be gathered together and dispersed over the waters of the rivers of Paradise, and it shall be said: 'O dwellers of Paradise pour water over them!' And they shall flourish like seedlings in a downpour.

61. It is reported from *Anas and Ibn Mas'ud* (may Allah be pleased with them) that the Messenger of Allah (Peace & blessings of Allah be with him) said: The last man to enter Paradise will be a man who will walk once and then stumble once and then be burnt by the Fire once, then when he gets beyond it he would turn towards the fires and say: 'Glory to The One Who has saved me from you, God Almighty has bestowed upon me that which He did not bestow to any in former or later times.' Then a tree will be brought before him and he will say: 'O my Lord, permit me to be nearer

to this tree that I may rest beneath its shade and drink its water.' God Almighty will say: 'O son of Adam, if I permit you, you will surely ask for something else.' He will say: 'No, by Your Glory I shall not ask for anything else.' And he will make many promises to God that he will not ask for anything else. So his Lord will pardon him and grant him his desire for what he sees and He will bring him near it, and he will rest beneath its shade and drink its water. Thereafter another tree more beautiful than the first will be brought before him and he will say: 'O my Lord, permit me to be nearer to this tree that I may rest beneath its shade and drink its water.' God Almighty will say: 'O son of Adam, if I permit you, you will surely ask for something else.' He will say: 'No, by Your Glory I shall not ask for anything else.' And he will make many promises to God that he will not ask for anything else. So his Lord will grant him his desire for what he sees and He will bring him near it, and he will rest beneath its shade and drink its water. Thereafter a tree of even greater beauty than the other two will be brought before him at the gate of Paradise and he will say: 'O my Lord, permit me to be nearer to this tree that I may rest beneath its shade and drink its water and I shall not ask You for anything else.' God Almighty will say: 'O son of Adam, did you not promise that you would not ask Me for anything else?' He will say: 'Yes, my Lord, indeed I will not ask You for anything else.' So his Lord will pardon him his temptation for what he cannot resist and He will bring him near to it. When he is brought near it he will hear the voices of the dwellers of Paradise and he will say: 'O my Lord, let me enter it.' God Almighty will say: 'O son of Adam, what will put an end to your desires? Would you be content with the entire world and all that is in it?' He will say: 'O my Lord, do You mock me even though You are the Lord of the Worlds?' Ibn Mas'ud laughed and asked: 'Why don't you ask me what I'm laughing at?' They said: 'Why are you laughing?' He said: 'The Messenger of Allah (Peace & blessings of Allah be with him) laughed likewise.' Then they asked: 'O Messenger of Allah! why are you laughing?' The Great Teacher replied: Because the Lord of the Worlds laughed when the man said: 'O my Lord! Do You mock me even though You are the Lord of the Worlds?' He will say: I am not mocking at you but I can command whatever I please.

62　　*Abu Zubayr* reported that when Jabir ibn Abd Allah was asked about the resurrection he said: "On the Day of Resurrection we will arrive in this manner, see and take heed, concerning those who will be raised up. The people will be gathered together one after the other with all the idols they worshipped. Then God Almighty shall ask: 'Who are you waiting for?' They will say: 'We are waiting for our Lord.' He will say: 'I am

your Lord.' They will say: 'We are unsure until we look at You directly.' And He will appear to them graciously and will go before them and they will follow Him, and all of humanity shall be given a light, and upon the bridge of Hell will be hooks and spikes that will ensnare whoever God pleases. Then the lights of the hypocrites will be extinguished and the believers will be saved, and the first to achieve salvation will be a group of seventy thousand, whose faces will shine with the brightness of the full moon, and they will not be called to render account. Then there will follow after them directly a group of people whose faces will shine as the brightest stars in the heavens. And so on, until the stage for intercession is reached, those who will be permitted to intercede will do so until the one who says: 'There is no god but Allah' and has in his heart goodness equal to the barley grain will be removed from the Fire. Then they will be taken to the courtyard of Paradise and the dwellers of Paradise will sprinkle water over them until they will flourish like seedlings in a downpour and their burnt skins will be restored. They will beseech their Lord until the bounty of the worlds will be granted them and ten times the like of it.

63.　*Yazid al Faqîr* is reported to have said that he had been anxious to learn about an opinion of the Khawarij, so he went along with a group to perform the Pilgrimage to

Makka and to ask the people there about it. He said: "We were passing through Medina where we met Jabir ibn Abd Allah seated beside a column speaking to the people about the Messenger of Allah (Peace & blessings of Allah be with him). When he spoke of the inhabitants of the Fire, I asked: 'O Companion of The Messenger of Allah (Peace & blessings of Allah be with him) what is this you are saying while God Almighty has said: '...Surely whosoever You admit into the Fire, You have indeed brought to disgrace, and there shall be no helper for the evildoers.' (Q. 3: 192) and '... whenever they attempt to come out of it, they shall be driven back to it...' (Q. 32: 20) So what are you saying?' He said: 'Do you read the Qur'an?' I said: 'Yes.' He said: 'Have you heard about the noble rank to which God Almighty will raise Muhammad?' I said: 'Yes.' He said: 'Indeed Muhammad will be raised to a noble rank by which Allah Almighty will permit whoever He pleases to be removed from it. Then he described the Path and how the people will cross it and said: 'I fear I cannot recall everything but I do remember that the people will come out of the Fire after having been in it.' He said: 'They will come out of it looking like the wood of the ebony tree; they will enter a river -one of the rivers of Paradise- and will bathe in it, and then they will emerge as white as paper.

64. *Abu Hurayra* is reported to have said that the Apostle of Allah (Peace & blessings of Allah be with him) one day said: On the Day of Resurrection I will lead mankind, do you know the reason for that. God Almighty will assemble all of humanity of all generations onto one plain on the Day of Resurrection. Then the sound of the proclaimer will be heard by all of them and the sight will penetrate all of them and the sun will come near. The people will be so agonized and fearful that they will not bear it and they will be unable to stand. Some of them will say to each other: 'Look at the anguish we are in, see what (misfortune) has overtaken us.. Look for someone to intercede for us with your Lord.' Some would say: 'Go to Adam.' And they will go to Adam and say: 'O Adam, you are the father of mankind, God created you with His Hand and breathed His spirit into you and commanded the angels to prostrate before you, so intercede for us with your Lord, look at what trouble we are in.' Adam would say: 'Verily my Lord is angry as He has never been before nor will be again. He forbade me to approach the tree and I disobeyed Him, I am fearful for myself, go to someone else, go to Noah. And they will go to Noah and say: O Noah (Nuh) you are the first Messenger sent on earth and God Almighty called you a 'grateful servant', so intercede for us with your Lord, look at what trouble we are going through.' He will say: 'Indeed my Lord is angry as He has never been before nor will be again. There is a curse that originated from me with which I cursed my people. I am fearful for myself. Go to someone else, go to Abraham. They will go to Abraham and say: O Abraham! you are the Messenger of God and the one He called His 'friend' from all the beings of the earth, so intercede for us with your Lord, look at what we are going through.' He will say: 'Indeed my Lord is angry as He has never been before nor will be again. I remember my misconceptions, I am fearful for myself, go to someone else, go to Moses.' And they will go to Moses and say: O Moses! you are the Messenger of Allah, God blessed you with His messages and conversed only with you of all the people. So intercede for us with your Lord, look at what we are going through.' Moses will say to them: 'Indeed my Lord is angry as He has never been before nor will be again. I slew a man without right, I fear for myself. Go to Jesus (peace be upon him).' And they will go to Jesus and say: O Jesus! you are the Messenger of God and you spoke to the people from the cradle, and you are His word which he sent down upon Mary and you are of His spirit, so intercede for us with your Lord, look at what we are going through.' Jesus will say: Indeed my Lord is angry as He has never been before nor will be again - he did not mention any of his sins - I am fearful for myself, I am fearful for myself. Go to someone else, go to Muhammad (Peace & blessings of Allah be with him)' and they will come to me and say: O Muham-

mad! you are the Messenger of Allah and the seal of His Messengers, God forgave you all your former and later sins, intercede for us with your Lord, look at what we are going through.' Then I will go and approach beneath the Throne and fall prostrate before my Lord, then God Almighty will reveal to me and inspire me to praise Him in praises which He has never before revealed, He will say: 'Muhammad, raise thy head and ask and it shall be granted, intercede and intercession will be permitted. I will raise up my head and say: 'O my Lord, my people, my people.' It will be said: 'O Muhammad, bring those of your people who have no account to render by the right gate of Paradise. They would share another door with the people.' The Prophet then said: 'By Him in Whose Hand is Muhammad's soul, the distance between the two doors of Paradise is as great as the distance between Makka and Hajar, or the distance between Makka and Basra.'

65. It is related from *Anas ibn Malik* that the holy Prophet (Peace & blessings of Allah be with him) said: On the Day of Resurrection I will approach the gate of Paradise and will ask for it to be opened, the gatekeeper will say: 'Who are you?' I will say: 'I am Muhammad.' He will say: 'I have been commanded regarding you that I should not open it to anyone before you.'

66. It is reported from *Abu Hurayra* that the Messenger of Allah (Peace & blessings of Allah be with him) said: Every Messenger has a prayer which will be granted and every Prophet would hasten to use his prayer. But I have kept my prayer to intercede for my people on the Day of Reckoning, and it would be granted, if Allah pleases, for everyone of my com-munity who dies without associating any partners with Allah.

67. *Abd Allah ibn Amr* is reported to have said: The Messenger of Allah (Peace & blessings of Allah be with him), recited the words of God Almighty which Abraham said: 'My Lord, they have led many people astray, then whoever follows me he is surely of mine...' (Q.14: 36) and Jesus (peace be upon him) said: 'If You chastise them, they are Your servants, and if You forgive them indeed You are the Almighty, the All Wise.' Then he lifted his hands up and said: 'O Lord, my people, my people' and he wept. So God Almighty said: 'O Gabriel go to Muhammad and ask him -although it is in God Almighty's knowledge-: 'Why do you weep?' Gabriel arrived and asked and the Apostle of Allah (Peace & blessings of Allah be with him), repeated what he had been saying. At this God Almighty commanded Gabriel to tell Muham-mad: 'Indeed We will please you concerning your people and will not disappoint you.'

68. *Abu Hurayra* is reported to have said that: When the verse was revealed 'And warn your nearest relations.' (Q. 26: 214) the Messenger of Allah (Peace & blessings of Allah be with him), summoned the Quraysh and he warned them all, then he warned certain tribes saying: 'O sons of Ka'b ibn Luayy, save yourselves from the Fire, O sons of Murra ibn Ka'b, save yourselves from the Fire, O sons of Abd Shams, save yourselves from the Fire, O sons of Abd Manaf, save yourselves from the Fire, O sons of Hashim, save yourselves from the Fire, O sons of Abd al Muttalib, save yourselves from the Fire, O Fatimah, save yourself from the Fire, for I have no power in anything from Allah except that I keep my bond of relationship with you.

69. *Hussain ibn Abd al- Rahman* has narrated that he was with Saeed ibn Jubair when he asked: 'Which of you saw a shooting star last night?' I said: 'I did.' Then Saeed said: 'I had not been awake at prayer but had been stung by a scorpion.' He said: 'So what did you do?' I said: 'I used magic.' He said: 'What made you do that?' I said: 'Because of the saying which Al Shu'ba related.' He said: 'What did Al Shu'ba relate to you.' I said: 'Buraida ibn Husaib al As'ari related to us, magic is of no use except in the case of envy or the sting of the scorpion.' He said: 'whoever acts according to what he has heard from the Prophet has acted correctly, but Ibn Abbas related that the Apostle of Allah (Peace & blessings of Allah be with him), said: The people were gathered before me and I saw a Messenger and a small group of his

followers with him. And another Messenger with one or two followers with him and yet another without any followers. When a large group was gathered before me I took it to be my community, then it was said to me: 'This is Moses and his people. Look at the horizon', and I saw a multitude. It was said to me: 'Look at the other horizon,' and there was also a multitude. And it was said: 'Look at the far side of the horizon,' and there was also a multitude. It was said to me: 'This is your community, and amongst them are seventy thousand people who will enter Paradise without any reckoning and without any chastisement.' Then he stood up and left to go to his house. The people started to talk about those who will enter Paradise without any reckoning or chastisement. Some of them said: 'may be they are those who were living at the time of the Messenger of Allah.' And others said: 'may be they are those who were born in the times of Islam and who never associated anything with God Almighty.' Others said other things. Then the holy Prophet (Peace & blessings of Allah be with him) came out and said: 'What is it that you are talking about?' They told him and he said: 'They are those who never used magic nor asked others to use it nor did they resort to omens, and they placed all their trust in their Lord.'

70. **Abd Allah ibn Mas'ud** is reported to have said: We were about forty men camped with The Messenger of Allah (Peace & blessings of Allah be with him), when he said: 'Are you not happy that you will amount to one fourth of the dwellers of Paradise?' He said: 'Yes.' He said: 'Are you not happy that you will amount to one third of the dwellers of Paradise?' They said: 'Yes.' At this he said: 'By Him in Whose Hands is my soul, I hope you will amount to one half of the dwellers of Paradise, this is because no one will enter Paradise except a believer and you amount to no more than a white hair on the skin of a black ox or a black hair on the skin of a white ox among the unbelievers.

71. It is related on the authority of **Abu Saeed al- Khudri** that the holy Prophet (Peace & blessings of Allah be with him) said: "On the Day of Resurrection God will say: 'O Adam.' summon the people of the Fire!' Adam will say: 'O God! How many are the people of the Fire?' God will say: 'From every one thousand, take nine hundred and ninety nine.' Then the children will turn white headed, every pregnant female will abort and you will see mankind as if they are intoxicated, but they will not be intoxicated, so awful will be the wrath of God.' The companions of the holy Prophet (Peace & blessings of Allah be with him) said: 'O Messenger of Allah! Who will be the one?' He said: 'Be glad at the good tidings, one person will be from you and one thousand will be from Gogg and Magog.' The holy Prophet (Peace & blessings of Allah be with him), also said: By

Him in Whose Hands is my life, I hope that you will be one-fourth of the people in Paradise. We called out: Allah is Great! and he said: 'I hope you will be one-third of the people of Paradise.' We called out: Allah is Great! and he said: 'I hope you will be one half of the people of Paradise.' We called out: Allah is Great!' He said: 'You are like a black hair on the hide of a white ox or a white hair on the hide of a black ox'.

72. *Musa ibn Sa'ad* Is reported to have said: Abd Allah, the son of Hadrat Umar Farouq visited Ibn Amr to enquire about his health when he was ill. He said: 'Umar why do you not pray to Allah for me?' Abd Allah said: I heard The Messenger of Allah (Peace & blessings of Allah be with him) say: 'Prayer is not accepted without purification, nor is charity accepted from impure wealth, and you were the governor of Basra'.

3

Book of Cleanliness, Purification and Ablution

1. It is reported from *Abu Malik al Ash'ari* that the Messenger of Allah (Peace & blessings of Allah be with him) said: Cleanliness is half of faith and 'Glory be to Allah' and 'Praise be to Allah' fill up what is between the heavens and the earth, and prayer is a light and charity is proof, and fortitude is brightness and the Qur'an is a proof for you or against you. Every man goes out in the morning and pledges allegiance for himself and thereby frees or destroys himself.

2. *Abu Hurayra* is reported to have said that the messenger of Allah (peace & blessings of Allah be with him) had warned that none should urinate in standing position nor wash himself in that position.

3. It is rseported from *Ibn Qatada* that his father told that the Messenger of Allah (Peace & blessings of Allah be with him) said: None of you should hold your organ with your right hand when passing urine, nor wipe yourself with it in the toilet, and you should not exhale into the drinking vessel.

4. It is reported from *Abu Hurayra* that the Messenger of Allah (Peace & blessings of Allah be with him) said: When any of you cleans himself with pebbles he must use an odd number of stones and when any of you performs ablution he must take water into his nose and expel it.

5. *Salman* is reported to have been told that: Your Messenger instructs you on all matters even about defecation? He said: Yes. He has forbidden us to face the Qibla when defecating or passing urine, and forbidden us to cleanse with the right hand or with less than three pebbles, or with dung or bone.

6. *Anas* has related that before the Messenger of Allah (peace & blessings of Allah be with him) used to enter the toilet he used to say: O Allah! I seek refuge in You from all wicked and offensive things.

7. *Abu Ayyub* is reported to have said that the Apostle of Allah (peace & blessings of Allah be with him) said that if anyone of you goes out into an open space to answer the call of nature you should neither face the *Qibla* nor turn your back in the direction of the *Qibla*.

8. *Abu Hurayra* is reported to have narrated that the Messenger of Allah (Peace & blessings of Allah be with him) said: When a servant washes his face every sin he thought of doing will be washed away from his face with the water, or with the last drop of water, and when he washes his hands every sin they committed will be erased from his hands by the water, or with the last drop of water, and when he washes his feet, every sin his feet have walked towards will be washed away with the water, or with the last drop of water, so that he will emerge pure from all sin.

9. According to *Abu Hurayra* the holy Prophet said: The five actions of purification are: circumcision, shaving the pubic hair, cutting the nails, shaving the hair of the armpits and trimming the moustache.

10. It is reported from *Ibn Abbas* that he stayed over one night at the house of the holy Prophet (Peace & blessings of Allah be with him). The Messenger of Allah (Peace & blessings of Allah be with him) left his bed for prayers in the latter part of the night, he went out and looked at the sky and recited: 'Indeed in the creation of the heavens and the earth and in the change of the night and day, there are signs for those who possess intelligence. Those who praise God standing, sitting or lying on their sides, and reflect upon the creation of the heavens and the earth: 'Our Lord, You have not created this in vain, glory be to You! So save us from the chastisement of the Fire.' (Q. 3: 190-191) Then he returned to his house and cleaned his teeth, performed ablution and then offered his prayers. Thereafter he rested upon his bed, and got up once again and looked towards the sky and repeated the same verse, and then returned and cleaned his teeth, performed ablution and offered prayers again.

11. *Hadrat Ayesha* (may Allah be pleased with her) is reported to have said that: Whenever the holy Prophet (Peace & blessings of Allah be with him) returned to his house he always cleaned his teeth. He always began with the right hand in performing ablution and in combing his hair and in putting on his shoes.

12. It is reported from *Abd Allah ibn Zayed al- Ansari*, who was a companion of the Apostle of Allah (Peace & blessings of Allah be with him) that he was asked: Show us how the holy Prophet (Peace & blessings of Allah be with him) performed ablution? He asked for a vessel and poured water from it over his hands and washed them three times, then he rinsed his mouth three times with water; then he drew water into his nose with his hand and exhaled it three times, then he poured water three times up to the elbow, then he wiped his head from front to back with his hands. Then he washed his feet up

to the ankles, and said: This is how The Messenger of Allah (Peace & blessings of Allah be with him) used to perform ablution.

13. It is related by *Abu Hurayra* that the Messenger of Allah (Peace & blessings of Allah be with him) said: When you performs ablution you should wash your nose by taking water into it, and then exhale it out. According to Abu Hurayra the holy Prophet said: When anyone of you awakes from sleep he should exhale from his nose three times as Satan spends the night on his nose. Al-Mujmir said: I saw Abu Hurayra performing ablution, he washed his face very well then he washed his right hand up to his arm, then he washed his left hand up to his arm, and then washed his right leg until the knee and then washed his left leg until the knee and said: This is how I saw the Messenger of Allah (Peace & blessings of Allah be with him) perform ablution. And according to him the holy Prophet (Peace & blessings of Allah be with him) had also said: Your faces, hands and feet will be bright on the Day of Resurrection due to your perfect ablution.

14. *Abu Hurayra* reported that the Apostle of Allah (Peace & blessings of Allah be with him) visited a graveyard and said: Peace be upon you, the resting place of the believers, and we, if Allah wills, shall soon join you. I wish to see my brothers. They said: O Messenger of Allah! are we not also your brothers? The holy Prophet (Peace

& blessings of Allah be with him) replied: You are my companions, and my brothers are those who have not yet come into the world. They said: O Mes-senger of Allah! how will you know the people of your community who have not yet been born? He said: If a man owned some horses which had white marks on their foreheads and whose legs were black, would he be able to recognize his own horses? They said: Yes indeed, O Messenger of Allah! He said: So they will come with white faces and arms and legs from their ablution and I will reach the fountain before them, some will be driven off from my fountain like the stray camel is driven off, and I will call out: 'Come, come.' Then it will be said: These people went astray after you. And I shall say: Go away, go away.

15. It is reported from *Humran*, the servant of Uthman ibn Affan that Uthman ibn Affan asked for a tumbler of water and poured water over his hands and washed them three times and then rinsed his mouth. Then he washed his face three times then he washed his right hand and forearms up to the elbows three times, then he washed his left hand in the same manner, then wiped his head and washed his right foot up to his ankles three times. Then his left foot in the same manner. Then he said: "I have seen The Messenger of Allah (Peace & blessings of Allah be with him) perform ablution in this way and the Messenger of Allah (Peace &

blessings of Allah be with him) said: 'If anyone performs ablution like this and offers two Rak'at in prayer at which they are not distracted then their past sins will be par-doned'.

16. According to *Humran*, his master Uthman ibn Affan told that the Messenger of Allah (Peace & blessings of Allah be with him) said: Whoever performs ablution perfectly as Allah Almighty has ordained then the prescribed prayer wipes out the sins they committed between them.

17. *Uthman* is reported to have said that he heard the Messenger of Allah (Peace & blessings of Allah be with him) say: 'Whoever performs ablution perfectly and then walks to offer the prescribed prayers in congregation or in the mosque, Allah will pardon his sins'.

18. *Abu Hurayra* reportedly said that the Messenger of Allah (Peace & blessings of Allah be with him) said: Shall I tell you the means through which Allah Almighty wipes out sins and raises mankind in rank? They said: Yes, O Messenger of Allah! The holy Prophet said: Performing ablution perfectly in spite of difficulty, walking a distance to the mosque, and waiting for the next prayer after having offered a prayer, such are the means.

19. It is reported from *Anas ibn Malik* that the holy Prophet (Peace & blessings of Allah be with him) performed ablution with one measure

of water and took a bath with up to five measures of water.

20 *Buraida* reported that the holy Prophet (Peace & blessings of Allah be with him) performed all prayers on the day of the Conquest with one ablution, and wiped his socks, so Umar said to him: You have done something today that you have never done before. The Great Seer said: O Umar I did it intentionally.

21. *Uqba ibn Amr* is reported to have heard the Messenger of Allah (Peace & blessings of Allah be with him) say: Any Muslim who performs his ablution perfectly then prays two Rak'at without being distracted, will be granted Paradise. I said: What a good thing I have just heard. And someone who was there before me said: What was said before this was even better. I looked and I saw Hadrat Umar who said: I just saw you arrive, then he said: Anyone of you who performs ablution perfectly and then says: 'I certify that there is no deity but Allah and Muhammad is His servant and Messenger' then eight gates of Paradise will be opened for him and he may enter through any one of them.

22. It is reported from *Hadrat Ali* (may Allah be pleased with him) that: I was a man whose seminal fluid used to discharge frequently and I felt shy to ask the Prophet about it, because I was married to his daughter, so I asked Al Miqdad ibn al- Aswad to ask him for me and

the Messen-ger of Allah (Peace & blessings of Allah be with him) said: He should wash his private parts and perform ablution.

23. It is reported from *Jabir ibn Samura* that a man asked the Messenger of Allah (Peace & blessings of Allah be with him): Do I have to perform ablution after eating lamb?' He replied: If you wish, do so, or if you do not wish, you do not have to. He asked: Do I have to perform ablution after eating camel? He replied: Yes, you should perform ablution after eating camel meat.

24. It is reported that *Umar ibn Abd al-Aziz* said that Abd Allah ibn Ibrahim told him that he found Abu Hurayra performing ablution in the mosque and he said: I am per-forming ablution because I have eaten butter (ghee) and I heard the Messenger of Allah (Peace & blessings of Allah be with him) say: Perform ablution after eating anything touched by fire.

2 *Affan ibn Amr ibn Umayya al Dammri* reported that his father said: I saw the Messenger of Allah (Peace & blessings of Allah be with him) slicing pieces of lamb shoulder and eating it, then the prayer was announced and he put down the knife and led the prayer without performing ablution.

26. *Affan* reported that Abu Musa said: A group of the Muhajirin and the Ansars were disputing regarding bathing, the Ansars said bathing was only obligatory when semen has been emitted. The Muhajirin said

bathing is obligatory if they have been intimate. Abu Musa said: I will find a solution for you both. Then he went to Hadrat Ayesha (may Allah be pleased with her) and sought permission to see her and she permitted him. He asked her: O, Mother of the Believers - I wish to ask you about something but I feel shy. She said: Do not be shy in asking me about something you could ask the mother who gave birth to you. I am your mother. I asked her: What obligates bathing? She replied: you have come to an expert on this. The Messenger of Allah (Peace & bles-sings of Allah be with him) said: If a husband sits between the four parts of his wife and their private parts touch then bathing becomes due.

27. *Ishaq ibn Abu Talha* reportetd that Anas ibn Malik said: Umm Sulaim - the grandmother of Ishaq – visited the Messenger of Allah (Peace & blessings of Allah be with him) while Ayesha was sitting with him, and asked him: O Messenger of Allah! if a woman sees what a man sees in his dream, then does she see for herself what a man sees? Hadrat Ayesha said: O Umm Sulaim, you are humiliating women, may your right hand be covered with dust. The holy Prophet told Ayesha: But it is your right hand that should be covered with dust. Yes, O Umm Sulaim, she should wash when she sees that.

28. *Maimuna*, the wife of the holy Prophet (Peace & blessings of Allah be with him) is reported to have

said that: I prepared water for the Messenger of Allah (Peace & blessings of Allah be with him) to bathe for Janaba (ritual impurity), he washed his hands two or three times, then he poured water over his private parts and washed them with his left hand, then he rubbed his hands well. Thereafter he performed ablution for prayers and poured three handfuls of water over his head and washed all of his body, then he washed his feet, and when I came to him with the towel and he refused it.

29. *Abu Sayeed al-Khudri* reported: the Apostle of Allah (Peace & blessings of Allah be with him) observed: Bathing is obligatory in case of seminal emission.

30. *Abu Hurayra* reported that the Messenger of Allah (Peace & blessings of Allah be with him) said: The people of Bani Israel used to bathe naked in full sight of each other. Moses (peace be upon him) used to bathe alone. They said: 'By God! Nothing prevents Moses from bathing with us except that he has a scrotal hernia.' So once Moses went out to bathe and put his clothes over a stone and then the stone rolled off with his clothes. Moses followed the stone saying: 'my clothes, O stone! My clothes, O stone! Until the people of Bani Israel saw him and said: 'By God, Moses has no imperfection in his body.'

31. It is reported on the authority of *Abu Sayeed al- Khudri* that the Messenger of Allah (Peace &

blessings of Allah be with him) said: A man should not look at the private parts of another man and a woman should not look at the private parts of another woman, and a naked man should not hug another naked man, and a naked woman should not hug another naked woman. (that is, the private parts of a man must not touch the private parts of another man and the private parts of a woman must not touch the private parts of another woman.)

32. *Hadrat Ayesha* (may Allah be pleased with her) is reported to have said: When the Messenger of Allah (Peace & blessings of Allah be with him) was in a state of *Janaba* (impurity) and wanted to eat or sleep, he used to perform ablution first.

33. *Abd Allah ibn Abu Qais* is reported to have said that: I asked Hadrat Ayesha (may Allah be pleased with her) What did the holy Prophet do when he was in a state of *Janaba*, did he used to wash before he slept or sleep before he washed?' She said: 'He used to do all of that, sometimes he washed and slept and sometimes perfor-med ablution and slept.'

34. *Abu Sayeed al- Khudri* is reported to have quoted the Messenger of Allah (Peace & blessings of Allah be with him) as having said: If anyone of you is intimate with his wife and wishes to return to do the same again he should perform ablution.

35. Hadrat *Ayesha* is reported to have

narrated that: We set off with the Messenger of Allah (Peace & blessings of Allah be with him) on one of his journeys until we reached Al-Baida or Dhat-al-Jaish, where my necklace was lost. The Messenger of Allah (Peace & blessings of Allah be with him) stayed on to search for it, and so did other companions with him. There was no water at that place so the people went to Abu Bakr al- Saeed and said: 'Look at what Ayesha has done, she has made the Messenger of Allah and others stay where there is no water and they have no supplies of water with them.' Abu Bakr came while the Apostle of Allah (Peace & blessings of Allah be with him) was asleep with his head resting upon my thigh, he said to me: 'you have kept the holy Prophet (Peace & blessings of Allah be with him) and the companions where there is no water and they have no supplies of it with them.' Thus he admonished me and slapped me on my flank. Nothing kept me from moving from the pain but the presence of the Messenger of Allah (Peace & blessings of Allah be with him) upon my thigh. The Messenger of Allah (Peace & blessings of Allah be with him) rose up at daybreak and there was no water. So Allah revealed the verses of Tayammum and they all performed ablution without water. Thereafter the camel on which I was riding moved from its place and the necklace was discovered beneath it.

36. **Abu Hurayra** is reported to have

met the Messenger of Allah (Peace & blessings of Allah be with him) on the way to Medina when he was in a state of impurity and he withdrew himself away and bathed. The holy Prophet (Peace & blessings of Allah be with him) looked for him and when he found him he said: O Abu Hurayra! where were you? He replied: O Messenger of Allah! when I met you I was unclean and I did not like to sit in your presence before bathing myself. The Apostle of Allah said: All praise be to Allah, indeed a believer is never unclean.

37. **Thabit** reported that Anas said: The Jews did not eat with women when they had their menses, nor did they live with them in their houses, so the companions of the Messenger of Allah (Peace & bles-sings of Allah be with him) asked the Prophet about it and Allah revealed: 'And they ask you about menstruation, say: 'It is a harm.' So keep away from women during their menstru-ation, and do not approach them until they become clean, so when they have cleansed themselves, then approach them as Allah has com-manded you. Surely Allah loves those who repent, and He loves those who are always pure.' (Q.2: 222). The Great Seer (Peace & blessings of Allah be with him) said: You may have contact except intercourse.

38. **Hadrat Ayesha** (may Allah be pleased with her) is reported to have said that Asma, the daughter of Shakal, asked the Messenger of Allah (Peace & blessings of Allah be

with him) regarding cleansing after menstruation. The holy Prophet (peace & blessings of Allah be with him) replied: You all should use water mixed with leaves of the Lote tree and wash yourselves well, and then pour water over your heads and rub it well until it reaches the roots of your hair, then pour water over it. Following that you should put musk in a piece of cotton and cleanse yourselves with it. Asma asked: How should she cleanse herself with it? The Messenger of Allah (Peace & blessings of Allah be with him) said: Praise be to Allah, she should cleanse herself with it. Ayesha said quietly that she should wipe away the traces of blood with it. Then Asma asked regarding bathing in the state of Janaba.. The Great Teacher replied: She should take water and cleanse herself well and complete ablution and rub her head well until the water reaches the roots and then pour water over herself. Ayesha said: It is good that the women of the Ansars are not too shy about learning about their religion.

39. *Abu Hurayra* is reported to have narrated that: When the Apostle of Allah (Peace & blessings of Allah be with him) was in the mosque he said: O Ayesha fetch me that garment. She said: I have my menses. He said: Your menses are not on your hands. And so she fetched his clothes for him.

40. *Hadrat Ayesha* is reported to have said that the Messenger of Allah (Peace & blessings of Allah be with him) used to rest on her lap even when she had her menses, and he would recite the Qur'an.

41. *Umm Salama* is reported to have said that when she was lying on a bedcover with the Messenger of Allah (Peace & blessings of Allah be with him) she began to menstruate, so she slipped away and put on the clothes for menses. The Apostle of Allah (Peace & blessings of Allah be with him) asked her if she was having her menses? She answered in the affirmative then he called her and she lay down with him on the bedcover. She is also reported to have said that the Messenger of Allah (Peace & blessings of Allah be with him) used to bathe from the same container with her after they had been intimate.

42. *Hadrat Ayesha* is reported to have said that: I used to drink (water) when I had my menses and then I would give the vessel to the holy Prophet (peace & blessings of Allah be with him) and he would put his mouth where my mouth had been and drink from it, and I used to eat meat from a bone when I had my menses and then give it to the Prophet and he would put his mouth where mine had been.

43. *Mu'athah* is reported to have said that: I asked Hadrat Ayesha why the menstruating woman has to recompense for fasting she missed but not for prayer? She said: It used to happen to us and we used to be ordered to recompense for our fasts and we were never ordered to recompense for prayers.

44. *Hadrat Ayesha* reported that the Messenger of Allah (Peace & blessings of Allah be with him) said: The ten actions of purification are: trimming the moustache, letting the beard grow, using *miswak* (tooth stick), aspi-rating water into the nose, cutting the nails, washing the finger nails, shaving the hair of the armpits, shaving the pubic hair.

45. *Ibn Umar* reported that the Messenger of Allah (Peace & blessings of Allah be with him) said: Distinguish (yourself) from the unbelievers by trimming your moustaches and letting your beards grow.

46. It is reported that *Anas ibn Malik* said: A period of time has been set for us in which we should trim our moustaches, cut our nails, pluck the hair under our armpits and shave our pubic hair, which should not exceed forty nights.

47. *Asma ibn Abu Bakr* is reported to have narrated that a woman came to the holy Prophet and asked if the menstrual blood stains our garments what should we do? The Apostle of Allah (peace & blessings of Allah be with him) said: Rub it first, then rub it with your hands under the water, and then dry it.

48. It is reported that Hadrat *Ayesha* said that the Apostle of Allah (Peace & blessings of Allah be with him) used to remember Allah at all moments.

49. *Abu Bakr* and *Ibn Umar* reported that Maimuna said that her freed slave girl was given a goat in charity but it died. The Messenger of Allah (Peace & blessings of Allah be with him) passed by it and said: Why do you not skin its hide? You could then tan it and use it. They replied that it was dead. The Great Master said: It is only prohibited to eat it.

50. It is narrated on the authority of *Abd Allah ibn Mughaffal* that the holy Prophet (Peace & blessings of Allah be with him) ordered the killing of dogs and then later he permitted the dogs that were used in hunting and the dogs that guard the flocks of sheep and goats and he is reported to have said that if a dog has licked a plate, wash it seven times and then rub it with sand and wash it for the eighth time.

4

Book of
Invitation to Prayers

1. *Abd Allah Ibn Umar* is reported to have said: When the Muslims first arrived in Medina they used to gather for the prayers and ask about the time it was due. At that time the practice of calling to prayer had not been introduced. On one occasion they discussed this problem, some of them suggested that they use a bell like the Christians, other proposed the use of a trumpet like the horn used by the Jews, but Umar was the first to suggest that a man should call for prayer, so the Messenger of Allah (Peace & blessings of Allah be with him) requested Hadrat Bilal to summon people to prayers.

2. It is reported that *Abu Mahthura* said that the holy Prophet (peace & blessings of Allah be with him) taught him the following call for prayer: Allah is Great, Allah is Great, I bear witness that there is no deity but Allah, I bear witness that there is no deity but Allah, I bear witness that Muhammad is the Messenger of Allah, I bear witness that Muhammad is the Messenger of Allah, then he repeated, I testify

that there is no deity but Allah, I testify that there is no deity but Allah, twice, I bear witness that Muham-mad is the Messenger of God, I bear witness that Muham-mad is the Messenger of Allah, twice, come to prayer, twice, come to prosper, twice." Ishaq, the son of Ibrahim, added, Allah is the Greatest, Allah is the Greatest, there is no deity but Allah."

3. It is reported from *Ibn Umar* that the Apostle of Allah (Peace & blessings of Allah be with him) had two muaddhins Abd Allah Ibn Umm Maktum, who was blind and Hadrat Bilal to perform the duty of summoning people to prayer.

4. *Anas ibn Malik* has reported that: "The Messenger of Allah (Peace & blessings of Allah be with him) would launch an attack against the enemy at dawn. And he would stop if he heard the call to prayer, otherwise he would continue to attack.

5. *Abu Hurayra* is reported to have said that the holy Prophet (peace & blessings of Allah be with him) said:

When the call to prayer is pronounced Satan takes to his heels and passes wind noisily as he flees in order not to hear the call to prayer. When the call to prayer is completed he returns and then takes to his heels once more when the Iqama is pronounced and when it is completed he returns to whisper into the hearts of the people to distract them from their prayer and he makes them recall things they had forgotten and thus causes them to lose count of their prayers.

6. *Isa ibn Talha* is reported to have said that he was sitting with Mu'awiya ibn Abu Sufyan when the caller pronounced the call to prayer. Mu'awiya said: I heard the Messenger of Allah (Peace & blessings of Allah be with him) say: Those who call to prayer will have the longest necks on the Day of Resurrection.

7. It is reported from *Abd Allah ibn Amr ibn al- A'as* that the Messenger of Allah (Peace & blessings of Allah be with him) said: When you hear the call to prayer, repeat the words, then invoke blessings upon me, for everyone who invokes blessings upon me will be granted ten blessings from God, then beseech God Almighty to reward me with a place in Paradise which will be given to only one of the servants of God, and I hope to be that one. And whoever beseeches God Almighty for that he will be certain of my intercession for him.

8. *Umar ibn al- Khattab* is reported to have said that the Messenger of Allah (peace & blessings of Allah be with him) said: When the caller says: 'Allah is Great, Allah is Great,' you should repeat: 'Allah is Great, Allah is Great,' and when he says: 'I bear witness that there is no god but Allah,' you should repeat: 'I testify that there is no god but Allah.' And when he says: 'I testify that Muhammad is the Messenger of Allah,' you should repeat: 'I testify that Muham-mad is the Messenger of Allah. When the he says: 'Come to prayer,' you should respond 'There is no strength or power but with Allah,' and when he says: 'Come to prosper,' you should respond: 'There is no strength or power but with Allah.' And when he says: 'Allah is the Greatest, Allah is the Greatest,' you should repeat: 'Allah is the Greatest, Allah is the Greatest.' And when he says: 'There is no god but Allah,' anyone of you who responds from his heart 'There is no god but Allah,' will be admitted to Paradise.

9. It is related from Sa'ad ibn Abu Waqqas that the Messenger of Allah (Peace & blessings of Allah be with him) said: If any one of you hears the caller pronouncing the call to prayer and says: 'I bear witness that there is no god but Allah, and that Muhammad is His servant and His Messenger, and that I am content with Allah as my Lord, with Muhammad as Mes-senger (of Allah) and Islam as my Religion,' his sins will be blotted out.

5

Book of Prayers

1. It is reported from *Anas ibn Malik* that a bedouin came and asked the holy Prophet (peace & blessings of Allah be with him): 'O Muhammad! Your emissary came to us and asserted that you claim that Allah has sent you?' He replied: 'He was truthful.' The bedouin asked: 'Who created the heavens?' He replied: 'Allah.' The bedouin asked: 'Who created the earth?' He replied: 'Allah.' The bedouin asked: 'Who created these mountains and what is in them?' He replied: 'Allah.' The bedouin asked: 'By The One Who created heavens and earth and created these mountains, did Allah send you?' He replied: 'Yes.' The bedouin asked: 'Your emissary asserts that there are five prayers due upon us in a day and night?' He replied: 'He was truthful.' The bedouin asked: 'By The One Who has sent you, did Allah command you with that?' He replied: 'Yes.' The bedouin asked: 'The emissary asserts that obligatory charity is due from our wealth?' He replied: 'He was truthful.' The bedouin asked: 'By The One Who has sent you, did Allah command you with that?' He

replied: 'Yes.' The bedouin asked: 'Your emissary asserts that we have to fast the month of Ramadan every year?' He replied: 'He was truthful.' The bedouin asked: 'By The One Who has sent you, did Allah command you with that?' He replied: 'Yes.' The bedouin asked: 'Your emissary asserts that we have to perform the pilgrimage to the House if we are able.' He replied: 'He was truthful.' Then he left saying: 'By The One Who sent you with the Truth, I will do no more nor less than that.' The holy Prophet (peace & blessings of Allah be with him) remarked: If he is true to his word he will be admitted to Paradise.

2. It is related that *Umar ibn Ruwaiba* claimed that his father said: "I heard The Messenger of Allah (Peace & blessings of Allah be with him) say: 'whoever offers prayer before sunrise and before sunset will not enter the Fire. A man from Basra asked: 'Did you hear that from the Messenger of Allah (Peace & blessings of Allah be with him)?' He said: 'Yes.' The man said: 'I bear

witness that I heard it from The Messenger of Allah (Peace & blessings of Allah be with him) my ears heard it and I kept it in my heart."

3. *Abu Bakr ibn Abu Musa al Ash'ari* is reported to have said that his father said that he heard the Messenger of Allah (Peace & blessings of Allah be with him) say: Who-ever observes the two prayers at the two cool hours will be admitted to paradise.

4. *Hadrat Ayesha* is reported to have said that: The Messenger of Allah (Peace & blessings of Allah be with him) did not neglect the two Rak'at after the afternoon prayer and that he said: 'Do not pray at the time of sunrise and at the time of sunset'.

5. *Anas ibn Malik* is reported to have narrated that: We used to offer the midday prayer with the Messenger of Allah (Peace & blessings of Allah be with him) when the heat was at its greatest, but some of us found it difficult to touch the ground with our foreheads, so we would spread out a garment and prostrate upon it.

6. *Abu Basra al-Ghafari* is reported to have narrated: The Messenger of Allah (Peace & blessings of Allah be with him) led us in the afternoon prayer and then said: This prayer was prescribed for those before you, but then abandoned. So whoever establishes it has a double reward and there is no prayer after it until the star has risen.

7. It is reported from *Abd Allah ibn Umar* that the Messenger of Allah (Peace & blessings of Allah be with him) said: Whoever intentionally misses the afternoon prayer, it is as if he has lost his family and his property.

8. *Abd Allah ibn Mas'ud* is reported to have said that the unbelievers delayed the Messenger of Allah (Peace & blessings of Allah be with him) from offering the afternoon prayer until the sun was red or yellow. The holy Prophet (Peace & blessings of Allah be with him) reportedly said: 'They have prevented us from offering the afternoon prayer, may God fill their stomachs and their graves with Fire.' Or he said: 'May God pack their stomachs and their graves with Fire'."

9. It is reported from *Abu Hurayra* that the Messenger of Allah (Peace & blessings of Allah be with him) forbade prayer after the afternoon (salat al-Asr) prayer until the sun had set and after the dawn (salat al-Fajr) prayer until the sun had risen.

10. *Abu Salaam* is reported to have asked Hadrat Ayesha about the two Rak'at that the Messenger of Allah (Peace & blessings of Allah be with him) used to offer after the afternoon prayer. She said: He used to offer them before the afternoon prayer then something kept him busy, or he forgot, so he offered them after the afternoon prayer thereafter he continued to do so, as he always liked to continue whatever he had established for himself.

11. *Anas ibn Malik* was reportedly

asked about voluntary prayer after the afternoon prayers, and he said: Umar used to punish those who used to pray after the afternoon prayer, and during the time of the Messenger of Allah (Peace & blessings of Allah be with him), we used to offer two Rak'at after sunset before the sunset (Maghrib) prayer.' So it was asked: 'Did the Messenger of Allah (Peace & blessings of Allah be with him) offer them?' He said: He used to see us offering them and he neither forbade us nor enjoined it upon us.

12. *Hadrat Ayesha* is reported to have said: The Prophet (peace & blessings of Allah be with him) once delayed the evening prayer until the people had left him and those in the mosque had slept, then he went out to pray and said: 'If I did not found it difficult for my followers I would have ordered them to pray the sunset prayer at this time.

13. *Abd Allah ibn Mas'ud* is reported to have asked the holy Prophet (Peace & blessings of Allah be with him) which deed is the dearest to God? The Messenger of Allah (peace & blessings of Allah be with him) replied: To offer the prayers at their due times. I asked: 'What is the next?' He replied: To be good and dutiful to your parents. I asked again: 'What is the next?' He replied: To strive in the way of Allah.

14. *Abu Hurayra* is reported to have said that the Messenger of Allah (Peace & blessings of Allah be with him) said: Whoever offers one Rak'at of prayer at its due time has been rewarded for the whole prayer.

15. *Abu Qatada* is reported to have narrated that the Messenger of Allah (Peace & blessings of Allah be with him) assembled us and said: You will journey this evening and night and you will reach near the water in the morning, God willing. So the people set off and Abu Qatada said: While the Messenger of Allah (Peace & blessings of Allah be with him) was riding through the night I was beside him and he slept, I saw him leaning sideways upon his mount so I tried to support him without disturbing him until he was sitting upright. We continued on until we were well into the night, I saw him leaning sideways upon his mount again so I tried to support him without disturbing him until he was sitting upright. We continued on until we reached the end of the hour of Sahr, then he leaned more than before until he almost slipped from his mount, so I went to him and supported him and he raised his head and asked: 'Who is that?' I said: 'I am Abu Qatada.' He asked: 'How long have you been at my side?' I said: 'Throughout the night.' He said: 'May God support you for supporting His Prophet.' Then he asked: 'Are we within sight of the people, do you see anyone?' I said: 'I can see a rider here and another there until we were about seven riders together.' The Messenger of

Allah (Peace & blessings of Allah be with him) went off the road to lie down to sleep and said: 'Do not let us miss our prayers.' Then the Messenger of Allah (Peace & blessings of Allah be with him) was the first one to awake with the sun on his back. We arose startled and he said: 'Mount.' So we journeyed on until the sun had fully risen, then he dismounted and asked for the water jar I had with me. He performed ablution and a little water remained in it, then he said to Abu Qatada: 'Keep your jar it will one day be the talk of the people.' Then Bilal pronounced the call to prayer and the holy Prophet (Peace & blessings of Allah be with him) offered two Rak'at and then offered the dawn prayer as usual. The holy Prophet (Peace & blessings of Allah be with him) then rode on and we rode along with him, and each of us was whispering to the other: 'How will we make up our missed prayers?' At this he said: 'why do you not take example from me? There is nothing wrong in sleeping, but the negligence is on the one who does not offer prayer at its due time and delays it until the time of the next prayer is due. So whoever misses a prayer from sleeping should pray it as soon as he awakes. And the following day he should offer it at its due time. He asked: 'What do you think the people will do when they find their Prophet not there in the morning.' So Abu Bakr and Umar said that the Messenger of Allah (Peace & blessings of Allah be with him) is still with you and he would not abandon you. But some of the people said: 'The Messenger of Allah (Peace & blessings of Allah be with him) is ahead of you.' So if you obey Abu Bakr and Umar you would have done the right thing. So we went on until we reached the people and it had become hot, and they said: 'O Messenger of Allah we are thirsting to death.' At this the Apostle of Allah (Peace & blessings of Allah be with him) said: 'You will not die.' Then he said: 'Fetch me my small cup and bring me the jar of water.' He began to pour the water into the cup and Abu Qatada passed it from one to the other to drink. When they saw that the water in the jar would not be sufficient for them all they rushed towards it, the holy Prophet (Peace & blessings of Allah be with him) said: 'Do not rush, each of you will get to drink, so they held back, while the Apostle of Allah (Peace & blessings of Allah be with him) continued pouring the water and I served them until no one remained except the holy Prophet (Peace & blessings of Allah be with him) and myself. He filled the cup and told me to drink.' I said: 'O Messenger of Allah, I will not drink before you.' At this he said: 'The one who serves the people is the last one of them to drink.' So I drank and the Messenger of Allah (Peace & blessings of Allah be with him) drank too and the people reached the watering place with comfort.'

16. *Hadrat Ayesha* is reported to have related that the holy Prophet (Peace

& blessings of Allah be with him) prayed in a square garment that had a pattern. During the prayer he looked at its pattern. So when he finished praying he said: 'Take this garment of mine to Abu Jam ibn Hudhaifa and bring me his garment that is without a pattern; as it has distracted my attention from the prayer.

17. *Abu Zarr* is reported to have asked the Messenger of Allah (Peace & blessings of Allah be with him) 'Which was the first mosque to be established on the earth?' He replied: 'The sacred Mosque.' I asked: 'Which one was next?' He replied: 'Al Aqsa Mosque.' I asked: 'How many years had been between the two?' He said: 'Forty years, and wherever you may be and if the prayer is due, pray at any mosque.'

18. *Anas ibn Malik* has reportedly narrated that when the Messenger of Allah (Peace & blessings of Allah be with him) arrived in Medina he stayed in the heights of Medina among the Bani Amr ibn Auf tribe. He rested there for fourteen nights, then he sent for Bani An- Najjar and they came armed with their swords. I remember that the Prophet (Peace & blessings of Allah be with him) was mounted upon his she-camel with Abu Bakr behind him and all the An-Najjar around him until he dismounted in the courtyard of Abu Ayyub's house. The Messenger of Allah (Peace & blessings of Allah be with him) used to love to pray wherever he was when the time for prayer was due,

even in the sheep pens. Later on he ordered a mosque to be built and summoned some of the Bani An-Najjar people saying: 'O Bani An-Najjar! Tell me the price of this piece of your land.' They replied: 'No, by God! We do not seek its price from God!' Anas added: 'There were the graves of some pagans in it and part of it was unleveled with some date-palms in it.' So the holy Prophet (Peace & blessings of Allah be with him) ordered the palm trees to be cut and the graves of the pagans to be removed and the unleveled land be leveled. They aligned the felled date palms along the *Qibla* of the mosque and they constructed two stone-walls on the sides. His companions carried the stones while reciting a rhyme. The Messenger of Allah (Peace & blessings of Allah be with him) was with them in saying: "There is no goodness except that of the Hereafter, O God! So please forgive the Muhajirin and the Ansars."

19. *Abu Salama ibn Abd al- Rahman* is reported to have narrated that Abd al- Rahman ibn Abu Saeed al-Khudri visited him and Abu Salama asked him: Have you heard what your father said about the mosque which is founded upon piety? He replied: My father said: I went to visit the Messenger of Allah (Peace & blessings of Allah be with him) at the house of one of his wives, and I asked him: O Messenger of Allah! which of the two mosques was founded upon piety? The holy

Prophet (Peace & blessings of Allah be with him) took a handful of pebbles and threw them at the ground and said: It is your mosque, the Mosque of Medina.

20. *Ibn Abbas* is reported to have related that a woman promised that if God Almighty relieved her of her pain she would pray at Al Aqsa Mosque. So when she was relieved she readied herself to travel, Maimuna, the wife of the holy Prophet came to greet her, and she informed her about it. Then Maimuna told her: 'Stay and eat what you have prepared for your journey and pray in the Mosque of the Prophet as I have heard him say: 'One prayer in it is one thousand times better than prayer in any other mosque except the Grand Mosque of Makka.'

21. It is reported that *Mahmoud ibn Labid* said that when Uthman ibn Affan intended to rebuild the Mosque the people disliked his intention and wished that it should be left as it was. So he said: "I heard the Messenger of Allah (Peace & blessings of Allah be with him) say: 'Whoever builds a mosque, God will build for him a similar place in Paradise'."

22. *Abu Hurayra* reportedly quotes the Messenger of Allah (Peace & blessings of Allah be with him) as having said: The places most liked by God Almighty are the mosques, and the places most disliked by God Almighty are the markets.

23. *Ubayy ibn Ka'b* is reported to have

narrated that one of the Ansars whose house was located at the farthest side of Medina never missed any prayer in the company of the Messenger of Allah (Peace & blessings of Allah be with him). We felt sympathy for him and said: 'If only you had a donkey you would not have to walk upon the scorching sand. He said: 'By God, I would not want my house to be closer to the house of the Messenger of Allah (Peace & blessings of Allah be with him).' I was angered at his words and told the holy Prophet what he had said. He summoned him and he repeated the same to him and told him that he was hoping for a reward for his long walk. The holy Prophet said to him: Indeed you will be rewarded with what you hoped for.

24. *Abu Hurayra* is reported to have said that the Messenger of Allah (Peace & blessings of Allah be with him) said: Whoever washes (performs ablution) in his house and then walks to a house of the houses of God to fulfill an obligation of the obligations of God, for every footstep he takes, a sin is blotted out and he is raised in rank.

25. *Zainab al Thaqafiyah* reportedly said that the Messenger of Allah (Peace & blessings of Allah be with him) said: If any one of you visits a mosque, she must not use perfume.

26. *Abu Humaid* or *Abu Saeed* reported that the Messen-ger of Allah (Peace & blessings of Allah be with him) said: When any of you enter the

mosque you should recite the following prayer: 'Please God open for me the gates of Your Mercy.' And when he leaves he should pray: 'Please God I ask You of Your Bounty.'

27. *Abu Qatada* is reported to have said that he entered the mosque while the holy Prophet (Peace & blessings of Allah be with him) was seated with the people, so he sat down, and the Apostle of Allah (Peace & blessings of Allah be with him) asked him: 'What prevented you from offering two Rak'at before you were seated?' Abu Qatada said: 'O Messenger of Allah, I saw you sitting with the people.' He said: 'when any of you enter a Mosque he should not be seated before he prays two Rak'at.'"

28. It is reported from **Umar ibn al-Khattab** that the holy Prophet (Peace & blessings of Allah be with him) said during the battle of Khyber: Whoever eats this herb - meaning garlic- must not come to the mosques.

29. *Jabir ibn Abd Allah* is reported to have said that the Messenger of Allah (Peace & blessings of Allah be with him) said: Whoever eats garlic or onion must keep away from us, or keep away from our mosques and he should stay in his house.

30. *Abu Talha* is reported to have said that Hadrat Umar ibn al- Khattab delivered the Friday sermon and said: I had a vision in which I saw a cock pecking me three times and I think my life is ending. Some people

have suggested that I should appoint a successor. By The One Who has sent His Prophet, if I am to die soon, the Caliphate will be decided by this Council (shura) of six with whom the Messenger of Allah (Peace & blessings of Allah be with him) was well pleased until he passed away. And I know there are people who plot against this Religion and I have fought them in the cause of Islam. If they continue in that they are the enemies of God and unbelievers who lead people astray. Then he said: 'O God, I ask You to be my witness over the rulers of the regions, I only appointed them to rule in justice, and to teach the people their Religion and the ordinances of the Prophet, and to share their booty with them and to ease their difficulties. O people, you eat two plants in which I see nothing bat evil, these are the onion and garlic, and I saw the Messenger of Allah (Peace & blessings of Allah be with him) ordering the eviction of anyone who smelt of them from the mosque to Al-Baqi. (The cemetery of the people of Medina) So whoever eats them he should first reduce them to nothing in cooking.

31. *Abu Hurayra* is reported to have narrated that the Messenger of Allah (Peace & blessings of Allah be with him) said: Whoever hears a man announcing in the mosque that he has lost something, should say: 'May God never enable you to find it,' the mosques were not established for that purpose.

32. It is reported from **Hadrat Ayesha**

and *Abd Allah ibn Abbas* that: When during the last illness of The Messenger of Allah (Peace & blessings of Allah be with him) (his condition) wor-sened he suddenly covered his face with his woolen wrap until, when he felt short of breath, he lifted it from his face and said: 'May Allah curse the Jews and the Christians because they took the graves of their prophets as places of prayer.' The holy Prophet (Peace & blessings of Allah be with him) was warning the Muslims about what the Jews and the Christians had done.

33. Hadrat *Ayesha* is reported to have related that Umm Habiba and Umm Salama mentioned having seen pictures in a church in Ethiopia. They informed the holy Prophet (Peace & blessings of Allah be with him) of it and he said: 'whenever a religious person dies people build a place of worship at his grave and draw such pictures upon it. On the Day of Resurrection they will be the most despicable of beings in the sight of God."

34. *Abu Hurayra* is reported to have narrated that the Messenger of Allah (Peace & blessings of Allah be with him) said: "Six things were bestowed upon me which were not bestowed on any prophet before me; I have been sent with the most concise expressions having the greatest meanings, I have been made victorious by casting terror into my enemy, war spoils have been made lawful to me, the earth has been made as a place of prayer

and purification, I have been sent to all mankind, and I am the seal of the Prophets."

35. It is related that *Abu Zarr* said that the Messenger of Allah (Peace & blessings of Allah be with him) said: "If any of you stands to pray and another man is standing in front of you in prayer then he is your cover. But if there is no one in front of you then your prayer would be annulled if a donkey, woman or a black dog passes in front of you." It was asked: "O Abu Zarr, what is the difference between a black dog or a red dog or a yellow dog?" He said: "O son of my brother, I asked the Messenger of Allah (Peace & blessings of Allah be with him) the same question and he said: 'the black dog is Satan."

36. It is reported that when it was mentioned to Hadrat *Ayesha* that three things_ dog, donkey and woman annul prayer she is reported to have remarked: You have compa-red us to donkeys and dogs, by God, I saw the Messenger of Allah (Peace & blessings of Allah be with him) praying while I was lying on my bed between him and the Qibla, and I did not move so as not to disturb the Messenger of Allah (Peace & blessings of Allah be with him) so I used to slip away by the side of his feet.

37. It is reported that the holy Prophet (Peace & blessings of Allah be with him) prayed facing Bait al-Muqad-das for sixteen months until the verse in Surah Al-Baqarah was revealed: "...Turn your faces in the direction of the Sacred Mosque and wherever you are turn you faces towards it..." (Q. 2: 144) It was revealed after the Prophet had offered his prayers.

38. *Abu Hurayra* is reported to have said that the holy Prophet (Peace & blessings of Allah be with him) said: "When the Iqama is pronounced no prayer is to be offered except the prescribed prayer."

39. *Jabir ibn Samura* is reported to have said: Bilal used to pronounce the call to prayer when he saw the sun disappear. But he never pronounced the Iqama until the Prophet came out (from his apartments). Whenever he saw him coming out he would pronounce it.

40. *Abu Musa* is reported to have said: The Messenger of Allah (Peace & blessings of Allah be with him) used to look at their feet as they stood aligned in rows and say: 'Straighten the rows and do not differ or your hearts will differ, and let the row closest to me be of those who are more knowledgeable. Then after them those with less knowledge and so on.'

41. *Abu Hurayra* is reported to have said that the holy Prophet (Peace & blessings of Allah be with him) said: Had the people known what is in the call to prayer and in the first row, they would have drawn lots for it. And if they had known what is the reward for the midday prayer, they would have raced for it. And if they had known the reward for the night and dawn prayers in congregation they would have joined them even if they led to crawl.

42. *Abu Hurayra* reported that the Messenger of Allah (Peace & blessings of Allah be with him) said: The best row for men in prayer is the first row and the least is the last one. And the best row for women in prayer is the last row and the least is the first.

43. *Ibn Umar* is reported to have said that the Messenger of Allah (Peace & blessings of Allah be with him) used to lift both his hands up to the height of his shoulders when opening the prayer and when he said 'Allah is Great' upon bowing. When he lifted his head after bowing he did the same. But he did not use to do that when prostrating.

44. *Hadrat Ayesha* is reported to have related that: The Messenger of Allah (Peace & blessings of Allah be with him) used to commence the prayer by pronoun-cing 'Allah is Great' and by reciting: 'All praise be to Allah, The Lord of the Worlds.' And when he bowed he did not lower his head exceedingly nor raise it up, but held it straight. And when he raised his head after bowing he never prostrated until he had stood upright fully, and when he raised his head after prostration he did not prostrate for the second time until he had sat upright. He used to recite 'at-Tahiyat' after every two Rak'at, and he used to sit upon his left leg with the sole of his right foot facing upwards. He used to forbid resting the buttocks upon the ground. And he also forbade the forearms from touching the ground as the lion sits. He used to end the prayer by pronouncing 'Peace be upon you.'

45. *Abu Hurayra* is reported to have narrated that: When the Messen-ger of Allah (Peace & blessings of Allah be with him) used to stand up during the prayer he would say 'Allah is Great' and the same upon bowing, then as he straightened from bowing he used to say 'Allah hears those who praise Him.' Then as he stood upright he said: 'Our Lord all praise is due to You'. Then he said 'Allah is Great' when he fell in prostration. Then he said 'Allah is Great' when he lifted his head up. Then he said 'Allah is Great' in the second prostration.

46. *Abu Hurayra* is reported to have related that the Messenger of Allah (Peace & blessings of Allah be with him) used to teach us saying: 'Do not be in advance of the Imam in your prayers, when he says 'God is Great' then you repeat it after him, and when he says 'nor those who go astray' then you say 'Amen.' When he bows then you bow, and when he says 'God hears those who praise Him' then you say 'Our Lord all praise is due to You.''

47. *Anas ibn Malik* narrated that the holy Prophet (Peace & blessings of Allah be with him) rode a horse and fell and his sight side was injured. So we went to visit him and the prayer became due so he led us in prayer seated and we prayed behind him seated. When he finished the prayer he said: 'The Imam should be followed, when he pronounces 'Allah is Great' then you repeat 'Allah is Great' and when he prostrates then you prostrate and when he rises up then you rise up and when he says 'Allah hears those who praise Him', then say 'Our Lord all praise is due to You.' And if he prays seated then you all pray seated."

48. It is reported from *Hammad* that he saw the Prophet (Peace & blessings of Allah be with him) raise his hands at the start of his prayer and pronounce 'Allah is Great' - Hammad said: "He raised his hands to the level of his ears" - then he wrapped his garment around him and placed his right hand over his left hand. When he made a bow he used to remove his hands from his garment and raise them up, then he pro-nounced 'Allah is Great' and bowed. When he said: 'Allah hears those who praise Him' he lifted his hands and when he prostrated he prostrated between his palms."

49. It is reported from *Ali ibn Abu Talib* that when the Messenger of Allah (Peace & blessings of Allah be with him) used to stand up for prayers he used to say 'I turn my face towards The One Who has created the heavens and earth in perfection and I am not of the polytheists, indeed my prayer and my offerings, my life and my death are to Allah, The Lord of the

Worlds, no partner has He. With this I was commanded and I am a Muslim. O Allah, You are The King, there is no god but You, You are my Lord and I am Your servant, I wronged myself and I confess my sins, so forgive me all my sins, indeed no one forgives sins except You, guide me to the best behaviour, no one can guide to the best of it but You, and turn the evil away from me, as no one can turn the evil away from me but You. I am at Your command and at Your pleasure, all goodness is in Your hands and the evil is not for You, I am from You and to You, Blessed and Exalted I seek Your forgiveness and repent to You.' And when he bowed down he said: 'O Allah to You I bow and I believe in You and to You I submit my hearing, my sight, my brain, my bones and my nerves all humble themselves to You. And when he rose up from bowing he said: 'My Lord all praise is due to You, filling the heavens and the earth and what is in between them and filling whatever You please after them.' And when he prostrated he said 'O Allah, to You I prostrate and in You I believe, and I submit to You, my face has prostrated to The One Who created and shaped me, and Who created my hearing and sight, blessed be Allah, The Best Creator' And finally between his testimony and his salutation he said: 'O Allah forgive me my former and later sins, and what I have concealed and what I have revealed, and

what I have been excessive in and what You know of me, You are the First and the Last, there is no god but You.'

50. It is reported from *Anas* that one day the Messenger of Allah (Peace & blessings of Allah be with him) drifted into a meditative state as we sat around him. Then he raised his head up smiling and we asked: 'O Messenger of Allah what makes you smile?' He said: 'A Surah has just been revealed to me.' Then he recited: 'In the Name of Allah, the Merciful, the Compa-ssionate, indeed We have given you 'Al Kauthar' (Heavenly Fountain) So pray to your Lord and sacrifice to Him * Surely he who hates you, is the one cut off.' (Q. 108) Then he said: 'Do you know what Al Kauthar is?' We said: 'Allah and His Messenger know best.' He said: It is a river my Lord, Most High, Exalted, promised me, it has much goodness and from it my community will drink on the Day of Judgment. The number of its drinking vessels is about the number of the stars. When one of them is driven away I will say: 'My Lord! He is of my community,' Allah Almighty would say 'you do not know what they did after you.'

51. *Abu Hurayra* is reported to have narrated that the holy Prophet (Peace & blessings of Allah be with him) said: Whoever offers any prayer without reciting 'The Opening' of the Qur'an in it, his prayer is lacking" It was said to Abu Hurayra: 'But we are led by the Imam.' He replied: 'Recite it by yourself, I have heard the Messenger of Allah (Peace & blessings of Allah be with him) say: 'Allah, Most High, Exalted said: 'The prayer is divided between Me and My servant and My servant receives what he asks for, when a servant says 'All praise be to Allah the Lord of the Worlds' God Almighty says 'My servant has praised Me' and when He says 'The Merciful, the Compassionate' God High Exalted says 'My servant has thanked Me' and when he says: 'Master of the Day of Judgment' God Almighty says 'My servant has glorified Me' - and once it was said: 'My servant has submitted to Me - and when he says 'You Alone do we worship, and You Alone do we turn to for help' God Says: 'This is between Me and My servant, and to My servant is what he asks for.' And when he says 'guide as to the Righteous Way, the way of those You have favored, not the way of those who earn Your wrath, not of those who go astray.' Allah says: 'this is to My servant and to My servant is what he asks.'"

52. *Abu Hurayra* is reported to have quoted the holy Prophet (Peace & blessings of Allah be with him) as having said: "Say, 'Amen' when the Imam pronounces it and if the 'Amen' of any one of you is spoken simultaneously with that of the angels then all his past sins will be forgiven."

53. *Anas ibn Malik* is reported to have related that: One day the Messen-

ger of Allah (Peace & blessings of Allah be with him) led us in prayer and when he had finished the prayer he turned towards us and said: "O people, I am your Imam, so do not bow or prostrate ahead of me nor precede me in standing and turning your faces, for I see you before me and behind me.' Then he said: 'By Him in Whose Hand is the soul of Muhammad, if you could see what I see you would have laughed only a little and wept a great deal.' They asked: 'O Messenger of Allah, what do you see?' He said: 'Paradise and Hell.'

54. *Hadrat Ayesha* is reported to have narrated that the Messenger of Allah (Peace & blessings of Allah be with him) often used to say when he bowed and prostrated: 'Glory be to You, O Allah, our Lord, and praise be to You, O Allah, forgive me.' In accordance with what is prescribed in the Qur'an."

55. It is reported from *Ibn Abbas* that: The Messenger of Allah (Peace & blessings of Allah be with him) drew back the curtain (of his apartments) and saw the people aligned in rows behind Abu Bakr, he said: 'There will be no more Revelation after this except for good visions which a Muslim may see or that may be shown to him, and I have been forbidden from reciting the Qur'an while bowing or prostrating, so when you bow you should glorify the Lord Most High, Exalted, and when you prostrate do your utmost in sincere suppli-

cation, it maybe that your supplication will be accepted.

56. It is reported from *Abu Saeed al-Khudri* that: When the Messenger of Allah (Peace & blessings of Allah be with him) used to raise his head after bowing he used to say: "Our Lord all praise is due to You, filling the heavens and the earth and what is in between them, and filling whatever You please after that. You are the Worthy of All Praise and Glory, most worthy of what a servant says - we are all Your servants - no one can withhold what You give and no one can give what You withhold, and wealth will in no way avail its possessor, wealth is from You alone.

57. It is reported from ibn *Abu Talha* that: I met Thauban, the freed slave of the Messenger of Allah (Peace & blessings of Allah be with him) and asked him to tell me of a deed I could do by which God would admit me to Paradise. He said: 'I asked The Messenger of Allah (Peace & blessings of Allah be with him) about that and he told me: 'Prostrate frequently before Allah Almighty as when you prostrate before Allah Almighty, for each prostration Allah will raise you up by one rank, and will blot out one of your sins. Ibn Abu Talha said: 'I met Abu Darda' and I asked him the same question, and he told me the same thing that Thauban had told me."

58. *Abu Hurayra* is reported to have narrated that the Messenger of Allah (Peace & blessings of Allah be with him) said: The closest a servant of Allah comes to his Lord is when he is prostrating, so increase your supplications at that time.

59. *Ibn Abbas* is reported to have related that: The holy Prophet (Peace & blessings of Allah be with him) said: I have been commanded to prostrate on seven bones, on the forehead, with the tip of the nose, and both hands, both knees and the toes of his feet.

60. *Anas* is reported to have related that: The holy Prophet (Peace & blessings of Allah be with him) said: Straighten up properly in your prostration and never put your forearms on the ground like a dog.

61. *Abd Allah ibn Malik* is reported to have reported that: When The Messenger of Allah (Peace & blessings of Allah be with him) used to prostrate he outstretched his hands from the armpits until I could see their whiteness.

62. *Abd Allah ibn Zubair* is reported to have narrated that his father said: When The Messenger of Allah (Peace & blessings of Allah be with him) used to sit in prayer, he used to put his left foot between his thigh and stretched his right foot and placed his left hand upon his left knee and his right hand upon his right thigh and lifted his finger.

63. *Abu Darda* is reported to have related that: The Messenger of Allah (Peace & blessings of Allah be with him) rose up to pray and we heard him say: 'I seek refuge in Allah from you', then he said: 'I invoke (for you) the curse of Allah.' He repeated this three times and stretched out his hand as if he was grasping at something. When he finished the prayer we asked: O Messenger of Allah! we heard you say something in your prayer which we never heard you say before, and we saw you stretching your hand.' He said: 'The enemy of God came with fire pointing at my face, so I said: 'I seek refuge in Allah from you,' three times then I said 'I invoke Allah's full curse' three times, but he did not withdraw, so I tried to seize him, but, by God, had it not been for the prayer of our brother Solomon, he would have been tied up and turned into a plaything for the children of Medina.

64. *Abd Allah ibn Zayed* is reported to have related that he was shown the call to prayer in a dream, that Mas'ud Al Ansari said: We were sitting in the company of Sa'ad ibn Ubada when the Messenger of Allah (Peace & blessings of Allah be with him) joined us. Bashir ibn Sa'ad said: O Messenger of Allah! God has commanded us to seek blessings upon you. How should we do that?' The holy Prophet remained silent and we wished he had not asked him.' Then the Messenger of Allah (Peace & blessings of Allah be with him) said: 'Say 'O Allah, bless Muhammad and the household of Muhammad as You blessed the household of Abraham, grant favour upon Muhammad and the household of Muhammad as You granted favour upon the household of Abraham in the world. You are Worthy of All Praise and Glory', and the salutation which you know."

65. *Abu Hurayra* is reported to have related that the Messenger of Allah (Peace & blessings of Allah be with him) said: Whoever praises Allah at the end of every prayer thirty three times and thanks Allah thirty three times and pronounces 'Allah is Great' thirty three times, this would be ninety nine and the completion of one hundred is to say 'There is no deity but Allah, all worship is due to Him Alone, to Him is the Dominion and all praises is for Him and He has power over all things,' his sins will be blotted out even if they were as much as the foam upon the ocean.

66. *Abu Mas'ud* is reported to have related that the Messenger of Allah (Peace & blessings of Allah be with him) said: The one who is most learned in the Book of Allah should be the Imam, but if they are equally learned in reciting it, then the one who is most learned in the Sunna, and if they are equally learned in the Sunna, then the one who emigrated first, and if they emigrated at the same time, then the one who was the first to embrace Islam. No one should lead the prayer in a place where another has authority, or set up his place of honor in his house except by his permission.

67. *Abu Musa Al Ansari* is reported to have narrated that: A man visited the holy Prophet (Peace & blessings of Allah be with him) and said: 'I avoid the dawn prayer because of so and so, as he detains us too long in it. I had never seen the Messenger of Allah (Peace & blessings of Allah be with him) admonish so angrily as he did on that day, he said: 'O people! Some of you are hindering the others, so whomsoever leads the people in prayer, he must be brief, for behind him are those who are weak or elderly and others have business to attend to.

68. *Ubayd Allah ibn Abd Allah* is reported to have narrated: I went to see Hadrat Ayesha and I asked her: 'Would you please tell me about the illness of the Messenger of Allah (Peace & blessings of Allah be with him).' She said: 'Yes, when the Prophet (Peace & blessings of Allah be with him) became gravely ill and he asked whether the people had prayed, we replied: 'No, O Messenger of Allah! They are waiting for you.' He said: 'Fill a tub of water for me.' Ayesha said:' we did so and he bathed in it and tried to get up but fainted. When he regained consciousness he again asked whether the people had prayed, we said: 'No, they are waiting for you Messenger of Allah.' He again said: 'Fill a tub of water for me.' He sat down and bathed in it again and tried to get up but fainted once again. Then he regained consciousness and enquired if people had prayed. We replied: 'No, they are waiting for you O Messenger of Allah.' He said: 'Fill a tub of water for me.' Then he sat down and bathed in it and tried to get up but he fainted. When he revived, he asked: 'Have the people prayed?' We said: 'No, they are waiting for you, O Messenger of Allah!' The people were in the mosque waiting for the Prophet (Peace & blessings of Allah be with him) to lead the evening prayer. The apostle of Allah (Peace & blessings of Allah be with him) sent for Abu Bakr to lead the prayer. The messenger went to Abu Bakr and said: 'The Messenger of Allah (Peace & blessings of Allah be with him) requests you to lead the prayer.' Abu Bakr asked Umar to lead the prayer, but Umar replied: 'your right to lead is more than mine. So Abu Bakr led the prayer that time. When the holy Prophet (Peace & blessings of Allah be with him) had recovered a little, he came out for the noon prayer aided by two people one of whom was Al Abbas. Abu Bakr was leading the prayer and when he saw The Prophet (prayers & peace be upon him) he moved to make place for the holy Prophet but the Apostle of Allah (Peace & blessings of Allah be with him) signaled for him to continue and sat beside Abu Bakr.. Abu Bakr was following The Prophet (Peace & blessings of Allah be with him) and the people were following Abu Bakr as the Prophet (Peace & blessings of Allah be with him) prayed sitting down.' Ebbed Allah said: 'I went to see Abd Allah ibn Abbas and related to him what

Ayesha had told me about the illness of the Messenger of Allah (Peace & blessings of Allah be with him). He did not deny any of it except that he asked: 'Did she name the man who was with Al Abbas?' I said: 'No.' He said: 'He was Ali (may Allah be pleased with him).

69. *Abu Hurayra* is reported to have narrated that a blind man visited the holy Prophet and said: 'O Messenger of Allah, I have no one to guide me to the mosque.' The Messenger of Allah (Peace & blessings of Allah be with him) gave him permission to pray in his house. So as he was leaving he called him back and asked him: 'Do you hear the call to prayer?' He said: 'Yes.' Then he said: 'you must respond to it.'"

70. The Messenger of Allah (Peace & blessings of Allah be with him) is reported to have said: The congregational prayer is better than the prayer offered alone by twenty five times.

71. *Abu Hurayra* reported that the Messenger of Allah (Peace & blessings of Allah be with him) said: The reward of the prayer of a man in congregation is twenty five times more than that of the prayer offered alone in one's house. This is because if you perform ablution and do it perfectly and then set off for the mosque with the sole intention of praying, for every step you take towards the mosque, you are upgraded by one degree of reward and one sin is blotted out from your record until you enter the mosque. When you enter the mosque and you offer the prayer the angels continue to seek God's Blessings and forgiveness for you as long as you stay in the place of prayer. And one is consi-dered in prayer for as long as you are waiting for the prayer.

72. *Abd al-Rahman ibn Abi Amr* is reported to have related that: Uthman ibn Affan entered the mosque after the sunset prayer and sat alone. I sat beside him and he said: 'O son of my brother, I have heard the Messenger of Allah (Peace & blessings of Allah be with him) say: Whoever offers the eve-ning prayer in congregation it will be counted for him as if he had stood half the night in prayer, and whoever offers the dawn prayer in congregation it will be counted for him as if he had stood the whole night in prayer'.

73. *Abu Hurayra* is reported to have related that the Messenger of Allah (Peace & blessings of Allah be with him) said: The most difficult prayers for the hypocrites are the night and dawn prayers. Had they known what is their reward, they would have attended them even if they had to crawl. And I was almost going to order the prayer to begin and order a man to lead the people in prayer, while I was going to go with a group of people to those who were not attending the prayer and set their houses on fire.

74. *Abd Allah ibn Mas'ud* is reported to

have said that the holy Prophet (Peace & blessings of Allah be with him) told people who did not attend the Friday prayer: I was almost going to order someone to lead the people in prayer and then go and burn the houses of those who were absent from the Friday prayer.

75. *Jabir* is reported to have related that the Messenger of Allah (Peace & blessings of Allah be with him) was asked: 'which prayer is the best?' He said: The one that you perform in humble submission.

76. *Mu'awiya ibn Al Hakam* is reported to have related that: While I was praying with the Messenger of Allah (Peace & blessings of Allah be with him) a man sneezed. I said: 'May Allah have mercy upon you.' The people looked at me and indicated for me to be quiet so I remained quiet. When the Messenger of Allah (Peace & blessings of Allah be with him) finished his prayer, he did not blame me nor hit me, but he said: 'This is prayer, so it is not fitting for people to speak during it, but it is for praising and glorifying Allah and for reciting Qur'an.' I said: 'O Messen-ger of Allah! I am newly in Islam and Allah Almighty has revealed Islam to us, and among us are soothsayers.' He said: Do not go to them.

77. *Zayed ibn Arqam* is reported to have said that: We used to speak during the prayers; a man spoke to his friend while he stood next to him in prayers until the verse was revealed: '...And stand in a devout manner before Allah' (Q. 2: 238) Then we were commanded to be silent and were forbidden from speaking during the prayers.

78. *Abu Hurayra* is reported to have related that: The Messenger of Allah (Peace & blessings of Allah be with him) said that people should desist from gazing at the sky during the prayers, otherwise they may lose their sight.

79. *Busr ibn Saeed* is reported to have related that according to Abu Juhaim the Messenger of Allah (Peace & blessings of Allah be with him) said: If a person passes in front of another person in prayer knew the magnitude of his sin, he would prefer to wait for forty years rather than pass in front of him." According to Abu al- Nadr: "I do not remember whether he said forty days, months or years.

80. *Abu Saleh* is reported to have related on the authority of Abu Saeed al- Khudri: I heard The Messenger of Allah (Peace & bles-sings of Allah be with him) say: If any of you are praying behind some object as a marker and someone tries to pass in front of you, then you should push him aside and, if he refuses, you should use force against him for he is a Satan.

81. *Talha ibn Abd Allah* is reported to have said that: We used to pray and (sometimes) animals used to pass in front of us, so we mentioned this to the Mes-senger of Allah (Peace &

blessings of Allah be with him) and he said: 'You should put something such as the back of a saddle, in front of yourself, then the one who passes in front of you will not harm you'.

81. **Ibn Umar** is reported to have related that: On the day of Feast when the Messenger of Allah (Peace & blessings of Allah be with him) went out to pray he would arrange a spear to be placed in front of him, and the people prayed behind him. He also used to do that during his journeys and so many amirs (Rulers) continued to do the same after him.

82. It is reported from **Ibn Umar** that the holy Prophet (Peace & blessings of Allah be with him) used to place his she camel in front of himself, and then pray facing it.

83. **Ibn Abu Zulhaifa** is reported to have said that his father saw the Messenger of Allah (Peace & blessings of Allah be with him) in a red leather tent, and saw Bilal bringing water for ablution. Then he saw the people vying with each other to take the water that the Prophet had used for his ablution. Whoever took some wiped it over him and the one who could not get any would wipe his hands with the hands of those who had. Then he saw Bilal bring out a staff and placing it into the ground. Then the Messenger of Allah (Peace & blessings of Allah be with him) came out hurriedly wearing a red garment and led the people in prayer facing the staff and

I saw the people and animals passing in front of the staff.

84. **Abu Hurayra** is reported to have related that the holy Prophet (Peace & blessings of Allah be with him) forbade a man to pray with his hands on his waist.

85. **Abu Saeed al- Khudri** is reported to have related that the Messenger of' Allah (Peace & blessings of Allah be with him) said: If any one of you yawns during his prayer let him stifle it as much as he can, as Satan enters. It is also related: Let him cover his mouth with his hand to prevent Satan from entering.

86. **Abu Qatada al Ansari** is reported to have related that he saw the holy Prophet (Peace & blessings of Allah be with him) leading the prayer while Umama, the daughter of Abu al As and Zainab the daughter of the Messenger of Allah (Peace & blessings of Allah be with him), was sitting upon his shoulders, when he bowed he put her down and when he rose up from prostration he lifted her up.

87. **Abd Allah ibn Abbas** is reported to have said that: "I saw Abd Allah ibn al Harith praying with his hair plaited behind him. So I undid it for him. When he finished his prayers he went to Ibn Abbas and asked him: 'What is wrong with my hair?' He replied: 'I have heard the Messenger of Allah (Peace & blessings of Allah be with him) say: The one who prays with plaited hair is like the one who prays while he is tied with a rope.

88. *Anas ibn Malik* is reported to have related that the Messenger of Allah (Peace & blessings of Allah be with him) said: If dinner is served when the prayer is due then eat before you pray the sunset prayer. And do not eat in haste.

89. *Abu Saeed al- Khudri* reported that the Messenger of Allah (Peace & blessings of Allah be with him) said: If any of you have doubts concerning your prayer, and do not remember if you prayed three or four (Rakahs), you should cast away your doubt by completing your prayer. Then offer two prostrations before ending the prayer.

90. *Ibn Umar* is reported to have said that: When the holy Prophet (Peace & blessings of Allah be with him) used to recite the Qur'an he recited a Surah which contained a prostration and he would prostrate and we all used to do likewise to the point that some of us were unable to find a place to perform it.

91. It is reported from *Hafsa* that the Messenger of Allah (Peace & blessings of Allah be with him) used to offer two brief Rak'at when call to prayer for the dawn prayer was pronounced.

92. *Hadrat Ayesha* (may Allah be pleased with her) is reported to have related that the holy Prophet (Peace & blessings of Allah be with him) said: The two Rak'at of the dawn prayer are better than this life and all that it in it.

93. *Jabir ibn Samura* is reported to have said that the holy Prophet (Peace & blessings of Allah be with him) never used to leave the place where he prayed the dawn prayer until the sun had risen, he used to leave after the sun had risen.

94. *Hadrat Ayesha* is reported to have said that the Messenger of Allah (Peace & blessings of Allah be with him) never prayed the forenoon prayer, but I used to. He used to refrain from doing a good deed even though he wished to do it, out of fear that people might make it an obligatory act for themselves.

95. *The holy Prophet* (peace & blessings of Allah be with him) is reported to have said that each one of you has to do an act of charity every morning, every glorifi-cation of Allah Almighty is charity, and every praise of Allah Almighty is charity, and every pronunciation of there is no god but Allah is charity, and every pronunci-ation of God is Great is charity, and every enjoining to good is charity, and every forbidding of evil is charity, and the highest reward of these are the two Rak'at of the forenoon prayer.

96. It is related from *Abu Hurayra* that: My friend (the holy Prophet) advised me to do three things; to fast for three days every month, to offer the forenoon prayer and to pray before going to sleep.

97. *Abu Hurayra* is reported to have narrated that the Messenger of Allah (Peace & blessings of Allah be with him) said: When the son of Adam recites 'The Prostration' and then he prostrates, Satan runs away weeping saying: 'O woe to me, the son of Adam was commanded to prostrate and so he prostrated, and he will be rewarded with Paradise, while I was commanded to prostrate but I refused and I shall be condemned to the Fire.

98. *Umm Habiba*, the wife of the holy Prophet, is reported to have said that she heard the Messenger of Allah (Peace & blessings of Allah be with him) say: Every Muslim who prays to God twelve Rak'at every day other than the obligatory prayer, God will build for him a house in Paradise. Or A house will be built for him in Paradise. Umm Habiba said: So I have never stopped praying them since.

99. *Abd Allah ibn Mughaffal al-Muzni* is reported to have said: The Messenger of Allah (Peace & blessings of Allah be with him) said: There is a prayer between the call to prayer and the Iqama, there is a prayer between the two calls to prayer. Then as he repeated it a third time he added: For the one who wishes to pray.

100. *Ibn Umar* is reported to have said that: I prayed with the Messenger of (Peace & blessings of Allah be with him) two Rak'at before the midday prayer and two after it. And two Rak'at after the sunset prayer and two after the evening prayer. And two after the Friday prayer. But the two Rak'at after sunset, night and Friday prayers, I prayed with the Prophet in his house.

101. *Abd Allah ibn Shaqiq* is reported to have said that: I asked Hadrat Ayesha (may Allah be pleased with her) about the prayers of the Messenger of Allah (Peace & blessings of Allah be with him) and she said: He used to offer four Rak'at in my house before the midday prayer, then he would go out and lead the congregation, then he returned and prayed two Rak'at. Then he used to lead the congre-gation in the sunset prayer and then return and offer two Rak'at. Then he led the congre-gation in the evening prayer and offered two Rak'at at home. He used to perform nine Rak'at at night one of which was Witr. And he used to pray at night for a long time standing and sitting, he used to recite the Qur'an standing, and then used to bow and then prostrate. When the dawn prayer was due he used to offer two brief Rak'at before going to the mosque.

102. *Zayed ibn Thabit* is reported to have said that the Messenger of Allah (Peace & blessings of Allah be with him) screened off an area for himself in the Mosque with date palm leaves. He went inside to pray and people followed him to pray with him. Next night they waited for him but the Messenger of Allah (Peace & blessings of Allah be with him) did not come out so they called out to him and

threw small stones at his door. The Messenger of Allah (Peace & blessings of Allah be with him) came out and angrily said: Because you have been doing this constantly I thought that this might be taken to be obligatory, so offer your prayer in your houses, for the prayer offered in the house is better, except for the prescribed prayers.

103. *Jabir* is reported to have said that the Messenger of Allah (Peace & blessings of Allah be with him) said: Establish your prayer in the mosque but offer some of your prayers at home, as God Almighty blesses the house in which prayer is offered.

104. *Anas ibn Malik* is reported to have said that: The Messenger of Allah (Peace & blessings of Allah be with him) said: you should pray for as long as you feel able and when you feel tired you should be seated (and pray).

105. *Hadrat Ayesha* is reported to have related that the Messenger of Allah (Peace & blessings of Allah be with him) said: Perform deeds that you are able to do regularly; God does not stop rewarding you until you cease.

106. *Ibn Abbas* is reported to have related that he slept one night in the house of the holy Prophet and saw him offer thirteen Rak'at before going off to sleep. Before dawn Bilal told the Prophet (Peace & blessings of Allah be with him)

of the approach of the dawn prayer, and the Prophet (Peace & blessings of Allah be with him) offered the dawn prayer without renewing his ablution. He used to say in his invocation: 'O God! Let my heart have light, and my sight have light, and my hearing have light, and let me have light on my right and light on my left, and have light above me, and have light beneath me, and have light before me and light behind me, and let me have light.

107. *Hadrat Ayesha* is reported to have said that when The Messenger of Allah (Peace & blessings of Allah be with him) used to stand for offering the night prayer, he would begin his prayer with two brief Rak'at.

108. *Ibn Abbas* is reported to have related that: When the Messenger of Allah (Peace & blessings of Allah be with him) stood up at night to offer the night prayers, he used say: 'O Allah! All praise is due to You, You are the Light of the heavens and the earth. All praise is due to You. You are the Master of the heavens and the earth. All praise is due to You. You are the Lord of the heavens and the earth and all that is in them. All praise is due to You. You are the Truth and Your promise is true, and Your word is the Truth and the meeting with You is true. And Paradise is true, and Hell is true. And the Hour is true. O Allah! I submit to You, I believe in You and depend upon You. And repent before You, and with Your help I confront those who reject (Your Message). And I take You as the Judge. Forgive me my past and future sins. And whatever I have concealed or revealed. You are my Allah, there is no deity but You.

109. Hadrat *Ayesha* is reported to have related that the Messenger of Allah (Peace & blessings of Allah be with him) used to offer thirteen Rak'at during night prayer, five of them in Witr, when he did not sit except towards the end.

110. *Hadrat Ayesha* is reported to have related that: I never saw the Messenger of Allah (Peace & blessings of Allah be with him) reciting the night prayers sitting except when he was in his old age and then he used to recite while sitting, and when-ever he wanted to bow he would get up and recite thirty or forty verses and then bow down.

111. Hadrat *Ayesha* reported that the holy Prophet (Peace & blessings of Allah be with him) said: If any of you feels sleepy during the prayer, he should sleep until he feels refreshed. Be-cause if any of you prays while he is sleepy he might mistakenly insult himself instead of seeking forgiveness.

112. Abu Hurayra reported that: The holy Prophet (Peace & blessings of Allah be with him) said: Satan ties three knots at the back of the head of the one who sleeps. Upon each knot he reads and blows the words: 'The night is long so remain sleeping.' When one wakes up and remem-bers God, one knot is untied, and when one performs ablution the second knot is untied, and when one prays the third knot is untied, and then one rises up with energy and in good spirit, failing this one gets up lethargic and in a bad mood.

113. *Jabir* is reported to have said that he heard the Apostle of Allah (Peace & blessings of Allah be with him) say that there is an hour in the night in which if any Muslim asks Allah for something good for this life or the Hereafter, Allah will grant it to him. And it is in every night.

114. *Abu Hurayra* is reported to have related that the Messenger of Allah (Peace & blessings of Allah be with him) said: Allah Almighty, glory be to Him, descends every night to the nearest heaven while the last third of the night still remains and says: 'I am The Lord, I am The Lord, is there anyone to invoke Me so that I may respond to his invocation? Is there anyone to ask Me so that I may grant him his request? Is there anyone who seeks My forgiveness so that I may forgive him?' And He continued to say this until the light of the dawn appeared.

115. *Hadrat Ayesha* is reported to have related that the Messenger of Allah (Peace & blessings of Allah be with him) used to offer the Witr prayer at different times of night, at the beginning of the night, in the middle of the night and up to the last hour of the night. He used to end his Witr at al-Sahar (predawn).

116. *Jabir* is reported to have related that the Messenger of Allah (Peace & blessings of Allah be with him) said: The one who fears he may miss the end of the night should offer his Witr prayer at the beginning of the night, and the one who hopes to offer Witr prayer at the end of the night, let him do so, as the prayer of the pre-dawn is witnessed, and that is better for you.

117. It is reported by *Abu Saeed al-Khudri* that the holy Prophet said: Offer Witr prayer before the dawn.

118. *Hadrat Ayesha* is reported to have related that the Messenger of Allah (Peace & blessings of Allah be with him) used to go out after the middle of the night and offered prayer in the mosque and the people at the mosque prayed too. In the morning the people talked about it and many more gathered there the following night and when the holy Prophet (Peace & blessings of Allah be with him) came out and prayed they prayed too. On the third night the mosque was filled with people, the Messenger of Allah (Peace & blessings of Allah be with him) came out and prayed and they also prayed. On the fourth night the mosque could not contain the number of people who came to pray, so the Messenger of Allah (Peace & blessings of Allah be with him) did not come out. Some people called out to him but he did not go out to the mosque until the dawn prayer was due. When he had finished the dawn prayer, he turned to the people and said: I know what you wished to do last night but I feared that the night prayer may become obligatory upon you then you would be unable to offer it.

119. *Abu Hurayra* is reported to have said that the Messenger of Allah (Peace & blessings of Allah be with him) used to urge the people to offer the night prayer during Ramadan, and he used to say to them: Whoever stands to offer the night prayer in Ramadan, seeking God's pleasure, all his former and later sins will be forgiven. After the holy Prophet (Peace & blessings of Allah be with him) left for his heavenly abode this practice continued after him until the beginning of the Caliphate of Hadrat Umar.

6

Book of Friday Prayers

1. *Abu Hurayra* is reported to have said that the Messenger of Allah (Peace & blessings of Allah be with him) said: "We are the last (community) but we will be the first on the Day of Judgment and we will be the first to enter Paradise although other communities were given the Scripture before us and we were given it after them. But they differed, so God guided us with the Truth about which they disputed. They were commanded to celebrate this day but they differed among themselves about it. So God guided us to it. He said: "Friday, is for us and tomorrow is for the Jews and after tomorrow is for the Christians."

2. *Abu Hurayra* is reported to have related that the holy Prophet (Peace & blessings of Allah be with him) said: "The best day upon which the sun rises is Friday, on that day Adam was created, and on it Adam was admitted to Paradise, and on it he was expelled from there, and the (last) Hour will be on a Friday."

3. *Abu Saeed al-Khudri* is reported to have said that the Messenger of Allah (Peace & blessings of Allah be with him) said: It is obligatory for every male Muslim who has reached the age of puberty to bathe on Friday and to cleanse the teeth with miswak, and to use perfume if he is able.

4. *Abu Hurayra* is reported to have said that the Messenger of God (prayers & peace be upon him) said: "On Friday the angels sit at the gates of the mosque recording those who arrive first, and so on, until when the Imam sits, they close their book of record and they sit to listen to the prayer, and the example of the one who arrives first is similar to the one who sacrificed a camel, the one who arrives next is as the one who sacrificed a cow, and then the one who comes after that is as the one who sacrificed a ram, and the one who comes after that is as the one who sacrificed a hen, and the one who comes thereafter is as the one who sacrificed an egg.

5. *Abu Hazem* is reported to have said that according to ibn Sa'ad Al-Saeedi the Messenger of Allah (Peace & blessings of Allah be with

him) sent for one Ansari woman and told her to ask her servant carpenter to make a pulpit for him to be used in the mosque. So he made the three steps and then the Messenger of Allah (Peace & blessings of Allah be with him) got it placed in the mosque. It was made of the wood of the tamarisk tree of the forest. Then I saw the holy Prophet (Peace & blessings of Allah be with him) standing upon it and pronouncing 'God is Great' and the people repeated the same after him while he stood upon the pulpit. Then he stepped back, descended and prostrated on the ground close to the foot of the pulpit and then again ascended it. After completing the prayers he turned to the people and said: 'O people! I have done this so that you may follow me and learn the way I pray'.

6. *Jabir ibn Abd Allah* is reported to have said that: When The Messenger of Allah (Peace & blessings of Allah be with him) used to deliver the sermon his eyes used to turn red and he would raise his voice and he became more vehement as if he was warning of an imminent attack, saying that they will surprise you in the morning or in the evening, and he used to say: "I was sent, and between me and the (final) Hour (the time) is as close as these two." He indicated by raising his index and middle fingers. He used to say: "After me the best of Hadith is the Book of God, and the best guidance is the guidance of Muhammad, and the worst of matters is the innovation in it, and every innovation implies going astray." Then he used to say: "I am more deserving to every believer than himself, and whoever leaves wealth for his family, and whoever leaves debt or children, I am responsible for that.

7. *Ammar* is reported to have said on the authority of Abu Wa'el that: 'I heard The Messenger of Allah (Peace & blessings of Allah be with him) say: 'The length of a man's prayer and the brevity of his speech is a sign of knowledge, so lengthen your prayer and shorten your sermon, for concise speech influences the audience.

8. It is related that *Jabir ibn Abd Allah* said that: "While the holy Prophet (Peace & blessings of Allah be with him) was delivering she Friday sermon, some camels (loaded with provisions) arrived from al- Sham. The camels distracted the people and only twelve people stayed in the mosque with the Prophet (Peace & blessings of Allah be with him) then the verse was revealed: 'But when they see merchandise or diversion, they run after it and leave you standing. Say: 'That which is with God is better than diversion and merchandise, and God is the Best of Providers.'"

9. It is related that *ibn Bashir* said that: "The Messenger of Allah (Peace & blessings of Allah be with him) used to recite in the prayer on the two Feast Days and during Friday prayer: "Glorify the Name of

your Lord, the Moss High." (Sarah 87) and "Have you heard the sidings of the Over-whelming Events?" (Sarah 88) He said: "If the Feast Day fell on a Friday he would recite both Surahs in the two prayers."

10. *Jabir ibn Samara* is reported to have said that: The Messenger of Allah (Peace & blessings of Allah be with him) used to deliver his sermon standing, then he would sit down, and stand up again and deliver his sermon. Whoever tells you that he used to deliver his sermon sitting has lied, by God, I have prayed with him more than two thousand times.

11. It was related that *Jabber ibn Samara* said: I used to pray with the Messenger of Allah (Peace & blessings of Allah be with him) and his prayer and his sermon were always of moderate length.

12. *Abu Hurayra* is reported to have said that the Messenger of Allah (Peace & blessings of Allah be with him) said: 'When the Imam is delivering the sermon, if you ask your companion to be quiet and listen you will have lost your reward'."

13. It is related from *Abu Hurayra* that the holy Prophet (Peace & blessings of Allah be with him) said: "Whoever bathes and then attends the Friday prayers and prays if he is destined to, then listens to the sermon until its end. Then prays with the Imam, then his sins between that Friday and the previous Friday will be expiated, and for three days after."

14. *Abu Hurayra* is reported to have said that the Messenger of Allah (Peace & blessings of Allah be with him) said: "When you complete the Friday prayers, then offer four (Rakahs)." It is also related that Suhail said: "If you are in a hurry to return home then offer two Rak'at in the mosque and two Rak'at when you return."

15. It is reported that *Abd Allah ibn Umar* used to offer the Friday prayers and then return to offer two Rak'at at his home." Then he said: "So did the Messenger of Allah. (Peace & blessings of Allah be with him).

16. It is reported from *Al- Hakim ibn Mina'* that Abd Allah ibn Umar and Abu Hurayra told him that they both heard the Messenger of Allah (Peace & blessings of Allah be with him) say while he was upon his pulpit: "The people must cease their neglect of the Friday prayers or God Almighty will seal their hearts, and then they will be heedless."

7

Book of Two Feasts
Eid al-Fitr and
Eid al-Adha

1. *Ibn Abbas* is reported to have said that he offered the Eid prayer with the Messenger of Allah (Peace & blessings of Allah be with him), Abu Bakr, Umar and Uthman; all offered the prayer before delivering the sermon. Then they delivered the sermon. The Prophet of Allah (Peace & blessings of Allah be with him) came down, (from the pulpit) and he walked up to the women, Bilal was with him and he said: 'O Prophet, when believing women come to you, taking oaths of allegiance to you, that they will not associate anything with God.' And he recited the verse until the end, then he said: 'Are you in accord with that?' Then only one woman replied: 'Yes, O Prophet of Allah.' At that time he did not know who she was. He said: 'Pay charity.' So Bilal spread out his cloak and said: 'Come and give your charity here, and the women all threw their jewelry and ornaments into Bilal's cloak.

2. *Ibn Abbas* is reported to have said that once the Messenger of Allah (Peace & blessings of Allah be with him) went out to the place of prayer to offer the prayer of Eid al Adha or Al Fitr. He offered two Rak'at; he did not offer any Rakahs before them nor after them. Then he took Bilal along and went to see the women and he requested them to give charity. The women vied with each other to give their earrings and necklaces."

8

Book of
Prayer for Travel

1. *Ibn Abbas* is reported to have said that: "God has made prayer obligatory for you, as your Prophet said: 'When you are not traveling four Rak'at, when you travel two Rak'at and if you fear attack then one Rak'at.'"

2. *Anas bin Malik* is reported to have said: "We traveled with The Messenger of God (prayers & peace be upon him) from Medina to Makka and we offered two Rak'at at each prayer time until we returned to Medina." It was asked: "Did you stay for some time in Makka?" He replied: "We stayed in Makka for ten days."

3. *Anas ibn Malik* is reported to have related that: "When The Messenger of Allah (Peace & blessings of Allah be with him) was in a hurry to travel, he would delay the midday prayer until the start of the afternoon prayer and then offer the two together, and he would delay the sunset prayer until the twilight had gone and then he offered it together with the evening prayer."

4. *Ibn Abbas* is reported to have said that: "The Messenger of Allah (Peace & blessings of Allah be with him) used to combine the midday and afternoon prayers together, and the sunset and evening prayers together when he was not in fear of attack or rain while he was in Medina." And it was asked why did he do that?' He said: 'So that he would not burden his community.

5. It is reported from *ibn Umar* that he called the people to prayer one cold, windy and rainy night, and said at the end of the call to prayer: 'Pray in your houses.' Then he said: Whenever it is cold and rainy the Messenger of Allah (Peace & blessings of Allah be with him) used to order the Caller (to the prayers) to say: pray in your houses.

6. *Ibn Umar* is reported to have said: The Messenger of Allah (Peace & blessings of Allah be with him) used so offer his praise to God when he was mounted regardless of the direction and he used to offer Witr prayer when he was mounted, but he never offered the obligatory prayer upon his mount.

7. *Jabir ibn Abd Allah* is reported to have said that: "We accompanied the Messenger of Allah (Peace & blessings of Allah be with him) in fighting some

people from Juhaina, and they fought us furiously. When we offered the midday prayer the unbelievers said: 'If we had attacked them suddenly we would have wiped them out.' Gabriel (peace upon him) informed the holy Prophet (Peace & blessings of Allah be with him) of that, so he told us: 'They are saying we will attack them during a prayer which is more dear to them than their own sons.' Then when the afternoon prayer was due, he aligned us in two rows, and the unbelievers were between the Qibla and us. The Messenger of Allah (Peace & blessings of Allah be with him) pronounced 'God is Great' then we pronounced 'God is Great' then he bowed and we bowed, then he prostrated and the first row prostrated with him, when they rose up the second row prostrated and the first row moved to stand behind, then the second row rose up in the place of the first. Then when the second row had prostrated they all sat down and the holy Prophet (Peace & blessings of Allah be with him) offered salutation to them all.' According to Abu al Zubair, Jabir mentioned that he said: Thus your commanders should offer prayer (in this manner).

8. *Hadrat Ayesha* is reported to have said that: During the Prophet's lifetime the sun eclipsed, so he led the people in prayer and stood up for a long time in prayer, then bowed for a long time. He stood up again for a long time in prayer but this time he stood less time than before. He bowed again for a long time but for less time than the first one, then he prostrated

and stayed a long time in prostration. He did the same in the second Rak'at and then completed the prayer; by that time the eclipse had ended. He gave a sermon and after praising and glorifying God he said: "The sun and the moon are two signs of the signs of God, they do not eclipse upon the death or birth of anyone. So if you witness an eclipse, remember God and say: 'God is Great', pray and give charity." The holy Prophet (Peace & blessings of Allah be with him) then said: "O followers of Muhammad! By God! There is no one who is worthy of respect more than Allah; He has prohibited adultery among His servants. O followers of Muhammad! By God! If you knew what I know, you would laugh little and cry much."

9. It is related from *Ibn Abbas* that: "The Messenger of Allah (Peace & blessings of Allah be with him) prayed eight Rak'at in four prostrations when the sun eclipsed."

10. It is related from *Abd Allah ibn Zayed al Ansari* that: "The Messenger of Allah (Peace & blessings of Allah be with him) went out to pray for rain. When he intended to beseech God Almighty he turned towards the Qibla and wrapped his garment around himself. It is also related that he turned his back to the people and faced the Qibla and asked God for rain. Them he turned his cloak inside out and led his followers in two Rak'at of prayer.

11. It is related from *Anas* that: "We were once with Messenger of Allah (Peace

& blessings of Allah be with him) when it was raining heavily, so the holy Prophet (Peace & blessings of Allah be with him) drew aside his garment until the rain soaked his skin, then we said: 'O Messenger of Allah, why did you do that?' He said: because it is sent *by my* Lord and I wish to be blessed by it.

12. It is related from *Hadrat Ayesha* that: "When the holy Prophet(Peace & blessings of Allah be with him) saw a strong wind he used to say: 'O God I ask you for the best of it and the good it contains and the good for which it was sent. And I seek refuge in You from the evil it contains and the evil for which it was sent.' And when he used to see a thunderstorm in the sky he would walk to and fro, and go in and out, and his face used to change, and then if it rained he used to feel relaxed. Ayesha asked him about that and the holy Prophet (Peace & blessings of Allah be with him) said: 'and how would I know, it maybe as the people of Aad said: "Then, when they saw it as a dense cloud coming towards their valleys they said: 'This is a cloud that shall give us rain.' But it is that which you did seek to hasten, a wind wherein is a painful torment." (Q.46: 24).

13. *Ibn Abbas* has related that the holy Prophet (Peace & blessings of Allah be with him) said: "I was granted victory with the easterly wind and A'ad were destroyed by the westerly wind."

Book of Funerals

1. It is related from **Umm Salama** that the Messenger of Allah (Peace & blessings of Allah be with him) said: "If you are present before a sick or dying person, then only say good words because the angels say: 'Amen' to whatever you say." And she said: "So when Abu Salama died, I went to the Prophet and said: 'O Messenger of Allah, AbuSalama has just died.' He said: 'Say: 'O God, forgive me and him and replace him for me with one better.' She said that she repeated those words, so God replaced him for her with one who is better than him, Muhammad."

2. *Hadrat Ayesha* has related that the Messenger of Allah (Peace & blessings of Allah be with him) said: "Whoever looks forward to meeting God, God looks forward to meeting him, and whoever dislikes to meet God, God dislikes to meet him.' So I asked: "O Prophet of Allah, is it the dislike of death? We all dislike death." The holy Prophet replied: "It is not that, but when the hour of a believer's death draws near, he is given the glad tidings of Allah's pleasure with him and His blessings, and thus nothing

is more dear to him than what lies before him. He looks forward to meeting Allah and Allah looks forward to meeting him. But when the hour of an unbeliever's death draws near, he is given the bad tidings of God's chastisement and His retribution, thus nothing is more hateful to him than what lies before him, and God hates to see him." It is also related from Abu Hurayra that the Messenger of Allah (Peace & blessings of Allah be with him) said: "Whoever looks forward to meeting God, God looks forward to meeting him, and whoever dislikes to meet God, God dislikes to meet him." He said: "I visited Hadrat Ayesha and said: 'O Mother of the Believers, I have heard Abu Hurayra mention a Hadith about the Messenger of Allah (Peace & blessings of Allah be with him), if that was true then we are in total loss.'" She said: "The one in total loss is the one who falsely attributes something to the Messenger of Allah (Peace & blessings of Allah be with him). And what is that?" He said that Abu Hurayra has narrated that the Messenger of Allah (Peace & blessings of Allah be with him) said: "Whoever looks forward to meeting God, God looks forward to meeting him, and whoever dislikes to meet God, God dislikes to meet him.' And we all dislike death." Then she said: "Yes, The Messenger of Allah (Peace & blessings of Allah be with him) said that, but that does not mean what you think it does. But it is when the sight is frozen upwards and breathing gets hard, and the skin retracts, at that time whoever looks forward to meeting God, God looks forward to meeting him, and whoever dislikes to meet God, God dislikes to meet him.'"

3. It is related from *Jabir* that three days before his death he heard the holy Prophet say: 'Each of you should be eager that death should not approach him except when he has good hope in God's mercy.'"

4. It is related from *Umm Salama* that: "The Messenger of Allah (Peace & blessings of Allah be with him) visited Abu Salama when his gaze was frozen, so he closed his eyelids and said: 'When the soul is seized the sight follows it.' As some people began to wail the holy Prophet: 'Do not say anything but good, as the angels say: 'Amen' to whatever you say.' Then he said: 'O God forgive Abu Salama and raise him in rank among the rightly guided and be the Guardian to his offspring, and forgive us and him O Lord of the Worlds, and make his grave spacious and give it light.'"

5. *Abu Hurayra* has related that: "When the soul of a believer is seized, two angels raise it up." And he said that its scent is musk, he also said: "The people of the heavens say: 'It is a good soul coming from the earth, God bless you and the body you dwelt in.' Then the soul will be taken up to his Lord Who shall say: 'Take him to furthest Lote tree.' He said: 'But when the soul of the unbeliever is seized, its scent is foul and it is cursed and the people of the heavens say: 'A bad soul comes from the earth.' Then it will be said: 'Take him to Sijjin at the base of the Hell Fire.'

6. It is related from *Anas ibn Malik* that: "The Messenger of Allah (Peace & blessings of Allah be with him) passed by a woman weeping at a graveside. He told her to fear God and to be patient. She said to him: 'Go away, for you have not suffered the affliction I have suffered.' Then after he left she was told he was the Messenger of Allah (Peace & blessings of Allah be with him) and she was stunned, so she went to his house and said: 'O Messenger of Allah I did not recognize you.' He said: 'Indeed, patience is gone at the first stroke of affliction when it strikes'."

7. It is related from *Abu Hurayra* that: "The Messenger of Allah (Peace & blessings of Allah be with him) said to some of the women of the Ansars: 'A woman whose three children die and she accepts what God has destined will be admitted to Paradise.' At that a woman asked: 'O Messenger of Allah what if only two die?' He replied: 'Even two.' Also it is related that Abu Hurayra said: "Any Muslim whose three children die, the Fire will only touch him, because God Almighty has decreed so."

8. It is related by **Umm Salama**, the wife of the Messenger of Allah (Peace & blessings of Allah be with him) said that the Messenger of Allah (Peace & blessings of Allah be with him) said: "Any Muslim who suffers affliction and says: 'To God we belong and unto Him is our return, O God, reward me for my distress and replace it with something better.' God Almighty will bestow some-thing better upon him in its place." She said: "When Abu Salama died I was ordered to say those words by the Messenger of Allah (Peace & blessings of Allah be with him) and I did so, and after-wards I was married to the holy Prophet (Peace & blessings of Allah be with him)."

9. It is related by **Abd Allah ibn Umar** that: "Sa'ad ibn Ubada was ill and the holy Prophet (Peace & blessings of Allah be with him) together with Abd al Rahman ibn Auf, Sa'ad ibn Abi Waqqas and Abd Allah ibn Mas'ud went to visit him to enquire about his health. When he arrived he asked: 'Has he died?' They said: 'No, O Messenger of Allah.' The holy Prophet (Peace & blessings of Allah be with him) began to weep and others wept too. The Apostle of Allah said: 'Listen. God does not mete out punishment for the tears you shed or for the grief you feel in your hearts, but he punishes or grants His mercy on account of this." And he pointed to his tongue and said: 'The deceased is punished for the lamentations that his family makes over him'."

10. It is related by **Abd Allah** that the holy Prophet (Peace & blessings of Allah

be with him) said: "The one who strikes his face, tears his clothes and follows the ways and traditions of the days of ignorance (on the death of a near one) is not of us."

11. It is was related from **Amr bint Abu Rahman** that she heard Hadrat Ayesha say when it was mentioned to her that Abd Allah ibn Umar had said that the deceased is punished by the weeping of his family. Then Hadrat Ayesha said: "May God forgive Abu Abd al Rahman! He is not a liar, but he might have forgotten or may have been confused. It happened that the Messenger of Allah (Peace & blessings of Allah be with him) once passed by the grave of a Jewess while her relatives were weeping and he said: 'They are weeping over her and she is being tortured in her grave'."

12. It is related from Hadrat *Ayesha* that: "The Messenger of Allah (Peace & blessings of Allah be with him) was shrouded in three pieces of white cotton cloth from Yemen."

13. It was related that **Jabber bin Abu Allah** said that The Messenger of God (prayers & peace be upon him) once mentioned in a speech that one of his Companions who

14. It is related on the authority of *Abi Saeed AlKhudri* that: "On Eid al Fitr or Eid al Adha the Messenger of Allah (Peace & blessings of Allah be with him) used to go out to the place of prayer and after completing the prayer he read out a sermon com-manding people to give charity saying: 'O people, give charity!' Then

he went over to the women and said: 'O women, give charity, for I have seen the Fire (of Hell) and the majority of its inhabitants are women.' They asked: 'Why, O Messenger of Allah?' He replied: 'you curse too much and are ungrateful to your husbands. I have not seen anyone of more fleeting memory and lessened in religion than you. Some of you could lead a sensible man to lose his senses.' Then he left and when he arrived at his house, Zainab, the wife of Ibn Mas'ud, came and she said: 'O Prophet of Allah! You ordered people this day to give charity and I had an ornament which I intended to give as charity, but Ibn Mas'ud said that he and his children were more deserving of it than anyone else.' The holy Prophet (Peace & blessings of Allah be with him) replied: 'Ibn Mas'ud has spoken in truth. Your husband and your children have more right to it than anybody else'."

15. *Harith ibn Wahab* has related that the Messenger of Allah (Peace & blessings of Allah be with him) said: "O people! Give charity for a time is approaching when a person would want to give alms and will not find anyone to accept it, and those who are offered it will say, "If you had offered it yesterday, I would have taken it, but today I have no need of it'."

16. *Zainab*, the wife of Abd Allah ibn Mas'ud related that: "I was in the Mosque and heard the Prophet (Peace & blessings of Allah be with him) say: 'O women! Give charity, even from your ornaments.' Zainab used to provide for Abd Allah and other orphans who were in her care. So she went to the Prophet (Peace & blessings of Allah be with him) and found an Ansari woman there who was standing at his door with a problem similar to hers. Bilal passed them by and they asked him: 'Ask The Prophet (Peace & blessings of Allah be with him) if it is permissible for me to spend the Zakat on my husband and the orphans in my care?' And we asked Bilal not to inform the Prophet (Peace & blessings of Allah be with him) of our presence. So Bilal went inside and asked the Apostle of Allah (Peace & blessings of Allah be with him) about our problem. The holy Prophet (Peace & blessings of Allah be with him) said: 'Yes, and she will receive a double reward, one for helping her relatives and the other for charity."

17. *Hadrat Ayesha* has related that someone came to the Messenger of Allah (Peace & blessings of Allah be with him) and asked: "My mother suddenly died without making a will, I think she would have given charity if she had time to speak. If I give charity on her behalf will it be accepted?" He said: "Yes."

18. It is related from *Jarir* that his father had said: "We were in the presence of the Messenger of Allah (Peace & blessings of Allah be with him) early one morning when some people came who had no shoes or clothes except woolen cloaks, wearing their swords around their necks. They all were from the tribe of Mudar. When the Messenger of Allah (Peace & blessings of Allah be with him) saw their plight his face changed, he commanded Bilal to pronounce the call to prayer. He pronoun-ced the call to prayer. Then the Prophet prayed with them and recited the verses: 'O mankind! Fear God the One Who fashioned you from a single person, and of the same kind He created his wife, and from the pair of them scattered many men and women. And fear God to whom you are answerable. Indeed God is ever watching over you.' (Q. 4: 1) Then he recited: 'O you who believe, fear God and let every soul consider what it has prepared for the hereafter (Q.58: 18). Thereafter some of the audience donated Dinars and some offered their Dirhams, others their garments and others gave a measure of wheat and yet others a measure of dates, until he said: "Even half a date." Then one of the Ansars came with a bag of money so large he could barely carry it, and they could hardly lift it. Then people kept coming until I saw two large piles of food and clothes, and I saw the face of the Messenger of Allah (Peace & blessings of Allah be with him) shining with joy as if his face was of gold. The holy Prophet (Peace & blessings of Allah be with him) said: "The one who sets a good example in Islam is rewarded for that and for whoever followed him in it, without their reward being dimi-nished at all. And the one who sets an evil example in Islam bears the consequences of it and the conse-quences of anyone who followed him in it, without their punishment being diminished at all."

19. It is related from *Abu Hurayra* that

the holy Prophet (Peace & blessings of Allah be with him) said: "While a man was standing in a plot of land, he heard a voice coming from a cloud saying: 'Water the orchard of so and so,' then the cloud burst straight away over a land where many black stones lay and a rivulet took the water away. The man followed the water until he saw another man standing in his garden, so he asked him: 'O servant of God, what is your name?' He replied: 'So and so.' And that was the name he had heard spoken from the cloud. And he asked him: "O servant of God, why do you ask me my name?' He said: 'I heard a sound in the cloud from where this water fell saying 'Water the garden of so and so,' and that is your name. So what do you do with this garden?' He said: 'Since you asked, I always look at what it produces and I pay Zakat one third, and I and my family eat one third, and I give away in charity one third.' It was related that he said: 'I give one third for the poor and the needy and the wayfarer.'"

20. It is related from *ibn Hatim* that: "While I was sitting with the Messenger of Allah (Peace & blessings of Allah be with him) two people approached him, one of them complained of poverty and the other complained about the prevalence of theft. The holy Prophet (Peace & blessings of Allah be with him) said: 'As for theft and waylaying, a time is approaching when caravans will go to Makka unguarded. And as for poverty, the final Hour will not come until a person will seek to give in charity and will not find anyone to accept it. And each one of you will stand before God and there will be neither a curtain nor an interpreter between you and God, and God will ask him: 'Did not I give you wealth?' He will answer: 'Yes.' Then God will ask: 'Did I not send a Messenger to you?' And again he will answer 'yes'. Then he will look to his right and he will see nothing but the Fire, and then he will look to his left and will see nothing but the Fire. And so you should all save yourselves from the Fire by giving even half of a date in charity. And if you do not have even half a date, then be charitable by saying a kind word to someone'."

21. *Abu Hurayra* has narrated that the Messenger of Allah (Peace & blessings of Allah be with him) said: "There are seven whom God Almighty will protect with His Shade on the Day of Reckoning; a ruler who was just, a youth who grew up wor-shipping God, the one whose heart yearns for the mosques, the two who love each other and meet each other and depart from each other only for God's sake, a man who spurns the advances of a beautiful woman of high rank because he fears God, the one who gives charity so secretly that his right hand does not know what his left hand has given and the one who remembers Allah when he is alone and his eyes weep in remembrance of Him."

22. *Abu Hurayra* has related that: "A man came to the holy Prophet (Peace & blessings of Allah be with him) and asked: 'O Messenger of Allah! Which

charity will earn the better reward?' He replied: 'the charity you perform when you are healthy, niggardly and fear poverty and wish to become wealthy. Do not put it off until death approaches and then say: 'Give something to so and so and some-thing to so and so.' It will be too late'."

23. It is related by *Abu Hurayra* that the Messenger of Allah (Peace & blessings of Allah be with him) said: "If any of you give in charity the equivalent of one date out of money that you earned honestly. Then God will take it into His right hand and increase its reward for the one who gives it, in the same way as you raise a young foal, until it grows to the size of a mountain."

24. *Abu Hurayra* has related that the Messenger of Allah (Peace & blessings of Allah be with him) said: "O people, God is Good and He accepts only that which is good, and God has commanded the believers as He commanded the messen-gers, He said: "O Messengers, eat of the good things and do righteous deeds, surely I am All Knowing of what you do.' (Q.23:51) And He said: 'O you who believe! Eat from the good things which We have bestowed on you, and be grateful to God, if He indeed is The One you worship."' And then he said: "If a man travels on a long journey until his hair is untidy and dusty, then lifts his hands towards the heavens and says: 'O Lord! O Lord!' while his food is unlawful, his drink is unlawful and his garments are unlawful and his sustenance is unlawful, how can his prayer be accepted?"

25. *Abu Mas'ud* has narrated that: "We were ordered to give charity even though we were porters. Abu Aquil gave a half measure and another came with more than that, the hypocrites said: 'God is not in need of this charity, and the other has only done it for show.' Then the verse was revealed: 'those who taunt the believers who give charity freely, and those who find nothing to give except the fruits of their endeavors, they deride them. God will throw back their derision upon them, and they shall have a painful chastisement.' (Q.9: 79)

26. *Abu Hurayra* has related that the Messenger of Allah (Peace & blessings of Allah be with him) said: "If any of you eat a pair of anything for the sake of God he will be invited to enter Paradise: 'O servant of God, it is good.' And those who parti-cipated in Jihad will be invited to enter by the Gates of Jihad, and those who gave charity will be invited to enter by the Gates of Charity, and those who fast will be invited to enter by the Gate of al-Rayyan." Abu Bakr said: 'O Messenger of Allah, will people be invited to enter through only one gate? Will anyone be invited to enter through all the gates?' The Messenger of Allah (Peace & blessings of Allah be with him) said: "Yes, and I hope you will be

27. *Abu Hurayra* has related that the Messenger of Allah (Peace & blessings of Allah be with him) said: "Which

of you is fasting today?" Abu Bakr said: "I am." He said: "Which of you accompanied a funeral today?' Abu Bakr said: 'I did." He said: "Which of you fed a poor man today?" Abu Bakr said: "I did." He said: "Which of you visited a sick person today?' Abu Bakr said: "I did." The Messenger of Allah (Peace & blessings of Allah be with him) said: "Whoever does such good deeds will certainly be admitted into Paradise."

28. It is related from *Hudhaifa* and *Abu Shihab* that the Messenger of Allah (Peace & blessings of Allah be with him) said: "Every good deed is charity."

29. It is related that some of the companions of the Messenger of Allah (Peace & blessings of Allah be with him) asked him: "O Messenger of Allah the wealthy people have all the rewards. They offer prayer as we do, they fast as we fast, they give charity from their extra wealth." He said: "Have you not been given the means to give charity? Every time you say 'Glory be to God' it is a charity, every time you say "God is Great' it is a charity, every time you say 'All thanks be to God' it is a charity, and every time you say 'There is no god but Allah' it is a charity. And enjoining others to do good is a charity, and prohibiting evil is a charity, and a man's intimacy with his wife is a charity." They said: "O Messenger of Allah, is there a reward for us when we satisfy our sexual passion?" He said: "Conver-sely, if he was to do it in a way which is prohibited, would it not be a sin?

So if he does it in a lawful way, should he not be rewarded?"

30. *Hadrat Ayesha* (may Allah be pleased with her) has related that the Messenger of Allah (Peace & blessings of Allah be with him) said: "Every son of Adam was created with three hundred and sixty joints, so whoever glorifies Allah, and praises Allah, and bears witness that Allah is One, and seeks forgiveness from Allah, and removes a stone or a thorn or a bone from the way of others, and enjoins good and forbids evil, three hundred and sixty four times, will have removed himself from the Fire on that Day."

31. *Abu Hurayra* has related that the Messenger of Allah (Peace & blessings of Allah be with him) said: "The similarity between a miser and the one who gives charity is like the similarity between two people dressed in cloaks of iron. When the charitable one wishes to give in charity, the Armour spreads out until it covers his whole body and hides even his fingertips and footprints. And whenever the miser wishes to give, it constricts and his hands are restrained and every ring tightens." And he said: "I heard the Messenger of Allah (Peace & blessings of Allah be with him) say: 'and even if he tries to loosen it, it does not get loose."

32. It is related from *Abu Hurayra* that the Messenger of Allah (Peace & blessings of Allah be with him) said: "Two angels come down from Heaven every day and one of them says: 'O God! Reward every person who spends in Your Cause,' and the other one says: 'O God! Annihilate the misers'."

33. It is from *Abu Musa al Ash'ari* that the holy Prophet (Peace & blessings of Allah be with him) said: "A Muslim storekeeper who honestly obeys his master and pays all that he has been ordered with a good heart and pays those who he has been ordered to pay, is one of the two kinds of charitable person."

34. It is related that *Asma' bint Abu Bakr al Siddiq* said that she went to the Apostle of Allah (Peace & blessings of Allah be with him) and said: "O Prophet of Allah, I have nothing except what al Zubair brings to the house. Is there any blame on me if I give some of it in charity?' The Messenger of Allah replied: "Give as much as you can afford, and do not tighten your purse, or God will withhold His blessings from you."

35. *Hadrat Ayesha* has related that the Messenger of Allah (Peace & blessings of Allah be with him) said: "When a woman gives some food in charity, she will receive the reward for what she has given and her husband will receive the reward for what he earned, and the storekeeper will receive a similar reward. The reward of one does not diminish the reward of others."

36. According to *Umair*, the freed slave of Abu al Lahm: "My master ordered me to cut some meat into slices, and a poor man came to me, so I gave him some of it to eat. My master heard about it and beat me. I went to the

Messenger of Allah (Peace & blessings of Allah be with him) and told him about the incident. The holy Prophet called him and said: 'Why did you beat him?' He replied: 'He gave food away without permission.' The Apostle of Allah remarked: 'both of you will earn rewards for it.' "

37. *Abu Hurayra* has related that the Messenger of Allah (Peace & blessings of Allah be with him) said; "A woman should seek the permission of her husband to fast when he is present, and she should not permit any Mahram into his house when he is present without his permission. And if she spends anything from his wealth without his permission, half of the reward is for him."

38. It is related by *Abu Saeed al-Khudri* that: "Some of the Ansars asked the Messenger of Allah (Peace & blessings of Allah be with him) for something and he gave it to them. They asked him again and he gave them. And then they asked him again and once more he gave them until all he had with him was finished. And then the holy Prophet said: 'if I had anymore I would not keep it from you. Whoever refrains from asking others, God will give him contentment, and whoever tries to make himself self-sufficient, God will make him self-sufficient. And whoever tries to be patient, God will make him patient. No one can be given a greater and better blessing than patience'."

39. It is related from *Amr ibn al-A'as* that the Messenger of Allah (Peace & blessings of Allah be with him) said:

"The successful one is the one who has accepted Islam, who has sufficient for his needs and who is content with what God has given him."

40. It is related from *Abd Allah ibn Umar* that the holy Prophet (Peace & blessings of Allah be with him) said: "A man persists in asking others for something until he faces God Almighty without any flesh on his face."

41. *Abu Hurayra* has reported that the Messenger of Allah (Peace & blessings of Allah be with him) said: "By Him in Whose Hand is my soul it is better for any of you to fetch a rope, cut and collect wood and carry it upon your back and sell it rather than to ask someone for something and that person may give it to him or may not." It is related from Al- Zubair ibn al-Awam that the holy Prophet (Peace & blessings of Allah be with him) said: "By Him in Whose hand is my soul it is better for any of you to fetch a rope and collect a bundle of wood upon your back and sell it and God will save his face because of that, rather than to ask people who may give him or may not."

42. *Abd Allah ibn Umar* has reported that he heard the Messenger of Allah (Peace & blessings of Allah be with him) speaking from the pulpit concerning charity and about begging, he said: 'The hand which gives is better than the hand which takes. And the hand which gives is the foremost and the hand which takes is the meanest."

43. *Hakim ibn Hizam* has reported: "I asked the holy Prophet (Peace & blessings of Allah be with him) and he gave it to me. I asked again and he gave me. I asked him once again and he gave me. And then he said: 'This property is like a succulent fruit and whoever takes it without greed, he is blessed in it, and whoever takes it with greed, he is not blessed in it, and he (the greedy) is like the one who eats but is never satisfied, and the hand which gives is better than the hand which receives'."

44. *Abu Hurayra* has reported that the Messenger of Allah said: "The poor person is not the one who demands a morsel or two or a date or two from others... "He (the poor) is the one who has nothing and is ashamed to beg from the people."

45. It is reported by *Abu Hurayra* that the Messenger of Allah (Peace & blessings of Allah be with him) said: "Fortune is not the wealth of the world but fortune is the wealth of the soul."

46. *Anas* has reported that the Messenger of Allah (Peace & blessings of Allah be with him) said: "The son of Adam grows old, but he retains two (lusts), the lust for wealth and the lust for life."

10

Book of Zakat

1. *Ibn Abbas* reported that Muaz related that the Messenger of Allah (peace & blessings of Allah be with him) sent me and said: 'You will come across people of earlier Scriptures, so call the people to bear witness that there is no deity but Allah, and that I am the Messenger of Allah, and if they obey you then educate them in the five compulsory prayers and if they listen to you then tell them that Allah has commanded them to pay Zakat from their property (and wealth) and that it is to be taken from the rich and given to the poor. And if they obey you in that, then do not take anything other than Zakat and fear the invocation of the one who is oppressed because there is no availing between it and Allah.

2. *Abi Sayeed al-Khudri* reported that the Messenger of Allah (peace & blessings of Allah be with him) said: No Zakat is due on property which amounts to less than five Uqiyas, and no Zakat is due on less than five camels, and no Zakat is due on less than five Wasqs.

3. It is reported from *Jabir ibn Abd Allah* that the Apostle of Allah (peace & blessings of Allah be with him) said: One tenth is due on the produce that is watered by rivers or rains, and one twentieth is due on that which is watered by camels.

4. *Abu Hurayra* reported that the holy Prophet (peace & blessings of Allah be with him) (prayers & peace be upon him) said: No Zakat is due on a horse or a slave belonging to a Muslim.

5. It is reported from *Abu Hurayra* that the Messenger of Allah (peace & blessings of Allah be with him) sent Umar to collect Zakat. It was said that Ibn Jamil, Khalid ibn al Walid and Abbas, the uncle of the Prophet (peace & blessings of Allah be with him) had refused to give Zakat. The Apostle of Allah (peace & blessings of Allah be with him) said: Why did Ibn Jamil refuse to give Zakat, he used to be poor but was made rich by Allah and His Messenger. However you should not have asked Khalid to pay Zakat as he is keeping his armour for the cause of Allah. As for Abbas ibn Abd al Muttalib, his Zakat is upon me.

6. *Abu Zarr* is reported to have said: I went to the holy Prophet (peace & blessings of Allah be with him) as he was sitting beneath the shade of the Ka'ba. When he saw me he said: 'By the Lord of the Ka'ba, they are the losers.' I stayed sitting there until I had to leave, then I rose up and asked: 'O Messenger of Allah! May my father and mother be redeemed for you, who are the losers?' He replied: Those who have enormous wealth except so and so who spend their wealth on those they find before them, behind them and to their right hand side and their left hand side, and they are only a few. And anyone who owns camels, cattle, goats or sheep and who does not pay its due Zakat will stand on the Day of Reckoning bigger than they were and the animals will jab him with their horns and trample him with their hooves, and every time one is through another will come upon him until the Judgment is completed.

7. *Abu Hurayra* reported that the Messenger of Allah (peace & blessings of Allah be with him) said: On the day of Judgment anyone who owned gold or silver and who did not pay its due Zakat will have sheets of Fire forged and heated in the Hellfire for him, and then his sides, his forehead and his back will be branded with them. And whenever they cool down it will be repeated on a Day whose length will be fifty thousand years, until the judgment of the people is completed. Then he will see his way, whether to Paradise or Hell. It was asked: O Messenger of Allah! What about the camels?' He said: On the Day of Judgment anyone who owned camels and who did not pay its due Zakat, and who did not give the due of its milk on the day he watered it, they will trample him with their feet and nibble him with their mouths, and when the last one has passed him it will be repeated on a Day whose length will be fifty thousand years, until the judgment of the people is completed. Then he will see his way, whether to Paradise or Hell. It was asked: O Messenger of Allah! What about the cattle and sheep? He said: On the Day of Judgment anyone who owned cattle or sheep and who did not pay its due Zakat, they will trample him with their feet and bite him with their mouths, and when the last one has passed him it will be repeated on a Day whose length will be fifty thousand years, until the judgment of the people is completed. Then he will see his way, whether to Paradise or Hell. It was asked: O Messenger of Allah! What about horses? He said: Horses are of three categories, to one man they are a burden, to another they are a cover and to another they are means of reward. As for the one to whom they are a burden, he is one who keeps horses just for show and in pride and as a means of causing harm to Muslims, and his horses will be a cause of sin for him. As for the one for whom they are a cover, he is the one who keeps horses in the cause of Allah, and he does not

forget the due right of Allah from what he earns through them, his horses are a cover for him. As for the one who keeps the horse as a means of reward, he is the one who keeps it for Allah's cause for the Muslims and who leaves it to pasture on a lengthy tether. Such a one will be rewarded to the extent that the tether permitted it to eat it in the pasture. If the horse breaks free of its rope and traverses the hills, every footstep it takes and every dung it drops will be considered a good deed for its owner, and if it comes to a river and drinks from it, that will also be considered a good deed for its owner even if he did not intend to water it then. The Apostle of Allah (peace & blessings of Allah be with him) was asked concerning donkeys and he said: I have not had a specific Revelation about donkeys but the verse which concerns all things applies: "Whoever does an atom's weight of goodness shall see it, and whoever has done an atom's weight of evil shall see it." (Q.99: 7-8).

8. It is reported from *Al Ahnaf ibn Qais* that he was sitting with a group of people from Quraysh when Abu Zarr passed by saying: 'Warn those who hoard treasures of the branding on their backs which will come out on their sides and the branding on the back of their necks which will come out on their foreheads. Then he went aside and sat down, I asked: 'Who is that?' They said: 'He is Abu Zarr.' Then I went to him and said: 'You said something which I have not heard

you say before.' He said: 'I did not say anything other than that which I heard from the Prophet.' I said: 'What would you say regarding the Ruler's gift?' He said: Take it, as it is help for today, but if it becomes the price for your Religion then refuse it.

9. *Jarir Ibn Abd Allah* is reported to have said: Some bedouin came to the Messenger of Allah (peace & blessings of Allah be with him) and said: 'Those who collect the Zakat come to us and treat us unfairly.' He said that the Apostle of Allah (peace & blessings of Allah be with him) said: 'Satisfy your collectors.' Jarir said: 'Since I heard that from The Messenger of Allah (peace & blessings of Allah be with him) I have never let any collector of Zakat leave without being satisfied with me.

10. *Abd Allah ibn Abi Aufi* said that when the Prophet (peace & blessings of Allah be with him) used to receive people coming to give their charity he used to say: O Allah! Bless the family of so and so." My father went to him with his charity, so he said: O Allah! Bless the family of Abi Aufi.

11. It is reported that *Anas ibn Malik* said: On the day of the battle of Hunayn, the Hawazin, Ghatafan and other tribes came with their children and animals, there were ten thousand troops with the Messenger of Allah (peace & blessings of Allah be with him) that day as well as the newly freed men

of Makka. They all took off and left the Prophet alone, he called out twice and then he looked to his right and said: O people of the Ansars! They responded: O Messenger of Allah! We are at your service, and well pleased to be with you." Then he looked to his left and said: O people of the Ansars! They responded: O Messenger of Allah! We are at your service, and well pleased to be with you. He dismounted from his white mule and said: "I am the servant and Messenger of Allah. " The unbe-lievers were (eventually) defeated and the Prophet (peace & blessings of Allah be with him) took much booty, and he distributed it between the Muhajirin and the people who had come from Makka, but he gave nothing to the Ansars. So the Ansars said: When threat is around it is we who are summoned, but the booty is given to others. When the Messenger of Allah (peace & blessings of Allah be with him) heard about their complaint he gathered them in a tent and said: What is it I hear from you? They remained silent, then he said: O people of the Ansars, do you not prefer that the people leave with worldly wealth while you leave with Muhammad and take him to your houses?" They said: O Messenger of Allah! Indeed we prefer that. He said: If the people walked along a spacious valley and the Ansars walked along a narrow terrain, I would take the narrow path with the Ansars.

12. It is reported that *Abu Sayeed al-*

Khudri said: Ali ibn Abu Talib sent to the Messenger of Allah (peace & blessings of Allah be with him) some gold mixed with clay from Yemen held in a leather pouch dyed with mimosa leaves. He shared it between four companions. One of the companions of the Prophet said: We have more right to this than they. When the Prophet (peace & blessings of Allah be with him) heard of his complaint he said: Have you no faith in me while I am the trustee of The One Who is in Heaven? Tidings come to me from heaven every morning and every evening. A man with deep set eyes and pronounced cheek bones, a high forehead, bushy beard, shaven head stood up and said: O Messenger of Allah! Fear God! He said: Woe to you! Am I not most deserving of the people of the world? The man left and Khalid ibn Walid said: O Apostle of Allah! Let me strike his neck! The Prophet said: He may be one who prays. Khalid said: Many people offer prayers with their tongues but there is nothing in their hearts. The Messenger of Allah (peace & blessings of Allah be with him) said: I have not been commanded to delve into the hearts of the people or to know what is inside them. He looked at him again as he was going away and he said: "There will come a people who will recite the Qur'an carelessly, and it will not go further than their throats, and their religion will slip through them as the arrow slips through its victim. I think he also said: If I were to see them, I would surely kill them like the people of Thamud were killed.

13. *Abu Hurayra* is reported to have said that when Hasan ibn Ali picked up a date from the dates of the Zakat and put it to his mouth, the Messenger of Allah (peace & blessings of Allah be with him) said: Spit it out! Spit it out! Do you not know that Zakat is not lawful for us.

14. *Abd al Muttalib ibn Rabi'a ibn al Harith* reported that Rabi'a ibn al Harith met Al Abbas ibn Abd Al Muttalib and said: 'By God, had we sent these two boys, meaning al Fadl ibn Abbas and myself, to the Messenger of Allah (peace & blessings of Allah be with him) to speak to him about appointing them as collectors who would collect and pay as the other people do and get a share as the other people get. While they spoke Ali ibn Abu Talib came and they told him about it, he said: Do not do that, by God, he (the Prophet) would not do that. Rabi'a ibn Harith turned to him and said: By God, you are only saying so out of jealousy because you are the son in law of the Messenger of Allah (peace & blessings of Allah be with him), while we harbor no jealousy for this reason. Ali said: Then send them if you want. So we left and when we went to his house we prompted each other to speak and one of us spoke and said: O Messenger of Allah! You are the most righteous one of man-kind who respects his blood relations. We have reached the age of puberty so

we have come to you for you to appoint us to collect Zakat, so we will pay you as the others pay and receive our share as the others receive. He remained silent for a long time, until we wanted to speak, then Zaynab indicated to us from behind the screen that we should not speak to him. Then he said: Zakat should not be for the family of Muhammad, as it is the means by which the people purify themselves.

15. *Anas* reported that the Prophet (peace & blessings of Allah be with him) was presented with some meat that had been offered to Buraira in charity. He remarked: 'This meat is a charity for Buraira, but for us it is a gift'.

16. *Abu Hurayra* reported that: If The Messenger of Allah (peace & blessings of Allah be with him) was offered food he would ask about it. If he were told it was a gift he would eat from it, and if he was told it was charity he did not eat from it.

17. It is reported from *Ibn Umar* that the Apostle of Allah (peace & blessings of Allah be with him) obligated the payment of one measure of dates or one measure of barley upon every Muslim whether free or slave, male or female, young or old, and he suggested that it should be paid before the Eid prayer.

18. *Abi Sayeed Al Khudri* is reported to have said: During the lifetime of the Messenger of Allah (peace & bles-

sings of Allah be with him) we used to go out on the morning of Eid al Fitr and give one measure of food, and Abu Sayeed said our food used to be, barley, raisins, ghee (cooking oil) and dates.

19. *Abd Allah ibn Umar* said: The Messenger of Allah (peace & blessings of Allah be with him) ordered the Zakat of the Feast (Al Fitr) to be paid before the Eid prayer.

20. *Abu Hurayra* is reported to have related that the Prophet said: I would like nothing better than to have a mountain like Uhud of gold, and (be left with) no Dinar with me except one Dinar which I would reserve to pay any debt.

21. *Abi Sayeed al-Khudri* is reported to have said: On Eid al-Fitr or Eid al-Adha the Messenger of Allah (peace & blessings of Allah be with him) went out to the place of prayer and after completing the prayer he gave the speech and told the people to give charity saying: O people, give charity!' Then he went over to the women and said:O women, give charity, for I have seen the Fire and the majority of its inhabitants are women.' They asked: 'Why, O Messenger of Allah?' He replied: 'You curse too much and are ungrateful to your husbands. I have not seen anyone of more fleeting memory and feeble in religion than you. Some of you could lead a sane man to lose his sanity.' Then he left and when he arrived at his house, Zainab, the wife of Ibn Mas'ud, came and asked permission to enter.

It was said: O Messenger of Allah! It is Zainab.' He asked: 'Which Zainab?' He was informed she was the wife of Ibn Mas'ud. He said: 'Yes, permit her to enter.' And she was allowed to come in. Then she said: 'O Prophet of Allah! You told people this day to give charity and I had an ornament which I intended to give as charity, but Ibn Mas'ud said that he and his children were more deserving of it than anyone else.' The Prophet (peace & blessings of Allah be with him) replied: 'Ibn Mas'ud has spoken in truth. Your husband and your children have more right to it than anybody else'.

22. *Abu Hurayra* reported that the Messenger of Allah (peace & blessings of Allah be with him) said: Allah Most High has said: O son of Adam spend and I shall spend on you. The Right Hand of God is full and unlimited and nothing will ever diminish it even by expending day and night.

23. *Haritha ibn Wahab* reported that the Messenger of Allah (peace & blessings of Allah be with him) said: O people! Give charity for a time is approaching when a person will seek to give in charity and will not find anyone to accept it, and any who are offered it will say: If you had offered it yesterday, I would have taken it, but today I have no need of it'.

24. It is reported from *Abu Hurayra* that the Messenger of Allah (peace & blessings of Allah be with him)

said: The earth will churn out lengths of its liver like pillars of gold and silver, and the murderer will say: I committed murder for this. And the one who severs blood relations will say: I severed my blood relations for this. And the thief will say: My hands were cut off for this. Then they will abandon it and take no more of it.

25. *Zainab*, the wife of Abd Allah ibn Mas'ud is reported to have said: I was in the Mosque and heard the Prophet (peace & blessings of Allah be with him) say: O women! Give charity, even from your ornaments.' Zainab used to provide for Abd Allah and other orphans who were in her care. So she said to Abd Allah: 'Will you ask the Messenger of Allah (peace & blessings of Allah be with him) if it will be sufficient for me to spend part of the Zakat on you and the orphans who are in my care?' He replied: Will you ask the Messenger of Allah (peace & blessings of Allah be with him) yourself?' So I went to the Apostle of Allah (peace & blessings of Allah be with him)) and found an Ansari woman there who was standing at his door with a problem similar to mine. Bilal passed us by and we asked him: 'Ask the Prophet (peace & blessings of Allah be with him) if it is permissible for me to spend the Zakat on my husband and the orphans in my care?' And we asked Bilal not to inform the Prophet (peace & blessings of Allah be with him) of our presence. So Bilal went inside and asked the Prophet (peace

& blessings of Allah be with him) about our problem. The Apostle of Allah (peace & blessings of Allah be with him) asked: 'Which two are they?' Bilal replied that she was Zainab. The Prophet (peace & blessings of Allah be with him) asked: 'Which Zainab?' Bilal said: 'The wife of Abd Allah.' The Messenger of Allah (peace & blessings of Allah be with him) said: Yes, and she will receive a double reward, one for helping her relatives and the other for giving Zakat.

26. *Anas ibn Malik* is reported to have said: Abu Talha owned more date palm tree gardens in Medina than any-one else of the Ansars, and his favorite was the Bairuha' garden which was in front of the Mosque of The Prophet (peace & blessings of Allah be with him). The Messenger of Allah (peace & blessings of Allah be with him) used to go there and drink its pleasant water." Anas also said: When the verses were revealed: 'You will not attain piety until you spend from what you love, and whatever you spend surely Allah knows of it,' (Q. 3: 92), Abu Talha said to the Prophet (peace & blessings of Allah be with him): 'O Messenger of Allah! God Almighty says: 'You will not attain piety until you spend from what you love,' and indeed the garden of Bairuha' is my favorite property, so I wish to give it in charity in the cause of Allah. I seek its reward from Allah. O Messenger of Allah! Use it as Allah guides you.' The

Prophet (peace & blessings of Allah be with him) said: 'It is indeed a valuable property, I hear what you have said and I deem it appropriate for you to give it to your close relatives.' Abu Talha said: 'I will do so, O Messenger of Allah! And Abu Talha divided the garden between his relatives and his cousins.

27. *Hadrat Ayesha* is reported to have said that someone came to the Messenger of Allah (peace & blessings of Allah be with him) and asked: My mother suddenly died without making a will, I think she would have given charity if she had time to speak. If I give charity on her behalf will it be accepted? He said: Yes.

28. *Jarir* reported that his father had said: We were in the presence of the Messenger of Allah (peace & blessings of Allah be with him) early one morning when some people came who had no shoes or clothes except woolen cloaks, wearing their swords around their necks. They all were from the tribe of Mudar. When the holy Prophet (peace & blessin-gs of Allah be with him) saw their plight his face changed, he went into his house and returned and ordered Bilal to pro-nounce the call to prayer. He pronounced the call to prayer. Then the Prophet prayed with them and recited the verses: O mankind! Fear Allah the One Who shaped you from a single person, and of the same kind He created his wife, and from the pair of them scattered many men and women. And fear Allah to whom you are answerable and the rights of the blood relationships. Indeed God is ever watching over you.' (Q.4: 1) Then he recited: O you who believe, fear Allah and let every soul consider what (provision) it has made for tomorrow.' (Q.58: 18) Some of them gave their Dinars and some gave their Dirhams, others their garments and others gave a measure of wheat and yet others a measure of dates, until he said: Even half a date. Then one of the Ansars came with a bag of money so large he could barely carry it, and they could hardly lift it. Then people kept coming until I saw two large piles of food and clothes, and I saw the face of the Prophet (peace & blessings of Allah be with him) shining with joy as if his face was of gold. The Messenger of Allah (peace & blessings of Allah be with him) said: The one who sets a good example in Islam is rewarded for that and for whoever followed him in it, without their reward being diminished at all. And the one who sets an evil example in Islam bears the consequences of it and the consequences of anyone who follo-wed him in it, without their punishment being diminished at all.

29. It is reported from *Abu Hurayra* that the Prophet said: While a man was standing in a plot of land, he heard a voice coming from a cloud saying: 'Water the orchard of so and so,' then the cloud burst straight away over a land where many black stones lay and a rivulet took the water away. The man

followed the water until he saw another man standing in his garden diverting the water with his hoe, so he asked him: O servant of Allah, what is your name?' He replied: 'So and so.' And that was the name he had heard spoken from the cloud. And he asked him: O servant of Allah, why do you ask me my name?' He said: 'I heard a sound in the cloud from where this water fell saying 'Water the garden of so and so,' and that is your name. So what do you do with this garden?' He said: 'Since you asked, I always look at what it produces and I pay Zakat one third, and I and my family eat one third, and I give away in charity one third.' He also said: 'I keep one third for the poor and the needy and the wayfarer.'

30. **Adi ibn Hatim** is reported to have said: While I was sitting with The Messenger of Allah (peace & blessings of Allah be with him) two people approa-ched him, one of them complained of poverty and the other complained about the prevalence of theft. The Apostle of Allah (peace & blessings of Allah be with him) said: 'As for theft and waylaying, a time is approaching when caravans will go to Makka unguarded. And as for poverty, the Hour will not come until a person will seek to give in charity and will not find anyone to accept it. And each one of you will stand before Allah and there will be neither a curtain nor an interpreter between you and Allah, and God will ask him: 'Did not I give you wealth?' He

will answer: 'Yes.' Then God will ask: 'Did I not send a Messenger to you?' And again he will answer 'yes'. Then he will look to his right and he will see nothing but the Fire, and then he will look to his left and will see nothing but the Fire. And so you should all save yourselves from the Fire by giving even half of a date in charity. And if you do not have even half a date, then be chari-table by saying a kind word to someone'.

31. **Abu Hurayra** is reported to have related that The Messenger of Allah said: The one who gives a family a she camel which produces a quantity of milk every morning and evening has a great reward.

32. It is reported from **Abu Hurayra** that the Messenger of Allah (peace & blessings of Allah be with him) said: There are seven whom God Almighty will protect with His Shade on the Day of Judgment; a ruler who was just, a youth who grew up worshipping Allah, the one whose heart yearns for the mosques, the two who love each other and meet each other and leave each other only for Allah's sake, a man who spurns the advances of a beautiful woman of high rank because he fears Allah, the one who gives charity so secretly that his right hand does not know what his left hand has given and the one who remembers Allah when he is alone and his eyes weep in remembrance of Him.

33. **Abu Hurayra** reportedly said: A man visited the Prophet (peace &

blessings of Allah be with him) and asked: 'O Messenger of Allah! Which charity will earn the better reward?' He replied: The charity you perform when you are healthy, stingy and fear poverty and wish to become wealthy. Do not put it off until death approaches and then say: Give something to so and so and something to so and so.' It will be too late'.

34. *Abu Hurayra* reported that the Messenger of Allah (peace & blessings of Allah be with him) said: If any of you give in charity the equivalent of one date out of money that you earned honestly. Then Allah will take it into His right hand and increase its reward for the one who gives it, in the same way as you raise a young foal, until it increases to the size of a mountain.

35. *Abu Hurayra* reported that the Apostle of Allah (peace & blessings of Allah be with him) said: O people, Allah is Good and He accepts only that which is good, and Allah has commanded the believers as He commanded the Messen-gers, He said: O Messengers, eat of the good things and do righteous deeds, surely I am All Knowing of what you do.' (Q.23: 51) And He said: O you who believe! Eat from the good things that We have bestowed on you, and be grateful to Allah, if He indeed is The One you wor-ship. And then he said: If a man travels on a long journey until his hair is untidy and dusty, then lifts his hands towards the heavens and says: O Lord! O

Lord!' while his food is unlawful, his drink is dishonest and his garments are illegiti-mate and his sustenance is illicit, how can his prayer be accepted?

36. *Abu Mas'ud* is reported to have said: We were told to give charity even though we were porters. Abu Aquil gave a half measure and another came with more than that, the hypocrites said: 'God is not in need this charity, and the other has only done it for show.' Then the verse was revealed: Those who taunt the believers who give charity freely, and those who find nothing to give except the fruits of their endeavors, they deride them. Allah will throw back their ridicule upon them, and they shall have a painful punishment.' (Q. 9: 79).

37. *Abu Hurayra* reported that the Messenger of Allah (peace & blessings of Allah be with him) said: If any of you eat a pair of anything for the sake of Allah he will be invited to enter Paradise: O servant of Allah, it is good.' And those who participated in Jihad will be invited to enter by the Gates of Jihad, and those who gave charity will be invited to enter by the Gates of Charity, and those who fast will be invited to enter by the Gate of al-Rayyan." Abu Bakr said: O Messen-ger of Allah! Will people be invited to enter through only one gate? Will anyone be invited to enter through all the gates?' The holy Prophet (peace & blessings of Allah be with him) said: Yes, and I hope you will be of them.

38. *Abu Hurayra* reported that the Messenger of Allah (peace & blessings of Allah be with him) asked: Which of you is fasting today? Abu Bakr said: "I am." He asked: "Which of you accompanied a funeral today?' Abu Bakr said: 'I did." He said: Which of you fed a poor man today? Abu Bakr said: "I did." He said: Which of you visited a sick person to-day?' Abu Bakr said: "I did." The Mes-senger of Allah (peace & blessings of Allah be with him) said: Whoever does such good deeds will certainly be admitted into Paradise.

39. *Hudhaifa* and *Abu Shaiba* reported that the Messenger of Allah (peace & blessings of Allah be with him) said: Every good deed is charity.

40. It is reported that *Abu Zarr* said: Some of the companions of the Prophet (peace & blessings of Allah be with him) asked him: O Messen-ger of Allah! The wealthy people have all the rewards. They offer prayer as we do, they fast as we fast, they give charity from their extra wealth. He said: Have you not been given the means to give charity? Every time you say 'Glory be to Allah' it is a charity, every time you say "Allah is Great' it is a charity, every time you say 'All thanks be to Allah' it is a charity, and every time you say 'There is no deity but Allah' it is a charity. And enjoining others to do good is a charity, and prohibiting evil is a charity, and a man's intimacy with his wife is a charity. They said: O Messenger of Allah! Is there a reward for us when we satisfy our sexual passion? He said: Conver-sely, if you were to spend it in a way that is prohibited, would it not be a sin? So if you expend it in a lawful way, should you not be rewarded?

41. It is reported from *Hadrat Ayesha* that the Messenger of Allah (peace & blessings of Allah be with him) said: Every son of Adam was created with three hundred and sixty joints, so who-ever glorifies Allah, and praises Allah, and bears witness that Allah is One, and seeks forgiveness from Allah, and remo-ves a stone or a thorn or a bone from the way of others, and enjoins good and forbids evil, three hundred and sixty four times, will have removed himself from the Fire (of Hell) on that Day.

42. *Abu Hurayra* reported that the Messenger of Allah (peace & blessings of Allah be with him) said: A man said he would give charity. He took his charity and went to find someone to give it to, but he put it in the hand of a thief, then the people said: 'He has given charity to a thief.' Then he said: All praise be to Allah! I will give another charity.' And he went out and gave charity to an adulteress. Then the people said: 'He has given charity to an adulteress.' So he said: All praise be to Allah! For my giving charity to an adulteress. I will give another charity.' So he went out and gave charity to a rich man. So the people said: 'He has given charity to a rich man.' So he said: All praise be to

Allah! For my giving charity to a thief, an adulteress and a rich man.' Someone came to him and said: The charity you gave to the thief may prevent him from stealing, as to the adulteress it may prevent her from committing adultery, and as for the rich man it may be an example he will take notice of so he would spend from what Allah has granted him'.

43. *Abu Hurayra* reported that the Messenger of Allah (peace & blessings of Allah be with him) said: The similarity of the miser and the one who gives charity is like the likeness of two people dressed in cloaks of iron. When the charitable one wishes to give in charity, the armour spreads out until it covers his whole body and hides even his fingertips and footprints. And whenever the miser wishes to give, it constricts and his hands are restrained to his neck and every ring gets fixed." And he said: "I heard The Messenger of Allah (peace & blessings of Allah be with him) say: And even if he tries to extend it, it does not extend'.

44. *Abu Hurayra* reported that the Messenger of Allah (peace & blessings of Allah be with him) said: Two angels come down from Heaven every day and one of them says: 'O Allah! Reward every person who spends in Your Cause,' and the other one says: O Allah! wipe out the misers'.

45. *Abu Musa al Ashari* reported that the Prophet (peace & blessings of Allah be with him) said: A Muslim storekeeper who honestly obeys his master and pays all that he has been ordered with a good heart and pays those who he has been ordered to pay, is one of the two kinds of charitable people.

46. *Asma' bint Abu Bakr al Siddiq* said that she went to the Prophet (peace & blessings of Allah be with him) and said: O Messenger of Allah! I have nothing except what al Zubair brings to the house. Is there any blame on me if I give some of it in charity?' He said: "Give as much as you can afford, and do not tighten your purse, or Allah will with-hold His blessings from you.

47. *Hadrat Ayesha* is reported to have related that the Messenger of Allah (peace & blessings of Allah be with him) said: When a woman gives some unspo-iled food in charity, she will receive the reward for what she has given and her husband will receive the reward of what he earned, and the storekeeper will receive a similar reward. The reward of one does not diminish the reward of others.

48. *Umair*, the freed slave of Abu al Lahm said: My master ordered me to cut some meat into slices, and a poor man came to me, so I gave him some of it to eat. My master heard about it and beat me. I went to The Messenger of Allah (peace & blessings of Allah be with him) and I told him about the incident. He called him and said: *Why* did you beat him? He replied: He gave food

away without permission. He said: You both will be rewarded for it.

49. *Abu Hurayra* reported that the Messenger of Allah (peace & blessings of Allah be with him) said: A woman should seek the permission of her husband to fast when he is present, and she should not permit any *Mahram* into his house when he is present without his permission. And anything she spends from his wealth without his permission, half of the reward is for him.

50. *Abu Sayeed al- Khudri* said: Some of the Ansars asked the Messenger of Allah (peace & blessings of Allah be with him) for something and he gave it to them. They asked him again and he gave them. And then they asked him again and once more he gave them until all he had with him was finished. And then he said: If I had anymore I would not keep it from you. Whoever refrains from asking others, Allah will give him contentment, and whoever tries to make himself self-sufficient, Allah will make him self-sufficient. And whoever tries to be patient, Allah will make him patient. No one can be given a greater and better blessing than patience'.

51. *Amr ibn Al A'as* reported that the Messenger of Allah (peace & blessings of Allah be with him) said: The successful one is the one who has embraced Islam, who has sufficient for his needs and who is content with what Allah has bestowed upon him.

52. *Mu'awiya* reported that the Messenger of Allah (peace & blessings of Allah be with him) said: Do not beg with impunity, by Allah, any of you who asks me for anything and because of his persistence I have to give it to him while I dislike his demand, he will be blessed in that which I gave him.

53. *Abd Allah ibn Umar* reported that the Prophet (peace & blessings of Allah be with him) said: A man persists in asking others for something until he faces Allah Almighty without any flesh on his face.

54. *Abu Hurayra* reported that the Apostle of Allah (peace & blessings of Allah be with him) said: By Him in Whose Hand is my soul it is better for any of you to fetch a rope, cut and collect wood and carry it upon his back and sell it rather than ask someone for something and that person may give it to him or may not. *Al Zubair ibn Al Awwam* reported that the Prophet (peace & blessings of Allah be with him) said: By Him in Whose hand is my soul it is better for any of you to fetch a rope and collect a bundle of wood upon his back and sell it and God will save his face because of that, rather than to ask the people who may give him or may not.

55. *Abd Allah ibn Umar* said: I heard The Messenger of Allah (peace & blessin-gs of Allah be with him) speaking from the pulpit concerning charity and refrai-ning from asking others for money, and about

begging, he said: 'The hand which gives is better than the hand which takes. And the hand that gives is the foremost and the hand that takes is the meanest.

56. *Hakim ibn Hizam* said: I asked the Prophet and he gave it to me. I asked again and he gave me. I asked him once again and he gave me. And then he said: 'This property is like a tender fruit and whoever takes it without greed, he is blessed in it, and whoever takes it with greed, he is not blessed in it, and he is like the one who eats but is never satisfied, and the hand that gives is better than the hand which receives'.

57. *Abu Hurayra* reported that the Apostle of Allah (peace & blessings of Allah be with him) said: The poor person is not the one who demands a morsel or two or a date or two from others. They asked: O Messenger of Allah! Who is the poor one? He said: He is the one who has nothing and is ashamed to beg from the people.

58. *Abu Hurayra* reported that the holy Prophet (peace & blessings of Allah be with him) said: Fortune is not the wealth of the world but fortune is the wealth of the soul.

59. *Anas* reported that the Messenger of Allah (peace & blessings of Allah be with him) said: The son of Adam grows old, but he retains two (things), the lust for wealth and the lust for life.

60. *Abu Sayeed Al-Khudri* reported that

the Prophet (peace & blessings of Allah be with him) was once seated upon a pulpit and we sat around him. Then he said: 'What I fear most for you is that you will indulge in the pleasures and delights of this worldly life.' Someone said: O Messenger of Allah! Can good produce evil?' The Prophet (peace & blessings of Allah be with him) remained silent for a while and it was said to that person: What is the matter with you? You speak to The Prophet (peace & blessings of Allah be with him) when he is not speaking to you?' Then we noticed that he was receiving Divine inspiration. The Apostle of Allah (peace & blessings of Allah be with him) then wiped away his sweat and said: Where is the one who asked the question?' It appeared that the Prophet (peace & blessings of Allah be with him) had liked his question. Then he said: 'Good never produces evil. It is as the growth upon the banks of a stream that either kills the animals or makes them ill, unless they eat their fill of it and face the sun and defecate and urinate and graze again. Indeed wealth is sweet and green, blessed is the wealth of a Muslim who gives from it to the poor, the orphan and those in need during their journeys. Indeed whoever takes it unlawfully is as the one who eats but is never satisfied and his wealth will bear witness against him on the Day of Reckoning.

61. *Umar ibn Al-Khattab* is reported to have said: The Messenger of Allah

(peace & blessings of Allah be with him) would give me something but I used to say to him: 'Please give it to someone more poor and needy than me.' The Prophet (peace & blessings of Allah be with him) said to me: Take it. If you are given something from this property without having asked for it or having a desire for it then take it, and if you are not given it, do not pursue it.

62. *Qabisa ibn Mukhariq al Hilali* said: I was in debt and I went to the Messenger of Allah (peace & blessings of Allah be with him) and asked him to pay it for me. He said: Wait until we receive the Zakat so that we may order it to be given to you. Then he said: O Qabisa, it is not permissible to beg except in three cases, for the one who is in debt, he may beg until he clears his debt, then he must desist, the one whose property has been destroyed in a disaster, he may beg until he obtains sufficient to live or enough to provide him with a reasonable suste-nance, and the one who has been impoverished, and his condition has been verified by three responsible persons from his people, he may beg until he obtains sufficient to live or enough to provide him with a reasonable sustenance. O Qabisa, other than those in these three situations, begging is forbidden, and the one who indulges in it consumes that which is unlawful.

11

Book of Fasting

1. *Abu Hurayra* has reported the Messenger of Allah (Peace & blessings of Allah be with him) as saying that God Almighty said: "Every deed of the son of Adam is for himself except for fasting which is for Me, and I will reward (him/her) for it." Fasting wards off the Fire (of Hell) and sin. On the day when any of you fasts, he should avoid approaching his wife intimately, and avoid arguing, and if anyone fights or argues with him he should say: 'I am fasting.' By Him in whose hand is Muhammad's soul! The smell that issues from the mouth of the fasting person is better than the scent of musk in the sight of Allah. There are two pleasures for the one who fasts, one when he breaks his fast, and the other when he meets his Lord, then he will rejoice because of his fasting."

2. *Abu Hurayra* has reported that the Messenger of Allah (Peace & blessings of Allah be with him) said: "When Ramadan starts, the gates of Paradise are opened."

3. It is related by *Abu Hurayra* that the holy Prophet (Peace & blessings of Allah be with him) said: "You should not fast a day or two before the month of Ramadan (commences) unless you habitually fast, then you may do so."

4. *Ibn Umar* has reported that: "I heard The Messenger of Allah (Peace & blessings of Allah be with him) say: 'When you see the crescent (indicating the beginning of the month of Ramadan) begin fasting, and when you see the crescent again, stop fasting, and if the sky is overcast then complete the month of Ramadan in thirty days."

5. *Umm Salama* has reported that the holy Prophet (Peace & blessings of Allah be with him) pledged to stay apart from his wives for a period of one month, and after the completion of twenty-nine days he went to his wives in the morning or in the afternoon. It was said to him: 'You pledged to stay apart from your wives for a month.' He said: 'The month is twenty-nine days'."

6. *Anas ibn Malik* has reported that the holy Prophet (peace & blessings of Allah be with him) said: "Take your pre-dawn (sahri) meal as there is blessing in it."

7. *Zayed ibn Thabit* has reported: "We took our pre-dawn meal with the holy Prophet (peace & blessings of Allah be with him). Then he rose up to pray. I asked: 'How long was the length of time between the predawn meal and the call to prayer?' He replied: 'the length of time was sufficient to recite fifty verses of the Qur'an, "

8. It is reported by *Samura ibn Jundab* that the Messenger of Allah (peace & blessings of Allah be with him) said: "You should not mistake Bilal's call to prayer as the signal to stop eating and begin your fast, nor the vertical streaks of light, but you should stop eating when the light spreads out." Hammad related that he indicated with his hand in a horizontal position.

9. It is reported from *Hadrat Ayesha* and *Umm Salama* that: "Sometimes the call to prayer at dawn was made while the Messenger of Allah (peace & blessings of Allah be with him) was in a state of ritual impurity from having approached his wife. Then he would bathe and fast."

10. It is reported that *Hadrat Ayesha* said: "A man came to the Messenger of Allah (peace & blessings of Allah be with him) and he asked: 'O Messenger of God, I am sometimes in a state of ritual impurity when the call to prayer is pronounced, should I still fast?' The Messenger of Allah (peace & blessings of Allah be with him) said: 'If the call to prayer is pronounced when I am in a state of ritual impurity, I fast.' He said: 'O Messenger of Allah, you are not like us for

God has forgiven your former and later sins.' The holy Prophet replied: 'By God, I trust I am the most God fearing of you and that I am the most knowledgeable amongst you to be aware of those things of which I should be aware."

11. *Abu Hurayra* has reported that the holy Prophet (peace & blessings of Allah be with him) said: "If any of you eat or drink in absentmindedness then let him complete his fast, as what he ate and drank was from God."

12. *Hadrat Ayesha* is reported to have said: "A man came to the Messenger of Allah (peace & blessings of Allah be with him) and said: 'I am in the fire.' The holy Prophet (peace & blessings of Allah be with him) asked the reason and he replied that he was intimate with my wife in the daytime during Ramadan.' The holy Prophet remarked: 'Give charity, give charity.' The man said: 'I have nothing.' He told him to sit down and he was brought two baskets of food, and the Apostle of Allah (peace & blessings of Allah be with him) said: 'give (away) these in charity.'"

13. *Hadrat Ayesha* is reported to have said that the holy Prophet (peace & blessings of Allah be with him) used to kiss and embrace his wives while he was fasting, and he was able to control his desire more than one else.

14. *Sahl ibn Sa'ad* is reported to have said that the Messenger of Allah (peace & blessings of Allah be with him) said: "The people will remain on the right path as long as they hasten to break their fast."

15. *Abu Atiyya* is reported to have said: "I went to Ayesha with Masruq and he asked her: "Two of the Companions of Muhammad are most righteous, but one of them hastens to offer the sunset prayer and to break his fast, and the other delays the sunset prayer and delays in breaking his fast." She asked: "Who hastens to offer the sunset prayer and to break his fast?" He replied: "Abd Allah." Hadrat Ayesha remarked: "That is what the Messenger of Allah (peace & blessings of Allah be with him) used to do."

16. *Abu Hurayra* is reported to have said: "The Messenger of Allah (peace & blessings of Allah be with him) prohibited continuous fasting. So one of the Muslims said: 'But you fast continuously O Messenger of Allah!' The holy Prophet (peace & blessings of Allah be with him) replied: 'Which of you is like me, I am given food and drink by my Lord during my sleep.' When the people refused to stop continuous fasting the holy Prophet (peace & blessings of Allah be with him) fasted day and night continuously with them for a day and then another day and then they sighted the crescent moon. The holy Prophet (peace & blessings of Allah be with him) told them: 'Had it (moon) not appeared, I would have made you fast longer.'

17. *Ibn Abbas* is reported to have said: "The Messenger of Allah (peace & blessings of Allah be with him) traveled during the month of Ramadan when he was fasting, until he reached Usfan where he ordered

a cup of something to drink and he drank it in front of everyone so that they would see, and he broke his fast until he arrived in Makka." Ibn Abbas added: "The Messenger of Allah (peace & blessings of Allah be with him) fasted and then broke his fast, so whoever wished fasted and whoever wished to break his fast did so."

18. *Jabir ibn Abd Allah* is reported to have said: "In the year of the Conquest of Makka the Messenger of Allah (peace & blessings of Allah be with him) was procee-ding towards Makka and he fasted until he reached Kura' al-Ghamim, and the people fasted with him. Then he asked for a cup of water and raised it aloft for the people to see, and he drank it. After that he heard that some people had continued fasting, so he said: 'they are disobedient, they are disobedient.'"

19. *Jabir ibn Abd Allah* is reported to have said: "The Messenger of Allah (peace & blessings of Allah be with him) was on a journey when he saw a crowd of people and they were shading a man. He asked what the matter was? They said: 'A man is fasting.' Then the holy Prophet (peace & blessings of Allah be with him) said: "It is not a good thing to fast while you are traveling."

20. *Abu Saeed al-Khudri* is reported to have said: "We set off on a foray with the Messenger of Allah (peace & blessings of Allah be with him) on the sixteenth of Ramadan. Some of us fasted and others broke their fasts, but

those who were fasting did not criticize those who broke their fast, nor did those who were not fasting criticize those were fasting."

21. *Anas* is reported to have said: "We were on a journey with The Messenger of Allah (peace & blessings of Allah be with him) and some of us were fasting and others were not. We dismounted at a place on a hot day and most of us shaded ourselves. Those who were fasting fainted and the others who were not fasting rose up and set up the tents and provided water to the mounts. The Messenger of Allah (peace & blessings of Allah be with him) said: "Those who broke their fast have gained reward this day."

22. *Abu Saeed al- Khudri* is reported to have said: 'We traveled to Makka with the Messenger of Allah (peace & blessings of Allah be with him) and we were fasting, when we stopped at a place the Messenger of Allah (peace & blessings of Allah be with him) said: 'You are approaching the enemy and if you break your fast you will have more energy.' And so we were permitted that concession, but some of us continued in their fast and some broke it. We dismounted at another place and he said: 'You will meet the enemy in the morning and if you break your fast you will have more energy, so break your fasts.' It had been our intention. We broke our fast. Later we fasted with the Messenger of Allah (peace & blessings of Allah be with him) when we were traveling.' "

23. *Hamza ibn Umar al-Aslami* is reported to have said that the Messenger of Allah (peace & blessings of Allah be with him) said: "God Almighty has given you a concession,(in not fasting during traveling) so whoever takes advantage of it, it is good and whoever prefers to fast there is no sin upon him." Harun related that the holy Prophet (peace & blessings of Allah be with him) said: "It is a concession" and he did not relate that he said 'From God Almighty.'"

24. *Abu al Darda'* is reported to have said: "We set off on a journey with the Messenger of Allah (peace & blessings of Allah be with him) on a day which was very hot, it was so hot we had to shade our heads with our hands from the heat. None of us was fasting except the holy Prophet (peace & blessings of Allah be with him) and Ibn Rawaha."

25. *Hadrat Ayesha* is reported to have said that the Messenger of Allah (peace & blessings of Allah be with him) said: "Who-ever has died and has missed days of fasting then his near of kin should fast for him."

26. *Abd Allah ibn Buraida* has narrated that his father said: "We were sitting in the presence of the Messenger of Allah (peace & blessings of Allah be with him) when a woman came to him and said: 'I gave my mother a servant girl as a gift and now my mother has died.' He said: 'The reward is for you and she has been returned to you as a legacy.' She said: 'She has fasts still due upon her, may

I make them up for her?' He said: "Fast on her behalf.' She said: 'She did not perform the pilgrimage, may I perform it for her?' He said: 'Perform the pilgrimage on her behalf.' "

27. *Abd Allah ibn Shaqiq* is reported to have said: "I asked (Hadrat) Ayesha: 'Did the Messenger of Allah (peace & blessings of Allah be with him) fast for a whole month?' She replied: 'I never saw him fast a whole month except during the month of Ramadan, and he used to fast a few days a month until he passed away.' "

28. *Abu Saeed al-Khudri* is reported to have said that the Messenger of Allah (peace & blessings of Allah be with him) said: "For every servant of God who fasts one day for the sake of Allah, then God Almighty will distance his face from the Fire (of Hell) by seventy years."

29. *Abu Hurayra* is reported to have said that the Messenger of Allah (peace & blessings of Allah be with him) said: "After the month of Ramadan, the best month to fast is the month of al Muharram, and after the prescribed prayers, the best prayer is the night prayer."

30. It is reported from Hadrat *Ayesha* that: "The Quraysh used to fast on the day of Ashura' before the advent of Islam, and the Messenger of Allah (peace & blessings of Allah be with him) also used to fast on that day. When he arrived in Medina he fasted on the day of Ashura and enjoined fasting on that day. Later when fasting during Ramadan became

obligatory, he ceased to fast on the day of Ashura' and whoever wished to fast on that day was free to do so and whoever did not, was free not to do so."

31. *Ibn Abbas* was asked about fasting on Ashura?' He said: 'When you see the new crescent of Muharram, then calculate the days and fast on the ninth day.' He was asked if the Messenger of Allah (peace & blessings of Allah be with him) used to observe the fast on that day?' He replied in the affirmative.

32. *Ibn Abbas* is reported to have said: "The holy Prophet (peace & blessings of Allah be with him) came to Medina and saw the Jews fasting on the day of Ashura'. He asked them: 'Why do you fast?' They said: 'This is a good day, it is the day on which God saved the Children of Israel from their enemy, so Moses fasted on this day.' The holy Prophet (peace & blessings of Allah be with him) remarked: 'I have better claim on Moses than you.' Thereafter he fasted during Ashura and enjoined the Muslims to do the same.

33. It is related that *Ibn Abbas* was asked about fasting on the day of Ashura, and he said: "I know of no other day which the Messenger of Allah (peace & blessings of Allah be with him) favored as the most excellent day to fast than this day, meaning Ashura, and this month, meaning Ramadan."

34. *Abu Salama* has reported that Hadrat Ayesha said: 'I never saw him (the holy Prophet -peace & blessings of Allah be with him) fasting more than in the month of Sha'ban. He almost fasted during the whole month of Sha'ban except a few days.'"

35. *Abu Ayyub al Ansari* is reported to have said that the Messenger of Allah (peace & blessings of Allah be with him) said: "Whoever fasts (during the month of) Ramadan and then fasts during the first six days of Shawwal, it will be as if he has fasted continuously."

36. *Abu Qatada* is reported to have said: "A man came to the Messenger of Allah (peace & blessings of Allah be with him) and asked: 'How do you fast?' The Apostle of Allah (peace & blessings of Allah be with him) was annoyed by his interruption. When Hadrat Umar perceived this he said: 'we are well pleased with Allah as our Lord, with Islam as our Religion, and with Muhammad as the Prophet of Allah. We seek refuge in Allah from the wrath of God and His Messenger.' Umar repeated this until his anger subsided. Then Umar said: 'O Messenger of Allah, what about the one who fasts continuously?' The holy Prophet (peace & blessings of Allah be with him) asked: 'He did not fast nor break his fast,' and he asked: 'Is anyone able to do that?' 'What about the one who fasts on alternate days?' 'That is the way David used to fast.' He asked: 'What about the one who fasts one day and breaks his fast for two days?' 'I wish I had the strength to do that.' Then he said: 'Fasting for three days every month and fasting in Ramadan is continuous fasting, I beseech Allah Almighty that fasting on the day of Arafat will blot out all

former and later sins, and I beseech Allah Almighty that fasting on the day of Ashura will blot out all the sins of the preceding year."

37. *Abu Ubaid*, the freed slave of Ibn Azhar, is reported to have said: "I offered the Feast prayer with Umar ibn al-Khattab and when he had prayed he spoke to the people saying: 'The Messenger of Allah (peace & blessings of Allah be with him) had forbidden fasting on two days, that is the Feast of Eid al-Fitr and the Feast (of Eid al-Adha) when you eat your sacrificial animals."

38. It is related from *Nubaisha al-Hudhali* that the Messenger of Allah (peace & blessings of Allah be with him) said: "The three days after the day of the sacrifice are days for eating and drinking."

39. *Abu Qatada* is reported to have said: "The Messenger of Allah (peace & blessings of Allah be with him) was asked about fasting on Mondays, so he said: 'It is the day I was born and the day Revelation was sent down upon me."

40. *Abu Hurayra* is reported to have said that the Apostle of Allah (peace & blessings of Allah be with him) said: "Do not consider Friday night a priority over other nights in offering prayer and do not consider Friday as a priority over other days in fasting, but only fast it if you usually fast on days which precede it."

41. *Hadrat Ayesha* was reportedly asked if the Messenger of Allah (peace & blessings of Allah be with him) had

fasted for three days every month. She said: 'Yes.' When asked on which days of the month he used to keep his fast, she replied: 'He did not choose particular days on which he would fast.' "

42. *Abd Allah ibn Umar ibn al-A 'as* is reported to have said: "The Apostle of Allah told me: 'O Abd Allah! Have I not told you that you fast every day and pray every night." Abd Allah answered: "Yes, O Messenger of Allah!" The holy Prophet (peace & blessings of Allah be with him) then said: "Desist from doing so, fast for a few days and leave it for a few days, offer prayers and sleep at night, for your body has a right upon you, and your wife has a right upon you, and your guest has a right upon you. And it is enough for you to fast for three days a month, as the reward of a good deed is multiplied ten times, thus it will be as if you fasted all year." I insisted upon fasting and so I said: "O Messenger of Allah! I have the ability." The holy Prophet (peace & blessings of Allah be with him) said: "Fast like Prophet David and do not exceed that." I asked: "What was the fasting of David, the holy Prophet of Allah?" He replied: "Half the year." Later when Abd Allah grew old he used to say: "It would have been better if I had taken the Prophet's advice."

43. *Abd Allah ibn Umar* (may God be pleased with them) is reported to have said that the Apostle of Allah (peace & blessings of Allah be with him) said: "The most liked fasting before God Almighty is the fasting of David

(peace be upon him), he used to sleep for half the night and stand in prayer for a third of it, and then sleep the sixth of it and fast on alternate days."

44. *Abu Saeed al-Khudri* (may God be pleased with him) is reported to have said: "The Messenger of Allah (peace & blessings of Allah be with him) used to retreat for prayers and meditation during the first ten days of Ramadan, thereafter during ten days in mid-Ramadan in a Turkish tent which had a rug over its door. He took the rug and put in a corner inside the tent. He put out his head and spoke to some people and they approached and he said: 'I went into retreat for the first ten nights to seek the Night of Power (Lailat al Qadr), then I went into retreat during the middle ten nights, then an angel was sent to me and I was informed that it (Lailat al-Qadr) was in the last ten nights of Ramadan. So any of you who wishes to go into retreat may do so.' The people joined him in retreat and he said: 'it was revealed to me upon a night of uneven number and I saw in the vision that I was prostrating in the morning in clay and water. So on the morning of the twenty-first night I rose up for the dawn prayer and it was raining and the water leaked into the mosque and I saw clay and water.' When he came out after the dawn prayer his head and his nose had traces of clay and water, and that was on the twenty first night of the last ten nights of Ramadan."

45. It is related that Hadrat *Ayesha*, the wife of the holy Prophet (peace & blessings of Allah be with him) said:

"The Apostle of Allah (peace & blessings of Allah be with him) used to go into retreat during the last ten days of Ramadan until his death, and thereafter his wives used to go into retreat."

46. It is reported that Hadrat *Ayesha* (may Allah be pleased with her) said that during the last ten nights of Ramadan the Messenger of Allah (peace & blessings of Allah be with him) remained awake at night, he woke his family and offered prayers.

47. *Ibn Umar* is reported to have said that the Apostle of Allah (peace & blessings of Allah be with him) said: "Look for the Night of Power (Lailat al Qadr) during the last ten nights. If any of you feel lethargic at the beginning, you should not permit yourselves to succumb to it in the last week."

48. *Abd Allah ibn Anas* is reported to have said that the Messenger of Allah (peace & blessings of Allah be with him) said: "I looked for the Night of Power (Lailat al Qadr) , then I was made to forget it, then I saw myself prostrating in water and clay the next morning." He said: "On the twenty third night it rained and The Messenger of Allah (peace & blessings of Allah be with him) led us in prayer and when he turned back, there were traces of water and clay upon his forehead and nose." He said: "Abd Allah ibn Anas said it was the twenty third."

49. *Abu Saeed al-Khudri* is reported to have said: "The Messenger of Allah (peace & blessings of Allah be with him) went into retreat in mid Ramadan to seek the Night of Power (Lailat al Qadr) before he was ordered to look for it. When the nights passed he ordered the tent to be taken down. Then he was ordered to look for it in the last ten nights and the tents were pitched again. He went to the people and said: "O people, the Night of Power was shown to me and I came out to inform you of it, but two people were arguing with each other and a devil was with them, and I forgot it. So look for it during the last tens nights of Ramadan, look for it on the ninth, on the seventh and on the fifth." I said: "O Abu Saeed, you know better about numbering.' He said: "Yes, indeed we know better than you." I said: "What is the ninth, seventh and fifth?" He replied: "When twenty one nights have passed and the twenty second begins, it is the ninth, and when twenty three have passed, there follows the seventh, and when twenty five nights have passed there follows the fifth."

50. *Ubayy ibn Ka'b* is reported to have sworn that it (Lailat ul Qadr) was on the twenty seventh night. When asked on what basis he says that, he replied: 'On the basis that The Messenger of Allah (peace & blessings of Allah be with him) said that it is on the day when the sun will rise without any rays of light'."

12

Book of Pilgrimage

1. *Abu Hurayra* is reported to have said that the Messenger of Allah (peace & blessings of Allah be with him) addressed us saying: "O people God has made the Pilgrimage obligatory upon you, so perform the Pilgrimage." A man asked: "O Messen-ger of Allah, every year?" The holy Prophet (peace & blessings of Allah be with him) remained silent and the man repeated his question three times, at that the Apostle of Allah (peace & blessings of Allah be with him) said: "If I say it is, it would become obligatory and you would not be able to do it." He then said: "Do not ask me more than I have told you, for people before you questioned excessively and they were destroyed for that, and for their rejection of their Prophets, so when I order you to do anything, just do it to the extent of your ability, and when I prohibit something, then desist from it."

2. *Abu Hurayra* is reported to have said that the Messenger of Allah (peace & blessings of Allah be with him) said: "From one Umrah to another is an expiation for sins committed between them. And the reward of a perfect Pilgrimage is nothing less than Paradise."

3. *Abu Hurayra* is reported to have related that the Messenger of Allah (peace & blessings of Allah be with him) said: "Whoever comes to this House (Ka'ba) to perform the Pilgrimage and abstains from sexual relations with his wife, and who does not utter any vulgarity, he will return like the day his mother gave birth to him."

4. It is related from *Hadrat Ayesha* that the Messenger of Allah (peace & blessings of Allah be with him) said: "The day of Arafat is the day upon which many people will be freed from the Fires of Hell. His Mercy nears and He lauds them before the angels and says: 'what do they beseech?'"

5. *Ibn Umar* (may Allah be pleased with him) is reported to have said: "When the Messenger of Allah (peace & blessings of Allah be with him) used to mount upon his she-camel for a journey, he would proclaim: 'God is Great' three times, and then he would say: 'Glory be to The One Who has subjected this (mount) for us and we have no power (to do so), and to our Lord is our return. O God, we seek Your goodness and piety and make our journey pleasing to You. O God, ease our journey and ease its distance for us, O God, You are our companion on this journey, protect our families. O God, I seek refuge in You from the perils and hardships of this journey, and from any loss in property or family upon my return.' He used to say this and then add: 'we return in repentance and in worship of our Lord and extolling His praises.'"

6. *Abu Saeed al-Khudri* (may Allah be pleased with him) is reported to have said that the Messenger of Allah (peace & blessings of Allah be with him) said: "It is not lawful for any woman who believes in Allah and the Hereafter to go on a journey which lasts for three days or longer, except when she is accompanied by her father, her son or her husband or her brother, or by another Mahram."

7. *Abu Hurayra* (may God be pleased with him) is reported to have said: "It is not lawful for any woman who believes in Allah and the Hereafter to go on a one day journey except with a Mahram."

8. *Ibn Umar* (may Allah be pleased with him) is reported to have narrated that: "I listened to the Messenger of Allah (peace & blessings of Allah be with him) when he was delivering a speech saying: 'No man may be alone with a woman except when a *Mahram* is with her, and no woman may go on a journey except with a *Mahram*.' A man stood up and said:

'O Messenger of Allah, my wife has set off on pilgrimage while I have enlisted to participate in a battle.' He said: 'Go and perform Pilgrimage with your wife.' "

9. *Ibn Abbas* is reported to have related that: "The holy Prophet (peace & blessings of Allah be with him) happened to meet some riders at Al Rauha, so he asked them who they were. They said they were Muslims and asked him: 'Who are you?' He said: 'I am the Messenger of Allah.' One woman raised a child up to him and asked: 'Is Pilgrimage due upon this child?' He said: 'Yes, and a reward is for you.

10. *Abd Allah ibn Abbas* has related that: "Al Fadl ibn Abbas was riding behind the Messenger of Allah (peace & blessings of Allah be with him) when a woman from the tribe of Khatham came to consult the Prophet. She said: 'O Messenger of Allah! The obligation of Pilgrimage commanded by God upon His devotees has become due upon my father while he is old and weak and he cannot sit upon a mount, so may I perform the Pilgrimage on his behalf?' He said: 'Yes.' This happened during the farewell Pilgrimage."

11. *Ibn Abbas* is reported to have said: "The Messenger of Allah (peace & blessings of Allah be with him) prescribed Dhul-Hulaifa as the starting point for the people of Medina to commence pilgrimage, Al-Juhfa for the people of al Sham; *(Syria, Palestine, Lebanon and Jordan)*, Qarn for the people of Najd, and Yalamlam

for the people of Yemen, these points are fixed for the people of those places, and for those who pass through them on their way to perform Pilgrimage and Umrah; and whoever comes from places other than these may commence pilgrimage from where he starts, even the people of Makka may start from Makka."

12. It is related that *Abu Zubair* said: "I heard Jabir ibn Abd Allah (may God be pleased with them), when he was asked about the location for entering the state of pilgrimage, say: 'The Prophet was asked this question, and I heard him say: 'Dhul-Hulaifa is the starting point for the people of Medina to commence pilgrimage, and the other way is Al-Juhfa. For the people of Iraq the starting point is from Irk and Qarn for the people of Najd, and Yalamlam for the people of Yemen.'''

13. According to *Abu Saeed al-Khudri* the Messenger of Allah (peace & blessings of Allah be with him) mentioned that musk is the best of perfumes.

14. *Abu Hurayra* is reported to have said: "The Messenger of Allah (peace & blessings of Allah be with him) said: 'Whoever is offered sweet basil should not refuse it, as it is light to carry and (has a) fragrant smell.' "

15. *Salim ibn Abd Allah* is reported to have said that he heard his father say: "The Messenger of Allah (peace & blessings of Allah be with him) never commenced pilgrimage from anywhere except at the Mosque of Dhul-Hulaifa, so your claim that the Messenger of Allah (peace & blessings of Allah be with him) commenced his Pilgrimage at the high hill is untrue."

16. It was related that *Jabir* has related that: "we went with the Messenger of Allah (peace & blessings of Allah be with him) intending to perform the Pilgrimage, and Ayesha intended to perform Umrah. When we reached Makka we circumambulated the Ka'ba and ran to and from Safa and Marwa, and the Messenger of Allah (peace & blessings of Allah be with him) ordered that whoever had no sacrificial animal with him should go out from his state of pilgrimage. We asked: 'What does this mean?' He said: 'Going out completely from the state of pilgrimage.' So we went to our wives and put on perfume and wore our everyday clothes, and we were four days out from Arafat. Then we went back into a state of pilgrimage on the eighth of Dhul Hijja. The Messenger of Allah (peace & blessings of Allah be with him) went to Ayesha and found her weeping, he asked her what the matter was?' She replied: 'my menses have commenced and the people have put off their state of pilgrimage, and so did I and I did not circumambulate the House. Now people are going to perform the Pilgrimage. He said: 'This is something that Allah has decreed for the daughters of Adam, so bathe and put on the state of pilgrimage and perform the Pilgrimage. She did so and stayed at the stations until her menses ceased, then she circumam-bulated the Ka'ba and went around Safa and Marwa. The holy Prophet (peace & blessings of Allah be with him) then said: 'Now both your Pilgrimage and Umrah are complete.' Hadrat Ayesha replied: 'O Messenger of Allah, I feel that I circumam-bulated the Ka'ba only for the Pilgrimage.' So he said: "O Abd Al Rahman, go with her and perform Umrah.'"

17. *Abd Allah ibn Umar* has related that when the Messenger of Allah (peace & blessings of Allah be with him) used to sit upon his mount at Dhul Hulaifa mosque on his way to pilgrimage, he used to recite: "I respond to Your call O God, I respond to Your call O God, and I obey Your command, You have no partner, I respond to Your call. All praise and blessings are for You. All sovereignty belongs to You. And You have no partner." And it is also related that Abd Allah ibn Umar used to repeat the same words and used to add to that: "I respond to Your call, I respond to Your call, I respond to Your call, and I obey Your command, all goodness is in Your Hands, and we seek Your pleasure in our deeds."

18. *Anas* is reported to have said: "I heard the Messenger of Allah (peace & blessings of Allah be with him) calling aloud the Name of God saying: 'I respond to Your call, I intend to perform Umrah and the Pilgrimage together.'"

19. *Musa Ibn Nafe'* is reported to have said: "I arrived in Makka intending to perform Umrah, it was four days prior to the day of Arafat, so the people said: 'Your pilgrimage will commence from Makka.' I asked Ata' ibn Abu Rabbah and he said: 'Jabir ibn Abd Allah al Ansari said: 'I performed the Pilgrimage with The Messenger of Allah (peace & blessings of Allah be with him) on the year he drove the camels with him. The people had intended only to perform Pilgrimage. The Messenger of Allah (peace & blessings of Allah be with him) ordered them to put off their state of pilgrimage after circumam-bulating the Ka'ba, and going to and fro between Safa and Marwa, and to cut their hair short and to remain there as those who were not on pilgrimage until the day of Tarwiya (one day before the day of Arafat) when they would go into a state of Pilgrimage and they were ordered to make the state of pilgrimage with which they had come before for Umrah alone.' They asked: "How can we perform Umrah when we intended to perform Pilgrimage?" The holy Prophet (peace & blessings of Allah be with him) told them to do as he had instructed: "Do as I order you. Had I not brought this sacrificial animal with me I would have done the same, but I cannot put off the state of pilgrimage until the sacrificial animal reaches its destination." So they did as the holy Prophet had instructed."

20. *Abu Musa* is reported to have said: "I went to the Messenger of Allah (peace & blessings of Allah be with him) while he was encamped at Batha'. He asked me about my intention. I replied: 'I intend as the

Prophet of Allah intends.' He asked me if I had brought any sacrificial animal with me. I answered in the negative. The Apostle of Allah (peace & blessings of Allah be with him) then said: 'Then circumam-bulate the House and go to and fro between Safa and Marwa and then come out from your state of pilgrimage.' So I circumam-bulated the House and went to and from between Safa and Marwa, then I went to a woman of my tribe and she washed and combed my hair, and I told the people of this during the reign of Abu Bakr and Umar. And it was during the time of Pilgrimage while I was addressing the people, a man came and said: 'You do not know what the Amir of the Believers has done with regard to the sacrificial animals.' So I said: 'O people, whoever we have advised regarding any matter should wait as the Amir of the Believers is coming to you, and you should follow him.' When he came I said: 'O Amir of the Believers, what have You advised regarding the sacrificial animals?' He said: 'We follow the Book of God and God Almighty has said: 'And perform the Pilgrimage (Hajj) and the Umrah for Allah, but if you cannot then make such offering as may be feasible, and do not shave your heads until the offering reaches its destination, and if any of you are ill or have an ailment in his scalp, then a compensation should be made by fasting or by offering charity or by offering sacrifice (slaughtering of a lawful animal for the needy) and when you are in peace, whoever enjoys the Umrah until the Pilgri-mage (Hajj), let his offering be such as may be feasible, or if he finds none, then a fast of three days during the Pilgrimage and of seven days when you return, that is ten days in all, this is only for those whose homes are not in the precincts of the Sacred Mosque. And fear Allah and know that Allah is severe in punishment.' (Q.2: 196) And we follow the ordinance of our Prophet Muhammad (peace & blessings of Allah be with him) indeed, he did not go out of the state of pilgrimage until he slaughtered the sacrificial animals."

21. *Abu Zarr* is reported to have said: "Umrah during the Pilgrimage was specially for the Companions of Muhammad (peace & blessings of Allah be with him)."

22. *Nafe* is reported to have said: "Abd Allah ibn Umar went to perform Umrah during the time of affliction (When Al Hajjaj fought Abd Allah ibn al Zubair) and he said: 'If I am hindered from visiting the House, I shall do as we did in the company of the Messenger of Allah (during the of Hudaybiyah).' Then he went out intending to perform Umrah and marched on until he reached al Baida'. (A place between Makka & Medina) He turned to his companions and said: 'The matter concerns one thing, and I call you to bear witness that I perform Pilgrimage and Umrah compulsory for myself.' And he went on until he reached the House and circumambulated it seven times and went to and fro between Safa and Marwa seven times, and he did nothing in addition to that, and he considered it sufficient, then he slaughtered the sacrificial animal."

23. *Abd Allah Ibn Umar* is reported by Salim ibn Abd Allah to have said: "The Messenger of Allah (peace & blessings of Allah be with him) performed Umrah and Pilgrimage during his Farewell Pilgrimage. He led a sacrificial animal from Dhul Hulaifa, the Messenger of Allah (peace & blessings of Allah be with him) performed Umrah and then Pilgrimage. And the people performed Umrah and Pilgrimage with him. Some of them had driven sacrificial animals with them and others had not. So when The Messenger of God (Prayers & peace be upon him) reached Makka he said to the people: "Whoever has driven a sacrificial animal should not leave his state of pilgrimage until he completes his Pilgrimage. And those who have not brought sacrificial animals with them should circumambulate the Ka'ba and go to and fro between Safa and Marwa, then cut their hair short and put off their state of pilgrimage, later they should again go into the state of pilgrimage for Pilgrimage then offer a sacrificial animal. And if anyone cannot afford to buy a sacrificial animal then they may fast for three days while on Pilgrimage and for seven days when they return home." When the Messenger of Allah (peace & blessings of Allah be with him) arrived in Makka, he kissed the Black Stone first while circumambulating the Ka'ba and he ran the first three rounds of the seven and then walked for the remaining four rounds. After completing his circumambulation of the House he offered two Rak'at of prayer at Abraham's station, then when he finished he went to and fro between Safa and Marwa seven times and he did not put off his state of pilgrimage until he had completed it. He slaughtered his sacrificial animal on the day of slaughtering and then came down from Mina and circumam-bulated the House, then went out from his state of pilgrimage.

24. *Hadrat Ayesha* is reported to have said: "We set off with the Messenger of Allah (peace & blessings of Allah be with him) in the year of the Prophet's Farewell Pilgrimage. Some of us had intended Umrah alone, and some had intended Pilgrimage alone. When we reached Makka the Messenger of Allah (peace & blessings of Allah be with him) said: 'Whoever intended Umrah and did not bring a sacrificial animal let him put off his state of Pilgrimage, and whoever intended Umrah and has brought a sacrificial animal should not leave his state of pilgrimage until he slaughters his sacrifice and whoever intended Pilgrimage let him remain in the state of pilgrimage until he completes his Pilgrimage.' Hadrat Ayesha (may Allah be pleased with her) said: ' I began menstru-ating and was menstruating until the day of Arafat, and I had intended to perform Umrah. The Messenger of Allah (peace & blessings of Allah be with him) told me: 'Untie and comb your hair and make your intention for Pilgrimage and give up your intention for Umrah.' I did so and when I completed my Pilgrimage the Messenger of Allah sent Abd al-Rahman ibn Abi Bakr with me and asked me to make an intention for Umrah from Al-Tan'im where my Pilgrimage had commenced.-'"

25. *Ibn Abbas* is reported to have said: "Duba'a bint Al Zubair ibn Abd al Muttalib came to the Messenger of Allah (peace & blessings of Allah be with him) and said: 'I am a woman afflicted with ill health, and I wish to perform Pilgrimage, what would you order me to do?' He said: 'Intend a state of pilgrimage, on the condition that the place where you feel unable to continue would be the place where you will leave the state of pilgrimage.' She managed to complete the Pilgrimage.'

26. *Ya'li ibn Monayah* is reported to have said: While the holy Prophet (peace & blessings of Allah be with him) was at Ju'raana a man came to visit him wearing a cloak scented with perfume and he asked: "What would you order me to do for my Umrah?" Then the Apostle of Allah (peace & blessings of Allah be with him) received Divine inspiration and was covered with a garment. Ya'li said: 'I always hoped to see the holy Prophet while he was receiving Revelation.' Umar asked him: 'Would it please you to see the Prophet receive Reve-lation?' So Umar raised the side of the garment and I looked under it and saw that the face of the Messenger of Allah (peace & blessings of Allah be with him) was red and his breathing was noisy. When this condition had passed the holy Prophet (peace &

blessings of Allah be with him) asked for the man who wanted to know about Umrah and told him to go and wash the perfume off from his body and remove the cloak and to do the same for Umrah as is done during pilgrimage.

27. *Ibn Umar* is reported to have said: "A man asked the Messenger of Allah (peace & blessings of Allah be with him) 'What should the one who is in a state of pilgrimage wear?' The Apostle of Allah (peace & blessings of Allah be with him) said: 'Do not wear shirts, nor turbans, nor trousers, nor head covers, nor socks except if you do not find sandals, then he may wear socks but he must cut them below the heel. And do not wear any dress which has perfume or saffron."

28. *Ibn Abbas* reportedly said: "I heard the Messenger of Allah (peace & blessings of Allah be with him) say while he was addressing the people: 'The Trousers are for those who cannot find a waist wrapper, and socks are for those who cannot find shoes.' He meant this was for those who were in a state of pilgrimage."

29. *Ibn Abbas* is reported to have said: "Zayed ibn Arqam came and Abd Allah ibn Abbas asked him: 'Do you remember what you told me regarding the meat of a hunt which was presented to the Messenger of Allah (peace & blessings of Allah be with him) while he was in a state of pilgrimage?' He replied: 'A part of the meat of the hunt was presented to the Messenger of Allah (peace & blessings of Allah be with him) but he declined

to accept it saying: 'We cannot eat it because we are in a state of pilgrimage.' "

30. *Abd Allah ibn Abu Qatada* is reported to have said that the Messenger of Allah (peace & blessings of Allah be with him) proceeded to perform Pilgrimage and we went along with him. According to Abu Qatada: 'He (the holy Prophet) sent some of his companions including Abu Qatada along the coastal route telling them to continue on until they met him.' So they went on ahead of the Prophet and they were all in a state of pilgrimage except Abu Qatada. On their way they saw a wild ass, so Abu Qatada killed it and cut off its back legs. They dismounted and ate from it, then they said: 'We have eaten ass while we are in a state of pilgrimage.' So they collected what remained of the ass and when they met with the Apostle of Allah they said: 'O Messenger of Allah, we intended Pilgrimage but Abu Qatada did not, then we saw wild ass and Abu Qatada killed one and we dismounted and ate from it, then we said, 'How can we eat flesh of the hunt while we are in a state of pilgrimage? We have brought with us what remained of its meat.' He said: 'Did any of you order him or indicate to him to do so?' They said: 'No.' Then he said: 'Then eat what remains of it.'

31. Hadrat *Ayesha* is reported to have said that the holy Prophet (peace & blessings of Allah be with him) said: "There are five types of animal which are harmful and which may be killed in the Sanctuary (of the Ka'ba)

whether you are in a state of pilgrimage or not. These are, the snake, the crow, the rat, the rabid dog and the kite."

32. *Ibn Umar* is reported to have said that the holy Prophet (peace & blessings of Allah be with him) said: "There is no blame on anyone who kills five types of animal which are harmful and which may be killed in the Sanctuary whether you are in a state of pilgrimage or not. These are, the rat, the scorpion, the crow, the kite and the rabid dog."

33. *Abd Allah ibn Hunan* reportedly said: "Abd Allah ibn Abbas and Al Miswar ibn Makhrama differed between themselves. Abd Allah ibn Abbas said that one in a state of pilgrimage could wash his head, while Al-Miswar held that he should not do so. Ibn Abbas sent me to Abu Ay al-Ansari to ask him about it. I found him bathing between the two wooden posts of the well and he was screened by a piece of cloth. I greeted him and he asked who I was. I said: "I am Abd Allah ibn Hunan and I have been sent to you by Abd Allah ibn Abbas to ask you how the Messenger of Allâh (peace & blessings of Allah be with him) used to wash his head while he was in a state of pilgrimage." Abu Ay caught hold of the piece of cloth and lowered it until I could see his head and then he told someone to pour water over his head. He poured the water on his head and Abu Ay rubbed his head with his hands by passing them from back to front and from front to back and said: "Thus I saw the holy Prophet

(peace & blessings of Allah be with him) do."

34. *Abd Allah ibn Ma'qil* reportedly said: "I sat in the mosque with Ka'ab and asked him regarding the verse: '...a compensation should be made by fasting or by charity or by offering sacrifice (slaughtering of a lawful animal for the needy) ... (Q.2: 196) Ka'ab said: "It was revealed on account of me. I had an affliction in my hair and I went to the Messenger of Allah (peace & blessings of Allah be with him) while great numbers of lice were falling on my face. The holy Prophet (peace & blessings of Allah be with him) remarked: "I did not know you were so afflicted as I see now. Can you find a sheep?" I said: "No." So the verse 'a compensation should be made by fasting or by charity or by offering sacrifice (slaughtering of a lawful animal for the needy)...' was revealed. So he said: 'Fast for three days or feed six needy people with a half measure of dates each' The verse was revealed on account of me but it is for you all."

35. *Ibn Abbas* is reported to have said: "A man fell from his camel and he broke his neck and died. The holy Prophet (peace & blessings of Allah be with him) said: "Wash him with water and lotus and shroud him in two pieces oz cloth, but do not perfume him or cover his head, for he will be raised on the Day of Resurrection saying: 'I respond to Your call'."

36. *Abd Allah ibn Umar* is reported to have said: "The Messenger of Allah (peace & blessings of Allah be with him) used to depart to Makka from the way of the tree and return from the way of Mu'arras. And whenever he entered Makka he used to enter from the heights and leave from the valley."

37. *Ibn Umar* is reported to have said: "When the Messenger of Allah (peace & blessings of Allah be with him) circumam-bulated the Ka'ba during the Pilgrimage and Umrah, he would run for the first three rounds and walk in the last four rounds. Then after circumambulating he used to pray two Rak'at and then go to and fro between Safa and Marwa."

38. *Jabir ibn Abd Allah* reportedly said: "I saw the Messenger of Allah (peace & blessings of Allah be with him) circumambulating quickly from the Black Stone three times."

39. *Abu Tufail* is reported to have said: "I asked Ibn Abbas (may Allah be pleased with him): 'Do you know if circumam-bulating the House quickly for three rounds and walking for four rounds is Sunna, for your people claim that it is the Sunna?' He said: 'They have spoken truthfully and they have lied.' I asked: 'What do you mean they have spoken the truth and they have lied?' He said: 'The Messenger of Allah (peace & blessings of Allah be with him) came to Makka and the unbelievers asserted that Muhammad and his Companions were so famished they would be unable to circumambulate the House, this was on account of their jealousy of him. So the Messenger of Allah

(peace & blessings of Allah be with him) told them to walk quickly for the first three rounds and then to walk for the other four rounds.' I asked him: 'Tell me if it is Sunna to go to and fro between Safa and Marwa when mounted, for your people regard it as the Sunna.' He said: 'They have spoken truthfully and they have lied.' I asked: 'What do you mean they have spoken the truth and they have lied?' He said: 'The Messenger of Allah (peace & blessings of Allah be with him) came to Makka and there was such a multitude of people gathered around him, and even the virgins had come out of their houses, and they were saying: 'It is Muhammad, it is Muhammad.' The Messenger of Allah (peace & blessings of Allah be with him) would not permit that the people be pushed back to make way for him, so when the crowd hovered around him, he rode on his she-camel. However to walk around or to go around at a brisk pace is better."

40. It is related from *Abd Allah ibn Sarjis* that: "I saw a bald man, that is Umar ibn al-Khattab (may Allah be pleased with him), kiss the Black Stone saying: "By God, I know that you are only a stone which can do no harm or benefit. Had I not seen the Messenger of Allah (peace & blessings of Allah be with him) kissing you I would not have done so."

41. *Ibn Umar* is reported to have said: "I have never missed touching the two corners of the Ka'ba, whether in a crowd or alone, from the time I saw the Apostle of Allah (peace & blessings of Allah be with him) touch them."

42. *Jabber* is related to have said: "During his last Pilgrimage the Apostle of Allah (peace & blessings of Allah be with him) circumambulated the Ka'ba mounted upon a camel and he touched the corner with his stick for the people to see him. He made himself noticeable so that they would be able to see him and question him for he was surrounded by crowds of people."

43. *Umm Salama* is reported to have said: "I complained to the Messenger of Allah (peace & blessings of Allah be with him) about my illness and he said: 'Circumambulate behind the people mounted.' She said: 'so I circumambulated and the Apostle of Allah (peace & blessings of Allah be with him) was praying at the side of the House and he was reciting: 'By the Mount Tur, and By a Scripture inscribed.' (Q. 52: 1-2).

44. *Urwa* is reported to have said: "I said to Ayesha: 'I see that there is no blame on me if I do not circumambulate between Safa and Marwa." She said: "How is that?" I said: "Because God Almighty has said: 'Indeed! Safa and Marwa are among the religious ceremonies of pilgrimage ordained by Allah, so whoever performs pilgrimage to the Sacred House or pays a visit to it (Umrah), there is no harm if he circumam-bulates them.'(Q.2: 158)." Then she said: "Had it been as you claim it to be then there is no harm for the one who does not go to and fro between them. But it was revealed regarding some of the Ansars who before becoming Muslims used to visit the idol of 'Manat', so it was embarrassing for them to go to and fro between Safa and Marwa when they became Muslims. They mentioned this to the holy Prophet, and then Allah Almighty revealed this verse. By God, God did not permit any pilgrimage to be completed without going to and fro between Safa and Marwa.'" It was also related that Hadrat Ayesha said: 'God does not accept a pilgrimage or Umrah from anyone who does not go to and fro between Safa and Marwa'."

45. *Jabbar ibn Abd Allah* is reported to have said: "Neither the holy Prophet (peace & blessings of Allah be with him) nor his companions went to and fro between Safa and Marwa except once."

46. *Ibn Umar* is reported to have said: "The Messenger of Allah (peace & blessings of Allah be with him) circumambulated the House seven times and prayed two Rak'at at the station of Abraham and then went to and fro between Safa and Marwa seven times, and there is an ideal for you in the Messenger of Allah (peace & blessings of Allah be with him)."

47. *Ibn Umar* is reported to have narrated: "The Messenger of Allah (peace & blessings of Allah be with him) arrived on the day of the conquest (of Makka) and stood in the courtyard of the Ka'ba and sent for Uthman ibn Talha. He came with the key, opened the gate and the holy Prophet (peace & blessings of Allah be with him), Bilal, Usama ibn Zayed and Uthman ibn Talha entered the Ka'ba, then the gate was closed on the instructions of the holy Prophet. They stayed there for some time and then the gate was re-opened." Ibn Umar added: "I was the first to meet the Messenger of Allah outside, Bilal was close behind him and I asked him: 'Did the Messenger of Allah (peace & blessings of Allah be with him) pray inside?' Bilal replied; "Yes, he prayed inside." I asked: "Where?" He replied: "Between the two pillars in front of him." Ibn Umar added: "I forgot to ask how many Rak'at the holy Prophet (peace & blessings of Allah be with him) had prayed."

48. *Jafar ibn Mohammed* is reported to have narrated that his father said: "We went to Jabir bin Abd Allah and he asked who I was and I said: 'I am Mohammed ibn Ali ibn Hussain.' So he put his hand upon my head and placed his hand on my chest. Then he said: 'Welcome son of my brother, ask me as you please.' I asked him: Tell me about the pilgrimage of the Messenger of Allah (peace & blessings of Allah be with him). He indicated nine with his fingers and began: The Messenger of Allah (peace & blessings of Allah be with him) stayed in Medina for nine years but did not perform the pilgrimage, then in the tenth year it was proclaimed that the Messenger of Allah (peace & blessings of Allah be with him) intended to perform the pilgrimage, so many people came to Medina, all of them seeking to follow the Messenger of

Allah (peace & blessings of Allah be with him) and copy his deeds. So we proceeded with him until we reached Dhul Hulaifa where Asma bint Umais gave birth to Muhammad ibn Abu Bakr, she sought the advice of the holy Prophet (peace & blessings of Allah be with him) and he counseled her to wash herself and wear a garment and make an intention for pilgrimage. Thereafter the holy Prophet (peace & blessings of Allah be with him) prayed in the mosque and mounted upon al-Qaswa (his she-camel). When she stood upright with him upon her back at al-Baida', as far as I could see in front of me and behind me and to my right and to my left were throngs of riders and people on foot. The Messenger of Allah (peace & blessings of Allah be with him) was amid us and receiving Revelation, and he knew its interpretation. And whatever he did we did likewise. He began with: I respond to your call O God, I respond to your call O God, and I obey your command, You have no partner, I respond to Your call. All praise and blessings are for You. All sovereignty belongs to You. And You have no partner'. The people were repeating it after him. Jabir said: when we reached the House with him, he touched the pillar and circumambulated quickly for three rounds and walked for the other four. Then he went to the Station of Abraham (peace be upon him) where he recited: and take Abraham's place of worship as your place of worship... (Q.2: 125). He stood with the station between himself and the House. My father said that the holy Prophet offered two Rakahs and recited: Say, He is Allah The One and Only...' (Q.112) And say, O unbelievers...' (Q.109) Then he returned to the pillar and touched it, then went out through the gate to Safa and when he reached near it he recited: 'Indeed Safa and Marwa are among the religious ceremonies ordained by Allah.. (Q.2: 158). And he said I will begin with which Allah started, then he started from Safa he ascended it until he could see the House, then he turned towards the Qibla and praised Allah and glorified Him, and said: There is no god but Allah, no partner is with Him, All praise and sovereignty is for Him, and He has power over all things, there is no god but Allah, the One and Only, He grants victory to His servants, and He alone defeats the parties.' Then he invoked between these words and repeated them three times, then he descended to Marwa and when he reached the valley he walked quickly until we mounted Marwa and so he walked until he reached Marwa. And he repeated the same he had done on top of Safa, and when he finished his going to and fro between Safa and Marwa at Marwa he said: 'Had I known before what I know now I would not have brought sacrificial animals with me and I would have performed Umrah, so if any of you have not brought sacrificial animals with him, then let him perform Umrah and put off his state of pilgrimage.' Suraqa ibn Malik ibn Ju'sham said: 'O Messenger of Allah (peace & blessings of Allah be with him), is it just for this year or from now on?' So the Messenger of Allah (peace & blessings of Allah be with him) intertwined his fingers and said: 'Umrah intertwines with the Pilgrimage.' And he repeated it twice and said: 'For ever and ever.' Ali returned from Yemen with the gift of a camel for the Prophet (peace & blessings of Allah be with him) and he found Fatimah was among those who had left the state of pilgrimage; she had dressed in colored garments and had put on perfume. He disapproved of this and so she said: 'My father ordered me to do that.' The narrator said: 'Ali used to say while he was in Iraq, I went to the Messenger of Allah (peace & blessings of Allah be with him) to incite him against Fatimah for what she did, asking the Messenger of Allah (peace & blessings of Allah be with him) about what she said he had told her to do, and I informed him I disapproved of what she did. But he said: 'She spoke the truth, she spoke the truth, and what did you say when you intended to perform Pilgrimage?' Ali said: 'O God, I intend to perform what Your Messenger has intended to perform.' He said: 'Since I have sacrificial animals with me I cannot go out from my state of pilgrimage.' He said: 'The number of sacrificial animals which Ali brought from Yemen together with those which the Prophet brought was one hundred in all.' Then all the people, except the Prophet and those who had brought sacrificial animals with them, went out from their state of pilgrimage and had their hair cut, and when it was the day of Tarwiya they went to Mina and went back into their state of pilgrimage for performing the Pilgrimage and the Messenger of Allah (peace & blessings of Allah be with him) rode and led the midday, afternoon and sunset, evening and dawn prayers. Then he stayed a little while until the sun had risen and ordered a tent of hide to be pitched at Namira. The Messenger of Allah (peace & blessings of Allah be with him) then walked until he reached Mash'ar al Haram and stopped there. The Quraysh thought he would stop there, since it was their practice before Islam. But he walked on until he reached Arafat and came to the tent that had been pitched for him at Namira. He stayed in it until sunset, then he asked for Qaswa to be brought to him, he rode it until he reached the depth of the valley and he addressed the people saying: 'O People, lend me an attentive ear, for I know not whether, after this year, I shall ever be amongst you again. Therefore, listen to what I am saying to you very carefully and take these words to those who could not be present today. O People, just as you regard this month, this day, this city as sacred, so regard the life and property of every Muslim as a sacred trust. Return the goods entrusted to you to their rightful owners. Hurt no one so that no one may hurt you. Remember that you will indeed meet your Lord, and that He will indeed take account of your deeds. God has forbidden you to take interest; therefore, all interest obligations shall henceforth be waived. Your capital, however, is yours to keep. You will neither inflict nor suffer inequity. God has judged that there shall be no interest and that all interest due to Abbas ibn Abd al Muttalib (the Prophet's uncle) shall henceforth be waived. Every right arising out of homicide in pre-Islamic days is henceforth waived and the first such right I waive is that arising from the murder of Rabi'a ibn Al-Harith (relative of the holy Prophet). O Men, the unbelievers indulge in tampering with the calendar in order to make permissible that which God forbade, and to forbid that which God had made permissible. With God the months are twelve; four of them are holy; three of these are successive and one occurs singly between the months of Jumadah and Shaaban. Beware of Satan, for the safety of your religion. He has lost all hope that he will ever be able to lead you astray in big things, so beware of following him in small things. O People, it is true that you have certain rights with regard to your women, but they also have rights over you. If they abide by your rights then to them belongs the right to be fed and clothed in kindness. Do treat your women well and be kind to them for they are your partners and committed helpers. And it is your right that they do not make friends with any one of whom you do not approve, as well as never commit adultery. O People, listen to me in earnest, worship God, perform your five daily prayers, fast during the month of Ramadan, and give your wealth in Zakat. Perform the Pilgrimage if you can afford to. All mankind is from Adam and Eve, an Arab has no superiority over a non Arab, nor a non-Arab has any superiority over an Arab; also a white has no superiority over a black, nor a black has any superiority over white except by piety and good action. Learn that every Muslim is the brother of another Muslim, and that Muslims constitute one brotherhood. Nothing shall be legitimate to a Muslim that belongs to a fellow Muslim unless it was given freely and willingly. Do not, therefore, do injustice to yourselves. Re-member, one day you will appear before God and answer for your deeds. So beware, do not stray from the path of righteousness after I am gone. O People, no Prophet or Messenger will come after me and no new faith will be born. Reason well, therefore, O People, and understand my words that I convey to you. I leave behind me two things, the Qur'an and my example, the Sunna, and if you follow these you will never go astray. All those who listen to me shall pass on my words to others, and those to others again; and may the last ones understand my words better that those who listen to me directly. Be my witness O God, that I have conveyed Your message to Your people.' He said this three times then Bilal pronounced the call to prayer and the Prophet led the midday prayer. Then he called later and the Prophet led the afternoon prayer and he prayed no other prayer between the two. The Messenger of Allah (peace & blessings of Allah be with him) mounted his camel Qaswa and led her towards the rocky side of the track facing the Qibla with those who were walking in front of him on the path. He stood there until the sun had set and the light had almost gone and the sphere of the sun had vanished. He made Usama sit behind him and he pulled Qaswa's reins to the extent that her head touched the saddle and he indicated to the people to keep an even pace. Whenever he passed over a high tract of sand he relaxed the reins until she climbed up and so he came to al Muzdalifa where he led the sunset and evening prayers with one call to prayer and he did not offer additional prayer in between the two. The Messenger of Allah (peace & blessings of Allah be with him) then lay down until dawn and offered the dawn prayer after the call to prayer and Iqama were pronounced when the morning light was appearing. He mounted Qaswa and went to Al Mash'ar al Haram and faced the Qibla, invoked God Almighty and glorified Him and bore witness to His Oneness. He stood there until the daylight was clear and then he left quickly before the sun rose, with Al Fadl ibn Abbas seated behind him. He reached Jamarat where he threw seven small stones with his hands while saying: 'God is Great' at every throw. Then he went on to the place of sacrifice and slaughtered sixty-three camels by his own hands, and he distributed his sacrifice. Then he ordered a piece of meat from each sacrificial animal to be put into a pot and cooked. When it was cooked he took some of the meat from it and drank some of the soup. The Messenger of Allah (peace & blessings of Allah be with him) mounted once

again and visited the House and offered the midday prayer at Makka. Thereafter he visited the family of Abd al Muttalib who were charged with the care of Zam Zam, and said: 'Draw water, O Bani Abd al-Muttalib! Had it not been   that the people would take this right from you, I would have drawn water with you.' So they drew a bucket for him and he drank it."

49. *Hadrat Ayesha* is reported to have said: "Quraysh and whoever believed in their creed, used to stand at Al Muzdalifah, and they called themselves 'Al Hums' while the rest of the Arabs used to stand at Arafat. When Islam came God Almighty commanded His Prophet to go to Arafat and stay there, and then to hasten on from there, and thus the saying of the High Exalted: "Then hasten on from where the people hasten." (Q. 2: 199).

50. It is related from *Umar* that his father said: "The Messenger of Allah (peace & blessings of Allah be with him) used to combine the sunset and evening prayers at Muzdalifah and he did not offer any additional prayers between them. He offered three Rak'at in the sunset prayer and two Rak'at in the evening prayer, and Abd Allah ibn Umar used to offer prayers the same way until he met his Lord."

51. *Abd Allah ibn Umar* is reported to have said: "I always saw the Messenger of Allah (peace & blessings of Allah be with him) offering prayers at their due time except for two, the sunset and evening prayers at Muzdalifah."

52. It is related from *Jabir* that: "I saw the holy Prophet (peace & blessings of Allah be with him) casting small stones while mounted upon his camel on the day of sacrifice, and he said: 'Learn from me the ceremonies of the Pilgrimage, as I do not know if I will perform another Pilgrimage after this one'."

53. *Jabir* is reported to have said: "The Messenger of Allah (peace & blessings of Allah be with him) used to cast stones in the forenoon of the day of sacrifice, and after that when the sun had set."

54. According to *Jabir* the Messenger of Allah (peace & blessings of Allah be with him) said: "An uneven number of stones should be used for cleansing after ans-wering the call of nature, and in throwing on the day of Arafat, and an uneven number should be performed in circumam-bulating. And when any of you needs to use stones he should use an odd number."

55. *Ibn Umar* has related that: "The Messenger of Allah (peace & blessings of Allah be with him) shaved his head during the Farewell Pilgrimage."

56. *Abu Hurayra* is reported to have said: "The Messenger of Allah (peace & blessings of Allah be with him) said: 'Please God! Forgive those who have shaved their heads.' They said: 'O Messenger of Allah, and those who cut their hair short.' He said: 'Please God! Forgive those who have shaved their heads.' They said: 'O Messen-ger of Allah, and those who cut their hair short.' He said three times: 'And those who cut their hair short'."

57. It is related from *Anas* that: "The Messenger of Allah (peace & blessings of Allah be with him) threw stones at the greater Jamarat. Then he offered sacrifice of an animal. The barber was sitting there so he had the right side of his head shaved, then he distri-buted it (his hair) among those who were around him, then he got the other side of his head shaved and gave his hair to Abu Talha.

58. *Abd Allah ibn Amr ibn al A'as* is reported to have said: "The Messenger of Allah (peace & blessings of Allah be with him) halted while mounted upon his camel and the people came to ask him, one said: 'O Messenger of Allah I did not know that stones should be thrown before slaughte-ring, so I slaughtered before casting the stones.' The holy Prophet (peace & bles-sings of Allah be with him) replied: 'Cast and do not worry.' Then another man asked: 'I did not know that slaughte-ring should be before shaving, so I shaved before I slaughtered.' He said: 'Slaughter and do not worry.' And whatever he was asked that day, his reply was: 'Do it and do not worry'."

58. *Amra bint Abd Al Rahman* is reported to have said that Zayed wrote to Hadrat Ayesha telling her that Abd Allah ibn Abbas had said: "Whoever sends his sacrificial animal to the Ka'ba, then whatever is unlawful for a pilgrim becomes unlawful for him until he slaughters it. I have sent my sacrificial animal so tell me what should I do?' According to Amra Hadrat Ayesha said: "It is not as Ibn Abbas has said, I twined the garlands of the sacrificial animals of the Messenger of Allah (peace & blessings of Allah be with him) with my own hands. Then the Mes-senger of Allah (peace & blessings of Allah be with him) put them around their necks with his own hands, and sent them with my father. But the Messenger of Allah (peace & blessings of Allah be with him) did not forbid anything which had been made lawful by God Almighty before the slaughtering the sacrificial animal."

59. *Hadrat Ayesha* is reported to have said that: "Once the holy Prophet (peace & blessings of Allah be with him) sent sheep as the sacrificial animals for his family and he garlanded them."

60. *Abu Hurayra* is reported to have said that the Messenger of Allah (peace & blessings of Allah be with him) saw a man leading his sacrificial camel. He said: "Ride it." The man said: "It is my sacrificial camel." The holy Prophet (peace & bles-sings of Allah be with him) repeated: "Ride it." He said: "It is my sacrificial camel." The holy Prophet (peace & blessings of Allah be with him) said for the third or second time: "Woe to you! Ride it."

61. *Al Zubair* is reported to have said that he heard Jabir ibn Abd Allah, when he was asked about riding animals say: I heard the Messenger of Allah (peace & blessings of Allah be with him) say: 'Ride it kindly, if you need to, until you find some-thing else to ride.'"

62. According to *Ibn Abbas, Zu'aib Abu Qabisa* told him that the Messenger of Allah (peace & blessings of Allah be with him) used to send the sacrificial animals with him and say: "If any of these falls from exhaustion and you think it is going to die, then slaughter it and dip its hooves into its blood and mark its hump with it, but none of you or your companions should eat it."

63. *Jabir ibn Abd Allah* is reported to have said: "We set off with the Messenger of Allah (peace & blessings of Allah be with him) intending to perform Pilgrimage, so the Messenger of Allah (peace & blessings of Allah be with him) ordered us to share the sacrificial animals, every seven of us to share in either a camel or one of the cattle."

64. It is related that *Jabir ibn Abd Allah* said: "The Messenger of Allah (peace & blessings of Allah be with him) slaughtered a cow on behalf of Hadrat Ayesha on the day of sac-rifice."

65. It is related that *Zayed ibn Zubair* said that Ibn Umar passed by a man who had made his sacrificial camel sit down in order to slaughter it. Ibn Umar said: "Slau-ghter it while it is standing tied up accor-ding to the tradition of your Prophet (peace & blessings of Allah be with him)."

66. *Hadrat Ali* is reported to have said: "The Messenger of Allah (peace & blessings of Allah be with him) asked me to supervise the slaughter of his sacrificial animals and to give their skins and covering sheets in charity

and not to give any part of it to the butcher, and he said: 'We will give him from what we have for ourselves'."

67. *Ibn Umar* is reported to have said: "The Messenger of Allah (peace & blessings of Allah be with him) circumambulated the House on the day of sacrifice, then returned and offered the midday prayer at Mina."

68. It is related that *Hadrat Ayesha* said: "We set off with the Messenger of Allah (peace & blessings of Allah be with him) in the year of Farewell Pilgrimage. Some of us had intended Umrah alone, and some had intended both the Pilgrimage and Umrah, and others had intended Pil-grimage. The Messenger of Allah (peace & blessings of Allah be with him) intended Pil-grimage. Thus whoever had intended Umrah then he puts off his state of pilgrimage, but those intended Pilgrimage or to combine Pilgrimage and Umrah did not leave their state of pilgrimage until the day of sacrifice."

69. It is related that *Ibn Umar* said: The Prophet (peace & blessings of Allah be with him) Abu Bakr and Umar (may Allah be pleased with them) used to stay at al Abtah (a place in the environs of Makka).

70. *Hadrat Ayesha* is reported to have said: The residing at al -Abtah was not mandatory, but the Messenger of Allah (peace & blessings of Allah be with him) stayed there because it was convenient for his travel.

71. It is related that *Bakr ibn Abd Allah*

al Muzani said: "A bedouin came to Ibn Abbas while I sat with him near the Ka'ba and asked: "Why is it that your uncle's children gave milk and honey while you give date water? Are you poor or are you misers?" Ibn Abbas said: "Praise be to God, we are neither poor not misers, but the Messenger of Allah (peace & blessings of Allah be with him) came here upon his she camel with Usama mounted behind him and asked for water, so we gave him a cup of date water and he drank it, and then he gave some to Usama, and the Prophet said: 'You have done well, you have done well, so continue doing this.' So we do not wish to do other than the Messenger of Allah (peace & blessings of Allah be with him) ordered us to do."

72. It is related that *Al Ala' ibn al Hadrami* said that the Messenger of Allah (peace & blessings of Allah be with him) said: "The pilgrim should remain in Makka for three days after completing the ordinances of the Hajj."

73. *Ibn Abbas* is reported to have said: "The people used to disperse in every direction, then the Messenger of Allah (peace & blessings of Allah be with him) said: 'No one should leave Makka except by way of the Ka'ba.'"

74. *Hadrat Ayesha* is reported to have said: "Safiyah bint Huyy began her menses after she had visited Arafat and circumambulated, so she mentioned this to the Messenger of God (prayers & peace be upon him) and he said: 'Is she going to delay us?' I said: 'O Messenger of God, she had already circumambulated the House upon returning from Arafat, then her menses began.' Then the Messenger of God (prayers & peace be upon him) said: 'Then she should depart.'"

75. *Ibn Abbas* is reported to have said: "The people were ordered to leave Makka by way of the Ka'ba, exemption was given only to the menstruating women."

76. According to *Ibn Abbas*: "We regarded Umrah during the month of Pilgrimage (in pre Islamic period) as one of the greatest sins, so we used to interchange the months of Muharram for Safar and said: 'When the backs of the camels have healed and the month of Safar is over then Umrah is permissible for any who wises to perform it.' When the Messenger of Allah (peace & blessings of Allah be with him), and his companions intended to perform Pilgrimage on the fourth he advised them to make an intention for Umrah instead. It was something incomprehensible to them, so they asked: 'Are we free to put off our intention for pilgrimage completely?' The holy Prophet (peace & blessings of Allah be with him) said: 'You are completely free to do so'.

77. It is related that *Abu Ishaq* said that he asked Zayed ibn Arqam: 'How many battles did you participate in with the Messenger of Allah (peace & blessings of Allah be with him)?' He said: 'Seventeen.' He also said: 'The Messenger of Allah (peace & blessings of Allah be with him) took part in nineteen battles, and he performed Pilgrimage once after his emigration (from Makka to Medina), and that was his Farewell Pilgrimage.' Abu Ishaq said: 'One more while he was in Makka'."

78. *Anas* is reported to have said: The Messenger of Allah (peace & blessings of Allah be with him) performed Umrah four times, all of which were in the month of Dhul Qada except for one which he com-bined with the Pilgrimage. He performed Umrah from Al Hudaybiyah in the month of Dhul Qada, and in the following year in the month of Dhul Qada, then he performed Umrah from Ji'rana where he had distributed the booty of Hunayn in the month of Dhul Qada, and then he performed Umrah together with the pilgrimage.

79. *Ibn Abbas* is reported to have said that Mu'awiya ibn Abu Sufian told him: 'I cut the hair of the Messenger of God (prayers & peace be upon him) with a blade when he was at Marwa' or 'I saw him having his hair cut with a blade when he was at Marwa.' "

80. *Hadrat Ayesha* is reported to have said: "We set off with the Messenger of Allah (peace & blessings of Allah be with him) at the beginning of the month of Dhul-Hijjah. The Messenger of Allah (peace & blessings of Allah be with him) said: 'whoever wishes to make an intention for Umrah may do so and whoever wishes to make an intention for Hajj may do so. And had I not brought the sacrificial animals with me I would have made an intention for Umrah.' Then I began menstruating before reaching

Makka and was menstru-ating until the day of Arafat. I complained to the Messenger of Allah (peace & blessings of Allah be with him) about it and he said: 'Give up your Umrah, untie and comb your hair and make your intention for Pilgrimage. I did so and when it was the night of Hasba the holy Prophet (peace & blessings of Allah be with him) sent Abd al Rahman with me to Al-Tan'im'." He let her ride behind him. And she intended Umrah to replace the one she had given up. God completed her Pilgri-mage and Umrah and no sacrificial animal or fasting or charity was due upon her." And it was related that she also said: "O Messenger of Allah! People are returning after having performed the two ceremonies, Pilgrimage and Umrah, while I return with one cere-mony of the Pilgrimage." It was said to her: "Wait until you purify yourself and then go to Al-Tan'im and announce your intention for Umrah. Then join at such and such a place, but it is according to your means or the hardships you can endure."

81. *Abd Allah Ibn Umar* is reported to have said: "Whenever the Messenger of Allah (peace & blessings of Allah be with him) returned from a battle, pilgrimage or Umrah he used to repeat 'God is Great' three times and then say 'There is no god but Allah, He is One and has no partner. All dominion is for Him, and all praise is for Him, and He is Omnipotent. We return repenting, worshipping, prostrating and praising our Lord. He has kept His promise and made His servant victorious, and He alone

defeated all the tribes of the unbe-lievers."

82. *Abu Hurayra* is reported to have said: "When God Almighty gave the Messenger of Allah (peace & blessings of Allah be with him) victory (against the Quraysh and pagan of Makka) he stood before the people and praised Allah and said: 'Indeed God Almighty restrained the elephant from (entering) Makka and subjected it to His Messenger and the believers, and it was inviolable to those before me and it was only made violable for me for one hour of one day, and it shall be for ever inviolable after me. Therefore do not hunt or cut the weeds (by mounting over it), and if you find anything that has been lost is not lawful for you to pick it up except by making public announce-ment of it. And for the one who is killed, his relatives are entitled to one of two things, to be paid blood money or retribution.' Abbas said: 'O Messenger of Allah but we use lemon grass for our graves and in our homes.' The holy Prophet (peace & blessings of Allah be with him) said: 'Except lemon grass.' Abu Shah, a man from Yemen said he wanted it in writing for him.' The Apostle of Allah (peace & blessings of Allah be with him) said: 'write that for Abu Shah.'

83. *Jabir* reportedly said that he heard the Messenger of Allah (peace & blessings of Allah be with him) say: "It is not lawful for any of you to carry weapons in Makka."

84. *Qutayba* is reported to have said:

"The Messenger of Allah (peace & blessings of Allah be with him) entered Makka in the year of the Conquest wearing a black turban but not dressed in the garments (prescribed for) pilgrimage.' "

85. It was related that *Anas ibn Malik* said: "The Messenger of God (prayers & peace be upon him) entered Makka in the Year of the Conquest wearing a turban and when he removed it a man came to him and said: 'Ibn Khattal is clinging to the covers of the Ka'ba.' The holy Prophet (peace & blessings of Allah be with him) said: 'Kill him.' Malik confirmed that this was true."

86. *Hadrat Ayesha* is reported to have said: "I asked The Messenger of Allah (peace & blessings of Allah be with him) if the circular wall was a part of the Ka'ba. He replied in affirmative. I asked him: "Why did they not include it in the building of the Ka'ba?" He said: " Your people ran short of funds?" I asked: "Why is its gate so high?" He replied: "Your people made it so to admit whoever they wished and to keep out whoever they wished. If your people had not been so close to the times before Islam and had I not been afraid that they would be disinclined, surely I would have included the wall inside the building of the Ka'ba and I would have lowered its gate to ground level."

87. *Ata'* is reported to have narrated that during the time of Yazid ibn Mu'awiya the House (Ka'ba) was burnt when the people of al Sham were fighting there. So it was fated for it. Ibn Zubair waited until the people came to perform the pilgrimage so that he could urge them to fight the people of al Sham. When they arrived he asked them: 'O people, tell me what to do about the Ka'ba, should I pull it down and rebuild it or should I repair the damage?' Ibn Abbas said: 'I believe you should only repair the damage and leave the House in which the people embraced Islam and which the Messenger of Allah (peace & blessings of Allah be with him) raised himself. Ibn Zubair said: 'If any of your houses are burnt, you would not be satisfied until you had rebuilt it, so what then of the House of your Lord? I shall seek guidance from my Lord three times and then decide about it.' Then he sought guidance three times and determined to demolish it. The people feared that they might be afflicted if they climbed to demolish it until a man threw down one of its stones, then they joined him and pulled it down until it was leveled to the ground. Then Ibn Zubair set up pillars and draped it with curtains and then the walls were built and ibn Zubair said: 'I heard (Hadrat) Ayesha say that the Messenger of Allah (peace & blessings of Allah be with him) had said: 'If the people had not been so close to the days of ignorance, and had I the means to rebuild it, I would have enclosed it within five cubits from Hijr and I would have built a door by which the people could enter and a door by which they could exit.' So now I have the means and I do not fear any opposition.' Then he added on five cubits to it on the side of Hatim where the ancient foundations lay, and the people saw it and the wall was built upon those foundations. The length of the Ka'ba was eighteen cubits with the additional building. Then ten cubits were added to it. Two doors were built, one for entrance and one for exit. When Ibn Zubair was killed, Hajjaj sent a letter to Abd al Malik informing him of his death and telling him that Ibn Zubair had rebuilt upon the foundations that were verified by the people of Makka. Abd al Malik replied to him: 'We do not wish to censure Ibn Zubair in anything, retain whatever he has added to its length, and whatever he has added on the side of Hijr revert it to its foundation, and close the door he has opened.' So it was demolished in part and rebuilt on its foundations.'

88. *Abu Qaza'ah* is reported to have said: "When Abd al Malik ibn Marwan was circumambulating the Ka'ba he said: 'May God Almighty destroy Ibn Zubair for falsely attributing to Ayesha that she said that the Messenger of Allah (peace & blessings of Allah be with him) said: 'Ayesha, if your people had not been so close to the days of ignorance I would have demolished the House and built on to it from the Hijr and pulled it down to its foundations.' Harith ibn Rabia said: 'O Amir of the Believers, do not say that, for I heard the Mother of the Believers say that.' He said: 'Had I known that before I demolished it I would have left it the way Ibn Zubair built it'."

89. *Abd Allah ibn Zayed ibn Assem* is

reported to have said that the Messenger of Allah (peace & blessings of Allah be with him) said: Abraham avowed Makka to be inviolable and invoked blessings upon those who dwell in it. I avow Makka to be inviolable as Abraham avowed it to be inviolable, and I invoke twofold measure of blessings upon those who dwell in it.

90. According to *Sa'ad* his father narrated that the Messenger of Allah (peace & blessings of Allah be with him) said: "I proclaim that the land between the two plains of Medina inviolable, its trees must not be felled nor its game (animals) killed." And he said: "Medina is better for them if only they knew, whoever departs from it out of aversion God Almighty replaces him there with one who is better. And whoever remains there in spite of misfortune and adversity, I will intercede for him on the Day of Resurrection."

91. *Anas ibn Malik* is reported to have said that the Messenger of Allah (peace & blessings of Allah be with him) said: "O God, bestow upon Medina twice the blessings You bestowed upon Makka."

92. *Abu Hurayra* is reported to have said that when the Messenger of Allah (peace & blessings of Allah be with him) was given the fruit of the first harvest he said: 'O God, bestow blessings upon us in this our city, and in our fruits, and in our measurements, blessings upon blessings.' And he gave it to the youngest children there with him.

93. *Abu Saeed Maula al Mahri* is reported to have said that he went to Abu Saeed al-Khudri to take his advice about leaving Medina. He complained that the prices there were too high and his family was large and he said he could not withstand the adversity of Medina and its desolate country. Al-Khudri said: 'Woe to you, I do not advise you to leave, for I heard the Messenger of Allah (peace & blessings of Allah be with him) say: 'whoever endures the adversity of Medina, if he is a Muslim, I will intercede for him on the Day of Resurrection.'

94. *Hadrat Ayesha* is reported to have said: "When we arrived in Medina it was an unhealthy and disagreeable place, Abu Bakr and Bilal both fell ill. When the Messenger of Allah (peace & blessings of Allah be with him) saw his companions unwell he said: 'O God, make Medina as favorable to us as You made Makka favor-able or even more so. Make it healthy and bless us in its measurements and banish its fever to Al Juhfa'."

95. *Abu Hurayra* is reported to have said that the Messenger of Allah (peace & blessings of Allah be with him) said: "Angels stand guard at the approaches of Medina so that neither plague nor the Antichrist shall gain entry into it."

96. *Abu Hurayra* is reported to have said that the Messenger of Allah (peace & blessings of Allah be with him) said: "There will come a time when the people will see a man invite his cousin and other relatives saying: 'Come to live where the life is cheaper and more bountiful, but Medina will be better for them if only they knew. By Him in Whose Hand is my soul, who-ever departs from his aversion of it God Almighty will replace him there with one who is better. Indeed, Medina is as a furnace that spews out its impurities. And the (final) Hour will not arrive until Medina has spewed out its evil as furnace reduces the impurities from iron."

97. *Abu Hurayra* is reported to have quoted the Messenger of Allah (peace & blessings of Allah be with him) as having said: "Between my house and my pulpit is a garden of the gardens of Paradise, and my pulpit is on the Fountain" (of Paradise).

98. *Abu Hurayra* is reported to have said that the holy Prophet (peace & blessings of Allah be with him) said: "Travel is for three mosques, my Mosque, the Sacred Mosque and Al Aqsa Mosque."

99. It is related from *Abu Hurayra* that the Messenger of Allah (peace & blessings of Allah be with him) said: "One prayer in my Mosque is one thousand times better than prayer in any other mosque except the Sacred Mosque.'

100. It is related from *Ibn Umar* that the Messenger of Allah (peace & blessings of Allah be with him) used to walk or ride to the mosque of Quba'a and pray two Rak'at there."

101. It is related that *Ibn Umar* used to come to the mosque of Quba'a every Saturday and he said: "I saw the Messenger of Allah (peace & blessings of Allah be with him) come here every Saturday."

13

Book of Marriage

1. It was related that *Alqama* said that he was walking with Abd Allah at Mina when they met Uthman; he stopped there and spoke to him. Uthman said: 'O Abu Abd Al Rahman, let us find for you a young girl to marry.' He said: 'If you say so, the Messenger of Allah (peace & blessings of Allah be with him) said: 'O young men, whoever among you can afford to support a wife then he should marry, for it keeps the eyes from glancing and prevents immorality, and whoever cannot afford to do so, then he should fast in order to control his desire'."

2. *Anas* is reported to have said: "Some of the Companions of the Messenger of Allah (peace & blessings of Allah be with him) asked his wives about his personal deeds and actions, some among them saying: 'I shall not marry women,' another said: 'I shall not eat meat' and another said: 'I shall not lie down to sleep.' " He praised and glorified Allah and said: "What is the matter with them that they say such things, while I pray and sleep as well, I fast and break my fast, and I marry women too? Whoever dislikes my Sunna is not from me."

3. It was reported that *Sa'ad ibn Abi Waqqas* said: "Uthman ibn Muz'un vowed never to marry, but the Messenger of Allah (peace & blessings of Allah be with him) advised him against it. And had he permitted him (not to marry) we would have had ourselves castrated."

4. It is reported that *Abd Allah ibn Amr* said that the Messenger of Allah (peace & blessings of Allah be with him) said: "The entire world is a bounty, but the best of bounties is the pious woman."

5. It is reported that *Abu Hurayra* said that the Prophet (peace & blessings of Allah be with him) said: "You may marry a woman for four things; her wealth, her family, her beauty and her Religion. But marry the religious woman or you will lose."

6. *Jabir Ibn Abd Allah* is reported to have narrated that when Abd Allah died he left nine or seven daughters behind. I married a woman who had been married before, the Messenger of Allah (peace & blessings of Allah be with him) asked me: 'O Jabir have you married?' I said: 'Yes.' He asked: 'A virgin or a woman previously

married?' I said: 'O Messenger of Allah (peace & blessings of Allah be with him), one who was married before.' He said: Why did you not marry a young girl so you could play with her and she could play with you? Or you could amuse her and she could amuse you?' I said: 'Abd Allah died and left nine or seven daughters behind, so I did not consider it right to marry one of their age, so I preferred to marry a woman who would look after them and teach them well.' The Messenger of Allah (peace & blessings of Allah be with him) said: 'May God bless you.'

7. *Uqba ibn Amer* reportedly stood upon the pulpit and said that the Messenger of Allah (peace & blessings of Allah be with him) said: A believer is the brother of another believer, so it is unlawful for him to seek to outstrip his brother, and he should not make a proposal after his brother has proposed, unless his brother first gives up his proposal.

8. It is reported that *Abu Hurayra* narrated that the holy Prophet (peace & blessings of Allah be with him) said: An unmarried matron should not be given in marriage without her consent and a virgin should not be given in marriage until she agrees to it. The people asked: 'O Messenger of Allah! How would we know if she hay agreed?' The holy Prophet (peace & blessings of Allah be with him) replied: 'By her silence'.

9. *Ibn Abbas* is reported to have narrated that the Messenger of Allah (peace & blessings of Allah be with him) said: An unmarried matron has more say concer-ning herself than her guardian, and a virgin must be consulted, and her silence is her consent.

10. It is reported that Uqba ibn Amer said that the Messenger of Allah (peace & blessings of Allah be with him) said: The commitment most worthy of fulfillment is that by which sexual relations become lawful.

11. *Abu Musa* is reported to have said that the Messenger of Allah (peace & blessings of Allah be with him) said: Whoever frees a slave woman and then marries her, he will be rewarded twice.

12. *Ibn Umar* is reported to have said: The Messenger of Allah (peace & blessings of Allah be with him) forbade for a man give his daughter in marriage in exchange for the daughter of another man without the payment of either dowry.

13. *Abd Allah ibn Mas'ud* is reported to have narrated that: "We went on an expedition with the Messenger of Allah (peace & blessings of Allah be with him) and we did not take our wives with us. We asked: 'Should we have ourselves castrated?' He prohibited us from doing so and then he gave us permission to contract a temporary marriage for a given term. Then Abd Allah recited: 'O you who believe, do not forbid the good things that God has permitted you, and do not commit excess, surely God does not love the excessive.' (Q. 5: 87).

14. *Jabir ibn Abd Allah* is reported to

have said: We contracted temporary marriage and gave a handful of dates and flour as a dowry during the lifetime of the Messenger of Allah (peace & blessings of Allah be with him) and Abu Bakr, but Umar forbade it in the case of Amr ibn Huraith.

15. *Ali ibn Abu Talib* is reported to have said: The Messenger of God forbade temporary marriages and the consumption of domestic Asses on the Day of Khyber.

16. *Rabi' ibn Sabra* is reported to have said: My father went on an expedition with the Messenger of Allah (peace & blessings of Allah be with him) during the conquest of Makka, and we stayed there for fifteen days, so the Messenger of Allah permitted us to contract temporary marriages. So I contracted a temporary marriage and did not break it until the Messenger of Allah (peace & blessings of Allah be with him) prohibited it.

17. It is reported that *Sabra al Juhanni* narrated that his father said: "When I was with the Messenger of Allah (peace & blessings of Allah be with him) he said: 'O people, I made temporary marriage permissible, but now God Almighty has prohibited it until the Day of Resurrection. So whoever has made such a contract should annul it and do not take back anything you have given to her'.

18. It was related that *Nubaih ibn Wahab* heard Uthman ibn Affan say: 'The Messenger of Allah (peace & blessings of Allah be with him) said: 'One who

is in a state of pilgrimage may not marry, or arrange the marriage for another person, nor should he make a proposal for marriage.'

19. It is reported that *Ibn Abbas* said: The Messenger of Allah (peace & blessings of Allah be with him) married Maimuna while he was in a state of pilgrimage.

20. It is reported that *Yazid ibn Al Assem* narrated that Maimuna bint al Harith said: 'The Messenger of Allah (peace & blessings of Allah be with him) married her after he had gone out of his state of pilgrimage.' He also said: 'She was my maternal aunt and the maternal aunt of Ibn Abbas.' "

21. *Abu Hurayra* is reported to have said that the Messenger of Allah (peace & blessings of Allah be with him) said: It is not permissible to marry a woman and her paternal aunt, nor a woman and her maternal aunt.

22. *Abu Salama ibn Abd al Rahman* is reported to have narrated that he asked Hadrat Ayesha, the wife of the Messenger of Allah (peace & blessings of Allah be with him): 'How much dowry did the Messenger of Allah give?' She replied: Twelve ounces and one Nash.' Then she asked: 'Do you know what a Nash is?' I said: 'No.' She said: 'It is half an ounce, which is equivalent to five hundred Dirhams, and that was the dowry that the Messenger of Allah gave his wives.

23. *Anas ibn Malik* is reported to have narrated that the Messenger of Allah (peace & blessings of Allah be with

him) noticed traces of saffron upon Abd al Rahman ibn Auf and asked: 'What is this?' He said: 'O Messenger of Allah, I have married a woman and given her gold of the weight of a date.' He said: 'May God Almighty bless you! Give a wedding feast, even if you have only one sheep.

24. *Hadrat Ayesha* is reported to have said: I used to feel jealous of the women who came and offered themselves in marriage to the Messenger of Allah, and said: 'How can a woman offer herself in marriage?' Then God Almighty revealed: 'You may put off any of them as you please, and you may receive any of them who you please, and if you seek any whom you had set aside, there is no blame on you. So it is more likely that they will be comforted and not grieve, and every one of them will be well pleased with what you give her. And God knows all that is in your hearts, and God is All-Knowing, All-Forbearing.' I said: 'By God, It seems to me that your Lord does not delay in fulfilling your wishes.' "

25. *Hadrat Ayesha* is reported to have said: The Messenger of Allah married me in the month of Shawwal and held my wedding in the month of Shawwal. It is reported that Hadrat Ayesha preferred her lady friends to have their wedding in the month of Shawwal.

26. *Anas ibn Malik* is reported to have narrated that: "The Messenger of Allah married and held the wedding for his wife. It was asked: 'How many

attended?' He said: 'About three hundred.' And 'the house became crowded with people to the point that the Messenger of Allah had to say: 'Sit in circles of tens people, and each one should eat from what is in front of him.' They began to eat until they had their fill. One group left and another came in, until they all had eaten. When all of them had finished their meals, he said to me: 'O Anas, clear it away.' He said: 'I did so, and it seemed that what I cleared away was more than what had been laid out.' Some of them remained there in the house of the Messenger of Allah talking, while the Messenger of Allah sat and his wife sat facing the wall. This bothered the Messenger of Allah and he went out and greeted his wives. Then he returned and entered his dwelling place. When the guests saw the Messenger of Allah had returned, they thought they had troubled him. He said: 'they left hurriedly, and then the Messenger of Allah drew a curtain and went in. I was sitting in his dwelling place and he stayed a short while, then he came to me and he was reciting the Verses: 'O you who believe! Do not enter the Prophet's houses, unless you have been invited for a meal, nor wait for the meal time, but if you are invited, then enter, and when you have had the meal leave promptly, do not linger to engage in familiar talk, for such behaviour is an annoyance to the Prophet, and he is shy of saying anything to you, but God does not hold back from the Truth. And when you ask his wives for something, ask them from behind a curtain, which is more pure for your hearts and their hearts. And it is not for you to annoy the Messenger of Allah, nor is it permissible for you to marry his wives after him ever, surely this, in the sight of Allah, is a grievous thing.' (Q. 33: 53) And thereafter the wives of the Messenger of Allah went into seclusion."

27. It is related that *Nafe'* quoted Ibn Umar as having said that the holy Prophet (peace & blessings of Allah be with him) used to say: If your brother invites you to a wedding or invites you to attend another occasion, you should accept it.

28. *Abu Hurayra* is reported to have said that the Messenger of Allah (peace & blessings of Allah be with him) said: If any of you is invited you should accept, and if you are fasting, you should continue, and if you are not fasting you should eat.

29. *Abu Hurayra* is reported to have related that the holy Prophet (peace & blessings of Allah be with him) said: "The worst kind of invitation is the invitation for a feast, the people who need its food are not invited, and only those who do not need it are invited. And the one who does not accept the invitation to it has disobeyed Allah and His Messenger.

30. *Ibn Abbas* reportedly narrated that the Messenger of Allah (peace & blessings of Allah be with him) said: "When any of you intends to be intimate with his wife, he should first recite: 'In the Name of God, O God, protect us from Satan and ward Satan away from that which You bestow upon us.' And if He has decreed a child for them, Satan will never be able to harm him."

31. *Abu Hurayra* is reported to have said that the Messenger of Allah (peace & blessings of Allah be with him) said: If a man calls his wife to his bed and she refuses so that he sleeps angry with her, the angels will curse her until the morning.

32. *Abu Saeed al Khudri* is reported to have narrated that the Messenger of Allah (peace & blessings of Allah be with him) said: The most evil of people in the sight of God on the Day of Judgment is the man who approaches his wife and she comes to him, and then he does not respect her privacy by disclosing it.

33. *Abu Hurayra* is reported to have said that he heard the Messenger of Allah (peace & blessings of Allah be with him) say: All my community will be pardoned except those who boast of committing a sin, and of that boasting is the servant who commits an act at night and his Lord, High Exalted, covers him from His mercy, then in the morning he boasts of it and says: 'O you, so and so, last night I did so and so.' While his Lord Almighty covered him at night and in the morning he blows the cover, which God Almighty gave him.

34. *Abu Saeed al- Khudri* is reported to have said that when anal sex was mentioned to the holy Prophet, he asked: "Why do you do it?" They said: "The wife of one man is suckling a

child and when he is intimate with her he does not wish her to conceive, another man has a slave girl and when he is intimate with her he does not wish her to conceive.' The Apostle of Allah (peace & blessings of Allah be with him) said: 'There is no harm for you in not doing so, for what is ordained will be.' Ibn Aun said: 'I related this to Al Hasan and he said: 'By God, it seems he rebuked them for it.' "

35. It is reported that *Judama bint Wahab al Asadiyyah* said that she heard the Messenger of Allah say: I had intended to forbid intimacy with nursing mothers until I saw that the Romans and Persians do so without detriment to their children.

36. *Anas* is reported to have related that the Messenger of Allah (peace & blessings of Allah be with him) had nine wives and he shared his time between them, so the turn of the first wife came every ninth day. They used to gather together in the dwelling place of the wife with whom he would stay. Once in Ayesha's house on her night while Zainab was present, he pointed his hand towards her, so Ayesha said: 'That is Zainab.' And the Messenger of Allah drew back his hand. An argument ensued between the two of them until their voices were raised at the time of the call to prayer. Then Abu Bakr passed by and hearing the voices said: 'O Messenger of Allah, come to pray and throw dust in their mouths.' So the Prophet left. Ayesha said: 'When the Messenger of Allah used to complete his prayer Abu Bakr used

to pass by like that. So when the Messenger of Allah had completed his prayer Abu Bakr came by and spoke to her sternly saying: Is this the way you behave?

37. *Umm Salama* is reported to have said: when the Messenger of Allah married me he stayed with me for three nights and said: 'Your husband is not lacking in his esteem for you, if you wish I can stay with you for a week, but in that case, I shall have to stay with all my wives for a week.'

38. It is related that *Jabir* said that the Messenger of Allah (peace & blessings of Allah be with him) saw a woman and then went to his wife Zainab while she was tanning leather and was intimate with her. Then he went to his companions and said: A woman comes and goes in the guise of a devil, so when any of you sees a woman, he should go to his wife, for that will assuage what is stirred within his heart.

39. It is reported that *Abu Hurayra* said that the Messenger of Allah said: Whoever believes in God and the Hereafter should either speak well of any matter he sees or keep silent. Be kind towards women.

40. *Jabir ibn Abd Allah* is reported to have said: "We went on an expedition with the Messenger of Allah, and when we returned I urged my camel on because it was lagging behind. I met a rider who came up from behind me and he prodded it with his metal tipped stick. My camel surged forward like the swiftest of beasts. I turned my face and saw the

Messenger of Allah, he said: 'O Jabir, why are you hurrying?' I said: 'O Messenger of Allah, I am newly married.' He said: 'Have you married a virgin or a woman who was married before?' I said: 'To a woman married before.' He said: 'Why did you not marry a young girl so that you could amuse her and she could amuse you?' Then when we reached Medina and were almost entering it he said: 'Wait until we enter by night so that the woman with untidy hair may comb it, and the woman who husband has been away may beautify herself, and when you enter you will enjoy your arrival."

41. *Abu Hurayra* is reported to have narrated that the Messenger of Allah (peace & blessings of Allah be with him) said: A believing man should not detest a believing woman, and if he dislikes her for one part of her nature, she may please him for another (part of her nature).

42. *Hammam ibn Munabbih* is reported to have said that one of the Hadith which Abu Hurayra related to us is that the Messenger of Allah said: 'Had it not been for the Children of Israel, food would never have spoiled, and meat would never have rotted, and had it not been for Eve, women would never have behaved unfaithfully towards their husbands'.

14

Book of Divorce

1. *Nafe'* is reported to have narrated that Ibn Umar divorced his wife while she was menstruating. Umar asked the holy Prophet (peace & blessings of Allah be with him) about it. He ordered him to take her back and keep her until she is clean and then to wait until she has her next period and then becomes clean, after that he may divorce her without being intimate with her, and that is the prescribed period of waiting decreed by God for women who you intend to divorce. When Ibn Umar was asked about the one who divorces his wife while she is menstruating, he said: If you pronounced the divorce once or twice, the Messenger of Allah (peace & blessings of Allah be with him) ordered that he should take her back and then wait until she has a second menses, and then wait until she purifies herself and then she may be divorced without being intimate with her during that period, and if a divorce is pronounced three times then 'you have disobeyed your Lord in what He has commanded you regarding divorcing your wife. Then what is between you and her is severed.

2. *Ibn Sirin* reportedly said: "I spent twenty years speaking about someone I do not accuse saying that Ibn Umar pronounced divorce to his wife three times while she was menstruating. He was ordered to take her back. I did not blame them nor accepted the Hadith until I met Abu Ghallab Yunus ibn Jubair al Bahili, who was reliable, and he told me that he had asked Ibn Umar about it, and he told him that he had divorced his wife once while she was menstruating, but he had been ordered to take her back.

3. *Ibn Abbas* is reported to have said: "In the time of the Messenger of Allah (peace & blessings of Allah be with him) and Abu Bakr after him, and for two years during the time of Umar, divorces were pronounced three times and counted as one. Then Umar ibn al Khattab said: 'the people hasten in a matter in which they should not hasten and should be rational. Should we subject them to what they say?' Then he subjected them to that."

4. *Hadrat Ayesha* is reported to have said: "Rifa'a al Qurazi divorced his wife irrevocably. Then she married

Abd al Rahman ibn al Zubair. She went to the holy Prophet (peace & blessings of Allah be with him) and said: 'O Messenger of Allah Rifa'a divorced me irrevocably, after him I married Abd al Rahman ibn Al Zubair who turned out to be impotent.' The Messenger of Allah (peace & blessings of Allah be with him) smiled and said: 'do you wish to return to Rifa'a? No, you cannot do so until you and Abd al Rahman consummate your marriage.' Abu Bakr was sitting with the Apostle of Allah while Khalid ibn Saeed ibn al As was sitting at the door of the chamber awaiting permission to enter. So Khalid called: 'O Abu Bakr! Would you not rebuke that woman for what she says out loud before the Messenger of God?' "

5. It is related that *Ibn Abbas* said: if a man swears to forsake his wife, that is just an oath which he may negate by means of charity or some other way. And he said: There is an ideal for you in the Messenger of Allah.

6. *Jabir ibn Abd Allah* is reported to have narrated that Abu Bakr came seeking permission to see the Messenger of Allah (peace & blessings of Allah be with him), and he found a group of people sitting at his door who had not been granted permission to see him. Permission was granted to Abu Bakr and he entered. Umar came and he was also granted permission. When he entered he found the Prophet (peace & blessings of Allah be with him) sitting silently with his wives around him, so Umar said: 'I have to say something to make the Prophet laugh.' So he said: 'O Messenger of Allah, when the daughter of Kharija (his wife) asked me for some money I nearly broke her neck.' Then the Messenger of Allah (peace & blessings of Allah be with him) laughed and said: 'And these around me are asking me for money.' Then Abu Bakr went over to Ayesha and slapped her neck, and so did Umar go over to Hafsa and slapped her neck, while they both said: 'How dare you ask the Messen-ger of Allah (peace & blessings of Allah be with him) for something he does not have.' They said: 'By God, we will never ask the Messenger of Allah for anything he does not have.' So he (Prayers & peace be upon him) stayed apart from his wives for a period of one month or twenty-nine days. Then the verse was revealed: 'O Prophet, say to your wives: 'If you desire the life of this world and its adornment, then come and I will make for you provision and set you free in kindness, but if you seek God and His Messenger, and the home of the Hereafter, surely God has prepared for those who do good among you a great reward.' (Q.33: 28-29) He said: 'He went back to Ayesha first and said: 'O Ayesha, I want to make an offer to you, and I would like you to think about it and not to hasten, and you should consult your parents first.' She said: 'O Messenger of Allah, what is it?' So he recited the verse to her. So she said: 'I consult my parents about you, O Messenger of Allah? But I choose God and His Messenger and the Hereafter, and I ask you not to tell any of your wives about what I just said.'

He said: 'if any of them asks me I have to tell her. Because God Almighty did not send me to cause difficulty, but He sent me to guide and to facilitate.'"

7. *Masruq* is reported to have said: "I would not worry if I gave my wife the opportunity to choose, once, or a hundred times, or a thousand times, after she had chosen me. I asked Ayesha and she said: 'The Messenger of Allah (peace & blessings of Allah be with him) gave us the choice, would you call that divorce?' "

8. *Abd Allah Ibn Abbas* is reported to have narrated that: "For a whole year I had the desire to ask Umar ibn Al Khattab about a Verse but I did not ask him because of my high regard for him. When he went to perform Pilgrimage I went along with him and upon our return journey I asked him. 'O Amir of the Believers! Who were the two who aided one another against the Messenger of Allah?' He said: 'They were Hafsa and Ayesha.' Then I said to him: 'By God, I wanted to ask you about this a year ago, but I could not do so due to my high regard for you.' Umar said: 'Do not refrain from asking me anything about which you think I have knowledge, and if I know I will tell you.' Then Umar added: 'By God, before Islam, we had no regard for women until God revealed what He has revealed regarding them and assigned for them what He has assigned. Once while I was contemplating a certain matter, my wife said: 'I think you should do so-and-so.' So I said to her: 'whom do you think you are to give an opinion on this matter? Why are you interfering in my affairs?' She said: How strange you are, O son of Al Khattab! You do not accept for anyone to argue with you while your daughter argues with the Messenger of Allah (peace & blessings of Allah be with him) until she upsets him for the whole day!' Umar said: 'I got dressed and went to Hafsa and said to her: 'O my daughter! Do you argue with the Messenger of Allah (peace & blessings of Allah be with him) until you have upset him for the whole day?' Hafsa said: 'By God, we do argue with him.' Umar said: 'then I warn you of the punishment of God and the anger of His Messenger, O my daughter! Do not be misled by the one who is proud of her beauty and of the love of the Messenger of Allah for her.' Then I went out to Umm Salama being my relative, and I talked to her. She said: 'How strange you are, O son of Al Khattab! You interfere in every matter, and now you interfere between the Messenger of Allah and his wives!' By God, I was so stunned by her words that my anger subsided. I left her, and I used to have a friend from the Ansars who brought me news when I was away and I brought him news if he was away. In those days we were afraid of one of the kings of Ghassan. We heard that he intended to move and attack us, so we were fearful. So my friend from the Ansars came and knocked at my door saying: 'Open Open!' I said: 'Has the king of Ghassan come?' He said: 'No, but something worse has happened. The Messenger of Allah has secluded himself away from his wives.' I said: 'In spite of Ayesha and

Hafsa.' Then I dressed and went to the house of the Messenger of Allah, and in a small room that was accessed by a ladder, a black servant of the Messenger of Allah was upon the first step. I said to him: 'This is Umar.' Then permission to enter was granted to me and I related the story to the Messenger of Allah. Until when I reached what Umm Salama had said, the Messenger of Allah smiled as he lay on a mat made of palm tree leaves with nothing between him and the mat. Beneath his head was a leather pillow stuffed with palm fiber and the leaves of a sauté tree were piled at his feet, and above his head hung a few water skins. I saw the marks of the mat imprinted on the side of the Messenger of Allah, so I wept. He said: 'O Umar, why are you weeping?' I said: 'O Apostle of Allah, Caesar and Khusrau are leading a life of luxury while you, the Messenger of Allah, are living in this condition.' The Apostle of Allah (peace & blessings of Allah be with him) said: 'Are you not content that the enjoyment of the life of this world is for them but for you is the Hereafter?'

15

Book of the Period of Waiting for Divorcees or Widows

1. *Ubayd Allah ibn Abd Allah ibn Utba* is reported to have related that: "My father wrote a letter to Umar ibn Abd Allah ibn al Arqam al Zuhri asking him to go to Subai'ah bint al Harith al Aslamiyya to ask her about what the Messenger of Allah (peace & blessings of Allah be with him) had told her. Umar ibn Abd Allah replied to Abd Allah ibn Utba saying that Subai'ah had said: 'I was married to Sa'ad ibn Khaula of Amer ibn Lu'ayy, who had participated in the Battle of Badr, and he died at the time of the Farewell Pilgrimage while I was pregnant. Soon after that I gave birth to a child and when I had recovered from childbirth I beautified myself to receive proposals of marriage. Abu al Sanabil ibn Ba'kak came to me and said: 'I see you have beautified yourself, do you intend to marry? By God, you may not marry before four months and ten days pass.' So I went to the Messenger of Allah (peace & blessings of Allah be with him) in the evening and asked him regarding it. The Messenger of Allah (peace & blessings of Allah be with him) said that I may marry after the birth of the child if I wished.' Ibn Shihab said: 'I saw nothing wrong in her marrying after giving birth to a child even if she is still bleeding, but her husband should not approach her until she purifies herself.' "

2. *Jabir bin Abd Allah* is reported to have said: "My maternal aunt was divorced and she wanted to pick her dates. A man reprimanded her for going outside, so she went to the Messenger of Allah (peace & blessings of Allah be with him) and he said: You may go out to pick your dates from your trees, and you may give in charity or perform some other kindness.

3. It is related that *Fatimah bint Qais* said that she asked the Messenger of Allah (peace & blessings of Allah be with him) that her husband had pronounced divorce to her three times and she feared that she might suffer. The holy Prophet said: "Move to another dwelling place." So she changed her home. Marwan refuted that divorcee may leave her house. According to Urwa Hadrat Ayesha rejected what Fatimah bint Qais related.

4. **Fatimah bint Qais** is reported to have said: My husband pronounced divor-ce to me three times and the Messenger of Allah made no provision for my mainte-nance and dwelling place. The Apostle of Allah (peace & blessings of Allah be with him) said: When your period of waiting is complete, inform me. So I informed him. Mu'awiya, Abu Jahm and Usama ibn Zayed had proposed marriage by that time, the Messenger of Allah (peace & blessings of Allah be with him) said: 'As for Mu'awiya, he is a poor man with no pro-perty, as for Abu Jahm, he is a wife beater, but Usama ibn Zayed.' I indicated with my hand that I disliked marrying Usama. But the Messenger of Allah (peace & blessings of Allah be with him) said: To obey Allah and to obey His Messenger is best for you. So I married him and in due course I was greatly envied."

5. **Zainab** is reported to have said: "I went to Umm Habiba, the wife of the Messenger of Allah (peace & blessings of Allah be with him) when her father Abu Sufyan had died. Umm Habiba asked for perfume or something similar. She put some on a girl and then rubbed her cheeks with it and said: 'By God, I am in no need of perfume but I heard the Messenger of Allah (peace & blessings of Allah be with him) say from the pulpit: It is forbidden for a woman who believes in God and the Hereafter to mourn for more than three days except for her husband, then she may mourn for four months and ten days.' It was also related that Zainab said: "Then I went to visit Zainab bint Jahsh when her brother had died. She asked for perfume and put some on and said: 'By God I am in no need of perfume but I heard the Messenger of Allah (peace & blessings of Allah be with him) say from the pulpit: "It is forbidden for a woman who believes in God and the Hereafter to mourn for more than three days except for her husband, then she may mourn for four months and ten days.' It is also related that Zainab said: "I heard my mother Umm Salama say: 'A woman went to the Apostle of Allah (peace & blessings of Allah be with him) and asked: 'O Messenger of Allah, my daughter's husband has died and she has an ailment in her eye, may we apply kohl to it?' The Messenger of Allah (peace & blessings of Allah be with him) said: 'No.' Then he said: It is only for four months and ten days; while before Islam you never threw dung until a year had passed.

6. **Umm Atiyya** is reported to have related that the Messenger of Allah (peace & blessings of Allah be with him) said: It is forbidden for a woman to mourn for anyone who has died for more than three days except in the case of her husband for whom she may mourn for four months and ten days. And she may not wear colored garments except those made of yarn, nor apply kohl, nor apply perfume, except for a little scent or incense when she may use to purify herself from her menses.

16

Book of Marital
Accusation of Infidelity

1. *Sahl ibn Sa'ad al Saeedi* reportedly narrated that: Uwaimir al Ajlani went to Assem ibn Adi al Ansari and said: Advise me what a man should do if he finds someone with his wife, should he kill him, and then you would put him to death, or what should he do? Assem asked the Messenger of Allah (peace & blessings of Allah be with him) and he disapproved of this question so much that Assem was upset at the reply that the holy Prophet (peace & blessings of Allah be with him) gave him. When Assem returned, Uwaimir asked: 'what did the Messenger of Allah say? Assem told Uwaimir: the Messenger of Allah (peace & blessings of Allah be with him) disliked advising on that subject. Uwaimir then said By Allah I shall not rest until I have asked him about it. He visited the Messenger of Allah (peace & blessings of Allah be with him) while he sat among some people and asked him: 'O Messenger of Allah, advise me what a man should do if he finds someone with his wife, should he kill him, and then you would put him to death, or what should he do?' The Great Seer (peace & blessings of Allah be with him) said:

Verses have been revealed concerning a man and his wife, so go and bring her here.' Sahl said that they both invoked curses and then said: I was with the people in the company of the holy Prophet (peace & blessings of Allah be with him) and when they had finished, Uwaimir said: 'O Messenger of Allah, I would have told a lie against her if I retain her.' So he pronounced divorce to her three times in the presence of the holy Prophet (peace & blessings of Allah be with him). According to Shihab, thereafter invoking curses became customary.

2. As related from *Abu Hurayra* that Sa'ad ibn Ubada said: O Messenger of Allah, if I were to find a man with my wife, am I not permitted to strike him before I bring four witnesses?' The Messenger of Allah (peace & blessings of Allah be with him) said: No. He said: 'On the contrary, by the One Who sent you with the Truth, I would strike him with my sword immediately. The Apostle (peace & blessings of Allah be with him) said: Listen to your leader, he is zealous for his honor, and I am more so than him, and God Almighty is more zealous than me.

3. According to *Saeed ibn Jubair* he was questioned concerning those who invoked curses, and whether they were permitted to separate. I did not know what to say, so I went to the house of Ibn Umar in Makka and I asked: 'O Abu Abd al Rahman, should those who invoke curses separate?' He said: 'Glory be to God! Yes, the Messenger of Allah (peace & blessings of Allah be with him) was asked about what should be done if any of us finds his wife committing adultery. If he let it be known it is a grievous matter and if he keeps it a secret then too it is a grievous matter? The Messenger of Allah (peace & blessings of Allah be with him) remained silent. After a while the man told the holy Prophet (peace & blessings of Allah be with him): 'I am one who has been affected by the matter about which I asked you.' Then God Almighty revealed the verses of Sura al-Nur: 'And those who accuse their own wives, and have no witness except themselves, the testimony of one of them is that he shall swear by God four times that he is truthful And the fifth time that the curse of God shall be upon him if he is lying. And it shall avert the punishment from her if she testifies four times by God that he is telling a lie. And the fifth time that the wrath of God shall be upon her if he is telling the truth.' (Q. 24:6-9) The holy Prophet (peace & blessings of Allah be with him) recited the verses to the man and warned him that the torments of life were less severe than he torments of the Hereafter. He said: 'By God, I did not tell a lie against her.' Then he summoned her and warned her that the torments of life were less severe than the torments of the Hereafter. She said: 'No, by God, he is lying.' The man had began to swear the oath and he swore four times in the name of God that he was telling the truth and upon the fifth he said: 'May the curse of God by upon me if I lie.' Then the woman was sum-moned and she swore four times in the name of God that he was lying and upon the fifth she said: 'May I be cursed if he is truthful.' So the holy Prophet (peace & blessings of Allah be with him) separated them from each other.

4. It was related that *Ibn Umar* said that the Messenger of Allah (peace & blessings of Allah be with him) told a man who had invoked a curse: Your reckoning is with Allah, for one of you is lying so now you have no right over your wife. The man said: O Messenger of Allah, what about my wealth? The holy Prophet remarked: You have no right to reclaim wealth from her. If you are telling the truth, then it is a recompense for the right you had of intimacy with her, and if you are lying, then it is more remote from you than she." Zuhair related: Sufyan reported to us on the authority of Amr that he had heard Saeed ibn Jubair say that he had heard Ibn Umar say that the Messenger of Allah (peace & blessings of Allah be with him) had said that.

5. It is reported that *Abu Hurayra* said: "A bedouin came to the Messenger

of Allah (peace & blessings of Allah be with him) and said: My wife has delivered a dark skinned child and I disown him. The Messenger of Allah (peace & blessings of Allah be with him) asked him if he had any camels? He said: 'Yes.' He again asked: 'what color are they?' He said: 'Red.' He asked: 'Are any of them dark?' He said: 'Yes.' The Messenger of Allah (peace & blessings of Allah be with him) asked him how could that be? He replied it could be a strain within them that has appeared. At this the holy Prophet (peace & blessings of Allah be with him) reportedly said that the black child might be due to a strain in him that has appeared.

17

Book of Suckling

1. *Hadrat Ayesha* is reported to have narrated that when the Messenger of Allah (peace & blessings of Allah be with him) was with her she heard a man's voice seeking permission to enter the house of Hafsa. Hadrat Ayesha reportedly said: O Messenger of Allah! A man is seeking permission to enter your house.' The holy Prophet (peace & blessings of Allah be with him) said: 'I believe he is so and so, the foster uncle of Hafsa.' Hadrat Ayesha asked: 'If so and so, her foster uncle, was alive, could he enter my house?' The holy Prophet (peace & blessings of Allah be with him) replied: Yes, for relationship in suckling renders unlawful everything that is unlawful by blood relationship.

2. *Hadrat Ayesha* is reported to have narrated that her foster uncle asked for permission to enter her house but she refused him until she had sought the opinion of the Messenger of Allah (peace & blessings of Allah be with him). When the holy Prophet (peace & blessings of Allah be with him) came she told him: My foster uncle asked permission to enter (the house) but I refused him. The Apostle of Allah

(peace & blessings of Allah be with him) said: Let your uncle enter. Hadrat Ayesha said: 'But it was his wife who suckled me not him.' The Great Seer said: He is your uncle; let him enter the house.

3. *Hadrat Ali* is reported to have asked: O Messenger of Allah why do you choose from the Quraysh but ignore us? The holy Prophet (peace & blessings of Allah be with him) replied: Do you have anything for me? Hadrat Ali said: Yes, the daughter of Hamza. The Apostle of Allah said that she was not lawful for him because she was the daughter of his brother in suckling.

4. *Umm Habiba* is reported to have related that she asked the Messenger of Allah (peace & blessings of Allah be with him) to marry her sister, the daughter of Abu Sufyan. The Apostle of Allah (peace & blessings of Allah be with him) asked: Would that please you? She said: Yes, for I am your only wife, and the dearest person to share good with me is my sister. The holy Prophet (peace & blessings of Allah be with him) remarked: 'But it is not lawful for me to marry two

sisters together.' Umm Habiba said: 'O Messenger of Allah! By God, we have heard that you wish to marry Durra the daughter of Abu Salama.' He said: By God! Even if she was not my step-daughter it would not be lawful for me to marry her, for she is my niece in suckling, as Thuwaiba suckled me and Abu Salama, so you should not offer your daughter or your sisters to me (in marriage).

5. *Umm Fadl* reportedly narrated that a bedouin came to the holy Prophet (peace & blessings of Allah be with him) and asked: 'O Messenger of Allah, I have a wife and I have married another one beside her, my first wife says that she has been suckled once or twice with my second wife.' The Apostle of Allah (peace & blessings of Allah be with him) said: Suckling once or twice does not invalidate the marriage.

6. *Hadrat Ayesha* is reported to have narrated that Salim, the freed slave of Abu Hudhaifa, lived with him and his family at their house. The daughter of Suhail visited the Messenger of Allah (peace & blessings of Allah be with him) and said: Salim is a grown up man and he understands what men understand, and he comes to our house, but I feel that the heart of Abu Hudhaifa is uneasy with this.' The Apostle (peace & blessings of Allah be with him) said: Suckle him and you will no longer be lawful for him and the heart of Abu Hudhaifa will be at rest. She later said that she suckled him and the heart of Abu Hudhaifa was at ease.

7. *Umm Salama*, the wife of the Messenger of Allah (peace & blessings of Allah be with him) reportedly said that all the wives of the holy Prophet (peace & blessings of Allah be with him) refuted the idea that someone who had been fostered in such a way should be permitted to enter their houses, and they told Ayesha: 'By God we see that this was only a concession which the Apostle of Allah (peace & blessings of Allah be with him) gave to Salim, but no one will be permitted to enter our houses through such a fosterage and we do not support such an opinion.

8. *Hadrat Ayesha* is reported to have said that the holy Prophet (peace & blessings of Allah be with him) returned to her house while a man was sitting with her, his face became angry as if he disliked that. She told him: This is my brother in suckling. The Apostle of Allah (peace & blessings of Allah be with him) said: Be certain as to who is your foster brother, for foster relationship is established only when milk is the sole food for a child.

18

Book of Expenditure

1. *Jabir ibn Abd Allah* is reported to have related that a man from Bani Ghudra freed a slave on the condition that he would only be free upon his death. So when the Messenger of Allah (peace & blessings of Allah be with him) was informed about it he asked: Do you possess anything other than him? He said: 'No, and who would buy him from me?' So Naim ibn Abd Allah al Adawi bought him for eight hundred Dirhams. He handed the money to the Apostle of Allah (peace & blessings of Allah be with him) who said: spend on yourself first, and if anything is left then on your family, and if anything is left, then on your close relatives, and if anything is left after that, then for so and so and so and so.'

2. It is related that *Khaithama* said that we were sitting with Abd Allah ibn Amr when a ruler came in and he asked him: 'Have you given the slaves their food?' He said: 'No.' so he told him to go and give them their food. Then he said that the Messenger of Allah (peace & blessings of Allah be with him) had said: the most grievous sin for a man is to withhold food from those whom he possesses.

3. *Thauban* is reported to have narrated that the Messenger of Allah (peace & blessings of Allah be with him) said: The best Dinar a man can spend is the Dinar he spends on his family, and a Dinar a man spends on his mount in the cause of God, and a Dinar he spends on his companion in the cause of God. Abu Qelaba reportedly said: He (the holy Prophet) started with the family and said who has a greater reward than the one who spends on his dependants.

4. *Abu Mas'ud Al Badri* is reported to have quoted the Apostle of Allah (peace & blessings of Allah be with him) that when a Muslim spends on his family in the hope of the reward of God it is considered a charity from him.

5. *Hadrat Ayesha* is reported to have narrated that Hind came to visit the Prophet (peace & blessings of Allah be with him) and said: 'O Messenger of Allah, by God! There was no family on the face of the earth that I wished to see God degrade more than yours, but today there is no family I wish to see God honor more than yours.' Then she said: 'O Messenger of Allah! Abu Sufyan is a miser, so is there any blame on me to take from his property without his permission to spend on his children?' The Apostle of Allah (peace & blessings of Allah be with him) said: There is no blame on you in spending on them in a fair and reason-able way.

6. *Fatimah bint Qais* is reported to have said that her husband pronounced divorce to her three times and the Messenger of Allah (peace & blessings of Allah be with him) made no provision regarding her dwelling place and alimony.

7. *Hadrat Ayesha* reportedly said that it was not right for Fatimah to say so and that there was (peace & blessings of Allah be with him) no provision for dwelling place or alimony.

8. *Abu Ishaq* is reported to have said that he was sitting with Al Aswad ibn Yazid in the great mosque together with Al Sha'bi. He related that Fatimah bint Qais said that the Messenger of Allah (peace & blessings of Allah be with him) had not made any provision regarding her dwelling place or alimony. Al Aswad picked up some small stones and threw them at him saying: 'Woe to you, that you relate it, while Umar said: 'We cannot forsake the Book of God and the Sunna of the Messen-ger of Allah on account of the words of a woman. We do not know if she remembers or forgets. He said: 'there is provision for a dwelling place and alimony. God Almighty has said: Do not expel them from their houses, nor shall they leave unless it is proven that they have committed an indecency. (Q. 65: 1).

19

Book of
Emancipation of Slaves

1. *Abu Hurayra* is reported to have narrated that the Messenger of Allah (peace & blessings of Allah be with him) said: Whoever frees a slave who believes, God will free his every limb from the Fire (of Hell) even his private parts for those of the slave.

2. *Hadrat Ayesha* is reported to have narrated that Buraira came to her to seek her help in securing his freedom from bondage. She said that five uqiyas of gold in five yearly payments were required for her emancipation. Hadrat Ayesha offered to pay the whole amount in one go so that she could be freed and her loyalty would be towards her. The owners of Buraira however demanded that they would not agree until her loyalty would not be towards them. Hadrat Ayesha told the holy Prophet (peace & blessings of Allah be with him) about it. The Apostle of Allah said: buy Buraira and free her and her loyalty will be for the liberator. Then he rose up and said: what of those who impose conditions which are not given in the Law of God? If anyone imposes conditions that are not given in the Law of God, then what he imposes is null and void. God's Laws are true and inviolable.

3. *Ibn Umar* is related to have said that the Messenger of Allah (peace & blessings of Allah be with him) prohibited the sale and making gift of the rights of inheritance of a slave.

4. *Abu Mas'ud al Ansari* is reported to have related: While I was beating one of my slaves, I heard a voice behind me saying: 'Abu Mas'ud, you should know that God has more power over you than you have over the slave.' So he looked behind and saw the Apostle of Allah (peace & blessings of Allah be with him) and he said: 'O Messenger of Allah, he is free for God's sake.' So the holy Prophet remarked: If you had not done that the Fire (of Hell) would have scorched you, or touched you.

5. It is related that *Zazan* said: Ibn Umar called one of his slaves and saw the signs of beating upon his back, so he said: 'Did I hurt you?' He said: 'No.' Then he said: 'You are free.' Then he picked up some earth and said: 'My reward is no more than the weight of this as I have heard the Messenger of

Allah (peace & blessings of Allah be with him) say: 'Whoever beats his slave for no cause or hits his face, its redemption is to free him.'

6. It is related that *Abu Hurayra* said: I heard Abu Al Qasim (peace & blessings of Allah be with him) say: If someone slanders his slave and the slave is innocent of it, he will be flogged on the Day of Reckoning unless the slave is guilty.

7. *Al Ma'rur ibn Suwaid* is reported to have narrated that: "We passed by Abu Zarr at Al Rabda and he was wearing a cloak while his slave wore a similar cloak, so we said: 'O Abu Zarr, if you had used the two together you could have made a full suit.' He said: 'I once had an argument with one of my companions whose mother was not Arab, so I embarrassed him for that, and he complained to the holy Prophet (peace & blessings of Allah be with him). When I met the Messenger of Allah(peace & blessings of Allah be with him) he said: 'O Abu Zarr, you are a man who retains some traits of ignorance.' I said: 'O Messenger of Allah, the one who insults another man has insulted his father and mother.' He said: 'O Abu Zarr, you are a man who retains some traits of ignorance. They are your brethren, God has subjected them to you, so feed them from what you eat, and clothe them from what you wear, and do not burden them beyond their capability, and if you burden them with anything you must help them.

8. It is related that according to *Abu Hurayra* the Apostle of Allah (peace & blessings of Allah be with him) said: When your servant brings your meals to you, and if you do not permit him to sit down to share the meal with you, then at least give him a mouthful or two of it.

9. *Abd Allah* is reported to have quoted the Messenger of Allah (peace & blessings of Allah be with him) as having said: If a slave serves his master sincerely and worships his Lord perfectly, he will be granted a double reward.

20

Book of Selling

1. *Mu'ammar ibn Abd Allah* is reported to have sent one of his slaves one day with a measure of wheat to sell it and to buy a measure of barley. The slave bought more than a measure of barley and when Mu'ammar was told he said to him: Why did you do that? Go quickly and sell it back, and do not take anything more than the same measure, as I have heard the Messenger of Allah (peace & blessings of Allah be with him) say: Food for food should be in equal measure. It was told to him: Barley and wheat are not the same. He replied: I fear that they may be the same.

2. *Ibn Abbas* reportedly quoted the Messenger of Allah (peace & blessings of Allah be with him) say: Whoever purchases grain should not sell it before taking possession of it.

3. It was reported that *Ibn Umar* said that the Messenger of Allah (peace & blessings of Allah be with him) said: Who-ever purchases grain should not sell it before he takes possession of it. It was also related that the Messenger of Allah (peace & blessings of Allah be with him) prohibited the resale of it before it had been transferred to another location.

4. *Abd Allah ibn Umar* is reported to have said that the Messenger of Allah (peace & blessings of Allah be with him) prohibited the sale of fresh dates for dried old dates by measure, and the sale of fresh grapes for dried old grapes by measure, and the sale of grain in the field for dry grain by measure. He prohibited all such transactions.

5. *Jabir ibn Abd Allah* is reported to have said that the Messenger of Allah (peace & blessings of Allah be with him) prohibited the sale of a pile of dates if its weight was not determined according to the known measure.

6. *Jabir* is also reported to have said that the Messenger of Allah (peace & blessings of Allah be with him) prohibited the sale of unripe and inedible fruit.

7. *Abu Bakhtari* is reported to have asked Ibn Abbas (may Allah be pleased with him) about the sale of dates, he said: The Messenger of Allah prohibited the sale of dates before they are edible or before they are

weighed.' Abu Bakhtari asked: 'What does before they are weighed mean?' A man who was with him said: 'Until they have been picked.' "

8. *Ibn Umar* is reported to have said that the Apostle of Allah (peace & blessings of Allah be with him) prohibited the sale of palm trees before their fruit had ripened, and the sale of grain before it was white and free of blight, and he forbade it to both the seller and the purchaser.

9. *Sahl ibn Hathma* is reported to have said that the Messenger of Allah (peace & blessings of Allah be with him) prohibited the exchange of fresh dates for dried dates, except in the case of those who make a donation of some trees.

10. *Zayed ibn Thabit* is reported to have said that the Messenger of Allah (peace & blessings of Allah be with him) permitted the exchange of dried dates for fresh dates by measure only for those households who did so in order to consume them.

11. *Abu Hurayra* is reported to have said that the Messenger of Allah (peace & blessings of Allah be with him) permitted the exchange of dried dates for fresh dates by measure only for less than five known measures or up to five known measures.

12. *Jabir ibn Abd Allah* is reported to have related that the Apostle of Allah (peace & blessings of Allah be with him) said: If you sell fruit to your brother and the pests blight it, then you have no right to seek money from him, how would you take your brother's money without right?

13. *Abd Allah ibn Umar* is reported to have related that the holy Prophet (peace & blessings of Allah be with him) said: Whoever buys a tree which bears fruit, then the fruit belongs to the one who sold it except when it has been stipulated by the buyer as his, and whoever buys a slave, then his property belongs to the one who sold him except when it has been stipulated by them as his.

14. *Jabir ibn Abd Allah* is reported to have said that the Messenger of Allah (peace & blessings of Allah be with him) prohibited the sale of fruit until it was ripe and fit for consumption, and the sale of crops still in the fields for grain by the known measure, and the sale of date palm for dried dates by known measure, and the leasing of land in return for one third or one fourth or similar amount of the crop.

15. *Jabir ibn Abd Allah* is reported to have said that the Apostle of Allah (peace & blessings of Allah be with him) prohibited the sale of fruit until it was ripe and fit for consumption, and the sale of crops still in the fields for grain by the known measure, and the sale of date palm for dried dates by known measure, and the leasing of land in return for one third or one fourth or similar amount of the crop, and he prohibited the sale of produce years before it had been grown, but he permitted the exchange of dried dates for fresh dates by measure only for those households who do so in order to eat them.

16. It is reported that *Jabir ibn Abd Allah* said that the Messenger of Allah (peace & blessings of Allah be with him) prohibited selling years in advance. And it was also reported that Ibn Abu Sheba said: That meant selling fruit years in advance.

17. *Abu Hurayra* is reported to have narrated that the Messenger of Allah (peace & blessings of Allah be with him) said: Anyone who purchases a sheep which has not been milked for a long time and then milks it, may retain it if he is satisfied, but if he is not satisfied he may return it within three days, but he should pay one measure of dates for the milk.

18. It is reported that *Abd al Rahman ibn Wa'ala al Saba'i*, who was from Egypt, asked Abd Allah ibn Abbas about grape juice. Ibn Abbas said that a man presented the Messenger of Allah (peace & blessings of Allah be with him) with a jar of wine, so the holy Prophet (peace & blessings of Allah be with him) asked him: Do you know that God Almighty has prohibited it?' He said: 'No.' Then he whispered to another man, so the Messenger of Allah (peace & blessings of Allah be with him) asked him: 'What did you tell him?' He said: 'I ordered him to sell it.' Then the Apostle of Allah (peace & blessings of Allah be with him) remarked: The One Who has prohibited the consumption of it has also prohibited its sale. And he opened the jar and poured the wine out on the ground.

19. *Jabir Ibn Abd Allah* is reported to have narrated that he heard the Messenger of Allah (peace & blessings of Allah be with him) saying while he was in Makka in the year of the Conquest: God and His Messenger prohibit the sale of intoxicants, carrion, the pig and idols. It was said: "O Messenger of Allah! What about the fat of the carrion, it is used for painting ships and hides, and it is used for lamps? The holy Prophet replied: No. It is prohibited. He added that the Apostle of Allah (peace & blessings of Allah be with him) then said: May God kill the Jews, when God prohibited fat to them, they melted it and sold it and devoured its price.

20. *Abu Mas'ud al Ansari* is reported to have said that the Messenger of Allah (peace & blessings of Allah be with him) prohibited the price of the dog, and money derived from prostitution and the earnings of a fortune teller.

21. *Rafi' ibn Khadij* is reported to have said that he heard the Apostle of Allah (peace & blessings of Allah be with him) say: The price of the dog is prohibited, and the earnings of prostitution are prohibited and the earnings of the cupper are prohibited."

22. *Ibn Umar* is reported to have said that the Messenger of Allah (peace & blessings of Allah be with him) prohibited the sale of an unborn animal, as was the custom before Islam when one would pay the price of a she-camel for the unborn offspring of a live she-camel.

23. *Abu Saeed* is reported to have said that the Apostle of Allah (peace & blessings of Allah be with him) prohibited two kinds of trading. He prohibited trading by touching the other's cloth without turning it over, and he prohibited trading by throwing the cloth to another without inspection or mutual agreement.

24. *Ibn Umar* is reported to have said that the Messenger of Allah (peace & blessings of Allah be with him) prohibited bartering.

25. *Abu Hurayra* is reported to have said that the Messenger of Allah (peace & blessings of Allah be with him) said: Do not go out to meet the seller while he is on his way (to the market) and trade with him, and whoever does that and buys from him, if the seller then comes to the marketplace and sees he has been underpaid then he has the right to nullify the transaction.

26. *Ibn Abbas* is reported to have narrated that the holy Prophet (peace & blessings of Allah be with him) said: Do not go to meet the caravan on the way to purchase their goods before it reaches the town. A town dweller should not sell the goods of a desert dweller on his behalf. Ibn Abbas was asked: What did the Prophet mean by a town dweller not selling the goods of a desert dweller? He replied: He should not be his broker.

27. *Mu'ammar* is reported to have narrated that the Messenger of Allah (peace & blessings of Allah be with him) said: The one who hoards up commits sin.

28. *Ibn Umar* is reported to have narrated that the Messenger of Allah (peace & blessings of Allah be with him) said:

When two men make a deal, they each have the right to cancel it provided they do not go apart from each other, unless one permits the other to cancel it. But if one permits the other the option, the deal is made on that provision and it is binding. And if they go apart from each other after striking the deal and neither cancels it, then the deal is binding.

29. *Hakim ibn Hizam* is reported to have said that the holy Prophet (peace & blessings of Allah be with him) said: The one who buys and the one who sells have the option to cancel or to confirm the deal, as long as they have not parted or until they part, and if they have been honest and described what they sell truthfully, then there will be blessings in their bargain. But if they were dishonest and concealed the truth, then the blessing of their dealing would be wiped out.

30. *Abd Allah ibn Dinar* is reported to have related that he heard Ibn Umar say: A man told the Messenger of Allah (peace & blessings of Allah be with him) that he had been cheated in a deal, at that the Apostle of Allah said: When you enter into a deal, say: 'Let there be no intention of deceit.'

31. *Malik ibn Aus* is reported to have said: "I asked: 'Who will exchange Dirhams for gold?' Talha ibn Ubaydallah said: 'Show us your gold and come back later and our servant will give you your Dirhams.' At this Umar ibn al Khattab said: 'Do not do so, by God you must either give him his Dirhams or return his gold to him, as the Messenger of Allah had said:

There is usury in the exchange of silver for gold unless it is done immediately, and wheat for wheat is usury unless it is handed over immediately, and barley for barley is usury unless it is handed over immediately, and dates for dates is usury unless it is handed over immediately.

32. *Abu al Minhal* is reported to have said that his partner sold some silver to be paid at the time of the Pilgrimage. He came to me and told me of it and I said: 'Such a way of trading is disliked.' He said: 'I sold it in the market and no one objected.' I went to Al Bara' ibn Aseb and asked him, and he said: The holy Prophet (peace & bles-sings of Allah be with him) came to Medina and we used to make such deals and he said: 'If the payment is made immediately there is no blame on you, but if it is deferred then it is usury.' You should go to Zayed ibn Arqam, as he trades more than I. So I went to him and asked him and he repeated the same.

33. *Uthman ibn Affan* is reported to have narrated that the Messenger of Allah (peace & blessings of Allah be with him) said: "Do not sell the Dinar for two Dinars, nor the Dirham for two Dirhams.

34. *Abu Saeed al Khudri* is reported to have met Ibn Abbas and asked him: 'what do you say regarding exchange, have you heard that from the Messenger of Allah (peace & blessings of Allah be with him) or seen it in the holy Book?' Ibn Abbas replied: you knew the Messenger of Allah (peace & blessings of Allah be

with him) better than I, as for the Book of God I have not seen that in it, but Usama ibn Zayed told me that the Messenger of Allah (peace & blessings of Allah be with him) said: There is no usury except in al- Naseeya' (interest on loan)'.

35. *Abu Nadra* is reported to have said: I asked Ibn Umar and Ibn Abbas about exchange and they did not disapprove of it. Then once when I was sitting with Abu Saeed al Khudri, I asked him about exchange. He said: 'If it is from the same kind the amount must be equal, and anything over that is usury.' I argued with him because of what they had both said. So he said: 'I shall tell you what I heard from the Messenger of Allah. A man who owned date palms came to him with a measure of good dates of the same type of dates that the Prophet (peace & blessings of Allah be with him) had. The Apostle of Allah (peace & blessings of Allah be with him) asked him: Where did you get these? He said: 'I bought one measure of these with two measures of my dates, as the market price for this type is equal to two of the other.' Then the Messenger of Allah (peace & blessings of Allah be with him) told him: 'Woe to you! You have dealt in usury, you should have sold yours and then bought with its price whatever you wished.' Abu Saeed said: 'Which is usury, a date for a date, or silver for silver?' He said: 'I went to Ibn Umar and informed him so he forbade exchange (of goods).

36. *Jabir* is reported to have said that the Messenger of Allah (peace & blessings of Allah be with him) cursed the one who devours usury and the one who pays it and the one who writes it down and the two witnesses to it. And he had said: "They are all equal."

37. *Al Numan ibn Bashir* is reported to have said that he heard the Messenger of Allah (peace & blessings of Allah be with him) say: The lawful and unlawful things are clear but between them are things of doubt of which most people have no knowledge. So whoever saves himself from doubtful things saves his Religion and his honor. And whoever indulges in doubtful things is like a shepherd who grazes his flocks near pasture belonging to someone else, at any moment liable to trespass it. O people! Beware, every king has a pasture and the pastures of God on earth are His forbidden things. Beware! There is a piece of flesh in the body, which if it is kept pure the whole body is purified, but if it is defiled the whole body is defiled, and this is the heart.

38. *Abu Hurayra* is reported to have narrated that a man came to the Apostle of Allah (peace & blessings of Allah be with him) demanding return of his debts in a rude manner. The companions of the Prophet (peace & blessings of Allah be with him) wanted to deal with him severely but the holy Prophet (peace & blessings of Allah be with him) said: Leave him alone; the creditor has a right to speak. Then he said: 'Give him a camel of the same age as the one he had.' The people said: 'O Messenger of Allah! The only camel we have is older than his.' The Apostle of Allah (peace & blessings of Allah be with him) said: Give it to him; the best of you is the one who returns the rights of others in a better way.

39. *Abu Qatada al Ansari* is reported to have said that the Messenger of Allah (peace & blessings of Allah be with him) said: Avoid swearing when negotiating a sale, it gains the sale but it negates the blessing in it.

40. *Abu Hurayra* is reported to have said that the Messenger of Allah (peace & blessings of Allah be with him) said: There are three people whom God will not speak to nor look at on the Day of Resurrection, nor will He purify them and they shall have a painful chastisement; the one who had surplus water on a way but he withheld it from the travelers. The one who offered his wares for sale after the afternoon prayer and said: 'By God, there is no deity but Him, I have been offered so much for my wares." Then someone believes him and buys them. The one who swore allegiance to a ruler only for worldly gain and was satisfied if he received anything from him, but if he got nothing from him he was dissatisfied.

41. *Jabir ibn Abd Allah* is reported to have narrated that: I was with The Messenger of Allah (peace & blessings of Allah be with him) on an expedition and my camel was tired and slow. He came back to me and said: What is the matter with your camel? I said: My camel is exhausted. He dismounted and poked the camel

with his stick and prayed for it, and thereafter it went faster than all the other camels. He asked me: How is your camel now? I replied: It is good, you have blessed it.' He asked: Will you sell it to me? I was too shy as I had no other camel, but I said: 'Yes.' And I sold it to him on the condition that I would hand it over on our return to Medina. When I arrived in Medina my uncle met me and asked me about the camel, I told him what I had done with it. He reprimanded me for what I had done. Jabir said: 'When the Messenger of Allah (peace & blessings of Allah be with him) arrived in Medina I took the camel to him; he paid me its price and returned the camel to me.

42. *Ka'b Ibn Malik* said: During the life time of the Messenger of Allah (peace & blessings of Allah be with him) I asked Ibn Abu Hadrad to pay me back the debt he owed me while I was in the mosque, and our voices were raised higher and higher. The Messenger of Allah (peace & blessings of Allah be with him) heard us from his apartments, so he came to us raising the curtain of his room and said: 'O Ka'b ibn Malik!' Reduce the debt to one half.' I said: 'O Messenger of Allah! I have done so.' Then the Messenger of Allah (peace & blessings of Allah be with him) said: pay the debt back to him.

43. *Abu Hurayra* is reported to have narrated that the Messenger of Allah (peace & blessings of Allah be with him) said: The procrastination of the wealthy man is unjust, and if a wealthy man owes any of you money, he should pay it back.

44. *Hudhaifa* is reported to have related that the holy Prophet (peace & blessings of Allah be with him) said: A man died and was admitted to Paradise, so he was asked: 'What did you to do?' He said: 'I used to sell goods to the people and I used to make it easy for the person who had difficulty in paying and I used to be lenient in accepting either a gold or silver.' So God forgave him his sins. Abu Mas'ud said: I heard the Messenger of Allah (peace & blessings of Allah be with him) say that.

45. It is reported that Abd Allah ibn Abu Qatada said that Abu Qatada sought repayment from a debtor who was hiding from him. When he found him he said: I am constrained. So he said: By God? The debtor replied: By God. So Abu Qatada said: I have heard the Messenger of Allah (peace & blessings of Allah be with him) say: 'The one who hopes that God will save him from distress on the Day of Judgment should give respite to the debtor or absolve him from it (the debt).

46. *Abu Hurayra* is reported to have narrated that the Messenger of Allah (peace & blessings of Allah be with him) said: If a man becomes bankrupt, and if his creditor finds the goods with him, he is entitled to have them back.

47. *Ibn Abbas* is reported to have said that when the holy Prophet (peace & blessings of Allah be with him) came to Medina the people were paying for the fruit a year or two in advance. Then he said: 'whoever pays in advance for dates should pay for a specified weight and measure and for an appointed time.

48. *Jabir ibn Abd Allah* is reported to have said that the Messenger of Allah (peace & blessings of Allah be with him) suggested preemption in all joint ownership, whether in a house or land. And he said that a partner has no right to sell without the permission of his partner. So if he wishes he may buy it or if he wishes he may leave it, and if one sells without the permission of the other, the other has the right to buy it back.

49. *Abu Hurayra* is reported to have narrated that the Messenger of Allah (peace & blessings of Allah be with him) said: No one should prevent his neighbor from fixing a wooden peg in his wall. He asked: Why is it that you are opposed to that? By God I will surely remind you of that saying.

50. *Urwa ibn al Zubair* is reported to have said: "Urwa bint Uwais argued with Saeed ibn Zayed saying that he had stolen some of her land, so she took her complaint to Marwan ibn Al Hakam. Saeed said: 'How could I take part of her land after I have heard what the Messenger of Allah (peace & blessings of Allah be with him) say: 'Whoever unfairly deprives another of his land, his neck will be tied down with it to the seven earths.' Marwan said to him: 'I would not ask you for any proof after that.' He said: 'O God, if she is lying, blind her eyes and kill her upon her land.' So she died after becoming blind and when she was walking upon her land she fell into a ditch and died.

21

Book of Agriculture

1. *Jabir ibn Abd Allah* was reportedly asked: Did the Messenger of Allah (peace & blessings of Allah be with him) say: Whoever has land should cultivate it himself, or allow his brother to cultivate it, and he should not rent it? He said: "Yes."

2. *Rafi' ibn Khadij* is reported to have said: In the lifetime of the Messenger of Allah (peace & blessings of Allah be with him) we used to cultivate the land and we rented it out in return for one third or one fourth of the produce together with a stated amount of grain. Then one of my uncles came and said: The Messenger of Allah (peace & blessings of Allah be with him) has prohibited sharecropping, we gain revenue from it, but to obey God and His Messenger is more beneficial to us. He has prohibited us to cultivate land in return for one third or one fourth of the produce together with a stated amount of grain, and he ordered that the landowner should cultivate it or permit it to be cultivated by others, and he disapproved renting it or anything other than that.

3. It is reported that *Hanzala ibn Qais al Ansari* said: I asked Rafi' ibn Khadij about renting land for gold and silver and he replied: 'There is no blame on those who rent out land near canals and by the ends of rivulets or parts of fields. But sometimes a part gave produce and another failed and so no rent was due to the owners except for the part that had borne produce. So The Messenger of Allah (peace & blessings of Allah be with him) forbade it, except in return for money.'

4. It is reported that Abd Allah ibn Al Sa'ib said: We visited Abd Allah ibn Ma'qil to ask him about sharecropping, and he said that according to Thabit the Apostle of Allah (peace & blessings of Allah be with him) prohibited sharecropping and ordered the leasing of land for money, and said: There is no blame in that.

5. It is reported that *Amr* told Tawus: 'I wish you would abandon sharecropping, as people say that the holy Prophet (peace & blessings of Allah be with him) prohibited it.' At that Tawus said: 'O Amr! I give the land to sharecroppers as assistance. Indeed the most knowledgeable one, Ibn

Abbas, told me that the Apostle of Allah (peace & blessings of Allah be with him) had not prohibited it, but had said: 'It is more beneficial for one to give his land free to his brother than to charge him a rent'.

6. *Abd Allah ibn Umar* is reported to have said that the Apostle of Allah (peace & blessings of Allah be with him) made a contract with the people of Khyber permitting them to use the land in return for half of the produce that it would bear. The holy Prophet (peace & blessings of Allah be with him) used to give his wives one hundred *Wasqs* each comprising eighty *Wasqs* of dates and twenty *Wasqs* of barley. When Umar was appointed as Caliph he offered the wives of the Prophet (peace & blessings of Allah be with him) the land and water as their share or to continue with the practice of the Prophet (peace & blessings of Allah be with him). Some of them chose the land and water and others opted for the *Wasqs*. Hadrat Ayesha chose land as her share.

7. *Anas ibn Malik* is reported to have said that the Messenger of Allah (peace & blessings of Allah be with him) said: Any Muslim who plants a tree or sows seeds and then a bird or a person or an animal eats from it, it is considered as if he has given in charity.

8. *Jabir ibn Abd Allah* is reported to have said that t he Messenger of Allah (peace & blessings of Allah be with him) prohibited the sale of superfluous water.

9. It is reported that *Abu Hurayra* said that the Messenger of Allah (peace & blessings of Allah be with him) said: Superfluous water may not be held back so that the cultivation of plants are prevented.

22

Book of Wills and Testaments

1. **Salim** is reported to have said that his father related that the Messenger of Allah (peace & blessings of Allah be with him) said: Any Muslim who has anything to bequeath should not let three nights pass without having his will written down. Abd Allah ibn Umar said: "And ever since I heard that from the Messenger of Allah (peace & blessings of Allah be with him) I have not let one night pass without having my will made.

2. **Amer ibn Sa'ad** is reported to have said that his father narrated that in the year of the Prophet's final Pilgrimage I was taken seriously ill and the holy Prophet (peace & blessings of Allah be with him) used to visit me to enquire about my health, I told him: 'I am beset with illness and I am wealthy but have no inheritors except one daughter, should I give two-thirds of my property in charity?' He replied: 'No.' I asked: 'Half then?' He said: 'No.' Then he added: 'One third, and even one third is a great deal. It is better to leave your inheri-tors wealthy rather than to leave them in poverty and obliged to beg from others. You will receive your reward for whatever you give for God's sake, even for what you put in the mouth of your wife.' I said: 'O Messenger of God! Will I be left alone after my companions have gone?' He said: 'if you are left behind, whatever good deeds you have done will elevate you. And perhaps you will live a long life so that some people will benefit because of you and others be harmed because of you. But the Messenger of Allah (peace & blessings of Allah be with him) grieved for Sa'ad ibn Khaula because he died in Makka.

3. **Ibn Abbas** is reported to have said that the people should reduce their will from one third to one fourth as the Messenger of Allah (peace & blessings of Allah be with him) had said: One third is more than enough.'

4. **Abd Allah ibn Abu Aufa** is reported to have asked: Did the Apostle of Allah (peace & blessings of Allah be

with him) draw up a will? He replied: "No." I asked: Why then is the making of a will enjoined upon the people? He answered: The holy Prophet (peace & blessings of Allah be with him) bequeathed the Book of God.

5. *Hadrat Ayesha* is reported to have said: The Messenger of Allah (peace & blessings of Allah be with him) did not leave any Dinars or Dirhams, or goats or camels. And he did not make a will bequeathing anything.

6. *Aswad ibn Yazid* is reported to have said that someone claimed in Ayesha's presence that the Messenger of Allah (peace & blessings of Allah be with him) had made a will nominating Ali, so she said: 'When did he make such a will? I was supporting him upon my chest and he asked for a tray and then he collapsed on my lap, and I had no idea that he had passed away, so when did he make any will to nominate him?

7. It is reported that *Ibn Abbas* said that the holy Prophet (peace & blessings of Allah be with him) was on his deathbed and gave three orders saying: 'Expel the unbelievers from the Arabian Peninsula, respect foreign emissaries, and give them gifts as you have seen me do'.

8. It is reported that *Ibn Abbas* said that the Apostle of Allah (peace & blessings of Allah be with him) said: The one who takes back his gift is like a dog that swallows (his own) vomit.

9. *Al-Numan ibn Bashir* is reported to have related that his father gave him a gift, but Amra bint Rawaha said that she would not agree to it unless he asked the Messenger of Allah (peace & blessings of Allah be with him) to witness it. So my father visited the holy Prophet (peace & blessings of Allah be with him) and said: 'O Messenger of Allah! I gave my son a gift from Amra' bint Rawaha but she requested me to make you a witness to it.' The Apostle of Allah (peace & blessings of Allah be with him) said: 'Have you given the same amount to your other sons?' He said: 'No.' the holy Prophet (peace & blessings of Allah be with him) said: 'Fear God and be fair to your children.' My father then returned and took back his gift'.

10. It is reported that *Numan ibn Bashir* said that his father took him to the holy Prophet (peace & blessings of Allah be with him) and said: 'O Messenger of Allah, witness that I have given Numan a gift of such and such from my wealth.' He asked: 'Have you given all your sons the same as you have given to Numan?' My father replied n the negative. Then the Apostle of Allah (peace & blessings of Allah be with him) said: 'Do you not wish for all your children to be good to you?' He said: 'Yes.' So he said: 'Then do not do such a thing.'

11. *Jabir ibn Abd Allah al Ansari* is reported to have said that the Messenger of Allah (peace & blessings of Allah be with him) said: Whoever gives a life grant to another and says: 'I give this to you and your heirs, then it belongs to him and his heirs, and it does not revert to the one who gave it as the law of inheritance applies regarding it.

12. It is reported that *Jabir ibn Abd Allah* said that the Messenger of Allah (peace & blessings of Allah be with him) said: Retain your property and do not waste it, for whoever gives a life grant to another, the property will belong to the recipient in life and in death, and will pass to his heirs.

23

Book of the Laws of Inheritance

1. *Usama ibn Zayed* is reported to have said that the Messenger of Allah (peace & blessings of Allah be with him) said: A Muslim may not inherit from a non-Muslim, and a non-Muslim may not inherit from a Muslim.

2. *Ibn Abbas* is reported to have related that the holy Prophet (peace & blessings of Allah be with him) said: Give the shares of inheritance as prescribed in the Qur'an to those who are entitled to receive them. Then whatever remains, should be given to the nearest male relative of the deceased person.

3. *Jabir* is reported to have said that the Messenger of Allah (peace & blessings of Allah be with him) came to visit him when he was ill and he soon fainted. The holy Prophet (peace & blessings of Allah be with him) performed ablution and sprinkled on him the water of ablution and he regained consciousness and said: 'O Messenger of Allah! To whom will my inheritance go as I have neither ascendants nor descen-dants?' He kept silent until the verses pertaining to inheritance were revealed: They ask you for a decision; say Allah gives you a decision concerning the person who has neither parents nor children. (Q.4: 76).

4. *Al Bara'* is reported to have said that the last final Surah to be revealed was Surah 'The Repen-tance' and the final verse to be re-vealed was the verse concerning al-Kalala (the person who has neither children nor parents).

5. *Abu Hurayra* is reported to have said: Whenever the body of a person, who had died in debt, was brought before the Messenger of Allah (peace & blessings of Allah be with him), he used to ask if he had left property to absolve his debt before the funerary prayer, if not he would say: You offer prayer for your companion. But when God Almighty granted him victory he would say: 'I am closer to the belie-vers than they are to their own selves, so if any of them dies in debt, I am responsible for it, and if any one of them leaves property behind, it must pass to his heirs.

6. It is reported on the authority of *Abu Hurayra* that the Apostle of Allah (peace & blessings of Allah be with him) had said: By Him in Whose hand is the life of Muham-mad, there is no believer on the earth with whom I am not the nearest among all the people. He who amongst you (dies) and leaves a debt, I am there to pay it, and he who amongst you (dies) leaving behind children I am there to look after them. And he who amongst you leave behind property that belongs to the inheritors whoever they are.

24

Book of
Religious Endowments

1. It is reported on the authority of *Abu Hurayra* that the Messenger of Allah (peace & blessings of Allah be with him) said: When anyone dies, his acts come to an end, except three, regular charity, knowledge which he has imparted to others, or a God fearing son who supplicates for his deceased father.

2. *Ibn Umar* is reported to have said that Hadrat Umar sought the opinion of the Apostle of Allah (peace & blessings of Allah be with him) about some property he had acquired in Khyber, saying: 'O Messenger of Allah, I have acquired land in Khyber which is more valuable than any land I have ever had, what should I do with it?' The holy Prophet (peace & blessings of Allah be with him) replied: 'You may keep the land if you wish and donate its produce as charity.' So Umar donated it as charity on the condition that it should not be sold or inherited or given away. He dedicated it to the needy and near of kin, to the emancipation of slaves and in the way of Allah and wayfarers and guests. And there is no blame on anyone who is charged with its administration if he eats from it in a reasonable amount, or if he feeds his friends from it and does not amass from it for himself. He said: 'I related this Hadith to Mohammed, but when I said 'does not amass from it for himself' he said: 'does not amass from it to enrich himself.' Ibn Aun said: 'the one who read the text told me that it is written therein 'does not amass from it to enrich himself.'

25

Book of Vows

1. **Ibn Umar** is reported to have said: Umar ibn al Khattab asked the holy Prophet (peace & blessings of Allah be with him): 'O Messenger of Allah, during the days of ignorance I had pledged to go into seclusion for one day at the Sacred Mosque, so what should I do?' The holy Prophet said: 'Go into seclusion for one day.'

2. **Ibn Abbas** is reported to have narrated that Sa'ad ibn Ubada went to the Messenger of Allah (peace & blessings of Allah be with him) to seek his opinion concerning a pledge his mother had made and not fulfilled before she died. The holy Prophet (peace & blessings of Allah be with him) said: Fulfill it on her behalf.

3. **Uqba ibn Amer** is reported to have narrated that his sister pledged that she would walk barefoot to the House of Allah, and she asked me to seek the opinion of the Messenger of Allah (peace & blessings of Allah be with him) about it, I asked him and he said: She should walk and ride as well.

4. **Anas** is reported to have said that the Messenger of Allah (peace & blessings of Allah be with him) saw an aged man walking supported by his two sons, so he asked: 'What is wrong with him?' They replied: 'He has taken a pledge to walk to the House of Allah.' The holy Prophet (peace & blessings of Allah be with him) remarked: God Almighty does not need him to put himself to hardship. And he advised him to ride.

5. **Ibn Umar** is reported to have said that the Messenger of Allah (peace & blessings of Allah be with him) disapproved the taking of pledges and said: It does not do any good, except that it makes the miser do something (which he otherwise wont do).

6. It is reported on the authority of **Abu Hurayra** that the Messenger of Allah (peace & blessings of Allah be with him) said: Pledges do not hasten anything for the son of Adam which God Almighty has not decreed for him, if the pledge is in accord with what is fated, then it is the means that the miser does

something which he was (other-wise) unwilling to do.

7. Imran Ibn Hussain is reported to have narrated that a woman of the Ansars had been taken prisoner and al-Adba' (the she-camel of the holy Prophet) had been caught as well. The woman was tied up with ropes and one night, while her captors were sleeping, she escaped on al-Adba' (the she-camel of the holy Prophet) and pledged to God Almighty that if she escaped to safety she would offer al-Adba as a sacrifice. When she reached Medina the people saw her and said: 'here is al- Adba, the she camel of the Messenger of Allah. The woman said that she has made a pledge that if God Almighty saves her on it she will sacrifice it.' The Messenger of Allah (peace & blessings of Allah be with him) was informed about it. He said: Praise be to God! How evil is the reward she pledges to God Almighty that if He saved her on it, she would sacrifice it! There is no obligation to fulfill a pledge made in disobedience or for something over which one has no control. It is reported that Ibn Hujr related that it was said: There is no pledge in disobedience to Allah.

8. It is reported that *Uqba ibn Amer* narrated that the Messenger of Allah (peace & blessings of Allah be with him) said: The expiation for breaking a pledge is the same as breach of an oath.

26

Book of Oaths

1. It is reported on the authority of **Umar ibn al- Khattab** that the Messenger of Allah (peace & blessings of Allah be with him) said: "God Almighty forbids you to swear by your fathers. Umar said: By God, since I heard the Apostle of Allah (peace & blessings of Allah be with him) forbidding it I have never taken such an oath.

2. *Abdullah ibn Umar* is reported to have narrated that the holy Prophet (peace & blessings of Allah be with him) found Umar ibn al-Khattab swearing by his father. The Messenger of Allah (peace & blessings of Allah be with him) called him and said: Our Allah, Most High and Exalted has forbidden you to swear by your father. He who wishes to swear must do so by Allah or keep quiet.

3. It is reported on the authority of Ibn Umar that the Messenger of Allah (peace & blessings of Allah be with him) said: Whoever swears an oath, must only swear by God. The Quraysh used to swear by their ethers, so the holy Prophet (peace & blessings of Allah be with him) said: Do not swear by your fathers.

4. It is reported on the authority of Abd al- Rahman ibn Samura that the Messenger of Allah (peace & blessings of Allah be with him) said: Do not swear by idols or by your fathers.

5. It is reported on the authority of *Abu Hurayra* that the Messenger of Allah (peace & blessings of Allah be with him) said that Solomon the son of David had sixty wives. One day he said that he would visit each one of them every night and they shall all deliver sons who will grow up as great horsemen and fight in the cause of Allah. His companion or the King told him: 'Say, if God wills.' But he did not remember to say so, and none of his wives delivered children except one who gave birth to a premature infant. The Messenger of Allah (peace & blessings of Allah be with him) said: had he said Insha Allah ('If God so wills') he would have been blessed with what he desired.

6. It is reported on the authority of

Abu Hurayra that the Messenger of Allah (peace & blessings of Allah be with him) said: Oaths are judged according to the intention they were made with.

7. It is reported on the authority of *Abu Umama al-Harith* that the Messenger of Allah (peace & blessings of Allah be with him) said: Whoever takes the right of a Muslim by oath, God will relegate him to the Hell Fire and prohibit Paradise for him. Then a man asked: "O Messenger of Allah, even for a little matter? The holy Prophet (peace & blessings of Allah be with him) replied: Even if it was for a tooth stick.

8. *Abu Musa al Ash'ari* is reported to have narrated that he visited the holy Prophet (peace & blessings of Allah be with him) along with a group of Asharites asking him for mounts, but he refused. Then we asked him again for mounts, so he swore that he would not provide us with mounts. After some time the holy Prophet (peace & blessings of Allah be with him) received some camels as war booty and he ordered that five be given to us. When we took the camels we said: 'The Apostle of Allah (peace & blessings of Allah be with him) forgot his oath and we will not prosper for that.' So I went to him and said: 'O Messenger of Allah! You swore an oath that you would not provide us with mounts, and now you have given them to us.' He said: It was not I who provided you with a mount, but Allah did it. As far as I

am concerned, by Allah, if He so wills I would not swear, but if, later on, I happen to see better than it, I (would break the vow) and expiate for it and do that which is better.

9. *Abu Hurayra* reportedly narrated that a man stayed with the Messenger of Allah (peace & blessings of Allah be with him) until late in the night and then returned to his family and found that his children had gone off to sleep without eating dinner. His wife offered him food but he swore that he would not eat because his children had slept hungry. Then he pledged to atone for the oath and he ate the food. Thereafter he visited the Messenger of Allah (peace & blessings of Allah be with him) and told him about it, the Apostle of Allah (peace & blessings of Allah be with him) said: 'Whoever makes an oath and then sees better than it, should do that and atone for (breaking the oath).

10. *Tamim ibn Tarafa* is reported to have said that he heard the Apostle of Allah (peace & blessings of Allah be with him) saying: He who took an oath but then found something moiré pious in the sight of Allah, he should break the oath and do what is more pious.

27

Book of Prohibition of Killing & Blood-Money

1. It is reported on the authority of *Abu Bakra* that (during his farewell address) the Apostle of Allah (peace & blessings of Allah be with him) said: 'Time has completed a cycle and come to the state of the day when God Almighty created the Heavens and the earth. The year is constituted of twelve months, of which four are sacred and three are consecutive: Dhu-l- Qada, Dhu-l-Hijjah and Muharram, and also Rajab the month of Mudar, which comes between Jumada and Sha'ban.' 'Which month is this?' the holy Prophet asked. We said: 'God and His Messenger know best.' So he remained silent and then he said: 'Is it not the Dhu-l-Hijjah?' We said: 'Yes.' He then asked: which city is this? We said Allah and His Prophet know best. He remained silent and then said: Is this not the city of Makka? We said: yes. He again asked: which day is this? We said Allah and His Messenger know best. He remained silent and then said: Is it not the Day of Sacrifice? We said: O Messenger of Allah yes it is. Thereupon the holy Prophet (peace & blessings of Allah be with him) said: your blood, your property, and your honor s sacred to you like the sanctity of this day in your town, in this month. And soon you will meet your Lord, and He will ask you about your deeds. So do not go astray after me, striking each other's necks. Behold! Let him who is present here convey to those who are not present, for many of you who conveyed a message are more tentative memory than the one who hears. Thereafter he said: Behold! Have I not delivered (the message) to you? We said: yes. Then the Apostle of Allah (peace & blessings of Allah be with him) said: O Allah bear witness.

2. It is reported on the authority of Abd Allah ibn Mas'ud that the holy Prophet (peace & blessings of Allah be with him) said: The first cases to be judged on the Day of Reckoning will pertain to bloodshed.

3. It is reported on the authority of Abd Allah ibn Mas'ud that the Messenger of Allah (peace & blessings of Allah be with him) said: The blood of a Muslim who swears that there is no deity but Allah and that I am His Messenger, cannot be spilled except in three cases: in retribution for murder, for adultery committed by a married person and for the one who reneges from Islam and abandons the community.

4. It is reported on the authority of Abu Hurayra that the Apostle of Allah (peace & blessings of Allah be with him) said: Whoever deliberately throws himself off a mountain and kills himself will enter the Fire falling down into it, and he will stay there forever, and whoever drinks poison and kills himself with it will carry the poison in his hand in the Fire and he will stay in it forever, and whoever kills himself with an iron instrument will carry the instrument in his hand and stab his belly with it in the Fire where he will stay for ever.

5. *Sahl ibn Sa'ad al-Saeedi* is reported to have narrated that the Messenger of Allah (peace & blessings of Allah be with him) fought the unbelievers and returned to his camp and the others returned along with him. From among the companions of the Prophet (peace & blessings of Allah be with him) was a man who could not resist pursuing any unbeliever to strike him with his sword. Someone said: No one had helped the Muslims today more than so and so. The Messenger of Allah (peace & blessings of Allah be with him) then remarked: 'Surely he is from the people of the Fire.' Another man said: 'I will go with him.' So he went and whenever he stopped, he stopped with him, and

wherever he went on, he went on with him. The man was then gravely wounded and in order to die quickly thrust his sword into the ground and put is point between his breasts and threw himself upon it and committed suicide. Thereafter the man following him returned to the Messenger of Allah (peace & blessings of Allah be with him) and said: 'I bear witness that you are the Messenger of Allah.' The holy Prophet (peace & blessings of Allah be with him) said: 'What makes you say so?' He said: 'Because of the man who you said was one of the people of the Fire. The people were astonished at your words and I said to them I will try to discover the truth about him for you.' So I went with him and then he was wounded and he hastened his own death by throwing himself upon his own sword.' The Apostle of Allah (peace & blessings of Allah be with him) said: 'A man may do what appears to the people to be the deeds of the people of Paradise but he may be from the people of the Fire and another man may do what appears to be the deeds of the people of the Fire but he may be from the people of Paradise.

6. It is reported that **Umm Haritha**, the sister of Al-Rubayyi, broke the front tooth of another woman and the Messenger of Allah (peace & blessings of Allah be with him) ordered retribution. At that Umm Rubayya said: 'O Messenger of Allah! By Him Who sent you with the Truth, her tooth shall not be

broken.' The holy Prophet (peace & blessings of Allah be with him) said: 'All Praise be to God, O Umm Rubayyi, it (retribution) is ordained in the Book of God.' She said: 'No, by God, her tooth shall not be broken.' And she repeated saying this until they accepted compensation instead of retaliation. So the Apostle of Allah (peace & blessings of Allah be with him) said: Among the servants of God there are some who, if they take an oath of Allah, He honors it.

7. It is narrated on the authority of **Alqama** that his father said that he was sitting in the presence of the holy Prophet (peace & blessings of Allah be with him) when a man came in dragging another man by a rope, saying: 'O Messenger of Allah! This man has killed my brother.' The Apostle of Allah (peace & blessings of Allah be with him) asked him: 'Did you kill him?' He said: 'Yes, I killed him.' He asked: 'Why did you kill him?' He replied: 'We were together felling leaves from a tree and he insulted me and made me angry, so I hit him on his head with my axe and killed him.' At this the holy Prophet (peace & blessings of Allah be with him) said: 'Have you anything with which to pay blood money?' He said: 'I have nothing but the garment I am wearing and my axe.' He the asked: 'Will your people pay ransom?' He said: 'I am not a prominent person among my people. Thereafter he said: Take him away.' The man took him away and as he turned his back

the Messenger of Allah (peace & blessings of Allah be with him) said: 'If he kills him, he will be like him.' He turned back and said: 'O Messenger of Allah, I heard you say: 'If he kills him, he will be like him.' The holy Prophet (peace & blessings of Allah be with him) said: 'Do you not wish that he should be burdened with your sins and the sins of your brother?' He said: 'O Messenger of Allah, indeed!' The holy Prophet (peace & blessings of Allah be with him) then said: Then release him and let him be.

8. It is reported that **Abu Hurayra** said that two women of Huthail fought with each other and one hit the other with a stone. The stone hit her in the belly and she was pregnant her unborn child was killed. They both took the matter before the holy Prophet (peace & blessings of Allah be with him) and he ruled that the blood money was due to her relatives for what she had in her womb and imposed an indemnity of a male or female slave of the highest quality to be given to the victim.

9. It is reported on the authority of Abu Hurayra that the Messenger of Allah (peace & blessings of Allah be with him) (prayers & peace be upon him) said: No atonement is due for a wound caused by an animal, or for falling down a well or into a mine, and one fifth is due from buried treasure.

10. **Sahl ibn Abu Hathma** is reported to have said that Abd Allah ibn Sahl and Muhaiyisa ibn Mas'ud ibn

Zayed departed for Khyber. At that time the inhabitants of Khyber had a peace treaty with the Muslims. They separated from each other and later on Muhaiyisa found Abd Allah ibn Sahl lying dead in a pool of blood. He buried him and returned to Medina. Abd Al Rahman ibn Sahl, Muhaiyisa and Huwaiyisa, the sons of Mas'ud went to the holy Prophet (peace & blessings of Allah be with him) and told him about the incident. The Apostle of Allah (peace & blessings of Allah be with him) said: 'If you swear that you know who had committed the murder it is your prerogative to take your rights from the murderer.' They said: 'How can we swear when we did not witness the murder or see the murderer?' The Messenger of Allah (peace & blessings of Allah be with him) said:

'Then the Jews may deny the charges by fifty of their men swearing that it was not them who committed the murder.' They said: 'How can we believe the oaths of unbelievers?' j So the holy Prophet (peace & blessings of Allah be with him) paid the blood money himself and sent one hundred camels to them.

11. Sulaiman ibn Yasar, the freed slave of Maimuna, the wife of the Messenger of God, is reported to have said that one of the Ansars said that the Messenger of Allah (peace & blessings of Allah be with him) used to continue the practice of Qasamah as it had been in the pre-Islamic period.

28

Book of Punishments

1. *Hadrat Ayesha* is reported to have said that during the lifetime of the Apostle of Allah the hand of the thief was not cut off for less than the theft of the value of a shield, iron coat or Armour and both of them were of great value.

2. *Ibn Umar* has reported that the Apostle of Allah used to order cutting off the hand of a thief (in case of theft) of a shield the price of which was three Dirhams.

3. It is reported on the authority of *Ubada ibn al Samit* that when revelation used to descend on the Messenger of Allah (peace & blessings of Allah be with him), he would feel its rigour and his complexion used to change. Once when a revelation descended upon him he underwent the same ordeal and when it had passed he said: 'Receive from me, receive from me. God Almighty has ordained a way for them. If a married male commits adultery with a married female and an unmarried male commits adultery with an unmarried female, then those who are married shall receive one hundred lashes and be stoned to death, and those who are unmarried shall receive one hundred lashes and banishment for a year.

4. *Abd Allah ibn Utba* is reported to have said that he heard Abd Allah ibn Abbas say: While lie was sitting on the pulpit of the Messenger of Allah, Umar ibn al Khattab said: 'God has sent Muhammad with the Truth and he sent down the Book to him, and the verse regarding stoning was revealed in that which was sent down to him. So we recited it and put it to heart. The Messenger of Allah ruled the punishment of stoning to death and after him we ruled the punishment of stoning to death. I fear that in time to come people may say: 'We cannot find stoning to death prescribed in the Book of Allah.' And so they may go astray from that which God Almighty has prescribed. Stoning is an obligation inscribed in the Book of Allah in the case of married men and women whose adultery has been proven, or when a pregnancy has resulted or a confession has been made.

5. It is reported on the authority of Jabir ibn Samura that a short man with thick untidy hair and muscular body wearing a waist wrapper was brought before the Messenger of Allah (peace & blessings of Allah be with him) on charges of commit-ting adultery. He sent him away twice to reconsider his confession, but he confirmed it so he pronounced the punishment of stoning upon him, and he was stoned to death. The Messenger of Allah (peace & blessings of Allah be with him) said: 'Every time we set off in the Cause of Allah to fight one of you lags behind and becomes excited like a male goat seeking a female goat, if God gives me the opportunity to catch any of them, I shall punish him and make an example of him.'

6. Buraida is reported to have narrated that *Ma'iz ibn Malik al Aslami* came to the Apostle of Allah (peace & blessings of Allah be with him) and said to him: " O Messenger of Allah, I have wronged myself and committed adultery and I wish that you could purify me. He sent him away to reconsider his confession. In the morning he returned and said: 'O Messenger of Allah I have committed adultery.' He sent him away again to reconsider his confession. At this the holy Prophet (peace & blessings of Allah be with him) asked his people: 'do you know if there is something wrong with his mind? Or is his behaviour unacceptable to you?' They said: 'We know that he

is of a sound mind and as far as we can see he is one of the righteous people among us.' Ma'iz returned to the Apostle of Allah a third time and again he sent for his people to ask about him. They confirmed that he had nothing wrong with his mind. When he asked them the fourth time, he ordered a hole to be dug for him and ordered him to be stoned to death, and so he was stoned. The narrator said: 'A woman of Ghamada came to him and said: 'O Messenger of Allah, I have committed adultery so purify me.' He sent her away to reconsider her confession. The next morning she returned to him and said: 'O Messenger of Allah, why do you send me away?' She said: 'I see that you intend to send me back as you sent back Ma'iz. By God, I am pregnant.' He said: 'Go away until you deliver.' So when she delivered she brought the boy wrapped in a cloth and said: 'This is what I have delivered.' He said: 'Go and suckle him until he is weaned.' So when he was weaned she brought him walking with a piece of bread in his hand and said: 'O Messenger of Allah, this is him and I have weaned him and he is eating food now.' The holy Prophet (peace & blessings of Allah be with him) handed the boy to one of the Muslims and ordered a hole to be dug for her unto her chest, and ordered the people to stone her.

7. It was reported on the authority of *Abd Allah ibn Umar* that a Jewish man and a Jewish woman were

brought to the Messenger of Allah (peace & blessings of Allah be with him) with charges of committing adultery. The holy Prophet said: 'What do you see in the Torah concer-ning punishment for adultery?' They said: ' We proclaim their crime and whip them.' He said: 'Bring the Torah if what you say is true.' They produced the Torah and read it and one of them put his hand over the verse regar-ding stoning and read only the verses before it and after it. Abd Allah ibn Salaam, who was with the Messenger of Allah, said: 'Order him to lift his hand up.' When he raised his hand the verse regar-ding stoning was there. The Messenger of Allah (peace & blessings of Allah be with him) then ordered that both of them should be stoned to death. Abd Allah ibn Umar said: 'I was among those who stoned them, and I saw the man trying to protect the woman with his body.

8. *Abu Hurayra* is reported to have said that the Messenger of Allah (peace & blessings of Allah be with him) was asked about the unmarried slave woman who had committed adultery. He said: 'If she commits adultery then whip her, and if she repeats it, then whip her again and sell her for as little as a length of rope.' Ibn Shihab said: 'I do not recall if he said that upon the third or fourth time.'

9. It is reported on the authority of Abd al Rahman that Hadrat Ali addressed the people saying: 'O people, punish your slaves accor-ding to the prescribed punishment, the married among them and the unmarried. One of the slave woman in the custodianship of the Messen-ger of Allah committed adultery and he ordered me to whip her, but as she had recently delivered a child I feared the whipping might have killed her. So I asked the Messenger of Allah about it and he said: 'You acted correctly.'

10. *Abu Hurayra* is reported to have narrated that the Messenger of Allah (peace & blessings of Allah be with him) said: May the curse of God be upon the one who steals an egg, and sever his hand, and the one who steals a rope, and sever his hand.

11. It is reported on the authority of *Hadrat Ayesha*, that the Quraysh were disturbed concerning a woman who had stolen during the Conquest of Makka and the people said: 'Who can intercede for her with the Messenger of Allah (peace & blessings of Allah be with him)?' No one dared to speak to him except Usama ibn Zayed who was beloved by the Prophet (peace & blessings of Allah be with him). So she was brought before the Messenger of Allah and his face changed and he said: 'Do you seek to intervene in the punish-ment prescribed by God Almighty?' he said: 'O Messenger of Allah, seek forgiveness for me!' Then when night fell he addressed the people saying: 'Concerning this matter, it has been the failing of people before you that if a person of noble rank

stole, they would forgive him, but if a poor man stole they would cut off his hand. But by Him in Whose Hand is my life, I would even cut the hand of Fatimah if she stole.' Then he ordered the hand of the woman to be severed." Ayesha also said: "She repented well and then married and she used to come to visit me thereafter, and I used to tell the Messenger of Allah about her needs.

12. *Hudain ibn al Munthir abu Sasan* is reported to have said that he saw Walid brought before Uthman ibn Affan after he had offered the dawn prayer and two men witnessed against him, one of them was Humran who said he had consumed wine, the other testified that he had seen him vomiting. Uthman said: 'He would not have vomited if he had not consumed it.' He asked Ali to whip him. Ali said: 'Hasan, get up and whip him.' Hasan asked Abd Allah ibn Jafar to whip him.' He began to whip him and Ali counted the lashes until they had reached forty, then he said: 'Stop.' And he said: 'The Messenger of Allah used to order forty lashes, and Abu Bakr ordered forty too, and Umar used to deliver eighty, and all of this is according to the Sunna, but I prefer his forty.'

13. *Ali Ibn Abu Talib* is reported to have said: I used to feel sorry for the one who died through legal punishment except for the drunkard, for if he died I would give blood money to his family because no fixed punishment has been ordered for drunkards by the Messenger of Allah.

14. It is related that *Abu Barda al-Ansari* said that the holy Prophet (peace & blessings of Allah be with him) used to say: No one should be flogged more than ten lashes unless he is guilty of a crime for which the legal punishment has been assigned by God.

15. *Ubada ibn al Samit* has narrated that the Messenger of Allah (peace & blessings of Allah be with him) accepted our pledge as he accepted from the women, that we would not associate any partners with Allah, that we would not steal, that we would not commit adultery, that we would not kill our children, and that we would not tell lies concerning one another. And whoever keeps his pledge his reward is with Allah, and whoever is subjected to the prescribed punishment his redemption is with Allah, and whoever is covered by God, his affair is with God, He may chastise him if He pleases or He may forgive him if He pleases.

29

Book of Judicial Decisions

1. *Hadrat Ayesha* is reported to have related that the Apostle of Allah (peace & blessings of Allah be with him) said: The quarrelsome are the most despised of people in the sight of Allah.

2. *Ibn Abbas* is reported to have related that the Messenger of Allah (peace & blessings of Allah be with him) said: if the people are awarded on the strength of their claims, then they would claim the lives and properties of the people, but the defendant must swear an oath.

3. *Ibn Abbas* is reported to have said that the Messenger of Allah (peace & blessings of Allah be with him) pronounced his verdicts on the basis of the oath and a witness (from the side of the plaintiff).

4. *Abd al- Rahman ibn Abu Bakr* is reported to have related that his father dictated a letter to Ubaydallah ibn Abu Bakra when he was a judge that he should not pronounce judgment between two persons in a state of anger, for the Messenger of Allah (peace & blessings of Allah be with him) used to say: No one should judge a dispute while he is angry.

5. It is reported on the authority of *Amr ibn al As* that the Messenger of Allah (peace & blessings of Allah be with him) said: When a judge delivers a verdict, after careful deliberation and if the decision is right, he has two rewards, and if he judged after careful deliberation but erred in his verdict then there is one reward for him.

6. It is reported that *Abu Hurayra* said that the Messenger of Allah (peace & blessings of Allah be with him) narrated that there were two women, each had a child. A wolf came and took one of the children away. Both women claimed that the child of the other had been taken away. So they brought the matter before David (Dawood) who ruled that the living child should be given to the older woman. So they both went to Hadrat Sulaiman (Solomon), the son of David and told him about it. He said; bring me a

knife to divide the child between the two.' The younger woman said: 'May God have Mercy upon you! Do not do it! For it is her child.' So he gave the child to the younger woman.

7. It is reported that *Zayed ibn Khalid al-Juhani* narrated that the Messenger of Allah (peace & blessings of Allah be with him) said: Shall I tell you who is the best witness? He is the one who produces his proof before he is asked for it.

30

Book of
Picking up Lost Things

1. *Zayed ibn Khalid al Juhani* is reported to have narrated that the Messenger of Allah (peace & blessings of Allah be with him) said: Whoever finds a stray article or goods then he himself is led astray if he does not pronounce his find.

2. *Zayed ibn Khalid al Juhani* is reported to have narrated that a man asked the Apostle of Allah (peace & blessings of Allah be with him) about stray articles (or stray gold or silver articles) that are found. The holy Prophet (peace & blessings of Allah be with him) replied: Recognize well its container and the strap with which it is tied, and then make an announcement about it for a year, then use it but it would be a trust with you; and if someone claims it some day then return it to its owner. Then the person asked what was to be done if a lost camel was found and the Messenger of Allah (peace & blessings of Allah be with him) said: You have no business with it as it has its water container and its feet and it will reach water and eat from the trees until its owner finds it.

Then the man asked about lost sheep. The holy Prophet (peace & blessings of Allah be with him) replied: It is either for you, for your brother or for the wolf.

3. *Abd al- Rahman ibn Uthman al Taimi* is reported to have said that the Messenger of Allah forbade the Pilgrims from picking up lost property.

4. It is reported on the authority of *Ibn Umar* that the Messenger of Allah (peace & blessings of Allah be with him) said: You may not milk your brother's animal without his consent, would any of you wish to have his house plundered and his safes broken into and his food taken away? Verily their wealth are the udders of their animals, so do not milk the animal of another without his permission.

31

Book of Hospitality

1. *Abu shuraih al-Adawi* is reported to have said that his ears heard and his eyes saw the Apostle of Allah (peace & blessings of Allah be with him) say: He who believes in Allah and the Hereafter should show respect to the guest with utmost kindness and courtesy. Some people asked: O messenger of Allah what is utmost kindness and courtesy? The holy Prophet (peace & blessings of Allah be with him) replied: it is for a day and a night. Hospitality extends for three days, and beyond that is charity.

2. It is reported that *Uqba ibn Amer* said that we asked the Messenger of Allah: 'You dispatch us to people who fail to offer us hospitality, what is you opinion on this?' The holy Prophet (peace & blessings of Allah be with him) replied: If you go to people who offer you suitable hospitality, then accept it, but if they do not, then take what is appropriate for you to take as a guest.

3. It is reported on the authority of *Abu Shuraih al Khuza'i* that the Messenger of Allah (peace & blessings of Allah be with him) said: The guest is entitled to three days hospitality, and to utmost courtesy for a day and a night. No Muslim should stay with his brother until he makes him sinful. It was asked: What would make him sinful? The holy Prophet replied: That he stays, with him (so long) until he has nothing left with him to entertain the guest.

4. *Iyas ibn Salama* is reported to have narrated on the authority of his father that we journeyed out with the Messenger of Allah (peace & blessings of Allah be with him) on an expedition and ran short of provisions and we thought of slaughtering some of our riding animals. The Messenger of Allah (peace & blessings of Allah be with him) commanded us to collect our entire foodstuff, which we did, on a sheet of leather. I figured out that the sheet was big enough to accommodate a goat over it. We were about fourteen hundred people and we all were satisfied and filled our bags with food. Then the Messenger of Allah asked for water for ablution. A man came with a small container of water; he poured it into a bowl and all fourteen hundred people performed ablution from that water.

32

Book of Holy Struggles

1. It is reported on the authority of *Salman* that he heard the Messenger of Allah (peace & blessings of Allah be with him) say: Striving one day and night in the way of Allah is better than fasting and praying for a whole month. And if he dies, his deeds will continue to be rewarded and his bounty will continue, and he will be spared from the sufferings of the grave.

2. *Abu Saeed al- Khudri* is reported to have said that a person asked the holy Prophet (peace & blessings of Allah be with him) who are the best of people?' The Messenger of Allah (peace & blessings of Allah be with him) answered: A believer who strives with all his effort, his life and his possessions in the way of Allah. He was asked: Who is the next best? The Apostle of Allah said: A believer who secludes himself on a rocky way worshipping Allah alone and keeping his mischief away from the people.

3. It is reported on the authority of *Abu Hurayra* that the Messenger of Allah (peace & blessings of Allah be with him) said: Whoever dies and did not strive in the way of Allah (during his lifetime) and did not intend to do so, then he would have died having a trait of hypocrisy.

4. It is reported on the authority of *Anas* that the Messenger of Allah (peace & blessings of Allah be with him) said: Going to and fro in the cause of Allah is much better than the life of this world and all that is in it.

5. *Masruq* is reported to have narrated that Abd Allah was asked regarding the verse of the Qur'an: 'And do not reckon as dead those who were killed in God's Cause, but they are alive with their Lord and well provided for.' (Q.3: 169) He replied that the Messenger of Allah (peace & blessings of Allah be with him) was asked to explain the meaning of this and he had said: The souls of the martyrs abide within green birds nesting in chandeliers that hang beneath the Throne of God Almighty, they eat from the fruits of Paradise as they please and rest within the chandeliers. Their Lord once looked down at them and asked: 'Do you wish for anything?' They answered 'what more would we wish for, we eat the fruit of Paradise as we please.' Their Lord asked them three times and when they realized that they will continue to be asked, they said: 'O our Lord, we wish to return to our bodies so that we may be martyred in the way of Allah again.' When He found that they did not desire anything else, they were left in their blissful state.

6. *Abu Hurayra* is reported to have narrated that the Messenger of Allah (peace & blessings of Allah be with him) said: Allah has promised to all those who strive in the way of Allah, believing in Him and His Messengers that they will be admitted to Paradise or He will return them to their homes with booty and rewards. By the One in Whose Hand is the soul of Muhammad, the wound a Muslim receives in the way of Allah will reappear on the Day of Resurrection as it was at the time of its infliction, blood will flow from it and its color will be the color of blood but its scent would be of musk'. By the One in Whose Hand is the soul of Muhammad, had I not found it difficult for my followers, I would never have missed any Jihad in the way of Allah and I would have loved to be martyred for the sake of Allah and then brought back to life and then martyred again and brought back to life and then martyred again in His way.

7. It is reported on the authority of *Abu Saeed al Khudri* that the Messenger of Allah (peace & blessings of Allah be with him) said: Abu Saeed whoever happily accepts Allah as his Lord, and Islam as his religion and Muhammad as his Messenger will be entitled to enter Paradise. Abu Saeed said: O Messenger of Allah, repeat it for me. The holy Prophet (peace & blessings of Allah be with him) did so and said: There is a deed that will raise anyone one hundred degrees in Paradise, and the raising of one degree is equal to the distance between heaven and earth. Abu Saeed asked: What is that deed? The Apostle of Allah (peace & blessings of Allah be with him) said: To strive in the way of Allah, to strive for the sake of Allah.

8. *Anas ibn Malik* is reported to have said that the Messenger of Allah (peace & blessings of Allah be with him) used to visit Umm Haram bint Melhan and she used to offer him food. Umm Haram was married to Obadiah ibn Samit, and one day the holy Prophet (peace & blessings of Allah be with him) visited her and she offered him food, and then began to search for lice in his head. Then the Apostle of Allah slept for some-time and woke up smiling. Umm Haram asked: What makes you smile, O Messenger of Allah?' He said: Some of my community were shown to me in my vision as fighters in the way of Allah, sailing in the midst of seas like kings on the throne or like kings seated upon thrones. Umm Haram said:

'O Messenger of Allah! I implore Allah to make me one of them.' So the holy Prophet prayed for her and again slept off. He woke up smiling again. Umm Haram said: 'what makes you smile, O Messenger of Allah?' He said: 'Some of my community were shown to me as fighters in the Cause of God.' He said the same as he had said before, Umm Haram said: 'O Messenger of Allah! Pray to God to make me one of them.' He replied: 'You are from the first of them.' Then Umm Haram sailed across the sea in the lifetime of Mu'awiya ibn Abu Sufyan and she fell from her mount upon coming ashore and died.

9. *Al Numan ibn Bashir* is reported to have said that he was sitting near the pulpit of the Messenger of Allah when a man said: I shall not bother to do any good deed after becoming Muslim other than giving water to the pilgrims.' Another man said: 'I shall not bother to do any good deed after becoming Muslim other than maintaining the Sacred Mosque.' Another said: 'To strive in the way of Allah is better than what you have said.' Hadrat Umar reprimanded them saying: 'Do not raise your voices near the pulpit of the Mes-senger of Allah on Friday.' When the prayer was completed I went in and asked his opinion on what they had said. Then the following verse of the Qur'an was revealed: 'Do you consider the giving of water to pilgrims and the maintaining of the Sacred Mosque as equal to believing in Allah and the Last Day and striving in Allah's cause? They are not equal in the sight of Allah, and Allah does not guide the evildoers.' (Q. 9:19).

10. *Sahl ibn Hunaif* is reported to have said that the holy Prophet (peace & blessings of Allah be with him) said: Whoever prays to Allah sincerely for martyrdom, Allah will make him dwell in the abode of the martyrs, even if he dies upon his couch.

11. It is reported on the authority of *Anas ibn Malik* that the Messenger of Allah (peace & blessings of Allah be with him) said: No one who is admitted to Paradise will ever wish to return to the life of this world even if he was offered everything upon the face of the earth, except the martyr who will wish to return to the world to be killed ten times for the great reward that is granted him.

12. It is reported that *Umar ibn al-Khattab* (May Allah be pleased with him) said that he heard the Messenger of Allah (peace & blessings of Allah be with him) saying: The reward for any deed depends upon the intention and everyone will be rewarded according to his intentions. So whoever emigrates for worldly benefit or to marry, his emigration is for what he emigrated for'.

13. *Anas* is reported to have narrated that some people requested the Messenger of Allah (peace & blessings of Allah be with him) to send some men to teach them the

Qur'an and Sunna. So the holy Prophet (peace & blessings of Allah be with him) sent seventy men from Ansars who were known as the Reciters. Among them was my uncle Haram, they used to recite the Qur'an and study it at night. During the day they fetched water at the Mosque and collected fire-wood to sell and buy food for the wayfarers and needy people living near the Mosque. The Apostle of Allah (peace & blessings of Allah be with him) sent them to those people but they were killed before they reached their destination. So they said: 'O God, please let our Prophet know that we have met You and that You are pleased with us and we are pleased with You.' Then the Messenger of Allah told his companions: 'your brothers have been killed and they said: 'O God, please let our Prophet know that we have met You (Allah) and that You (Allah) is pleased with us and we are pleased with You (Allah).

14. It is reported on the authority of *Abu Hurayra* that the Messenger of Allah (peace & blessings of Allah be with him) said: If a man walking along a way finds a thorny branch upon the road, and he moves it away from the road, God will appreciate it and forgive him. The holy Prophet (peace & blessings of Allah be with him) also said that martyrdom is for five things; the one who dies of the plague, the one who dies of an intestinal disease, the one who drowns, the one who dies under a fallen structure and the

one who is martyred in the way of Allah.

15. *Amr ibn al- A'as* is reported to have said that the Messenger of Allah (peace & blessings of Allah be with him) said: A martyr is forgiven all his sins except debt.

16. *Abu Qatada* is reported to have said that the Apostle of Allah (peace & blessings of Allah be with him) addressed his companions and told them that to strive in the way of Allah and to believe in Him are the best of deeds. A man stood up and asked: 'O Messenger of Allah, if I am killed in the cause of Allah, will all my sins be wiped out?' The holy Prophet (peace & blessings of Allah be with him) said: 'Yes, if you are killed in the cause of Allah and you have been patient and sincere and have always stood and faced the enemy without ever taking flight.' Then he asked: 'What did you say?' He repeated: 'If I am killed in the cause of Allah, will all my sins be forgiven?' The Messenger of Allah (peace & blessings of Allah be with him) said: 'Yes, if you are killed in the cause of Allah and you have been patient and sincere and have always stood and faced the enemy without ever taking flight, except debt (that is if the debts have been cleared). Gabriel told me of this.

17. It is reported that *Abu Hurayra* said that a man came to the Messenger of Allah (peace & blessings of Allah be with him) and said: " O Messenger of Allah, what do you say if a man comes to take my money

from me?' He said: 'Do not give him your money.' He said: 'What do you say if he fights me?' He said: Fight him. He asked: 'What do you say if he kills me?' The holy Prophet (peace & blessings of Allah be with him) replied: Then you are a martyr. He asked: 'What do you say if I kill him?' He said: He is in the Hell Fire.

18. *Anas* is reported to have narrated that: My uncle, after whom I was named, missed the Battle of Badr. He said: 'O Messenger of Allah! I missed the first battle you fought against the unbelievers, if God permits me another chance to fight the unbelievers, without doubt, God will see how valiantly I will fight.' Then on the day of Uhud when the Muslims deserted and fled he said: 'O God! I seek Your forgiveness for what they have done and I denounce what the unbelievers have done.' Then he went forward and Sa'ad ibn Mu'adh met him, he said: 'O Sa'ad ibn Mu'adh! By the Lord of Al Nadr, Paradise is near. I perceive its scent from the side of Uhud.' Later Sa'ad said: 'O Messenger of Allah! I cannot do what he did. We found him with over eighty wounds in his body inflicted by swords and arrows. He was dead when we found him and his body was so badly mutilated that no one could identify him except his sister from his fingers.' We thought that this verse was revealed about him and others like him: 'Of the believers are men who have been true to their pledge to God.' (Q. 33: 23)

19. *Abu Musa* is reported to have narrated that a man came to the holy Prophet (peace & blessings of Allah be with him) and said: 'One man fights for war spoils, another for fame and another to show off, which of them fights in the way of Allah?' The Apostle of Allah (peace & blessings of Allah be with him) replied: 'he one who fights so that Islam is triumphant is the one who fights in the way of Allah.

20. *Sulaiman ibn Yasar* is reported to have said that Abu Hurayra was surrounded by people and he was asked to recount Hadith that he may have heard from the Messenger of Allah (peace & blessings of Allah be with him).' Abu Hurayra said: 'Yes, I heard the Messenger of Allah (peace & blessings of Allah be with him) say: The first of mankind to be judged on the Day of Reckoning will be a man who was martyred, he will be summoned forward and God Almighty shall make him recall his blessings and he will recall them. Then God Almighty will say: 'What did you do for them?' He will say: 'I fought in Your cause until I was martyred.' God Almighty will say: 'You have lied, but you fought so that the people would call you daring, and they did so.' He will be ordered to be dragged upon his face and cast into Hell. Then a man who acquired knowledge and imparted it to others and recited the Qur'an will be summoned forward and God Almighty shall make him recall his blessings and he will recall them.

Then God Almighty will say: 'What did you do for them?' He will say: 'I acquired knowledge and imparted it to others and recited the Qur'an for Your sake.' He will say: 'You have lied, but you acquired knowledge so that it would be said of you, you are knowledgeable, and you recited the Qur'an so that it would be said of you, you are a reciter (of the holy Qur'an), and so it was.' He will be ordered to be dragged upon his face and cast into Hell. Then an affluent man will be summoned forward and God Almighty shall make him recall his blessings and he will recall them. Then God Almighty will say: 'What did you do for them?' He will say: 'I spent in every cause for Your sake.' He will say: 'You have lied, but you did so that it would be said of you, you are generous, and so it was.' He will be ordered to be dragged upon his face and cast into Hell.

21. *Bara'* is reported to have said that a man from Bani Nabit (tribe) visited the holy Prophet (peace & blessings of Allah be with him) and said: 'I bear witness that there is no deity but Allah and that you are His servant and Messenger.' Later he went out in the cause of Allah and fought and was killed. The Apostle of Allah (peace & blessings of Allah be with him) remarked: He has done little but his reward is great.

22. *Abd Allah ibn Amr* is reported to have related that the Messenger of Allah (peace & blessings of Allah be with him) said: When a battalion of fighters, whether great or small in number, fight in the cause of Allah and take their booty and return safely, they have received two thirds of their reward in advance, and when a battalion of fighters, whether great or small in number, returns wounded and empty handed, their reward is with Allah and they will receive it in full.

23. *Zayed ibn Khalid Al Juhni* is reported to have narrated that the Messenger of Allah (peace & blessings of Allah be with him) said: The one who prepares a fighter going to fight in the cause of Allah is himself given the reward of a fighter, and the one who safeguards the property of the dependants of a fighter who fights in the cause of Allah is himself given the reward of a fighter.

24. It is reported on the authority of *Thauban* that the Messenger of Allah (peace & blessings of Allah be with him) said: A group of my community will remain on the right path and no one will be able to divert them. Whoever deserts them will not cause them any harm, and they shall remain so until the Day of Judgment.

25. *Abd Al Rahman ibn Shumasa al Mahri* is reported to have said that he went to visit Maslama ibn Mukhallad and found Abd Allah ibn Amr ibn al A 'as with him. So Abd Allah said: 'The (final) Hour will not come except when only the worst kind of people remain on the earth, they will be worse than the people of the days of ignorance.

Whatever they desire God will give them.' While they were sitting Uqba ibn Amer came, and Maslama told him: 'O Uqba, listen to what Abd Allah is saying.' So Uqba said: 'He is well aware, but I have heard the Messenger of Allah (peace & blessings of Allah be with him) say: 'A group of my community will continue to fight in the cause of Allah, they will conquer their enemies, and whoever deserts them will do them no harm, and they will remain so until the Day of Judgment.'

26. *Sa'ad ibn Abu Waqqas* is reported to have narrated that the Messenger of Allah (peace & blessings of Allah be with him) said: The Arabs will remain on the right path until the Day of Judgment.

27. *Abu Hurayra* is reported to have narrated that the Messenger of Allah (peace & blessings of Allah be with him) said: They will not be gathered together in the Fire to harm each other. It was asked: Who are they, O Messenger of Allah? He replied: A believer who killed an unbeliever, but then he repented.

28. *Abu Mas'ud al Ansari* is reported to have narrated that the Messenger of Allah (peace & blessings of Allah be with him) said: 'whoever directs towards good is rewarded like the one who does good.

29. It is reported that Abu Ishaq heard Al Barra' speaking about the verse: 'Those people from among the believers who stay at home without any genuine excuse, are not equal in rank with those who exert their utmost with their lives and wealth in Allah's cause. For God has assigned a higher rank to those who exert their utmost with their lives and wealth than to those who stay at home. Although God has promised a rich reward for all, He has a far richer reward for those who fight in His cause than for those who stay at home.' (Q.4: 95) The Messenger of Allah (peace & blessings of Allah be with him) asked Zayed to write it down. Ibn Maktoum complained to him of blindness, so the verse was revealed: 'Those people from among the believers who stay at home without any genuine excuse, are not equal in rank with those who exert their utmost with their lives and wealth in the way of Allah.

33

Book of Expeditions

1. It is reported on the authority of *Zayed ibn Arqam* and *Buraida* that the Apostle of Allah (peace & blessings of Allah be with him) participated in nineteen battles and after Hijra performed only one pilgrimage called Hajjat ul Wida.

2. It is reported on the authority of *Abu Hurayra* and *Jabir* that the Messenger of Allah (peace & blessings of Allah be with him) said: War is a strategy.

3. *Hadrat Ayesha* is reported to have narrated that the Messenger of Allah (peace & blessings of Allah be with him) set out for Badr, when he reached Harrah he met a man who was famous for his bravery. The companions of the holy Prophet (peace & blessings of Allah be with him) were happy to see him and he said: 'I have come to join you so that I may take a share of the war spoils.' The Apostle of Allah (peace & blessings of Allah be with him) asked him: 'Do you believe in Allah and His Messenger?' He said: 'No.' The Messenger of Allah (peace & blessings of Allah be with him) told him to go away as he did not need the help of an unbeliever. So he continued on until we reached Sharjara, and there he met the same man again, and he asked him the same question and the man gave the same reply. The holy Prophet (peace & blessings of Allah be with him) again told him to go away. The man returned and was asked the same again, and this time he said that he believed in Allah and His Messenger so the Apostle of Allah (peace & blessings of Allah be with him) said: Then join us.

4. It has been reported on the authority of Umar ibn al-Khattab that on the day the Battle of Badr took place, the Apostle of Allah (peace & blessings of Allah be with him) cast a glance at the enemy, and they were one thousand while his own compa-nions were three hundred and nineteen. The holy Prophet turned his face towards the Qibla and prayed: O Lord, O Allah, accomplish for me what Thou hast promised to me. O Allah if this small band of Muslims is destroyed, Thou wilt not be worshipped on this earth. He continued his suppli-

cations until his mantle slipped off his shoulders. Thereafter it was revealed: When ye appealed to your Lord for help, He responded to your call (saying): I will help you with one thousand angels coming in succession. And succour cometh not but from Allah. Verily Allah is Mighty, Wise. (Q. 8:10).

5. It is reported that on one of the days when the Messenger of Allah (peace & blessings of Allah be with him) was waiting to meet the enemy, (on the eve of the Battle of Badr) he waited until the sun had declined and then he stood up and said: 'O people! Do not desire to encounter the enemy and ask God to save you, but if you do encounter the enemy, then be firm and patient and know that Paradise is under the shade of the sword.' Then the holy Prophet (peace & blessings of Allah be with him) said: 'O God! The Revealer of the Book, the Disperser of the clouds, the Defeater of the hordes, vanquish our enemy and grant us victory.

6. *Anas* is reported to have narrated that on the day of the battle of Hunayn Umm Sulaim had a dagger with her, Abu Talha saw it and told the Messenger of Allah about it. The holy Prophet (peace & blessings of Allah be with him) asked: 'What is this dagger?' She replied that she was carrying it so as to cut open the belly of any unbeliever who dared to come near her. The Apostle of Allah (peace & blessings of Allah be with him) smiled and said: 'O Umm Sulaim, God Almighty is sufficient (against the mischief of the unbelievers) and He will be kind to us. (So there was no need to carry the dagger).

7. It is reported that *Umm Atiyya* of the Ansars said that she participated in seven battles with the Messenger of Allah, staying behind at the men's campsite and cooking their food and treating their wounds and nursing the sick.

8. *Abd Allah Ibn Umar* is reported to have said that in one of the battle a woman was found killed, so the Messenger of Allah (peace & blessings of Allah be with him) prohibited the killing of women and children.

9. It is reported from Sulaiman ibn Buraid on the authority of his father that when the Messenger of Allah (peace & blessings of Allah be with him) appointed anyone as leader of an army or detachment he used to advise him to fear Allah and to be good to the Muslims who were with him. He used to say: Fight in the name of Allah and in the way of Allah. Fight against those who disbelieve in Allah. Fight and do not exceed the limits. Do not embezzle the spoils of war, do not mutilate (dead bodies of the enemy), and do not kill any child. When you encounter your enemy from the unbelievers, invite them to three things. If they respond to any one of these, accept it from them and do not fight them. Invite them to Islam; if they respond to you, accept it from them and desist from fighting

against them. Then invite them to migrate from their lands to the land of the Muhajirs and inform them that, if they do so, they shall have all the privileges and obligations of the Muhajirs. If they refuse, tell them that they will have the status of bedouin Muslims and will be subjected to the Ordinances of Allah like the believers, but they will not receive any share from the booty except when they participate in fighting alongside the Muslims. But if they refuse to accept Islam, demand from them the poll tax (Jizyah). If they agree to pay, accept it from them and do not fight them. If they refuse to pay the tax, then seek the help of Allah and fight them. And when you lay siege to a fortress and the besieged appeal to you for protection in the name of Allah and His Prophet, do not give them the guarantee on behalf of Allah and His Prophet, but give them your own guaran-tee and the guarantee of your companions. It is a lesser sin that the security given by you or your companions be disregarded than the security given in the name of Allah and His Prophet. When you besiege a fortress and the besieged want you to let them out in accordance with Allah's Command, do not let them come out in accordance with His Command, but do so at your own command, for you do not know whether or not you will be able to carry out Allah's Will regarding them.

10. *Abu Musa* is reported to have

narrated that the holy Prophet (peace & blessings of Allah be with him) sent him and Muaz to Yemen and told them: Be easy with the people and do not be difficult with them, and give them glad tidings and do not repel them and obey each other and do not dispute with one another.

11. *Abu Saeed al-Khudri* is reported to have narrated that the Messenger of Allah (peace & blessings of Allah be with him) said to Bani Lahyan: 'Let one man out of every two, come out to strive in the way of Allah.' Then he said to those who were left behind: 'Anyone of you who takes care of the family and wealth of the one who went out to strive in the cause of Allah will be receive half of his reward.

12. *Ibn Umar* is reported to have said that the Messenger of Allah (peace & blessings of Allah be with him) summoned me on the day of the Battle of Uhud, I was fourteen years old at that time and he did not permit me to participate in the battle, but he summoned me again on the day of the Battle of the Trench when I had reached fifteen years of age and he permitted me to participate in that battle." Nafe' said: When I visited caliph Umar ibn Abd al Aziz, I related this Hadith to him, and he said: 'That is the difference between the child and the youth.' So he wrote to his rulers to give salaries to all who had reached the age of fifteen. And whoever was less than that, he was to be considered a child.

13. It is reported on the authority of *Abu Hurayra* that the Messenger of Allah (peace & blessings of Allah be with him) said: When you travel through a fertile land, you should allow the camels to graze. And when you travel through a barren land you should hurry on. And if you need to rest for the night, you should keep away from the road, as it is the path of harmful things at night.

14. It was related that *Abu Hurayra* is reported to have narrated that the Apostle of Allah (peace & blessings of Allah be with him) said: Traveling is a form of hardship as it prevents you from food, drink and sleep. So when you have completed the purpose of your journey, you should hurry back to your family.

15. *Anas* is reported to have said that the holy Prophet (peace & blessings of Allah be with him) never returned to his wives from a night journey. He used always to return in the morning or in the afternoon.

16. *Ibn Abbas* is reported to have narrated that he heard the tradition from Abu Sufyan that Heraclius had sent a messenger to him while he was accom-panying a trade caravan from Quraysh going to do business in al Sham (Syria, Palestine, Lebanon and Jordan), at the time when the Messenger of Allah (peace & blessings of Allah be with him) had a truce with Abu Sufyan and the infidels of the Quraysh. So Abu Sufyan and his compa-nions went to Heraclius at Aelya (Jeru-salem). Heraclius invited them to his court while he sat among the Roman notables. He summoned his translator and asked them: "Which one of you is the closest relative to the man who claims to be a pro-phet?" Abu Sufyan said, I replied I am the closest relative." Heraclius said: "Bring him nearer to me and make his companions stand behind him." Then Heraclius said to his translator: "Tell them I will ask him about that man, so if he lies to me you must say so." Abu Sufyan said: "By God if I had not been afraid of my companions calling me a liar, I would not have spoken any word of truth about him, the first question he asked me was: "What is his family status amongst you?" and I answered: "He is from a noble family." Then Heraclius asked: "Has any one of your people ever claimed the same before him?" I replied: "No." He asked: "Were any of his ancestors kings." I replied: "No." He said: "Do the nobles or the meek follow him?" I replied: "The meek follow him." He asked: "Are his followers increasing or decreasing?" I replied: "They are increasing." Then he asked: "Do any of his followers renounce the religion after having embraced it?" I replied: "No." Heraclius then said: "Have you ever accused him of telling lies before his claim to prophet hood?" I replied: "No." Heraclius said: "Does he break his promises?" I replied: "No, we are at truce with him but we do not know what he will do in it." And so I could not find any oppor-tunity to say anything against him except that. Heraclius asked: "Have you ever fought him?" I replied: "Yes." Then he said: "What was the outcome of the battles." I replied: "The battles between us had their ups and downs, we fought each other with alternate success." Heraclius said: "What does he tell you to do?" I said: "He tells us to worship God alone and not to worship anything besides God, and to renounce all the practices of our ancestors. He enjoins us to pray, to be truthful, to be chaste and to keep good relations with our kin." Heraclius told the translator to convey the following to me: "I asked you about his family and your reply was that he came from a very noble family. Indeed all the prophets came from the noble families. I asked you whether anyone else among you had made similar claims and you replied no. If the answer had been in the affirmative, I would have thought that this man was following the statement of the previous man. Then I asked you whether anyone of his ancestors was a king. Your reply was no, and if it had been in the affirmative, I would have thought that this man wanted to regain his ancestral kingdom. I then asked you whether he was ever accused of telling lies before saying what he now says, and your reply was no. So I wondered how a person who never tells lies about others could lie about God. I then asked you whether the rich people followed him or the poor. You replied that it was the poor who followed him. Indeed the poor have followed all the prophets. Then I asked you whether his followers were increasing or decreasing. You replied that they were increasing. Indeed this is the way of true faith until it is complete in all respects. I further asked you whether anyone had renounced his religion after embracing it. Your reply was no. Indeed this is a sign of true faith when its delight enters the heart and is instilled in it. I asked you whether he had ever betrayed anyone, and you answered no. Indeed prophets never commit betrayal. Then I asked you what he ordered you to do. You replied that he ordered you to worship God alone and not to worship any besides Him and he forbade you to worship idols and he asked you to pray and speak the truth and to be chaste. If what you have said is true, he will very soon occupy this place beneath my feet and I knew (from the Scriptures) that he was going to appear but I did not know that he would be from your people, and if I could reach him definitely, I would go immediately to meet him and if I were with him I would most certainly wash his feet." Heraclius then asked for the letter addressed by the Messenger of Allah (peace & blessings of Allah be with him) that was delivered by Dihya Kalbi to the governor of Basra, who had forwarded it to Heraclius. The letter read as follows: "In the name of Allah, the Merciful, the Compassionate, this letter is from Muhammad, the servant of God and His Messenger, to Heraclius the ruler of Byzantine. Peace be upon him, who follows the right path. I invite you to Islam and if you become Muslim you will be safe and Allah shall double your reward, but if you reject this invitation to Islam you would be committing a sin by misguiding your people. God Almighty has said: "Say, 'O people of the Book! Let us reason together, that we worship none but Allah and we ascribe no partners unto Him, and that we do not set up from among ourselves lords other than God.' But if they turn away, then say, 'Bear witness that we are Muslims.' " (Q. 3: 64) Abu Sufyan then added: "When Heraclius had finished his speech and had read this letter, there was a great uproar in the royal court. So we were turned out of the court. I told my companions that Ibn Abu Kabsha (a derogatory nickname which Abu Sufyan gave the holy Prophet) has now come to wield great power that even the King of Romans now fears him. Then I became certain that the influence of the Messenger of Allah (peace & blessings of Allah be with him) would triumph in the near future.

17. It is reported that *Usama ibn Zayed* narrated that before the battle of Badr, he and the Apostle of Allah (peace & blessings of Allah be with him) rode a donkey to visit Sa'ad ibn Ubada in Bani Al Harith. They passed by a gathering in which Abd Allah ibn Ubayy was present, and that was before Abd Allah ibn

Ubayy became Muslim. In the gathering there were people from different religions, Muslims, pagans, idol worshippers and Jews, and Abd Allah ibn Rawaha was also there. When a cloud of dust kicked up by the donkey reached the people, Abd Allah ibn Ubayy covered his nose with his clothes and said: 'Do not cover us with dust.' Then the Messenger of Allah (peace & blessings of Allah be with him) greeted them and stopped and dismounted and invited them to embrace Islam, he recited the Qur'an to them. At that, Abd Allah ibn Ubayy said: 'O man! There is nothing better than what you say, if it is the truth, then do not bother us with it in our gatherings, go back to your mount and if anyone comes to you, tell it to him.' At that Abd Allah ibn Rawaha said: 'Yes, O Messenger of Allah, bring it to us in our gathering, as we love it.' Thereafter the Muslims, the pagans and the Jews began to insult each other until they almost came to blows. The holy Prophet (peace & blessings of Allah be with him) tried to calm them and then he rode away until he reached Sa'ad ibn Ubada. The Apostle of Allah (peace & blessings of Allah be with him) said: 'O Sa'ad, did you hear what Abu Hubab and Abd Allah ibn Ubayy - said: 'So and so.' Sa'ad ibn Ubada replied: 'O Messenger of Allah! Pardon him, for by He Who revealed the Book to you, God brought the Truth that was sent to you at the time when the people of this town had decided to crown him (as the chief) and tie a turban upon his head. But when Allah opposed that through His Truth he felt jealous and aggrieved and that was the reason for his behaviour.' So the holy Prophet (peace & blessings of Allah be with him) pardoned him.

18. *Abu Saeed* is reported to have related that the Messenger of Allah (peace & blessings of Allah be with him) said: Every traitor will have an ensign raised for him on the Day of Resurrection according to the degree of his treason, but there is no greater treason than the treason of a ruler or an Amir.

19. It is reported that *Mus'ab ibn Sa'ad* said that his father related: Four verses of the Qur'an were revealed on account me. I found a sword among the booty and it was taken to the Apostle of Allah (peace & blessings of Allah be with him). I said: 'O Messenger of Allah, give it to me.' The holy Prophet (peace & blessings of Allah be with him) said: 'Put it there.' Then I stood up and he said: 'Put it back where you found it.' I asked again: 'O Messenger of Allah (peace & blessings of Allah be with him), give it to me, am I to be treated as one who has no share of the booty?' The holy Prophet (peace & blessings of Allah be with him) said: 'Put it back where you found it.' Then the verse was revealed: 'They ask you about the spoils of war, say: 'Spoils are at the disposal of God and His Messenger...' (Q. 8: 1).

20. *Ibn Umar* is reported to have said that the Messenger of Allah (peace & blessings of Allah be with him) sent a company of soldiers to Najd with Abd Allah Ibn Umar. They brought many camels as war booty, each one of them got a share of eleven or twelve camels, and they were each given an additional camel.

21. *Abd Aliah ibn Umar* reportedly said that the Messenger of Allah (peace & blessings of Allah be with him) used to give a slighter larger share of the booty to the small forces he sent out on expeditions than to the larger forces. And one fifth of the booty was always kept for Allah and His Messenger.

22. *Abu Qatada* is reported to have narrated that: We set off on a journey with the Messenger of Allah (peace & blessings of Allah be with him) on the day of Hunayn. When we confronted the unbelievers some Muslims retreated and I saw an unbeliever throwing himself over a Muslim. I turned around and came upon him from behind and struck him with my sword on his shoulder, he advanced towards me and took hold of me so brutally that it seemed as if death was near. But death overtook him and his grip upon me was released. I followed Umar ibn Al Khattab and asked him: 'What is the matter with the people?' He replied: 'This is the Will of God.' Then the people came back and the holy Prophet (peace & blessings of Allah be with him) sat down and said: 'Anyone

who has killed the enemy and can prove it will be given his posse-ssions.' I got up and asked: 'Who will bear witness for me?' Then I sat down. The Prophet (peace & blessings of Allah be with him) again said: 'Anyone who has killed the enemy and can prove it will be given his possessions.' I got up and again asked: 'Who will bear witness for me?' Then I sat down. Then The Prophet (peace & blessings of Allah be with him) said the same a third time. I got up again and the Apostle of Allah said: 'O Abu Qatada! Tell us your tale.' So I related the epi-sode to him. A man said: 'O Mes-senger of Allah! He is telling the truth, and the possessions of the man he killed are with me. So please compensate him on my behalf.' At this Abu Bakr Siddiq said: 'No, by God, he will not agree to give you the booty gained by one of Allah's warriors who fought in the way of Allah and His Mes-senger. 'The holy Prophet (peace & blessings of Allah be with him) said: 'Abu Bakr has spoken the truth.' So the booty was given to me. I sold the armor and I bought a garden at Bani Salima with the money from it, and this was the first property I gained after I embraced Islam.

23. *Abd Al Rahman ibn Auf* is reported to have said that he was aligned in the ranks on the day of Badr, when he saw two young boys of the Ansars, and one of them surprised him by saying: 'O Uncle! Do you know Abu Jahl?' I said: 'Yes, what do you want from him, my ne-phew?' He said: 'I have been told that he insults the Messenger of Allah, by He in Whose Hands is my life, if I should see him, I will not leave his body until one of us meets his fate.' I was astounded at his speech, and then the other boy surprised me by saying the same as the other had said. After some time I saw Abu Jahl and I said to the boys: 'look! There is the man you enquired about.' So both of them set upon him with their swords and struck him until he died and then returned to the Messenger of Allah (peace & blessings of Allah be with him) to tell him about it. The Apostle of Allah (peace & blessings of Allah be with him) asked as to which one of them had killed Abu Jahl. Both claimed they had killed him. The holy Prophet looked at their swords and agreed that they both had killed him and the spoils of the deceased were given to both of them.

24. *Abu Hurayra* is reported to have narrated that the Messenger of Allah (peace & blessings of Allah be with him) said: Whatever village you reach and you stay therein you have a share in it. And whatever village disobeys Allah and His Messenger one-fifth of it is for Allah and His Messenger and the rest is for you.

25. *Malik ibn Aus* is reported to have said that Umar ibn Al Khattab summoned him, so he visited him and found him lying upon a couch made of palm fiber, there was nothing between the palm fiber and

his body, and he reclined upon a leather cushion. He said: 'O Malik, some of your people who have families came to me and I have ordered that they should receive a gift. So take it and distribute it between them.' I said: 'O Leader of the Believers! I wish you would order someone else to do that.' He said: 'Take it!' As I sat there with him his usher Yarfa came in and said: 'Uthman, Abd Al Rahman ibn Auf, Al Zubair and Sa'ad ibn Abu Waqqas seek your permission to come in, may I admit them?' Umar said: 'Yes.' So they were admitted and they entered and greeted him and were seated. A while later Yarfa came in again and said: 'May I admit Ali and Abbas?' Umar said: 'Yes.' So they were admitted. Then Abbas said: 'O Leader of the Believers! Decide the dispute between Ali and me' - and he said something. Malik ibn Aus said: 'I thought they were coming for that purpose.' Umar said: 'Patience! I implore *you by Allah* by Whose permission the Heaven and Earth exist, do you not know that the Messenger of Allah (peace & blessings of Allah be with him) said: 'Our property will not be inherited and anything we leave is for charity.' They said: 'He did say so.' Umar turned to Ali and Abbas and said: 'I implore you by Allah, by Whose permission the Heaven and Earth exist, do you not know that the Apostle of Allah (peace & blessings of Allah be with him) said that his property will not be inherited and anything he leaves is

for charity?' They both said: 'Yes.' Umar then recited the Verse: "And whatever spoils of war Allah bestowed upon His Messenger from them, you urged not any horse or riding camel for the sake thereof but God prevails His Messengers over whom He pleases." (Q. 59: 6). - I am not sure if he read the verse before it as well or not, - Umar also said: 'The Messenger of Allah (peace & blessings of Allah be with him) distributed the property of Bani an-Nadir amongst you until this is all that was left from it. And by God, he did not prefer himself in it nor exclude you. The Messenger of Allah (peace & blessings of Allah be with him) used to provide for the expenses of his family from it every year and used to keep the remainder as funds to be spent in the way of Allah. I ask you by God, by Whose permission the Heavens and earth exist, do you not know that?' They said: 'Yes.' Umar then said the same to Ali and Abbas asking them: 'Do you not know that?' They said: 'Yes.' Umar also said: 'When Allah called His Prophet back to Him, Abu Bakr said: 'I am the successor of the Messenger of Allah, and you went to him demanding your inheritance from the son of your brother and this one went to ask for the inheritance of his wife from her father. Abu Bakr then said that the Messenger of Allah (peace & blessings of Allah be with him) had said that his property would not be inherited and whatever remained of it would be given in charity. Do you see him as a liar or a traitor while

God knows that he was truthful, God-fearing and rightly guided, and he followed what is right. Then God called Abu Bakr back to Him and I became the successor of the Messenger of Allah and that of Abu Bakr, do you see me as a liar or a traitor while God knows that I have been truthful, God-fearing and have followed what is right, and I kept the property in my possession for the first two years of my Caliphate, I dealt with it in the same way as the Messenger of Allah (peace & blessings of Allah be with him) had done. So now you both come to me putting forward the same claim and offering the same argument, and asking me to give it to you. If you wish I will give it to you both on condition that you promise by Allah that you will use it in the same way as the Messenger of Allah used to do. Then you will take it upon that condition. He said: 'Do you agree?' They both said: 'Yes.' He said: 'Then Umar said: 'You both came to me for a decision between yourselves, by God, I will not do so other than this until the Hour comes to pass, and if you are unable to look after it then return it to me, and I will manage it for you'.

26. *Hadrat Ayesha* is reported to have related that: Fatimah, the daughter of the Apostle of Allah (peace & blessings of Allah be with him) made a request to Abu Bakr for her share in the property of her father, the holy Prophet (peace & blessings of Allah be with him) that he had left in Medina and Khyber. Abu Bakr replied that the Messenger of Allah (peace & blessings of Allah be with him) had said: Our property will not be inherited; whatever we leave is for charity. But the family of Muhammad will continue to live off this property.' And Abu Bakr said: 'I would never change anything of the charity of the Messenger of Allah, and I shall leave it (in the same situation) as it had been in his lifetime. I would manage it in the same way as the Messenger of Allah had done.' Abu Bakr refused to give anything to Fatimah. This made the beloved daughter of the holy Prophet (peace & blessings of Allah be with him) angry with Abu Bakr and she did not speak to him until she died. And she died six months after the Messenger of Allah. On her death, Ali had her buried during the night and he did not inform Abu Bakr or permit him to attend her burial. During Fatimah's lifetime, Ali did not make allegiance to Abu Bakr, but after she had left for her heavenly abode; Ali realized that Muslims did not approve of his non-allegiance to Abu Bakr, so he requested Abu Bakr to visit him alone, as he did not wish that Umar ibn al Khattab should accompany Abu Bakr to his house. Umar said to Abu Bakr: 'By God, you will not go to their alone.' Abu Bakr said: 'why, what can they do to me? By God, I will visit them.' Abu Bakr kept his appointment and Ali said to the venerable caliph: 'We acknowledge your virtue and what Allah has granted you, and we do not envy you in anything good that Allah has

given you, but you did not consult us regarding your appointment, and we feel that we have a right to be consulted due to our relationship to Muhammad, the Messenger of Allah.' He continued to speak to Abu Bakr until Abu Bakr's eyes were filled with tears. Then Abu Bakr spoke and said: 'By The One in Whose Hand is my soul, the relationship with the Messenger of Allah (peace & blessings of Allah be with him) is dearer to me than the relationship with my own people. But as for the dispute that has arisen between you and I regarding the properties, I have not deviated from the right way nor have I failed to deal with them in the way of the Messenger of Allah.' So Ali said to Abu Bakr: 'We shall meet tonight to give allegiance to you.' After the noon prayers Abu Bakr ascended the pulpit and spoke about the situation with Ali and what had kept him from allegiance, and he appreciated his reasons. Then he sought Allah's forgiveness. Then Ali replied: "I certify that there is no deity but Allah and Muhammad is His servant and Messenger and I praise Abu Bakr greatly, and it was not envy that delayed us from making allegiance to Abu Bakr nor a denial of his virtue or the position Allah has granted him, but we consider that we have the right to be consulted, that is why we were upset.' The Muslims were pleased with that and said: 'You have done the right thing.' And once again the Muslims became close to Ali after he had offered his allegiance as the rest of the companions of the holy Prophet (peace & blessings of Allah be with him) had done.

27. *Abu Hurayra* is reported to have narrated that the Messenger of Allah (peace & blessings of Allah be with him) said: My inheritors will not share in as little as a Dinar, whatever I leave is for the maintenance of my wives and salary for my servants, and the rest is for charity.

28. *Yazid ibn Hurmuz* is reported to have related that Najdah wrote to Ibn Abbas asking him five questions. Ibn Abbas said: Had it not been that I would be concealing knowledge, I would not have written to him. Najdah wrote to him saying: Tell me did the Messenger of Allah (peace & blessings of Allah be with him) permit women to participate with him in battles? Did he allot them a regular share from the booty? Did he permit the killing of children? How long would an orphan be considered an orphan? Who is entitled to a fifth of the booty? Ibn Abbas wrote to him: You have written to me asking did the Messenger of Allah (peace & blessings of Allah be with him) permit women to participate with him in battles. He did permit them to participate in the battles and sometimes he fought alongside them. They used to treat the wounded and were rewarded from the booty, but he did not assign any regular share for them. The Messenger of Allah (peace & blessings of Allah be with him) did not kill

children, so you should not kill the children. Also you have written to me asking me how long would an orphan be considered and orphan. By my life, if a young man has become bearded but is still incapable of obtaining his due from others as well as fulfilling his obligations towards them, but when he is able to take care of his interests, he is no longer an orphan. You have written to me asking who is entitled to one fifth of the booty. We, as the family of the Messenger of Allah, used to say: It is for us, but our people have rejected that it be given to us.

29. *Abu Hurayra* is reported to have said that the Apostle of Allah (peace & blessings of Allah be with him) sent some cavalry to Najd and they brought a man from Bani Hunaifa called Thumama ibn Uthal, the chief of the people of Yamama. They tied him to a pillar in the Mosque. The holy Prophet (peace & blessings of Allah be with him) asked him: 'what do you have, O Thumama?' He said: 'I have a good idea, O Muhammad! If you kill me you will kill someone who deserves to be killed, and if you release me you will do a favour to one who will be grateful, and if you wish for property then ask me for anything you want.' The Messenger of Allah (peace & blessings of Allah be with him) left him until the following day and then again said to him: 'what do you have, O Thumama?' He said: 'As I told you, you would do a favour to one who will be grateful, if you kill me you will kill someone who deserves to be killed, and if you wish for property then ask me for anything you want.' The Messenger of Allah (peace & blessings of Allah be with him) left him there until the following day, and then he said: 'what do you have, O Thumama?' He said: 'I have as I told you, you would do a favour to one who will be grateful, if you kill me you will kill someone who deserves to be killed, and if you wish for property then ask me for anything you want.' At that the holy Prophet (peace & blessings of Allah be with him) freed Thumama.' So he went to a garden of date trees close by the mosque and bathed and then entered the mosque and said: 'I testify that there is no deity but Allah and Muhammad is His servant and Messenger. O Mohammed! By God! There was no face on the surface of the earth that I hated more than your face, but now your face has become the most beloved face to me. By God, there was no religion that I hated more than your Religion, but now your Religion is the most beloved Religion to me. And by God, there was no city that I hated more than your city, but now, your city is the most beloved city to me. Your troops arrested me when I wanted to perform Umrah, so what do you think?' The Messenger of Allah (peace & blessings of Allah be with him) gave him the glad tidings and permitted him to perform Umrah. When he reached Makka someone said to him: 'You have changed your religion?' He

said: 'No! But by God! I have become Muslim with Muhammad the Messenger of Allah, by God! You will not get from Al Yamama one grain of wheat unless the Messenger of Allah (peace & blessings of Allah be with him) permits me to do so.

30. *Abu Hurayra* is reported to have said: While we were in the Mosque the Messenger of Allah (peace & blessings of Allah be with him) came to us and said: 'Go to the Jews.' So we went out with him and went to them. The Messenger of Allah (peace & blessings of Allah be with him) stood up and addressed them: 'O you gathering of Jews, embrace Islam and you will be secure.' They replied: 'O Abul Qasim, you have conveyed the Message of Allah to us.' The Apostle of Allah (peace & blessings of Allah be with him) said: That is what I want, embrace Islam and you will be secure.' They said: 'O Abul Qasim, you have conveyed the Message of Allah to us.' The holy Prophet (peace & blessings of Allah be with him) said: 'That is what I want,' And he repeated his words a third time and added: 'Know that the earth belongs to Allah and His Messenger, and I want to expel you from this land, any of you who have property should sell it, or know that the earth belongs to God and His Messenger.'

31. *Umar ibn Al Khattab* is reported to have said that the Messenger of Allah (peace & blessings of Allah be with him) said: I shall expel the Jews and Christians from the Arabian Peninsula and I shall not leave any (one) except Muslims.

32. It is reported that Hadrat Ayesha said: Sa'ad was wounded on the day of the Battle of the Trench (Khandaq). A man of the Quraysh named Ibn al Ariqah shot an arrow at him and it struck the artery of his forearm. The Messenger of Allah (peace & blessings of Allah be with him) had a tent set up for him in the Mosque and he used to ask about him whenever he was nearby. When he returned from the Trench and laid down his arms and bathed, the Archangel Gabriel appeared before him as he was removing dust from his hair. He said: 'you have laid down your arms, by God, we have not done so yet. Go out against them.' The Messenger of Allah (peace & blessings of Allah be with him) asked: 'Where to?' He (Gabriel) indicated towards Bani Quraiza. So the Messenger of Allah (peace & blessings of Allah be with him) proceeded to fight against them, and they surrendered to the Messenger of Allah (peace & blessings of Allah be with him) at his command, but he gave Sa'ad the decision regarding their fate and he said: 'I declare that those of them who can fight should be put to death, and their women and children should be taken prisoner, and their property should be distributed.'

34

Book of Military Expeditions and Emmigration

1. *Al-Bara' ibn Azib* is reported to have said that Abu Bakr visited his father at home and bought a saddle from him. He said to Azib. 'Tell your son to carry it with me.' So I carried it with him and my father followed us to collect its price. My father asked Abu Bakr: Tell me what happened when you traveled at night with the Messenger of Allah (during the flight from Makka to Medina).' He said: 'Yes, we traveled the entire night and into the following day until noon, when no one could be seen on the way. Then we came across a large rock casting shade beneath it, and the sun had not hit it yet, so we dismounted there and I leveled a place and covered it with an animal hide or dried grass for the Messenger of Allah (peace & blessings of Allah be with him) to sleep upon. Then I said: 'O Messenger of Allah, sleep, and I will stand guard over you.' So he slept and I stood guard for him. Suddenly I saw a shepherd coming towards the rock with his sheep, seeking the shade as we had done. I asked: 'O boy, who do you belong to?' He replied: 'I belong to a man from Medina or Makka.' I asked: 'Do your sheep have milk?' He said: 'Yes.' I said: 'Will you milk them for us?' He said: 'Yes.' The shepherd milked a little milk into a wooden container and I had a leather container that I carried for the Messenger of Allah (peace & blessings of Allah be with him) to drink (from) and perform the ablution from. I went to the holy Prophet (peace & blessings of Allah be with him) disliking to awaken him, but when I got there, the Apostle of Allah (peace & blessings of Allah be with him) was awake, so I poured water over the center of the container of milk until the milk was cool. Then I said: 'O Messenger of Allah, drink.' He drank until I was happy. Then he asked: 'Is it time for us to leave?' I said: 'Yes.' So we left (around noon time). Suraqa ibn Malik followed us and I said: 'O Messenger of Allah, we have been discovered.' He said: 'Do not worry for God is with us.' The Apostle of Allah (peace & blessings of Allah be with him) prayed to God to hinder him and the legs of his horse sank into the earth unto its belly. Suraqa said: 'I perceive you have invited harm upon me. Please invoke good for me, and by God, I will cause those who are pursuing you to go back.' The Messenger of Allah (peace & blessings of Allah be with him) invoked good for him and he was saved. Then, whenever he met anyone upon the way, he used to say: 'I have looked for him here to no avail.' So he caused whomever he met to go back. In this way Suraqa fulfilled his promise.

2. It was related that *Anas ibn Malik* said: " When the Messenger of God (prayers & peace be upon him) heard that Abu Sufyan was leading an army and advancing he consulted his companions. The narrator said: Abu Bakr voiced his opinion but he ignored his words. Then Umar voiced his opinion but he ignored his words (too). Then Sa'ad ibn Ubada stood up and said: 'O Messenger of Allah, you wish us to speak. By God in Whose Hand is my life, should you command us to plunge into the sea on horseback, we would do so. If you order us to urge our horses to the most far off place, such as Bark al-Ghimad, we would do so.' The narrator said: Now the Messenger of Allah (peace & blessings of Allah be with him) summoned the people. So they set out and camped at Badr. Then the water bearers of the Quraysh arrived, among them was a black slave belonging to Bani al-Hajjaj. The companions of the Prophet (peace & blessings of Allah be with him) seized him and questioned him about Abu Sufyan and his comrades. He said: 'I

know nothing about Abu Sufyan, but Abu Jahl, Utbah, Shaybah and Umayya ibn Khalaf are there.' When he told them this they beat him. Then he said: 'All right. I shall tell you about Abu Sufyan.' They ceased beating him and then questioned him about Abu Sufyan. He repeated: 'I know nothing about Abu Sufyan, but Abu Jahl, Utbah, Shaybah and Umayyah ibn Khalaf are there.' When he said this, they beat him again. The Messenger of Allah (peace & blessings of Allah be with him) was standing in prayer and when he completed his prayer he said: 'By God in Whose Hand is my life, you beat him when he tells you the truth, and you let him go when he lies to you. The narrator said: Then the Messenger of Allah (peace & blessings of Allah be with him) placed his hand on certain portions of the ground and said: 'In this place so and so will be killed.' Not one of them was struck down on any other place except where the Apostle of Allah (peace & blessings of Allah be with him) had indicated on the ground with his hands.

3. It is reported on the authority of *Anas ibn Malik* that the Messenger of Allah (peace & blessings of Allah be with him) sent Busaysah to report on the caravan of Abu Sufyan. He returned while no one was there the Messenger of Allah and myself. He related to him the news of the (arrival of the) caravan. The Apostle of Allah (peace & blessings of Allah be with him) rushed out and addressed the people saying: 'We need more men, whoever has an animal with him, ready to ride,

should ride with us.' People started to seek his permission to bring their mounts that they had left to graze near Medina. He said: 'No, only those who have their mounts ready.' So the holy Prophet (peace & blessings of Allah be with him) and his companions set off towards Badr and arrived there before the unbelievers. When the unbelievers (the Quraysh of Makka) arrived then the Messenger of Allah (peace & blessings of Allah be with him) said: 'none of you should advance unless I am ahead of you. The unbelievers advanced and the Apostle of Allah (peace & blessings of Allah be with him) said: 'Rise up to enter Paradise which is equal in width to the Heavens and the Earth.' Umar ibn al Humam al Ansari said: 'O Messenger of Allah, is Paradise equal in extent to the Heavens and the Earth?' He said: 'Yes.' Umar said: 'My goodness!' The Messenger of Allah (peace & blessings of Allah be with him) asked him: What caused you to say those words.' He said: 'O Messenger of Allah only my wish to be among its inhabitants.' The holy Prophet remarked: 'Indeed you are among its inhabitants.' Umar Ansari took out some dates from his saddlebag and began to eat them. Then he said: 'If I live until I had eaten all these dates, I would have lived a long life.' Then he discarded all the dates and he went out to fight against the unbelievers until he was martyred.

4. It was related that *Ibn Abbas* said that Umar ibn Al Khattab said: "On the day of the Battle of Badr, the Messenger of Allah (peace & blessings of Allah be with him) looked towards the unbelievers and they were one thousand while his companions numbered three hundred and nineteen. The holy Prophet (peace & blessings of Allah be with him) turned towards the Qibla and raised his hands in supplication to his Lord: 'O God, accomplish for me what You have promised me, O God, fulfill what You have promised me. O God, if this small group of Muslims perish, You will not be worshipped on this earth.' And he continued in his supplication to his Lord, raising his hands and facing the Qibla, until his cloak slipped from his shoulders. Abu Bakr came and picked up his cloak and put it back over his shoulders, then he embraced him and said: 'O Apostle of Allah! Your prayer to your Lord will surely suffice you, and He will fulfill what He has promised you.' Then it was revealed: 'When you appealed to your Lord for succour, He responded to your call, I shall assist you with one thousand angels in succession.' So God assisted him with angels. Abu Zumail said that Ibn Abbas told him on that day while a Muslim man was chasing one of the unbelievers, he heard the voice of a knight saying: 'Faster Hizoum!' So he looked at the unbeliever who he was pursuing and saw him fall down to the ground. He looked at him and saw that his nose had been cut and his face was slashed as if a whip had struck it. Ansari came and related this to the Messenger of Allah and he said: 'You have spoken the truth, that was assistance from the third Heaven.' On that day they killed

seventy, and took seventy as war captives. Abu Zumail said that Ibn Abbas said: 'When they caught the war captives the Messenger of Allah asked Abu Bakr and Umar: 'What should we do with these war captives?' Abu Bakr said: 'O Prophet of Allah, they are relatives and from the Tribe (of Quraysh), I see that you should take a ransom from them, then we shall have power over the unbelievers, and may Allah guide them to Islam.' The Apostle of Allah said: 'O, Ibn al Khattab, what do you think?' He replied: 'O Messenger of Allah, no, by God, I do not agree with what Abu Bakr proposes. I see that you should permit us to strike their necks, let Ali strike the neck of Uqail and let me strike the neck of the man who is related to Umar by marriage, for they are the leaders of the unbelievers.' But the Messenger of Allah liked what Abu Bakr had proposed and did not like what I had proposed, and then following morning I went to the Messenger of Allah and found him sitting with Abu Bakr and they both were weeping. I asked: 'O Messenger of Allah, tell me what makes you and your companion weep, so that I too shall weep, and if I do not find it deserves weeping, then I shall weep in empathy with you.' The Apostle of Allah said: 'I weep for what the companions have suggested to me in taking ransom, for it has just been revealed to me that their punishment is closer to them than this tree.' - a tree was nearby to where the Messenger of Allah was sitting. - Then Allah revealed: "It is not fitting for a Prophet to take prisoners of war, but the unbelievers should be killed until they are wiped out from the land, and the believers have the upper hand. You desire the gains of this world, but God wishes for you the Hereafter, and God is Almighty, All Wise. Had it not been for a Decree already given by God, you would have incurred a severe punishment in consequence of what you have taken. So eat of what you have taken as spoils of what is lawful and good, and fear God, surely God is All-Forgiving, All Merciful." (Q.8: 67-69). Then God made war spoils lawful for them (Muslims).

5. It was related that *Anas ibn Malik* said: "On the day of the Battle of Uhud, the Messenger of God (prayers & peace be upon him) was left with only seven men from the Ansars and two men from the Quraysh. When the enemy advanced towards him and overwhelmed him, he said: 'Whoever repels them from us will attain Paradise or will be my companion in Paradise.' One of the Ansars came forward and fought until he was killed. The enemy advanced and overwhelmed him again and he repeated the words: 'Who-ever repels from us will attain Paradise or will be my companion in Paradise.' Another man from the Ansars came forward and fought until he was killed. And thus it continued until seven of the Ansars were killed in succession. Then the Messenger of Allah (peace & blessings of Allah be with him) said to his two companions (from the Quraysh): We have not done justice to our com-

panions (the Ansars who were martyred).

6. *Abd Al Aziz ibn Abu Hazem* is reported to have related that his father said: When Sahl ibn Sa'ad was asked about the injury inflicted upon the Messenger of Allah (peace & blessings of Allah be with him) on the day of the Battle of Uhud, he said: 'The face of the Messenger of Allah (peace & blessings of Allah be with him) was wounded and his front teeth were broken and his helmet was smashed. Fatimah, the daughter of the holy Prophet, was washing the blood away and Hadrat Ali poured water on it from a shied. When Fatimah saw that the bleeding was increasing with the water, she took a piece of mat fiber and burnt it to ashes, and then applied the ashes upon the wound, and the bleeding stopped.

7. *Anas* is reported to have said that the Messenger of Allah (peace & blessings of Allah be with him) had his front teeth broken on the day of the Battle of Uhud, and his head was injured. So he was wiping the blood and saying: 'How will they win when they have injured their Prophet and broken his front teeth while he was inviting them to God?' Then God Almighty revealed the Verse: "The matter is not in your hands, whether God turns to them or chastises them, for surely they are evildoers." (Q. 3: 128).

8. *Sa'ad ibn Abu Waqqas* is reported to have said that on the day of Uhud I saw a man on the right of the Messenger of Allah (peace & bles-

sings of Allah be with him) and another on his left, wearing white clothes, I never saw them before that or afterwards. He means Gabriel and Michael (peace be upon them). It is also related that they were fighting ferociously.

9. *Abu Hurayra* is reported to have related that the Messenger of Allah (peace & blessings of Allah be with him) said: The wrath of God was increasing upon those who did this to the Messenger of Allah, and he indicated towards his front teeth. And the Apostle of Allah (peace & blessings of Allah be with him) said: The wrath of God, Most High, is upon the one who is killed by the Messenger of Allah (peace & blessings of Allah be with him) in the cause of God.

10. *Hadrat Ayesha* is reported to have narrated that she asked the Apostle of Allah (peace & blessings of Allah be with him): "O Messenger of Allah! Have you encountered a day worse than the day of Uhud?' The holy Prophet (peace & blessings of Allah be with him) replied: 'Your tribes have aggrieved me much and the worse distress was the distress on the day of Aqaba when I went to Ibn Abd Yalail ibn Abd Kulal and he did not res-pond to my demand. So I left overtaken with grief and bewildered and could not rest until I found myself at Qarnath Tha'alib where I glanced towards the sky and saw a cloud shading me all of a sudden. I looked up and saw Gabriel, he said to me: 'Allah has heard what your people said to you,

and He has heard the response. God has sent the Angel of the Mountains to you for you to command him to do whatever you desire to do with them.' The Angel of the Mountains greeted me and said: 'O Muhammad, command whatever you wish. If you so desire I will let the two mountains fall upon them.' The holy Prophet (peace & blessings of Allah be with him) said: 'No, I only hope that Allah will permit them to beget children who will worship Allah alone, and none beside Him'.

11. *Jundab ibn Sufyan* is reported to have said that one of the fingers of the Messenger of Allah was injured in one of the battles and he said: You are only a finger that has been wounded in the cause of God.

12. *Ibn Mas'ud* is reported to have related that once The Messenger of Allah (peace & blessings of Allah be with him) was offering prayers at the Ka'ba. Abu Jahl was seated with some of his companions. One of them said to the others: 'Who of you will bring me the intestines of a camel which was slaughtered yesterday?' So Abu Jahl said: 'Which one of you will bring me the intestines of the camel of Bani so and so and put them upon the shoulders of Muhammad when he prostrates?' The most depraved of them went and brought them, he waited until the holy Prophet (peace & blessings of Allah be with him) prostrated and then placed them on his shoulders. They started laughing and falling upon one another. I was watching but was unable to do anything. I wished I had some people with me to remove it from the back of the Messenger of Allah. The holy Prophet (peace & blessings of Allah be with him) was in prostration and he did not lift his head up until someone went and told Fatimah and she came and threw the intestines away from his back, then she turned towards them and insulted them. When the holy Prophet had completed his prayers he raised his voice and prayed to God against them. He always used to invoke three times and when he made his supplications to Allah he used to do so three times, so he said three times: 'O God! Punish Quraysh.' When they heard the Prophet (peace & bles-sings of Allah be with him) invoking God's wrath against them they were worried, then he said: 'O God, punish Abu Jahl ibn Hisham, Utba ibn Rabia, Sheba ibn Rabia, Al Walid ibn Uqba, Umayyah ibn Khalaf and Uqba ibn Abu Mu'ait.' And he mentioned the seventh but I do not recall his name. By God Who sent Muhammad with the Truth, I saw the corpses of those persons whom he named lying on the day of Badr, then they were dragged into the old well of Badr. Abu Ishaq said: The mention of the name of Al Walid ibn Uqba in this Hadith was incorrect.

13. *Anas ibn Malik* is reported to have narrated that the Messenger of Allah (peace & blessings of Allah be with him) said: Who will go and see what Abu Jahl is doing? So Ibn

Mas'ud went out and found that the two sons of Afra had inflicted a fatal wound to Abu Jahl. He grabbed him by the beard and said: 'Are you Abu Jahl?' Abu Jahl said: 'Can there be a man greater than the one you have killed or one who his own people have killed?'

14. *Jabir* is reported to have said that the Messenger of Allah (peace & blessings of Allah be with him) said: Who will kill Ka'b ibn Al Ashraf as he has harmed God and His Messenger. So Muhammad ibn Maslama got up and said: 'O Messenger of Allah, would you like me to kill him?' He said: 'Yes. So Mohammed ibn Maslama went to Ka'b and told him: 'That man (Prophet Muhammad) has asked us to give charity and has bothered us, and I have come to ask you to lend me something.' Ka'b said: 'By God! You will be fed up with him.' Mohammed ibn Maslama said: 'we have followed him and we do not like to leave him until we see how he will end. And we want you to lend us one or two camel loads of food.' Ka'b said: 'Yes, but you must mortgage something to me.' They said: 'What do you want?' He said: 'Mortgage your women.' They said: 'How can we mortgage you our women while you are the most handsome of the Arabs?' He said: 'Then mortgage me your sons.' They said: 'How can we mortgage our sons, then someone insults and tells them: 'You have been mortgaged for a camel load or two,' that is shameful for us. But we can mortgage our

weapons. And he promised Ka'b that they would return. They returned to him at night together with Ka'b's foster brother, Abu Na'ila. Ka'b invited them to come down to his fortress and then he went to them. His wife asked: Where are you going at this hour?' Ka'b said: 'It is only Mohammed ibn Maslama and my brother Abu Na'ila.' She said: 'I hear a voice that sounds like death.' Ka'b said: 'It is only my brother Mohammed ibn Maslama and my foster brother Abu Na'ila. The noble man should respond to a call at night even if he is being invited to be stabbed in the dark.' He said: 'Mohammed ibn Salama entered with two men.' It was related that they were Abu Abs ibn Jabr and Al Harith ibn Aus and Abbad ibn Bisher. Then he said: 'When Ka'b arrives I will make a remark upon his hair and smell it, then I will let you smell it, so when you see me hold his head then strike him.' He came down wearing his best clothes, and his sword. They said: 'We can smell your nice perfume.' So he said: 'Yes I have married so and so and she is the best Arab woman who knows the best perfumes.' So he said: 'Will you permit me to smell your head.' Ka'b said: 'Yes.' So he smelled. Then he said: 'Will you permit me to smell it again?' He said; 'Yes.' Then he held his head firmly and said: 'Get him!' So they killed him.

15. *Ibrahim al Timi* is reported to have related that his father said: "We were sitting in the company of

Hudhaifa when a man said: 'Had I been living at the time of the Messenger of Allah (peace & blessings of Allah be with him) I would have fought by his side and would have striven hard for his cause.' Hudhaifa said: 'You might have done that.' I was with the Messenger of Allah (peace & blessings of Allah be with him) on the night of the battle of Ahzab (The Allies) and a violent wind and bitter cold struck us. The Messenger of Allah (peace & blessings of Allah be with him) said: 'Whichever man will go and bring me news of the enemy God Almighty will make him my companion on the Day of Judgment.' We all remained silent and none of us responded to him. He repea-ted: 'Whichever man will go and bring me news of the enemy God Almighty will make him my companion on the Day of Judgment.' We all remained and none of us responded to him. He again said: 'Whichever man will go and bring me news of the enemy God Almighty will make him my companion on the Day of Judg-ment.' Then he said: 'O Hudhaifa, go and bring me news of the enemy.' When he called me by name, I had no alter-native but to go. He said: 'Go and bring me news about the enemy, and do nothing that may provoke them against me.' When I left him, I felt warm as if I was walking in a heated bath, until I reached them. When I saw Abu Sufyan warming his back against the fire, I put an arrow in the middle of the bow, intending to

shoot him, but I recalled the words of the Messenger of Allah; 'Do not provoke them against me.' Had I shot him, I would have hit him. But I returned and felt warm as if I was walking in a heated bath. I returned to him and told him the news of the enemy and when I had done so, I began to feel cold, so the Messenger of Allah (peace & blessings of Allah be with him) wrapped me up with his cloak while he prayed.

16. *Bara'* is reported to have said that the Messenger of Allah (peace & blessings of Allah be with him) was carrying sand with us on the Day of Ahzab and. the whiteness of his skin was covered with sand. Meanwhile he recited with us: 'O God! Without You we would not have been guided to the right path, nor would we have given in charity nor would we have prayed, so please forgive us what we have committed, let us all be redeemed in Your Cause. And send Your sere-nity upon us to make our feet firm when we encounter our enemy, and if they beckon us to something unjust we will refuse, the unbelie-vers have made a commotion in seeking the help of others against us. And at that he raised his voice.

17. *Anas ibn Malik* is reported to have related that on the Day of the Battle of the Trench the companions of the holy Prophet (peace & blessings of Allah be with him) were saying: 'We are those who have given allegiance to Muhammad to follow Islam as long as we live.' Or they

said: 'to fight in the cause of Allah as long as we live.' - Hammad was uncertain - and the Apostle of Allah (peace & blessings of Allah be with him) said: 'O God, the true goodness is the goodness of the Hereafter, so forgive the Ansars and the Muhajirin.

18. *Iyyas ibn Salama* said that his father said that: We arrived at Huday-biyah with the Messenger of Allah (peace & blessings of Allah be with him) and we were about fourteen hundred men. We had fifty goats with us and insufficient water for them to drink, so the Messenger of Allah (peace & blessings of Allah be with him) sat on the brink of the well. Then he prayed or spat into the well and the water swelled up. We drank and gave water to the animals. Then the Messenger of Allah (peace & blessings of Allah be with him) summoned us to swear oaths of allegiance to him as he sat beneath a tree. I was the first man to swear the oath, and then others took the oath. When half of the people had done so, he asked me: Did you take the oath, Salama. I said: 'I was among the first to take it.' He said: 'Do so again.' Then the Messenger of Allah (peace & blessings of Allah be with him) noticed I had no weapons, so he gave me a large or a small shield. Then he continued to take pledge from the people until the last group of them came and the holy Prophet said: 'Will you not swear the oath of allegiance, Salama?' I said: 'O Messenger of Allah I was among the first to take

it and then I took it again while you were in the midst of the people.' He said: 'You may do so again.' So I took the oath of allegiance three times. Then he said to me: 'Salama, where is the shield which I gave you?' I said: 'O Messenger of Allah, my uncle Amir met me and he had no weapons, so I gave the shield to him.' The Messenger of Allah (peace & blessings of Allah be with him) laughed and said: 'you are like someone of days of old who said: O God, I seek a friend who is dearer to me than myself.' The unbelievers then conveyed messages of peace and the people could move from our encampment to camp of the Mak-kans and vice versa. Then at last the peace treaty was concluded. I was a dependant of Talha ibn Ubaydallah. I watered his horse and groomed its back, and I served Talha and shared with him in his food. I had left my family and my property as an immigrant in the cause of Allah and His Messenger. When we sealed a peace treaty with the people of Makka and the people of each party began to mix with each other, I went to a tree, brushed off its thorns and lay down beneath it. As I lay there four unbelievers from Makka came to me and began to speak disrespectfully about the Messen-ger of Allah. I became very angry with them and moved away to another tree. They hung their weapons up and lay down. Then someone called out from the depths of the valley; 'Come up, O immi-grants! Ibn Zunaym has been mur-dered.' I drew my sword and attacked the four, as they lay asleep. I seized their arms, picked them up with my hands saying: 'By the One Who has bestowed honor upon Muhammad if any of you raises his head I shall strike it off.' I led them towards the Prophet (peace & blessings of Allah be with him) and my uncle Amir came with a man from Abalat named Mikraz. Amir dragged him upon a horse whose back was covered with thick cover, and they had seventy unbelievers with them. The Messenger of Allah (peace & blessings of Allah be with him) looked at them and said: 'Release them so they may break the trust once more.' So the Messenger of Allah (peace & blessings of Allah be with him) forgave them. Then God revealed the verse: 'God is The One Who restrained their hands from you, and your hands from them in the valley of Makka, after He had granted you a victory over them. And God sees well all that you do.' (Q. 48: 24). Then we proceeded towards Medina, and stopped where there was a mountain between us and Bani Lahyan who were unbelievers. The Messenger of Allah (peace & blessings of Allah be with him) sought forgiveness for whoever went up the mountain at night to keep a watch for the Messenger of Allah (peace & blessings of Allah be with him) and his compa-nions. I went up the mountain two or three times that night. When we arrived in Makka, the Apostle of Allah (peace & blessings of Allah be with him) sent his camels with his servant Rabbah, and I was with him. I went to the pasture with Talha's horse and the camels. When day broke, Abd al Rahman al-Fazari laun-ched a raid and took away all the camels of the Messenger of Allah (peace & blessings of Allah be with him) and killed the man who looked after them. I said: 'Rabbah, mount this horse and take it to Talha ibn Ubaydallah and inform the Mes-senger of Allah that the unbelievers have taken away his camels.' Then I turned my face towards Medina and called out three times: 'Come to help us!' Then I set off in pursuit of the raiders and shot arrows at them while praising myself in Iambic poetry; 'I am the son of al-Aqwa. And today is the day of defeat for the low. I shall overcome one of their men, shoot at him with an arrow which, penetrating the saddle, will pierce his shoulder, and I shall say: Take it, while intoning the verse: 'I am the son of al-Aqwa. And today is the day of defeat for the low.' By God, I continued shooting at them and harassing their animals and whenever a horseman turned upon me, I went and sat beneath a tree. Then I shot him and hamstrung his horse. Then they entered a narrow mountain pass and I went up the mountain and held them off casting stones at them. I continued to chase them in this manner until I took back all the camels of the Messenger of Allah (peace & blessings of Allah be with him) and none remained with them. They retreated and I pursued them shooting at them until they dropped over thirty cloaks and thirty spears, relieving themselves of their burden. I marked everything they dropped with a stone so that the Messenger of Allah (peace & blessings of Allah be with him) and his companions would recognize them. When they reached a narrow valley, the son of Badr al-Fazari joined them. They sat down to take their lunch and I sat upon the summit of a sloping rock. Al-Fazari said: 'Who is that man I see?' They said: 'this man has harassed us. By God, he has not left us since nightfall and he has shot at us until he has taken everything out of our hands.' He said: Four of you should go to fight him.' So four of them went up the mountain and came towards me. When they came near I told them: 'Do you know who I am?' They said: 'No, and who are you?' I said: 'I am Salama ibn al-Aqwa. By the One Who has honored the countenance of Muhammad, I am able to kill any of you as I like but none of you will be able to kill me. One of them said: 'I think so.' So they retreated and I did not move from my position until I saw the horsemen of the Messenger of Allah (peace & blessings of Allah be with him) come riding through the trees. Akhram al- Asadi was the first of them and behind him was Abu Qatada al- Ansari and behind him was al Miqdad ibn al Aswad al-Kindi. I took hold of the reins of Akhram's horse and they took flight. I said: 'Akhram, be on your guard against them until the holy Prophet (peace & blessings of Allah be with him) and his companions reach you.' He said: 'O Salama, if you

believe in Allah and the Last Day and know that Paradise is as true and Hell is true, you should not stand between me and martyrdom.' So I let him go. Akhram and Abd al Rahman met in combat. Akhram hamstrung Abd al Rahman's horse and he struck him with his spear and killed him. Abd al Rahman turned around riding Akhram's horse. Abu Qatada, a horseman of the Apostle of Allah (peace & blessings of Allah be with him) fought Abd al Rahman and struck him with his spear and killed him. By the One Who honored the counte-nance of Muhammad, I ran behind them so fast I could not see the companions of the Prophet behind me or even the dust kicked up by their horses, until they reached a valley before sunset where there was a spring of water called Dhu Qarad. So there they could have a drink, for they were thirsty. When they saw me running at them I made them take flight from the valley before they were able drink a drop of its water. They fled from the valley and ran down a slope, I pursued them running and overtook one of their men and shot him with an arrow through the shoulder blade and said: 'take this. I am the son of al-Aqwa. And today is the day of defeat for the people who are low.' The man said: 'May his mother weep for him! Are you the Aqwa who has been chasing us since the morning?' I said: 'Yes, O enemy of yourself, the same Aqwa.' They aban-doned two exhausted horses and I led them along to the Messenger of Allah. I met Amir who had a container of milk diluted with water with him and another container of water. I performed ablution with the water and drank the milk. Then I reached the Messenger of Allah (peace & blessings of Allah be with him) when he was at the spring of water where I had chased them off. The Messenger of Allah (peace & blessings of Allah be with him) had captured the camels and everything else I had captured, and all the spears and cloaks I had seized from the unbelievers. Bilal had slaughtered a she-camel from the camels I had seized and was roasting its liver and hump for the Apostle of Allah. I said: 'O Messenger of Allah let me pick one hundred men from our people and I will pursue the raiders and I will finish them all off so that none remains to convey their tidings. The Messenger of Allah (peace & blessings of Allah be with him) laughed so much that his molar teeth were visible in the fire light and he said: 'Salama, do you think you can do that?' I said: 'Yes, by the One Who has honored you.' He said: 'They have reached the land of Ghatafan now and they are being feted there.' Then a man from the Ghatafan arrived and said: 'so and so slaughtered a camel for them.' When they were skinning it they saw dust in the distance and said: 'it is Aqwa and his compa-nions, so they took flight. In the morning, the Messenger of Allah (peace & blessings of Allah be with him) said:

'Now our best horseman is Abu Qatada and our best infantryman is Salama.' Then he gave me two shares of the booty, one share kept for the horseman and the other share kept for the infantryman. He intended to return to Medina and he made me mount behind him on his she-camel named al-Adba. As we were riding, a man from the Ansars who had never been beaten in a race asked: 'Is there anyone who will race with me up to Medina?' Is there any com-petitor? And he continued repeating this. On hearing this, I said: 'Why do you not show deference to a dignified person and respect a noble man?' He said: 'No, unless he is the Messenger.' I said: 'O Messenger of Allah, may my father and mother be sacrificed for you, let me dismount to defeat this man. He said: 'If you wish.' I said: 'I am coming.' Then I sprang to my feet, jumped up and ran and panted, when one or two high places were left and then again followed at his heels and again panted when one or two high places were left and again sprinted until I reached him and knocked him between his shoulders. I said: 'You have been overtaken, by God.' He said: 'That is so.' So I reached Medina before him, by God, we had stayed there only three nights when we set off for Khyber with the Messenger of Allah (peace & blessings of Allah be with him) reciting the following poetry:

'By God, if You had not guided to the Right, We would have neither practiced charity nor offered prayers.

(O God!) We cannot do without Thy favors;

Keep us steadfast when we counter the enemy, and descend tranquility upon us.'

The Messenger of Allah (peace & bles-sings of Allah be with him) asked: 'Who is this?' Amir said: 'It is I, Amir.' He said: 'May God forgive you!' The narrator said: 'Whenever the Messenger of Allah (peace & blessings of Allah be with him) used to invoke forgiveness for a specific person that person was certain to be martyred. Umar ibn al Khattab, riding on his camel, called out: 'O Prophet of God, I wish that you had let us enjoy that from Amir. Salama related: 'When we reached Khy-ber, its king, who was named Marhab, came out wielding his sword and chan-ting: Khyber knows that I am Marrab, a well armed, and tested warrior, When the war comes and outspreads its flames.

My uncle, Amir, advanced to fight him, saying: Khyber surely knows that I am Amir, well armed and seasoned who charges into battles. Then they fought with each other. Marhab's sword struck Amir's shield and he leaned onward to attack his adversary from below, but his sword sprang back at him and severed the main artery in his forearm and caused him to die. Salama said: 'I came out and heard some people among the companions of the Prophet (peace & blessings of Allah be with him) saying: 'Amir's deed has gone waste; he has killed himself.' So I went to the Prophet (peace & blessings of Allah be with him) weeping and said: 'O Messenger of Allah, has Amir's deed been wasted?' The Messenger of Allah (peace & blessings of Allah be with him) said: 'Who said that?' I said: 'Some of your companions.' He said: 'The one who said that has lied, for Amir has a double reward.' Then he called for Ali who eyes were sore, and said: 'I will give the standard to someone who loves Allah and His Messenger and whom Allah and His Messenger love.' So I went to Ali, and led him along, as his eyes were sore, I took him to the Mes-senger of Allah, who applied his saliva to his eyes and he recovered. The Messenger of Allah (peace & blessings of Allah be with him) handed him the standard. Marhab advanced chan-ting: 'Khyber knows that I am Marrab, a well armed, and tested warrior, when the war comes and outspreads its flames. Ali chanted in reply:

'I am the one whose mother named him Haydar, as a lion of the forest whose appearance instills terror. I respond to my opponents' force with a measured response.' The narrator said: 'Ali struck Marhab's head and killed him, so the victory was because of him.'

19. *Al-Bara' ibn Azib* is reported to have said when the holy Prophet (peace & blessings of Allah be with

him) was prevented from going to the Ka'ba, the people of Makka did not permit him to enter Makka until he had settled the matter with them by pledging to stay there for only three days and that no weapons will be brought into Makka except in their boxes, and none of the people of Makka will be permitted to go with him even if they wish to follow him, and he will not prevent any of his companions from staying in Makka if they wish to stay. When the treaty was written down it was specified in it: 'These are the conditions upon which Muham-mad, the Messenger of Allah (peace & blessings of Allah be with him) has agreed.' They said: 'We do not agree to that, for if we believed that you are the Messenger of Allah (peace & blessings of Allah be with him) we would not prevent you, but you are Muhammad ibn Abd Allah.' The Prophet (peace & blessings of Allah be with him) said: 'I am the Mes-senger of Allah and I am also Muham-mad ibn Abd Allah.' Then he said to Ali: 'Erase the words 'Messenger of Allah,' but Ali said: 'No, by God, I will never erase your name.' The Messenger of Allah (peace & blessings of Allah be with him) asked where it was written and he was shown and he erased the words, and then Ali wrote: 'This is what Muhammad ibn Abd Allah has agreed upon.' When the holy Prophet (peace & blessings of Allah be with him) entered Makka after three days the Makkans told Ali: 'Tell your friend to leave since the period has elapsed.' So the holy Prophet (peace & blessings of Allah be with him) left Makka.

20. *Anas ibn Malik* is reported to have said: "When we were overtaken with grief and distress on his return from Hudaibiyah where he had slaughtered his sacrificial beasts the following verses were revealed: 'Surely We have granted you a manifest victory. That God may forgive you your mistakes of the past and those to follow, and to perfect His blessing upon you, and guide you to the Straight Path. And God will make you victorious with a mighty victory. God is The One Who sent down serenity on the hearts of the believers that they may increase in their faith, and to God belongs the forces of the heavens and the earth, and God is All-Knowing, All Wise. That He may admit the believing men and the believing women into Gardens beneath which rivers flow, to dwell therein for-ever, and remove from them their evil deeds, this in the sight of God is the greatest triumph.' (Q. 48: 1-5.) The Apostle of Allah (peace & blessings of Allah be with him) said: 'A verse has been revealed to me that is dearer to me than the whole world.

21. *Abu Hurayra* is reported to have said: We went with the holy Prophet (peace & blessings of Allah be with him) during the battle of Khyber and Allah granted us victory. We did not gain any gold or silver as booty, but we gained sheep, food and clothing. So we went with it to the valley where the

Messenger of Allah (peace & blessings of Allah be with him) was together with his slave who had been granted to him by a man from Guzam. When we reached them, the slave of the Messenger of Allah (pe-ace & blessings of Allah be with him) got up to remove the saddles and an arrow wounded him and he died from his wounds. So we said: 'O Messenger of Allah 'He must be happy with his martyr-dom.' The Messenger of Allah (peace & blessings of Allah be with him) said: 'No, by The One in Whose Hand is the soul of Muhammad, the garment he is wearing is burning with the Fire of Hell upon him because he took it from the booty of Khyber, before it had been distri-buted.' So the people were terrified, and a men ran off and brought one or two bridles and said: 'O Mes-senger of Allah, I took these on the Day of Khyber.' Then the Messenger of Allah (peace & blessings of Allah be with him) asked: 'A Bridle of Fire or two bridles of Fire.

22. *Abu Hurayra* is reported to have said: 'Shall I tell you one of your tradi-tions, O gathering of the Ansars?' He then related the account of the Conquest of Makka and said: 'The Messenger of Allah (peace & blessings of Allah be with him) advanced until he reached Makka, then he stationed Zubair on his right flank and Khalid on the left, and he dispatched Abu Ubaydah with the force that had no Armour. They advanced to the midst of the valley. The Messenger

of Allah (peace & blessings of Allah be with him) was amid a large body of fighters. He saw me and said: 'O Abu Hurayra: 'permit no one to come to me except the Ansars, so summon only the Ansars to me. Abu Hurayra said: 'so they assem-bled around him. The Quraysh also ga-thered their villains and their degene-rates, and said: 'we shall send these on ahead, if they are successful, we shall be with them, and if misfortune befalls them, we shall recompense for whatever we are asked.' The Messenger of Allah (peace & blessings of Allah be with him) said: 'You see the villains and the degenerates of the Quraysh.' And he indicated with one hand over the other that they should be killed, and said: 'Join with me at al Safa.' Then we proceeded on and if anyone of us wished for a particular person to be killed, he was killed, and no one was able to withstand us. Then Abu Sufyan came and said: 'O Messenger of Allah the blood of the Quraysh has been made cheap, there will be no Quraysh from now on.' Then the holy Prophet said: 'Whoever enters the house of Abu Sufyan will be secure.' Some of the Helpers Ansars whispered among themselves that he had been moved by his compa-ssion for his city and tenderness towards his relations. Then Reve-lation came to The Prophet (peace & blessings of Allah be with him) and we knew when he was about to receive Revelation. As he received it, none of us would dare raise our eyes towards the Messenger of

Allah (peace & blessings of Allah be with him) until the Revelation came to an end. When the Revelation ceased, the Apostle of Allah (peace & blessings of Allah be with him) said: 'O you gathering of the Ansars!' They said: ' we are here at your command O Messen-ger of Allah.' He said: 'You were saying that I have been moved by compa-ssion for my city and tenderness towards my relations.' They said: 'That is so.' He said: 'No, never. I am a servant of Allah, and His Messen-ger. I migrated to God and to you and I shall live with you and die with you.' So they turned towards him tearfully saying: 'By God, we said that because of our closeness to God and His Messen-ger.' The holy Prophet said: Surely, God and His Messenger bear witness to your explanation and accept your apology.' People went to the house of Abu Sufyan and others locked their doors. The Messenger of Allah (peace & blessings of Allah be with him) proceeded on until he neared the Stone; he kissed it and circumam-bulated the Ka'ba. Then he went towards an idol by the side of the Ka'ba, which the people worship-ped. The Messenger of Allah (peace & blessings of Allah be with him) held a bow in his hand, and he took it from one corner. When he reached the idol, he stabbed its eyes with the bow and said: 'Truth has come and falsehood has vanished.' Upon completing his circum-ambulation, he went to Safa and ascended its height from where he could see the Ka'ba, raised his hands and praised Allah and offered prayers.

23. It is reported that *Abd Allah ibn Mas'ud* said: When the holy Prophet (peace & blessings of Allah be with him) entered Makka there were three hundred and sixty idols surrounding the Ka'ba, he lunged at them with his stick and said: 'Truth has come and falsehood has vani-shed. Indeed falsehood is bound to vanish.' (Q. 17: 81) Truth has come and falsehood can neither create anything nor can it return anything to life.

24. *Mujashi ibn Mas'ud al Sulaimi* is reported to have narrated that he brought his brother, Abu Ma'bad, to the Messenger of Allah (peace & blessings of Allah be with him) after the Conquest of Makka, and said: 'O Messenger of Allah, permit him to swear the oath of migra-tion to you.' The holy Prophet (peace & blessings of Allah be with him) replied: 'The time of migration is over for those who had to do so.' l said: 'For what then may he pledge his oath to you?' He said: 'In the cause of Islam, to strive in the cause of God, and for fighting in the cause of piety.'

25. *Hadrat Ayesha* is reported to have said that the Messenger of Allah (peace & blessings of Allah be with him) was asked about migration and he replied: 'there is no migration after the Conquest (of Makka), but striving in the way of Allah and sincerity of intent. So

when you are asked to go out in the cause of God, you should go out.

26. *Abu Saeed al Khudri* is reported to have said that a bedouin asked the Messenger of. Allah (peace & blessings of Allah be with him) about migrating, so he said: 'you speak of migration? The matter of migration is difficult, do you have any camels?' The bedouin said: 'Yes.' He asked: 'Do you pay the due charity for them?' He said: 'Yes.' Then the holy Prophet (peace & blessings of Allah be with him) said: 'Continue doing good deeds, indeed God does not leave any good deed to go waste.

27. *Kathir ibn Abbas ibn Abd al Muttalib* is reported to have narrated that Al Abbas said: I was with the Messenger of Allah (peace & blessings of Allah be with him) on the Day of Hunayn. Abu Sufyan ibn Harith ibn Abd al Muttalib and I remained with the Messenger of Allah (peace & blessings of Allah be with him) and we did not part company from him. The Apostle of Allah (peace & blessings of Allah be with him) rode his white mule. When the Muslims confron-ted the unbelievers in battle, the Muslims took flight, but the Messenger of Allah (peace & blessings of Allah be with him) urged his mule towards the unbelievers. I was holding the holy Prophet's mule by the reins to prevent it from going too fast. Abu Sufyan was holding stirrup and the Apostle of Allah (peace & blessings of Allah be with him) was saying: 'Abbas, summon the people of al

Samurah.' Abbas called out in a loud voice: 'Where are the people of al Samurah?' And by God, when they heard my voice, they returned as the cows return to their calves, and said: 'Here we are, here we are!' Abbas said: They started to fight the unbelievers. Then there was a call to the Ansars. Bani al-Harith ibn al-Khazraj were the last to be called. Then the call was made: 'O Bani al-Harith ibn al-Khazraj! O Bani Harith ibn al-Khazraj!' And the Messen-ger Allah who was riding his mule, looked at them fighting, stretching his neck forward and he was saying: 'This is the moment when the fighting rages like fire.' Then the holy Prophet (peace & blessings of Allah be with him) picked up some stones and cast them at the faces of the unbelievers. Then he said: 'By the Lord of Muhammad, the unbelievers are vanquished.' Abbas said: 'I went around and saw that the battle was at the same stage in which I had seen it, and By God, it remained at the same stage until he (the holy Prophet) threw the pebbles. I continued to watch until I saw that they had been vanquished and were in flight.

28. *Abu Ishaq* is reported to have related that Al-Bara'was asked: 'O Abu Umara! Did you all retreat on the Day of Hunayn?' He replied: 'By God, no! The Messenger of Allah (peace & blessings of Allah be with him) did not take flight, but his young companions who were unarmed went along with the

archers of the tribe of Hawazin and Bani Nasr and their arrows rarely missed a target, and they shot their arrows at them seldom missing their target. So the Muslims retreated towards the Prophet (peace & blessings of Allah be with him) who was riding his white mule led by his cousin Abu Sufyan ibn Al Harith ibn Abd al Muttalib. The Apostle of Allah (peace & blessings of Allah be with him) dismou-nted and prayed to Allah for victory and then he said: 'I am the Prophet in truth, I am the son of Abd al- Muttalib, and then he re-grouped his companions in rows.

29. *Salama ibn al Aqwa* is reported to have narrated: we fought beside the Messenger of Allah (peace & blessings of Allah be with him) at Hunayn and when we encountered the enemy, I noticed a group of people appear from the other side. They fought with the companions of the Prophet (peace & blessings of Allah be with him), but the companions retreated and I too took flight. I had two cloaks, one of which I was wrapping round the waist and the other I was wearing around my shoulders. My waist wrapper became loosened and I held the two cloaks together. Thus I went towards the Messenger of Allah (peace & blessings of Allah be with him) who he was riding on his white mule. When the companions assembled around him from all sides, the Messenger of Allah (peace & blessings of Allah be with him) dismounted from his mule, picked up a handful of dust from the ground and threw it into the faces of the enemy saying: 'May their faces be deformed!' Their eyes, without exception, were filled with the dust from this one handful, and they took flight. Thus God Almighty, defeated them, and the Messenger of Allah (peace & blessings of Allah be with him) distributed their booty among the Muslims.

30. *Abd Allah ibn Amr* is reported to have said: When the Messenger of Allah (peace & blessings of Allah be with him) attacked Tayef but could not overcome the enemy he said: We will go back if Allah pleases. The companions of the Prophet (peace & blessings of Allah be with him) were distressed at this and said: shall we leave without victory?' The Apostle of Allah (peace & blessings of Allah be with him) said: 'Let us return (and we shall) Fight tomorrow.' They fought and many were wounded at which the holy Prophet (peace & blessings of Allah be with him) said: We shall return tomorrow if God pleases.' They were pleased at this and the holy Prophet (peace & blessings of Allah be with him) smiled.

35

Book of Governance

1. It has been related on the authority of **Abdullah Ibn Umar** that the Apostle of Allah (peace & blessings of Allah be with him) said: The caliphate will remain with the Quraysh even if only two of them are left (on the face of the earth).

2. **Abu Hurayra** is reported to have said that the Messenger of Allah (peace & blessings of Allah be with him) said: The Quraysh must lead the people in this matter, Muslims should lead the Muslims, and unbelievers should lead the unbelievers.

3. **Jabir ibn Samurah** is reported to have said that he heard the Messenger of Allah said: 'Islam will continue until the (last) Hour is established, or you will be ruled by twelve Caliphs, and they all shall be from the Quraysh.' I also heard him say: 'A small party of Muslims will capture the white palace, the palace of the Persian Emperor or his descendants.' I also heard him say: 'Before the Day of Judgment imposters will appear. Beware of them.' I also heard him say: 'When God blesses any one of you with

wealth, you should first spend it on yourself and your family.' And I heard him say: I shall be before you at the Fountain (in Paradise).

4. **Abu Hazem** is reported to have said: I was in the company of Abu Hurayra for five years and I heard him relate that the holy Prophet (peace & blessings of Allah be with him) said: 'The Children of Israel were ruled by their Prophets. Whenever one Prophet died another succeeded him, but since I am the last Prophet there will be many successors.' They asked: 'What do you command us to do?' He said: 'Fulfill your allegiance to the first and the subsequent ones who follow and respect their rights, God will surely ask them about what He entrusted them.

5. **Abd al Rahman ibn Abd al Rabb** is reported to have said that he entered the mosque and saw Abd Allah ibn Amr ibn al A'as seated in the shade of the Ka'ba with the people gathered around him. I joined them and sat near him. Abd Allah said: 'I went with the Messenger of Allah (peace & blessings of Allah be with him) on a journey and we stopped at a place. Some of us started to pitch our tents and others began to compete with one another in archery, and others left their mounts to graze, Then prayers were announced, we gathered around the Messenger of Allah (peace & blessings of Allah be with him) and he said: Every Prophet who has gone before me was entrusted with the duty of guiding his followers to what he knew to be good for them and to warn them against what he knew to be bad for them. However, your community will enjoy its days of peace and security at its beginning, and in the final phase of its existence it will be afflicted with adversity and with things you will find odious. At that time there will be great trials, one after the other. In such conditions of adversity, the believers will say: 'This will cause my destruction.' When it passes, they will be afflicted with more adversity and the believers will say: 'This must surely be my end.' Whoever seeks to be saved from the Fire (of Hell) and to be admitted into the Garden (of Paradise) should die with faith in God and the Last Day and should treat the people, as he would wish to be treated by them. He who swears allegiance to a Caliph should give him the pledge of his hand and the sincerity of his heart. He should obey him to the best of his ability and if another man seeks to dispute his authority, they should behead that man.' I went up to him and asked him:

'Can you swear on oath that you heard this from the Messenger of Allah?' He indicated to his ears with his hands and towards his heart and said: 'My ears heard it and my heart put it to memory.' I said: 'your cousin Mu'awiya orders us to devour our wealth falsely among ourselves and to kill one another, while God Almighty has said: 'O you who believe! Do not devour your wealth among yourselves falsely, but trade fairly by your mutual consent, and do not kill yourselves. Surely, God is All-Merciful to you.' (Q. 4: 29). Abd Allah ibn Amr ibn al A 'as remained silent for a while and then said: 'obey him in so far as he is obedient to God but disobey him in matters where disobedience to God is involved.

6. *Ibn Umar* is reported to have related that the Apostle of Allah (peace & blessings of Allah be with him) said: Beware, each of you is a shepherd and each of you is answerable for his flock. The Caliph is a shepherd for his people and he will be questioned concerning them. A man is a shepherd over his family and he will be questioned concer-ning them. A woman is a shepherd over the household of her husband and his children and she will be questioned concerning them. A slave is a shepherd over his master's property and he will be questioned concerning it. Beware, each of you is a shepherd (guardian) and each of you will be questioned regarding your trust.

7. *Abd Al Rahman ibn Samura* is reported to have narrated that the Messenger of Allah (peace & blessings of Allah be with him) told him: 'O Abd Al Rahman do not seek authority, for if you get it due to your demand, you will be left alone without God's help. But if you get it without seeking it for yourself, then you will be helped.

8. *Abu Zarr* is reported to have said: I asked the Messenger of Allah: 'Will you not appoint me to a position of authority?' He stroked my shoulder with his hand and said: 'O Abu Zarr, you are weak and authority is a trust, and on the Day of Judgment it will be a cause of disgrace and repentance except for those who fulfill the obligations and duties pertaining to it.

9. *Abu Barda* is reported to have related that Abu Musa said: I visited the Apostle of Allah (peace & blessings of Allah be with him) together with two men from the tribe of Ash'ar. One of them was at my right and the other on the left, they both asked for positions of authority as the holy Prophet (peace & blessings of Allah be with him) was brushing his teeth with a tooth stick. He said: 'O Abu Musa, what do you think?' I said: 'By God Who sent you to convey the Truth, they did not tell me what they intended, and I did not know that they would ask for positions.' The holy Prophet replied: 'We shall never appoint those who seek positions of public authority, but you may leave Abu Musa.' Abu Musa was sent to Yemen as gover-nor, then Muath ibn Jabal was deputed to assist him. When Mu'ath arrived at the camp of Abu Musa, he welcomed him and said: 'Kindly dismount.' And he laid a mattress out for him while there was a man there bound in hand and in foot. Mu'ath said: 'Who is this?' Abu Musa replied: 'He is a Jew and he embraced Islam and then he returned to his creed and became a Jew.' Mu'ath said: 'I shall not be seated before he is put to death in accordance with the Law of God and His Messenger.' Abu Musa said: 'Be seated, so it shall be done.' He again said: 'I shall not be seated before he is put to death in accordance with the Law of God and His Messenger.' And he repeated his words three times. Then Abu Musa conveyed orders and he was put to death.

9. It is related on the authority of *Abu Hurayra* that the Apostle of Allah (peace & blessings of Allah be with him) said: Imam (religious-political leader) is a shield for the Muslims, they fight behind him and he protects them. If he is God fearing and just, he will be rewarded and if he enjoins other than that, it will rebound against him.

10. *Abd Allah ibn Umar* is reported to have said that the Messenger of Allah (peace & blessings of Allah be with him) said: Behold! The dispensers of justice will be seated on pulpits of light beside God Almighty, on the right side of The Most Merciful, Exalted and Glorious. Either side of His Presence is

the right side and is equally meritorious. They (the dispensers of justice) are those who have acted justly concerning their families and in all they undertook to do.

11. *Abd al Rahman ibn Shumasa* is reported to have said: I paid a visit to Hadrat Ayesha to ask her about something. She asked: 'Which country are you from?' -1 said: 'I am from the people of Egypt.' She said: 'How did your governor act towards you in your time of war?' I said: 'we did not see anything bad from him. If one of our men's camels died, he used to give him another camel. If any one of us lost his slave, he would give him another slave. If anybody was in need of the necessities of life, he would provide them with necessities.' She said: 'see! The way my brother, Mohammed ibn Abu Bakr, was treated, does not prevent me from telling you what I heard from the Messenger of Allah. He said in this my house: 'O God, whoever acquires some authority over the affairs of my people and is severe with them, be severe with him, and whoever acquires some authority over the affairs of my people and is kind to them, be kind to him.

12. *Tamim al Dari* is reported to have related that the holy Prophet (peace & blessings of Allah be with him) said: The Religion is advice." We said: "Concerning what?" He said: "Concerning Allah and His Book and His Messenger and leaders of the Muslims, and the people.

13. *Jarir* is reported to have said that he made the pledge of allegiance to the Messenger of Allah (peace & blessings of Allah be with him) for the following: "To establish prayer, to pay obligatory charity and to be sincere and faithful to every Muslim. He also reportedly said: I paid a visit to the holy Prophet (peace & bles-sings of Allah be with him) and said: I make the pledge of allegiance for Islam on the condition that I will be sincere and faithful to every Muslim.

14. It is narrated on the authority of *Hasan* who said that Ubaid Allah ibn Ziyad visited Ma'qil ibn Yasar al Muzni during his final illness before his death, so Ma'qil said: "I shall relate to you a Hadith I heard from the Messenger of Allah, had I thought that I would survive I would not narrate it to you, I heard the Messenger of Allah say: 'if God entrusts His people to a ruler and he dies being treacherous to them, God will prohibit his entry into Paradise.

15. *Abu Hurayra* is reported to have said: The Prophet (peace & blessings of Allah be with him) spoke of the theft of war spoils before their distribution, he stressed the gravity of it and said it was a great sin, he said: 'Do not steal the war spoils before distribution, for I should not like to see anyone of you on the Day of Resurrection carrying a bleating sheep around his neck or a grunting camel.

Such a one will say: 'O Messenger of God! Intercede with God for me!'

And I shall say: 'I cannot help you for I conveyed the Message of God to you.' Or one carrying garments which will flutter and he will say: 'O Messenger of God! Intercede with God for me!' And I will say: 'I cannot help you for I conveyed the Message of God to you'.

16. *Al-Kindi* is reported to have said: I heard the Messenger of Allah (peace & blessings of Allah be with him) say: 'Whoever of you is appointed by us to a position of authority and he conceals from us a needle or anything smaller than that, it would be embezzlement and he will be made to produce it on the Day of Judgment.' A dark-skinned man from the Ansars stood up and said: 'O Messen-ger of Allah, rescind my appoint-ment. He said: 'What is the matter?' The man said: 'I have heard you say such a thing.' He said: 'I say it again: Whoever of you is appointed by us to a position of autho-rity, he should produce everything, large or small, and he should take whatever he is right-fully given to him, and he should restrain himself from taking that which is forbidden.

17. *Abu Humaid al Saeedi* is reported to have said: The Messenger of Allah (peace & blessings of Allah be with him) appointed a man of the Azd tribe as in charge of the charity from the Bani Sulaim. When he returned, the Messen-ger of Allah (peace & blessings of Allah be with him) asked him to render account of it, he said: 'This amount is for you and this is a gift to me.' The Apostle of Allah (peace & blessings of Allah be with him) said: 'You should have stayed at the home of your father and mother and waited until your gift came to you, if what you say is true.' Then he spoke to us. He said: 'I appointed one of your men to a position of trust to share in the authority that God Almighty has entrusted me with and then he came to me saying 'This amount is for you and this is a gift to me.' Why did he not stay at the home of his father and mother until his gift came to him, if what he said was true? By God, if any of you takes anything from it without due right, he shall meet his Lord while his is burdened with it on the Day of Judgment. I shall not know you when you have to face Allah carrying a grunting camel or a bellowing cow or a bleating sheep.' Then he raised his hands so high that one could see the whiteness of his armpits, and he said: 'O my Lord! I have conveyed it.' I saw him do so and my ears heard it.

18. *Jabir ibn Abd Allah* is reported to have said: We were one thousand and four hundred on the Day of Hudaibiyah. We swore allegiance to him and Umar was holding his hand as he sat under the Tree. We swore an oath to the effect that we would not desert the battle, but we did not swear an oath to fight until death.

19. *Yazid ibn Abu Ubaid* said that he asked Salama: For what did you swear allegiance to the Messenger of Allah (peace & blessings of Allah be

with him) on the Day of Hudai-biyah?" he said: "To death."

20. *Junada ibn Abu Umayya* is repor-ted to have said: We went to see Ubada ibn Samit when he was ill, and we said: 'Tell us a Hadith you have heard from the Messenger of Allah (peace & blessings of Allah be with him) so that we may benefit with it.' He said: 'The Messenger of Allah (peace & blessings of Allah be with him) called us and we pledged our oaths of allegiance to Islam and among the injunctions he made binding upon us was that we would listen and obey the orders (of the Amir) in busy times and during times of leisure, and in times of difficulty and in times of ease, and to be obedient to the ruler and give him his right even if he did not give us our rights, and not to fight him unless we saw him in open unbelief for which we would have proof before Allah.

21. *Hadrat Ayesha* is reported to have narrated that when believing women emigrated (from Makka to Medina) to the Prophet (peace & blessings of Allah be with him) he used to test them according to the Command of God Almighty. 'O you who believe! When believing women come to you as emigrants, examine their faith. Then if you find them to be belie-ving women, do not return them to the unbelievers, neither are these women lawful for them, nor are those unbelievers lawful for them. And give them what they have spent, and there is no blame on you if you marry them

when you have given them their dowries. And do not hold fast to the ties of marriage with unbelieving women, and ask for what you have spent, and let them ask for what they have spent. This is the Judgment of God, He judges bet-ween you, and God is All-Knowing, All-Wise.' (Q. 60: 10) So if any of such believing women accepted those conditions, she accepted the condi-tions of faith. When they agreed to those conditions and confirmed it with their tongues, the Messenger of Allah (peace & blessings of Allah be with him) used to tell them: 'Go, I have accepted your oath of allegiance.' By God, the hand of the Apostle of Allah (peace & blessings of Allah be with him) never touched the hand of any woman; he only used to take their pledge of alle-giance orally. By God, the Messen-ger of Allah did not take the pledge of allegi-ance from the women except in accor-dance with what God had com-manded him. When he accepted their pledge of allegi-ance he would tell them: I have accepted your oath of allegiance.

22. *Abu Hurayra* is reported to have related that the Prophet (peace & blessings of Allah be with him) said: Whoever obeys me he has obeyed God, and whoever disobeys me he has diso-beyed God, and whoever obeys the Ruler he has obeyed me, and whoever disobeys the Ruler he has disobeyed me.

23. *Yahya ibn Hussain* is reported to have related that his grandmother Umm Al Hussain said that she

heard the Apos-tle of Allah (peace & blessings of Allah be with him) delivering his sermon at his Fare-well Pilgrimage, and he said: If a slave is appointed over you and he conducts your affairs according to the Book of God, you should listen to him and obey him.

24. *Hadrat Ali* is reported to have narrated that the Messenger of Allah (peace & blessings of Allah be with him) sent an army and appointed a man as its commander, so he lit a fire and ordered his soldiers to enter it, some of them moved to enter it and others escaped from going into it. When the holy Prophet (peace & blessings of Allah be with him) was informed about it he said to those who moved to enter it: Had you gone into it (the fire) you would have remained in it until the Day of judgment, and he told the others they had acted correctly and said: There is no obedience in wrong doing, but obedience is obli-gatory only in what is good (reasonable).

25. *Ibn Umar* is reported to have related that the Apostle of Allah (peace & blessings of Allah be with him) said: The Muslim has to hear and to obey in what he likes and in what he dislikes, unless he is ordered to wrongdoing, as if he is ordered to wrongdoing, then there is no listening nor obedience.

26. *Ibn Yazid al Ju'afi* is reported to have asked the holy Prophet (peace & blessings of Allah be with him): "O Apostle of Allah! What do you

advise if we have rulers who demand that we fulfill our obli-gations towards them, but they do not fulfill their own responsi-bilities towards us? What do you order us to do?' The Messenger of Allah (peace & blessings of Allah be with him) did not answer. He was asked again and again for the second time or third time, then he said: Listen to them and obey them, for on them will be their burden and on you will be your burden.

27. *Auf ibn Malik* is reported to have related that the Messenger of Allah (peace & blessings of Allah be with him) said: 'The best of your rulers are those whom you love and who love you, who invoke God's bles-sings upon you and you invoke His blessings upon them. And the worst of your rulers are those whom you hate and who hate you and whom you curse and who curse you. It was asked: 'Should we not depose them by force?' He said: 'No, not as long as they establish prayer among you. If you then find anything detestable in them, you should hate their administration, but do not disobey them.

28. *Umm Salama* is reported to have related that the Messenger of Allah (peace & blessings of Allah be with him) said: A time is approaching soon in which there will be Amirs and you will like their good deeds and dislike their bad deeds. The one who witnesses their bad deeds and objects to them openly is absolved from blame, the one who hates their bad deeds and only objects in his

heart also has no blame. But one who approves of their bad deeds and imitates them is lost. The people asked: 'Should we not fight against them?' He replied: 'No, not as long as they establish prayer.

29. *Hudhaifa ibn al -Yaman* is reported to have narrated that people used to ask the Messenger of Allah (peace & blessings of Allah be with him) about good times, but I used to ask him about the bad times fearing that they might overtake me. I told the holy Prophet (peace & blessings of Allah be with him): 'O Messenger of Allah, we were in the depths of igno-rance and evil, and then Allah brought us good. Is there any bad time after this good one?' He said: 'Yes.' I asked: 'Will there be a good time again after that bad time?' He said: 'Yes, but there will be hidden evil in it.' I asked: 'What will that hidden evil be?' He said: People will arise who will adopt ways other than mine and seek guidance other than mine, and you will see good together with bad.' I asked: 'Will there be a bad time after that good one?' He said: 'Yes.' A people will arise who will stand and invite at the gates of Hell. Whoever responds to their call will be cast into the Fire.' I said: 'O Messenger of Allah, describe them to us.' He said: 'Very well. They will be a people with the same complexion as ours and who will speak our language.' I said: 'O Messenger of Allah, what do you advise if I happened to be alive in such times? He replied: 'You should adhere to the Muslims and their leader.' I said: 'What if there are no Muslims and no leader?' He said: 'Distance yourself from them even if you have to eat the roots of trees until death comes to you.

30. It is related on the authority of *Abu Hurayra* that the Messenger of Allah (peace & blessings of Allah be with him) said: Anyone who disobeys the leader and distances himself from the Muslims and then dies in that condition, will die the death of one who dies in the days of ignorance. Anyone who fights for a cause of the people, who is arrogantly proud of his family and who invites to fight for their family honour, and who fights in the cause of his relatives and tribe, if he is killed he will die the death of one who died in the days of ignorance. Whoever attacks my community and kills both the righteous and the wicked of them, and does not spare even the faithful, and does not honour the pledge he made with those who have been given a pledge of security, he is not from me and I have nothing to do with him.

31. *Nafe'* is reported to have said: Abd Allah ibn Umar visited Abd Allah ibn Muti' in the days (when atrocities were perpetrated on the people of Medina during the reign of Yazid ibn Mu'awiya) at Harra. Ibn Muti' said: 'Lay down a cushion for Abu Abd al Rahman.' But he said: 'I have not come to sit with you, I have come to tell you a Hadith I have heard from the Messenger of Allah. I heard him say: 'Anyone who disobeys the leader will have no excuse when he stands before God on the Day of Judg-ment, and one who dies without having sworn an oath (of allegiance) will die the death of one who died in the days of ignorance.

32. *Arfaja* is reported to have related that the Messenger of Allah (peace & blessings of Allah be with him) said: Various evils will appear in the near future. Whoever attempts to divide this community while they are united, you should strike him down with the sword no matter whom he happens to be.

33. It is reported on the authority of *Abu Hurayra* that the Messenger of Allah (peace & blessings of Allah be with him) said: Whoever raises his arms against us is not one of us, and whoever cheats us is not one of us.

34. It is reported on the authority of Abu Hurayra that the Messenger of Allah (peace & blessings of Allah be with him) said: God likes three (things) for you and dislikes three (things) for you, he likes that you worship Him and not associate any partners with Him, and that you are unified and not divided, and He dislikes gossip and begging and squandering of wealth.

35. *Hadrat Ayesha* is reported to have said that the Apostle of Allah (peace & blessings of Allah be with him) said: whoever performs a deed that does not conform to the Qur'an and the Sunna is unlawful.

36. *Usama ibn Zayed* is reported to have related that the Messenger of Allah (peace & blessings of Allah be with him) said: A man will be summoned on the Day of Resurrection and cast into the Fire, so that his intestines will come out and he will go round as a donkey goes round a millstone. The people of the Fire will gather around him and say: 'O so and so, what is the matter with you? Did you not enjoin us to do good deeds and forbid us from doing bad deeds?' He will say: 'Yes, I used to enjoin others to do good deeds but I did not do them myself, and I used to forbid you from doing bad deeds but I used to do them myself.

37. *Sa'ad ibn Abu Waqqas* is reported to have narrated that the Apostle of Allah said: The people of the West (Ma-ghreb) will continue to triumphantly follow the truth until (the final) Hour arrives.

38. *Abd Allah ibn Umar* is reported to have narrated that he was present with his father when he was wounded. People praised him and said: may Allah give you a great reward. Hadrat Ali said: I am hopeful of Allah's mercy and fearful of His wrath. People said appoint anyone as your successor. He rep-lied: should I carry the burden of conducting your affairs in my life as well as in death? I wish I could (as far as Caliphate is concerned) acquit myself before (the Almighty Allah) in a way that there is neither anything to my credit nor anything to my discredit. If I leave you alone (I would do so) because the Messen-ger of Allah did the same.

36

Book of Hunting and Slaughtering

1. **Adi Ibn Hatim** is reported to have related that the holy Prophet (peace & blessings of Allah be with him) said: when you set off your trained hounds for hunting you (should) recite the Name of Allah, and if your hound catches the animal and kills it, you may eat it. But if the hound eats some of it, you may not eat it as the dog caught it for itself. And if your hunting hound meets up with other dogs over which the Name of God has not been recited and they catch an animal, then you should not eat it, as you will not know which of them killed it. And if you shoot an arrow at an animal or bird and find it two or three days later and it has no sign of a wound except that of your arrow, then you may eat it. But if you find it dead in water then do not eat it.

2. **Abu Tha'laba al-Khushani** is reported to have narrated that he said to the holy Prophet (peace & blessings of Allah be with him): O Messenger of Allah! We live in a land governed by people of the Book, may we eat from their plates?' In that land there is much game (of hunting) and I hunt with my bow and arrow and with my untrained dog and my trained hunting dog, so what is lawful for me to eat?' He said: 'Regarding what you mention about the people of the Book, if you can use plates other than theirs do not eat from their places, but if you can not get other than theirs then wash their plates and eat from them. If you hunt an animal with your bow after reciting the Name of Allah eat it, and if you hunt something with your untrained dog, slaughter it and then eat it.

3. It is reported that **Adi ibn Hatim** said that he asked the holy Prophet (peace & blessings of Allah be with him) concerning game killed by spears. He said: 'If it is killed with its sharp edge, then eat it, but if it is killed by its shaft it is unlawful as an animal killed with a piece of wood.' I asked him concerning game killed by a hunting dog, he said: 'if the hunting dog catches the game for you, eat it, for killing the game by the hunting dog is similar to slaughtering it. But if you see

your hunting dog or dogs with other dogs, and you fear that bet may have shared in hunting the game with your dog and may have killed it, then do not eat bet because you have recited the Name of Allah on your hunting dog, but you have not recited it on the other dog.

4. *Abu Thalami* is reported to have related that the holy Prophet (peace & blessings of Allah be with him) said regarding the one who searches for his game for three days: Then eat it if is not rotten.

5. It is reported from *Ibn Umar* that the holy Prophet (peace & blessings of Allah be with him) said: Whoever keeps a dog for a purpose other than as a watch dog or the hunting dog he will lose two quirt from his good deeds every day.

6. It is reported from *Abu Hurayra* that the Messenger of Allah (peace & blessings of Allah be with him) said: Whoever keeps a dog except for guarding sheep or the farm or for hunting, loses one quirt every day of the reward for his good deeds. Al Zuhri reportedly said: When what Abu Hurayra said was mentioned to ibn Umar, he said: May God have mercy upon Abu Hurayra, he had a farm.

7. *Jabir bin Abu Allah* is reported to have said: The Messenger of Allah (peace & blessings of Allah be with him) ordered us to kill the dogs, so when any woman came from the desert with her dog we used to kill it, then the holy Prophet (peace & blessings of Allah be with him)

forbade its killing and said: Kill the black dog because it is Satan.

8. *Hisham ibn Zayed ibn Anas ibn Malik* reported to have said: My grandfather Anas ibn Malik and I visited Al Hikam ibn Ayyub and Anas saw some boys shooting at a tethered hen and said: 'The holy Prophet (peace & blessings of Allah be with him) has prohibited the shooting of animals (and birds) that are tied.

9. *Jabir ibn Abd Allah* reported that the Apostle of Allah (peace & blessings of Allah be with him) had forbidden that any beast should be killed after it has been tied.

10. *Shaddad ibn Aus* is reported to have said: I recall two things that the Messenger of Allah (peace & blessings of Allah be with him) said: 'Indeed God has enjoined upon you to be kind to all that you slaughter, so slaughter in a kind manner and when you slaughter, slau-ghter well. Every one of you should keep his knife sharp and permit the animal to die in comfort.

11. It is reported from *Rafi ibn Khadij* that the Messenger of Allah (peace & blessings of Allah be with him) said: If the instrument used to slaughter causes blood to flow out, and if Allah's Name is recited, then eat it. But do not slaughter with a tooth or a nail. I shall explain why, as for the tooth, it is a bone; and as for the nail, it is the knife of Abyssinians. Then we took some camels and sheep as booty and one of the camels ran off, a man shot an

arrow at it and halted it. The Messenger of Allah (peace & blessings of Allah be with him) said: Some of these camels are as wild as wild beasts, so if one of them escapes and makes you exhausted, then deal with it in this way.

12. *Ibn Abu Aufa* reported: we went on seven expeditions with the holy Prophet (peace & blessings of Allah be with him) and ate locusts.

13. *Ibn Umar* reported that a man asked the Messenger of Allah about eating lizard, whereupon he said: I neither eat it nor do I prohibit (eating) it.

14. *Jabir ibn Abd Allah* reported that The Apostle of Allah (peace & blessings of Allah be with him) prohibited eating the flesh of domestic Asses on the Day of Khyber, and permitted the cooking of the flesh of horses.

15. *Ali Abu Talib* reported that the holy Prophet (peace & blessings of Allah be with him) had forbidden temporary marriages (Muta') and eating of the flesh of the domestic Asses.

16. *Ibn Umar* has reported that the Apostle of Allah said: Two dead things and two bloods have been made lawful for us, as far as dead things are concer-ned; one is fish and the other is locust. So far as two bloods are concerned one is that of liver and the other is that of spleen.

37

Book of Sacrifice

1. **Umm Salama** is reported to have related that the Messenger of Allah (peace & blessings of Allah be with him) said: When any one of you intends to offer sacrifice (during Eid al-Adha) he should not get his hair trimmed or nails cut until he has offered sacrifice.

2. **Ibn Sufyan** is reported to have related that: During the lifetime of the Messenger of Allah (peace & blessings of Allah be with him) we once offered some animals for sacrifice, some of the people slaughtered their animals before the prayer (of Eid al-Adha) so when the Prophet (peace & blessings of Allah be with him) had completed his prayer, he noticed that they had slaughtered them before the prayer and he said: 'Whoever has slaughtered before the prayer should slaughter another in its place, and whoever did not slaughter before the prayer should slaughter in the Name of Allah.

3. **Al Bara ibn Aazib** is reported to have related that the holy Prophet (peace & blessings of Allah be with him) said: Upon this day of ours (Eid al-Adha) the first thing we must do is to offer the prayer and then return to slaughter the sacrifice. Whoever does so has acted according to our Sunna, and whoever has slaughtered before the prayer, his offering is only the meat he gives to his family, and it will not be considered as a sacrifice.

4. **Jabir ibn Abd Allah** is reported to have related that the Messenger of Allah (peace & blessings of Allah be with him) said: Sacrifice only fully-grown animals unless it is difficult for you, in which case sacrifice a ram (of over six months of age).

5. **Anas** is reported to have said: The Messenger of Allah (peace & blessings of Allah be with him) slaughtered two rams, one was black and the other was white, and I saw him putting his foot on their flanks and reciting the Name of Allah and reciting 'God is Great' over them. Then he slaughtered them with his own hands.

6. **Hadrat Ayesha** is reported to have narrated: The Messenger of Allah (peace & blessings of Allah be with

him) asked for a black legged ram with black flanks and black patches about the eyes to be brought to him for sacrifice. He took a large knife, had it sharpened, and then he took up the knife and held the ram and placed it upon the ground and sacrificed it reciting the following: *Bismillah, Allah-humma Taqabbal min Muhammadin wa a'ali-I Muhammadin, wa min ummati Muhammadin.* ('In the Name of Allah, O Allah accept this from Mu-hammad and the family of Muhammad and the community of Muhammad).

7. It is reported that *Abu Ubaid*, the freed slave of Ibn Azhar said: I was present on the day of the Feast of al Adha with Umar ibn al Khattab, then I was present with Ali ibn Abu Talib when he offered the prayer for the Feast and then the sermon before the people and he said: The Messenger of Allah (peace & blessings of Allah be with him) has prohibited you from eating the meat of your sacrificial animals beyond three days.

8. *Abd Allah ibn Waqid* is reported by Abd Allah ibn Abu Bakr to have said: The Messenger of Allah (peace & blessings of Allah be with him) prohibited eating the flesh of the sacrificial animals for longer than three days. Abd Allah ibn Abu Bakr said: 'I told Amra about it and she said: 'He has told the truth, as I have heard Ayesha say: 'the needy people of the nomads used to come on the Feast Day of al Adha during the lifetime of the Messenger of Allah (peace & blessings of Allah be

with him) and he said: 'Keep what remains with you for three days and whatever is left from it give as charity.' Then they said: 'O Messenger of Allah, the people make water skins from the hides of their sacrificial animals and they melt fat from them.' Then he said: 'What then?' They said: 'You have forbidden us from eating the flesh of the sacrificial animals for longer than three days.' So he said: 'I only prohibited you because of the nomads who come on that day, so you should eat and save and give charity.

9. *Jabir ibn Abd Allah* reportedly said: we did not eat the flesh of sacrificed animal beyond three days but then the Apostle of Allah (peace & blessings of Allah be with him) commanded us to make it a provision for journey and eat it beyond three days.

10. Messenger of Allah (peace & blessings of Allah be with him) is repor-ted by Abu Hurayra to have said: Fara and Atira are forbidden. Fara is the first-born of a she-camel that the unbelievers used to slaughter to their deities.

11. *Abu Tufail Amir ibn Wathila* is reported to have said: I was with Ali ibn Abu Talib when someone asked him: 'What did the Messenger of Allah (peace & blessings of Allah be with him) tell (you) in secret?' Ali became angry and said: 'The Messenger of Allah (peace & blessings of Allah be with him) did not tell me anything secretly which

he did not tell the people, except four things.' He said: 'O Commander of the Faithful what were they?' Ali replied: 'God curses the one who curses his father, God curses the one who sacrifices in the name of anyone else besides Allah or who invokes any-thing besides Allah, and God curses the one who accommodates anyone who innovates in the Religion, and God curses the one who changes the boundaries of the land (he possesses).

38

Book of Drinks

1. *Ibn Umar* is reported to have said that the Messenger of Allah (peace & blessings of Allah be with him) said: Every intoxicant is forbidden.

2. *Ali ibn Abu Talib* is reported to have said: There fell to my lot an old she-camel from the spoils of Badr and Allah's Messenger (peace & blessings of Allah be with him) gifted me another camel. When I intended to marry Fatimah, the daughter of the Messenger of Allah (peace & blessings of Allah be with him), I had arran-ged with a goldsmith from the tribe of Bani Qainuqa to go with me to bring Idhkhir (dry grass) and sell it to the gold-smiths and use its money for my wedding feast. I was gathering saddles, sacks and ropes for my she-camels while my two she camels were kneeling down beside the room of an Ansar. I returned after collec-ting whatever I could and returned to find the humps of my two she-camels severed and their flanks cut open and a part of their livers disgorged. When I saw the condition of my two she-camels, I could not prevent myself from weeping. I asked: 'Who has done this?' The people replied: 'Hamza ibn Abd al Muttalib who is staying with some Ansar drunkards in this house.' I went to the Prophet (peace & blessings of Allah be with him), Zayed ibn Haritha was with him. The holy Prophet (peace & blessings of Allah be with him) asked. 'What is the matter with you? I replied: 'O Messenger of Allah, I have never seen such a day like today. Hamza attacked my two she-camels, severed their humps, and ripped open their flanks, and he is sitting there in a house in the company of some drun-kards.' The Prophet (peace & blessings of Allah be with him) set off towards the house where Hamza was followed by Zayed ibn Haritha and me. He asked permission to enter, and they allowed him, and they were drunk. The Messen-ger of Allah (peace & blessings of Allah be with him) rebuked Hamza for what he had done, but Hamza was drunk and his eyes were red. Hamza first looked at his knees, then he looked at his waist, and looked at his face and said: 'Are you not but the slaves of my father?' The Messen-ger of Allah

(peace & blessings of Allah be with him) realized that he was drunk, so he turned to leave and we left with him.

3. *Jabir* is reported to have related that a man came from a town of Yemen called Jayshan, and asked the Prophet (peace & blessings of Allah be with him) about the wine they used to drink in their land which was made from millet and was known as Mizr (modern beer). The Apostle of Allah (peace & blessings of Allah be with him) asked if it was intoxicating. He said: 'Yes.' At that the Messenger of Allah (peace & blessings of Allah be with him) said: all intoxicants are prohibited. Indeed God Almighty made a promise to those who drink intoxicants that they will be made to drink Tinat al Khabal. They asked: 'O Messenger of Allah, what is Tinat al Khabal?' He said: it is the sweat of the inhabitants of Hell or the discharge of the inhabitants of Hell.

4. *Hadrat Ayesha* is reported to have said: The Messenger of Allah (peace & blessings of Allah be with him) was asked about al Biti (an intoxicating drink prepared from honey). He said: all drinks that intoxicate are prohibited.

5. *Ibn Umar* is reported to have related that the Messenger of Allah (peace & blessings of Allah be with him) said: Whoever takes alcoholic drinks in the world and dies without repenting will be deprived of it in the Hereafter.

6. *Anas ibn Malik* is reported to have related that: As I was serving Abu Talha, Abu Dujana and Mu'az ibn Jabel among a group of Ansars with alcoholic drinks, it was announced that alcoholic drinks had been prohibited. So they told me to throw it away and I threw it away. It was made from ripe dates and unripe dates. Qatada reportedly said that Anas ibn Malik said: Alcoholic drinks were prohibited. At that time such drinks used to be prepared from unripe and ripe dates.

7. *Ibn Umar* is reported to have said: I delivered a sermon from the pulpit of the Messenger of Allah (peace & blessings of Allah be with him) saying that alcoholic drinks were prohibited by Divine Com-mand, and these drinks used to be pre-pared from five things, i.e., grapes, dates, wheat, barley and honey. Alcoholic drink is that and it disturbs the mind.' I wish the Mes-senger of Allah (peace & blessings of Allah be with him) had not left us before giving us definite verdicts concerning three matters, how much a grandfather may inherit, the inheritance of al Kalala (inhe-ritors such as brothers and paternal uncles) and the different kinds of usury.

8. *Jabir ibn Abd Allah Al Ansari* is reported to have said: The holy Prophet (peace & blessings of Allah be with him) prohibited the drinking of alcoholic drinks made from raisins, dates, and unripe or fresh dates.

9. *Buraida* is reported to have related that the Messenger of Allah (peace

& blessings of Allah be with him) said: "I have prohibited Nabith (mixture of the drink prepared with grapes and fresh dates and dry dates and fresh dates) in containers, but a container is just a container and it does not make things lawful or unlawful. And all intoxicants are unlawful.

10. *Ibn Abbas* reportedly said: Nabith was prepared for the Messenger of Allah (peace & blessings of Allah be with him) at the beginning of the night and he would drink it in the morning and the following night and the following day and the night after that up to the after-noon. If anything was left after that he gave it to his servant, or had it thrown away.

11. *Anas* is reported to have said: The Prophet (peace & blessings of Allah be with him) was asked about the use of alcohol from which vinegar is prepared. He said: It is prohibited.

12. *Wa'il al Hadrami* is reported to have related that the Messenger of Allah (peace & blessings of Allah be with him) was asked about alcohol and he said: It is not a medicine, but a malady.

13. It was related that *Jabir ibn Abd Allah* said that the Messenger of God (prayers & peace be upon him) said: At dusk stop your children from going out, for the devils come out at that hour. But when an hour of the night has passed, let them go and close the doors and recite the name of Allah, for Satan does not open a closed door. Tie the mouth

of your waterskin and recite the Name of Allah. Cover your containers and utensils and recite the Name of Allah. And cover them even by placing something across it, and put out your lamps (at night before going off to sleep).

14. *Anas* is reported to have said: I served a drink to the Messenger of Allah (peace & blessings of Allah be with him) in this cup of mine, it was honey, Nabith, water and milk.

15. *Abu Hurayra* is reported to have said: On the night (of Ascension) when the Messenger of Allah (peace & blessings of Allah be with him) was taken on a Night Journey (to the heavens) from Jerusalem, two cups were offered to him, one contained wine and the other contained milk. He looked at them and took the cup of milk. Gabriel said: 'Praise be to God Who has guided you to the Right Path, if you had taken the wine, your community would have gone astray.

16. *Hudhaifa* is reported to have said that the Messenger of Allah (peace & blessings of Allah be with him) said: 'do not drink from containers of gold or silver nor wear clothes of silk or Dibaj. These things are for them (unbelievers) in this world and for you in the Hereafter, on the Day of Resurrection.

17. *Umm Salama*, the wife of the holy Prophet, reportedly related that the Messenger of Allah (peace & blessings of Allah be with him) said: Whoever drinks from silver containers is only filling his stomach with

the Fire of Hell. It is also reported that she said: Whoever eats or drinks from silver or gold utensils...

18. *Anas ibn Malik* is reported to have related that: Once the Messenger of Allah (peace & blessings of Allah be with him) visited us in our house and asked for a drink. We offered him sheep milk mixed with water. Abu Bakr was sitting on his left side and Umar in front of him and a bedouin on his right side. When the Messenger of Allah (peace & blessings of Allah be with him) had finished, Umar said: 'O Messenger of Allah, give it to Abu Bakr.' But the holy Prophet (peace & blessings of Allah be with him) offered the remaining milk to the bedouin and said twice, 'to those on the right side! So, start from the right side.' Anas added: 'it is a Sunna. And he repeated it three times.

19. *Abu Qatada* is reported to have said: The Prophet (peace & blessings of Allah be with him) forbade exhaling in the drinking cup.

20. *Anas* is reported to have said: The Messenger of Allah (peace & blessings of Allah be with him) used to take a drink in three breaths, and he is reported to have said: It is more satisfying, healthier and better.

21. *Abu Hurayra* reportedly related that the Messenger of Allah (peace & blessings of Allah be with him) said: None of you should drink while standing; and if anyone forgets, he should vomit.

22. *Ibn Abbas* is reported to have said: I served the Messenger of Allah (peace & blessings of Allah be with him) with water from Zam Zam and he drank it while standing, he asked for it while he was at the Ka'ba.

23. *Abu Barda* has reported that the Messenger of Allah (peace & blessings of Allah be with him) was told that the people of Yemen are fond of a drink made from honey and Mizr which is made from Barley, The holy Prophet (peace & blessings of Allah be with him) replied: every intoxicant that detains you from prayer is forbidden.

39

Book of Food

1. *Hudhaifa* is reported to have said: We went to a dinner with the Messenger of Allah (peace & blessings of Allah be with him) and we did not touch the food before the Messenger of Allah (peace & blessings of Allah be with him) had laid his hand and started to eat. Once we went out with him to a dinner when a girl came rushing in as if someone had been pursuing her. She was about to lay her hand on the food, when the Messenger of Allah (peace & blessings of Allah be with him) restrained her. Then a bedouin entered as if someone had been pursuing him. He restrained his hand, and then the Apostle of Allah (peace & blessings of Allah be with him) said: 'Satan considers that food upon which the Name of God is not mentioned to be lawful. He had brought this girl so that the food might be made lawful for him and I restrained her hand. And he had brought a bedouin so that it might be lawful for him. So I restrained his hand. By Him, in Whose Hand is my life; in her hand was the hand of Satan.

2. *Jabir ibn Abd Allah* is reported to have related that the Messenger of Allah (peace & blessings of Allah be with him) said: When a person enters his house and recites the name of Allah and when he eats the food, Satan tells himself: 'You have nowhere to pass the night and no evening meal.' But when he enters without reciting the name of Allah, Satan says: 'You have found a place to pass the night, and when he does not take the name of Allah while eating food, he (Satan) says: You have found a place to pass the night and an evening meal.

3. *Ibn Umar* has reported that the Messenger of Allah (peace & blessings of Allah be with him) said: When any of you intends to eat, he should eat with his right hand, and when he drinks he should drink with his right hand, for Satan eats with his left hand and drinks with his left hand.

4. *Umar ibn Abu Salama* is reported to have related: I was a child in the care of the Messenger of Allah (peace & blessings of Allah be with him) and my hand used to move about the dish as I ate. So the Apostle of Allah (peace & blessings of Allah be with him) said: 'O boy! Recite the Name of Allah and eat with your right hand, and eat from whatever is nearest to you in the dish.

5. *Ka'b ibn Malik* is reported to have said: The Messenger of Allah (peace & blessings of Allah be with him) used to eat using three fingers and licked them before wiping them.

6. *Jabir* is reported to have said that the holy Prophet (peace & blessings of Allah be with him) recommended the licking of fingers and the dish, saying: You do not know in what portion the blessing lies.

7. *Jabir* is reported to have said that he heard the Apostle of Allah (peace & blessings of Allah be with him) say: When any one of you drops a mouthful he should remove dirt from it and then eat, and should not leave it for a Satan.' He also recommended that the dish should be wiped clean, and he said: You do not know in what portion of your food the blessing (may) lie.

8. *Anas ibn Malik* is reported to have related that the Messenger of Allah (peace & blessings of Allah be with him) said: Allah is pleased with the servant who thanks Him after taking his meals or drinking a drink and praises Allah for it.

9. *Abu Hurayra* is reported to have related that the holy Prophet (peace & blessings of Allah be with him) went out one day or night, met Abu Bakr and Umar outside and asked: 'What has brought you out of your houses at this hour?' They said: 'O Messenger of Allah, hunger.' He said: 'By Him in Whose Hand is my life, what has brought you out has brought me out too, stand up.' They stood up with him, and went to the house of one of the Ansars, but he was not home. When his wife saw them she said: 'Most welcome.' The Messenger of Allah (peace & blessings of Allah be with him) asked her: 'Where is so and so?' She said: 'He has gone to fetch some fresh water for us.' When the man of the Ansars came and saw the Messenger of Allah (peace & blessings of Allah be with him) and his two companions, he said: 'Praise be to God, no one has more honorable guests today than I. Then he went out and brought for them a cluster of ripe dates, some dry dates and fresh dates, and said: 'Eat of them.' He then took out his long knife and the Messenger of Allah (peace & blessings of Allah be with him) told him: 'Beware of killing an animal which gives milk.' He slaughtered a sheep for them and they ate of it and some of the dates and drank." When they had eaten q sufficiently and had satisfied their thirst, the Messenger of Allah (peace & blessings of Allah be with him) said to Abu Bakr and Umar: 'By Him in Whose Hand is my life, you will surely be questioned concerning this bounty on the Day of Judgment. You left your house due to hunger and you did not return before receiving this bounty.

10. *Anas* is reported to have related that the Messenger of Allah (peace & blessings of Allah be with him) had a Persian neighbor who was good at making a delicious soup. He made some for the Messenger of Allah (peace & blessings of Allah be with him) and then came to invite him. The holy Prophet asked: 'What about Ayesha?' He said: No. He repeated his invitation, and the Messenger of Allah (peace & blessings of Allah be with him) again asked: 'what about Ayesha? He said: 'No.' He repeated his invitation and the Apostle of Allah (peace & blessings of Allah be with him) again said: 'What about Ayesha?' He said: 'Yes' on the third time So both of them stood up and followed one another until they reached his house.

11. *Abu Hurayra* is reported to have related that the Messenger of Allah (peace & blessings of Allah be with him) said: The food for two is sufficient for three and the food for three is sufficient for four.

12. *Jabir ibn Abd Allah* is reported to have related that the Messenger of Allah (peace & blessings of Allah be with him) said: The food for one is sufficient for two and the food for two is sufficient for four, and the food for four is sufficient for eight.

13. *Jabir and Ibn Umar* have reported that the Messenger of Allah (peace & blessings of Allah be with him) said: A believer eats with one stomach but an unbeliever eats with seven stomachs.

14. *Abu Hurayra* is reported to have said that a man used to eat much, but when he embraced Islam, he started eating less. That was mentioned to the Prophet (peace & blessings of Allah be with him) who then said: A believer eats with one stomach and an unbeliever eats with seven.

15. *Talha ibn Nafe'* related that he heard Jabir ibn Abd Allah say: The Messenger of Allah (peace & blessings of Allah be with him) held my hand once and took me to his house; he brought some bread and asked his family for condiment. They said: 'We have nothing here but vinegar.' He asked for it and then said: 'Vinegar is a good condiment; vinegar is a good condiment.

16. *Abd Allah ibn Busr* is reported to have related: The Messenger of Allah (peace & blessings of Allah be with him) visited my father and we offered him a meal of a mixture of dates, cheese and butter. He ate some of that. Then he was offered dates that he ate. Then a drink was brought for him and he drank it, and then gave it to one who was on his right side.' He (the narrator) said: 'my father took hold of the rein of his riding animal and requested him to pray for us. So he said: 'O Allah, bless them in what You have provided for them as sustenance and forgive them and have mercy upon them.

17. *Hadrat Ayesha* is reported to have related that the holy Prophet (peace

& blessings of Allah be with him) said: O Ayesha, a house (that is) without dates its people will suffer hunger. O Ayesha, a house (that is) without dates, its people will suffer hunger. Or he said: Its people will be hungry. He said it two or three times.

18. *Jabala ibn Suhaim* is reported to have said that at the time of Ibn Al Zubair we were afflicted by famine, and he provided us with dates to eat. Abd Allah ibn Umar used to pass by us while we were eating, and say: 'Do not eat two dates at once, for the Messenger of Allah (peace & blessings of Allah be with him) forbade the taking of two dates at once.' Ibn Umar used to add: except with the permission of your companions.

19. *Abu Saeed* is reported to have related that a bedouin visited the Messenger of Allah (peace & blessings of Allah be with him) and said: I reside in a low land where lizards are plentiful, and my family usually eats them. The holy Prophet did not react, so we said: 'Repeat it, and he repeated it, but he gave no answer. Then the Messenger of Allah (peace & blessings of Allah be with him) replied: 'O dweller of the desert, indeed Allah Almighty cursed and was angered with one of the tribes of Bani Israel and changed them into creatures that move upon the earth. I do not know if the lizard is one of them, so I do not eat it, but I do not prohibit it from being eaten.

20. *Jabir ibn Abd Allah* is reported to have said that on the day of Khyber the Messenger of Allah (peace & blessings of Allah be with him) prohibited the con-sumption of donkey meat and allowed the consumption of horsemeat.

21. *Anas* is reported to have related that when The Messenger of Allah (peace & blessings of Allah be with him) was victorious at (the battle of) Khyber, we caught the asses outside the village and cooked their meat. Then it was proclai-med: 'Beware! Indeed Allah and His Mes-senger have prohibited you from it (meat of asses), it is an evil deed of Satan's works.' Then the clay pots were over-turned with their contents and they were filled to the brim.

22. It was related that *Abu Tha'laba* is reported to have said that the Messenger of Allah (peace & blessings of Allah be with him) prohibited the consumption of donkey meat

23. *Asma'* is reported to have said that during the lifetime of the Messenger of Allah (peace & blessings of Allah be with him) we slaughtered a horse and ate it.

24. *Abu Hurayra* is reported to have related that the Messenger of Allah (peace & blessings of Allah be with him) said: The eating of all animals with fangs is prohibited.

25. *Ibn Abbas* is reported to have said that the Messenger of Allah (peace & blessings of Allah be with him) prohibited (the eating of) all animals

with fangs, and all birds with talons.

26. *Abu Ayyub* is reported to have said: The Messenger of Allah (peace & blessings of Allah be with him) came to my house and stayed on the lower floor while I lived on the upper floor. One night I got up and thought 'How is it that we walk above the head of the messenger of Allah,' so we moved aside and spent the night in a corner, and then told the holy Prophet of God (peace & blessings of Allah be with him) about it. So The Messenger of Allah (peace & blessings of Allah be with him) said: 'The lower floor is more comfortable for me.' But I said: 'Who would not prefer to be under the roof over which you live.' So The Apostle of Allah (peace & blessings of Allah be with him) moved to the upper floor and I moved to the lower floor. I used to prepare food for the Messenger of Allah (peace & blessings of Allah be with him) and when it was brought back to me I used to ask what part of the food had his fingers touched and I used to move my fingers around the parts where his fingers had touched. Then I made some food with garlic and when it was brought back I was told that he had not eaten it. I was worried and went up to ask him saying: 'Is it prohibited?' But the Messenger of Allah (peace & blessings of Allah be with him) said: 'No, but I do not like it.' I said: 'I too do not like what you do not like.' Angels visited the Messenger of Allah (peace & blessings of Allah be

with him) who brought him the Message of God Almighty.

27. *Abu Hurayra* is reported to have said that the Messenger of Allah (peace & blessings of Allah be with him) never adversely commented about food, but if he liked it he ate it, and if he disliked it he left it.

28. *Umm Salama*, the wife of the holy Prophet is reported to have related that the Apostle of Allah (peace & blessings of Allah be with him) said: He who drinks in the vessels of gold or silver in fact drinks down in his belly the fires of Hell.

40

Book of Clothes and Adornment

1. *Ibn Umar* is reported to have said: Umar saw Utrid al-Tamimi selling silk garments in the market. He used to go to the royal courts and fetch a good price for them. Umar informed the Messenger of Allah about it and asked: would you buy and wear one to receive the delegations from the Arabs when they come to visit you?' I think he also said: 'So you may wear it on Friday.' The Messenger of Allah (peace & blessings of Allah be with him) said: Whoever wears silk in this life has no share of it in the Hereafter. When silk garments were presented to the Apostle of God (peace & blessings of Allah be with him) later, he gave one to Umar and one to Usama ibn Zayed and one to Ali ibn Abu Talib, saying: 'cut them and make veils for your wives (out of it). Umar came with his garment and said: 'O Messenger of Allah, you gave this to me while yesterday you told us about the silk garments of Utrid.' He said: 'I did not send it to you for you to wear, but so that you may obtain some benefit from it.' And Usama wore the garment given to him and seemed to be excited and The Messenger of Allah (peace & blessings of Allah be with him) seemed to be agitated and he looked at him with disapproval and displeasure. Usama asked: 'O Messenger of Allah, why are you looking at me that way while you gave it to me?' He said: I did not give it to you for you to wear, but to use it as a veil for your wives.

2. *Abd Allah ibn Zubair* is reported to have said: Beware! Do not dress up your women in silk as I have heard it from Umar ibn Khattab that he heard the Messenger of Allah (peace & blessings of Allah be with him) say: Do not wear silk, for whoever wears it will not wear it in the Hereafter.

3. *Uqba ibn Amer* is reported to have said: A silk cloak was gifted to the Messenger of Allah (peace & blessings of Allah be with him) and he wore it and offered prayer in it. When he completed the prayer, he pulled it off violently as if he hated it and said: such a robe is unseemly for one who fears Allah.

4. *Abu Uthman* is reported to have related that: While we were at Adhar-bijan, Umar wrote to us: 'O Utba ibn Farqad, these funds are not of your own earning nor the earning of your father nor your mother, so feed the Muslims from what you eat and avoid indulgence and the garments of the unbelievers and avoid wearing silk, The Messenger of Allah (peace & blessings of Allah be with him) prohibited wearing silk except to the extent of two or three or four fingers width of it.

5. *Jabir ibn Abd Allah* is reported to have said: The Prophet (peace & blessings of Allah be with him) once wore a cloak of brocade that had been given to him as a gift. He took it off quickly and sent it to Umar ibn Al Khattab, so someone asked him: 'O Messenger of Allah, why did you remove it so quickly?' He replied: Gabriel forbade me from (wearing) it. Then Umar came to him weeping and said: 'O Messenger of Allah, you disapproved of something and gave it to me, so what of me?' He said: I did not give it to you for you to wear it, but I gave it to you so that you could sell it. And Umar sold it for two thousand Dirhams.

6. *Abd Allah*, the freed slave of Asma' bint Abu Baker, reportedly said: Asma' sent me to Abd Allah ibn Umar asking: 'I have heard that you prohibit three things; the garment threaded with silk, the stuffed bright red saddle cloth and fasting in the month of Rajab?' Abd Allah replied:

'As for what you mention about fasting in the month of Rajab, how would it be for the one who fasts all the time? As for the garment threaded with silk, I have heard Umar ibn al Khattab say that he heard The Messenger of Allah (peace & blessings of Allah be with him) say: 'Only those who dress in silk are those who will have no share of it.' So I fear that the threaded silk may be among that. As for the stuffed bright red saddle cloth, it is the saddle of Abd Allah and it is just a saddle.' So I returned to Asma' and infor-med her what Ibn Umar had said and she said: 'Here is a cloak of the Mes-senger of Allah, and she brought out a cloak for me which was made of Persian cloth with a brocade edging and its sleeves edged in brocade and she said: 'This was with Ayesha until she died, and when she died I got it, and the Prophet (peace & blessings of Allah be with him) used to wear it, and we used to wash it for the sick people to heal themselves with it.

7. *Ali ibn Abu Talib* is reported to have said: The Messenger of Allah (peace & blessings of Allah be with him) prohi-bited the wearing of silk and yellow garments, gold rings, and the reciting of the Qur'an while kneeling.

8. *Abd Allah ibn Amr ibn al-As* is reported to have related that the Messen-ger of Allah (peace & blessings of Allah be with him) saw

me wearing two clothes dyed in saffron, whereupon he said: These are the clothes of the unbelievers, so do not wear it.

9. *Anas* reportedly said: The Messenger of Allah (peace & blessings of Allah be with him) prohibited men to wear clothes dyed with saffron.

10. *Jabir ibn Abd Allah* is reported to have related that when Abu Quhafa came on the Day of the Conquest of Mak-ka his head and his beard were white like hyssop, The Messenger of Allah (peace & blessings of Allah be with him) said: Change this with something (dye it with color) but avoid black.

11. *Abu Hurayra* reportedly said that the holy Prophet (peace & blessings of Allah be with him) said: Jews and Chris-tians do not dye their hair so you should do the opposite of what they do.

12. *Qatada* is reported to have said: I asked Anas ibn Malik: 'What kind of garments did the holy Prophet (peace & blessings of Allah be with him) prefer?' He replied: the cloth from Yemen.

13. *Abu Barda* is reported to have said: Ayesha showed us a square piece of cloth and a waist wrapper and said: The Prophet (peace & blessings of Allah be with him) died wearing these.

14. *Jabir ibn Abd Allah* reportedly said that the Messenger of Allah (peace & blessings of Allah be with him) said to him: There should be a couch for a man and a couch for his wife and a third one for the guest, but the fourth is for Satan.

15. *Hadrat Ayesha* is reported to have said: The pillow on which the Messenger of Allah (peace & blessings of Allah be with him) reclined was of leather stuffed with palm fiber.

16. *Jabir ibn Abd Allah* is reported to have said that the holy Prophet (peace & blessings of Allah be with him) said: None of you should recline on his back raising one leg over the other.

17. *Abbad ibn Tamim* reportedly said that his uncle told him: I saw The Messenger of Allah (peace & blessings of Allah be with him) reclining upon his back in the Mosque with one leg raised over the other.

18. *Mohammed ibn Ziyad* related on the authority of Abu Hurayra that when he was Amir of Bahrain he heard the Messenger of Allah (peace & blessings of Allah be with him) say: On the Day of Resurrection God Almighty will not look at the one who drags his garment behind himself in pride.

19. *Abu Zarr* is reported to have related that the holy Prophet (peace & blessings of Allah be with him) said: There are three whom Allah will not speak to or even look at or purify on the Day of Re-surrection and they shall have a grievous chastisement. Abu Zarr said: They are doomed

and lost, who are they O Mes-senger of Allah? He said: The one who leaves his garment to be too long, and the one who hurts the people by reminding them of his charity, and the one who swears false oaths in order to sell his goods.

20. *Abd Allah ibn Umar* reportedly said that the Messenger of Allah (peace & blessings of Allah be with him) said: On the day of Resurrection God Almighty will not look at the one who drags his garments on the ground in pride.

21. *Hadrat Maimuna* is reported to have said: The Apostle of Allah was silent with grief one morning so I asked: 'O Messenger of Allah! I see your mood is different today?' The holy prophet (peace & blessings of Allah be with him) said: Gabriel promised me that he would visit me last night, but he did not appear, by God he never broke his promise.' And so the Messenger of Allah (peace & blessings of Allah be with him) remained in that mood. Then he thought that there might have been a puppy under their couch, so he asked that it be removed, and then he sprinkled some water over the place. In the evening Gabriel appeared and he asked him: 'You promised you would meet me last night.' He said: 'Yes, but we do not enter a house where there is a dog or a picture.' The following morning he ordered the dogs to be killed, including the dogs kept for the orchards, but he permitted the dogs used to guard large areas of land to be left alive.

22. *Abu Hurayra* is reported to have related that the Messenger of Allah said: The angels do not enter premises where there are images or pictures.

23. *Hadrat Ayesha* is reported to have said: The Messenger of Allah (peace & blessings of Allah be with him) returned from a journey when I had hung a thick curtain having pictures in front of a door. He ordered me to remove it and I remo-ved it.

24. *Hadrat Ayesha* is reported to have related: I bought a cushion with drawings on it. When The Mes-senger of Allah (peace & blessings of Allah be with him) saw it he remained standing in the door-way of the house and did not enter. I saw a look of disapproval on his face so I said: 'O Messenger of Allah! I repent to God and His Messenger, what sin have I done?' The Messen-ger of Allah (peace & blessings of Allah be with him) said: What cushion is that? I said: 'I bought it for you to recline upon.' The Apostle of Allah (peace & blessings of Allah be with him) said: Those who draw these pictures will be punished on the Day of Resurrec-tion. It will be said to them: 'Make the images you drew come alive.' The Pro-phet (peace & blessings of Allah be with him) also said: The angels do not enter a house where there are pictures.

25. It is reported that *Abu Zur'a* said: 1 entered the house of Marwan with Abu Hurayra, and he saw pictures at the top of the house. He said: 'I heard The Messenger of Allah (peace & blessings of Allah be with him) saying that God said: who would be more unjust than the one who tries to create the like of My crea-tures? Let them create a grain; let them create a gnat.

26. *Abd Allah ibn Abbas* is reported to have related: The Messenger of Allah (peace & blessings of Allah be with him) saw someone wearing a gold signet ring on his finger, so he pulled it off from his finger and said: 'do you seek the hot coals of Hellfire to be put on your hand'. It was said to the man take your ring and obtain some benefit from it.' So he said: 'No, by God, I will never take it back after the Messenger of Allah (peace & blessings of Allah be with him) has cast it away.

27. *Abd Allah ibn Umar* has related that the Messenger of Allah (peace & blessings of Allah be with him) at one time wore a ring of gold or silver engra-ved with 'Mohammed the Messenger of Allah, and he used to turn its stone in towards the palm of his hand. Then the people started to wear similar rings and the Prophet (peace & blessings of Allah be with him) cast it aside and said: 'I shall never wear it again.' Thereafter he wore a silver ring and the people started to wear silver rings. After The Prophet (peace & blessings of Allah be with him) Abu Bakr wore the ring, and then Umar and them Uthman, until it fell from Uthman ibn Umar into the well of Aris.

28. *Ibn 'Umar* is reported to have said that the Messenger of Allah (peace & blessings of Allah be with him) had a silver ring made for himself and used to wear it. Afterwards it was worn by Abu Bakr, and then by 'Umar, and then by 'Uthman till it fell in the Aris well. On that ring was engraved: Muhammad is the Messenger of God.

29. *Anas ibn Malik* is reported to have said that Messenger of Allah (peace & blessings of Allah be with him) took a silver ring and had 'Muham-mad the Messenger of Allah' engraved upon it. The Prophet (peace & blessings of Allah be with him) then said: I have a silver ring engraved with Muhammad the Messenger of Allah', so none of you should have the same engraved on his ring.

30. *Anas* is reported to have said that the Prophet (peace & blessings of Allah be with him) wanted to write letters to the Roman and Persian emperors. He was informed that they do not accept any unstamped letter. So the Apostle of Allah (peace & blessings of Allah be with him) had a silver ring made with the engraving 'Muhammad, the Messenger of Allah'.

31. *Anas ibn Malik* is reported to have

said that the ring of the Messenger of Allah (peace & blessings of Allah be with him) was made of silver and had a stone from Abyssinia fixed into it.

32. It is reported by *Anas* that the Messenger of Allah (peace & blessings of Allah be with him) used to wear his ring in his little finger on his left hand.

33. *Ali ibn Abu Talib* is reported to have said: The Prophet (peace & blessings of Allah be with him) prohibited me from wearing any ring on my forefinger or on the finger next to it.

34. *Abu Hurayra* is reported to have related that the Messenger of Allah (peace & blessings of Allah be with him) said: When you put on your shoes, put on the right shoe first, and when you remove them, remove the left one first. Let the right shoe be the first to be worn and the last to be removed.

35. *Asma' bint Abu Baker* has narrated that a woman came to visit the Prophet (peace & blessings of Allah be with him) and said that her daughter had just married, but she had fallen sick and all her hair had fallen off. And she asked whether her daughter could use artificial hair?' The holy Prophet (peace & bles-sings of Allah be with him) remarked that Allah curses such women who artificially lengthen their hair or have their hair lengthened artificially.

36. *Jabir ibn Abd Allah* reportedly said: The Messenger of Allah (peace & blessings of Allah be with him) disappro-ved for a woman to add anything artifi-cial to her hair.

37. *Abd Allah ibn Mas'ud* is reported to have said: Allah curses the women who practice tattooing and those who remove hair from their faces and those who create spaces between their teeth artificially to look beautiful, who change what Allah has created. Umm Yaqub said: 'What is that?' Abd Allah said: 'Why should I not curse those who were cursed by The Messenger of Allah (peace & blessings of Allah be with him) and are referred to in the Book of God Almighty?' She said: 'I have read the whole Qur'an but I have not found such a thing.' Abd Allah said: 'If you had read it you would have found it, God Almighty says: 'And whatever the Messenger gives you accept it, and whatever he forbids you desist from it.' (Q.59: 7) So the woman said: 'But I see something of this on your wife now.' He said: 'Go and see.' So she went to the wife of Abd Allah and she did not see anything. So she returned to him and said: 'I have seen nothing.' He said: 'had she had what you said, I would not have kept her as a wife.

38. *Abu Hurayra* reportedly narrated that the Apostle of Allah (peace & blessings of Allah be with him) said: There are two kinds of people who are the denizens of Hell whom I

have not (yet) seen. People having whips like the tails of an ox with which they beat people, and women who well be dressed and yet (appear) naked, who will be inclined to evil and lure their husbands to evil. Their heads well be as the humps of camels, inclined to one side. They well not enter Paradise nor will they ever smell its scent although its scent can be smelled from such and such a distance.

39. *Abu Hurayra* is reported to have said that the Messenger of Allah (peace & blessings of Allah be with him) said: Angels do not accompany the travelers who have with them a dog and a bell.

40. *Abu Hurayra* is reported to have said that the Messenger of Allah (peace & blessings of Allah be with him) said: The bell is the musical instrument of Satan.

41

Book of
General Behaviour

1. *Ibn Umar* is reported to have narrated that the Messenger of Allah (peace & blessings of Allah be with him) said: The names dearest to God Almighty are Abd Allah and Abd Al Rahman.

2. *Abu Hurayra* is reported to have related that the Apostle of Allah said: The vilest name in the sight of Allah is Malik al-amlak (king of kings). Sufyan said that similarly the word Shahenshah is also of vilest applications. The Messen-ger of Allah said: The most wretched person in the sight of Allah on the Day of Reckoning and the worst person and target of His wrath would be the person who is called Malik al-Amlak for there is no King but Allah.

3. *Jabir ibn Abd Allah* is reported to have narrated that a man named his newborn son as Mohammed. The people said that they would not permit him to call his son by the name of the Messenger of Allah, so he took the matter to the holy Prophet (peace & blessings of Allah be with him) and said: 'O Messenger of Allah, a son has been born to me and I have named him Mohammed, my people are not permitting me to name him after the name of the Messenger of Allah.' The holy Prophet (peace & blessings of Allah be with him) replied: 'Name yourselves (after my name) but do not use my Kunya, for I am Al-Qasim and I disburse the blessings of Allah (knowledge of religion, spoils of war and Zakat) amongst you.

4. *Ibn Umar* reportedly said that Hadrat Umar had a daughter named Asiya (disobedient), so The Messenger of Allah (peace & blessings of Allah be with him) changed her name to Jamila (meaning beautiful).

5. *Mohammed ibn Amr ibn Ata'* is reported to have said: I named my daughter Barrah, then Zainab bint Abu Salama told me that The Messenger of Allah (peace & blessings of Allah be with him) forbade us to use that name, as my name was Barrah, but the Apostle of Allah (peace & blessings of Allah be with him) said that she prided herself with piety in that name. So

the holy Prophet (peace & blessings of Allah be with him) changed her name to Zainab.

6. It is reported from Samurah ibn Jundab that the Messenger of Allah (peace & blessings of Allah be with him) prohibited us to give our servants these four names, Aflah (Successful), Rabbah (Profit), Yasar (Wealth), and Nafe' (Bene-ficial).

7. *Samurah ibn Jundab* is reported to have said: The most beloved words to Allah Almighty are four: Subhan Allah (Glory be to Allah), Alhamd lillah (Praise be to Allah), La ilaha illallah (there is no deity but Allah), and Allâhu Akbar (Allah is Great). There is no harm for you as to the order in which you say them." And he also said: Do not name your servants, Yasar and Rabbah and Nafe and Najih.

8. *Jabir ibn Abd Allah* is reported to have said: The Messenger of Allah (peace & blessings of Allah be with him) decided to name people as Ya'la (Elevated), Barakah (Blessing), Aflah (Successful), Yasar and Nafe', but he kept silent after that and did not say anything (regarding it) until he left for his heavenly abode. And he did not prohibit these (names), then Umar decided to prohibit the use of these names, but later on he abandoned his decision.

9. *Abu Hurayra* is reported to have narrated that the Messenger of Allah (peace & blessings of Allah be with him) said: Do not say 'Feed your lord, help your lord' when performing ablution, or 'give water to your lord', instead you should use words such as 'master' or 'guardian' (instead of lord). And do not say 'my slave' or 'my slave-girl', but say 'my boy' or 'my girl'.

10. *Mughirah ibn Shu'bah* is reported to have said: No one questioned the Messenger of Allah (peace & blessings of Allah be with him) more about the Anti-Christ than I, but he used to reply: 'My son, why are you worried because of him? He will not harm you.' I said: 'The people think that he will have rivers of water and mountains of bread with him.' At this he said: 'He will be more insigni-ficant in the sight of Allah Almighty than all these.

11. It is reported from *Abu Hurayra* that the holy Prophet (peace & blessings of Allah be with him) said: The most despised name in the Sight of Allah is a man calling himself the king of kings.

12. *Abu Hurayra* is reported to have said: I heard the Messenger of Allah (peace & blessings of Allah be with him) say: 'the rights of a Muslim upon his Mus-lim brother are, to accept his invitation and to reply the sneezer, and to follow the funeral processions.

13. It is reported that *Abu Hurayra* said: The rights of a Muslim upon the Muslims are six: to visit the sick, to accept invitations, to help the oppressed, to fulfill the oaths, to return the greeting and to reply to the sneezer and to follow the funeral procession.

14. *Abu Saeed al-Khudri* is reported to have related that the Prophet (peace & blessings of Allah be with him) said: Beware! Avoid sitting on the thorough-fares." The people said: "We have no option as we need to sit there to conduct our discussions." The Apostle of Allah (peace & blessings of Allah be with him) said: If you have to sit there, then observe the rights of the thoroughfare. They asked: What are the rights of the tho-roughfare? He said: To lower your gaze, to avoid causing harm to people, to return salutations, to enjoin the good and to forbid evil.

15. It is reported on the authority of *Abu Hurayra* that the holy Prophet (peace & blessings of Allah be with him) said: The young should greet the old, the passer by should greet the one who is seated, and the smaller group should greet the more numerous group.

16. *Abu Barda* has reported from Abu Musa Ash'ari that Abu Musa paid a visit to Umar ibn al Khattab and said: 'Peace be upon you, this is Abd Allah ibn Qais.' But he did not let him enter. Then he said: 'Peace be upon you,' and said: 'this is Abu Musa, peace be upon you. This is al Ash'ari.' Then he left. So Umar said: come back come back. So he returned and Umar said: 'O Abu Musa, what made you go away, while we were busy?' He said: 'I heard the Messenger of Allah (peace & blessings of Allah be with him) say: 'Seek permission three times. And if you are permitted, enter, otherwise go away' He (Umar) said:

'Bring a witness for that or I shall have to do so and so.' Abu Musa left and Umar said: 'If he brings a witness he should meet near the pulpit in the evening and if he does not bring a witness you will not find him there.' When it was evening he found him there. He said: 'O Abu Musa, what do you say, have you found a witness?' He said: 'Yes, Ubayy ibn Ka'b.' Ubayy said: 'Yes, he is right.' Umar said: 'O Abu Tufail, what about what this man says?' He said: 'O Ibn al Khattab, I heard the Messenger of Allah (peace & blessings of Allah be with him) say so. Do not be a burden upon the companions of the Messenger of Allah.' So he said: 'Praise be to Allah, I had heard something and I wished to verify it.

17. *Jabir ibn Abd Allah* is reported to have said: I sought permission to see the Prophet (peace & blessings of Allah be with him) so he asked: 'Who is it?' I said: 'It is I.' The Prophet (peace & blessings of Allah be with him) said: 'it is I; it is I? It was reported that he disliked that (expression).

18. *Sahl ibn Sa'ad al-Sa'di* is reported to have related that a man peeped through a hole in the house of the Messenger of Allah (peace & blessings of Allah be with him) when the Prophet (peace & blessings of Allah be with him) was combing his hair with an iron comb. The Apostle of Allah (peace & blessings of Allah be with him) said: 'If I had known you were spying I would have stabbed your eyes with it.'

Indeed, the command to seek permission to enter has been enjoined because of that, and one should not spy upon others.

19. *Abu Hurayra* is reported to have narrated that the Messenger of Allah (peace & blessings of Allah be with him) said: If anyone peeps into your house without your permission, and you throw a stone at him and put out his eyes, there is no blame on you.

20. *Jarir ibn Abd Allah* is reported to have asked the Messenger of Allah (peace & blessings of Allah be with him) about a quick glance at the face. He advised me to turn away my eyes (in that event).

21. *Abu Waqid Al Laithi* is reported to have narrated that while the Messenger of Allah (peace & blessings of Allah be with him) was sitting in the mosque with some people, three men came in. Two of them stood in front of the Prophet (peace & blessings of Allah be with him) and the third one went away. The two kept standing in front of the Prophet (peace & blessings of Allah be with him) for a while and then one of them found a place in the circle and sat there while the other sat behind the gathering and the third went away. When the Messenger of Allah (peace & blessings of Allah be with him) had finished speaking he said: Shall I tell you about these three people? One of them sought Allah, so Allah took him into His grace and mercy and accommo-dated him, the second felt shy of Allah, so Allah sheltered him in His mercy and did not punish him, while the third tur-ned his face away from Allah, so Allah turned His face away from him likewise.

22. It is reported on the authority of *Abd Allah ibn Mas'ud* that the Prophet (peace & blessings of Allah be with him) said: If you are three persons seated toge-ther, then two of you should not converse secretly from the third person until others have joined you, as that would offend him.

23. *Abu Hurayra* is reported to have related that the Messenger of Allah (peace & blessings of Allah be with him) said: Do not initiate a greeting to a Jew or Christian, and if you meet one of them on a way, force him to its narrowest place.

24. *Jabir ibn Abd Allah* is reported to have narrated that some Jews greeted the Messenger of Allah (peace & blessings of Allah be with him) saying: 'Al Sam (death be) upon you O Abu-l-Qasim.' So he replied: 'And upon you.' Ayesha got very angry and said: 'Have you not heard what they said?' He said: 'Yes, and I replied to them and our invocation against them is accepted but theirs will never be.

25. *Hadrat Ayesha* is reported to have related that the wives of the Prophet (peace & blessings of Allah be with him) used to go out at night to Al-Manas'a, a vast open place near Medina, to answer the call of nature. Umar used to say to the Prophet (peace & blessings of Allah be with

him) Order your wives to wear the veil. But The Messenger of Allah (peace & blessings of Allah be with him) did not do so. One night Sauda bint Zam'a, she wife of the Prophet (peace & blessings of Allah be with him) went out around the time of the evening prayer and she was a tall lady. Umar recognized her and said: "I have recognized you, O Sauda!" He said so in the hope that God might reveal a commandment regarding she veil. So God revealed the verses of the veil.

26. *Hadrat Ayesha* is reported to have related that Sauda went out to answer the call of nature after the veil was made obligatory. She was a large fat lady and everyone who knew her before could recognize her. So Umar ibn al khattab saw her and said: 'O Sauda! By God, you cannot hide yourself from us, so think of a way by which you should not be recog-nized by us when you go out. Sauda returned while the Messenger of Allah (peace & blessings of Allah be with him) was in the house taking his supper and bone of meat was in his hand. She entered and said: 'O Messenger of Allah! I went to answer the call of nature and Umar said so and so to me." Then Allah inspired him and when that state was over, the bone was sill in his hand and he said: 'You women have been permitted to go out for your needs'

27. *Safiya bint Huyyi* is reported to have related: I visited the Apostle of Allah (peace & blessings of Allah be with him) while he was in seclusion in the mosque during the last ten days of Ramadan. I spoke with him for a while and then got up to return home. The holy Prophet (peace & blessings of Allah be with him) came with me and when we reached the gate of the mosque opposite the door of Umm Salama, two men from the Ansars were passing by and they greeted the Messenger of Allah. He said to them: 'Do not run away, she is my wife Safiya bint Huyyi.' They both said: 'Glory be to Allah, O Messenger of Allah, we did not think any evil.' The Prophet (peace & blessings of Allah be with him) told them: 'Satan reaches everywhere in the body of mankind just as the blood reaches everywhere in it, I feared Satan might cast an evil thought into your minds'

28. *Jabir* is said to have reported that the Messenger of Allah (peace & blessings of Allah be with him) said: A man should not spend the night (in the dwelling of) a married woman except if he is the husband or a Mahram.

29. *Uqba ibn Amer* is said to have reported that the Messenger of Allah (peace & blessings of Allah be with him) said: Beware do not enter (the dwellings) of the ladies. A man from the Ansars asked: 'O Messenger of Allah! What about the wife's in-laws?' The Prophet (peace & blessings of Allah be with him) said: the in-laws are death to the wife.

30. *Abd Allah ibn Amr ibn Al As* is

reported to have narrated that some people from Bani Hashim paid a visit to visit Asma' bint Amis while she was married to Abu Bakr al Siddiq and he came in and saw them and disliked that. He mentioned it to the Messenger of Allah (peace & blessings of Allah be with him) and said: 'I did not see anything wrong.' The Messenger of Allah (peace & blessings of Allah be with him) said: 'God has purified her from that.' Then the Apostle of Allah (peace & blessings of Allah be with him) went up the pulpit and said: From this day on, no man should visit a woman while her husband is absent except if he has with him another man or two other men.

31. *Hadrat Ayesha* is reported to have said: An effeminate man used to (come to) see the wives of the Prophet (peace & blessings of Allah be with him), and they used to consider him as one who has no sexuality. He said: 'One day The Prophet (peace & blessings of Allah be with him) came while he was with some of his wives, and he was describing a woman to them, he said: 'She shows four rings of flesh when she faces you and eight when she turns away.' The Prophet (peace & blessings of Allah be with him) said: 'Do I not see that he knows all that, such men should not enter (your house). She said: so he was banned.

32. *Abu Musa* is reported to have related that a house in Medina was burnt down at night along with its occupants. The Prophet (peace & blessings of Allah be with him) said: The fire is indeed your enemy; so whenever you go to bed, put it off to protect yourselves.'

33. *Al Mughirah ibn Shu'bah* is reported to have related that when he came to Najran the Christians of Najran asked him: You recite 'O sister of Aaron' in the Qur'an, while Moses was born long before Jesus. When I visited the Messenger of Allah (peace & blessings of Allah be with him) I asked him about it and he said: 'People of the past used to name themselves after the Messengers and pious persons who had lived before them.

34. *Abu Musa* is reported to have said: I had a son and I took him to The Prophet (peace & blessings of Allah be with him) who named him Ibrahim, and he put the chewed juice of a fresh date into his mouth.

35. *Anas* is reported to have related that when the Messenger of Allah happe-ned to pass by young children he would greet them.

42

Book of Healing

1. *Hadrat Ayesha* is reported to have said: Whenever The Messenger of Allah (peace & blessings of Allah be with him) suffered an ailment, Gabriel (peace be upon him), used to perform Ruqya upon him, saying: 'In the Name of God, He relieves you from every ailment, and from the evil of every envier when he envies, and from the evil of every eye.

2. *Abu Saeed* is reported to have said: Gabriel (peace be upon him) came to the Prophet (peace & blessings of Allah be with him) and said: 'O Muhammad, are you suffering?' He said: 'Yes.' Gabriel said: 'In the Name of God, I perform Ruqya upon you from everything that harms you and from the evil of every soul, or from every envying eye. God relieve you in the Name of God, I perform Ruqya upon you.

3. *Hadrat Ayesha* is reported to have said: Labid ibn al A'sam of the tribe of Bani Zaraiq worked magic on the Messenger of Allah (peace & blessings of Allah be with him) until he began to imagine he had done a thing that he had not really done.

One day, or one night when he was with us he prayed for a long while, and then said: 'O Ayesha! Do you know that God has directed me concer-ning the matter I have asked him about? Two men visited me; one of them sat near my head and the other near my feet. One asked the other: 'what is this man's malady?" The other replied: 'He is suffe-ring from magic.' The first one asked: 'Who has done magic upon him?' The other replied: 'Labid ibn Al A'sam.' The first one asked: 'What did he use for it?' The other replied: 'A comb with hair in it and the pollen skin of a male date palm.' The first one asked: 'Where is it?' The other replied: 'In the well of Dharwan.' So The Messenger of Allah (peace & blessings of Allah be with him) together with some of his companions went there and after returning said: 'O Ayesha, the color of its water is like an infusion of Henna leaves and the tops of the date palm trees near it are like the heads of the devils.' I asked: 'O Messenger of Allah, why did you not display it?' He said: 'Since

Allah has cured me, I did not wish to let evil spread among the people.' Then he had the well filled with sand.

4. *Hadrat Ayesha* is reported to have said: Whenever a wife of The Messenger of Allah (peace & blessings of Allah be with him) fell ill, he used to recite Surah Al-Falaq and Surah Al-Nas and then blow his breath over her body. When he became seriously ill, I used to recite the same and rub his hands over his body in the hope of its blessings.

5. *Uthman ibn Abu Al As Al Thaqafi* is reported to have said: When I became Muslim, I complained to The Messenger of Allah (peace & blessings of Allah be with him) of pain in my body. So the Prophet (peace & blessings of Allah be with him) said: 'Put your hand where you feel the pain and say 'In the name of Allah' three times and say 'I seek refuge in Allah and in His Power from the evil I find and the evil I fear' seven times.

6. It was related that *Uthman ibn Abu Al As* said: "I went to The Messenger of God (prayers & peace be upon him) and said: 'O Messenger of God, Satan disturbs my prayer and my recitation of the Qur'an and confuses me.' The Messenger of God (prayers & peace be upon him) said: 'That is the work of he who is known as Khinzab, and when you feel it, seek refuge in God from it three times and spit three times to your left side.' I did so and

God warded it away from me."

7. *Abu Saeed Al Khudri* is reported to have narrated that the companions of the Messenger of Allah (peace & blessings of Allah be with him) set out on a journey until they reached one of the Arab tribes. They expected hospitality but were refused. The leader of the tribe was bitten by a snake or stung by a scorpion and they tried to cure him without success. Then they came to the Companions and said: 'Our leader has been bitten by a snake or stung by a scorpion and we have tried everything without success. Have you anything?' One of them said: 'yes, by God! I can heal him with a Ruqya, but by God! Since we sought your hospitality and you refused, I will not do so until you agree to give something for it in return.' So they agreed to give them a flock of sheep, and he performed the Ruqya and read: 'All praise be to Allah the Lord of the Worlds,' then the leader was imme-diately healed and he stood up as if he had never been ill and said: 'Pay them what you agreed to pay them.' Some of them said: 'Let us divide it between ourselves.' So the one who performed the Ruqya said: 'Do not do so until we reach the Prophet (Prayers & peace be upon him) and tell him what happened, then we shall see what he orders us to do.' So when they arrived and informed him of the matter he said: Who told you that it was Ruqya?' Then he said: 'you were right, divide and make a share for me as well.

Then The Messenger of Allah (peace & blessings of Allah be with him) smiled.

8. *Jabir* is reported to have said: The Messenger of Allah (peace & blessings of Allah be with him) prohibited invoca-tions. Then the kinfolk of Amr ibn Hazem paid a visit to The Prophet (peace & blessings of Allah be with him) and said: 'We know an invocation which we used to cure the scorpion sting but you have prohibited it.' They repeated the words to him and he said: I see no harm in that, so whoever of you is able to do good to his brother should do so.

9. *Abu Hurayra* is reported to have narrated that a man came to The Prophet (peace & blessings of Allah be with him) and said: 'O Messenger of Allah! Last night a scorpion stung me, the Prophet replied: If you say in the evening: 'I seek refuge in the complete words of Allah from the evil of what He has created,' nothing will harm you.

10. *Ibn Abbas* is reported to have said that the Messenger of Allah (peace & blessings of Allah be with him) said: The effect of the evil eye is true, if anything were to alter destiny it would be the evil eye, and when you are told to bathe from the effect of an evil eye, you should do so.

11. *Jabir ibn Abd Allah* is reported to have said: The Messenger of Allah (peace & blessings of Allah be with him) permitted the family of Hazem to use invocations for snakebite, and he said to Asma' bint Umais: 'Why do I see the children of my brother so thin, are they under-nourished?' She said: 'No, but they are suffering from the effect of an evil eye.' He said: 'Use invocation.' She recited it and he said: 'yes, use this invocation for them.

12. *Umm Salama* is reported to have related that the Messenger of Allah (peace & blessings of Allah be with him) saw a girl in her house whose face had a black spot. He said: 'She has been harmed by an evil eye so treat her by reciting verses of the Qur'an.

13. It is reported that *Hadrat Ayesha* said: The Messenger of Allah (peace & blessings of Allah be with him) used to recite: In the Name of Allah.' The earth of our land and the saliva of one of us may cure an unwell person by the permission of our Lord.

14. It is reported from *Khaula bint Hakim al Sulmiya* that she heard the Messenger of Allah (peace & blessings of Allah be with him) say: Whoever stays in a different place and then says: 'I seek refuge in the complete words of Allah from the evil of what He has created,' nothing will harm him until he leaves that place.

15. *Hadrat Ayesha* is reported to have said: Whenever the Messenger of Allah (peace & blessings of Allah be with him) wished to treat some of

his wives by passing his right hand over the place of ailment, he used to say: 'Remove the affliction, O Lord of the people! Cure her, as You are the One Who Cures. There is no cure except Your cure which leaves no ailment.'

16. It is reported on the authority of *Hadrat Ayesha* that whenever the Messenger of Allah (peace & blessings of Allah be with him) visited an unwell person, or some sick person was brought to him, he used to invoke God and say: 'Remove the affliction, O Lord of the people! Cure him as You are the One Who Cures. There is no cure except Your cure which leaves no ailment.'

43

Book of
Illness and Medicine

1. *Jabir* is reported to have related that the Messenger of Allah (peace & blessings of Allah be with him) said: For every ailment is a cure. If the remedy is correct the ailment will be cured by the leave of God Almighty.

2. *Abd Allah ibn Mas'ud* is reported to have related that he visited the Prophet (peace & blessings of Allah be with him) when he was ill and he suffered greatly. Abd Allah said: 'You are suffering grea-tly, is this because you will have a double reward?' The Apostle of Allah replied: 'Yes, no Muslim is afflicted with any harm but Allah will drop his sins like the leaves drop from a tree'

3. *Thauban* is reported to have quoted the Prophet (peace & blessings of Allah be with him) as having said: When a Muslim visits his sick Muslim brother; he will remain in a garden of Paradise until he returns.

4. *Abu Hurayra* is reported to have narrated that the Messenger of Allah (peace & blessings of Allah be with him) said: On the Day of Judgment God Almi-ghty will say:

'O son of Adam, I was ill and you did not visit me.' So he will say: 'O my Lord, how would I visit You while You are the Lord of the Worlds?' He will say: 'Did you not know that My servant so and so was ill, and you did not visit him? Did you not know that if you visited him you would find Me with him? O son of Adam! I asked you for food and you did not feed Me.' He will say: 'O my Lord, how would I feed You while You are The Lord of the Worlds?' He will say: 'did you not know that when My servant so and so asked you for food and you did not feed him? Did you not know that if you had fed him you would have found Me with him? O son of Adam! I asked you for a drink but you did not give Me to drink.' He will say: 'O my Lord, how would I give You to drink while You are The Lord of the Worlds?' He will say: 'My servant so and so asked you for a drink and you did not give him to drink, if you had given him to drink, you would have found Me with him.

5. It was related that Asma' used to invoke God and then sprinkle water

over herself upon her chest saying: 'The Messenger of Allah (peace & blessings of Allah be with him) told us to douse the fever with water.

6. *Jabir ibn Abd Allah* is reported to have related that the Messenger of Allah (peace & blessings of Allah be with him). 'Do not insult the fever, for it removes the sins of the son of Adam as the bellows remove the dross from the iron.

7. *Ibn Abbas* is reported to have related that a black woman went to the Prophet (peace & blessings of Allah be with him) and said: 'I suffer from epilepsy and my body becomes uncovered, so please invoke God for me.' The Apostle of Allah (peace & blessings of Allah be with him) said to her: 'you may endure it and enter Paradise or if you wish I will invoke God to cure you." She said: 'I will endure it.'

8. It is reported from *Hadrat Ayesha* that the Messenger of Allah (peace & blessings of Allah be with him) said: The cooked flour and honey comforts the heart of the infirm and takes away some of the sadness.

9. *Abu Saeed* is reported to have related that a man visited the Apostle of Allah (peace & blessings of Allah be with him) and said: 'My brother has an ailment in his stomach.' The Prophet (peace & blessings of Allah be with him) said: 'Let him drink honey.' The man came back to the Prophet (peace & bles-sings of Allah be with him) and he told him a second time: 'Let him drink honey.'

He came back a third time and the Pro-phet (peace & blessings of Allah be with him) again said: 'Let him drink honey.' He came back once again and said: 'I have done as you said.' The Prophet (peace & blessings of Allah be with him) said: 'God has spoken the truth, but your brother's stomach has lied. Let him drink honey.' So he made him drink honey until he was cured.

10. *Abu Hurayra* is reported to have heard the Prophet (peace & blessings of Allah be with him) say: This black seed is a cure for everything except Al Saam.' Ayesha asked: 'What is Al Saam?' He said: 'Death'.

11. It is reported that *Sa'ad ibn Abu Waqqas* said that The Messenger of Allah (peace & blessings of Allah be with him) said: The one who eats seven squashed dates every morning then no poison nor magic can harm him that day.

12. *Hadrat Ayesha* is reported to have related that the Messenger of Allah (peace & blessings of Allah be with him) said: "Indeed, there is a remedy in the squashed dates taken from the date palms of the heights, and it is a healing for all poisons.

44

Book of Plague

1. *Usama ibn Zayed* is reported to have said that The Messenger of Allah (peace & blessings of Allah be with him) said: The plague is a punishment, some communities before you were punished by it. Then it remained on the earth, and it returns from time to time. Whoever hears of it in a land, he should not go there, and if it occurs in the land where he is, he should not flee from it.

2. *Abd Allah ibn Abbas* is reported to have narrated that Umar ibn Al Khattab left for al Sham and when he reached Sargh, the commanders of the (Muslim) army, Abu Ubaida ibn al Jarrah and his companions met him and told him that an epidemic had broken out in al Sham. Umar then summoned the first Muhajirin and consulted them and told them that an epidemic had broken out in al Sham. They differed amongst themselves, some of them said: 'You have set out for a purpose and we do not think that it is proper to give it up.' Others said: 'You have other people with you and the companions of the Messenger of Allah, so do not advise us to take them into this epidemic.' Umar said to them: 'Leave me now.' Then he called the Ansars and he consulted them and they did as the Muhajirin had done and differed amongst them. Then he said to them: 'Leave me now,' and summoned the aged people of Quraysh and they all agreed saying: 'We advise that you return with the people and do not take them to the epidemic.' So Umar announced to the people: 'I will ride back to Medina in the morning, and you should do likewise.' Abu Ubaida ibn Al Jarrah asked: 'Are you fleeing from God's fate?' Umar said: 'If only someone else had said such a thing, O Abu Ubaida! - Yes, we are flee-ing from the fate of God to the fate of God. Do you see that if you had camels that descended into a valley in which there was a height at each end, one lush and the other arid, is it not that if you grazed them in the lush one it would be by God's fate, and if you grazed them in the arid one it would be by God's fate?" At that moment Abd al Rahman ibn Auf, who was not there at that time,

arrived and said: 'I have some knowledge concer-ning this matter, I have heard The Mes-senger of Allah (peace & blessings of Allah be with him) say: 'If you hear of a plague in a land, do not go to it, but if a plague breaks out in the land where you are, do not flee from it. He said: 'Then Umar thanked Allah and returned.

45

Book of Warnings of Diseases

1. *Ibn Shihab* is reported to have said that Abu Salama ibn Abd Al Rahman ibn Auf told him that the Messenger of Allah (peace & blessings of Allah be with him) said: There is no contagious disease. And he said that the Apostle of Allah (peace & blessings of Allah be with him) said: Do not put a sick person with a healthy per-son. Abu Salama said that Abu Hurayra related both as from the Messen-ger of Allah, then he ceased saying: There is no contagious disease, but continued saying: Do not put a sick person with a healthy person. Then Abu Hurayra was asked: we used to hear you relating another Hadith with this but you ceased relating it. You used to say: " The Messenger of Allah (peace & blessings of Allah be with him) said: "No contagious disease." Abu Hurayra said: 'The Prophet (peace & bles-sings of Allah be with him) said: Do not put a sick person with a healthy person.

2. *Al Sharid* is reported to have narrated that a delegation of Thaqif came and among them was a leper, so the Prophet (peace & blessings of Allah be with him) sent for him and said: 'We have acknowledged you so return back.'

3. *Abu Hurayra* reported that the Prophet (peace & blessings of Allah be with him) said: There is no bird of evil omen and the best portent is the Fa'l.' It was asked: 'what is the Fa'l, O Messenger of Allah?' He said: 'it is the good word that any of you hears."

4. *Ibn Umar* reported that the Prophet (peace & blessings of Allah be with him) said: If there is any evil portent, it is only in three; a horse, a woman and a house.

5. *Jabir ibn Abd Allah* reported that the Messenger of Allah (peace & blessings of Allah be with him) said: If there is any evil portent, it is in the house, the servant and the horse.

46

Book of Fortune Telling

1. *Safiya bint Abu Ubaid* is reported to have related that some of the wives of The Prophet (prayers & peace be upon him) said that the Prophet (peace & bles-sings of Allah be with him) Whoever brings a fortune teller and asks him for anything, his prayer will not be accepted for forty nights.

2. *Hadrat Ayesha* is reported to have said: Some people asked the Messenger of Allah (peace & blessings of Allah be with him) about fortu-netellers. So the Prophet (peace & blessings of Allah be with him) said: 'They are nothing.' They said: 'O Messenger of Allah, they some-times tell you something which turns out to be true.' The Apostle of Allah said: 'the word that turns out to be true was snat-ched by Jinn and poured it into the ears of his ally repeatedly clucking it like a hen. Then they add to it more than one hundred lies.

3. *Abd Allah ibn Abbas* is reported to have said: A man of the Ansars who was from the companions of the Prophet (peace & blessings of Allah be with him) said that one night while they sat with the Messenger of Allah (peace & blessings of Allah be with him) they saw a shooting star with a flame of fire, so the Prophet (peace & blessings of Allah be with him) asked them: 'What did you say about this before Islam?' They said: 'Allah and His Messenger know, but we used to say; 'Tonight a great man has been born and a great man has died.' Then the Messen-ger of Allah (peace & blessings of Allah be with him) said: 'The stars are not cast on account of the birth or death of any one, but when our Lord, Blessed High Exalted be His Name, decrees a matter the bearers of His Throne give praise to Him, then the people of the heavens follow them in prai-sing until the praise reaches the people of the lowest heaven, then those who nearest to the bearers of the Throne ask the bearers of the Throne; 'What has your Lord said?' They will tell them what He has said, and then the dwellers of the heavens ask each other until the news reaches the lowest heaven. There the Jinn snatch a word or two and cast it to their allies, so what they snatch is the truth but they add falsehood to it.

47

Book of Snakes and Other Things

1. The holy Prophet was asked: "O Messenger of Allah! Is there a reward for us in serving animals?" The Apostle of Allah replied: "Yes, there is a reward for serving every living thing.

2. *Ibn Umar* is reported to have said that he heard the Messenger of Allah (peace & blessings of Allah be with him) order the killing of dogs saying: Kill the dogs and kill the snakes and kill the one with two white marks on its back and the one with a stunted tail, as they blind the sight and induce abortion. Abd Allah ibn Umar said: 'Ever since that time I kill any snake I see. One day while I was chasing a snake of the type that live inside the houses, Zayed Ibn al Khattab passed me by- or Abu Lubaba, and said: 'O Abd Allah, wait.' I said: 'The Messenger of Allah (peace & blessings of Allah be with him) ordered us to kill the snakes.' He said: 'The Messenger of Allah (peace & blessings of Allah be with him) prohibited the killing of snakes that live inside the houses.

3. *Abu Sa'b ibn Hisham ibn Zuhrah,* said that he visited Abu Saeed al-Khudri at his house and found him praying, so he sat waiting for him until he completed his prayer. Abu Sa'b heard something moving between the date staves inside his house, so he looked and found a snake and tried to kill it but Abu Saeed indi-cated to him to sit down, and so he sat. When he finished he took him to the middle of his house and said: 'Do you see this house?' I said: 'Yes.' He said: 'There used to be one of our young men here who had just married, we went with the Messenger of Allah (prayers & peace be upon him) to the (battle of the) Trench and that young man used to seek the per-mission of the Messenger of Allah (peace & blessings of Allah be with him) to return to see his wife every midday. One day he sought permission and the Apostle of Allah (peace & blessings of Allah be with him) said to him: 'Take your wea-pons with you as I fear for you from Quraiza.' The man took his weapons and returned and he found his wife standing at the gate, so he felt

jealous and tried to stab her with a spear. But she told him: 'Keep your spear away from me and come to the house to see what made me go out.' So he went in and found a huge snake that had coiled itself upon their bed. He stabbed it with the spear and the spear pierced through it and he took it out to the middle of the house and the snake turned towards him, and until now we do not know which of them died faster, the snake or the young man.' He said: 'so we went to the Messenger of Allah (peace & blessings of Allah be with him) and told him about it and asked him to pray to God to revive him, so he said: 'Seek forgiveness for your companion.' Then he said: 'There are in Medina, jinn who have become Muslim, so if you see any of them, warn it to leave within three days, and if it is seen after that, then kill it, because it will be a Satan.'

4.   *Abd Allah ibn Mas'ud* is reported to have related that: We were with The Prophet (peace & blessings of Allah be with him) in a cave when Surah al -Mura-salat was revealed. As we were listening to the first recitation of it, a snake came out at us. Then he said: 'Kill it.' We mo-ved to kill it and it slid away and escaped from us, so the Messenger of Allah (peace & blessings of Allah be with him) said: God has protected it from your harm as He has protected you from its harm.

5.   *Abu Hurayra* is reported to have

related that the Prophet (peace & bles-sings of Allah be with him) said: One of the prophets was resting beneath a tree when an ant bit him. So he ordered for his baggage to be removed from under it and then ordered it to be burnt. Then God Almighty revealed to him: 'would one ant not have been sufficient?

6.   *Abd Allah ibn Umar* is reported to have narrated that the Messenger of Allah (peace & blessings of Allah be with him) said: A woman was tortured and cast into Hell because of a cat she had kept locked up until it died of hunger. She did not feed it nor give it water when she locked it up, nor did she set it free to eat from the creatures of the earth.

7.   It is reported from *Abu Hurayra* that the Apostle of Allah (peace & bles-sings of Allah be with him) said: Some of the Children of Israel were lost. Nobody knows what they did. But I do not see other than they were cursed and changed into rats, do you not see that if you put the milk of a she camel in front of a rat, it will not drink it, but if you put the milk of a sheep in front of it, it will drink it." Abu Hurayra said: I told Ka'b of this Hadith and he asked me: 'Did you hear it from the Messenger of Allah?' I said: 'Yes.' Ka'b kept repeating the question so I said: 'Do I read the Torah?' or he said: 'was the Torah revealed to me?

8.   It is reported from *Abu Hurayra* that the Messenger of Allah (peace &

blessings of Allah be with him) said: While a man was walking he felt thirsty and went down a well and drank water from it. On coming out of it, he saw a dog panting and eating mud due to excessive thirst. The man said: 'It is suffering as I was suffering.' So he went down again and filled his shoe with water, holding it with his teeth and climbed up and gave the dog to drink. God thanked him for his deed and forgave him. The people asked: "O Messenger of Allah! Is there a reward for us in serving animals?" He replied: "Yes, there is a reward for serving every living thing.

48

Book of Poetry

1. *Al- Sharid* is reported to have said: One day as I rode behind the Messenger of Allah, (peace & blessings of Allah be with him) he said: 'Do you remember any of Umayyah ibn Abu Al Salut's poetry?' I said: 'Yes.' He said: 'Then go on.' I recited two stanzas and he said: 'Carry on.' So I recited another two stanzas and he said: 'Carry on.' Until I recited one hundred couplets of rhyme.

2. *Abu Hurayra* is reported to have related that the Messenger of Allah (peace & blessings of Allah be with him) said: The truest word that has been uttered by a poet is the word of Labid (an Arab poet during the times of the holy Prophet): 'everything other than Allah is falsehood.

3. *Sa'ad ibn Abu Waqqas* is reported to have related that the Prophet (peace & blessings of Allah be with him) said: It is better for the belly of any of you to be filled with pus rather than to fill his head with poetry.

4. *Hammam ibn al-Harith* is reported to have narrated that a man praised Uthman, so Al Miqdad, who was a very huge man, threw sand into his face. Uthman asked him: 'What is the matter with you?' He replied I heard the Messenger of Allah (peace & blessings of Allah be with him) say: When you hear someone praising another then throw dust into the face of the one who praises him.

5. *Abu Bakra* is reported to have related that someone spoke about a man and praised him excessively in the pre-sence of the Prophet (peace & blessings of Allah be with him). The Apostle of Allah said: 'May God have Mercy upon you! You have cut the neck of your friend.' He repeated this several times and said: 'If you have to praise someone then say: 'I think he is so and so,' if he really thinks that he is such a person. Allah will bring him to account and no one can exalt anyone else before Allah.'

6. *Buraida* is reported to have related on the authority of his father that the Apostle of Allah (peace & blessings of Allah be with him) said: The one who plays chess is like one

who stained his hand with the flesh and blood of swine.

7. *Abu Saeed Khudri* reported: we were going with the Messenger of Allah (peace & blessings of Allah be with him) and as we reached a place called Arj there we came across a poet who was reciting poetry. Thereupon the Apostle of Allah (peace & blessings of Allah be with him) said: catch (or detain) the Satan, for filling the belly of a man with puss is better than stuffing his brain with poetry.

49

Book of Visions

1. The holy Prophet is reported by *Abu Qatada* to have said: A good vision comes from Allah and a (bad) dream from devil.

2. *Anas ibn Malik* is reported to have related that the Messenger of Allah (peace & blessings of Allah be with him) said: In the night I saw that a person sees while sleeping as if we were in the house of Uqba ibn Rafi' where we were offered the fresh dates of Ibn Tab. I interpreted it as meaning our elevation in this life and good in the Hereafter and that our religion is good.

3. *Abu Musa al-Ash'ari* reported that the Prophet (peace & blessings of Allah be with him) said: I saw in a dream that I was migrating from Makka to a land where there were date palm trees. I thought that it might be the land of Al Yamama or Hajar, but it turned out to be Medina. And I saw cattle there, but the reward given by Allah is best. Then the cattle turned out to symbolize the believers on the Day of Uhud, and the good I had seen was the good and the reward and the truth that Allah granted to us after the Battle of Badr.

4. *Ibn Abbas* has related that Musailama, the Liar came to Medina with a band of his people during the lifetime of the Prophet (peace & blessings of Allah be with him), and proclaimed: 'If Muham-mad appoints me as his succes-sor, if will follow him.' So the Prophet (peace & blessings of Allah be with him) went to him with Thabit ibn Qais ibn Shams, carrying a piece of the stalk of a palm leaf. He confronted him while he sat among his band and said to him: 'if you ask me for this piece, I would not give it to you, and I will not exceed the limits of God regarding you. If you reject, God will destroy you, and I see that which I have been shown about you, and this is Thabit who will respond to you on my behalf.' Thereafter the Prophet (peace & blessings of Allah be with him) left. Ibn Abbas said: 'I asked about the Prophet's words: 'I see that which I have been shown about you.' So Abu Hurayra told me that the Prophet (peace & blessings of Allah be with him) said: 'While I

was sleeping I saw two gold bracelets upon my hands and I was worried about them, so it was revealed to me as I slept, 'Blow them away.' So I blew them away and they both disappeared. I interpreted it to signify that two liars will come after me -al Ansi of Sana'a and Musailama of Yamama.

5. It is reported that Abu Hurayra said: I heard the Messenger of Allah (peace & blessings of Allah be with him) say: Whoever sees me in a vision will see me in reality, and Satan cannot imper-sonate me. Abu Salama and Abu Qatada said that the Apostle of Allah (peace & blessings of Allah be with him) said: Whoever sees me in a vision then he has indeed seen me.

6. *Abu Salama* related that according to Abu Qatada the Messenger of Allah (peace & blessings of Allah be with him) said: A vision that comes true is from Allah, and a bad dream is from Satan, so if anyone of you sees a bad dream, he should seek refuge with Allah from Satan and should spit to his left, so the bad dream will not harm him. He also said: I used to see a bad dream as heavy as a mountain, until I heard this Hadith, then I did not worry after that.

7. *Abu Salama* is reported to have said: I used to see a dream which made me sick until I met Abu Qatada and he said: 'I also used to see a dream which made me sick until I heard the Messenger of Allah (peace & blessings of Allah be with him) say:

'A vision is from Allah, so if anyone of you sees a vision he likes, he should not speak of it to anyone except to those he loves, and if he sees a dream he dislikes, then he should seek refuge with Allah from its evil and from the evil of Satan, and spit three times to his left side and should not speak of it to anyone, so it will not harm him.

8. *Jabir* is reported to have related that the Messenger of Allah (peace & blessings of Allah be with him) said: If anyone of you sees a bad dream which he dislikes, he should spit to his left three times and he should seek refuge with Allah from Satan three times, and turn over to his other side.

9. *Ubada ibn Al Samit* is reported to have related that the Messenger of Allah (peace & blessings of Allah be with him) said: The vision of a believer is one of the forty-six parts of the Prophetic traits.

10. *Ibn Umar* reported that the Mes-senger of Allah (peace & blessings of Allah be with him) said: The good vision is one of the seventy parts of the Pro-phetic traits.

11. *Abu Hurayra* is reported to have related that the Prophet (peace & bles-sings of Allah be with him) said: When the (final) Hour draws near, the visions of a Muslim will almost always come true, and the most truthful one of you will have the most true visions, and a vision of a Muslim is one of the forty-five parts of Prophecy. The dreams are three: The good vision is glad tidings from

Allah, or what is suggested by Satan to frighten the dreamer, or the reflection of what is in one's mind, So, if any of you sees what he dislikes, he should not speak of it to others, but offer a prayer.

12. *Ibn Abbas* is reported to have narrated that a man came to the Messen-ger of Allah (peace & blessings of Allah be with him) and said: 'I saw a dream in which there was cloud giving shade, butter and honey were dropping from it and I saw the people collecting it with their hands, some took a little and some took much. And then a rope extended from the earth to the sky, and I saw you take hold of it and go up, and then another man held it and went up, and then another man held it and went up and then a fourth man held it and it broke and was then rejoined.' Abu Bakr said: O Messenger of Allah! Permit me to interpret this dream. The holy Prophet (peace & blessings of Allah be with him) said: "Interpret it." Abu Bakr said: "The cloud giving shade is Islam, and the butter and honey dropping from it is the Qur'an with its sweetness dropping and some people learn much of it and some people learn little. The rope extended from the earth to the sky is the Truth which you follow and Allah will raise you high with it, then another man will follow it and will rise up with it and another will follow it and then another man will follow it but it will break and then be rejoined for him and he will rise up with it. O Messenger of Allah! Am I correct?' The Prophet (peace & blessings of Allah be with him) said: 'You are correct in part and wrong in part.' Abu Bakr said: 'By God, tell me where I was wrong?' The Prophet (Prayers & peace be upon him) said: 'Do not swear.'

13. *Jabir ibn Abd Allah* reported that a bedouin came to the Prophet (peace & blessings of Allah be with him) said: 'O Messenger of Allah! I have seen a dream that my head was severed and rolled off, so I ran after it.' The Apostle of Allah (peace & blessings of Allah be with him) said: 'Do not speak to the people about what Satan plays in your mind when you sleep.' He said: 'I heard The Prophet (prayers & peace be upon him) addres-sing the people saying: 'none of you should speak about what Satan plays in his mind when he sleeps.

50

Book of Merits

1. *Wathila ibn al-Asqa'* is reported to have said that he heard the Messenger of Allah (peace & blessings of Allah be with him) say: 'Verily Allah Most High gran-ted eminence to Kinana from the descendants of Ishmael and He made the Quray-sh eminent amongst Kinana and He granted eminence to the Quraysh from Bani Hashim and He chose me from Bani Hashim.

2. *Abu Hurayra* has related that the Messenger of Allah (peace & blessings of Allah be with him) said: I shall be the foremost of the descendants of Adam on the Day of Resurrection and I will be the first to intercede and the first whose intercession will be accepted (by Allah).

3. *Abu Musa al-Ash'ari* has related that the holy Prophet (peace & blessings of Allah be with him) said: The example of guidance and know-ledge with which God has sent me is like abundant rain falling on the earth, some of which Was fertile soil that absorbed rainwater and brou-ght forth vegetation and grass in abundance. Another portion of it was hard and held the rainwater and Allah benefited the people with it and they utilized it for drinking, making their animals drink from it and for irrigation of the land and cultivation. A portion of it was barren which could neither hold the water nor bring forth vegetation. The first is an example of the person who compre-hends God's Religion and gets benefit from the knowledge that God has revea-led through me; and the second an example of a person who learns and then teaches others. The last example is that of a person who does not care for it and does not take God's guidance revealed through me.

4. *Abu Musa* reported that the Prophet (peace & blessings of Allah be with him) said: My position and the position of the message with which Allah has sent me is as that of a man who came to his people and said: 'O my people! I have seen the enemy in ranks with my own eyes, and I am but a Warner to you, so save yourselves!' Some of them believed his words and left at night in secrecy and were safe, while

Sahih Muslim — 274

others did not believe him and then the army overtook them in the morning and they perished. Thus the similarity of the one who obeys me and follows that with which I have been sent and the likeness of the one who disobeys me and rejects the Truth with which I have come.

5. It is reported from *Abu Hurayra* that the Messenger of Allah (peace & blessings of Allah be with him) said: My position as compared to other prophets before me is like that of a man who const-ructed a house perfectly except for one brick in the corner. The people look at it and marvel at its beauty and say: 'If only that brick was put in its place!' So I am that brick, and I am the final Prophet.

6. *Jabir ibn Samura* reported that the Messenger of Allah (peace & blessings of Allah be with him) said: I know a stone in Makka that used to greet me before I was sent, and I still know it now.

7. *Anas ibn Malik* has related that he saw the holy Prophet (peace & blessings of Allah be with him) and his companions at al- Zawra, a place near the market in Medina where the Mosque is situated, he asked for a pot of water. He put his hand into the pot and asked the people to per-form ablution from it. I saw the water rushing out from beneath his fingers and all his companions performed their ablution. I asked: 'O Abu Hamza, how many were they?' He said: 'They were about three hundred.'

8. *Muaz ibn Jabir* is reported to have related: We set out with the Messenger of Allah (peace & blessings of Allah be with him) in the year of the Battle of Tabuk, and he used to perform the prayers toge-ther, so he prayed the noon prayer and the afternoon prayer together, and the sun set prayer and the evening prayer together. Another day he delayed the prayer, then he came out and prayed the noon prayer and the afternoon prayer together, then he went in and came back out and prayed the sun set prayer and the evening prayer together, then said: 'Tomorrow, God willing, you will reach at the spring of Tabuk, but you will not reach there until late morning. So who-ever reaches there should not touch its water until I have arrived.' So we arrived there and two men reached it before us, and the spring is just like a shoestring, its water issuing in small amounts. The Messenger of Allah (peace & blessings of Allah be with him) asked them both: 'Have you touched any of its water?' They said: 'Yes.' So the Prophet rebuked them. He said: 'then they scooped up water with their hands from the spring little by little, until they had collected some in a pot. The Apostle of Allah (pe-ace & blessings of Allah be with him) washed his hands and face, and poured the water back into the spring, then the spring gushed forth with abundant water.

9. *Jabir* is reported to have related that a man came to the Prophet (peace &

blessings of Allah be with him) and asked him for some food, so he gave him a half measure of barley. The man and his wife and his guest ate from it until they had satisfied their hunger. Then he came to the Prophet, so he said: 'had you not stopped eating from it, it would have continued to provide for you.

10. *Jabir ibn Abd Allah* is reported to have said: When the Trench was being dug (on the eve of the Battle of the Tren-ch), I saw the Messenger of Allah (peace & blessings of Allah be with him) looking very hungry. I went to my wife and asked her: 'do you have any food? I have seen the Messenger of Allah (peace & blessings of Allah be with him) loo-king extremely hungry. She fetched a bag of provisions that contained a measure of barley. We had a lamb with us as well, so I slaugh-tered it and she did the flour. She finished her work and I mine, and then returned to the Messenger of Allah (peace & blessings of Allah be with him). She said: 'do not embarrass me in front of the Prophet (peace & blessings of Allah be with him) and the people with him. I whispered to the Apostle of Allah: 'O Messenger of Allah, we gave slaughtered a lamb for you, and she has done a mea-sure of barley we had with us. So come with some of the people. So the Messen-ger of Allah (peace & blessings of Allah be with him) called out: 'O people of the Trench! Come, Jabir gas prepared a meal for you. The Messenger of Allah (peace

& blessings of Allah be with him) said: do not remove your pot from the fire nor bake the bread from the dough until I come.' So I came and the Messenger of Allah (peace & blessings of Allah be with him) came and he was ahead of the people. I went to my wife and she said: 'You will be embarrassed.' I said: 'I did what you asked me to do.' So she brought out the dough for him and he spat in it and blessed it. Then he spat in the pot and blessed it and then said: 'Call another baker to bake with you and cook it but do not remove it from the fire.' There were one thousand of us. He swore by Allah that they all ate and left but our pot was still as full as it had been, and the dough was the same.

11. *Abd Al Rahman ibn Abu Bakr* is reported to have related: The Muhajir companions were needy and the holy Prophet (peace & blessings of Allah be with him) said: 'whoever has food enough for two should feed a third from the Muhajirs. And whoever has food enough for four should take a fifth or sixth of them.' Abu Bakr fed three and the Prophet (peace & blessings of Allah be with him) fed ten of them. Abd Al Rahman said: 'the three were my father, my mother and myself. Abu Bakr took his supper with The Prophet (peace & bles-sings of Allah be with him) and remained there until the evening prayer was offered. Abu Bakr returned and stayed with the

Prophet until he took his meal and then Abu Bakr went back to his house after most of the night had passed. Abu Bakr's wife said: 'What kept you from your guests?' He replied: 'Have you not served them yet?' She replied: 'They refused to eat until you came, the food was served to them but they refused it.' Abd Al Rahman said: 'I went away and hid and meanwhile Abu Bakr shouted at me and reprimanded me and said: 'Eat! You are undeserving, and he said, 'by God I will not touch this food at all.' So by God, whenever any of us took any-thing from the food, it increased from beneath. We all ate our fill and the food was more than it had been before being served. Abu Bakr looked at the food and found it as it was before being served or even more in quantity. He spoke to his wife saying: 'O sister of Bani Firas! What is this?' She said: 'O what delight! The food is now three times more than it was.' Abu Bakr ate from it and said: 'My oath was from Satan.' Then he took another bite from it and then took the rest of it to the Apostle of Allah (peace & blessings of Allah be with him). There was a treaty between some people and us and when the time of its expiry was reached, The Prophet (peace & blessings of Allah be with him) divided us into twelve groups each under the command of one man. God knows how many men were under the command of each leader. And all of them ate from that meal.

12. It is reported on the authority of *Abd Allah ibn Mas'ud* that: While we were with the Messenger of Allah (peace & blessings of Allah be with him) at Mina, the moon was split into two, one half was behind the mountain and the other before it, and the Apostle of Allah (peace & blessings of Allah be with him) said: Bear witness to this (event).

13. *Anas ibn Malik* is reported to have said: The people of Makka asked the Messenger of Allah (peace & blessings of Allah be with him) to show them a miracle, so he showed him the splitting of the moon twice.

14. *Abu Hurayra* is reported to have related that Abu Jahl said: Are you going to permit Muhammad to prostrate upon the dust in front of you? They said: "Yes." He said: "By Lat and by Uzza, if I see him do so, I shall put my foot on his neck or I shall wipe his face in the dust." He went to the Messenger of Allah (peace & bles-sings of Allah be with him) while he was praying intending to stand on his neck but they were surprised to see Abu Jahl turning back upon his heels in fright, trying to protect himself with his hands. They asked him: 'What happened to you?' He replied: I found between him and me the trench of Hell Fire and a terri-fying thing and wings.' The Messen-ger of Allah (peace & blessings of Allah be with him) said: 'Had he come closer the angels would have snatched him part by part.' So Allah Most Exalted revealed: 'No indeed, mankind is

surely ever insolent, for he deems himself self-sufficient. Surely to your Lord is the return, have you seen he who forbids the servant of God when he prays, have you considered if he were guided, or enjoins to piety? Have you seen if he denies the Truth and turns away? Does he not realize that God sees all? No indeed, if he does not desist, We shall drag him by the forelock, a lying sinful forelock, let him then call his henchmen, We shall call the guards of Hell. No indeed, never obey him.' (Q. 96: 6-19).

15. *Anas ibn Malik* is reported to have related that a Jewess offered (the meat of) a poisoned sheep to the Messenger of Allah (peace & blessings of Allah be with him) and he ate from it. Then she was brought to the Prophet so, he asked her about it and she said: 'I wanted to kill you.' He said: 'Allah would not permit you to do that.' Then they asked him: 'Shall we kill her?' He said: 'No.' There-after I saw the effect of the poison on the palate of the Messenger of Allah's mouth.

16. *Abu Humaid* is reported to have related: "We marched out with the Messenger of Allah (peace & blessings of Allah be with him) to participate in the battle of Tabuk and when we reached Wadi al Qura we found a woman in her garden. The Apostle of Allah (peace & blessings of Allah be with him) asked his companions to estimate the quantity of fruit in the garden, he estimated it to be ten measures

and said to the woman: Assess what your garden will produce until we return to you if Allah wills.' When we reached Tabuk the Messenger of Allah (peace & blessings of Allah be with him) said: There will be a strong wind blowing tonight, so none of you should go out and whoever has a camel should secure it well.' So we secured our camels. A strong wind raged that night and a man who stood up was blown away to the mountains. An envoy from the King of Ayla came to the Messenger of Allah with a letter and presented him a white mule. The holy Prophet (peace & blessings of Allah be with him) sent him a cloak. We marched on until we reached Wadi al Qura and the Messenger of Allah (peace & blessings of Allah be with him) asked the woman how much her garden had produced. She said: 'Ten measures.' So the Apostle of Allah said: 'I am in a hurry to reach Medina, so whoever of you wishes to hurry there let him come with me, and whoever wishes to stay let him stay.' So we marched until we reached Medina and the Messenger of Allah (peace & blessings of Allah be with him) said: 'this is Taba and this is Uhud. This mountain loves us and we love it.' Then he said: 'The best family of the Ansar is the family of Bani al Najjar, and then the family of Bani Abd al Ashal, then Bani Al Harith ibn Al-Khazraj and the family of Bani Saeeda. And there is goodness in all the families of the Ansar.' Sa'ad ibn Ubada arrived and Abu Asid said:

'Do you not see that the Messenger of Allah (peace & blessings of Allah be with him) said that there is goodness in all the families of the Ansars, and he mentioned us last?' So Sa'ad visited the holy Prophet (peace & blessings of Allah be with him) and said: 'O Messenger of Allah, you have mentioned that there is goodness in all the families of the Ansars and mentioned us last?' He said: 'is it not enough for you that you are among the best?

17. *Sa'ad* reported that: on the Day of Uhud I saw on the right side f the Apostle of Allah and on his left side two men dressed in white clothes and whom I did not see either before or afterwards, and they were Gabriel and Michael (may Allah be pleased with them).

18. *Abu Hurayra* is reported to have related that the Messenger of Allah (peace & blessings of Allah be with him) said: My position and the position of the people is akin to a person who lit a fire and let the butterflies and insects fall into it. He continued to ward them from it but they overwhelmed him and plunged into it. He said: This is my situation and yours. I ward you from the fire, but you overwhelm me and dive into it.

19. *Hadrat Ayesha* is reported to have related that the Messenger of Allah (peace & blessings of Allah be with him) permit-ted a matter for some people, but some others refused it, when the Prophet was informed about it he got very angry and it showed upon his face, and he said: 'What is wrong with those people, they refuse what I am allowed to permit, by Allah, I know better than they and I am more God fearing than they are.

20. *Hadrat Ayesha* is reported to have said: Whenever the Messenger of Allah (peace & blessings of Allah be with him) was given a choice bet-ween two matters he would choose the easier one as long as it was not sinful. If it were sinful he would be the furthest from it. The Apostle of Allah (peace & blessings of Allah be with him) never sought to take revenge for him, except when the sanctity of God Almighty was violated.

21. *Al Mughira ibn Shu'abah* is reported to have related that the Prophet (peace & blessings of Allah be with him) used to stand in prayer until both his feet or legs were swollen. He was asked why and he replied: Should I not be a thankful servant.

22. *Jundab* is reported to have said that he heard the Prophet say: I will be before you at the Fountain (in paradise) in readiness for you.

23. *Abd Allah ibn Amr ibn al A'as* is reported to have related that the Messenger of Allah (peace & blessings of Allah be with him) said: My Fountain is a month's journey to traverse, its water is more white than silver, and its scent is more pleasing than musk, and its drin-

king cups are as the stars in the sky, and whoever drinks from it, will never thirst." Abd Allah also reported that on the authority of Asma bint Abu Bakr that the Messenger of Allah (peace & blessings of Allah be with him) said: I will wait for you at the Fountain (of Paradise) to see which one of you comes, some people will be taken away before they reach me, and then I will say: 'My Lord! They are from me and of my community.' Then it will be said: 'did you not perceive what they did after you, by God, they almost turned back after you.'

24. *Haritha ibn Wahab* is reported to have said that he heard the Prophet (peace & blessings of Allah be with him) say that the Fountain (of Paradise) was about the distance between Medina and Sana.

25. It is reported from *Ibn Umar* that the Prophet (peace & blessings of Allah be with him) said: There will be a Fountain (or my Fountain) before you as wide as the distance between Jarba and Adruh. And Ubaid Allah reportedly said: "I asked him (Nafe') about Jarba and Adruh- he said: 'they are two villages in al-Sham, the distance between them is three nights (or three days) walk.

26. It is reported from *Jabir ibn Samura* that the Messenger of Allah (peace & blessings of Allah be with him) said: I will be before you at the Fountain in readiness for you, and the distance between its two sides is the distance between Sana and Ayla, and the drinking cups are like the stars.

27. *Abu Zarr* reportedly asked the Messenger of Allah: What are the drinking cups of the Fountain?' He said: 'By The One in Whose Hand is the soul of Muhammad, its cups are more numerous than the stars in the sky and the planets on a dark night, cups from Paradise, whoever drinks from it will never thirst. Two rivers run into it from Paradise, whoever drinks from it will never thirst, its width is like its length and the distance between them is as Amman and Ayla, and its water is more white than milk and sweeter than honey.

28. *Uqba ibn Amir* is reported to have related that the Messenger of Allah (peace & blessings of Allah be with him) offered the funeral prayer for the martyrs of Uhud and then ascended the pulpit and said: I will pave the way for you as your predecessor and I will be a witness for you. By God! I have just seen my Heavenly Fountain and I have been given the keys of the treasures of heaven and earth.' By God! I do not fear that you will take others in worship besides Allah after I die, but I do fear that you will fight each other for the things of this life and you would be destroyed as other communities were destroyed before you. Uqba also reported that it was the last occasion I saw the Messenger of Allah (peace & blessings of Allah be with him) on the pulpit.

29. *Anas ibn Malik* is reported to have described the holy Prophet (peace & blessings of Allah be with him) saying: He was of middle height, neither too short nor too tall, his complexion was of rosy colour, neither completely white nor deep brown, his hair was neither completely curly nor straight. Divine Inspiration was revealed to him when he was forty years of age. He stayed ten years in Makka receiving Divine Inspi-ration and in Medina for another ten years. When he died, he had fewer than twenty white hairs in his hair and beard." Rabi'a said: I saw some of his hair and it was red, when I asked about that I was told it had become red from perfume. And Anas also related that: The Messenger of Allah (peace & blessings of Allah be with him) was neither comp-letely white nor deep brown; his hair was neither curly nor straight. God chose him for His mission when he was forty years old; thereafter he stayed in Makka for ten years and then in Medina for another ten years. When God called him back to Him, there were fewer than twenty white hairs in his hair and beard.

30. *Al Bara' Ibn Aazib* is reported to have said: The Messenger of Allah (peace & blessings of Allah be with him) was of medium height and had broad shoulders and long hair that reached the lobes of his ears. I saw him once wearing a red cloak and I have never seen a more handsome man than he.

31. *Abu al Tufail* is reported to have said: I saw the Messenger of Allah (peace & blessings of Allah be with him) and no man on the surface of the earth saw him as I saw him. He was asked: 'How did you see him?' He said: 'He had a white handsome face.' Muslim said: 'Abu al Tufail who died in the year 100 Hijra was the last of the companions of the Messenger of Allah (peace & blessings of Allah be with him).

32. *Al Sa'ib ibn Yazid* is reported top have related that his aunt took him to the Apostle of Allah (peace & blessings of Allah be with him) and said: 'O Messen-ger of Allah! This son of my sister has an ailment in his legs.' So he passed his hands over my head and prayed for Allah's blessings, then he performed ablution and I drank from the remaining water. I stood behind him and saw the seal of Prophet-hood between his shoul-ders; it was like the button of a small tent.

33. It is reported that *Abdullah ibn Sarjis* said: I saw the Messenger of Allah (peace & blessings of Allah be with him) and ate bread and meat (or bread soaked in soup) with him. He was asked: 'Did the Prophet invoke forgiveness for you?' He said: 'Yes, and then he recited: '...and ask forgiveness for yourself and for the believing men and believing women...' (Q.47: 19) Then I followed him and saw the Seal of Prophethood between his shoulders on the left side of his shoulder with mole-like spots around it.

34. *Jabir ibn Samurah* is reported to have said: The face of the Messenger of Allah (peace & blessings of Allah be with him) was broad and ruddy and his heels were slender. '

35. *Anas ibn Malik* is reported to have said: I hate to see any man pluck out the whites hairs from his head or beard, and the Messenger of Allah (peace & blessings of Allah be with him) never colored his hair. The white hair was under his lower lips and on his cheeks and upon his head was a sprinkling of white hair.

36. *Abu Juhaifa* is reported to have related that he saw the Messenger of Allah (peace & blessings of Allah be with him) glowing and some of his hair was white and Al Hasan ibn Ali looked like him.

37. *Anas* has reported that the hair of the Messenger of Allah (peace & blessings of Allah be with him) used to reach up to his shoulders.

38. *Anas* is reported to have said: The hair of the Messenger of Allah (peace & blessings of Allah be with him) used to reach to his ear lobes.

39. It is reported that *Ibn Abbas* said: The Messenger of Allah (peace & blessings of Allah be with him) used to leave his hair hanging down because the unbelievers used to part their hair. The People of earlier Scriptures used to leave their hair hanging down and the Messenger of Allah (peace & blessings of Allah be with him) liked to do the same in all that about which there were no guidance from Allah, and then later he parted his hair.

40. *Abu Saeed Al Khudri* is reported to have said: The Prophet (peace & blessings of Allah be with him) was more bashful than a virgin girl in a veil. And it is also reported: If he disliked a thing, it would be show on his face.

41. It is reported from *Anas ibn Malik* that: The Messenger of Allah (peace & blessings of Allah be with him) had a glowing complexion and his sweat was like pearls. His gait was slanted. I have never felt fine silk or heavy silk softer than the hands of the Messenger of Allah (peace & blessings of Allah be with him), and I have never smelt a scent or a sweat sweeter than the scent of the holy Prophet (peace & blessings of Allah be with him).

42. *Jabir ibn Samura* reportedly related that he prayed with the Messenger of Allah (peace & blessings of Allah be with him) the first prayer, then he returned to his family and I left with him, he met two boys and he rubbed the cheeks of both of them one after the other, when he rubbed my cheeks and I found his hands very cold - or scented - as if he had just removed them from a jar of perfume.

43. It is reported on the authority of *Hadrat Ayesha* that: Surely I saw The Messenger of Allah (peace & blessings of Allah be with him) receiving Revelations on a very cold

morning and I noticed the sweat dropping from his forehead.

44. *Hadrat Ayesha* is reported to have related that Al-Harith ibn Hisham asked the Prophet: 'How does the Revelation come to you?' The holy Prophet (peace & blessings of Allah be with him) replied: Sometimes it comes to me like the ringing of a bell, this form of Revelation is the hardest of all and then this state passes off after I have grasped what is revealed. Sometimes the angel comes in the form of a man and talks to me and I grasp whatever he says.

45. It is reported from *Anas* that the Prophet (peace & blessings of Allah be with him) came to visit us. He sweated profusely and my mother collected his sweat in a bottle. The Prophet woke up and asked: 'O Umm Sulaim, what are you doing?' She replied: This is your sweat that I have added to my perfume and it is the best of perfumes.

46. It is reported on the authority of *Anas ibn Malik* that: The Prophet used to visit the house of Umm Sulaim. One day he arrived and slept upon a piece of cloth and when she came she was told the Prophet is sleeping in your house on your cloth. He sweated profusely until the cloth was drenched in it, so she opened her vanity box and took the cloth and squeezed it into her bottles, the holy Prophet (peace & blessings of Allah be with him) was amazed and asked her: 'O Umm Sulaim, what are you doing?' She replied: 'O Messenger of Allah, we hope for its blessing for our children.' He remarked: You are right.

47. *Anas ibn Malik* is reported to have said: The Messenger of Allah (peace & blessings of Allah be with him) used to pray the dawn prayer, and the servants of Medina used to assemble with their containers full of water, he used to dip his hand in every container placed before him, and even when it was cold he would dip his hand in it.

48. *Anas ibn Malik* is reported to have related that he saw the Messenger of Allah (peace & blessings of Allah be with him) have his hair trimmed by the barber and his companions gathered around him, vied with each other so that no hair would fall except into their hands.

49. *Anas ibn Malik* is reported to have said: I have never seen anyone more kind to his family than the Messenger of Allah (peace & blessings of Allah be with him). Ibrahim was sent to the outskirts of Medina to be suckled and he used to go there and we used to go along with him. He entered the house, which was filled with smoke, as his foster-father was a blacksmith. He picked him up and kissed him and then returned. Amr said that when Ibrahim died, the Messenger of Allah (peace & blessings of Allah be with him) said: Ibrahim my son has died as a suckling infant, and now he has two foster-mothers who will complete his period of suckling in Paradise.

50. *Anas ibn Malik* is reported to have said: The Messenger of Allah (peace & blessings of Allah be with him) was the best of people, and the most generous of them, and the bravest. One night the people of Medina were frightened, and they ran towards the sound and the Apostle of Allah (peace & blessings of Allah be with him) met them as he was returning, so he rushed before them to the sound and he was mounted upon the horse of Abu Talha without a saddle. He hung the sword over his neck and said: 'Why are you frightened, why are you frightened?' They said: 'we saw a Bahr running, or 'It is Bahr.' He said: It was a horse walking slowly.

51. *Anas ibn Malik* is reported to have said: The Messenger of Allah (peace & blessings of Allah be with him) had the kindest nature of all people. One day he sent me on an errand and I said: 'By God I will not go.' Although I thought to myself I would do what the prophet asked me to do and I went out and met with some children who had been playing in the street. Then the Apostle of Allah (peace & blessings of Allah be with him) came and caught me by the back of my neck and when I looked at him I saw that he was smiling, and he asked: 'Unais, did you go where I asked you to go?' I replied: 'O Messenger of Allah! I am just going.' Anas added: 'I attended him for nine years and he never asked me why I had done a thing or why I had not done a thing.

52. *Jabir ibn Abd Allah* is reported to have related that whenever the Messen-ger of Allah (peace & blessings of Allah be with him) was asked for something, he never said: No.

53. *Ibn Shihab* is reported to have said: The Messenger of Allah (peace & bles-sings of Allah be with him) set out with the Muslims on an expe-dition for the conquest of Makka and they fought at Hunayn, and God Almighty granted victory. Thereafter the Messenger of Allah (peace & blessings of Allah be with him) gave one hundred camels to Safwan ibn Umayyah and then gave him another one hundred camels, and then again gave him one hundred camels. Ibn Shihab said that Saeed ibn al Musayyib reported that Safwan said: The Messen-ger of Allah gave me and he was the most disliked person of all people in my eyes. But he continued giving to me until now he is the most beloved of people to me.

54. *Jubair ibn At'im* is reported to have related that the Messenger of Allah (peace & blessings of Allah be with him) said: I have names; I am Muhammad and Ahmad, I am Al-Mahi through whom God will eradicate unbelief, I am Al- Hashir who will be the first to be resur-rected before the people, and I am the Al- Aaqib after whom there will be none (messenger or prophet from Allah). And God has named him: 'Benevolent and compassionate.'

55. *Abu Musa al Ash'ari* is reported to have said: The Messenger of Allah (peace & blessings of Allah be with him) used to tell us his names: 'I am Muhammad, and Ahmad, and al Muqaffi, the Last of the Prophets, and al Hashir, the one who gathers the people, and the Prophet of Repentance and the Prophet of Mercy.

56. *Ibn Abbas* has reported that the Messenger of Allah (peace & blessings of Allah be with him) stayed in Makka for thirteen years and received Divine Inspiration in Medina for ten years and he died at the age of sixty-three.

57. It is reported that *Ibn Abbas* said: The Apostle of Allah (peace & blessings of Allah be with him) stayed in Makka for fifteen years, listening to the sound and seeing the light for seven years, and he did not see anything. And eight years receiving Revelation, and he stayed in Medina for ten years.

58. *Anas ibn Malik* is reported to have related that the holy Prophet (peace & blessings of Allah be with him) died at the age of sixty-three, and so did Abu Bakr, and so did Umar, who was also sixty-three (at the time of his death).

59. It is reported on the authority of *Anas ibn Malik* that the Messenger of Allah (peace & blessings of Allah be with him) was told something about his companions, so he addressed us saying: 'Paradise and the Fire were displayed to me, but I do not see a day like today of good or evil. If you know what I know you would have laughed a little and wept a lot.' He said: 'the companions of the Prophet (peace & blessings of Allah be with him) did not see a more difficult day than that day. They covered their heads and they were weeping deeply.' Then Umar ibn Khattab stood up and said: 'We are pleased with Allah as our Lord, and with Islam as our Religion and with Muhammad as our Prophet.' Then the verse was revealed: 'O you who believe! Do not question things which if they were revealed to you would only vex you...' (Q.5: 101).

60. *Sa'ad ibn Abu Waqqas* has reported that the holy Prophet (peace & blessings of Allah be with him) said: The most grievous wrong that a Muslims commits to the other Muslims is by the one who questions something that was not prohi-bited to the Muslims, then it be-comes unlawful to them due to his questioning.

61. It is reported on the authority of *Abu Hurayra* that the Messenger of Allah (peace & blessings of Allah be with him) said: Shun what I have prohibited to you and do what I have told you to do to the utmost of your ability. The people before you were destroyed because they questioned excessively, and disagreed with their Prophets.

62. *Talha ibn Ubaid Allah* is reported to

have said that the holy Prophet (peace & blessings of Allah be with him) and he passed by some people near the date-palm trees and he asked: 'What are they doing?' They said: 'they are grafting, they are combining the male and female part of the tree. So the Messenger of Allah (peace & blessings of Allah be with him) said: 'I do not see it will do anything.' The people were told about that and they gave up this practice. The Apostle of Allah (peace & blessings of Allah be with him) was informed of that so he said: 'If there is any use in it, let them do it, it was just a thought I had, so do not charge me for it, but if I tell you anything regarding Allah then you must accept it, as I do not attribute lies to God Most High.

63. It is reported on the authority of *Abu Hurayra* that the Messenger of Allah (peace & blessings of Allah be with him) said: The people to whom I would be the most beloved would be the people who will come after (my death), any of them would wish to see me, even at the cost of his family and his wealth.

51

Book of the Prophet

1. *Abu Hurayra* is reported to have said: The Messenger of Allah (peace & blessings of Allah be with him) held my hand and said: 'God Most High, created the earth on Saturday and the mountains in it on Sunday, and created the trees on Monday, and created the disliked on Tuesday, and created the light on Wed-nesday, and spread the creatures upon it on Thursday, and created Adam on the afternoon of Friday and he was the last to be created on the last hour of Friday between the afternoon and the night.

2. *Anas ibn Malik* has reported that a person visited the Messenger of Allah (peace & blessings of Allah be with him) and said: O, the best of creation; there-upon the holy Prophet remarked: That (best of creation) is Ibrahim.

3. It is reported on the authority of *Abu Hurayra* that the Messenger of Allah (peace & blessings of Allah be with him) said: Abraham only lied on three occa-sions. Twice in the cause of God when he said: 'I

am ill,' and when he said: 'I did not do it but the big idol has done it.' And when Abraham and Sarah were on a journey when they entered the land of a tyrant. It was said to the tyrant: 'This man has a beautiful woman with him.' So he sent for Abraham and asked him about Sarah, saying: 'Who is the lady?' Abra-ham said: 'She is my sister.' Abraham went to Sarah and said: 'O Sarah! There are no believers on the face of the earth except you and me. This man has asked me about you and I have told him that you are my sister, so do not contradict me. The tyrant summoned Sarah and she went to him, he tried to grab her with his hand but he was thwarted. He asked Sarah: 'Pray to God for me and I shall not hurt you.' So Sarah prayed to God for him and he went. He tried to grab her a second time but he was thwarted again. He asked Sarah again: 'Pray to God for me and I will not hurt you.' Sarah prayed to God again and he went. Then he sum-moned one of his guards and said: 'You did not bring me a human but a devil.' The tyrant then gave her Hajar to serve her. So she returned to Abraham while he was praying, Abraham indicated with his hand asking: 'What happened?' She replied: 'God has thwarted the evil plot of the tyrant and has given me Hajar to serve me.

4. *Abu Hurayra* is reported to have related that: Moses was a shy man and was never seen naked. 'The children of Israel said: 'He has a scrotal hernia.' 'Moses took off his clothes and put them on a stone to wash, but the stone rolled away with his clothes; Moses picked up his stick and ran after the stone beating it and saying: 'O stone! Give me back my clothes!' when he reached near a group of the children of Israel, it was revealed: 'O you who believe! Do not be as those who annoyed Moses, then God freed him of what they said of him, and he was highly honored with God.   (Q. 33: 69).

5. *Ibn Abbas* is reported to have narrated on the authority of Ubayy ibn Ka'b that the holy Prophet (peace & bles-sings of Allah be with him) said: 'Once Moses stood up and addressed Bani Israel and he was asked who was the most learned man among the people. He said: 'I.' God Almighty admonished him because he failed to attribute absolute knowledge to Him. So, God said: 'At the confluence of the two seas there is

one of My servants who is more learned than you.' Moses said: 'O my Lord! Where shall I find him?' God Almighty said: 'Carry a fish in a basket and where you lose the fish you will find him.' So Moses set off with his boy, Yusha ibn Nun, and carried with him a fish in a basket and reached the rock where they rested, and the fish wriggled out of the basket and fell into the sea. He said: 'God Almighty calmed the water and made it appear as an arch.' So it was for the fish a way to go through and for Moses and his boy a wonder, so they set off and journeyed the rest of the day and night, and Moses' boy forgot to mention it to him, in the morning Moses said to his boy: 'Bring us our meal, we have faced much weari-ness on our journey.' His boy said to him: 'Did you see when we were resting at the rock, then I forgot the fish, and nothing made me forget it but Satan, and it took it away into the sea, what a wonder!' Moses said: 'this is what we were seeking and so they returned tracing their footsteps. He said: 'they retraced their steps back until they reached the rock. There they saw a man lying covered with a garment. Moses greeted him and al-Khidr replied saying: 'How can there be peace in your land?' He said: 'I am Moses.' He asked: 'Moses of the Children of Israel?' Moses said: 'Yes, I have come to you so that you may teach me from the knowledge of God which He has taught you.' He said: 'O Moses! I have some of the Knowledge of God which God has taught me, and which you do not know, while you have some of the Knowledge of God which God has taught you and which I do not know." Moses asked: 'Shall I follow you so that you may teach me of what you have been taught of right knowledge?' He said: 'Surely you will not be able to bear with me patiently, and how should you bear patiently that which you have never encompassed in your knowledge.' He said: 'If God pleases, you will find me patient, and I will not disobey you in any matter.' So Al-Khidr told him: 'Then if you follow me, question me not on anything until I myself explain it to you.' He said: 'Yes.' So they both set out walking along the seashore, and a boat passed by them and they asked the crew of the boat to take them on board. The crew recognized Al-Khidr and so they took them on board without pay-ment. Al Khidr intentionally pulled out one of the boat's boards, and Moses said to him: 'The people carried us without payment and you are intentionally destroying their ship to drown those in it, you have indeed done a grievous thing?' He replied: 'Did I not say that you would not be able to bear with me patiently?' Moses replied: 'Excuse me I forgot about it and do not make it difficult for me.' So they left the boat and as they were walking upon the shore they saw some boys playing. Al-Khidr pulled off one of the boy's head and killed him. Moses said: 'have you killed an innocent soul who has not killed any soul? You have indeed done an evil thing.' Al-Khidr said: 'Did I not say to you that you would not be able to bear with me patiently?' He said: 'This is worse than the first.' Moses said: 'If ever I question you about anything after this then keep me no more in your company. So they left until they reached the people of a town, they asked them for food but they refused any hospitality. There they found a wall about to collapse so Al-Khidr repaired it up. Moses said: 'those people who neither gave us food, nor hospitality. If you had wished, you could surely have exacted payment for that. He said: This is where you and I will part; but before that I will explain to you that which you could not bear patiently.' The Messenger of Allah (peace & blessings of Allah be with him) said: 'May God bestows His Mercy on Moses! I wish he had remained patient, so that we would have been told more of their narrative.' The holy Prophet (peace & blessings of Allah be with him) said: 'The first time it was from that Moses forgot.' He said: 'A sparrow came and fell upon the edge of the boat, then it dipped its beak into the sea, so Al Khidr said: 'My knowledge and your knowledge do not diminish the Knowledge of God by even as much as this sparrow has diminished from the sea with its beak.' Said ibn Jubair said: 'Ibn Abbas used to recite: 'As a king was pursuing them who was seizing every good ship forcibly.' And he also said (about the boy who was killed by Al-Khidr): 'And indeed the boy was an unbeliever.'

6. It is narrated on the authority of *Abu Hurayra* that once while a Jew was selling something; he was offered a price that displeased him. So, he said: 'No, by Him Who gave Moses superiority over all humanity.' Hearing this, a man of the Ansars slapped his face and said: 'you say: 'By Him Who gave Moses superiority over all humanity, while the Prophet is present amongst us!' The Jew went to the Prophet and said: 'O Abu Al Qasim! I am under the pledge and agreement of secu-rity, so what right does so-and-so have to slap me?' The Prophet asked the Ansar: 'Why did you slap him?' He related what had happened to him, and the Prophet became angry so that his anger was apparent in his face, he said: 'Do not attribute superiority to any Prophet of the Prophets of God, for when the trumpet will be blown, everyone on the earth and in the heavens will fall un-conscious except those whom God will exempt. The trumpet will be blown for the second time and I will be the first to be resurrected to see Moses holding the Throne of God. I shall not know if the uncons-ciousness

that Moses suffered on the Day of al Tur was deemed commen-surate for him, or whether he was revived before me. And I do not say that there is anybody who is better than Yunus ibn Matta.

7. *Abu Hurayra* is reported to have narrated that: The angel of death was sent to Moses and when he approached him Moses struck him violently putting out one of his eyes. The angel went back to his Lord and said: You had sent me to a servant who does not want to die. God restored his eye and said: Go back and tell him to put his hand upon the back of an ox and he will be permitted to live for as many years as there are hairs under his hand.' Then Moses asked: 'O my Lord! What will be after that?' He said: 'Death will come to you.' He said: 'Let it be now.' He asked God to bring him to within a stone's throw of the Sacred Land. The Messenger of Allah (peace & blessings of Allah be with him) said: If I were there I would have shown you the grave of Moses on the wayside close to the red hillock of sand.

8. It is reported from *Anas ibn Malik* that the Messenger of Allah (peace & blessings of Allah be with him) said: I happened to pass by Moses on the occasion of the Night Journey (Night of Ascension) near the red mound (and found him) saying his prayer in his grave.

9. It is reported from *Abu Hurayra* that the Prophet (peace & blessings of Allah be with him) was asked: Who is the most honorable person? He replied: The one who is the most God fearing. The people said: We do not mean that. He said: The most honorable person is Yusuf (Joseph), the Prophet of God, the son of the Prophet of God, the son of the Friend of God. The people said: We do not mean that. He said: Then you mean to ask me about the origins of the Arabs? People are of various origins. The best in the times before Islam are the best in Islam, as long as they are knowledgeable in their Religion.

10. *Abu Hurayra* is reported to have claimed that the Messenger of Allah (peace & blessings of Allah be with him) said: In this world and in the Hereafter, I am the closest of all the people to Jesus, the son of Mary. The Prophets are paternal brothers, they have different mothers, but their Religion is one.

52

Book of the Merits of the Companions of the Prophet

1. *Abu Said Al- Khudri* is reported to have said that the Apostle of Allah (peace & blessings of Allah be with him) addressed the people saying: God has given a servant the choice of this world or that, which is with Him, and the servant has chosen what is with God. Abu Bakr began to weep, and we were surprised that he wept at the Prophet saying that a servant of God had been offered a choice, but later we got to know that it was the Messenger of Allah (peace & blessings of Allah be with him) who had been given the choice, and Abu Bakr had known better than all of us. The holy Prophet (peace & blessings of Allah be with him) also said: The one who has favored me most of all with both his company and wealth, is Abu Bakr. And if I were to take a friend besides my Lord, I would have taken Abu Bakr, but we are brothers in Islam and in friendship. Close all the gates of the Mosque except the gate of Abu Bakr.

2. *Abu Uthman* is reported to have related that Amr ibn al A'as said that he asked the Messenger of Allah: Who is the most beloved person to you?" The holy Prophet replied: Ayesha. I asked: Among the men? He said: Her father. I said: Who then? He said: Then Umar. He then named other men.

3. It is reported from *Abu Hurayra* that the Messenger of Allah (peace & blessings of Allah be with him) said: While a man was taking a cow with a load on it, it turned towards him and said: I have not been created for this purpose, but for ploughing. The people said: 'Glory be to God! A speaking cow? The Apostle of Allah (peace & blessings of Allah be with him) said: 'But I believe in it and so do Abu Bakr and Umar.' Abu Hurayra said that the holy Prophet said: 'while a shepherd was with his sheep a wolf attacked them and took away a sheep. When the shepherd chased the wolf, the wolf turned towards him and asked: Who will guard it on the day of wild animals when nobody except I will be its shepherd?' The people said: 'Glory be to God.' The Messenger of Allah (peace & blessings of Allah be with him)

said: but I believe in it and so do Abu Bakr and Umar.

4. *Ibn Abbas* is reported to have said: As I stood with the people while they were invoking God Almighty for Umar ibn al Khattab who lay upon his bed, a man behind me rested his elbows on my shoulders and said: 'May God have mercy upon you, I always hoped that God would keep you with your two compa-nions, as I often heard the Prophet say: 'I, Abu Bakr and Umar were in such a place. I, Abu Bakr and Umar did so and so. I, Abu Bakr and Umar set off together.' So I hoped that God would always keep you with both of them.' I turned around and saw that the speaker was Ali ibn Abu Talib.

5. *Ibn Abu Mulaikah* is reported to have said that he heard Hadrat Ayesha say when she was asked whom would the Messenger of Allah (peace & blessings of Allah be with him) have nominated as his successor if he had to nominate some-one. She said: 'Abu Bakr.' Then she was asked: 'Then whom after Abu Bakr?' She said: 'Umar.' Then she was asked: 'Then whom after Umar? She said: Abu Ubaida ibn Jarrah. And then she mentioned no one else after that.

6. *Mohammed ibn Jubair ibn Mutim* is reported to have related that his father said: A woman came to the Prophet and he requested her to return later. She asked: 'What if I come and do not find you?' as if she meant to say What if I find you have died? The Prophet said: If you do not find me, then go to Abu Bakr.

7. It is reported on the authority of *Hadrat Ayesha* that she said: During the final illness of the Messenger of Allah (peace & blessings of Allah be with him), he asked me to call Abu Bakr, my father, and my brother as well, so that he might dictate a document, for he feared that someone else might make a claim to succeed him. While God Almighty and the Believers will not approve any claim except that of Abu Bakr.

8. *Abu Said Al Khudri* is reported to have related that the Messenger of Allah (peace & blessings of Allah be with him) said: While I was sleeping I saw some people wearing shirts of which some covered only their breasts while others were even shorter than that. Umar ibn Al Khattab was shown to me wearing a shirt that was dragging. The people asked: How do you interpret it, O Messenger of Allah? He rep-lied: It is the Religion.

9. *Abd Allah ibn Umar* is reported to have related that the holy Prophet (peace & blessings of Allah be with him) said: When I slept I saw myself drinking milk and I was content to the point that I saw milk leaking from my fingertips. Then I gave it to Umar. They asked: How do you interpret that? He replied: It is know-ledge.

10. *Abu Hurayra* is reported to have related that the Messenger of Allah (peace & blessings of Allah be with

him) said: As I slept I saw myself standing at a well that had a bucket upon it. I drew water from the well as much as God Almighty plea-sed. Then Ibn Abu Quhafa took the bucket from me and pulled out one or two bucketful's but he drew the water weakly. May God forgive him his weak-ness. Then the bucket grew very large and Ibn Al Khattab took it, and I had never seen such a powerful man as he in carrying out such heavy work, until the people drank to their satisfaction and gave it to their camels that rested there.

11. It is reported on the authority of *Abu Hurayra* that the Prophet said: As I slept I saw myself in Paradise and a woman was performing ablution beside a palace. I asked: 'Who is this for?' she replied: 'It is for Umar ibn al Khattab.' I thought of Umar's feelings and left. Abu Hurayra said: 'Umar wept as we were with the Messenger of Allah there, and Umar said: O Messenger of God, may my father and mother be sacrificed for you. How could I feel jealous of you?

12. *Sa'ad ibn Abu Waqqas* is reported to have said: Umar ibn al-Khattab sought the permission of the Messenger of Allah (peace & blessings of Allah be with him) to enter as some women of the Quraysh were speaking to him asking him for more expenses. When Umar sought per-mission to enter, the women hurried to veil them-selves. The Apostle of Allah (peace & blessings of Allah be with) per-mitted him to enter and as

Umar came in the Messenger of Allah (peace & bles-sings of Allah be with him) was smiling, Umar said: 'O Messenger of Allah, May God always make you smile.' The Prophet said: These women here amazed me, for as soon as they heard your voice, they hurried to veil themselves. Umar said: 'O Messenger of Allah, they should more rightly fear you than I.' Then Umar add-ressed the women saying: 'O you women! Do you fear me more than you fear the Messenger of Allah?' They said: 'Yes, be-cause you are more harsh and severe than the Messenger of Allah.' Then the holy Prophet (peace & blessings of Allah be with him) said: O Ibn al-Khattab! By Him in Whose Hands is my soul! Never does Satan find you taking a way, but he takes a different way than yours.

13. It is reported on the authority of *Hadrat Ayesha* that the Messenger of Allah (peace & blessings of Allah be with him) said: Before you there were people who received inspiration, and if there is such a one among my community it is Umar ibn al Khattab. (Ibn Wahab inter-preted that the word *'Muhaddathun'* refers to those who receive enligh-tenment from the Almighty).

14. *Ibn Umar* is reported to have related that Umar said: My Lord concurred with me on three occasions: in the matter of the Station of Ibrahim, in the matter of veiling (of women) and in matter of the prisoners of Badr.

15. It is reported from *Ibn Umar* that when Abd Allah ibn Ubayy died, his son Abd Allah ibn Abd Allah went to the Messenger of Allah (peace & blessings of Allah be with him) who gave him his shirt and told him to shroud his father in it. Then he stood up to offer the funeral prayer for the deceased, but Umar ibn Al Khattab grabbed his garment and said: 'will you offer the funeral prayer for him, he was a hypocrite and God has forbidden you to ask forgiveness for hypocrites.' The Prophet said: 'God Almighty has informed me: 'Whether you ask forgiveness for such people or not, God will not forgive them, even if you ask for forgiveness for them seventy times...' (Q.9: 80) Then he said: 'I shall ask more than seventy times.' So the Messenger of Allah (peace & blessings of Allah be with him) offered the funeral prayer for him and we too, offered the prayer with him. Then God revealed: 'And never pray for any one of them when they are dead, nor stand over their grave. They disbelieved in Allah and His Messenger, and died while they were transgressors.' (Q. 9: 84).

16. It is reported that *Hadrat Ayesha* said: The Messenger of Allah (peace & blessings of Allah be with him) was reclining in his house while his legs were uncovered. Then Abu Bakr sought permi-ssion to enter, so he permitted him to enter and he spoke to him. Then Umar sought permi-ssion to enter, so he was per-mitted likewise, and he spoke to

him as well while he continued to recline. Then Uthman came and sought permi-ssion to enter, so the Prophet sat up and covered his legs and straigh-tened his garments. Then Uthman was permitted to enter and he spoke to him. When he left, Ayesha said to the Messenger of Allah (peace & blessings of Allah be with him): 'Abu Bakr came and you did not move, and Umar came and you did not move, but when Uthman came you sat up and straighte-ned your garments?' He said: Should I not feel shy before a man whom the angels feel shy of?

17. *Abu Musa Al Ash'ari* is reported to have said: I performed ablution in my house and then went out intending to stay beside him all day.' I went to the Mosque and asked about the Prophet (peace & blessings of Allah be with him). They said: 'He has gone this way.' So I followed that way asking about him until I found he had entered a place called Bi'r Aris, I sat at its gate until the Prophet (peace & blessings of Allah be with him) had answered the call of nature and performed ablution. Then I went unto him and saw him sitting at the well of Aris on the middle of its wall with his legs hanging into the well. I saluted him and went back and sat at the gate, I said: 'Today I will be the Prophet's (peace & blessings of Allah be with him) gate keeper.' Abu Bakr came and pushed the gate, I asked: 'Who is it?' He said: 'Abu Bakr.' I told him to wait and I went in and said: 'Abu Bakr seeks permission to enter.' He said: 'Let him come in and tell him the glad tidings that he will be admitted to Paradise.' So I went out and said to Abu Bakr: 'Come in and the Mes-senger of Allah gives you glad tidings that you will be admitted to Paradise.' Abu Bakr entered and sat at the right hand side of the Messenger of Allah (peace & blessings of Allah be with him) upon the edge of the well and hung his legs into it like the Prophet (Prayers & peace be upon him). Then I went back and sat at the gate. Then someone moved the door, I asked: 'Who is it?' He said: 'Umar ibn Al Khattab.' I asked him to wait and I went to the Messenger of Allah (peace & blessings of Allah be with him) saluted him and said: 'Umar ibn Al Khattab seeks permission to enter.' He said: 'Let him in and tell him the glad tidings that he will be admitted to Paradise.' I went to Umar and said: 'Come in and the Messenger of Allah gives you glad tidings that your will be admitted to Paradise.' So he came in and sat next to the Messenger of Allah (peace & blessings of Allah be with him) on the edge of the well on the left hand side and hung his legs into the well. I went back and thought: 'If God intends good for so and so He will bring him here.' Someone came and moved the door, I asked: 'Who is it?' He said: 'Uthman ibn Affan.' I asked him to wait and I went to the Prophet (peace & blessings of Allah be with him) and told him. He said: 'Let him in and give him the glad tidings that he will be admitted to Paradise after a tragedy happens to him.' So I went

to him and said: 'Come in, the Messenger of Allah gives you glad tidings that you will enter Paradise after a tragedy has struck you.' Uthman came in and found the edge of the well occupied, so he sat on the other side facing the Pro-phet (peace & blessings of Allah be with him).

18. *Sa'ad ibn Abu Waqqas* reportedly related that the Apostle of Allah (peace & blessings of Allah be with him) was lea-ving for Tabuk (on a military expedition) and he told Ali to guard the women and children while the Muslims were away from Medina. So Ali said: Will you leave me with the women and children? The holy Prophet (peace & blessings of Allah be with him) replied: Does it not please you that you are to me as Aaron was to Moses? Except that there will be no prophet after me.

19. *Sahl ibn Sa'ad* is reported to have related that he heard the Apostle of Allah (peace & blessings of Allah be with him) say on the day of Khyber: I will give the flag to someone at whose hands God will grant victory. So the companions of the Prophet (peace & blessings of Allah be with him) rose up expectantly to see which of them would be given the flag. The holy Prophet (peace & blessings of Allah be with him) asked for Ali. Some-one told him that he was suffering from an ailment in his eye, but he told them to bring Ali before him. The Messenger of Allah (peace & blessings of Allah be with him) then applied some of his saliva in his eyes and his eyes were

immediately cured. Ali said: 'We will fight them until they become Muslim.' The Apostle of Allah (peace & blessings of Allah be with him) said: Have patience, until you con-front them and invite them to Islam and tell them of what Allah has enjoined upon them. By God! If one person embra-ces Islam at your hands it will be better for you than the best of all blessings.

20. *Sahl ibn Sa'ad* is reported to have related that there was a ruler of Medina from the family of Marwan who summoned Sahl ibn Sa'ad and ordered him to insult Ali. Sahl refused so he said to him: 'Since you have refused, may God curse Abu al Turab.' Sahl said: 'the best name I liked for Ali was the name Abu al Turab." He said: 'Tell me why Ali was called Abu Turab?' He said: 'The Mes-senger of Allah (peace & blessings of Allah be with him) went to Fatimah's house but did not find Ali there. He asked her: 'Where is your cousin?' She replied: 'we had an argument and he was angry with me and left. He did not take his mid afternoon rest in the house.' The Apostle of Allah (peace & blessings of Allah be with him) asked someone to look for him. That person came back and said: 'O Messenger of Allah! He is sleeping in the mosque.' The holy Prophet (peace & blessings of Allah be with him) went to the mosque and found Ali lying there. His shoulder wrap had fallen down to one side of his body and he was covered in dust. The Messenger of Allah (peace & blessings of Allah be with him) wiped the dust from his body saying: 'get up! O Abu Turab (dust), get up O Abu Turab (dust)'.

21. *Abu Uthman* is reported to have said that no one remained with the Messenger of Allah (peace & blessings of Allah be with him) during the battles in which he took part except Talha and Sa'ad.

22. *Jabir ibn Abd Allah* is reported to have related that the Messenger of Allah (peace & blessings of Allah be with him) asked his men on the day of the Trench (Battle of the Trench) if anyone can bring him news of the unbelievers. So no one except Al- Zubair volunteered. Then he asked them again, and again Al-Zubair volunteered. Then he asked again, and Al-Zubair volunteered. Then the Prophet remarked: For every Prophet there are disciples, and Al-Zubair is my disciple.

23. *Abu Hurayra* is reported to have said: The Messenger of Allah (peace & blessings of Allah be with him) was on the mountain of Hira' along with Abu Bakr, Umar, Uthman, Ali, Talha and Zubair, when the mountain shook. So the Apostle of Allah (peace & blessings of Allah be with him) said: Be still, for there is none upon you but a Prophet, a true believer (Siddiq) and a Martyr.

24. *Hadrat Ayesha* is reported to have narrated that the Messenger of Allah (peace & blessings of Allah

be with him) was at vigil during a night and when he arrived in Medina he said: 'If only a God fearing man from my companions would stand guard for me tonight!' All of a sudden the sound of clattering Armour was heard. He asked: 'Who is there?' He said: 'I am Sa'ad ibn Abu Waqqas.' The Messenger of Allah (peace & blessings of Allah be with him) asked him: 'What has brought you here?' He said: 'I feared for the Messenger of Allah and so I have come to stand guard for him.' So the holy Prophet (peace & bles-sings of Allah be with him) prayed for him and slept.

25. *Musab ibn Sa'ad* is reported to have related that his father said: There are verses of the Qur'ân that were revea-led regarding me." He said: 'Umm Sa'ad swore that she would never speak to him, nor eat or drink until he renegades on his religion. And she said: 'You claim hat God Almighty has enjoined upon you to be good to your parents, so I am your mother and order you to renegade.' He said: She persisted for three days, and then fell uncons-cious from weariness. Then her son Umara gave her a drink, and she invoked against Sa'ad. Then God Almighty revealed: 'And We have enjoined upon mankind to be kind to parents...' (Q. 29: 8) And: 'And if they try to force you to associate (partners) with Me that whereof you have no knowledge, do not obey them. And keep company with them in this life in kindness...'

(Q.31: 15). He said: 'The Messenger of Allah (peace & blessings of Allah be with him) gained much booty and there was a sword among it. So I took it to the Prophet (peace & blessings of Allah be with him) and said: 'Give me this sword as me booty as I am the only one who can appreciate it.' He said: 'Return it back to where you got it.' I took it back until I was going to throw it with the rest of the booty, but my soul restrained me, so I went back to him and said: 'Let me have it.' He spoke to me harshly saying: 'Return it back to where you took it.' So God Almighty revealed: 'They ask you about the spoils of war...' (Q. 8: 1). He said: 'I felt ill and I sent for the Apostle of Allah (peace & blessings of Allah be with him) and he came to me, and I said to him: 'Let me divide me wealth as I wish.' But he refused. I said: 'Then the half.' But he refused. So I said: 'Then the third.' He did not say anything. Since then the third became permissible. He said: 'I passed by some of the Ansars and Muhajirin and they said: 'Come, we will feed you and give you alcohol to drink.' This was before alcohol was prohibited. So I went with them and they were in a garden and I found a roasted camel head and a con-tainer of alcohol. He said: 'So I ate and drank with them.' And he said: 'We talked about the Ansars and Muhajirin, so I said that the Muha-jirin are better than the Ansars. One man took up a jaw-bone of the camel and struck me with it and cut me nose. I went to the Messen-ger of Allah (peace & blessings of Allah be with him) and told him about it, then God Almighty revealed regarding me: 'O you who believe! Most certainly intoxi-cants and gambling and idol worship and fortunes telling are an abomination of Satan's handiwork, so shun it... (Q. 5: 90).

26. *Hudhaifa* is reported to have related that the people of Najran visited the holy Prophet (peace & blessings of Allah be with him) and said: O Messen-ger of Allah! Send with us a trustworthy man. He said: I will send with you a trust-worthy man, truly a trustworthy man. So the people looked around to see who that would be. He said: He sent Abu Ubaida ibn Jarrah.

27. *Salama ibn al Aqua* is reported to have related that he was privileged to lead the white mule upon which the Messenger of Allah (peace & blessings of Allah be with him) was mounted, and Al-Hasan and Al-Hussain were with him, until it reached the house of the Prophet (peace & blessings of Allah be with him). One of them was seated in front of him and the other one was seated behind him.

28. *Abu Hurayra* is reported to have related that he went with the Messenger of Allah (peace & blessings of Allah be with him) in the daytime and they did not speak with each other until they reached the market of Bani Qainuqa, then he sat in the compound of Fatimah's

house and asked about his young grandson, but Fatimah kept the boy inside for some time. We thought she was changing his clothes or bathing him. After some time the boy came running until he reached the Prophet (peace & blessings of Allah be with him) and they embraced and kissed each other, so the Messenger of Allah (peace & blessings of Allah be with him) said: 'O God! I love him and so love him and love whoever loves him'.

29. *Al Miswar ibn Makhrama* is repor-ted to have related that Ali proposed to the daughter of Abu Jahl, when Fatimah heard about it she went to the Messenger of Allah (peace & blessings of Allah be with him) and said: Your people assert that you do not get angry for the sake of your daughters, and now Ali is going to marry the daughter of Abu Jahl.' So the Apostle of Allah (peace & blessings of Allah be with him) rose up and I heard him say: 'I gave one of my daughters to Abu Al- As ibn Al Rabi', and he was tru-thful to his word. And Fatimah is a part of me and I hate anything that upsets her. By God, the daughter of the Messenger of Allah will not be with the daughter of the enemy of Allah with one man.' So Ali put off the proposal.

30. *Hadrat Ayesha* is reported to have said: All the wives of the Prophet were with him when Fatimah came walking, and her gait resembled the gait of the Messenger of Allah (peace & blessings of Allah be with him). When he saw her, he welcomed her and said: 'Welcome

my daughter!' Then he made her sit on his right or on his left side, and then whis-pered to her and she cried. When he saw her distress, he whispered to her again, and she laughed. So I asked her: 'The Messenger of Allah has favored you above his wives when he whispered to you, so why did you cry? She said: I will never disclose the secrets of the Apostle of Allah. When the holy Prophet left for his heavenly abode I again asked Fatimah about it and she said: When he whispered to me for the first time that every year Gabriel used to revise the Qur'ân with me once but this year he has done it twice. I see that my death is near, so be God fearing and patient. So I cried as you saw and when he saw my grief he whispered to me again and said: O Fatimah, are you not happy to know that you shall be the first lady of the believing women of this com-munity? So I laughed as you saw.

31. It is reported from *Zayed ibn Arqam* that the Apostle of Allah (peace & blessings of Allah be with him) said: As for our purposes, o people, I am a human being. I may be about to receive a message from my Lord, and I shall respond to the sum-moning of God. But I leave you with two momentous things, one is the Book of Allah in which there is right guidance and light, so hold fast to the Book of Allah ...and the second are the members of my family. I remind you concerning the members of my family. 'Zayed was asked: Who are the members of his family? Are not his wives the members of his family?' So he said: 'His wives are the members of his family, the members of his family are those for whom acceptance of Zakat is forbid-den.' And he said: 'Who are they?' So he said: 'Ali and the offspring of Ali, Aqil and the offspring of Aqil, the offspring of Jaa'fer and the offspring of Abbas.' Hussain said: 'Are they those for whom the acceptance of Zakat is for-bidden? Zayed said: yes.

32. *Hadrat Ayesha* is reported to have said: The Messenger of Allah (peace & blessings of Allah be with him) told me: 'you were shown to me in a dream. An angel brought you to me, wrapped in a piece of silken cloth, and said to me: 'This is your wife.' I lifted the piece of cloth from your face, and there you were. I said to myself. If this is from God, then it will surely come to pass.

33. It is reported on the authority of *Hadrat Ayesha* that the people used to do their best to find out which day was my day and then send their gifts on that day, and they thereby sought the pleasure of the Messen-ger of Allah (peace & blessings of Allah be with him).

34. *Hadrat Ayesha* is reported to have related that the wives of the Messenger of Allah (peace & bles-sings of Allah be with him) sent Fatimah, the daughter of the Prophet (peace & blessings of Allah be with him). She sought permission to enter as he had been lying with me in my blanket. He gave her permission and she said:

'O Messen-ger of Allah! Your wives have sent me to ask you to give equal treatment to them with the daughter of Abu Quhafa.' I remained silent. Then the Apostle of Allah (peace & blessings of Allah be with him) said: 'O daughter, do you not love whom I love?' She said: 'Yes.' Then he said: 'I love this one.' Fatimah left and told the wives of Prophet what she had said to him and what she had been told by the Prophet (peace & blessings of Allah be with him).' So they said to her: 'we see you have not assisted us. So go back to the Messenger of Allah and tell him that his wives seek equal treatment with the daughter of Abu Quhafa.' Fati-mah said: 'By God, I shall never speak to him again concerning that.' The wives of the Prophet then sent Zainab bint Jahsh, the wife of the Messenger of Allah (peace & blessings of Allah be with him) as she was the nearest to me in standing with the Messenger of Allah (peace & blessings of Allah be with him).I had never seen a more pious woman than Zainab, no one more God fearing, more truthful, more conscious of the ties of blood relations, more generous, more self-sacrificing in her daily life and with a kinder nature which brought her closer to God Almighty. She was quick to anger but equally quick to forgive. The Prophet (peace & blessings of Allah be with him) permitted her to enter. I was with the Messenger of Allah (peace & blessings of Allah be with him) in my blanket, in similar circumstances as when Fatimah

had entered. She said: 'O Messenger of Allah, your wives have sent me to you, seeking equal treatment with the daughter of Abu Quhafa.' Then she came near me and showed harshness towards me. I looked at the eyes of the Prophet (peace & blessings of Allah be with him) to see if he would permit me to speak. Zainab continued until I realized that the Messenger of Allah (peace & blessings of Allah be with him) would not be annoyed if I replied. Then I exchanged words with her until she became silent. So the Apostle of Allah (peace & blessings of Allah be with him) smiled and said: 'She is the daughter of Abu Bakr. Zuhri also related this Hadith with some varia-tion.

35. *Hadrat Ayesha* is reported to have said: I heard the holy Prophet speaking before his death while he was resting his back on me and saying: O Allah! Forgive me, and confer Your Mercy upon me, and let me meet the companions.

36. It is reported that *Hadrat Ayesha* said: When the Prophet was in good health he used to say: 'No soul of any prophet is taken before he is shown his place in Paradise and then he is given a choice.' When death approached him while his head was on my thigh, he became unconscious and then recovered his consciousness. Then he looked at the ceiling of the house and said: O God! The highest companions.' I thought: 'He has not chosen us.' Then I realized that what he had said was what he had told us before when he was in good health. The last words he said were: 'O God! The highest companions.'

37. It is reported that *Hadrat Ayesha* related that the Messenger of Allah (peace & blessings of Allah be with him) said to her: O Ayesha! This is Gabriel and he sends his salutations to you. Ayesha said: Salutations to him, and May Allah have Mercy upon him and bless him. And she said to the Prophet (peace & blessings of Allah be with him): You can see what I do not see.

38. *Abu Musa* is reported to have related that the Messenger of Allah (peace & blessings of Allah be with him) said: Many men attained perfection but of women none attained perfec-tion except Mary, the daughter of Imran, and Asiya the wife of Pharaoh. And the superiority of Ayesha over other women is like the superiority of Tharid (bread with soup) to other meals.

39. *Abu Musa* is reported to have related that the Messenger of Allah (peace & blessings of Allah be with him) said: Many men attained perfection but of women none attained perfection except Mary, the daugh-ter of Imran, and Asiya the wife of Pharaoh. And the superiority of Ayesha over other women is like the superiority of Tharid (bread with soup) to other meals.

40. *Abd Allah ibn Jafar* is reported to have said that he heard Ali saying at al Kufa: 'I heard the Messenger of

Allah (peace & blessings of Allah be with him) say: 'The best of women is Mary the daughter of Imran, and the best of its women is Khadija bint Khuwailid.'

41. *Abu Hurayra* is reported to have related: Gabriel came to the Prophet (peace & blessings of Allah be with him) and said: 'O Messenger of Allah, Khadija comes to you brin-ging a dish of cooked stew, or food or drink, so when she comes tell her that her Lord, Most High and I, send our salutations to her. And give her the glad tidings of a house in Para-dise made of engraved pearls. There is neither disturbance there nor weariness.

42. *Hadrat Ayesha* is reported to have said: I never felt jealous of any of the wives of the Prophet except Khadija, although I never saw her. And the Messenger of Allah used to say whenever he slaughtered a sheep: 'Send it to the friends of Khadija.' So one day I annoyed him by saying: 'Khadija!' Then he said: 'I had the privilege of loving her'.

43. *Hadrat Ayesha* is reported to have said: The Messenger of Allah (peace & blessings of Allah be with him) did not marry any other women till Khadija died.

44. It is reported that *Hadrat Ayesha* said: Hala bint Khuwailid, the sister of Khadija, came seeking permission to enter to see the Messenger of Allah (peace & blessings of Allah be with him). He felt pleased to see her and said: 'O God, Hala bint Khuwailid.' I felt jealous and said: 'You still

remember an old woman of the old women of Quraysh, with red gums, who died a long time ago while God has compensated you with better than her.

45. It is reported that *Hadrat Ayesha*, the mother of the believers, said that the Messenger of Allah (peace & blessings of Allah be with him) said: The first of you to follow me will be the one who has the longest hand. She said: So we vied (in charity) with each other to be the one with the longest hand. Zainab had the longest hand because she used to make things with her own hands and give them in charity.

46. *Anas ibn Malik* is reported to have said: The Prophet never visited any woman other than his wives, except Umm Sulaim. They asked him about it so he said: I am only being kind to her because her brother was killed with me.

47. *Anas ibn Malik* is reported to have related that the Prophet said: I entered Paradise and heard the sound of footsteps, so I said: 'Who is it?' They said: 'it is Ghumaisa bint Milhan, the mother of Anas ibn Malik.

48. *Anas* is reported to have related that after that death of the Messenger of Allah (peace & blessings of Allah be with him), Abu Bakr told Umar: Let us visit Umm Aiman as the holy Prophet (peace & blessings of Allah be with him) used to visit her. When they visited her, she began to weep. They asked her: 'why are you weeping? What awaits the Messen-

ger of Allah (peace & blessings of Allah be with him) in the Hereafter is better.' She said: I am not weeping because I am unaware that what awaits the Messenger of Allah (peace & blessings of Allah be with him) is better, but I am weeping because the Revelation that was sent down from Heaven has been terminated. They were both moved to tears by this and wept with her.

49. *Ibn Umar* is reported to have said: We did not call Ibn Haritha by any name other than Zayed ibn Mohammed, until the verse in the Qur'an was revealed: 'Call them by the names of their fathers, that is more just in the sight of God...' (Q.33: 5).

50. It is reported from *Ibn Umar* that the Messenger of Allah (peace & blessings of Allah be with him), said while he was on the pulpit: If you reject his appoint-ment as commander- he meant Usama ibn Zayed - you have rejected the Imara of his father before him. By God he was the best one for it, and by God he is the most beloved one of the people to me, and by God, this one is the best one for it - he meant Usama ibn Zayed - and by God, he is the most beloved one to me after him. So I commend you to look after him, he is one of your righteous people.

51. *Abu Hurayra* is reported to have related that the Messenger of Allah (peace & blessings of Allah be with him) said to Bilal at the dawn prayer: O Bilal! Tell me of the best deeds you have done in the cause of

Islam, as I heard tonight the sound of your footsteps before me in Paradise. Bilal said: I did not do any deed for Islam which I liked better than that whenever I perform ablution at any hour of the day or night, I pray that God will permit me to pray as much as He pleases.

52. *Anas* is reported to have related: My mother Umm Anas took me to the Apostle of Allah (peace & blessings of Allah be with him). She wrapped her veil around me as a waist wrapper and covered the rest of my body with the other half of it and said: 'O Messenger of Allah! This is my son Anas, I have brought him to serve you, so pray to God for him.' He said: 'O God! Confer upon him wealth and sons.' Anas said: 'By God, my wealth is too much, and my sons and the sons of my sons are more than a hundred today.

53. *Abu Musa* is reported to have said that: we received news of the Prophet's (peace & blessings of Allah be with him) migration when we were in Yemen. So we decided to migrate too. We were my two brothers and myself and I was the youngest, and one was Abu Barda and the other was Abu Ruhm. We numbered fifty three or fifty two men from our people, we boarded a boat to take us to Negus (Ethiopia) and there we met Jafar ibn Ali Talib who was with his compa-nions, then Jafar said: The Messenger of Allah sent us here and told us to stay, so stay with us, so we stayed with him. Then we all left and visited the Messenger of Allah (peace & blessings of Allah be with him) and he allocated shares for us, or he said, he gave us a part, but he did not allocate any shares for anyone who had not participated in the conquest of Khyber other than for those who had participated in the Battle with him. But for the people of our boat and Jafar and his companions he allocated shares. Some of the people on the boat said: 'We migrated before you.' Asma' bint Umais who was among us, went to visit Hafsa, the wife of the Prophet (peace & blessings of Allah be with him). She had migrated to Negus with other Muslims. Umar visited Hafsa when Asma' bint Umais was with her, Umar saw Asma' and said: 'Who is that?' She said: 'Asma' bint Umais.' Umar said; 'Is she the lady from Habash (Ethiopia) who journeyed by sea?' Asma' said: 'Yes.' Umar said: 'We emigrated before you so we have more right than you towards the Messenger of Allah.' Asma' was angry at this and said: 'No, by God, when you were with the Messenger of Allah (peace & blessings of Allah be with him) who was feeding the hungry among you, and teaching the ignorant among you, we were in the far land of Habash (Ethiopia) for the cause of God. By God, I will not eat or drink until I tell the Apostle of Allah (peace & blessings of Allah be with him) what you have said. We suffered harm and fear there, I will tell this to the Prophet (peace & blessings of Allah be with him) and ask him. So when the Prophet (Prayers & peace be

upon him) came she said: 'O Prophet of God! Umar said so and so.' The Messenger of Allah (peace & blessings of Allah be with him) said: He has no more right towards me than you, for he and his companions have emigrated once, and you people of the boat emigrated twice'. Later Asma' said: Abu Musa and the other people of the boat asked me about this Hadith many times in groups, and to them nothing in the world was more joyous and greater than what the Prophet had said about them.' Abu Barda said that Asma' said: Abu Musa asked me to repeat this Hadith again and again.

54. *Abd Allah ibn Jafar* is reported to have related that when the Messenger of Allah (peace & blessings of Allah be with him) used to return from a journey, the children of his family would go out to welcome him. Once when he returned from a journey I was the first to meet him. He put me before him on his mount and then one of the two sons of Fatimah came and he put him behind him on his mount and in this way the three of us entered Medina riding upon the animal.

55. *Abd Allah ibn Umar* is reported to have narrated that during the lifetime of the Messenger of Allah (peace & blessings of Allah be with him) if anyone had a dream he would relate it to the Prophet (peace & blessings of Allah be with him). I wished to have a dream to relate to the Prophet. When I was an unmarried youth I used to sleep in the Mosque during the lifetime of

the Apostle of Allah (peace & blessings of Allah be with him) and I had a dream in which I saw two angels holding me and taking me to the Fire. It was surrounded with walls like the sides of a well with two poles in its midst and I recognized the people there. I began to say: 'I seek refuge in Allah from the Fire, I seek refuge in Allah from the Fire, I seek refuge in Allah from the Fire.' Then I met another angel who told me not to fear. I related the dream to Hafsa who related it to the Messenger of Allah (peace & bles-sings of Allah be with him). He said: 'Abd Allah is a good man; I wish he would pray the night prayer. Salim said: Thereafter Abd Allah would only sleep a little during the night.

56. *Abd Allah ibn Mas'ud* is reported to have said: When the verse was revea-led: 'There is no blame upon those who believe and do good deeds, for what they have eaten before if they abstain from it now, and they are certain in their faith.' to the end. The Messenger of Allah (peace & blessings of Allah be with him) said: you are of them.

57. It is reported that *Abu al Ahwas* said: We were in the house of Abu Musa together with some of the companions of Abd Allah and they were looking at the Book. Abd Allah rose up and Abu Mas'ud said: I do not know if the Messenger of Allah (peace & blessings of Allah be with him) left anyone more know-ledgeable after him than the man who is standing now.' Abu Musa said: what you say is correct, for he was present when we were absent, and he was permitted when we were denied.

58. *Abd Allah ibn Mas'ud* reportedly said: The verse: '...and whoever commits betrayal will be brought on the Day of Resurrection carrying what he has betrayed...' (Q.3: 161) Then he asked: What kind of citation do you wish me to cite? I memo-rized more than seventy Surah directly from the Messenger of Allah (peace & blessings of Allah be with him) the companions of the Prophet came to know that I am one of the most knowledgeable of the Book of Allah, and if there was one of them more know-ledgeable than I then I would have gone to him." And Shaqiq said: I sat among the circle the companions of Muhammad and I heard no one oppose or refute what he said.

59. *Masruq* is reported to have said: Abd Allah was mentioned before Abd Allah ibn Amr and the latter said: 'He is a man I shall always love because I heard the Messenger of Allah (peace & blessings of Allah be with him) say: 'Memorize the recitation of the Qur'an from these four, Abd Allah ibn Mas'ud, Salim, the freed slave of Abu Hudhaifa, Ubayy ibn Ka'b, and Muaz ibn Jabal.

60. *Jabir ibn Abd Allah* is reported to have said: On the day of the Battle of Uhud, my father was killed and he was carried and placed in front of the Messenger of Allah (peace & blessings of Allah be with him) covered with a sheet. I moved to uncover my father but people prevented me, then I moved again to uncover him but my people prevented me. The Messenger of Allah (peace & blessings of Allah be with him) gave the order and he was moved away. Then he heard the voice of a weeping woman and asked: 'Who is that?' They said: 'It is the daughter or the sister of Amr.' He said: why is she weeping for the angels were shading him with their wings until he was moved away.

61. *Amer ibn Sa'ad* reportedly related on the authority of his father who said: I never heard the Messenger of Allah (peace & blessings of Allah be with him) say to any living soul that he would go to Paradise, except to Abd Allah ibn Salaam.

62. *Khrasha ibn al Hurr* is reported to have related that he was sitting in a circle in the Medina Mosque where there was a handsome scholar; he was Abd Allah ibn Salaam. He addressed them in a good way and when he had left the people said: Whoever wishes to gaze upon one of the inhabitants of Paradise, them let him cast his eyes upon this man.' So I said: 'By God, I shall follow him to know his house.' I followed him as he set off towards the outskirts of Medina, then he entered his house, and I sought per-mission to see him and I was admitted. Then he said: 'O son of my brother, what can I do for you?' I said: 'I heard the people say when you rose up: 'Whoever wishes to gaze upon one of the inhabi-tants of Paradise, them let him cast his eyes upon this man.' So I liked to be with you.' He said: God knows of the inha-bitants of Paradise, and I shall tell you concerning that which they have said. While I was asleep I saw a man coming to me saying: 'Get up!' He took my hand and I went with him, and I saw a path upon my left, so I intended to go on it but he said to me: 'Do not take it, for it is the way of the people of the Left.' Then I saw a straight path upon my right, he said to me: 'Take it.' Then I reached a mountain and he said to me: 'Ascend it.' So I intended to ascend it but I fell back. And I repeated that several times, then he took me with him on until we reached a place, whose summit was in the sky and whose base was upon the ground. At the top of it I saw a ring, he said to me: 'Climb it.' I asked: 'How can I ascend this while its summit is in the sky?' He took my hand and pushed me up until I found myself holding the ring, then he struck the pillar and it fell while I remained holding on to the ring until the morning. I went to the Prophet and related this to him, so he said: 'As for the path you saw on your left, it is the path of the people of the left, but the path which you saw on your right, it is the path of the people of the right. The moun-tain is the place of the martyrs and you will not attain it. But as for the pillar it is the pillar of Islam, and as for the ring, it is the ring of Islam, and you will remain holding on to it until you die.

63. It is reported from *Jabir ibn Abd Allah* that the Messenger of Allah (peace & blessings of Allah be with

him) said: When the bier of Sa'ad ibn Muaz was placed before them, the Throne of the Most Merciful shook.

64. *Al Bara'* is reported to have related that a silk cloak was presented to the Messenger of Allah (peace & blessings of Allah be with him), his Companions touched it and admi-red its softness, so he said: You are amazed by its softness? The hand-kerchief of Sa'ad ibn Muaz in Paradise is much better and softer that this.

65. *Anas* is reported to have narrated that one of Abu Talha's sons was taken ill and died while Abu Talha was not at home. His wife washed and shrouded him and laid him somewhere in the house. When Abu Talha came home he asked: 'How is the boy now?' She replied: The child is quiet and I hope he is in peace. Abu Talha supposed she had told him the truth so he passed the night and in the morning he bathed and got ready to go out, then she told him his son had died. Abu Talha offered the prayer with the Prophet (peace & blessings of Allah be with him) and told him what had happened. The Messenger of Allah (peace & blessings of Allah be with him), said: May Allah bestow His blessings on you for your night.

66. It is reported from *Anas* that the holy Qur'an was compiled during the life time of the Messenger of Allah (peace & blessings of Allah be with him) by four persons who belonged to the Ansar: Muaz ibn

Jabal, Ubayy ibn Ka'b, Zayed ibn Thabit and Abu Zayed. Qatada said: I asked Anas: Who is Abu Zayed? He said: One of my uncles.

67. *Abd Allah ibn al Samit* is reported to have related that Abu Zarr said: We departed from our tribe Ghifar who regard the prohibited months as permis-sible months. My brother Unais, our mother and I stayed with our maternal uncle who treated us well. The men of his tribe felt jealous and they said: 'when you are away from your house, Unais commits adultery with your wife. Our maternal uncle came and he accused us of the sin he had been told of. I said: 'you have undone the good you did for us; we cannot remain with you any longer. We loaded our baggage and our maternal uncle began to weep, and wrapped himself by a cloth. We went on until we camped near Makka. Unais played lots on the camels and it fell to an equal number. They both went to a fortuneteller and he made Unais win and Unais came with our camels and an equal number beside them. He said: 'My nephew, I used to offer prayer three years before I met the Messenger of Allah (peace & blessings of Allah be with him). I asked: 'To whom did you offer your prayer?' He said: 'To Allah.' I said: 'In which direction did you turn your face?' He said: 'I used to turn my face as God commanded me to turn my face. I used to observe the night prayer towards the end of night and I fell down in prostration like a cloak until the sun rose over me.' Unais said: 'I have business in Makka, so you had better stay here.' Unais went on until he reached Makka and he returned to me late. I said: 'What did you do?' He said: 'I met a man in Makka who is from your Religion and he claims that God has sent him.' I said: 'What do the people say about him?' He said: 'They say that he is a poet or a fortune teller or a magician.' Unais was a poet himself and he said: 'I have heard the words of a fortu-neteller but his words are not like that. I also compared his words with the verses of poets but any poet cannot utter such words. By God, he is truthful and they are liars.' Then I said: 'You stay here while I go to see him.' He said: 'I went to Makka and I asked an un-important man of the people there: 'Where is the one you call a Sabi'?' He pointed towards me, saying: 'He is a Sabi'.' Then the people of the valley atta-cked me with chunks of sand and bows until I fell down unconscious. I regained consciousness and found that I looked like a red image. I went to Zam Zam, washed the blood from myself and drank its water. O son of my brother, I stayed there for thirty nights or days and there was no food for me but the water of Zam Zam, and I became so thin that my stomach got wrinkled, but I did not feel any hunger in my stomach. It was during this time that the people of Makka slept during the moonlit night and no one used to circum-ambulate the House except two women who had been invoking the name of Isafa and Na'ilah. They came to me as they went round and I said: 'Let one marry the other.' But they did not desist from their invocation. They came towards me and I said to them: 'Put wood inside them.' I was unable to express it figuratively. The women went away crying and saying: 'If any of our people had been here he would have taught you a lesson.' The women met the Messenger of Allah (peace & blessings of Allah be with him) and Abu Bakr who had also been coming down the hill. He asked them: 'What is the matter with you?' They said: 'It is Sabi', who has hidden himself between the Ka'ba and its curtain.' He said: 'What has he said to you?' They said: 'We cannot repeat the words he said to us.' The Messenger of Allah (peace & blessings of Allah be with him) came and he kissed the Black Stone, circumam-bulated the House with his companion and then offered prayer. Abu Zee said: 'When he had completed his prayer, I was the first to greet him with the saluta-tion of peace and I said: 'O Messenger of Allah, peace be upon you.' He said: 'May it be upon you too, and the mercy of God.' Then he asked: 'Who are you?' I said: 'I am from Ghifar.' He raised his hand and placed his finger on his forehead and I thought to myself: 'Perhaps he does not like that I am from Ghifar.' I tried to take hold of his hand but his friend, who knew him better than I, prevented me from doing so. He then raised his head and asked: 'How long have you been here?' I said: 'I have been here for the last thirty nights or days.' He said: 'Who has been feeding you?' I said: 'I have had no food, only the water of Zam Zam and I have become so thin that my stomach is wrink-led but I do not feel any hunger.' He said: 'It is blessed and it is like food.' Then Abu Bakr said: 'O Messenger of Allah, let me offer him hospitality tonight. Then the Apostle of Allah (peace & blessings of Allah be with him) left and so did Abu Bakr, and I went along with them. Abu Bakr opened the door and brought us raisins from Tayef, and that was the first food I ate there. Then I stayed as long as I needed. Then I visited the Messenger of Allah (peace & blessings of Allah be with him) and he said: 'I have been shown a land luxuriant with trees and I think it must be Yathrib. You go and teach the people from my side and I hope God will enable you to be of benefit for them and He will reward you.' I returned to Unais and he asked: 'What have you done?' I said: 'I have embraced Islam and I have borne witness.' He said: 'I am not averse to your Religion and I also embrace Islam and I bear witness.' Then we both went to our mother and she said: 'I am not averse to your Religion and I also embrace Islam and I bear witness that Muhammad is the Messenger of Allah.' We then loaded our camels and returned to our people of Ghifar and half of them embraced Islam and their leader was Ayma ibn Rahada Ghifari and he said: 'We will embrace Islam when the

Mes-senger of Allah comes to Medina.' So when the Prophet (peace & blessings of Allah be with him) came to Medina the other half of them also embraced Islam. Then the tribe of Aslam came to the Prophet and said: 'O Messe-nger of Allah, we also have accepted Islam like our brothers who have embraced Islam.' And they also converted to Islam. Then the Messenger of Allah (peace & blessings of Allah be with him) said: God forgave the tribe of Ghifar and God saved the tribe of Aslam.

68. *Ibn Abbas* is reported to have narrated that when Abu Zarr heard of the advent of the holy Prophet, he said to his brother: Ride to the valley and bring me the news of the man who claims to be a Prophet recei-ving inspiration from Heaven. Hear what he says and then return to me. His brother set out until he met the Prophet and listened to his speech and returned to Abu Zarr and said: I have seen him admonishing the people to good and his speech was not as poetry. Abu Zarr said: You have not done as I wished. So he set off for Makka. When he arrived there he went to the Mosque looking for the Prophet, and he did not know whom he was nor did he like to question anyone about him. After part of the night had passed Ali saw him and realized that he must be a stranger. Abu Zarr followed him but they did not question each other about anything until the morning, when he took his water-skin and food and went to the Mosque. He passed the day without the Prophet noticing him until the night, then when he returned to the place he was sleeping, Ali saw him again and asked: 'Has that man not found anyplace to stay as yet?' So Ali took him to his house, but they did not question each other about anything, until the third day when Abu Zarr stayed with him again. Then Ali asked: Tell me why you have come here? He replied: If you promise me that you will direct me I will tell you. After Ali promised to do so, Abu Zarr told him the reason. Ali said: it is the Truth, and he is the Messenger of Allah. Follow me in the morning, and if I think that there is any danger to you, I will warn you by pretending to go to the latrine. But if I continue walking, follow me until you enter the place I will enter. Abu Zarr agreed and followed Ali until he entered the place where the Prophet was, and Abu Zarr entered with him. Then he listened to the speech of the Prophet and embraced Islam there and then. The Prophet said to him: Return to your people and teach them until you receive my word. Abu Zarr said: By Him in Whose Hands is my soul; I shall annou-nce my Islam aloud before them all. He went out to the Mosque and announced as loudly as he could: 'I bear witness that there is no god but Allah and Muhammad is His servant and Messenger.' The people then beat him up until they knocked him down. Al-Abbas came and threw himself over him saying:

Woe to you, do you not know he is from Ghifar upon the high-way your tradesmen take to al Sham? So he saved him from them. Abu Zarr did the same the following day and the people beat him again, and Al Abbas threw himself over him once again.

69. *Abu Musa* is reported to have narrated: I was with the Prophet (peace & blessings of Allah be with him) when he camped at Al Ja'ana between Makka and Medina with Bilal. A bedouin visited the Apostle of Allah (peace & blessings of Allah be with him) and said: Will you honour your promise to me? The Prophet (peace & blessings of Allah be with him) said: Be glad. The bedouin said: 'Be glad,' many times. Then the Messenger of Allah (peace & blessings of Allah be with him) got angry, turned towards Bilal and me and said: The bedouin has rejected the good news. So you both accept it. Bilal and I said: 'We accept.' Then the Prophet (peace & blessings of Allah be with him) asked for a drinking vessel of water and washed his hands and face in it and took a mouthful of water and returned it to us saying: Drink some of it and pour some of it over your chests and faces and be glad at the good news. So they both took the drinking vessel and did as they were directed. Umm Salama called from behind the screen: Keep some for your mother. So they saved some of it for her.

70. *Abu Musa* reported that when the Prophet (peace & blessings of Allah be with him) was through with the Battle of Hunayn he sent Abu Amir to Autas as commander of an army. He met Duraid ibn Al Summa and Duraid was killed and God defeated his companions. The Prophet (peace & blessings of Allah be with him) sent me with Abu Amir. Abu Amir was hit in the knee by an arrow that got embedded in his knee. I went to him and said: O uncle! Who hurt you? He pointed out the man saying: That is my killer. So I set off towards him and caught up with him, when he saw me he fled and I pursued him saying: Stop, are you not ashamed? He stopped and we exchanged blows with our swords and I killed him. Then I said to Abu Amir: God has killed your murderer. He said: Remove this arrow. I removed it and water oozed from the wound. He said: 'O son of my brother! Give my salutations to the Prophet (peace & blessings of Allah be with him) and ask him to pray to God to forgive me.' Abu Amir made me his successor in command. He lived for a short while and then died. I returned to the Apostle of Allah (peace & blessings of Allah be with him) and told him about Abu Amr and that he had requested him to ask from God to forgive him. The Prophet (peace & blessings of Allah be with him) performed ablution and then lifted his hands saying: 'O God! Forgive Ubaid Abu Amir.' 'O God! Make him superior on the Day of Resurrection over many of Your servants.' I said: 'Will you ask for God's Forgiveness for me?' He said: O God, forgive the sins of Abd

Allah ibn Qais and admit him in good admittance on the Day of Recko-ning.

71. It is reported that Abu Hurayra said: I invited my mother, who was a polytheist, to Islam. One day I invited her and she said something about the Messenger of Allah (peace & blessings of Allah be with him) that I did not like. I came to the Prophet (peace & blessings of Allah be with him) weeping and said: 'O Messenger of Allah, I invited my mother to Islam but she rejected it. Then I invited her today and she said something about you that I did not like, so please invoke God Almighty to guide the mother of Abu Hurayra to the Right Path. Then the Apostle of Allah (peace & blessings of Allah be with him) said: 'O God, guide the mother of Abu Hurayra to the Right Path. I returned happily and when I reached home I found that the door was locked from inside. My mother heard the sound of my footsteps and she said: 'O Abu Hurayra, wait a moment.' I heard the splashing of water. She took a bath, put on her dress, quickly covered her head with a shawl opened the door and then said: 'Abu Hurayra, I bear witness that there is no god but Allah and Muhammad is His servant and Messen-ger.' I returned to the Prophet (peace & blessings of Allah be with him) weeping with joy. I said: 'O Messenger of Allah! Rejoice for God has answered your invocation and He has guided the mother of Abu Hurayra to the Right Path.' He praised Allah and extolled Him and spoke kind words. I said: 'O Messenger of Allah, invoke God to instill love in the hearts of the believers for my mother and me and let our hearts be filled with love for them. Then the Messenger of Allah (peace & blessings of Allah be with him) said: O God, let there be love for these of Your servants in the hearts of the believers and let their hearts be filled with love for the believers. God Almighty granted this so much that every believer ever born, who heard of me and who saw me did not fail to love me.

72. *Urwa* is reported to have related that Hadrat Ayesha said: Do you dislike Abu Hurayra? He came and sat beside my room relating about the Prophet so that I could hear him, and I was busy in my prayers and he left before I could complete my supplication. Had I seen him I would have refuted what he was saying. The Messenger of Allah (peace & bles-sings of Allah be with him) never related any Hadith as he (Abu Hurayra) did. Ibn Shihab reported on the authority of Ibn Masib that Abu Hurayra said: They say Abu Hurayra has related too much and our appointment is with God. And they also say: Why do the Muhajirin and the Ansars never relate as much as he does? I shall explain that for you. My brethren of the Ansars were busy working in their fields and my brethren of the Muhajirin were busy trading in the markets, but I was always near the Messenger of Allah (peace & blessings of Allah be with him), to be able to find something to eat.

While they were absent, I used to memo-rize while they forgot, and one day the Messenger of Allah (peace & blessings of Allah be with him) said: Any of you who spreads out his garment to take from my Hadith, and then gathers it to his chest, will never forget anything he hears. So I spread out my garment until he finished his Hadith, then I gathered it to my chest and I have not for-gotten anything he has related to me. Had it not been for two verses which God Almighty revealed of His Book, I would never have spoken of anything: 'Surely those who conceal the manifest Revelations and the guidance which We have revealed, after We have made it clear for the people in the Book, those it is who shall be cursed by God and by those who curse. Except those who repent and amend themselves, and made known the Truth, to them I turn in Mercy, indeed I am The Relenting, The All-Merciful.' (Q.2: 159-160).

73. It is reported from *Abu Zumayil* that Abd Allah ibn Abbas said: The Muslims did not have any regard for Abu Sufyan nor did they like his company. He said to the Prophet (peace & blessings of Allah be with him): 'O Messenger of Allah, grant me three things.' He said: 'Yes.' He said: 'I have the best and most beautiful woman with me Umm Habiba, the daughter of Abu Sufyan, so marry her.' He said: 'Yes.' And Abu Sufyan asked: 'Permit Mu'awiya to serve as your scribe.' He said: 'Yes.' Then he asked: 'Appoint me as commander so that I may fight against the unbelievers as I fought against the Muslims.' He said: 'Yes.' Abu Zumayil said: If he had not asked for these three things from the Messenger of Allah (peace & blessings of Allah be with him), he would have never granted them to him of his own wish, but he used to grant the requests made to him.

74. *Abu Barza* is reported to have said: The Prophet was in one of the battles when God Almighty bestowed booty upon him, then he said to his compa-nions: 'Is there someone missing?' They said: 'Yes, so and so, and so and so, and so and so.' Then he asked: 'Is there some-one missing?' They said: 'Yes, so and so, and so and so, and so and so.' Then he said: "Is there someone missing?' They said: 'No.' He said: 'But I have not seen Julaibibiaba, so find him. They looked for him and found him among the dead, with seven others whom he had killed. The Prophet came and stood over him and said: He killed seven then they killed him, he is of me and I am of him, he is of me and I am of him. Then he carried him in his arms and dug a grave for him and buried him in it.

75. *Abu Hurayra* is reported to have narrated that Umar ibn Al Khattab passed by Hasan ibn Thabit when he was reciting poetry in the Mosque. So he rebuked him saying: Remember where you are! He said: I used to say poetry here when the one who is better than you was present. Then he looked at Abu Hurayra and said: I ask you by

God, to answer me if you heard the Messenger of Allah (peace & blessings of Allah be with him) pray for me: O God strengthen him with the Holy Spirit. He replied: 'By God, yes.'

76. *Masruq* is reported to have related: We visited Hadrat Ayesha when Hasan ibn Thabit was reciting some of his poetry to her, saying: 'A virtuous wise lady of whom nobody can have suspicion. She rises with an empty stomach because she never eats the flesh of the indiscreet.' Ayesha said to him: 'But you are not like that.' I said to her: 'Why do you permit him to enter when God Almighty has said: '...and the one who took the lead and the greater part in it, for him there awaits a severe chastisement.' (Q.24: 11). Hadrat Ayesha replied: 'And what punishment is worse than blind-ness?' And she said: Hasan used to recite poetry for the Messenger of Allah (peace & blessings of Allah be with him).

77. It is reported on the authority of *Hadrat Ayesha* that the Messenger of Allah (peace & blessings of Allah be with him) said: Ridicule the Quraysh, as that is more injurious to them than the injury of an arrow. So Ibn Rawaha was asked to ridicule them. He composed a parody, but he was not satisfied with it so he sum-moned Ka'b ibn Malik and Hasan ibn Thabit. When Hasan entered he said: Now you have summoned a lion that strikes with its tail. He put out his tongue and moved it about and said: By Him Who has sent you with Truth; I shall rent them asunder with my tongue, as leather is rent asunder. The Messenger of Allah (peace & blessings of Allah be with him) said: Be not in such haste, permit Abu Bakr who is the most knowledgeable of the lineage of the Quraysh outline my lineage for you, as my lineage is the same as theirs. Hasan then went to him and enquired about it and then returned and said: O Messenger of Allah, he has out-lined your lineage. By Him Who has sent you with the Truth, I shall extract your name as a hair is extracted from flour. Ayesha said: I heard the Messenger of Allah (peace & blessings of Allah be with him) say to Hasan: Indeed, Gabriel will continue to assist you for as long as you defend Allah and His Messen-ger. And she said: I heard the Apostle of Allah (peace & blessings of Allah be with him) say: Hasan ridiculed them and made the Muslims pleased and tormen-ted the others. You ridiculed Muham-mad, But I respond for him, And God Almighty re-wards for that. You ridiculed Muham-mad, the virtuous, The righteous, the Messenger of Allah (Peace & bles-sings of Allah be with him), Whose very nature is truth. So indeed my father, his father and my honour is a protec-tion to the honour of Muhammad. May I lose my beloved daughter if you do not see her? Brushing off the dust from both sides of Kada. They pull the reins up. On their shoulders are spears thirsting. Our steeds are sweating, and our women wipe them with their cloaks. Had you not barred us, we would have performed the Lesser Pilgrimage. Then there was the victory, and the darkness lifted away. So wait for the confrontation on the day when God will honour whom He pleases. God Almighty has said: "I have sent a servant who speaks the Truth wherein is no ambi-guity." God has said: "I have readied an army of the Ansars who are intent on fighting. Each day there comes from Mu'adh abuse, fighting or ridicule. Whoever of you ridicules the Messenger of Allah, or praises him and helps him it is all the same, and Gabriel and the Messenger of Allah are with us, and The One who has no equal.

78. It is reported from *Jarir* that the Messenger of Allah (peace & blessings of Allah be with him) said: Will you get rid of Dhul-Khalasa for me? Dhul-Khalasa was a pagan shrine of the tribe of Khath'am known as Al Ka'ba Al Yama-niya. So, I set off with one hundred and fifty cavalrymen from the tribe of Ahmas, who were excellent horse-man. It happe-ned that I could not sit well upon horses, so the Prophet stroked my chest until I saw his fingerprints on my chest and he said: 'O God! Make him firm and make him one who guides and one who is rightly guided.' Jarir set off towards the shrine, demolished it and burnt it. Then he sent a mes-senger to the Prophet (peace & blessings of Allah be with him) to inform him of it. Jarir added: 'The Prophet invoked the blessing of Allah for the horses and the men of Ahmas five times.

79. *Umm Mubashshir* is reported to have said that she heard the Messenger of Allah (peace & blessings of Allah be with him) say in the presence of Hafsa: God willing, the people of the Tree will never enter the Fire of Hell. - one of them owed allegiance under it. She said: O Messenger of Allah! Why not?' He reprimanded her. Hafsa said: And there is none of you who shall not go down to it...'(Q.19: 71). Then the Apostle of Allah (peace & blessings of Allah be with him) said: God Almighty has said: Then We shall save those who were pious and shall leave the evildoers therein on their knees. (Q.19: 72).

80. It is reported on the authority of *Ali ibn Abu Talib* that the Messenger of Allah (peace & blessings of Allah be with him) sent him along with Al- Zubair and Al-Miqdad to Raudat to get a letter from a woman. Ali said: So we went and our horses ran at full speed until we reached Al- Raudat where we found the woman, we told her to give us the letter. She said: 'I have no letter.' So we said: Either you give us the letter or take your clothes off. So she took out the letter from her plaits. We took the letter to the Prophet (peace & blessings of Allah be with him) and it was from Hatib ibn Abu Balta'a addre-ssed to some unbe-lievers in Makka informing them of the Prophet's (peace & blessings of Allah be with him) affairs. The Apostle of Allah (peace & blessings of Allah be with him) said: 'O Hatib, what is this?' He replied: 'O Messen-ger of Allah! Do not be hasty with me. I was a

man from Quraysh but I was not of their people, and the Muhajirs who are with you have relatives there to protect their families and wealth in Makka. I only wanted to do them a favour so that they would protect my relatives in Makka. And I did not do that out of disbelief or to renege on my Religion.' So the Prophet (peace & blessings of Allah be with him) said: He has spoken the truth. Umar then said: 'O Messenger of Allah! Let me strike his neck. The Prophet (peace & blessings of Allah be with him) said: He fought in Badr, and how would you know, maybe God has looked at the people of Badr and said: Do as you please, I have forgiven you. The narrator said: This verse was revealed regarding him: 'O you who believe! Do not take my enemies and yours for friends, offering them friend-ship when they have rejected the Truth that has come to you, and expelling the Messenger and you only because you believe in Allah your Lord. If you go forth to strive in My Cause and seeking My pleasure, (take them not as friends) hol-ding secret communication of friendship with them, while I am best aware of what you hide and what you reveal, and whoever of you does that, has truly gone astray from the Right Path.' (Q. 60: 1)

81. It is reported from *Abu Hurayra* that the Prophet said: The tribes of Quraysh, Al-Ansar, Juhaina, Muzaina, Aslam, Ghifar and Ashja' are my helpers, and they have no protector but Allah and His Mes-senger.

82. *Abu Hurayra* is reported to have said that he heard the Messenger of Allah (peace & blessings of Allah be with him) say: Of all the women who ride camels, the ladies of Quraysh are the best, they have compassion and consideration for their children and they are the best guar-dians of their husband's property.

83. *Zayed ibn Arqam* is reported to have related that the Messenger of Allah (peace & blessings of Allah be with him) said: 'O God! Forgive the Ansars and the children of the Ansars and the grand-children of the Ansars.'

84. *Anas* is reported to have related that the Prophet (peace & blessings of Allah be with him) saw the women and children (of the Ansar) coming. The Apostle of Allah (peace & blessings of Allah be with him) stood up and said three times: By God! You are the dearest of people to me.

85. It is reported from *Anas ibn Malik* that the Messenger of Allah (peace & blessings of Allah be with him) said: Al- Ansar are my nearest and dearest and my most trusted, surely the people will say, more or less, but acknowledge their goodness and forgive them their wrong.

86. *Abu Asid al-Ansari* is reported to have said: I bear witness that the Messenger of Allah (peace & blessings of Allah be with him) said: The homes of the Bani An-Najjar are the best homes of the Ansars and thereafter those of the

Bani Abd Al Ash-hal, and thereafter those of the Bani Al Harith ibn al Khazraj and thereafter the Bani Saeeda, and there is good in all the homes of the Ansars. According to Abu Salama Abu Asid said: Do I accuse the Apostle of Allah? Had I been a liar, I would have begun with my own people of Bani Saeeda.' When Sa'ad ibn Ubada heard this he became angry and said: He made us the last of the four. I will visit the Messenger of Allah (peace & blessings of Allah be with him).' But the son of his brother, Sahl, said to him: 'are you going to say such a thing to the Messenger of Allah, while he knows better! Is it not sufficient for you to be the fourth of the four?' So he changed his mind and said: Allah and His Messenger know better.

87. *Abu Musa* is reported to have related that the Prophet (peace & blessin-gs of Allah be with him) said: When some of the Al Ashariyun recite the Qur'an I recognize their voices, and when they enter their homes at night I recognize their houses by their voices as they recite the Qur'an, although I do not see their houses as they enter them during the day. Of these is Hakim, who used to say when he encountered the enemy, or cavalry: My compa-nions order you to wait for them.

88. *Abu Hurayra* is reported to have related that the Messenger of Allah (peace & blessings of Allah be with him) said: May God protect the tribe of Aslam, and may God pardon the tribe of Ghifar!

89. *Abu Hurayra* is reported to have said: I have loved the tribe of Bani Tamim from the time I heard the Prophet (peace & blessings of Allah be with him) say about them: These people will stand firm against the false Messiah. When the gifts of charity came from them, the Messenger of Allah (peace & blessings of Allah be with him) said: These are the gifts of charity from our people.' Ayesha had a slave girl from that tribe and the Prophet (peace & blessings of Allah be with him) told her: Free her, for she is a descendant of Ishmael.

90. *Abu Barda'* is reported to have related on the authority of his father that he said: We prayed the sunset prayer with the Messenger of Allah (peace & blessings of Allah be with him) then we decided to stay put for the evening prayer with him. The Apostle of Allah (peace & blessings of Allah be with him) came out and asked: Are you still here? We said: O Messenger of Allah! we have prayed the sunset prayer with you, then we decided to sit until we pray the evening prayer with you.' He said: 'You have done the right thing.' - or 'You are right.' Then he raised his head towards the sky, as he used to do it many times, and said: 'the stars are safety for the sky. If the stars go, then the sky will bring to you what you have been promised. And I am security for my companions, when I go, my companions will get what they have been promised. And my companions are prote-ction for my

community, if my compa-nions go, my community will get what it has been promised.

91. **Abu Saeed Al- Khudri** is reported to have related that the Apostle of Allah (peace & blessings of Allah be with him) said: There will be a time when groups of people will go for Jihad and it will be asked: Were any of you in the company of the Prophet (peace & blessings of Allah be with him)?' They will say yes and they will be given victory because of that. Then there will be a time when it will be asked: 'Were any of you in the company of the companions of the Prophet (peace & blessings of Allah be with him)?' They will say yes and they will be given victory because of that. Then there will be a time when it will be said: Were any of you in the company of the companions of the companions of the Prophet (peace & blessings of Allah be with him)?' They will say yes and they will be given victory because of that.

92. **Imran ibn Hussain** is reported to have related that the Prophet (peace & blessings of Allah be with him) said: The best of all people are the people of my generation, then those who come after them, then those whom come after them. Imran said- I do not recall if he men-tioned two or three generations after his generation. - Then the Prophet said: Thereafter, there will come people whose witness will precede their oaths and their oaths will precede their witness, and obesity will appear among them.

93. **Abu Hurayra** is reported to have related that the Messenger of Allah (peace & blessings of Allah be with him) said: People are of different natures. Those who were the best in the times before Islam are also the best in Islam if they are know-ledgeable in the Religion. You see the best of such people are those who disdain to rule. And you see that the worst of people are the two faced, who appear to some with one face and to others with another face.

94. It is reported from **Abu Hurayra** that the Messenger of Allah (peace & blessings of Allah be with him) said: Do not hate my companions. Do not hate my Companions. By Him in Whose Hand is my soul, if any of you spends as much gold as the mountain of Uhud it would not amount to as much as one measure of theirs or even half of it.

95. It is reported from **Abu Zarr** that the Messenger of Allah (peace & blessings of Allah be with him) said: You will soon conquer Egypt, which is a land whose people are in the habit of using foul language. So when you conquer it, be good to its people because the rights of marital bond (Mariam, the wife of the holy Prophet was from Egypt) are due to them - so if you see any two of them disputing for the space of a brick, then get out of there.

96. It is reported on the authority of **Ibn Umar** that the Apostle of Allah (peace & blessings of Allah be with him) said: People are like camels; from one hundred of them you can hardly find one camel suitable to ride.

53

Book of Virtues, Manners and Relations

1. *Abu Hurayra* reported that the holy Prophet (peace & blessings of Allah be with him) said: Do not insult Time, as God is Time.

2. *Abu Hurayra* reported that the Messenger of Allah (peace & blessings of Allah be with him) was asked to invoke a curse upon the polytheists. He replied: I have not been sent to invoke curses, but I have been sent as a mercy.

3. *Abd Allah ibn Mas'ud* reported that the holy Prophet (peace & blessings of Allah be with him) said: Perished are those who are excessive in their words and deeds. He repeated it three times

4. *Nawwas ibn Sim'an* is reported to have related that he asked the Messenger of Allah (peace & blessings of Allah be with him) about virtue and vice. The holy Prophet replied: Virtue is a kind nature and vice is what festers in your heart and which you dislike to reveal to others.

5. *Abu Hurayra* is reported to have related that a man came to the holy Prophet (peace & blessings of Allah be with him) and said: O Messenger of Allah! Who deserves my best care and atten-tion?' The holy Prophet (peace & blessings of Allah be with him) replied: 'Your mother.' The man said: 'Who after that?' The Apostle of Allah (peace & blessings of Allah be with him) said: 'Your mother.' The man said: 'Who after that?' The Prophet (Prayers & peace be upon him) said: 'Your mother.' The man asked a fourth time: 'Who after that?' The Messen-ger of Allah (peace & blessings of Allah be with him) said: 'Then your father.'

6. *Abd Allah ibn Amr ibn al A'as* is reported to have related that a man visited the holy Prophet and said: 'I pledge my allegiance for emigration and Jihad, seeking the reward from Allah Most High.' He asked: 'Are your parents alive?' He replied in the affirmative. The Prophet said: 'Do you wish to seek the reward from Allah?' He said: 'Yes.' The Apostle of Allah said: Go back to your parents and look after them.

7. It is reported from *Al Mughirah ibn Shu'ba* that the Prophet (peace & blessings of Allah be with him) said: God has pro-hibited you to be undutiful to-wards your mothers, to bury your daughters alive, to neglect the rights of others. And God disapproves that you beg from people, engage in vain talk or ask persis-tently or be extravagant.

8. It is reported from *Abu Hurayra* that the Messenger of Allah (peace & blessings of Allah be with him) said: Let him be humbled into dust, let him be humbled into dust. It was asked: O Messenger of Allah! Who is that? He replied: The one who sees either of his parents reach old age or he sees both of them, but does not enter Paradise.

9. *Abd Allah ibn Umar* is reported to have related: When I used to travel out of Makka, I used to ride on a donkey when I felt tired of riding camels. And I covered my head with a turban. One day while I was on the donkey a bedouin passed me by and I said: 'Are you not the son of so and so?' He said: 'Yes.' So I gave him the donkey and told him to ride on it.' And also gave the turban to cover his head. Some of my companions said to me: 'May God forgive you, you have given the bedouin the donkey you ride upon and the turban you wrap around your head?' I said to them, I have heard the Messen-ger of Allah (peace & blessings of Allah be with him) say: The best of virtues are that a man maintains ties with those who loved his father after his father has died. My father was a friend of Umar.

10. It is reported on the authority of Hadrat Ayesha that she said: A lady and her two daughters came asking for charity, but I had nothing with me except one date which I gave her and she divided it between her daughters and did not eat anything herself. When the Prophet (peace & blessings of Allah be with him) came in and I told him what had happe-ned. He said: Whoever is given daughters and treats them kindly then they will be as a shield for him from the Fire (of Hell).

11. It is reported from *Anas ibn Malik* that the Messenger of Allah (peace & blessings of Allah be with him) said: Whoever brings up two daugh-ters well until they reach maturity, he and I will be this close on the Day of Resurrection. And he intertwined his fingers.

12. *Anas ibn Malik* is reported to have related that the Messenger of Allah (peace & blessings of Allah be with him) said: Whoever desires more wealth and wishes for a long life should care for the ties of blood relationship.

13. It is reported from *Abu Hurayra* that someone asked the Prophet: 'O Messenger of Allah! I have relatives with whom I try to keep good relationship, but they sever it. I treat them well, but they ill-treat me. I am kind to them but they are

harsh with me.' The Apostle of Allah said: If it is as you say, then throw blistering ash at them and there would always remain with you on behalf of God who would keep you dominant over them so long as you keep to this.

14. *Abu Hurayra* is reported to have related that the Messenger of Allah (peace & blessings of Allah be with him) said: God fashioned His creation, and when he had completed it the womb rose up and reached out for God, so God said: 'What is the matter?' It said: 'I seek refuge in You from those who sever the ties kinship.' God said: 'Will you be content if I grant My favour on those who preserve your ties and withhold My favour from those ho sever them?' It said: 'Yes, my Lord!' Then God said: 'So it is for you.' Abu Hurayra said: 'If you wish you can recite: 'Would you then, if you held authority, work corruption in the land and sever ties of kinship.' And it was related that Abu Hurayra said: 'then the Messenger of Allah (peace & blessings of Allah be with him) said: 'If you wish recite: 'would you then, if you held authority, work   corruption in the land and sever ties of kinship.

15. It is reported from *Jubair ibn Mut'im* that the Prophet said: The one who severs the bond of womb rela-tionship will not enter Paradise.

16. *Abu Hurayra* is reported to have related that the Messenger of Allah (peace & blessings of Allah be with him) said: The ward of the orphan or of another, shall be as near to me as this in Paradise. And Malik indicated with his index and middle fingers.

17. It is reported from *Abu Hurayra* that the Messenger of Allah (peace & blessings of Allah be with him) said: The one who cares for a widow or a needy person is like a fighter in God's Cause or like the one who prays all night and fasts all day.

18. *Abu Hurayra* is reported to have related that the apostle of Allah (peace & blessings of Allah be with him) said: On the Day of Resurrection God will say: Where are those who have loved each other for My sake? Today I shall protect them in My shade when there is no other shade but Mine.

19. *Abu Hurayra* is reported to have related that the Prophet (peace & blessings of Allah be with him) said: A man visited his brother in another town and God appointed an Angel to wait for him on the way, when he appeared to him he asked: 'Where do you intend to go?' He said: 'I am going to my brother in the town.' He said: 'Have you done him any favour?' He said: 'No, I only love him for the sake of God Almighty.' Then he said: 'I am a messenger from God and have come to tell you that God loves you as you love for His sake.

20. *Anas* is reported to have related that a man asked the Messenger of

Allah (peace & blessings of Allah be with him) about the (final) Hour saying: 'When will it come to pass?' The Prophet (peace & blessings of Allah be with him) said: 'What have you prepared for it?' He said: 'Nothing except that I love God and His Messenger.' The Apostle of Allah (peace & blessings of Allah be with him) said: 'You will be with those you love.' We never had been so happy as we were when we heard the Prophet (peace & blessings of Allah be with him) say: 'You will be with those you love.' So I love the Prophet (peace & blessings of Allah be with him), Abu Bakr and Umar and I hope I will be with them all even though my deeds are not as great as theirs.

21. *Abu Hurayra* is reported to have related that the Prophet (peace & blessings of Allah be with him) said: If God loves someone, He calls Gabriel and says: 'God loves so and so, O Gabriel, love him.' Gabriel will love him and announce before the dwellers of Heaven: 'God loves so and so, so you should love him as well.' And so all the dwellers of the Heaven will love him, and then he is granted the pleasure of the people on the earth. If God hates someone, He calls Gabriel and says: 'God hates so and so, O Gabriel, hate him.' Gabriel will hate him and announce before the dwellers of Heaven: 'God hates so and so, so you should hate him as well.' And so all the dweller of the Heaven will hate him, and then he will earn the hatred of the people on the earth.

22. *Abu Hurayra* reportedly said: People are like silver and gold, the best of you in the times before Islam are the best of you in Islam if they are knowledgeable in their Religion. And the souls are gathered in all their forms, what is akin to the other in morality is drawn to its like, and what differs from it is repelled from it.

23. *Abu Musa* is reported to have related that the Messenger of Allah (peace & blessings of Allah be with him) said: A believer to another believer is like a building whose different parts buttress each other.

24. *Al Numan ibn Bashir* is reported to have related that the Messenger of Allah (peace & blessings of Allah be with him) said: You see the believers as regards their being merciful among themselves and showing love among themselves and being kind, resembling one body, so that, if any part of the body is not well then the whole body shares the sleeplessness and fever with it.

25. It is reported on the authority of *Abu Hurayra* that the Messenger of Allah (peace & blessings of Allah be with him) said: Do not harbour a grudge against another and do not outbid him to increase the price and do not harbour dislike or hatred and do not seek to do a deal when others have already entered into that deal and be as brothers and servants of God. A Muslim is the brother of a Muslim. He does not oppress, nor humiliate, nor disdain

his brother. Piety is here, and he indicated towards his chest three times. It is a grievous sin for a Muslim to disdain his brother Muslim. Everything pertaining to a Muslim is inviolable for his brother in Islam- his blood, his wealth and his integrity.

26. *Abu Hurayra* reported that the Apostle of Allah (peace & blessings of Allah be with him) said: God does not look at your outward appea-rance nor your wealth, but He looks at your hearts and your deeds.

27. *Abu Hurayra* reported that the Messenger of Allah (peace & bles-sings of Allah be with him) said: The servant of God covers in this world, God will also cover on the Day of Resurrection.

28. *Abu Musa* is reported to have related that whenever a beggar approa-ched the Messenger of Allah (peace & blessings of Allah be with him) or he was asked for anything, he would say: Help him and listen to him, and you will be rewarded, and God will bring to bear what He pleases through His Prophet's tongue'.

29. *Abu Musa* reported that the holy Prophet (peace & blessings of Allah be with him) said: The similarity between the righteous companion and the evil compa-nion is as the man who carries musk and another who blows bellows. The one who carries musk will give you some or you will buy some from him, or you will find a nice smell on him but the one who blows bellows will either burn your clothes or you will find a bad smell on him.

30. It is reported on the authority of *Hadrat Ayesha* that she heard the Messenger of Allah (peace & bles-sings of Allah be with him) say: 'Gabriel conti-nued to advise to me about treating the neighbors kindly and politely so much so that I thought he would order me to make them my heirs.

31. *Abu Zarr* reported that the Prophet said to him: Do not consider any good deed trivial even if it is only that you meet your brother with a smile.

32. *Jarir* is reported to have related that the Messenger of Allah (peace & blessings of Allah be with him) said: He who is devoid of kindheartedness is devoid of any goodness.

33. It is reported on the authority of *Hadrat Ayesha* that the Prophet said: Kindness is never seen in anything except that it increases its beauty and it is not removed from anything but it renders it defiled.

34. *Hadrat Ayesha* reported that the holy Prophet (peace & blessings of Allah be with him) said: Ayesha, indeed God is Kind and He loves kindness and confers upon kindness that which he does not confer upon harshness and does not confer upon anything else other than it.

35. *Abu Saeed al Khudri* reported that

the Messenger of Allah (peace & blessings of Allah be with him) said: God Almighty, High Exalted, has said: 'Glory is His garment and Majesty is His cloak and whoever contends with Me in this regard shall suffer.

36. *Abu Hurayra* reported that the Messenger of Allah (peace & blessings of Allah be with him) said: There are three with whom God will not speak on the Day of Judgment nor will He purify them- Abu Mu'awiya said - Nor will He look at them, and for them is a painful punish-ment— an old man who is adul-terous, a King who lies, and a poor man who is arrogant.

37. *Hadrat Ayesha* is reported to have related that a man sought per-mission to see the Prophet. He said: 'permit him, what an evil son of his tribe! Or 'What an evil man of this tribe!' When he entered, the Prophet spoke to him kindly. I said: O Messenger of Allah! You said about him what you said, then you spoke to him kindly.' He said 'O Ayesha! On the Day of Resurrection, the worst people in the sight of God will be those whom the people have ignored because of their wickedness.

38. *Abu Hurayra* reported that the Messenger of Allah (peace & blessings of Allah be with him) said: Charity never decreases wealth. Whenever a servant of God pardons another, God increases him in might, and whenever anyone is modest for the sake of God, God elevates him.

39. *Abd Allah ibn Mas'ud* reported that the Apostle of Allah (peace & blessings of Allah be with him) said: Whom do you consider Raqub? They said: The one who has no children. The holy Prophet said: He is not, but a Raqub is one whose child does not precede him. Then he asked: Who do you consider a wrestler?" We said: The one who wrestles with others. He said: No, it is not he, but one who controls himself when he is angry.

40. *Anas ibn Malik* reported that the Messenger of Allah (peace & bles-sings of Allah be with him) said: When God created Adam in Paradise, He formed him as He pleased, then Iblees walked around him to see what he was and when he found him hollow inside, he perceived that he had been created with a nature over which he would have no self-control.

41. *Abu Hurayra* reported that the Messenger of Allah (peace & blessings of Allah be with him) said: A man passed by a felled tree on the roadway, so he said: 'By God, I shall have to remove this from the path of the Muslims so that it will not harm them.' Then he was admitted to Paradise.

42. *Abu Barza* reportedly asked the Messenger of Allah to teach him some-thing so that he may derive benefit from it. He said: remove any obstacle from the paths of the Muslims.

43. *Al Aswad* reported that some youth from the Quraysh visited Ayesha while she was in Mina and they were laughing. She asked: 'Why are you laughing?' They said: 'So and so tripped over the rope of the tent and nearly broke his neck or lost his eyes.' She said: 'Do not laugh, for I heard the Messenger of Allah (peace & blessings of Allah be with him) say: If a thorn or something worse stabs a Muslim, he is awarded a higher rank and his sins are blotted out.

44. It is reported from *Abu Saeed al Khudri* and *Abu Hurayra* that they heard the Messenger of Allah (peace & blessings of Allah be with him) say: If a believer is afflicted by weariness, disease, worry, sorrow, harm or distress, God will blot out some of his sins because of that.

45. *Abu Hurayra* reportedly related that when this verse was revealed: '...Whoever does evil shall be recom-pensed for it...' (Q. 4: 123.) And when this was conveyed to the Muslims they were much pertur-bed. So the Messenger of Allah (peace & blessings of Allah be with him) said: Be calm and stand resolute in the face of aff-liction, as for the Muslims it is an expia-tion, even tripping over on the road or the pricking of a thorn.

46. *Anas ibn Malik* reported that the Messenger of Allah (peace & blessings of Allah be with him) said: Do not hate each other and do not be jealous of each other and do not abandon each other, and, O wor-shippers of God! Be brotherly, for it is not permissible for any Muslim to aban-don his brother for more than three days.

47. *Abu Ayyub Al Ansari* reported that the Messenger of Allah (peace & blessings of Allah be with him) said: It is not lawful for anyone to abandon his brother in Islam for more than three nights, that when they meet he ignores the other, and the other ignores him, and the better of the two is the one who greets the other first.

48. *Abu Hurayra* reported that the Messenger of Allah (peace & blessings of Allah be with him) said: The gates of Paradise are opened only on two days, that is, Monday and Thursday, and then every servant, who does not associate any partners with Allah, is forgiven except the one in whose heart there is hatred for his brother. And it is said: Look towards both of them until there is reconciliation; look towards both of them until there is reconciliation; look towards both of them until there is reconciliation.

49. *Abu Hurayra* reported that the Messenger of Allah (peace & blessings of Allah be with him) said: Refrain from suspicion, for suspicion is the most evil of falsehood, and do not look for faults in others, and do not spy on each other, and do not be jealous of each other, and do not despise each other, and do not aban-don each other. And, O worshippers of Allah! Be brotherly.

50. *Jabir* reported that he heard the Prophet say: Satan lost any hope that those who pray to God Almighty in the Arabian Peninsula would ever worship him. But he still tries to incite them against each other.

51. It is reported that *Hadrat Ayesha*, the wife of the Prophet, said: The Messen-ger of Allah (peace & blessings of Allah be with him) left my house one night and I felt jealous, so when he returned he saw that I was upset, and he said: 'O Ayesha, what is the matter, are you jealous?' I said: 'And why, as your wife, should I not feel jealous for you?' The Messenger of Allah (peace & blessings of Allah be with him) said: 'Has your Satan come to you?' She asked: 'O Messenger of Allah! Do I have a Satan?' He said: Yes.' I said: 'Does everyone have one?' He said: 'Yes.' I said: 'O Messenger of God, do you have one?' He said: 'Yes, but my Lord has enabled me over him until he became Muslim.

52. *Abu Hurayra* reported that the Messenger of Allah (peace & blessings of Allah be with him) said: Do you know what is denigration? They said: God and His Messenger know best. Then he said: Denig-ration is when you speak about your brother in a way he would not Ike. It was said to him:

What do you say if I find my brother has the fault of which I had spoken? He said: If he is as you say, you have denigrated him, and if not you have slandered him.

53. *Abd Allah ibn Mas'ud* reported that the Prophet said: should I tell you about slandering, it is telling of untruths that create strife between people. And he said: A person tells the truth until he is recorded as truthful, and he tells a lie until he is recorded as a liar.

54. *Abd Allah ibn Mas'ud* reported that the Messenger of Allah (peace & blessings of Allah be with him) said: Be truthful, as truthfulness leads to righteous-ness, and righteousness leads to Paradise. And a man keeps being truthful until he beco-mes a truthful person. Falsehood leads to wickedness and wickedness leads to the Fire, and a man keeps lying until it is written for him before God that he is a liar.

55. *Umm Kulthum* reported that she heard the Messenger of Allah (peace & blessings of Allah be with him) say: The one who makes peace between people by inventing good or by saying good things is not a liar. Ibn Shihab said: I have not heard that the people were prohibited from lying except in three cases— war, reconciliation between people and the conversation of a man and his wife and the conversation of a wife and her hus-band. Umm Kulthum said: I have not heard him permitting lies in anything of what the people say except in three (situations).

56. *Jabir* is reported to have related that: We were with the Prophet (peace & blessings of Allah be with him) during a battle, a great number of Muhajirin joined him and among them was one who liked to jest, so he struck a man from the Ansars on his hip. The Ansars became angry and both sides summoned their people, the Ansars said: 'help! O Ansars.' And the Muhajirin said: 'help! O Muhajirin.' The Prophet (peace & blessings of Allah be with him) came out and said: 'What is the matter with the people of ignorance?' Then he said: 'What is wrong with them?' So he was told about the incident and he said: 'Stop it, for it is a call for harm.' Abd Allah ibn Ubayy ibn Salul said: 'The Muhajirin have rallied against us, so when we return to Medina the most noble people will expel the inferior from there.' At that Umar said: 'O Messenger of Allah! Let us kill this evil man.' The Prophet (peace & blessings of Allah be with him) said: No, in that case people shall say that Muhammad kills his companions.

57. *Abu Hurayra* reported that the Messenger of Allah (peace & blessings of Allah be with him) said: When two people take to insulting each other, the first is the sinner on condition that the oppressed does not exceed the limits.

58. *Abu Hurayra* reported that the Messenger of Allah (peace & blessings of Allah be with him) said: God Most High said: The son of Adam annoys Me by saying 'It is a bad time.' None of you should call time bad for I alternate its nights and days and if I wish I may seize them.

59. *Abu Hurayra* reported that the Messenger of Allah (peace & blessings of Allah be with him) said: None of you should point at his Muslim brother with his weapon, for he does not know, maybe Satan will prompt him to strike him and then he would fall into a pit of Fire.

60. *Abu Hurayra* reported that the Messenger of Allah (peace & blessings of Allah be with him) said: If any of you fights his brother, he should not hit him on the face.

61. *Abu Hurayra* reported that the Apostle of Allah (peace & blessings of Allah be with him) said: If any of you fights his brother he must avoid his face, indeed God Almighty created Adam in that form.

62. *Abu Al Darda* reported that he heard the Messenger of Allah (peace & blessings of Allah be with him) say: The one who invokes a curse will neither intercede nor bear witness on the Day of Resurrection.

63. *Abu Hurayra* reported that the Messenger of Allah (peace & blessings of Allah be with him) was asked to invoke a curse upon the

polytheists. He replied: I have not been sent to invoke curses, but I have been sent as a mercy.

64. *Abu Hurayra* reported that the Messenger of Allah (peace & blessings of Allah be with him) said: When anyone says that someone else is ruined he is himself ruined.

65. *Abd Allah ibn Mas'ud* reported that the holy Prophet (peace & blessings of Allah be with him) said: Perished are those who are excessive in their words and deeds. He repeated it three times.

66. *Hadrat Ayesha* is reported to have related that two people came to visit the Messenger of Allah (peace & blessings of Allah be with him), and they both spoke about a matter, of which she do not know, but it annoyed him and he invoked curses upon both of them and denounced them, and when they had left Ayesha said: 'O Messenger of Allah! Goodness will extend to everyone but it will not extend to these two.' He asked: 'Why is that?' I said: 'Because you have invoked curses and denounced both of them.' He said: 'Do you not know that I have made a provision with my Lord saying: 'O God, I am a human, so if I invoke a curse or denounce a Muslim make it a cause for virtue and reward.

66. *Anas ibn Malik* related that there was an orphan girl living with Umm Sulaim. The Messenger of

Allah (peace & blessings of Allah be with him) saw the orphan girl and said: 'O, it is you! you have grown up. May you not grow older!' The slave-girl returned to Umm Sulaim, weeping. Umm Sulaim said: 'O daughter, what is the matter?' She said: 'The Messenger of Allah has invoked a curse upon me that I may not grow older and so I will never grow older.' - or she said - 'live longer.' So Umm Sulaim went out to meet the Messenger of Allah (peace & blessings of Allah be with him). He asked her: O Umm Sulaim, what is the matter with you?' She said: 'O Messenger of Allah! You invoked a curse upon my orphan girl. He said: 'Umm Sulaim, what is that?' She said: 'She says you have cursed her, saying that she may not grow older or live longer.' The holy Prophet (peace & blessings of Allah be with him) smiled and then said: 'Umm Sulaim, do you not know that I have made this proviso with my Lord that I am a human and I am pleased as a human is pleased and I lose my temper as a human loses his temper. So if I curse any one of my community and if he does not deserve it, let that, O Lord, be made a cause of purification, virtue and nearness on the Day of Resurrection.

54

Book of Oppression

1. *Abu Zarr* is reported to have related that the Messenger of Allah (peace & blessings of Allah be with him) said: Allah has made oppression unlawful; so do not resort to oppression against one another. All of you are liable to do wrong except those whom I guide to the right path, so seek right guidance from me so that I may direct you to the right path. Allah Most High says: O My servants, all of you are hungry except those whom I feed, so beg food from Me, that I may give it to you. O My servants, all of you are naked except those whom I provide with garments, so beg clothes from Me, that I may clothe you. O My servants, you commit error night and day and I am there to pardon your sins, so seek My pardon that I may pardon you. O ye servants, even if the first among you, the last among you, even if the whole of the human race, and that of the jinn too become in unison like the heart of a single person, it will cause no loss to my power. O My servants, even if the first among you and the last among you, the whole human race,

and that of the jinn's also stand in one place and you ask Me and I confer on every person what he asks for, it will not in any way cause any loss to Me than that which is caused to the ocean by dipping a needle in it. My servants, for your deeds that are being recorded you shall be rewarded. So he who finds good should praise Allah and he who does not find it should not blame anyone but himself.

2. *Jabir ibn Abd Allah* reported that the Apostle of Allah (peace & blessings of Allah be with him) said: Beware of committing oppression, for oppression is a darkness on the Day of Resurrection, and beware of being narrow-minded for narrow-minded-ness destroyed those who were before you, as it incited them to shed blood and consider those things legiti-mate that were illicit for them.

3. It has been reported from *Ibn Umar* that the Messenger of Allah (peace & blessings of Allah be with him) said: The Muslims are brothers to

one another, so they should not oppress each other, nor hand over any Muslim to an opp-ressor. Who-ever meets the needs of his brother, God will meet his need, whoever helps his brother in time of distress, God will rescue him from the distress of the Day of Reckoning, and whoever protects a Muslim, God will protect him on the Day of Resurrection.

4. **Abu Musa** reported that the holy Prophet (peace & blessings of Allah be with him) said: Verily God respites the oppressor until He seizes him, and when He seizes him He never releases him.

5. **Jabir ibn Abd Allah** is reported to have said: Two youth, one from the Muhajirin and the other one from the Ansars quarreled with each other and both called out for help from their own people. Then the Messenger of Allah (peace & blessings of Allah be with him) arrived and asked: What is this, an incidence of the days of ignorance?' They said: O Messenger of Allah! It is not serious. So he said: 'one should assist his brother whether he is an oppressor or the oppressed. If he is the oppressor he should prevent him from it, that is his assistance, and if he is the oppressed he should be helped.

6. **Urwa ibn Zubair** reported: 'I heard the Messenger of Allah (peace & blessings of Allah be with him) say: God will torture those who torture the people in this life.

7. **Abu Hurayra** is reported to have related that the Messenger of Allah (peace & blessings of Allah be with him) asked: Do you know who is needy? They said: 'The needy man is one who has neither Dirhams nor wealth.' He said: The needy of my community will be those who will come on the Day of Judgement with prayers and fasts and charity but will find themselves ruined that day because they insulted others, slandered others, consumed the wealth of others without right and shed the blood of others, and all their good deeds will be credited to the account of those they oppressed. And they would be thrown in the Fires of Hell.

55

Book of Fate

1. It is reported from *Abu Hurayra* that when the disbelievers of the Quraysh came to argue with the Messenger of Allah (peace & blessings of Allah be with him) regarding Fate, then this verse was revealed: 'On the day when they are dragged into the Fire upon their faces, taste the touch of Fire. Surely, We have created everything according to measure.

2. *Abd Allah ibn Umar* reported that the Messenger of Allah (peace & blessings of Allah be with him) said: There is a measure for everything - even for incapa-bility and capability.

3. It is reported from *Abu Hurayra* that the Prophet (peace & blessings of Allah be with him) said: The strong believer is better and is more dear to Allah than a weak believer, and there is good in everyone, but appreciate that which gives you benefit and seek help from Allah and do not lose heart, and if anything comes to you, do not say: 'If only I had not done that, it would not have happened,' but say:

'Allah ordained what He has ordai-ned.' For 'if' opens the way for the Satan.

4. *Abu Hurayra* is reported to have related that the Messenger of (peace & blessings of Allah be with him) said: Adam and Moses argued with each other. Moses said to Adam: 'O Adam! You are our father who let us down and had us banished from Paradise.' Then Adam said to him: 'O Moses! God privi-leged you with His direct speech and He inscribed for you with His Own Hand. Do you blame me for the fate that God had written in my destiny forty years before I was created?

5. *Abu Al Aswad Al Duthaly* reported that Imran ibn Hussain asked him: 'What is your opinion on what the people do today in the world, and strive for, is it something decreed for them or preordai-ned for them or will their fate in the Hereafter be determined by the fact that their Prophets conveyed to them tea-chings that they did not take heed of?' I said: 'Of course, it is something which is predetermined

for them and preordained for them.' He said: 'Then, would it not be unfair?' I felt most disturbed about that, and said: All things are created by God and lie in His Power. He will not be questioned regarding what He does, but they will be questioned.' Then he said to me: 'May Allah have mercy upon you, I only meant to ask you in order to test your intelligence.' Two men of the tribe of Muzaina came to the Prophet (peace & blessings of Allah be with him) and said: O Messenger of Allah! What is your opinion on what the people do in the world and strive for, is it something decreed for them, or preordained for them or will their fate in the Hereafter be determined by the fact that their Prophets conveyed to them teachings which they did not take heed of and thus they deserve punish-ment?' Then he said: 'Of course, it is decreed by Destiny and it is preordained for them, and this opinion is borne out by this verse in the Book of God: 'By the soul and He Who balanced it, then He inspi-red it to knowledge of wickedness and piety.' (Q. 91: 7-8).

6. *Hadrat Ali* is reported to have related: We were in Baqi-l-Gharqad accompanying a funeral procession and the Messenger of Allah (peace & blessings of Allah be with him) came and sat down and we sat around him. He held a small stick in his hand and began to scratch the ground with it, then he said: 'All of

you and all created souls have a place in Paradise or Hell assigned for them and it is decreed for each of you whether you will be blessed or condemned.' A man said: 'O Messenger of Allah! Then should we not rely upon what is decreed for us and ignore our deeds as whoever is blessed will do the deeds of the blessed and whoever is wretched will commit the deeds of the wretched?' The Prophet (peace & blessings of Allah be with him) said: 'The good deeds are facilitated for the blessed and the evil deeds are facili-tated for the wretched.' Then he recited the verses: 'So he who gives and is God fearing, and believes in that which is best, We shall facilitate for him the easy way....'. (Q. 92: 5-7).

7. It is reported on the authority of *Abu Hurayra* that the Messenger of Allah (peace & blessings of Allah be with him) said: Indeed one does deeds consistently like the deeds of the people of Paradise. Then his deeds are terminated like the deeds of the people of Hell, and indeed, a person does deeds consistently like the inhabitants of the Fire, then his deed is finally followed by the deeds of the people of Paradise.

8. *Abu Allah ibn Mas'ud* reported that Umm Habiba said: "O God, enable me to gain benefit from my husband, from the Messenger of Allah, and from my father, Abu Sufyan, and from my brother, Mu'awiya." The Messenger of

Allah (peace & blessings of Allah be with him) said: 'You have asked God concerning life spans that have been preordained, the length of days already decreed, and bounty the share of which has been allotted. God will not cause anything before its due time, nor will He delay anything be-yond its due time. And if you were to ask God to give you refuge from the torment of Hell Fire, or from the torment of the grave, it would further good for you and be better for you too.

9. *Abu Allah ibn Mas'ud* is reported to have related that the Apostle of Allah (peace & blessings of Allah be with him) said: Each one of you abides in the womb of his mother for forty days, and then turns into something which clings for an equal period and then turns into a piece of chewed flesh for a similar period and then God sends an angel and orders him to write four things_ his sustenance, his age, and his happiness or unhappiness. Then the soul is breathed into him. And by God, any of you may do deeds of the people of the Fire until there is only a cubit's distance between him and the Fire, but then the decree which God ordered takes precedence and he does the deeds of the people of Paradise and enters it; and any of you may do the deeds of the people of Paradise until there is only a cubit or two between him and Paradise, and then that decree takes prece-dence and he does the deeds of the people of the Fire and enters it.

10. *Hudhaifa ibn Usaid* reported that the Messenger of Allah (peace & blessings of Allah be with him) said: When the drop of sperm remains in the womb for forty or fifty days or forty nights, the angel comes and asks: 'My Lord, will he be good or bad?' And this will be written down. Then the angel asks: 'My Lord, will he be male or female?' And this will be written down. And his deeds and actions, his death and his suste-nance are also written down. Then his document of destiny taken up and nothing is added to it nor erased from it.

11. It is reported from *Amer ibn Wathila* that the Messenger of Allah (peace & blessings of Allah be with him) said: When the small quantity of sperm remains in the womb for forty two nights, God sends an angel to it to shape it and fashion its hearing, sight, skin, flesh and bones, then he asks: 'My Lord! Will it be male or female?' Your Lord ordains what-ever he pleases and the angel writes it. Then he asks: O my Lord! What age will he attain?' Your Lord ordai-ns whatever He pleases, and the angel writes it. Then he asks: 'What will his sustenance be?' Your Lord will ordain whatever He pleases and the angel writes it. Then the angel leaves with his document of destiny and nothing is added or erased from it. It was also reported: "It will be asked: 'Is he good or bad?' Then God will make him good or bad.

12. *Abd Allah ibn Amr ibn al A'as* is reported to have related that he heard the Messenger of Allah (peace & blessings of Allah be with him) say: 'The hearts of all the sons of Adam are between the two fingers of the fingers of the Most Merciful as one heart. He directs it wherever He pleases. Then the Apostle of Allah (peace & blessings of Allah be with him) said: 'O God, the Turner of the hearts! turn our hearts towards Your obedience.

13. *Abu Hurayra* reported that the Messenger of Allah (peace & blessings of Allah be with him) said: Every child is born a Muslim but his parents convert him to Judaism, Christianity or Paganism, just as the animals bring forth perfect offspring, do you see any imperfections?' Then Abu Hurayra recited the verses: 'So set yourself steadfast to the Religion on a True Path. The instinctive Religion that God has created in mankind. There is no alteration in God's creation. This is the right Religion, but most of the people do not know'. (Q. 30: 30).

14. *Hadrat Ayesha*, the Mother of the Believers, related that the Messenger of Allah was invited to attend the funeral of a child of the Ansar, so she said: 'O Messenger of Allah! There is happiness for this child as it is one of the birds of Paradise. He had not committed any sin nor reached the age of puberty." Then the Prophet (peace & blessings of Allah be with him) said: O Ayesha, what else? Indeed God Almighty has created dwellers for Paradise while they were still in the loins of their fathers, and He has created inhabitants for Hell while they were still in the loins of their fathers.

56

Book of Knowledge

1. *Anas ibn Malik* is reported to have said that he will relate a Hadith that no one else can relate. He said: I have heard the Messenger of Allah (peace & blessings of Allah be with him) saying: The Signs of the Hour are that Religious knowledge will be diminished, ignorance will prevail, adultery will be committed openly, women will outnumber men until there will be one man to every fifty women.

2. *Abu Hurayra* id that the Prophet (peace & blessings of Allah be with him) said: Religious knowledge will be erased, ignorance and affliction ill appear and Harj will increase. It was asked: "What is Harj, O Mes-senger of Allah?" He plied by indicating with his hand: murder.

3. *Abd Allah ibn Amr ibn al A'as* reported that he heard the Messenger of Allah (peace & blessings of Allah be with him) say: God does not take away know-ledge, by taking it away from (the hearts of) the people, but takes it away by the death of the religious, learned men till none of them (religious learned men) remain, then people will take as their leaders the ignorant ones who when consulted will give their verdict without knowledge. So they will go astray and will lead the people astray.

4. *Jarir ibn Abd Allah* reported that some bedouin wearing garments of wool visited the Messenger of Allah (peace & blessings of Allah be with him). He realized that they were needy and he requested to the people to give charity, but they were reluctant until his face showed signs of anger. Then one of the Ansars came with some silver. Then another came and then others followed them one after the other until his face showed signs of joy. Then the Apostle of Allah (peace & blessings of Allah be with him) said: 'Who-ever introduces a good custom in Islam and it is followed after him, he will be assured of the like reward like those who followed it, without any reduction in their own rewards. And whoever introduces an evil custom in Islam

and it is followed thereafter, he will be made to bear the like burden of those who followed it without any reduction of their own burdens.'

5. *Abu Hurayra* reported that the Messenger of Allah (peace & blessings of Allah be with him) said: Whoever urges people towards righteousness, he will be rewarded the like of the rewards of those who heeded him, without any reduction of their own reward. And whoever urges people to sin, he will bear the like of their sin, without any reduction in their own punishment.

6. *Abu Saeed al- Khudri* reported that the Apostle of Allah (peace & blessings of Allah be with him) said: Do not write about me, and whoever writes about me anything other than the Qur'an he should erase it. There is no blame on you in relating about me, but whoever attributes a lie to me - Hammam

said: I thought he used the word - intentionally, then he has indeed secured his place in the Fire (of Hell).

7. *Al Mughira ibn Shu'aba* reported that he heard the Messenger of Allah (peace & blessings of Allah be with him) say: Attributing falsehood to me is not the same as attributing falsehood to anyone else. Whoever attributes a lie to me intentionally has indeed secured his place in the Fire.

57

Book of Supplication

1. *Abu Hurayra* is reported to have related that the holy Prophet (peace & blessings of Allah be with him) said: God has ninety-nine Names, whoever memori-zes them will be admitted to Paradise. God is One, and He loves the uneven number.

2. *Hadrat Ayesha* is reported to have related that the Messenger of Allah (peace & blessings of Allah be with him) used to invoke God Almighty by saying: 'I seek refuge in You from the evil of what I have done and from the evil of what I have not done.'

3. *Ibn Abbas* reported that the Messenger of Allah (peace & blessings of Allah be with him) said: "O God! I submit myself to You, and I believe in You and I rely upon You, and I repent to You and with You I stand against my enemies, I seek refuge in Your Power, all worship is due only to You, and no death can reach You, while Jinn and mankind both die."

4. *Abu Hurayra* is reported to have related that when the Prophet used to travel, he would wake up at dawn and say: All praise be to God for His favour to us, our Lord! accompany us and favour us, we seek refuge in God from the Hell-Fire.

5. *Abu Musa Al- Ash'ari* reported that the Prophet (peace & blessings of Allah be with him) used to invoke God saying: 'O God! Forgive my mistakes and my igno-rance and my exceeding the limits of righteousness in my deeds, and forgive whatever You know better than I. O God! Forgive the wrong I have done in jest or seriously, and forgive my uninten-tional and intentional mistakes, all that is present with me. O God! Forgive me for my past sins and those to come, and what I have concealed and what I have revea-led and forgive whatever You know better than I. You are the The First and The Last, and You have Power over all things.'

6. *Abd Allah ibn Mas'ud* reported that the Messenger of Allah (peace & blessings of Allah be with him)

used to recite the following prayer: 'O God, I beg of Your Right Guidan-ce, security from evil, virtue and liberty from need.'

7. *Zayed ibn Arqam* reported that the Messenger of Allah (peace & blessings of Allah be with him) used to invoke: 'O God! I seek refuge in You from inability, from laziness, from cowardliness, from miserliness, senility and from the punish-ment of the grave. O God! Bestow upon my soul the sense of righteousness and purify it, for You are The One Who Purifies. You are The Protector of it, and The Guardian of it. O God! I seek refuge in You from the knowledge which does no good, from the heart that does not fear, from the soul that is not content and the invocation that is denied.'

8. *Abu Malik al Ashja'i* reported that when anyone embraced Islam, the Messenger of Allah (peace & blessings of Allah be with him) used to ask him to recite: 'O God! Forgive me, have mercy upon me, guide me to the path of right-teousness and provide me with suste-nance.'

9. *Abu Al Aziz ibn Suhaib* reported that Qatada asked Anas: What was the most frequent invocation that the Prophet used to make? He replied: The most frequent invo-cation that the Prophet (peace & blessings of Allah be with him) made was: 'O God! Give us good in this life and good in the Hereafter

and save us from the penalty of the Fire.

10. *Hadrat Ali* reported that the Messenger of Allah (peace & bles-sings of Allah be with him) told him: "Say: 'O Allah! Guide me and enable me, and with Your guidance lead me to the Right Path. And guide me straight to the target.'

11. *Abd Allah ibn Umar* is reported to have related that he heard the Messenger of Allah (peace & blessings of Allah be with him) say: 'Once three men set off together until they reached a cave at night and they entered it. It happened that a rock rolled down the mountain-side and blocked the entrance of the cave. They said: 'Our only hope to be saved from this rock is to beseech God to have mercy upon us because of the good deeds we did for His sake.' So the first one said: 'O God! When my parents were old I never gave milk to my wife, children or slaves before first giving them. Once I was late and by the time I came they had slept. I milked the animals for them and took the milk to them, but I found them asleep. I could not bring myself to give my family and slaves before them, so I waited with the bowl of milk in my hand until the dawn broke. Then they awakened and drank the milk. O God! If You see that I did so for Your Sake alone, then save us from the danger were are facing because of this rock.' Then the rock moved

slightly, but they still could not get out of the cave. The Prophet (peace & blessings of Allah be with him) said: The second man said: 'O God! My uncle had a daughter who I loved. I desired to be intimate with her but she refused me. Later when she suffered hardship during a year of famine she came to me and I offered her one hundred and twenty Dirhams. But when I tried to be intimate with her she said: 'It is unlawful for you to violate my chastity except by marriage. So I deemed it a sin to be intimate with her and I left although I loved her more than anyone and I left to her the gold I had given her. O God! If You see that I did so for Your sake alone, then save us from the danger we are facing." Then the rock moved again slightly, but they still could not get out of the cave.' Thereafter the Prophet (peace & blessings of Allah be with him) said: 'The third man said: 'O God! I hired some people and I paid them their wages except for one man who went away without taking his money.' I invested his wages and I made much gain from that. He came to me and said: 'O servant of God! Pay me my wages.' I told him: 'All the camels, cows, sheep and slaves before you are your.' He said: 'O servant of God! Do not tease me.' I said: 'I am not teasing you.' So he took them all off, leaving nothing behind. O God! If You see that I did so for Your sake alone, then save us from the danger

we are facing.' Then the rock rolled away from the entrance of the cave and they were able to walk out safely.

12. *Ibn Abbas* reported that the Apostle of Allah (peace & blessings of Allah be with him) used to invoke God in times of distress, saying: 'There is no god but Allah; the Majestic, the Most Forbearing, there is no god but Allah, the Lord of the heavens and the earth, and the Lord of the fabulous Throne'.

13. *Abu Hurayra* reported that the Messenger of Allah (peace & blessings of Allah be with him) said: The invocation of the servant of God will be fulfilled as long as he does not pray for aggression or to sever the womb relations, and as long as he does not make haste. It was asked: 'O Messenger of Allah! What is making haste?' He said: 'that you say, 'I have invoked God and my request has not be fulfilled,' then you abandon invocation.

14. *Abu Hurayra* reported that the Messenger of Allah (peace & blessings of Allah be with him) said: You should not say: 'O God, forgive me if You please, O God, have mercy upon me if You please,' but you should plead with vigor as no one can compel Allah to do anything against His Will.

15. *Jabir* reported that he heard the Prophet say: 'There is one hour during the night when if any Muslim asks for anything good for

this life or the Here-after, God will grant it to him.

16. *Abu Hurayra* reported that the Messenger of Allah (peace & blessings of Allah be with him) said: During the final third of the night, our Lord, the Blessed, the Most High, descends to the heaven of the world each night and asks: 'Is there anyone invoking Me so that I may res-pond to his invocation, is there anyone who asks Me for something so that I may bestow it upon him, is there anyone who seeks My forgiveness so that I may forgive him?'

17. It is reported on the authority of *Abu Hurayra* that the Prophet (peace & blessings of Allah be with him) said: When you hear the cock crow, seek God's blessings for it has seen an angel. And when you hear a donkey bray seek refuge with God for it has seen a devil.

18. *Anas* is reported to have related that the Messenger of Allah (peace & blessings of Allah be with him) visited one of the Muslims who had become weak due to ill health to ask about him. The Prophet (peace & blessings of Allah be with him) said: 'Did you pray for anything or invoke Him?' He said: 'yes. I used to say: 'Give me the punishment in this life which You would punish me with in the Hereafter.' Then the Messenger of Allah (peace & blessings of Allah be with him) said: 'Glory be to Allah! You have

no power nor should you invoke such a thing for yourself. Why did you not say: O God, grant us good in the world, and good in the Hereafter, and save us from the penalty of the Fire?' He invoked this for him and he recovered.

19. *Anas* reported that the Apostle of Allah (peace & blessings of Allah be with him) said: None of you should make an invocation for death, because of diffi-culties. If you intend to invoke, you should say: 'O God, give me life if life is better for me, or give me death if death is better for me.'

20. *Abu Hurayra* is reported to have related that the Messenger of Allah (peace & blessings of Allah be with him) said: None of you should make an invocation for death, and do not summon it before it comes, as when anyone dies, his deeds come to an end and the life of a believer is not extended except to do good.

58

Book of Remembrance

1. It is reported on the authority of *Abu Hurayra* that the Apostle of Allah (peace & blessings of Allah be with him) said: God has said: I am with My servant as he thinks I am, and I am with him if he remembers Me. If he remembers Me by himself, I remember him by Myself, and if he remembers Me among the people, I remember him among those who are better than they, and if he comes nearer to Me by one hand span, I go nearer to him by one cubit, and if he comes nearer to Me by one cubit, I go nearer to him by two arms lengths, and if he comes to Me walking, I go to him running.

2. *Abu Uthman al-Nahdi* reported that Hanzalah al Usaidi, who was one of the scribes of the holy Prophet (peace & blessings of Allah be with him) said: I met Abu Bakr al Siddiq, and he asked me: 'O Hanzalah, how are you?' I said: 'Hanza-lah has become a hypocrite!' He said: 'Glory be to Allah! What is that you say?' I said: 'when we are with the Messenger of Allah, he admonishes us about the Fire and Paradise as if we see if with our eyes. But when we are away from him we play with our wives and children and concern ourselves with our affairs, so we forget.' Abu Bakr said: 'By God, I also experience the same.' So Abu Bakr and I proceeded to see the holy Prophet (peace & blessings of Allah be with him) and I said: 'O Messenger of Allah! Hanzalah has become a hypocrite!' The Prophet (peace & blessings of Allah be with him) said: 'How is that?' I said: 'O Messenger of Allah! When we are with you, you remind us of the Fire and Paradise until it is as if we see it with our eyes, when we leave you we play with our wives and children and concern ourselves with our affairs, so we forget.' The Apostle of Allah (peace & blessings of Allah be with him) said: 'By the One in Whose Hand is my soul, if you continuously abide with me in that remembrance, the angels would shake hands with you on your beds and on every way you take. But O Hanzalah, let it be one hour for each.' He repeated it three times.

3. *Abu Hurayra* reported that the Messenger of Allah (peace & blessings of Allah be with him) said: Whoever relieves another Muslim from the afflictions of this world; God will relieve his affliction on the Day of Resurrection. Whoever facilitates something for another, Allah will facilitate things for him in the Hereafter. God supports His servants as long as His servant supports his fellow Muslims. Whoever seeks knowledge, God will ease the path for him and lead him to Paradise, and whoever gathers in the houses of God and recites the Book of God, and learns and teaches the Qur'an, serenity and mercy will descend on them and cover them, the angels will sur-round them and God will mention them to those near Him. And who-ever is slow in doing good deeds; he is only impeded by his reluctance.

4. *Abd Allah ibn Mas'ud* reported that the Messenger of Allah (peace & blessings of Allah be with him) used to invoke at night: 'we have encountered the night and the entire Kingdom of God has also encoun-tered the night, all praise be to God. There is no god but Allah, the One with Whom there is no partner.' Hasan said that Zubaid told him that he had memorized these words from Ibrahim: 'His is the Sovereignty and all Praise is due to Him, and He is Potent over everything. O God! I beg of You the good of this night and I seek refuge in You from the evil of this night and the evil which follows it. O God! I seek refuge in You from

laziness, from the evil of vanity. O God! I seek refuge in You from agony of the Fire and from ordeal in the grave.'

5. *Ali ibn Abu Talib* is reported to have related that: Fatimah complained about the blisters on her hand because of using the millstone. She went to ask the Prophet for a servant, but she did not find him and so told Ayesha of her need. When he returned Ayesha told him about it. The Prophet came to us after we had gone to our beds. When I moved to get up he said: 'Stay as you are.' And he sat between us, until I felt the coolness of his feet on my chest. The Prophet then said: 'shall I tell you of something that is better for you than a servant? When you go to your bed, say 'God is Great' thirty-four times, and 'All Praise be to God' thirty-three times, 'All thanks be to God' thirty-three times, for that is better for you than a servant.'

6. *Al Bara' ibn Aazib* reported that the holy Prophet (peace & blessings of Allah be with him) said to him: Whenever you go to bed, perform ablu-tion as you do for prayer, lie on your right side and say: 'O God! I submit myself to You and I entrust all matters to You and on You I depend for Your blessings in both fear and hope of You. There is no eluding You, and there is no refuge except with You. O God! I believe in Your Book which You have revealed and in Your Prophet

whom You have sent.' So if you die during the night you will die a believer. Let these words be your last words. '

7. It is reported from *Al Bara' ibn Aazib* that: When the Messenger of Allah (peace & blessings of Allah be with him) used to go to bed, he would say: 'O God! With Your Name I live and with Your Name I die.' And when he used to wake up he would say: 'All praise be to God, Who gives us life after our death and to You is the Resurrection.'

8. *Abd Allah ibn Umar* reported that: Ibn Umar said that when one goes to bed (for sleep) he should say: O God! You created me and it is for You to take me to my destiny. And death and life is at Your command, and if You give life, protect it, and if You send death, forgive me. O God! I implore Your protection.' Someone asked: 'Did you hear this from Umar?' So he said: 'I heard it from one who is better than Umar, the Messenger of Allah (peace & blessings of Allah be with him).

9. It is reported from *Suhail* that: Abu Saleh used to tell us that when any one of you intends to go to sleep, he should lie in bed on his right side and then say: 'O God! Lord of the Heaven, Lord of the Earth and the Lord of the Magnificent Throne, our Lord! And the Lord of all things, the One Who Splits the grain of corn and the date-stone, the Revealer of the Torah, the Bible and the Qur'an, I seek refuge in You from the evil of all things, You have power over

them. O God! You are The First, there is nothing before You and You are The Last and there is nothing after You. You are Manifest and there is nothing above You. You are Unseen and there is nothing beyond You. Relieve us from the burden of debt and relieve us from need.' Abu Saleh related that Abu Hurayra said that the Messenger of Allah (peace & blessings of Allah be with him) related this to him.

10. *Abu Hurayra* reported that the Prophet (peace & blessings of Allah be with him) said: When anyone of you go to bed he should clean out his bed as you do not know what has gone into it, and then he should say: 'O my Lord! In Your Name I put my body over this bed and with Your Name I will lift it up from it again. If You take my soul, grant me Your Mercy upon it, and if You return it, protect it as You protect Your righteous servants.'

11. *Anas ibn Malik* reported that the Messenger of Allah (peace & blessings of Allah be with him) said: When you go to bed, say: 'All Praise be to God, Who feeds us, provides us with drink, nourishes us and provides us with shelter, for there are many a people for whom there is none to suffice and none to provide shelter.

12. *Juwhariya* reported that: The Messenger of Allah (peace & blessings of Allah be with him) went out in the morning while I was occupied in offering the dawn prayer in my place of worship. He

returned in the forenoon and I was still sitting there. He asked me if I had remained in the same place since he left?' I said: 'Yes.' Then the Messenger of Allah (peace & blessings of Allah be with him) said: 'I recited four words three times after I left you and if these are to be weighed against what you have recited since the morning they would over-shadow them, they are: 'Glory be to Allah, and All Praise be to Him according to the entirety of His creation and accor-ding to the pleasure of His Self and accor-ding to the weight of His Throne and according to the ink of the words praising Him.'

13. It is reported on the authority of *Abu Hurayra* said that the Messenger of Allah (peace & bles-sings of Allah be with him) said: Whoever says in the morning and in the evening: 'Glory be to God and all praise is due to Him,' one hund-red times, he will not bear anything better than this on the Day of Resurrection other than the one who says these words more or says more than these words.

14. *Abu Hurayra* reported that the Messenger of Allah (peace & blessings of Allah be with him) said: There are two words which are light upon the tongue, but heavy upon the scale, and beloved to The Most Merciful, and these are: 'Glory be to God,' 'All Praise be to Him, Glory be to God The Great.'

15. *Abu Hurayra* reported that the Apostle of Allah (peace & blessings of Allah be with him) said: The pronounce-ment of 'Glory be to God, all praise be to God, there is no god but Allah and God is Great,' is dearer to me than all things over which the sun rises.

16. It is reported that a bedouin visited the holy Prophet (peace & blessings of Allah be with him) and said to him: 'Teach me the words that I should repeat most often.' The Apostle of Allah said: 'There is no god but Allah, the One; there is no partner with Him. God is the Greatest of the great and all praise be to Him. Glory be to God, the Lord of the Worlds, there is no Might and Power but with God, the All-Powerful and the All-Wise.' He said: 'That is all praise to my Lord, but what should I say for myself?' He said: 'you should say: 'O God! Forgive me and have mercy upon me, guide me to the right way and bestow upon me my sustenance.' Musa added: I think he also said: 'Grant me security.' But I cannot vouch that he said so.

17. *Abu Zarr* reported that the Mes-senger of Allah (peace & blessings of Allah be with him) said: Shall I tell you what are the most beloved words to God Almighty?' I said: 'O Messenger of Allah! Tell me what are the most beloved words to God Almighty.' Then he said: The most beloved words to God Almighty are: 'Glory be to God and All Praise be to Him'.

18. *Abu Hurayra* reported that the Apostle of Allah (peace & blessings of Allah be with him) said:

Whoever says: 'There is no god but Allah, He has no partner, to Him belongs the Kingdom, and for Him all praise is due, and He has power over all things,' one hundred times will get the same reward as that of freeing ten slaves, and one hundred good deeds will be written down for him in his record, and one hundred sins will be deducted from his record, and it will shield him from Satan on that day until the night, and no one will be able to do a better deed except the one who repeats it more than him.

19. *Sa'ad ibn Abu Waqqas* is reported to have related: We were sitting with the Messenger of Allah (peace & blessings of Allah be with him) when he said: Are you unable to gain one thousand virtues each day?' One of those who were sitting there asked: 'How can any of us can gain one thousand virtues each day?' He said: Say: 'Glory be to Allah,' one hundred times, and one thousand virtues will be added in your account and one thousand sins will be erased.

20. *Ibn Abbas* reported that Allah's Apostle (peace & blessings of Allah be with him) used to supplicate during the difficult times: There is no God but Allah, the Great, and The Tolerant. There is no God but Allah, the Lord of the Splendid Throne. There is no God but Allah, the Lord of the Heaven and the Earth, the Lord of the Magnificent Throne.

21. It is reported on the authority of *Hadrat Ayesha* that the holy Prophet used to say: O Allah! I seek refuge in You from laziness and the weakness of old age, from all sins and from being indebted, from the ordeal of the Fire (of Hell) and from the punishment of the grave and from the evil of the burden of wealth, and I seek refuge in You from the misery of poverty and I seek refuge in You from the trouble of anti-Christ. O Allah! Purify my sins with the water of snow and hail, and wash my heart from all sins as white cloth is cleansed from dirt, and let there be as great a distance between my sins and me as the distance between the east and the west.

22. *Anas ibn Malik* reported that the Apostle of Allah (peace & blessings of Allah be with him) used to invoke God by saying: O Allah! I seek refuge in You from incapacity and laziness, from cowardice and senility and miserliness, and I seek refuge in You from the torture of the grave, from the temptations of life and from an evil end.

23. *Abd Allah ibn Umar* is reported to have related that the Apostle of Allah (peace & blessings of Allah be with him) used to invoke God Saying: O Allah! I seek refuge in You from the denial of Your bounty, the loss of Your support, from Your sudden punishment and from all Your wrath.

24. *Abu Musa* reported that the holy Prophet (peace & blessings of Allah be with him) said: Allah stretches out His Hand (metaphorical expression) during the night so that people repent for the sins committed during the day and He stret-ches out His Hand during the day so that the people repent for the sins committed during dusk to dawn.

25. *Abdullah ibn Mas'ud* reported that a man visited the Messenger of Allah (peace & blessings of Allah be with him) and told him that he had kissed a woman or touched her or had done something alike. He enquired about its expiation. It was on this occasion that the verse was revealed: And observe prayer at the (two) ends of the day and in the first hour of the night. Surely good deeds take away evil deeds. That is a reminder for the heedful (Q. XI: 14). The man asked does this concern me only? The holy Prophet (peace & blessings of Allah be with him) replied: It concerns every one of my people.

59

Book of Repentance

1. It is reported on the authority of *Abu Hurayra* that the Apostle of Allah (peace & blessings of Allah be with him) said: Whoever seeks forgiveness before the rising of the sun from the west, God will turn to him with Mercy.

2. *Abu Musa* reported that the Messenger of Allah (peace & blessings of Allah be with him) said: Allah stretches out His Hand during the night so that the people may repent for the sins they committed from dawn till dusk and He stretches out His Hand during the day so that the people may repent for the sins they committed from dusk to dawn, until the day the sun rises in the west.

3. *Abu Hurayra* is reported to have related that the holy Prophet (peace & blessings of Allah be with him) said: By The One in Whose hand is my soul, had you not committed sin, Allah would get rid of you and replace you with another people who would sin and then they would seek Allah's forgiveness, so He would forgive them.

4. *Abu Hurayra* reported that the Apostle of Allah (peace & blessings of Allah be with him) said: When God ordained the Creation, He inscribed in His Book that is with Him: My Mercy transcends My Wrath.

5. *Abu Barda'* reported that he heard al-Aghar- who was one of the companions of the Prophet - spea-king to Ibn Umar and saying that the Messenger of Allah (peace & blessings of Allah be with him) said: O people! Repent to Allah, for I repent to Allah one hundred times each day.

6. *Al Harith ibn Suwaid* reported on the authority of Abd Allah that the Messenger of Allah (peace & blessings of Allah be with him) said: God is more pleased with the repentance of His servant than a man who camps at a place where his life is threatened but has his mount and his food and water, then takes rest and sleeps for a while and then wakes to find his mount gone. He suffers from heat and thirst or whatever God wished him to endure. Then he decides to return to his place sleeps again and then gets up to find his mount standing beside him.

7. It is reported from *Ibn Shihab* that the Messenger of Allah (peace & blessings of Allah be with him) proceeded to Tabuk to fight the Romans and the Christian Arabs of Al Sham. Ibn Shihab said that Abd Al Rahman ibn Abd Allah ibn Ka'ab ibn Malik said that Abd Allah ibn Ka'ab ibn Malik - who was one who led Ka'ab when he became blind - said: 'I heard Ka'ab ibn Malik speaking about the time he remai-ned behind from the Battle of Tabuk, saying: I did not remain behind from any battle in which the Messenger of Allah (peace & blessings of Allah be with him) took part except the campaign of Tabuk, but I remained behind in the battle of Badr, and no one was blamed for not participa-ting in it as the Apostle of Allah (peace & blessings of Allah be with him) had departed in search of the caravan of Quraysh. I saw the night of Al -Aqaba with the Prophet (peace & blessings of Allah be with him) when we pledged in Islam, and I would not exchange that for the Battle of Badr even though the Battle of Badr is dearer to the people than it. I was neither stronger nor weal-thier than I was when I stayed behind the Prophet (peace & blessings of Allah be with him) in that Battle. By God, I never had two she-camels before that, but I had them at the time of this Battle. Whenever the Apostle of Allah (peace & blessings of Allah be with him) wished to go out in battle he used to conceal his intention by seeming to speak of other battles; until it was the time for that campaign in which the Messenger of Allah (peace & blessings of Allah be with him) fought in severe heat after a long journey in the desert, and against a formidable enemy. So the Prophet (peace & blessings of Allah be with him) announced to the Muslims so that they may prepare for their battle. He told them exactly where they were going. With the Messenger of Allah (peace & blessings of Allah be with him) were such a number of Muslims that their names could not be listed except in a register. The Prophet (peace & blessings of Allah be with him) fought the campaign when the fruits had ripened and the shade was pleasant. He and his companions prepared for battle and I began to leave to prepare myself to be ready with them, but I returned without doing anything. I said to myself: 'I can do that.' So I kept on delaying until the Messenger of Allah (peace & blessings of Allah be with him) and other Muslims had left while I had not prepared for my departure. I said: 'I will prepare myself to leave in one or two days, and then join them.' In the morning after their departure, I went out to get ready but came back having done nothing. Then again the following morning I went out to get ready but came back having done nothing. Thus the battle was missed but

even then I had the intention of joining them. I wish I had done so, but it was not to be. So after the Messenger of Allah (peace & blessings of Allah be with him) had left whenever I went out and walked among the people I was saddened that I could see no one around me but one accused of hypocrisy or those weak men who were exempted. The Prophet (peace & blessings of Allah be with him) did not remember me until he reached Tabuk, so as he sat with the people in Tabuk he said: 'What did Ka'b do?' A man from Bani Salama said: 'O Messenger of Allah! He has been prevented by his two garments and by his looking at himself in pride.' Then Muaz ibn Jabal said: 'what a bad thing you are saying! By God! We know only good of him.' The holy Prophet (peace & blessings of Allah be with him) remained silent." Ka'b ibn Malik said: 'When I heard that he was on his way back to Medina I made myself busy and began to think up excuses, saying to myself: 'How can I defer his anger tomorrow?' When it was said that the Prophet (peace & blessings of Allah be with him) had arrived in the vicinity of Medina, all the excuses I had thought up left my mind and I knew very well that I could not rescue myself from this problem by inventing an untruth. So I decided to tell the truth. The Messenger of Allah (peace & blessings of Allah be with him) arrived in the morning and whenever he used to return from a journey he used to visit the Mosque first and offer two Rak'at of prayer in it and then sit with the people. So when he was through with the routine, those who had failed to join the campaign came and began to offer excuses and swear oaths before him. They were more than eighty men. The Apostle of Allah (peace & blessings of Allah be with him) accepted the excuses, took their pledges of allegiance and prayed to Allah to forgive them. I came to him and when I gave him my salutation he smiled the smile of an angry man and said: 'Come in.' so I sat before him. He asked: 'what prevented you from joining us? Had you not bought an animal as your mount?' I said: 'Yes, O Messenger of Allah! But by God if I were sitting before anyone of the people of this life other than you I would have liked to avoid his anger with an excuse. By God, I have been blessed with eloquent speech, but by God, I know all too well that if I tell lies to you today to win your favour, God will surely make you angry with me in the near future, but if I tell you the truth, you will be angry with me now, I hope for Allah's forgiveness, indeed, by God, I had no excuse. By God! I had never been stronger and wealthier than I was when I stayed with you. The Messenger of Allah (peace & blessings of Allah be with him) said: As for this man, he has indeed told the truth, so rise up until God decides the matter.' I got up and many men of Bani Salama followed me and said: 'By God, we never witnessed you doing any sin before this. Indeed you failed to offer excuses to the Messenger of Allah (peace & blessings of Allah be with him) as the others who did not join him did. The prayer of the holy Prophet to forgive you would have been sufficient for you.' By God they continued blaming me so much that I wanted to return and accuse myself of telling a lie, but I said to them: 'Is there anyone else who has met the same fate as I?' They said: 'Yes, there are two men who have said the same thing as you and both of them were told the same thing you were told.' I said: 'Who are they?' The ones they mentioned were two God fearing men who had participated the Battle of Badr. So I did not change my mind when they told me about them. The Apostle of Allah (peace & blessings of Allah be with him) prohibited all the Muslims to speak to all the three who had remained behind in that campaign. So we distanced ourselves from the people and they changed towards us until the land we lived in itself seemed strange as if I did not know it. We stayed in this state for fifty nights; the two other fellows stayed inside their houses and wept. But I was the youngest and more resolved, so I used to go out and witness the prayers with the Muslims and walk around in the markets, but no one would speak to me, and I came to the Messenger of Allah (peace & blessings of Allah be with him) and gave him my salutation while he was in his assembly after the prayer, and I wondered whether the Prophet (peace & blessings of Allah be with him) did move his lips in response to my salutation or not. Then I would offer my prayer near him. When I was occupied in prayer he would turn his face towards me, but when I turned my face towards him, he would turn his face away. When this treatment by the people continued, I climbed the wall of the garden of Abu Qatada, my cousin and dearest person to me. I offered him my salutation; by God he did not respond. I said: 'O Abu Qatada! I implore you by Allah! Do you not know that I love Allah and His Messenger?' He remained silent, I asked him again, but he remained silent. Then I asked him again. He said: 'God and His Messenger know best.' At that my eyes filled with tears and I returned and jumped over the wall.' Ka'b said: 'as I walked in Medina I suddenly saw a Christian farmer in the market from Al- Sham, who had come to sell his grain in Medina. He said: 'Who will lead me to Ka'b ibn Malik?' The people began to point me out to him until he approached me and handed me a letter from the king of Ghassan in which it was written: 'To start with I have been informed that your friend has treated you harshly, anyhow, God does not let you live in a place where you feel inferior and where your rights are lost. So join us and we will comfort you.' When I read it I thought: 'This is a trap.' Then I burnt the letter. After forty days had passed, an envoy of the holy Prophet (peace & blessings of Allah be with him) came to me and said: 'The Messenger of Allah commands you to keep away from your wife.' I said: 'Should I divorce her, or what should I do?' He said: 'No, only keep away from her and do not live with her.' The Prophet (peace & blessings of Allah be with him) sent the same message to the other two fellows. Then I said to my wife: 'Go to your parents and stay with them until God gives His Command in this matter.' Ka'b said: The wife of Hilal ibn Umayya went to the Messenger of Allah (peace & blessings of Allah be with him) and said: 'O Messenger of Allah! Hilal ibn Umayya is a weak old man who has no servant to wait on him, do you not wish for me to serve him?' He said: 'No, but he must not approach you.' She said: 'O Mes-senger of Allah, he has no desire for anything. By God, he has not ceased weeping from that day to this.' At that some of my family said: 'Will you ask the Messenger of Allah to permit your wife to serve you as he has permitted the wife of Hilal ibn Umayya to serve him?' I said: 'By God, I will not ask the permission of the Messenger of Allah concerning her, for I do not know what the Apostle of Allah would say if I asked him to permit her while I am a young man.' Then I stayed in that state for ten more nights after that the first fifty nights was completed, counting from the time when the Prophet (peace &

blessings of Allah be with him) had forbidden the people from speaking to us. When I had offered the dawn prayer on the fiftieth morning on the roof of my house and as I sat my soul seemed to have narrowed and even the earth seemed narrow for all its extensiveness. Then I heard a voice of one who had ascended the mountain of Sal' calling at the top of his voice: 'O Ka'b ibn Malik! Good news! I fell prostrate in joy before Allah, knowing that relief had come. After the dawn prayers the Mes-senger of Allah (peace & blessings of Allah be with him) had proclaimed that God had accepted our repen-tance. The people came out to congratulate us, and a horseman came to me hurriedly and a man of Bani Aslam came running and climbed the mountain and his voice was faster than his horse. When he whose voice I had heard, came to me conveying the good news, I took off my garments and dressed him in them, and by God, I owned no other garments than those. Then I borro-wed garments and wore them and went to the Messenger of Allah (peace & blessings of Allah be with him). The people came and cong-ratulated me and when I entered the Mosque I saw the Messenger of Allah (peace & blessings of Allah be with him) sitting with the people around him. Talha ibn Ubaydallah came quickly to me shook my hand and congratulated me. By God, none of the Muhajirin got up for me but him, and I will never forget that.'

Ka'b said: 'When I gave my salutation to the Messenger of Allah (peace & blessings of Allah be with him) his face was bright with joy and he said: Rejoice for the best day of your life since the day your mother delivered you.' Ka'b said: 'I said to the Prophet (peace & blessings of Allah be with him): 'Is this forgiveness from you or from Allah?' He said: 'It is from Allah.' Whenever the Messenger of Allah (peace & blessings of Allah be with him) was happy his face would shine like the moon, and we all knew that about him. When I sat before him I said: 'O Messenger of Allah! I will give up all my wealth because of the acceptance of my repentance as charity in the Cause of Allah and His Messenger.' The holy Prophet (peace & blessings of Allah be with him) him) said: 'Keep some of your wealth, as it is better for you.' I said: 'I will keep my share from Khyber.' And I said: 'O Messenger of Allah! God has saved me for telling the truth, so it is a part of my repentance that I will only ever tell the truth for as long as I live, by God, I do not know any of the Muslims who God has favoured for telling the truth as much as I. Since I told the truth to the Messenger of Allah I have never intended to tell a lie. I pray that God will save me also for the rest of my life, so God revealed the verses: 'Allah has relented towards the Prophet and the Muhajirin and the Ansars who followed him in his hour of distress, after the hearts of some of them had nearly swerved, but He relented towards them, surely He is to them All Compassionate, All Merciful. O you who believe! Fear Allah and be with those who are truthful.' (Q. 9: 117 & 119) By God! Allah has never granted me other than His guiding me to Islam, a greater blessing than keeping me from telling a lie to the Messenger of Allah which would have caused me to perish as those who lie perished. For Allah described those who lie as the worst beings when He said: They swear to you by Allah when you return to them, that you might leave them alone, so leave them alone, they are an abominable people, and Hell is their abode, a recompense for what they have earned. They will swear to you that you may be pleased with them, but if you are pleased with them, surely Allah will not be pleased with those who are wicked.' (Q. 9: 95-96). Ka'ab said: 'We three persons were completely different from those whose excuses were accepted by the Messenger of Allah (peace & blessings of Allah be with him) when they swore their oaths to him, he took the pledges and asked Allah to forgive them, but the Prophet (peace & blessings of Allah be with him) left our matter to rest until Allah gave His judgement, and Allah said: 'And for the three who stayed behind, until when the earth became narrow for them, for all its vastness, and their souls became narrow for them, and they thought there was no shelter from Allah except in Him, then He relented towards them, that they might repent, surely He is the Relenting, the All Merciful.' (Q. 9: 118) What God said in that verse does not refer to our failure to take part in the campaign but refers to the Prophet's (peace & blessings of Allah be with him) decision to put the matter in the court of Allah as against the cases of those who had made excuses and sworn oaths before him and he had excused them by accepting their excuses.

8. *Abu Hurayra* reported that the Messenger of Allah (peace & blessings of Allah be with him) said: There are one hundred parts of God's mercy and from that He has sent down one part of mercy upon the Jinn and mankind and the insects and it is because of this that they love one another and treat each other kindly, and even the creatures treat their offspring with love, and God has kept ninety-nine parts of mercy with Him with which He will deal with His servants on the Day of Resurrection.

9. *Abu Hurayra* reported that the Apostle of Allah (peace & blessings of Allah be with him) said: If the believer had known of all the punishment held with God, he would never have any hope of entering Paradise and if the unbeliever had known of all the Mercy which is in the Hands of God he would never lose hope of entering Paradise.

10. *Umar ibn Al Khattab* is reported to have related that some Sabian war captives were brought before the Apostle of Allah (peace & blessings of Allah be with him) and one of the women was breast-feeding the children of the cap-tives. Whenever she saw a child she took it to her breast and nursed it. The Prophet (peace & blessings of Allah be with him) said: 'Do you consider that woman capable of throwing her child into the fire?' We said: 'No, if she can resist throwing it.' The Messenger of Allah (peace & blessings of Allah be with him) said: 'God is more merciful to His servants than that woman is to her son.'

11. It is reported on the authority of *Hadrat Ayesha* that the Messenger of Allah (peace & blessings of Allah be with him) said: So inculcate the habit of doing good deeds, sincerely and modestly, None of your deeds will save you from the Fire. It was asked: "Even you, O Messenger of God?" He said: Even I will not be saved unless God has Mercy upon me. And know that the deeds are most loved by God are the deeds which are established and done constantly even if they are few in number.'

12. *Abu Hurayra* reported that the Messenger of Allah (peace & blessings of Allah be with him) said: God is jealous and the believers are jealous, but the jealousy of God is when the believer commits that which is forbidden to him.

13. *Abu Hurayra* is reported to have related that people asked: 'O Messenger of Allah Will we see our Lord on the Day of Judgment?' He replied: 'Do you doubt that you will see the sun when there are no clouds?' They replied: 'No.' He said: 'Do you doubt that you will see the full moon on a clear night?' They replied: 'No.' He said: 'By The One in Whose Hand is my soul, you will not doubt seeing your Lord, Most High, unless you doubt that you will see either of those.' He said: 'Our Lord will ask His servant: 'Did I not honour you and raise you in rank and cause you to marry and subjec-ted horses and camels to you, and I permitted you to have authority and you were obeyed and took a quarter of the spoils from your people?' He will reply: 'Yes, my Lord.' The Messenger of Allah said: 'Then God Almighty will ask: 'Did you think that you would meet Me?' He will reply: 'No.' Then God Almighty will say: 'I shall disregard you as you disregarded Me.' Then He will ask another: 'Did I not honour you and raise you in rank and cause you to marry and subjected the horses and camels to you, and I permitted you to have authority and you were obeyed and took a quarter of the spoils from your people?' He will reply: 'Yes, my Lord.' The Messen-ger of Allah said: 'Then God Almighty will ask: 'Did you think that you would see Me?' He will reply: 'No.' Then God Almighty will say: 'I shall disregard you as you disregarded Me.' Then He will ask others the same and he will reply: 'My Lord, I believed in You and Your Books and Your Messengers, and I prayed and fasted and gave in charity.' Then he will praise God as much as he is able. The Messenger of Allah said: 'God Almighty will say: 'That will suffice.' The Messenger of Allah said: 'Then it will be said to him: 'Now We shall raise you as Our witness over yourself.' So he will think to himself, who is that who shall witness over me?' Then his mouth will be sealed and it will be said to his thighs, his flesh and his bones: 'Speak!' Then his thighs, flesh and bones will speak of his deeds, so that he will find no way to excuse himself. Such a one is a hypocrite with whom God Almighty is most wrathful.

14. *Abu Hurayra* reported that the Messenger of Allah (peace & blessings of Allah be with him) said: A man commit-ted innumerable sins and when he was about to die, he left this will that his corpse should be burnt and ashes thrown to the wind and in the ocean. For he feared that if his Lord takes hold of him, He will chastise him as He has never chastised any other.' So they did accor-dingly. Then Allah said to the earth: 'Return what you have.' And so he was restored. He asked him: 'What caused you to do this?' He said: 'My Lord, I did it in fear and awe of You.' Then Allah forgave him because of that.

15. *Abu Hurayra* reported that the Apostle of Allah (peace & blessings of Allah be with him) said: A servant committed a sin and then said: 'O my Lord! I have sinned, please forgive me!' And his Lord says: 'My servant knows that he has a Lord Who forgives sins and chastises for them, so I forgive My servant.' Then he does not commit another sin for a while and then commits another sin and says: 'O my Lord! I have committed another sin, please forgive me,' and God says: 'My servant knows that he has a Lord Who forgives sins and chastises for them.' So I have forgiven My servant. Then he does not commit another sin for a while and then sins a third time and says: 'O my Lord, I have committed another sin, please forgive me,' and God says: 'My servant knows that he has a Lord Who forgives sins and chastises for them.' So I have forgiven My servant, he may do what he pleases.

16. *Abu Umama* is reported to have said: We were sitting in the mosque with the holy Prophet (peace & blessings of Allah be with him) when a man entered and said: 'O Messenger of Allah! I have committed a sin that deserves due punishment of God, so order it upon me. The Apostle of Allah (peace & blessings of Allah be with him) remained silent. He repeated it and said: 'O Messenger of Allah! I have committed a sin that deserves due punishment of God, so order it upon me. He remained silent, and then the Iqama was pronounced. When the Messenger of Allah (peace & blessings of Allah be with him) had completed the prayer, the man followed him. Abu Umama said: 'I also followed the Messenger of Allah (peace & blessings of Allah be with him) after he had conclu-ded the prayer, to see what his response would be. The man stayed beside the Prophet (peace & blessings of Allah be with him) and said: 'O Messenger of Allah! I have commit-ted a sin that deserves due punish-ment of God, so order it upon me.' Abu Umama said that the holy Prophet (peace & blessings of Allah be with him) told him: 'Did you not see that when you left the house, you had performed ablution perfec-tly?' He said: "O Messenger of Allah! Indeed I did.' Then he said to him: 'Then you offered prayer with us.' He said: 'O Messenger of Allah, indeed that it so.' Then the Prophet (peace & blessings of Allah be with him) said to him: Indeed, God Almighty has excused you from His punishment.' Or he said: from your sin.

17. It is reported from *Abu Musa* that the Messenger of Allah (peace & blessings of Allah be with him) said: On the Day of Resurrection God will deliver to every Muslim, a Jew or a Christian and say: 'This is your redemption from the Hell Fire.'

60

Book of Hypocrites

Allah Most High has said:

When the hypocrites' come to you they say: 'We bear witness that you indeed are the Messenger of Allah.' And God knows that you are indeed His Messenger, and God bears witness that the hypocrites are surely liars. They have taken their oaths as a screen, so they hinder from the way of Allah, surely evil is that which they do. This is because they have believed then disbelieved. So a seal has been set on their hearts and they do not understand. And when you see them, their appea-rance pleases you, and when they speak to you, you listen to their words; they are as worthless as hollow pieces of timber propped up, unable to stand on their own. They think that every cry is against them; they are the enemies, so beware of them. The curse of Allah be upon them! How perverted they are ! And when it is said to them: 'Come, the Messenger of Allah will ask for forgiveness for you,' they shake their heads, and you see them turning away in arrogance. It is the same with them, whether you ask for forgive-ness for them, or you do not ask for forgiveness for them, Allah will not forgive them, surely God does not guide the wicked people. They are the ones who say: 'do not spend on those with the Messenger of Allah until they break away from him. (Q.63: 1-7).

1. *Zaid ibn Arqam* reportedly said: I was fighting in a battle when I heard Abd Allah ibn Ubayy say: 'Do not spend on those with the Messenger of Allah until they break away from him, and if we return to Medina, the stronger ones will expel there from the weaker ones.' I mentioned that to my uncle or to Umar, who reported it to the Apostle of Allah (peace & blessings of Allah be with him). So he called me and I told him about it. So the Prophet (peace & blessings of Allah be with him) sent for Abd Allah ibn Ubayy and his friends and they swore that they had not said it. So it was said that the Messenger of Allah (peace & blessings of Allah be with him) disbe-lieved Zaid. I was more upset than I had ever

been. So Allah revealed: 'When the hypo-crites come to you.' Then the Prophet (peace & blessings of Allah be with him) summoned them to pray to Allah for forgiveness for them, but they turned their heads away.

2. *Jabir ibn Abd Allah* reported that the Messenger of Allah (peace & blessings of Allah be with him) said: Whoever climbs this hill, the hill of Murar, his sins will be washed off as were the sins of the Children of Israel blotted out. So the first to mount their horses were the people of Bani Khazraj. Then there was a continuous flow of people and the Messenger of Allah (peace & blessings of Allah be with him) said to them: All of you will be forgiven except the owner of a red camel. We went to him and said: 'Come with us to the Messenger of Allah so that he may seek forgiveness for you.' But he replied: By God, as far as I am concerned, I prefer to look for something lost rather than to have your companion seek forgiveness for me.' And he stayed on to look for what his lost things.

3. *Qais ibn Ubad* reportedly related: I asked Ammar: What do you think about your fight with Ali? Is this matter of your own doing, then it is subject to being right or wrong, or did the Prophet direct you about it?' Ammar said: The Messenger of Allah (peace & blessings of Allah be with him) did not express anything that he did not express to the rest of the people to.' He said

that the Apostle of Allah (peace & blessings of Allah be with him) said: 'There is among my community...' Shuba said: 'I thought he said that Hudhaifa said that he said: 'Twelve hypocrites who will not enter Para-dise nor recognize its scent before a camel would be able to pass through the hole of a needle. For eight of them, a flame of fire will enter into their shoulders and come out burning through their chests.

4. *Abu Al Tufail* is reported to have said: There was a man from the people of al Aqbah, and there was a trust between him and Hudhaifa. So he said to Hudhaifa: I ask you in the Name of Allah, how many people participated in al Aqbah?' He replied: We used to say we were fourteen, so if you were one of them, then, they were fifteen. And I ask Allah to bear witness that twelve of them were enemies of Allah and His Messenger in this life and on the Day of Judgment. And three of them were pardoned because they said: We did not hear the call of the Messenger of Allah, nor did anyone inform us.' He was walking on a black stony land and he said: 'The water is scant, so no one should go there before me.' He found that people had reached the water before him, so he cursed them on that day.

5. *Ibn Umar* reported that the holy Prophet (peace & blessings of Allah be with him) said: The similarity of a hypocrite is that of a sheep which

roams aimlessly between two flocks. She goes to one at one time and to the other at another time.

6. *Jabir* reportedly narrated that the Messenger of Allah (peace & blessings of Allah be with him) returned from a journey and as he neared Medina, there was a high wind that almost buried the riders. The Apostle of Allah (peace & blessings of Allah be with him) said: This wind has been sent for the death of a hypocrite. When he arrived in Medina a renowned hypocrite had passed away.

7. *Salama ibn al Aqwa* is reported to have said: We went with the Messenger of Allah (peace & blessings of Allah be with him) to visit a sick man. When I placed my hand upon him, I said: 'By God! I have never seen ever before, a man who is hot like this. So the Apostle of Allah said: Shall I tell you who will be hotter than him on the Day of Judgment? Those two men riding upon their camels and turning their backs to the Muslims. They were two men from among his Companions.

8. *Anas ibn Malik* is reported to have related: There was a man from Bani al Naggar who read Surah Al Baqarah and 'Al-I- Imran, and he who used to write for the Messenger of Allah (peace & blessings of Allah be with him). Then he ran away and joined the people of earlier Scrip-tures, so they admired him and raised him in rank and said: 'This man used to write for Muhammad.' Then God Almighty destroyed him while he was with them. So they dug his grave and buried him, but the next morning they saw that the earth had cast his body out. They said: This is the doing of Muham-mad and his companions. So they dug the grave even deeper and buried him again but the next morning they saw that the earth had cast his body out. They dug the grave again more deeply and buried him again but in the morning they saw that the earth had cast his body out. So they left him to his fate.

61

Book of Depiction of the Day of Judgment

1. *Ibn Umar* reported that the Messenger of Allah (peace & blessings of Allah be with him) said: On the Day of Resurrection, God Almighty will fold the heavens, then hold it with His Right Hand, and then say: 'I am The King, where are the tyrants? Where are the arrogant?' Then He will fold the earth with His Left Hand and then say: 'I am The King, where are the tyrants, where are the arrogant?'

2. *Sahl ibn Sa'ad* reported that the Apostle of Allah (peace & blessings of Allah be with him) said: The people will be gathered on the Day of Resurrection on reddish-white land like a loaf of bread, it will be devoid of any landmark.

3. *Jabir* is reported to have said: I heard the Messenger of Allah (peace & blessings of Allah be with him) say: 'Every servant will be resurrected and judged according to his deeds.'

4. *Abd Allah Ibn Umar* said: I heard the holy Prophet (peace & blessings of Allah be with him) say: 'If God wishes to punish a community it affects the entire population without discrimination, then they will all be resurrected and judged according to their deeds.

5. It is reported on the authority of *Hadrat Ayesha* that she heard the Apostle of Allah (peace & blessings of Allah be with him) say: 'On the Day of Resurrection people will be gathered barefoot, naked and uncircumcised.' I said: 'O Messenger of Allah! Will the men and the women see each other?' He said: 'Their plight would be so severe that they will not look at each other.'

6. *Abu Hurayra* is reported to have said: The people will be gathered (on the Day of Reckoning) in three ways, the first will be those who will hope for Paradise and fear puni-shment. The second will be those who will ride two or three on a camel or ten on a camel. The third will be the remainder of the people who will be urged to assemble near the Fire which will go with them at the time of their afternoon rest and stay with them wherever they spend the night, and it will be with them in the morning wherever they

may be, and it will be with them in the afternoon wherever they may be.

7. *Anas ibn Malik* reported that a man said: O Messenger of Allah! How will the unbeliever be gathered upon his face on the Day of judgment?" The Prophet replied: Do you not see that The One Who made him walk upon his feet in this life is able to make him walk upon his face on the Day of Judgment? Qatada said: Yes! Indeed, by the might of our Lord.

8. *Sulaim ibn Amer* said: Al Miqdad ibn al Aswad told me that he heard the Messenger of Allah (peace & blessings of Allah be with him) say: 'On the Day of Resurrection the sun will come closer to the people until it is only one mile away.' By God I do not know what this mile will be, if it is a distance upon the earth or a stick which applies the kohl to the eye.' He said: 'Then the people will be standing in their sweat according to the measure of their deeds, some will be covered in it until their heels, and some will be covered in it until their knees, and some will be covered in it until their shoulders, and some will be covered in it until the sweat will be a restraint to them.' And he indicated with his hand towards his mouth.

9. *Abu Hurayra* reported that the Messenger of Allah (peace & blessings of Allah be with him) said: On the Day of judgment the sweat will cover the land to the depth of seventy cubits and it will reach the mouths of the people, or to their ears.

62

Book of Depiction of Paradise

1. It is reported from *Abu Hurayra* that the Messenger of Allah (peace & blessings of Allah be with him) said: Whoever is admitted to Paradise will enjoy such eternal bliss and he will neither become needy, nor will his garments become shabby, nor will his youth ebb away.

2. *Abu Hurayra* reported that the Messenger of Allah (peace & blessings of Allah be with him) said: The faces of the first party to be admitted into Paradise will shine like the moon on the night when it is full. Those who follow them will shine like the brightest star. Their hearts will be as if they are one heart, They will not dispute · nor hate each other, For each one of them will have two wives, the bone marrow of their wives' legs will be visible through the flesh from its beauty. They will not feel ill, nor spit or blow their noses. Their utensils will be of gold and silver, their combs will be of gold, the fuel of their braziers will be of scented wood and their sweat will be musk.

3. *Abu Hurayra* is reported to have related that the Messenger of Allah (peace & blessings of Allah be with him) said: God Almighty created Adam in his form and his height was sixty cubits. So when He had created him, He told him: 'Go to greet those there.' And there was a group of angels sitting, 'Listen to how they will salute you, for it will be your salutation and the salutation of your offspring.' He said: 'so he went and said: 'Peace be upon you.' Then they replied: 'Peace be upon you and the Mercy of God be upon you.' Thus they added 'And the Mercy of God.' So all who shall be admitted to Paradise will look like Adam (peace be upon him) and their height will be sixty cubits, ever since the creation has diminished in stature until today.

4. *Abu Hurayra* reported that the Apostle of Allah (peace & blessings of Allah be with him) said: Some people will enter Paradise whose hearts will be like the hearts of birds.

5. *Abu Saeed Al Khudri* reported that the Messenger of Allah (peace & blessings of Allah be with him)

said: God will say to the people of Paradise: 'O people of Paradise!' They will say: 'At Your Command, O our Lord and we obey!' God will say: 'Are you well pleased?' They will say: 'How would we not be pleased when You have given us such as You have given to no other of Your creation?' God will say: 'I will give you something even better.' They will say: 'O our Lord! And what is better than this?' God will say: 'I will grant My pleasure and satisfaction upon you so that I will never be wrathful with you for ever after.

6. **Abu Saeed Al Khudri** is reported to have related that the holy Prophet (peace & blessings of Allah be with him) said: The people of Paradise will look at the dwellers of the lofty mansions as the way one gazes at a distant shining star on the eastern or western horizon, for they are superior over one another. At that the people said: "O Messenger of Allah! Are the lofty mansions the mansions of the Prophet (peace & blessings of Allah be with him) which no one else can attain?" The Apostle of Allah (peace & blessings of Allah be with him) said: By God in Whose Hand is my life, some who believe in God and trust His Messenger will get them.

7. **Jabir ibn Abd Allah** said that he heard the Messenger of Allah (peace & blessings of Allah be with him) say that the inhabitants of Paradise will eat and drink but will not spit, nor urinate, nor defecate, nor blow their noses. It was asked:

'What will happen to their food?' He said: They would eructate and sweat and their sweat will be of musk and they will glorify and praise God as easily as you breathe.

8. **Thauban** related that he was serving the Messenger of Allah (peace & blessings of Allah be with him) when a Jewish Rabbi came and said: 'O Mohammed, peace be upon you.' I came to ask you.' The Prophet (peace & blessings of Allah be with him) said: 'Would that benefit you anything?' He said: 'I am attentive.' The Apostle of Allah (peace & blessings of Allah be with him) scratched a stick in the dust and said: 'Ask.' The Jew said: 'Where will the people be when the earth is changed into other than the earth and the heavens?' The Messenger of Allah (peace & blessings of Allah be with him) said: 'They will be in the dark below the bridge.' He asked: 'Who will be the first people to pass?' He said: 'The poor people of the Muhajirin.' The Jew asked: 'What shall they be given to eat?' He said: 'The caudal lobe of fish liver.' He asked: 'What will be their meal after that?' He said: 'The ox of Paradise which grazed on its sides, will be slaughtered for them.' He asked: 'What will be their drink?' he said: 'It will be from the spring named Salsabil.' He said: 'You have said the truth.' He said: 'I have come to ask you of a matter which no one of this earth knows except a Prophet or one or two men.' He said: 'Would that benefit you?' He

said: 'I am attentive.' He said: 'I came to ask you regarding (birth of) a child.' He said: 'The water of a man is white and the water of a woman is yellow, if a man is intimate with his wife and his discharge is first, the child will be a male by the permission of God, and if the woman's discharge is first the child will be a female, by the permission of God.' The Jew said: 'You have said the truth, and you are the Prophet.' Then he left. Then the holy Prophet (peace & blessings of Allah be with him) said: He asked me about things of which I had no knowledge until God inspired me.

9. *Abu Musa* reported that the Messenger of Allah (peace & blessings of Allah be with him) said: In Paradise there is a pavilion formed of a single hollow pearl sixty miles in width, at each of its corners are families who will not see the other, and the believers will visit them.

10. *Abu Hurayra* reported that the Messenger of Allah (peace & blessings of Allah be with him) said: Saihan, Jaihan, Euphrates and the Nile are all of the rivers of Paradise.

11. *Anas ibn Malik* reported that the Messenger of Allah (peace & blessings of Allah be with him) said: Paradise is surrounded by trials and Hell Fire is surrounded by temp-tations.

12. *Haritha ibn Wahbin Al Khuza'i* said: I heard the Prophet (peace & blessings of Allah be with him) say:

'shall I tell you of the people of Paradise? Whenever the weak and those deemed defenceless ask God for something, it is fulfilled. Shall I tell you of the people of the Fire? Every violent and cruel one who is arrogant and proud.'

13. *Iyad ibn Himar* reported that one day the Messenger of Allah (peace & blessings of Allah be with him) said: 'My Lord has commanded me to teach you that which you do not know and that which He has taught me today: 'The property which I have bestowed upon them is lawful for them. I have created My servants with an innate nature to worship God but Satan make them deviate from the right Religion. He makes unlawful that which has been declared lawful for them and he commands them to ascribe partners to Me although he has no authority.' God turned towards the people of the world and He showed abhorrence for the Arabs and the non-Arabs, with the exception of some who remained from the People of the Book. And He said: 'I have sent you to put you to the test and put them to the test through you. I sent down the Book to you, which cannot be washed away by water, so that you may recite it while you are awake or asleep.' God commanded me to burn the Quraysh. I said: 'My Lord, they would tear off my head as if it were bread.' God said: 'you evict them as they evicted you, you fight against them and We shall assist you, you spend and you will be given more. You dispatch a force

and I shall send a force five times greater than that. Fight alongside those who obey you against those who disobey you. The inhabitants of Paradise are of three kinds; one who hold authority that is just and fair; one who is truthful and has been enabled to do good deeds; and the one who is merciful and kindhearted towards his relatives and to every God fearing Muslim, and who does not stretch out his hand even if he has many to support. The denizens of Hell are of five kinds; the weak who are devoid of power, the careless who do not care for their family or for their wealth, the dishonest whose greed is evident even in the smallest matters; and the third kind, is he who betrays you morning and evening, in regard to your family and your property.' He also mentioned the miser and the liar and those who habitually insult others with obscenity and profanity.

14. *Abd Allah ibn Umar* reported that the Messenger of Allah (peace & blessings of Allah be with him) said: When the people of Paradise have entered Paradise and the people of the Fire have entered the Fire, Death will be brought near and placed between the Fire and Paradise, and then it will be slaughtered and a herald will call: 'O people of Paradise, no more death! O people of the Fire no more death!' So the people of Paradise will rejoice with even more happiness and the people of the Fire will grieve in even more distress.

15. It is reported from *Abu Saeed* that ibn Sayyad asked the Prophet about the soil of Paradise. So he said: It is luminous white and its scent is pure musk.

63

Book of Depiction of Hell

1. *Abu Hurayra* reported that the Prophet (peace & blessings of Allah be with him) said: Your fire which the son of Adam kindles is one part of seventy parts of Hell Fire." It was said: O Apostle of Allah! Our fire is sufficient. The Messen-ger of Allah (peace & blessings of Allah be with him) said: Hell Fire has sixty nine more parts than the fire of this world, each part is as hot as the fire of this world.

2. *Abu Hurayra* is reported to have related that: We were with the Messenger of Allah (peace & blessings of Allah be with him) when we heard a terrible sound. Then the Prophet (peace & bles-sings of Allah be with him) said: 'Do you know what that is?' We said: 'Allah and His Messenger know best.' He said: 'That was a stone which was thrown seventy years ago into Hell and ever since it has been slipping downwards and now it has fallen to the depths of it.'

3. *Al Numan ibn Bashir* reported that the Messenger of Allah (peace &

blessings of Allah be with him) said: The one in the Fire who receives the least punishment will be a man with two smoldering embers under the arches of his feet, and his brain will boil because of them like a pot boiling with water.

4. *Samura ibn Jundab* reported that the Messenger of Allah (peace & blessings of Allah be with him) said: The Fire will reach unto the ankles of some, and it will reach the knees of some, and it will reach the waists of some, and the Fire will reach up to the collar bones of others.

5. *Abu Hurayra* reported that the Prophet (peace & blessings of Allah be with him) said: Paradise and the Fire argued, and the Fire said: 'I have been allocated the arrogant and the tyrants.' Paradise said: 'Why do only the weak and humble people enter me?' At that God Blessed and High Exalted said to Paradise: 'You are My Mercy by which I am Mer-ciful to whoever I please of My servants.' Then God said to the Fire: 'You are My

punishment by which I punish whoever I please of My servants. And both of you will have your fill.' As for the Fire it will not be filled until God puts His Foot over it and it will say: 'Enough! Enough! Then it will be filled and its parts will draw near to each other, and God will not wrong any of His creation. As for Paradise, God will assign a creation for it.'

6. *Abu Hurayra* reported that the Messenger of Allah (peace & blessings of Allah be with him) said: The molar teeth of an unbeliever or the canine teeth of an unbeliever will be as the mountain of Uhud and the thickness of his skin will be (about the length of) three night's journey.

7. *Abu Hurayra* reportedly said: The distance between the two shoulders of an unbeliever will be equal to the distance covered by a fast rider during three days of travel.

8. *Abu Hurayra* reported that the **Messenger** of Allah (peace & blessings of Allah be with him) said: The denizens of the Fire will be of two kinds and I have yet not seen them. One will have whips like the tails of oxen and they will flog people with them. The women will appear naked although they will be dressed; they invite to transgression and allure others to it with hair like the humps of camels. These women will never **be** admitted to Paradise nor will they smell the fragrance of Paradise, although its fragrance can be smelled from a far distance.

9. It is reported from *Abu Hurayra* that the Messenger of Allah (peace & blessings of Allah be with him) said: If you live longer you will surely see a people who will have whips in their hands like the tails of oxen. They will rise every morning under the wrath of God and they will reach the evening under the wrath of God.

10. *Anas ibn Malik* reported that the Messenger of Allah (peace & blessings of Allah be with him) said: One of the denizens of Hell who had led a life of comfort and abundance among the people of this world will be made to plunge into the Fire only once on the Day of Resurrection and then he will be asked: 'O, son of Adam! Did you find any comfort, did you receive any bounty?' He will say: 'By God, no my Lord.' And then a person of the people of the world will be brought, who had suffered hardship in the life of this world, who will be of the inhabitants of Paradise and he will be made to plunge only once into Paradise and then he will be asked: 'O, son of Adam! Did you suffer any hardship? Or did any affliction beset you?' And he will say: 'By God, no my Lord! Never did I suffer any hardship nor was I beset by any misery.

64

Book of Afflictions

1. *Usama ibn Zayed* said: The Prophet ascended one of the fortresses of Medina, then said: 'Do you see what I see?' I see the places of suffering through your homes as falling rain.

2. *Hudhaifa* is reported to have related: Once I was sitting with Umar and he said: 'Who of you remembers what the Messenger of Allah (peace & blessings of Allah be with him) said about the trials?' I said: 'I know it. The trials for a man are his wife and children, money and neigh-bors which are expiated by prayers, fasting, charity and by enjoining what is good and forbidding what is evil.' Umar said: 'I did not mean that but I was asking about the trials that will outspread like the waves in the sea. I said: 'O Emir of the believers! You do not need to fear be-cause there is a closed door between you and it." Umar asked: 'Will the door be broken or opened?' I replied: 'It will be broken.' Umar said: 'Then it will never be closed again.' I was asked whether Umar knew that door, I replied that he knew it as

one who knows there will be night before the morning." This Hadith was clear of misstatement. He added that they sent Masruq to ask Hudhaifa about the door, he said: The door was Umar himself.

3. *Thauban* reported that the Messenger of Allah (peace & blessings of Allah be with him) said: God Almighty drew the ends of the world together for my sake. I have seen its eastern and western extremities. The dominion of my commu-nity will extend to those extremities that have been drawn together before me and I have been granted the red and the white treasures. I implored my Lord that my community would not be ravished by famine, nor be dictated to by a foreign enemy who will kill them and destroy them root and branch. My Lord said: 'Mohammed, whenever I decree a thing, there is no changing it. So I grant you that your community will not be ravished by famine, nor will it be dictated to by a foreign enemy who will kill them and destroy them root and branch, even if all the people from the different parts of the world amass together. But, it will be some from among your community who will kill or imprison them.

4. *Amer ibn Sa'ad* reported that his father said that once the Messenger of Allah prayed in the mosque of Bani Mu'awiya and invoked Allah for a long time. Then he came to us and said: I asked my Lord three things and He has granted me two but has withheld one. I begged my Lord that my community should not e ravished by famine and He granted me this. And I begged my Lord that my community should not perish by drowning and He granted me that. And I begged my Lord that there should be no bloodshed among the people of my community, but He did not grant me that.

5. *Abu Hurayra* reported that the Messenger of Allah (peace & blessings of Allah be with him) said: The (final) Hour will not come to pass until two great parties fight each other and it will be a great war. They both will be Muslim.

6. *Abu Hurayra* reported that the Messenger of Allah (peace & blessings of Allah be with him) said: By The One in Whose Hand is my soul, the world will not come to an end until a man passes by a grave of someone and rolls himself upon it and says: 'I wish I was in his place.' And nothing will drive him to that but affliction.

7. *Abu Hurayra* reported that the Messenger of Allah (peace & blessings of Allah be with him) said: The Hour will not come to pass until will be much al Harj. They asked: "O Messenger of Allah! What is al Harj?" He said: "Killing! Killing!"

8. *Abu Hurayra* reported that the Messenger of Allah (peace & blessings of Allah be with him) said: By Him in Whose Hand is my soul, a time will come when the murderer will not know why he committed the murder, and the victim will not know why he has been killed.

9. *Abu Hurayra* reported that the Messenger of Allah (peace & blessings of Allah be with him) said: The Hour will not be arrive until a fire comes out of Hijaz, and it will illuminate the necks of the camels at Basra.

10. *Hadrat Ayesha* reported that the Messenger of Allah (peace & blessings of Allah be with him) said: The rotation of night and day will not cease until the people begin to worship Lat and Uzza. I said: "O Messenger of Allah! I think when God revealed: 'God is The One Who sent His Messenger with the Gui-dance and the Religion of truth to make it prevail over all religion, even though the unbelievers may detest it,' (Q. 9: 33.) means that will be fulfilled." Then he said: 'It will come to pass as God pleases. Then God will send a soft scented wind by which everyone who has even a mustard grain of

faith in Him will die, and only those who have no goodness in them will survive. And they will revert to the creed of their ancestors.

11. *Abu Hurayra* related that the Messenger of Allah (peace & blessings of Allah be with him) said: Have you heard of the city, which is inclined upon one side and the other is upon the shore?' They said: 'Yes, O Messenger of Allah!' Then he said: 'The Hour will not come to pass until seventy thousand people from the Children of Israel attack it. When they land there, they will not fight with weapons nor fire arrows but will only say: 'There is no god but God and God is Great,' and one side of it will fall." Thawr said: "I think that he said: 'the area by the shore, then they will say a second time: 'There is no god but God and God is Great,' and the other side will also fall. They will say: 'There is no god but God and God is the Great,' and the gates will be opened for them and they will enter. They will amass the booty and distribute it among themselves when a noise will be heard and it will be said: Indeed, the Anti-Christ has come. Then they will drop everything and confront him.

12. *Abu Hurayra* related that the Messenger of Allah (peace & blessings of Allah be with him) said: The Hour will not come to pass until the Euphrates will reveal a moun-tain of gold and when the people hear of it they will rush towards it but the people who own

it will say: 'If we permit them to remove it they will take all of it.' So they will fight and ninety-nine from one hundred will be killed.

13. *Abu Hurayra* reported that the Messenger of Allah (peace & blessings of Allah be with him) said: The river Euphrates will soon give up its treasure of gold, *so whoever is there at that time* should not take any of it.

14. *Abu Hurayra* reported that the Messenger of Allah (peace & blessings of Allah be with him) said: Before the Hour you will fight a people who wear shoes of hair who have small eyes, reddish faces and flattened noses, and their faces will appear to be like flat shields.

15. *Abu Hurayra* reported that the Prophet (peace & blessings of Allah be with him) said: The days and the nights will not pass away until a man called Aljehjah becomes a king.

16. *Anas* reported that the Messenger of Allah (peace & blessings of Allah be with him) said: The Hour will not come to pass until no one remains on the earth to give praise to God.

17. It is reported from *Abu Hurayra* that the Messenger of Allah (peace & blessings of Allah be with him) said: God will send a wind from Yemen which will be softer than silk, and it will not leave anyone who has as much as the weight of a mustard seed or an atom of faith in

his heart, but will seize his soul.

18. *Abd Allah ibn Mas'ud* reported that the Messenger of Allah (peace & blessings of Allah be with him) said: The Hour will not come to pass except when only the evildoers are left alive.

19. *Abu Hurayra* reported that the Messenger of Allah (peace & blessings of Allah be with him) said: The Hour will not come to pass until imposters and liars, about thirty of them, will appear, each one of them will claim to be a Messenger of God.

20. *Jabir ibn Samura* reported that the Messenger of Allah (peace & blessings of Allah be with him) said: Before the Hour comes to pass many liars will appear.

21. *Abu Hurayra* reported that the Messenger of Allah (peace & blessings of Allah be with him) said: The Hour will not come to pass before the Muslims fight the Jews, and the Muslims will kill them until the Jews will seek to hide themselves behind a stone or a tree, and then the stone or tree will say: 'O Mus-lim,' or 'O servant of Allah,' there is a Jew behind me, come and kill him.' Except for the tree of al-Gharqad, for it is the tree of the Jews.

22. *Musa ibn Ali* reported from his father that Mustawrid al Qurayshi said: I heard the Apostle of Allah say: 'The Hour will come to pass when the Romans are the majority of the people.' Amr said: 'What are you saying?' He said: 'I say what I heard from the Messenger of Allah.' Then he said: If that is so, then they have four traits. They have the patience to withstand a trial and forthwith restore themselves after their distress and then re-attack after taking flight. They are good to the needy and the orphans and the weak, and lastly their good trait is that they oppose the tyranny of kings.

23. *Ibn Jabir* narrated that once a red storm appeared in Kufa and Abd Allah ibn Mas'ud said: the Hour has come. A man was sitting reclining against something, and he said: The Hour will not come to pass before the people divide inheritance and rejoice over war spoils. Then he gestured towards al Sham and said: 'The enemy will assemble against the Muslims and the Muslims will assemble against them.' I said: 'Do you mean al Sham?' He said: 'yes, and there will be a great battle. The Muslims will assemble an army that will resolve never to return without victory. They will fight until the darkness of night. Both sides will return without victory and both will be obliterated. Then the Muslims will organize another army to fight to the death and resolve never to return without victory. On the fourth day, a new army from the remaining Muslims will assemble and God will decree that the enemy will be vanquished. They will fight a battle the like of which has never

been witnessed before, so ferocious that if even a bird were to *fly by* their flanks, it would fall down dead before reaching the other side. And then when they will count only one from every hundred men will be found alive who will be related to each other. What war spoils could be enjoyed after such a war and what inheritance could be shared out? They will be in this condition when they will hear of an affliction more frightful than this. They will be told: 'The Anti-Christ is lodging among your children. Then they will cast aside what is in their hands and set off, dispatching ten cavalrymen to recon-noiter.

24. *Jabir ibn Samura* reported that Nafi' ibn Utbah said: We were with the Messenger of Allah (peace & blessings of Allah be with him) on an expedition when some people clothed in wool came to the Messenger of Allah (peace & blessings of Allah be with him) from the west, they stood near a dune and met the Prophet (peace & blessings of Allah be with him) while he was sitting there. I thought that I should go to them and stand between him and them in case they attack him. Then I thought that perhaps there were secret negotiations going on between them. But, I went over to them and stood between them and him and I recall four things that the Messenger of Allah (peace & blessings of Allah be with him) said on that occasion; 'You will attack Arabia and God will enable you to

vanquish it, then you will attack Persia and He will cause you to vanquish it. Then you will attack al-Sham and God will enable you to vanquish it, then you will attack the Anti-Christ and God will enable you to vanquish him. Nafi' said: Jabir, we thought that the Anti-Christ will appear after al- Sham is vanquished.

25. *Abu Hurayra* reported that the Messenger of Allah (peace & blessings of Allah be with him) said: The Hour will not come to pass before the Romans land at al Amaq or in Dabiq. An army comprising of the best of the people on the earth at that time will set out from Medina. When they align themselves in rows, the Romans will say: 'Do not stand between us and those who took prisoners from among us, but let us confront them.' The Muslims will say: 'No, by God, we shall never turn away from you or from our brethren and leave you to fight them.' Then they will fight and one third of the army, whom God will never forgive, will flee. Another third comprising the most excellent martyrs in the sight of Allah will be killed. And the third that will never be put on trial will have victory and they will be the vanquishers of Constantinople. While they are occupied in sharing the booty, after propping up their swords beside the olive trees, Satan will cry out: 'The Anti-Christ is dwelling with your families.' They will then set off, but it will be of no avail. When they reach al Sham, he

will appear while they are still readying themselves for battle. Then, for certain, prayer will become due and then Jesus son of Mary will descend and lead them in prayer. When the enemy of God sees him, he will vanish as the salt dissolves in water and even if he were not to confront them at all, it would dissolve completely. God will kill them by his hand and he would show them their blood on his spear.

26. *Abu Hurayra* reported that the Apostle of Allah (peace & blessings of Allah be with him) said: A short-legged Abyssinian will destroy the Ka'ba.

27. *Abu Hurayra* reported that the Messenger of Allah (peace & blessings of Allah be with him) said: Iraq will withhold its Dirhams and Qafiz, Syria will withhold its measurement and Dinar and Egypt will withhold its Irdab and Dinar and you will return to the way you were when you began and will return to the position you were in when you began and the bones and the flesh of Abu Hurayra shall bear witness to it.

28. It is reported from *Abu Hurayra* that the Messenger of Allah (peace & blessings of Allah be with him) said: Famine will not break out because of drought, but there would be famine in spite of heavy rainfall, because nothing will grow from the earth.

29. *Hudhaifa* is reported to have narrated that the holy Prophet (peace & blessings of Allah be with him) related two Hadiths to us, one of which I have seen fulfilled and the other I am still waiting for. The Prophet said that God Almighty placed the virtue of honesty into the hearts of mankind. Then they learned it from the Qur'an and then they learned it from the Traditions of the Prophet. The Prophet then said how that honesty would be removed. He said: 'Mankind will sleep and honesty will be removed from his heart and only a trace of it will remain in their heart like the trace of a dark spot, then mankind will sleep, and honesty will decrease yet more, so that its trace will resemble the trace of blister when an ember is dropped on one's foot and it would appear swollen but there will be nothing inside it. People will continue with their business but there will be hardly anyone who would be trustworthy. It will be said: In the tribe of so and so there is still an honest man. Thereafter it will be said of another man: 'What a wise, polite and strong man he is!' Although he will not have faith equal even to a mustard seed in his heart.'

30. It is reported that *Hudhaifa ibn Usaid al Ghifari* said: The Messenger of Allah (peace & blessings of Allah be with him) came to us unexpectedly while as we were speaking together. He asked: 'What are you discussing?' We said: 'We are discussing the Hour.' Then he

said: 'It will not come to pass before you see ten signs.' And he mentioned smoke, the Anti-Christ, the beast, the rising of the sun from the west, the descent of Jesus, son of Mary (may Allah be pleased with him), Gog and Magog, and landslides in three places, one in the east, one in the west and one in Arabia, after which a *burning* fire will emerge from the Yemen which will drive the people to the place they will all be gathered.

31. *Abu Hurayra* reported that the Messenger of Allah (peace & blessings of Allah be with him) said: Hasten with good deeds, as afflic-tions will fall like pieces of a dark night. A man will believe in the morning and by the evening he will disbelieve. And he will believe in the evening and in the morning he will disbelieve. He will sell his Religion for worldly gain.

32. *Abu Hurayra* reported that the Apostle of Allah (peace & blessings of Allah be with him) said: Hasten in doing good deeds before six things happen, the rising of the sun from the west, the smoke, the Anti-Christ, the beast, your death or the time of calamity.

33. *Abd Allah ibn Umar* reported that the Apostle of Allah (peace & blessings of Allah be with him) addressed the people, praised Allah and mentioned Anti-Christ saying: No Prophet was ever sent who did not warn his followers against the one- eyed liar. Beware he is blind in one eye, and your Lord is not,

and it will be written between his eyes-unbeliever.

34. *Hudhaifa* reported that the Messenger of Allah (peace & blessings of Allah be with him) said: I know more of the Anti-Christ than the Anti-Christ knows of himself. He has two flowing rivers with him, the water of one of them appears white and the other appears to be flaming with fire. If anyone encounters him, he should go into the river he sees as fire and shut his eyes and bend his head and drink from it, because it is cool water. The Anti-Christ's eyes are squinted and upon it is a thick nail and between his eyes is the word 'Kafir' (unbeliever) written and every believer-literate or illite-rate- will be able to read it.

35. *Hudhaifa* reported that the Messenger of Allah (peace & blessings of Allah be with him) said: The Anti-Christ has a squinted left eye, his hair is heavy and he has with him a Paradise and a Fire. His Fire is Paradise and his Paradise is Fire.

36. *Al Nawwas ibn Sam'an* reported that the Prophet (peace & blessings of Allah be with him) mentioned the Anti-Christ one morning. At times he men-tioned him as inconsequen-tial and sometimes of great conse-quence until we felt as if he was lurking within the cluster of date palm trees. When we visited him in the evening and he saw fear on our faces, he said: 'What is the matter?' We said: 'O Messenger of Allah! You men-tioned the Anti-

Christ this morning as sometimes inconsequen-tial and sometimes of great conse-quence until we felt as if he was lurking within the cluster of date palm trees.' So he said: 'I fear for you in so many things other than the Anti-Christ.' If he appears while I am among you, I shall deal with him for you, but if he appears after me, each of you must deal with him for yourselves and God will protect every Muslim on my behalf. He will be a young man with wiry, cropped hair, and a blind eye. I liken him to Abdul Uzza ibn Qatan. Whoever lives to see him should recite the opening verses of Surah 'The Cave' over him (Surah 18). He will appear on the way between Syria and Iraq and will spread mischief right and left. O servant of God! Be firm.' We said: 'O Messenger of Allah! How long will he abide upon the Earth?' He said: 'For forty days, one day will be like a year, one day will be like a month, one day will be like a week, and the rest of the days will be like your days.' We said: 'O Messenger of Allah! Will the prayer of one day be sufficient for the prayers of the day equal to one year?' Then he said: 'No, you must estimate the time.' We said: 'O Messenger of Allah! How fast will he move over the earth?' He said: 'As fast as the clouds driven by the winds, he will appear to the people and invite them, they will pledge their faith in him and hearken to him. Then he will command the sky and rain will fall upon the

Earth and crops will grow. Then in the evening, their grazing animals will come to them with their humps very high, their udders full of milk and their flanks bloated. Then he will go to another people and invite them. But they will reject him so he will leave them; they will face a drought and no wealth will remain with them. Then he will traverse the desert and say: 'Bring out your treasures.' And the treasures will come out and assemble before him like a swarm of bees. Then he will summon a youth and strike him with the sword, cut him into two distant pieces. Then he will summon the youth and he will arise laughing, his face aglow. At that moment God Almighty will send Jesus, son of Mary. He will descend at the white minaret on the eastern side of Damascus, wearing two garments lightly dyed with saffron and placing his hands on the wings of two Angels. When he lowers his head, beads of perspiration will fall from his head, and when he raises it up, beads like pearls will scatter from it. Every unbeliever who smells the scent of his body will die and his breath will reach as far as his sight. He will then search for him until he catches hold of him at the gate of Ludd and kill him. Then a people whom God has protected will come to Jesus, son of Mary, and he will wipe their faces and inform them of their ranks in Paradise. So it will be when God reveals to Jesus: 'I have brought forth from among My servants such people against whom none will be able to fight; you take these people safely to Tur, and then God will send Gog and Magog and they will slide down from every slope. The first of them will pass lake Tiberias and drink it. And when the last of them passes, he will say: 'There used to be water there.' Jesus and his companions will then be attacked so that the head of an ox would be dearer to them than one hundred Dinars. The Messenger of Allah (peace & blessings of Allah be with him), Jesus (peace be with him) and the companions will invoke God Almighty and He will send to them insects and in the morning they would perish at once. The Messenger of Allah (peace & blessings of Allah be with him), Jesus, and his companions, will then descend to the Earth and they will not find space of even a single span that is not filled with decay and foul odor. The Messenger of Allah (peace & blessings of Allah be with him), Jesus, and his companions will then invoke God, and He will send birds whose necks would be like the necks of Bacteria camels and they will lift them away and cast them where God pleases. Then God will send rain that no house of mud-bricks or camel hair will repel and it will wash the Earth until it shines like a mirror. Then the Earth will be told to bring forth its fruit and restore its blessings and then a pomegranate will grow so large that a party of people will be able

to eat it and seek shelter under its skin, a dairy cow will give so much milk that a whole party will be able to drink it. The milking camel will give so much milk that a whole tribe will be able to drink from it, and the milking sheep will give so much milk that a whole family will be able to drink from it. Then God will send a gentle wind that will touch them even under their armpits. And He will take the soul of every Muslim and only the wicked will be left alive and will fornicate like Asses and then the Hour will arrive.

37. *Abu Saeed al Khudri* reported that one day the Messenger of Allah (peace & blessings of Allah be with him) addressed us regarding the Anti-Christ and among the things he spoke of was that the Anti-Christ will come, and he will be forbidden to enter the mountain passes of Medina. He will encamp in one of the salt areas in the environs of Medina and on that day a man from the best of the people will appear to him and say: 'I bear witness that you are the Anti-Christ which the Messenger of Allah (peace & blessin-gs of Allah be with him) told us of.' The AntiChrist will say: 'If I kill this man and bring him back to life, would you doubt me?' They will reply: 'No.' Then he will kill him and bring him back to life, and then the man will say: 'By God I was not so certain about you as I am now.' The Anti-Christ will try to kill him but will not be able to do so. Abu Ishaq said: This man

is Al Khidr (peace be with him).

38. *Al-Mughira ibn Shu'ba* reported that: No one **asked** the Prophet as many questions about the Anti-Christ as I. The Prophet asked me: 'What makes you worry about him?' I said: 'The people say that he will have a mountain of bread and a river of water.' The Prophet said: 'No! He is too ordinary that God would permit him to have such things.

39. *Al Numan ibn Salem* reported that he heard Yaqub ibn Asim ibn Urwa ibn Mas'ud al Thaqafi say that he heard Abd Allah ibn Amr say that someone came to him and asked: 'What is that Hadith you relate in which the Hour will come to pass after a certain time?' Then he said: 'Glory be to God, there is no god but Allah. I have resolved never to relate anything to anyone. I related only that after some time an momentous event will occur, the House will be burnt and it will certainly come to pass.' Then he said that the Messenger of Allah (peace & blessings of Allah be with him) said: 'The Anti-Christ will appear to my community and he will stay for forty,' - I do not know if he meant forty days, forty months or forty years. -'Then God will send Jesus, the son of Mary, who will look like Urwa ibn Mas'ud. He will pursue him and kill him. Then mankind will live for seven years, during which time there will be no dissent between any people. After that God Almighty will send a cold wind from the direction of Syria. No one who has as much as a grain of goodness in him will survive on the Earth. And even if you were to enter the deepest recess of the mountain, the wind will reach it and cause you to die.' I heard the Messenger of Allah (peace & blessings of Allah be with him) say: Only the wicked people will be left alive and they will be as carefree as the birds and have the nature of animals. They will neither value piety nor condemn evil. Then Satan will appear to them in the guise of a human being and say: 'Will you obey?' They will ask: 'What do you order us to do?' Then he will order them to worship idols, and despite that they will still enjoy ample sustenance and comforts. Then the trumpet will be blown and the heads of all who hear it will reel. The first to hear that trumpet will be the one who is busy repairing the water trough for the camels. He will faint and the other people will also faint. Then God will send, or He will cause a rain to be sent, which will be like dew and the bodies of mankind will emerge from it. Then the second trumpet will be blown and they will stand up and gaze around. Then it will be said: 'O mankind, go to your Lord. They will be made to stand there and they will be questioned. Then it will be said: 'Bring a group for the Hell Fire.' It will be asked: 'How many?' It will be said: 'Nine hundred and ninety-nine from every thousand for the Hell Fire.'

That Day the children will become old from its terror and that will be the Day about which it has been said: 'On the Day when the flanks will be uncovered.'

40. *Abd Allah ibn Amr ibn Al A'as* said: I memorized a Hadith from the Messenger of Allah (peace & blessings of Allah be with him) and I never forgot it after I had heard the Prophet say: The first Sign will be the rising of the sun from the west, then the appearance of the beast before mankind in the forenoon, and whichever of the two occurs first, the second will follow immediately there-after.

41. It is reported from *Fatimah, daughter of Qais,* that she heard the Messenger of Allah say in the mosque: 'Everyone who is praying here should stay in his place, then he said: 'Do you know why I asked you to congregate?' They said: 'God and His Messenger know best.' He said: 'By God, I did not ask you to gather here to exhort you or to warn you.' I have kept you here because Tamim Dari, who was a Christian has embraced Islam, and he told me something which corresponds with what I told you about the Anti-Christ.' He told me that he had set-sail in a ship with thirty men of Bani Lakhm and Bani Judham and it had tossed about by waves in the ocean for a month. Then they reached near the land in the ocean at the time of sunset. They took a small rowing boat to the shore of the island. There they saw

a beast with such long thick hair that they could not make out its face from his back. They said: 'Woe to you, who are you?' It said: 'I am al -Jassasah.' They said: 'What is al-Jassasah?' It said: 'O people, go to a man in a monastery as he is eagerly awaiting you.' When it named the man we feared it might be a Devil. Then we hurried on until we reached the monastery and found a well-built person there with his hands tied to his neck and iron shackles upon his ankles. We said: 'Woe to you, who are you?' He said: 'You soon will come to know about me, but tell me who you are.' We said: ' We are from Arabia and we set sail in a boat but the waves carried us off for one month and brought us near the island, so we took to the rowing boats and came ashore on the island. Then a beast with bushy hair met us and its hair was so thick we could not make out its front from its back. We said to it: 'Woe to you, who are you?' It said: 'I am al Jassasah.' We said: 'What is al Jassasah?' It said: Go to the monastery as a man is eagerly waiting for you. So we came to you in hurriedly fearing that it might be the Devil. He said: 'Tell me about the date-palm trees of Baysan.' We said: 'What do you wish to know about them?' He said: 'I wish to know if they bear fruit or not.' We said: 'Yes.' Then he said: 'I think they will not bear fruit.' He said: 'Tell me about lake Tiberias?' We said: 'What do you wish to know about it?' He said: 'Is there water in it?' They said: 'There is plenty of water in it.' Then he said: 'I think it will soon be dry.' Then he said: 'Tell me about the spring of Zughar.' They said: 'What do you wish to know about it?' He said: 'Is there water in it and does it provide irrigation?' We said: 'Yes, there is plenty of water in it and people irrigate by it.' He said: 'Tell me about the unlettered Prophet, what has he done?' We said: 'He has left Makka and settled in Medina.' He said: 'Are the Arabs fighting against him?' We said: 'Yes.' He said: 'How does he deal with them?' We told him that he had vanquished those in the vicinity and they had pledged allegiance to him. Then he said: 'Has it already happened?' We said: 'Yes.' Then he said: 'If that is so then it is better for them that they pledge allegiance to him. Now I will tell you about myself. I am the AntiChrist and soon I shall be allowed to leave this place.' Then I shall leave and travel about the land, and shall not leave any town without staying for forty nights except Makka and Medina, as these two are forbidden to me and I will not attempt to enter either of them. An angel bearing a sword in his hand will confront me and prevent me and there will be angels to guard every road leading to them.' Then the Messenger of Allah (peace & blessings of Allah be with him) struck the pulpit with the end of his staff and said: 'Did I not tell you of this?' The people said: 'Yes.' And I like what Tamim Dari related as it corroborates with what I told you about him in Makka and Medina. Indeed, the Anti-Christ is in the Mediterranean Sea or the Arabian Sea. No, to the contrary, he is in the east, he is in the east, he is in the east.' And he pointed his hand towards the east. I said: 'I memorized this from the Messenger of Allah (peace & blessings of Allah be with him).

42. *Anas ibn Malik* reported that the Messenger of Allah (peace & blessings of Allah be with him) said: The Anti-Christ will appear and camp near Medina, and Medina will have two angels at each gate. Then Medina will be shaken three times and every unbeliever and hypocrite will be expelled from it towards him.

43. *Anas ibn Malik* reported that the Apostle of Allah (peace & blessings of Allah be with him) said: seventy thousand Jews of Isfahan wearing Persian cloaks will follow The Anti-Christ.

44. *Usama ibn Zayed ibn Haritha* and Sayeed ibn Zaid ibn Amr ibn Nafil reported that the Messenger of Allah (peace & blessings of Allah be with him) said: No affliction will remain after me more harmful to men than women.

45. *Abu Sayeed al Khudri* reported that the Prophet (peace & blessings of Allah be with him) said: This life is sweet and green, and God has assigned you to dwell in it to see how you will act, so beware of the life and beware of women, as the first affliction to the Children of Israel were the women.

65

Book of Asceticism

1. It is reported on the authority of *Abu Hurayra* that the Messenger of Allah (peace & blessings of Allah be with him) said: This life is a prison for the believers and a Paradise for the unbelievers.

2. *Suhaib* reported that the Messenger of Allah (peace & blessings of Allah be with him) said: The ways of a believer are different, for he sees goodness in all that happens to him, and this is not so with other than a believer, for if he has reason to be happy, he gives thanks to Allah, and so there is goodness for him in it. And if he suffers affliction, he endures it with patience, and so there is goodness for him in it.

3. *Al Mustawrid* reported that the Messenger of Allah (peace & blessings of Allah be with him) said: By God, what is in this life compared to what is in the Hereafter is just as if one of you dipped his finger into the sea. So let him see what he draws out with it.

4. *Abu Hurayra* reported that the Messenger of Allah (peace & blessings of Allah be with him) said: Look at the people who have less than you and do not look at those who have more than you, it is better for you that you do not despise the blessings of Allah.

5. It is reported from *Urwa* said that Hadrat Ayesha used to say: By God, O son of my sister! We used to see three crescents in two months, and no fire used to be lit in the houses of the Messenger of Allah (peace & blessings of Allah be with him). Urwa said: "O my aunt, what did you survive on?" She said: "The two (things) which are black, dates and water, but the Messenger of Allah (peace & blessings of Allah be with him) had neighbors from the Ansars who used to send milk to the Messenger of Allah (peace & blessings of Allah be with him) to drink and he used to make us drink it.

6. It is reported from *Hadrat Ayesha* that when the Messenger of Allah (peace & blessings of Allah be with him) died, he had never filled his stomach twice in a day with bread and oil.

7. *Hadrat Ayesha* (may Allah be pleased with her) is reported to have said: The family of Muhammad never ate two meals in one day, but one of the two was of dates.

8. *Abu Hazem* reported: I saw Abu Hurayra indicating repeatedly with his finger saying: 'By The One in Whose Hand is the soul of Abu Hurayra, the Prophet of Allah and his family never ate their fill of wheat bread for three successive days until he died.

9. *Hadrat Ayesha* is reported to have said: When the Prophet died, nothing that could be consumed by any living creature remained on my shelf except some barley grain.

10. It is reported from *Al Numan ibn Bashir* that Umar mentioned what the people have gained of this life, and he said: 'I saw the Messenger of Allah (peace & blessings of Allah be with him) suffering pangs of hunger the whole day and he could not find even a date to fill his stomach.'

11. It is reported from *Abu Abd al Rahman al Hubuli* that Abu Abd al Rahman said that three people came to Abd Allah ibn Amr ibn al As while I was sitting with him and said: 'By God, we have nothing at all with us as provision or mount or wealth. Then he said: 'I will do whatever you like. If you join us, we will give you whatever God provides for you, and if you like I can inform the ruler of your situation. If you wish you can be patient as well, for I have heard the Messenger of Allah (peace & blessings of Allah be with him) say:

The needy of the Muha-jirin will be admitted to Paradise forty years before the wealthy ones on the Day of Resurrection.' So they said: We shall be patient and we do not ask for anything.

12. *Usama ibn Zaid* reported that the Messenger of Allah (peace & blessings of Allah be with him) said: I stood by the gate of Paradise and saw that the majority of the people who entered it were the poor, while the rich were stopped at the gate. But the companions of the Fire were ordered to be taken to the Fire, then I stood by the gate of the Fire and saw that the majority of those who entered it were women.

13. *Jabir ibn Abd Allah* reported that the Messenger of Allah (peace & bles-sings of Allah be with him) walked through the market and he saw a dead lamb there that had stunted ears. He held its ear and asked: 'Which of you would take this for a Dirham?' They said: 'We would not want it for even less than that as it is useless.' He said: 'Would you like it free?' They said: 'By God, not even if it were living, for it is defective with stunted ears and now it is dead as well. Then the Apostle of Allah (peace & blessings of Allah be with him) said: 'By God, this world is of less significance in the Sight of Allah than this is to you.'

14. *Amr ibn Auf* reported that the holy Prophet (peace & blessings of Allah be with him) sent Abu Ubaida ibn Al Jarrah to Bahrain to collect the Jizya. The Messenger of Allah

(peace & blessings of Allah be with him) had made peace with the people of Bahrain and appointed Al Ala' ibn Al Hadrami as governor. When Abu Ubaida returned from Bahrain with the money the Ansars came to know of his arrival that coincided with the time of the Morning Prayer. When the Apostle of Allah (peace & blessings of Allah be with him) led the morning prayer and completed it, the Ansars approached him and he looked at them and smiled at seeing them and said: 'I feel you have heard that Abu Ubaida has returned with something?' They said: 'Yes, O Messenger of Allah.' He said: Be glad, and hope for what pleases you! By God I do not fear poverty for you, but I fear that you will lead a life of luxury as former communities did, and you will vie with each other for it, as they vied for it, and it will destroy you as it destroyed them'.

15. *Khalid ibn Umair Al Adawy* reported that Utbah ibn Ghazwan addressed the people and praised and glorified Allah and said: Indeed, the world has been told the tidings of its end too soon. Nothing will be left of it except the water left by its owner in the container. You are going to an eternal abode, and you should go forwarding good for yourself, for we have been told that a stone which is cast on one side of Hell will slip down for seventy years and still not reach its depths. By God, it will be overflowing. Do you find that strange? It has been

mentioned that there stretches a distance, which one can cover in forty years, from one end of Paradise to the other, and a day will come when it is overflowing. You must know that I was the seventh of seven who were with the Messenger of Allah (peace & blessings of Allah be with him) and we had no food except the leaves of the tree which we ate until the corners of our mouths were sore. We found a cloth and tore it into two and divided it between Sa'ad ibn Malik and myself. I made a waist wrapper with one half and Sa'ad also made a waist wrapper with the other half. This day there is not one of us who has not been appointed governor of one of the cities. I seek refuge with Allah that I do not deem myself important while I am insignificant in the Sight of Allah. Prophethood does not abide forever and its imprint fades until it evolves into kingship. You will soon come to know and suffer from rulers who will succeed us.

16. *Anas ibn Malik* reported that the Messenger of Allah (peace & blessings of Allah be with him) said: There are three who follow the deceased, two of them return, while one only remains with him. His family, his wealth and his deeds, follow him. His family and his wealth return, but his deeds remain with him.

17. *Abu Hurayra* reported that the Messenger of Allah (peace & blessings of Allah be with him) said: God Most High, Exalted said: 'I am far Superior to having

partners, whoever does any deed and shares in it with other than Me, I abandon him to what he associates.

18. *Ibn Abbas* reported that the Messenger of Allah (peace & blessings of Allah be with him) said: Whoever heeds, God will hear him, and whoever acts only for show, God will let the people see his reality.

19. It is reported from *Suhaib* that the Messenger of Allah said: Once there was a king in times before you and he had a magician. When he grew old, he said to the king: 'I have grown old, so bring me a youth that I may instruct him in magic.' He sent for a youth so that he could instruct him in magic. On his way there the youth happened upon a monk sitting on the way and he sat to listen to him, and was impressed by him. So he used to meet the monk every time he went to the magician until one day he was late in meeting the magician. He beat him because of his sluggishness, so the youth complained to the monk about it and he said to him: 'When you fear the magi-cian's anger, then say: 'My family de-tained me.' And when you fear your family's anger then say: 'The magician detained me.' Then a huge beast came and hindered the people on the way. He said: 'Now I shall see which is the greater of the two, the magician or the monk.' He picked up a stone and said: 'O God, if the monk is more beloved to You than the magician, then cause the beast to die so that the people may move as they wish.'

And he threw the stone at it and killed it and the people began to move about. He then went to the monk and told him of it. The monk said: My son, now you are better than I. You have attained a degree (of faith) where I see you will soon be tested. So in that case do not disclose who I am. The youth began to treat the blind and those suffering from leprosy and began to cure people of many complaints. When one of the king's companions, who had become blind, heard about him, he went to him with many gifts and said: 'If you cure me, all these will be yours.' He said: 'I myself do not cure anyone, but it is God Who cures. If you have firm faith in God, I will invoke God to cure you.' He affirmed his faith in God and God cured him. He returned to the king and sat beside him as he used to do and the king asked him: 'Who restored your sight?' He said: 'My Lord.' He said: 'You say that your Lord is one other than me!' He said: 'My Lord and your Lord is God.' Then he seized him and tortured him until he spoke of the youth. The youth was then brought before the king and he said to him: 'O boy, I have been told that you have become so skilled in your magic that you cure the blind and those suffering from leprosy and many things besides.' He said: I do not cure anyone, it is God Who cures.' He seized him and tortured him until he spoke of the monk. The monk was then brought and he was told: 'Renege from your religion.' But he refused. He ordered a saw to be brought and he had it placed over his head and sawed until it fell off. Then the courtier of the king was brought and it was said to him: 'Renege from your religion.' But he refused. So the saw was placed over his head and sawed until it fell off. Then youth was brought and it was said to him: 'Renege from your religion.' He refused and he was handed to some of his courtiers. He said to them: 'Take him to a certain mountain and make him climb it and when you reach its summit order him to renege and if he refuses, then throw him off. So they took him and made him climb the mountain and he said: 'O God, rescue me from them as You please.' The mountain began to shake and they all fell down. The youth returned to the king and the king asked him: 'What became of your companions?' He said: 'God rescued me from them.' So he handed him over to his courtiers again saying: 'Take him and carry him away in a small boat and when you reach the middle of the ocean order him to renege from his religion, and if he refuses, throw him into the sea.' So they seized him and he said: 'O God, rescue me from them and what they wish to do.' Soon the boat capsized and they were drowned, but he returned to the king and the king asked him: 'What happened to your compa-nions?' He said: 'God rescued me from them.' Then he told the king: You will not be able to kill me unless you do as I say. He asked: 'What is that?' He said: Assemble the people on a level ground and hang me on a tree trunk. Then take an arrow from its quiver and say: In the name of God, the Lord of the Worlds, then shoot an arrow and thus you will be able to kill me.' So he assembled the people on a level ground and tied him on a tree trunk. Then he took an arrow from its quiver and put it in the bow and said: 'In the name of God, the Lord of the youth.' He then shot an arrow and it hit his temple. He put his hands on his temple where the arrow had hit. The people said: 'We believe in the Lord of this youth, we believe in the Lord of this youth, we believe in the Lord of this youth.' The courtiers went to the king and asked: 'Do you not see that they have believed in the Lord?' He ordered trenches to be dug at strategic points on the road. When the trenches were dug, and a fire was kindled in them, they were told: Whoever does not renege from the religion of the youth will be cast into the fire or forced to jump into it.' They refused until when a woman came with her child she hesitated to jump into the fire with her child, so the child said to her: 'O mother endure it for it is the Truth.'

20. *Abu Hurayra* reported that he heard the Messenger of Allah (peace & blessings of Allah be with him) say: God intended to test three Israelis, one was a leper, one was blind and one was bald. So He sent an angel to the leper saying: 'What do you wish for most of all?' He said: 'I would like to be a good colour and have a healthy skin as the people find me most loathsome." The angel touched him and his malady was cured, his colour became good and his skin became healthy. The angel asked him: 'What kind of property do you prefer?' He said: 'Camels.' Or he said: 'Cows.' So he was given a pregnant she-camel and the angel said: 'May God bless you in it.' The angel then went to the bald man and said: 'What do you wish for most of all?' He said: 'I would like good hair and to be cured of this malady for the people find me most loathsome.' The angel touched him and his malady was cured, and he was given good hair.' The angel asked him: 'What kind of property do you prefer?' He said: 'Cows.' So the angel gave him a pregnant heifer and said: 'May God bless you in it.' The angel went to the blind man and said: 'What do you wish for most of all?' He said: 'I would like God to restore my sight so that I may see the people.' The angel touched his eyes and God restored his sight. The angel asked him: 'What kind of property do you prefer?' He said: 'Sheep.' The angel gave him a pregnant sheep. There-after the three pregnant animals gave birth to their young and their numbers increased so that the men had a herd of camels filling the valley, and a herd of cows filling the valley and a herd of sheep filling the valley. Then the angel disguised himself as a leper and visited the leper and said: 'I am a poor man who has lost all means of livelihood while I was traveling. So no one will fill my needs but God and you. In the Name of He Who has given you a good colour and healthy skin and great property, I ask you to give me one camel so that I may reach my destination. The man said: 'I regret, I have so many commitments.' The angel said: 'I think I know you, were you not a leper whom the people found most loathsome? Were you not poor and then God gave you all this?' He said: 'I gained this property from the inheritance of my forebears.' The angel said: 'If you are lying, then let God return you to your former state.' Then the angel disguised himself as a bald man and appeared to the bald man and said the same as he had said to the first one. The angel said: 'If you are lying, then let God return you to your former state.' The angel disguised himself as a blind man and appeared to the blind man and said: 'I am a poor man on a journey and my livelihood has been exhausted while I was traveling. I have no one to help me except God and after Him, you. I ask you in the Name of He Who has restored your sight, to give me one sheep, so that I may reach my destination.' The man said: 'Indeed I was blind and God restored my sight, I was poor and God made me rich, so take whatever you need of my property. By God I will not acclaim you if you leave anything of my property which you need in the cause of God.' The angel said: 'Keep your property, you have been tested and God is well pleased with you but angry with your two companions'.

66

Book of Merits of the Qur'an

1. *Ibn Abbas* reported: While Gabriel was sitting with the Prophet he heard a noise from above him, so de raised his head and said: This is a gate in Heaven which has just opened today, and it never opened before today, and an angel has descended from it.' He also said: This is an angel who has come down to earth and he had never come down before today.' So he greeted them and said: 'Glad tidings of two lights you have been given which no prophet before you had been given- Surah 'The Opening,' and the end of Sura' 'The Heifer.' Every letter you recite of the two, God will grant it to you.

2. *Abu Amama al Bahly* reported that he heard the Messenger of Allah (peace & blessings of Allah be with him) say: 'Recite the Qur'an because on the Day of Judgment it will intercede for its companions. Recite the ever blossoming two Suras of 'The Heifer' and 'Al-e-Imran' as on the Day of Judgment it will come as a shade above you or as two flocks of birds spreading

their wings to protect its companions. Recite Sura 'The Heifer,' because doing it is a blessing and leaving it is a sorrow and no one can memorize it but those who have strong faith.'

3. It is reported from *Ubayy ibn Ka'ab* that the Messenger of Allah (peace & blessings of Allah be with him) said: O Abu al Munthir, do you know which of the verses that you have memorized from the Book of Allah is the greatest?' I said: 'Allah and His Messenger know best.' He said: 'O Abu al Munthir, do you know which verse you have memorized from the Book of Allah is the greatest?' I said: 'Allah, there is no god but He, The Ever-Living, The Eternal Power...' (Sura' 2 verse 255) He patted me on my chest and said: 'O Abu al Munthir, congratulations for the knowledge that you have been given.

4. It was related that *Abu Mas'ud* said that the Prophet said: Whoever recites the last two Verses of Sura 'The Heifer' at night, it will suffice him.

5. *Abu Darda* reported that the Prophet of Allah said: Whoever memorizes ten verses from the beginning of Sura 'The Cave' will be protected from the afflictions of the Anti-Christ. It was also reported that it is from the end of Surah 'The Cave.'

6. According to *Abu Darda* the holy Prophet said: Is any one of you unable to recite a third of the Qur'an in one night?' They said: 'How can we recite one third of the Qur'an?' He said: "Say: He is Allah the One and Only.' It is equal to one third of the Qur'an.

7. *Hadrat Ayesha* related that the Apostle of Allah (peace & blessings of Allah be with him) appointed a man as commander of a company, and he used to recite to his companions during the prayer and end with: 'Say, He is Allah the One and Only.' Then when they returned they mentioned that to the Prophet (peace & blessings of Allah be with him) and he told them to ask him why he did that?' So they asked him and he said: Because it is the attribute of Allah, Most Merciful. And I like to recite it.' Then the Mes-senger of Allah (peace & blessings of Allah be with him) said: Inform him that Allah loves him.

8. *Uqba ibn Amer* reported that the Apostle of Allah (peace & blessings of Allah be with him) said: Do you know that this night verses have been revealed which no one has ever seen the like of?' 'Say, I seek refuge in the Lord of the daybreak,' and 'Say, I seek refuge in the Lord of mankind.'

9. *Abu Musa* reported that the Messenger of Allah (peace & blessings of Allah be with him) said: The believer who reads the Qur'an and acts upon it, is like a citron which tastes nice and smells nice.' And the believer, who does not recite the Qur'an but acts upon it, is like a date; it tastes nice but has no smell. And the similarity of the hypocrite who recites the Qur'an is a fragrant herb that smells nice but tastes bitter, and the likeness of the hypocrite who does not recite the Qur'an is as the colocynth that tastes bitter or bad and has a foul smell.

10. It is reported on the authority of *Hadrat Ayesha* that the Messenger of Allah (peace & blessings of Allah be with him) said: The similitude of the one who recites the Qur'an from memory will be with the noble righteous scribes. And such a one who reads the Qur'an to learn it and is eager has double rewards.

11. *Al Bara ibn Aazib* reported that a man recited Surah 'The Cave' and a mount in the house was frightened and began to jump. The man completed the prayer with the salutation but suddenly a cloud hung around him. He told the Prophet (peace & blessings of Allah be with him) about it and he said: 'O so and so, recite, for that was a sign of peace descending due to the recitation of the Qur'an.

12. *Abu Sayeed Al Khudri* reported that Usaid ibn Hudayr said: When he was reciting Surah 'The Heifer' at night, his horse was tethered beside him and the horse began to be frightened. When he stopped reciting the horse became calm, and when he started again the horse was frightened. Then he stopped reciting and the horse became calm. He started reciting again and the horse was nervous again. Then he stopped and his son Yahya was beside the horse. He feared the horse might trample him, so he took the boy away and gazed at the sky, he could not see it. The next morning he told the Prophet (peace & blessings of Allah be with him) who said: 'Recite O ibn Hudayr!' Ibn Hudayr said; O Messenger of Allah! My son Yahya was near the horse and I feared it might trample him, so I looked at the sky and went to him. When I gazed at the sky, I saw something like a cloud containing lamps, so I went out so as not to see it.' The Prophet (peace & blessings of Allah be with him) said: 'Do you know what that was?' He said: 'No.' The Prophet (peace & blessings of Allah be with him) said: They were angels who came near you to hear your voice, and if you had continued until dawn, it would have remained there until the morning and the people would have seen it.

13. *Salim* reported on the authority of his father that the Prophet said: There is no envy except of two men. A man to whom God has given the knowledge of the Book and he recites it during the hours of the night, and a man whom God has given wealth, and he spends it in charity during the night and the hours of the day.

14. *Abd Allah Ibn Umar* reported that the Messenger of Allah (peace & blessings of Allah be with him) said: The similarity of one who puts the Qur'an to heart is as the one who owns tethered camels. If he keeps them tethered, he will control them, but if he releases them, they will run away.

15. *Abd Allah Ibn Mas'ud* reported that the Apostle of Allah (peace & blessings of Allah be with him) said: It is wrong for any of you to say: 'I have forgotten such and such verse of the Qur'an.' Because he has been caused to forget it, so you should keep reciting the Qur'an because it escapes from the heart of man faster than camels.

16. *Abu Hurayra* reported that the Messenger of Allah (peace & blessings of Allah be with him) said: God does not listen to a prophet as He listens to a prophet who recites the Qur'an in a loud and pleasant tone.

17. It is reported from *Hadrat Ayesha* that the holy Prophet (peace & blessings of Allah be with him) heard a man reciting the Qur'an at night, and said: May God bless him with His Mercy, he has reminded me of such-and-such Verses of such-and such Suras, which I had forgotten.

18. *Umar ibn Al Khattab* is reported to have related: I heard Hisham ibn Hakim reciting Surah 'The Criterion' during the lifetime of the Messenger of Allah (peace & blessings of Allah be with him) and I listened to his recitation and noticed that he recited in several different ways which the Apostle of Allah (peace & blessings of Allah be with him) had not taught me. I was going to jump upon him in the prayer, but I controlled my anger, and when he had finished his prayer I put his upper garment around his neck and grabbed him by it and said: 'Who taught you this Surah you have just recited?' He said: 'The Messenger of Allah taught me.' I said: 'You lie, the Messenger of Allah taught it to me in a different way.' So I dragged him to the Prophet and said: 'I heard this man recite Surah the Criterion in a way you have not taught me.' The Apostle of Allah (peace & blessings of Allah be with him) said: Let him go! O Hisham! Recite.' Then he recited in the same way I had heard. Then the Messenger of Allah (peace &

blessings of Allah be with him) said: 'It was revealed in that way,' and said 'Recite O Umar!' So I recited it as he had taught me. The Prophet (peace & blessings of Allah be with him) said: It was revealed in that way. This Qur'an has been revealed to be recited in seven diffe-rent ways, so recite it in whichever way is easier for you.

19. *Anas ibn Malik* reported that the Messenger of Allah (peace & bles-sings of Allah be with him) said to Ubayy ibn Ka'b: Allah has ordered me to recite upon you: Those who disbelieve among the people of earlier Scripture will never depart (from their error) until their had come to them Clear Evidence.' (Q. 98: 1.). He asked: 'God named me?' The Prophet replied in the affirmative and Ubayy ibn Ka'ab wept.

20. *Amer al–Shubi* reported that he asked Alqama: 'Was ibn Mas'ud with the Messenger of Allah on the night of the jinn?' Alqama said: 'I asked ibn Mas'ud: 'Were any of you with the Messenger of Allah on the night of the jinn.' He said: 'No, but one night we were with the Prophet (peace & blessings of Allah be with him) then we missed him, so we looked for him in every valley and place. Then we said: 'Has he flown away or has someone assassinated him?' So we passed a troubled night the like of which no one has ever seen. In the morning we saw him coming from Hara', so we said:

'O Messenger of Allah! We missed you and we could not find you anywhere so we passed a troubled night the like of which no one has ever seen.' He said: One of the jinn came to invite me, so I went with him and I recited the Qur'an to them. Then he took us to the place and he showed us their tracks and the embers of their fire, and they asked him for food, and he said: You may have every bone over which the name of God has been mentioned which comes to your hand, it is more plentiful than meat, and the dung of the camels is food for your animals. Then the Messenger of Allah (peace & blessings of Allah be with him) told us: So do not wipe yourselves with it, as it is the food of your brethren.

21. *Abd Allah ibn Mas'ud* is reported to have related that the Messenger of Allah (peace & blessings of Allah be with him) told him to recite the Qur'an to him.' I said: 'O Messenger of Allah! Should I recite the Qur'an to you while it was revealed to you?' He said: 'I like to hear it from others.' So I recited Surah 'The Women,' until I reached: 'How will it be for them when We bring from every nation a witness and bring you to witness over them all?' (Q. 4: 41). Then I raised my head up and saw his tears flowing.

22. *Abd Allah ibn Amr* reported that one day he visited the Messenger of Allah (peace & blessings of Allah be with him) early in the morning and he heard the voices of two men arguing about a verse, so the Prophet (peace & blessings of Allah be with him) came out in great anger and he said: Those before you were destroyed because of their arguing about the Book.

23. *Jundab ibn Abd Allah* reported that the Apostle of Allah (peace & blessings of Allah be with him) said: Recite the Qur'an as much as your hearts accepts, but when you feel differently, then stop.

67

Book of Prophetic Commentary on the Qur'an

The Interpretation of Surah Al Baqarah

"And enter the gate prostrating and say: We enter imploring Allah for forgiveness."'

(Q. 2: 58)

1. It is reported on the authority of *Abu Hurayra* that the Messenger of Allah (peace & blessings of Allah be with him) said: It was said to the Children of Israel: Enter the gate prostrating and say: 'We enter begging God's forgiveness.' So they entered crawling on their backsides, and so they substituted it and said: 'A grain of wheat in a hair.'

2. *Al-Bara* is reported to have said: In the days before Islam, when the people intended to perform Pilgrimage, they would enter their houses from the back. So God revealed:'... Righteousness is not to enter houses from the back, but righteousness is that you fear God and enter the houses from their doors and fear God that you may succeed.' (Q. 2: 189)

3. *Abu Hurayra* is reported to have

related that when it was revealed to the Messenger of Allah (peace & blessings of Allah be with him): Whether you disclose what is in your hearts or hide it, God will charge you for it. So he forgives whom He pleases and chastises whom He pleases, and God has power over all things.' The companions of the Messenger of Allah (peace & blessings of Allah be with him) were troubled, so they came to the Prophet (peace & blessings of Allah be with him) said: 'O Messenger of Allah! Order us to do the deeds we can bear, prayer, fasting, charity and Jihad, but this verse which has just been revealed to you we cannot bear.' The Apostle of Allah (peace & blessings of Allah be with him) said: 'Do you wish to say as the people of earlier Scripture said: 'We hear and we disobey.' But say: 'We hear and we obey, we implore Your forgiveness our Lord and to You is the destiny.' (Q. 2: 285) So when they did so, God Almighty abrogated it, and revealed: 'God does not impose on any soul a burden greater than it can bear, it receives every good that it earns and it suffers every evil that it earns. Our Lord! Pardon us if we forget or commit an error, he said: 'Yes,' our Lord! Do not subject us to hardship as you did subject those before us. He said: 'Yes,' our Lord do not subject us to more than we can bear, he said; 'Yes,' pardon us and forgive us, have mercy on us. You are our Guardian, so grant us victory over the unbelievers.' He said: 'Yes.' (Q. 2: 286).

The Interpretation of Surah Al-I- Imran

"God is the One Who revealed the Book (Qur'an) to you Some of its verses are definitive." (Q. 3: 7)

4. *Hadrat Ayesha* reported that the Messenger of Allah (peace & blessings of Allah be with him) recited the verse: 'God is The One Who revealed The Book (Qur'an) to you, some of its verses are definitive, these are the essence of the Book, and others are metaphorical. Those who have deviation in their hearts adhere to what is metaphorical desiring sedition through their own interpretation, but only God knows its interpretation. And those who are deeply rooted in knowledge: 'We believe in it, it is all from our Lord.' Yet only those who possess minds remem-ber." She said that the Messenger of Allah (peace & blessings of Allah be with him) said: If you see those who follow what is metaphorical of it, then

those are the ones whom God has named, so beware of them.

5. *Abu Sayeed Al Khudri* reported: In the lifetime of the Apostle of Allah (peace & blessings of Allah be with him) some men from among the hypocrites used to stay behind when he went out for a battle, and they would be content to remain at home behind the Prophet (peace & blessings of Allah be with him). When the Messenger of Allah (peace & blessings of Allah be with him) used to return they would offer excuses and swear oaths, with a view to be praised for what they had done, so it was revealed: 'Do not think that those who rejoice for what they have been given and love to be praised for what they have not done, so do not think that they can escape the punishment, and for them there is a painful chastise-ment.' (Q. 3: 188)

6. *Humaid ibn Abd al Rahman ibn Auf* reported that Marwan said to Rafe': "Go to Ibn Abbas ask him: 'If everyone who rejoices in what he has done and likes to be praised for what he has not done, will be punished, then all of us will be punished.' Ibn Abbas said: 'What do you have to do with that matter?' It was only when the Prophet (Prayers & peace be upon him) called the Jews and asked them about some-thing, and they hid the truth and said something else, and desired praise for the favour of telling him the answer to the question, and they were pleased with what they had concealed'.

The Interpretation of Surah An- Nisa

God High Exalted said: " And if you fear that you will not be fair to the orphans" (Q. 4: 3)

They consult you concerning women..."

(Q.4: 127)

7. **Urwa ibn Al Zubair** reported that he asked Ayesha concerning the saying of Allah: 'And if you fear that you will not be fair to the orphans.' She said: 'O son of my sister! This concerns the orphan girl who is under the care of a guardian, she involves him in her property, her guardian is attracted by her wealth and beauty and he desires to marry her without being fair in her dowry. So he should give her as he would give anyone else. Thus guardians were forbidden from marrying them unless they were fair to them and gave them the maximum dowry that their peers might expect to receive. They were permitted to marry women of their choosing.' Urwa said that Ayesha said: The people asked the Messenger of Allah (peace & blessings of Allah be with him) for his opinion after the revelation of that verse, and so Allah revealed: 'They consult you concerning women...' (Q. 4: 127) Ayesha also said: 'And Allah said: 'And yet you desire to marry them...' (Q. 4: 127). They refrain from marrying an orphan who lacks property and beauty. She said: They are forbidden from marrying orphan girls for their wealth and beauty except fairly, and that was because they used to refrain from marrying them if they did not have wealth or beauty.

8. It is reported that **Hadrat Ayesha** said concerning the saying of Allah: "But if he is poor, let him have for himself what is just and reasonable (according to his work). This Verse was revealed regarding the orphan's property. If the guardian is poor, he can take from the property of the orphan, what is just and reasonable according to his work and the time he spends on managing it.

9. **Zaid ibn Thabit** is reported to have said: When the Prophet set out for the Battle of Uhud, some of his troops returned back, then companions of the Prophet were divided regarding them. Some of them said: 'We should kill them.' And others said: 'No.' So Allah revealed the verse: 'Why are you divided into two sides concerning the hypocrites.'

10. **Sayeed ibn Jubair** said: I asked Ibn Abbas: 'Is there repentance for the one who intentionally kills a believer?' He said: 'No.' So I recited to him the verse of 'The Criterion': 'And they do not invoke with Allah any other god, nor kill any soul Allah has forbidden except by right, nor commit adultery, and whoever does this shall get the wages of sin. The punishment shall

be doubled for them on the Day of Resurrection, and he shall abide therein in disgrace. Except he who repents and believes and does righteous deeds, those Allah shall change their evil deeds into good deeds, and Allah is the All Forgiving, The Merciful.' (Q. 25: 68-70) He said: These verses were revealed at Makka, and they were abrogated by a verse revealed later in Medina, which says: 'And whoever kills a believer intentionally, has punishment in Hell, he shall abide in it forever.'

11. *Ibn Abbas* reported that a group of Muslims pursued a man among his sheep and he said: 'Peace be on you.' But they killed him and took his sheep. So the verse was revealed: 'O you who believe! When you go to war in God's Cause, differentiate between friend and foe, and if one greets you with a salutation of 'peace', do not say to him abruptly 'you are not a believer,' if you seek worldly gain by this, God has abundant spoils for you.' (Q. 4: 94) Ibn Abbas used to recite: 'Al salaam.

12. *Hadrat Ayesha* said concerning the verse: And if a wife fears cruelty or desertion from her husband, there as no blame on them if they recon ciliate between themselves, and reconciliation between them is far better, and souls are prone to greed." (Q.4: 128) She said: It was revealed for the wife whose husband might have had enough of

her, but because of her children and has company, she does not want him to divorce her, and she wishes to remain with him, so she says to him: 'You are free of any responsibility towards me.

13. *Tariq ibn Shihab* said: The Jews said to Umar: 'You recite a verse, and had it been revealed to us, we would have taken the day of its revelation as a day of celebration.' He asked: 'Which verse is that?' They said: 'Today I have perfected for you your Religion and completed My Grace on you.' Umar said: 'I know very well when and where at was revealed. It was revealed upon the Messenger of Allah (peace & blessings of Allah be with him) on the day of Arafat on a Friday.'

14. *Abd Allah ibn Mas'ud* said: When the Verse: "Only those who have believed and have not polluted their faith by associating others with Allah (Q. 6: 82) was revealed, the companions of the Messenger of Allah (peace & blessings of Allah be with him) felt troubled and said: 'Which of us has not wronged himself?' So the Prophet (peace & blessings of Allah be with him) said: It is not as you think, but it is as Luqman said to has son: 'And when Luqman said to his son, admoni-shing him, O my son, do not associ-ate others with God, surely po-lytheism is a grievous iniquity.' (Q. 31: 13).

15. *Abu Hurayra* reported that the

Apostle of Allah (peace & blessings of Allah be with him) said: There are three Signs—-the rising of the sun from the West, the coming of the AntiChrist, and the beast that will speak. When they appear it shall not profit a soul to believe who did not believe before, or has earned in its faith any goodness.

16. *Abu Zarr* said: At sunset the Prophet (peace & blessings of Allah be with him) asked me: 'Do you know where the sun goes to when it sets?' I said: 'Allah and His Messenger know best.' He said: 'It goes down until its prostrates itself under the Throne and then takes permission to rise again, and it is permitted and then it will be about to prostrate itself but its prostration will not be accepted and it will seek permission to continue its course but it will not be permitted, but it will be comman-ded to return to where it came from and so it will rise in the West. And that is the meaning of the verse: "And the sun runs its course to a settled place, this is the Decree of The Almighty, the All-Knowing." The Apostle of Allah (peace & blessings of Allah be with him) said: Do you know where that will be? On the day it happens:'... it shall not profit a soul to believe who did not believe before, or has earned in its faith any goodness. (Q. 6: 158).

17. It is reported from *Abu Sayeed Al-Khudri* and *Abu Hurayra* that the Prophet said: A caller will call, you will be so healthy and never feel ill, and you will live forever, you will not die. And you will be young and never be old, and you will have enjoyment and never feel misery. That is the saying of Allah Most High: And they shall hear a call: This is your Paradise that you have inherited for your righteous deeds. (Q. 7: 43).

18. *Abd Allah Ibn Mas'ud* reported that a man came to the Apostle of Allah (peace & blessings of Allah be with him) and said: 'O Messenger of Allah! I have unlawfully kissed a woman at the reaches of Medina and all I did was kiss her. So here I am, pass judgment upon me as you deem appropriate.' Umar said: 'Allah has covered you, so why do you not cover yourself?' The Prophet did not reply. So the man left and the Messenger of Allah sent a man to call him back, then he recited to him: 'And establish regular prayers at the (two) ends of the day and when the night approaches, surely the good deeds blot out the evil deeds. This is a reminder for those who remember Allah.' (Q. 11: 114.) A man asked: 'O Prophet of Allah is that for him?' He said: 'It is for all my followers'.

19. *Abd Allah ibn Mas'ud* said: While I was walking with the Prophet (peace & blessings of Allah be with him) in a field some Jews passed by. They said: Let us ask him about the spirit. Some of them said: And how will you know that he

will not answer you with something that will expose your arrogance and cause you to regret your question. Then they said: Ask him. Some of them came to him and asked him about the spirit. The Prophet remained silent and said nothing in reply, I realized that he was receiving Reve-lation, so I got up and went away. When the Revelation had been completed, he said: And they question you concerning the soul, say: The soul is the concern of my Lord, and knowledge that you have been given is very little. (Q.17: 85).

20. *Abd Allah ibn Mas'ud* said: There used to be a group of people who worshipped a group of the Jinn, so the group of Jinn became Muslim, but the group of people continued worshipping them. Then it was revealed: Those they invoke are themselves seeking the means to please their Lord. (Q.17: 57).

21. *Ibn Abbas* said concerning the verse: "And do not be loud in your prayer, nor be silent therein, but seek a way between." He said: This was revea-led while the Messenger of Allah (peace & blessings of Allah be with him) was still hiding in Makka. And when he used to lead his compa-nions in prayer he used to raise his voice in recitation of the Qur'an, so when the unbelievers heard that, they insulted the Qur'an and The One Who send it, and the one who came with it. So Allah said to His Prophet: 'And do not be loud

in your prayer,' or the unbelievers will hear your recitation. 'Nor be silent therein,' from your companions, let them listen to the Qur'an and do not recite it so loudly. 'But seek a way between,' he said: Between loudly and silently.

22. Hadrat Ayesha explained concer-ning the verse: "And do not be loud in your prayer, nor be silent there-in..." She said: This was revealed for invocations.

23. *Abu Hurayra* reported that the Messenger of Allah (peace & blessings of Allah be with him) said: On the Day of judgment, the huge fat man will not weigh as much as the wing of a gnat in the Sight of Allah. "And on the Day of Resur-rection We shall not assign to them any weight." (Q.18: 105).

24. *Abu Sayeed al-Khudri* reported that the Messenger of Allah (peace & blessings of Allah be with him) said: Death will be brought out in the form of a black and white ram. Then a herald will call: 'O people of Paradise!' At that they will stretch their necks and look intently. The herald will say: 'Do you know this?' They will say: 'Yes, it is Death.' By that time they all would have seen it. Then it will be said: 'O people of Hell! They will stretch their neck and look intently. The herald will say: 'Do you know this?' They will say: 'Yes, it is Death.' And by that time they all would have seen it. Then the ram

will be slaughtered and the herald will say: 'O people of Paradise! Eternity for you and no death; O people of Hell! Eternity for you and no death.' Then the Apostle of Allah (peace & blessings of Allah be with him) recited: 'And warn them of the Day of Sorrow, when the matter is decided, while they are heedless and they do not believe.' (Q.19: 39) And he indicated with his hands to this life.

25. *Khabbab* said: Ibn Wa'il owed me some money, so I went to him to ask for it. He said: 'I will not pay you unless you disbelieve in Muham-mad.' I said: 'I will not disbelieve in Muhammad until Allah kills you and then you are resurrected.' He said: 'Leave me until I die and am resurrected, then I will be given wealth and children and I will pay you back your debt.' Then the verses were revealed: "Have you seen him who disbelieves in Our Revelations and says: 'I shall certainly be given wealth and children.'? Has he observed the Unseen or taken a covenant with Allah Most Compassionate?" (Q. 19: 77).

26. *Ibn Abbas* reported that the Messenger of Allah (peace & blessings of Allah be with him) addressed us saying: 'O mankind, you will be summoned before Allah Almighty barefoot, naked and uncircumcised: 'As We originated the first creation, so shall We bring it back again. A promise binding on Us, truly We shall fulfill it.'(Q. 21: 104) But the first of the people to be covered on the Day of Judgment will be Abraham (peace be upon him). Some men of my community will be driven to the Left, so I will say: 'O my Lord! My followers!' Then it will be said: 'You do not know what they did after you.' Then I will say as the righteous servant said: 'I was a witness over them while I remained among them, but when You ended my term on earth, You were the Watcher over them, You are The Witness over all things. If You chastise them, they are Your servants, and if You forgive them, indeed You are The Almighty, The All-Wise.' (Q. 5: 117-118) Then it will be said to me: They are still turned upon their heels since you left them.

The Interpretation of Surah Al-Nur

"Those who invented the slander are a band from among you."

(Q. 24: 11)

27. It is reported from Al Zuhri on the authority of Sai'd ibn al Masib, Urwa ibn al Zubair, Alqama ibn Waqqas and Abd Allah ibn Utba ibn Mas'ud that Hadrat Ayesha, the wife of the holy Prophet said: When the Messenger of Allah (peace & blessings of Allah be with him) wished to proceed on a journey he would draw lots between his wives and take the one along to whom the lot fell. Once during a battle he drew lots between us and the lot fell to me, and I set off with him

after Allah had commanded the women to wear veils. When we were returning home after the battle and were near the city of Medina, the Messenger of Allah (peace & blessings of Allah be with him) decided to travel during the night. When the order to set off was given I walked on until I had gone beyond the army to answer the call of nature. When I was through with it I returned to the camp and realized that my necklace was missing. So I went back to search for it and got delayed. The people who used to bear my Howdah to the camel lifted it up upon the back of the camel thinking I was inside it. At that time women were light being thin and lean because they ate little. So they did not notice any difference in the weight of the Howdah when they raised it up and put it upon the camel. I was a young lady at that time. They went on they way with the camels. I found my necklace and returned to the camp to find everyone gone. So I went to the place I was staying at thinking they would find me missing and come back to search for me. While there I felt drowsy and fell asleep. Safwan ibn Mu'attal Al-Sulami Al-Dhakwani was journe-ying behind the army and he hap-pened to see me in the morning. I got up when I heard him say 'We belong to Allah and to Him is our return'. He made his camel sit and he dismounted and put his leg on the camel's front legs, then I rose and sat upon it. Safwan set off walking leading the camel by its reins until we reached the army where they had stopped to rest at noon. Then false accusations were cast against me, and the leader of slanderers was Abd Allah ibn Ubayy ibn Salul. After that we returned to Medina and I was ill for one month while the people repea-ted the false accusations spread by Ubayy and others. While I was ill I felt that the Prophet (peace & blessings of Allah be with him) was not behaving in his usual way towards me as he used to do when-ever I was unwell. But he used to come with a salutation and say: 'How is that girl?' I was not aware of what was happening until I felt better and went out with Umm Mistah to answer the call of nature, and we only used to go to answer the call of nature at night before we had lavatories close to our houses. In this way our custom was the same as that of the Arabs in rural areas. So I and Umm Mistah bint Ruhm set off walking, Umm Mistah tripped upon her long dress and said: 'May Mistah be ruined.' I said: 'That is a bad thing to say, why do you abuse a man who participated in the Battle of Badr?' She said: 'O Hanata, did you not hear what they are saying?' Then she told me about the slander of the lying accusers. My difficulty worsened and when I returned home, the Messenger of Allah (peace & blessings of Allah be with him) visited me and after salutation he said: 'How is that girl?' I asked him to let me go to my parents; I wanted them to verify the news to me. The Prophet permitted me to go and I went to my parents and asked my mother: 'What are the people saying?' She said: 'O daughter! Do not fret over this matter, by God, whenever an attractive woman is loved by her husband and he has other wives, the women invent such slander about her.' I said: 'Glory be to Allah! Do the people really talk about that?' That night I wept continuously and did not sleep until the morning. The Messenger of Allah (peace & blessings of Allah be with him) called Ali ibn Abu Talib and Usama ibn Zaid in the morning when he saw a pause in Divine Inspiration, and he consulted with them about divorcing his wife. Usama ibn Zaid said what he knew of the good reputation of his wives and said: 'O Messenger of Allah! Keep your wife, for by God, we know only good about her.' Ali ibn Abu Talib said: 'O Messenger of Allah! God has not imposed restrictions upon you, and there are many women besides her, yet you may ask the servant woman who can tell you the truth.' At that the Prophet (peace & blessings of Allah be with him) called Buhaira and said: 'O Buhaira! Did you ever witness anything which gave rise to your suspicion about her?' Buhaira said: 'No, by God, Who sent you with the Truth, I have never seen any fault in her except that she is still a young girl who sometimes sleeps and lets the goats eat the dough.' At that the Messenger of Allah (peace & blessings of Allah be with him) ascended the pulpit and asked for someone to support him in punishing Abd Allah ibn Ubayy ibn Salul. The Apostle of Allah said: 'Who will support me in punishing the one who has injured me by slandering the reputation of my family?' By Allah, I know nothing but good from my family, and they have accused someone of whom I have known nothing but good, and he never entered my house except in my presence.' Sayeed ibn Muaz rose up and said: 'O Messenger of Allah! By God, I will relieve you of him. If he is from the tribe of Aus, then we will cut his head off, and if he is from our brothers the Khazraj, then command us and we will fulfill your command. At that Sa'ad ibn Ubada, the leader of the Khazraj, who before this incident had been a God fearing man, rose up zealously and said: 'By God, you have lied, you cannot kill him and you will never be able to kill him.' At that Usaid ibn Al-Hadir rose up and said: 'By God! You are the liar, by God, we will kill him, and you are a hypocrite who defends the hypocrites.' At this the two tribes of Aus and Khazraj were riled and almost fought each other while the Messenger of Allah (peace & blessings of Allah be with him) stood on the pulpit. He descended and calmed them down until they were silent. That day I wept so much that I could not sleep. My parents were with me in the morning and I had been weeping for two nights and one day, until I felt that my liver would burst from weeping. While they were sitting with me as I wept, an Ansari woman asked my permission to come in, and I let her enter. She sat down and began to weep with me. As we were in this state, the Messenger of Allah (peace & blessings of Allah be with him) came and sat down and he had not sat with me since the day of slander. For a month no Revelation had come to him about my case, he recited: 'There is no god but Allah and Muhammad is the Messenger of Allah', and then he said: 'O Ayesha! I have been told something about you, if you are innocent, then God will soon reveal your innocence, and if you have committed a sin, then repent to Allah and ask Him to forgive you, as when someone confesses his sins and asks Allah for forgiveness, Allah accepts his repentance.' When the Apostle of Allah (peace & blessings of Allah be with him) finished speaking my tears dried, not one tear fell. I asked my father to reply to the Prophet on my behalf. My father said: 'By God, I do not know what to say to the Messenger of Allah.' I said to my mother: 'Speak to the Messenger of Allah on my behalf.' She said: 'By God, I do not know what to say to the Messenger of Allah.' I was a young girl and did not know very much of the Qur'an. I said: 'By God, I know that you have heard what people have said and that has been placed in your mind and taken as true. Now if I say that I am innocent and God knows that I am innocent, you will not believe me, and if I confess to you falsely that I am guilty and God knows that I am innocent, you would believe me. By God, I do not see my plight except in comparison to the plight of Joseph's father, who said: 'Patience is best for me against that which you assert and no help can be sought except the help of God.' Then I turned to the other side of my bed hoping that God would reveal my innocence. By God I never thought that God would reveal His Inspiration concerning me, as I saw myself too insignificant to be spoken of in the Qur'an. But I did hope that the Messenger of Allah (peace & blessings of Allah be with him) might have a dream in which God would prove my innocence. By God, the Prophet (peace & blessings of Allah be with him) did not rise and no one left the house before Divine Inspiration came to him. Thus was he overtaken by the same condition he always underwent upon receiving Divine Inspiration. He was perspiring so mach that the beads of sweat dropped as if they were pearls, although it was a winter's day. When the Apostle of

Allah (peace & blessings of Allah be with him) emerged from this condition, he smiled and the first words he spoke were: 'Ayesha, thank Allah for He has declared your innocence.' My mother told me to go to the Prophet but I said: 'By God, I will not go to him and I will thank none but Allah.' Then Allah revealed: Those who invented the slander are a band from among you...' (Q. 24: 11). When Allah gave the declaration of my innocence, Abu Bakr, who used to provide for Mistha ibn Uthatha as he was related to him, said: 'By God, I will never provide for him because of what he said about Ayesha.' But Allah revealed later: "And let not those among you who are endowed with bounty and plenty, swear by oath against giving near of kin and the poor and those who have emigrated in the cause of Allah, but let them pardon and forgive. Do you not love that Allah should forgive you? And Allah is All Forgiving, Most Merciful." Thereafter, Abu Bakr said: Yes, by God! I love that God would forgive me.' Thereafter he continued to help Mistah as he had done before. The Messenger of Allah (peace & blessings of Allah be with him) asked Zainab bint Jahsh about me saying: 'What do you know and what did you see?' She said: 'O Messenger of Allah! I do not claim to have heard or see what I have not heard or seen. By God, I know nothing but good of Ayesha.'

Hadrat Ayesha said: 'Zainab was vying with me but Allah protected her because she was God fearing'.

28. *Jabir* is reported to have related that Abd Allah ibn Ubayy used to force his two slave girls into prostitution. So they complained about it to the holy Prophet. Then Allah Most High revealed: Force not your maids into prostitution, when they desire to keep themselves chaste, in order that you make a gain in the goods of this life. (Q.24: 33).

29. *Ibn Abbas* reported that some of the unbelievers killed many people and committed much adultery and then came before the holy Prophet and said: 'That which you are calling for is good, will you tell us is there any atonement for our sins?' Then it was revealed: 'And those who invoke not with Allah any other god, or slay such life that Allah has made sacred, except for just cause, nor commit fornication, and who-ever does this shall meet the price of sin.' (Q. 25: 68) Then it was revea-led: Say: O My servants who have transgressed against their souls, despair not of the Mercy of Allah, surely Allah forgives all sins, surely He is Oft - Forgiving The Most Mer-ciful."' (Q.39: 53).

30. It is reported from *Abu Hurayra* that the Messenger of Allah (peace & blessings of Allah be with him) said: Allah Most High said: I have prepared for My righteous servants

something the eye has never seen nor ear heard of nor entered the thoughts of any of mankind.' This is over and above that which Allah has described. Then he recited: 'No soul knows what delight of the eye has been kept hidden for him as a reward for their (good) deeds.' (Q. 32: 17).

31. *Abd Allah* is reported to have said: O people fear Allah! You should only speak of things you know of, and if you do not know you should say: Allah knows best.' It is better for you to say, when you do not know something that Allah knows best. As God Almighty has said to His Prophet: 'Say, I do not ask you for a reward for it, nor am I one of those who speaks of his own accord.' When the Messenger of Allah (peace & blessings of Allah be with him) saw the people reject Islam he said: 'O God! Send them years of famine like the seven years of Joseph.' So they were plagued with famine for one year and all kinds of life were destroyed to the extent that they were reduced to eating hides, carcasses and decaying animals. So Abu Sufyan visited the Prophet (peace & blessings of Allah be with him) and said: O Muhammad! You order people to obey Allah and to preserve blood relations. The people of your tribe are perishing so please pray to Allah for them.' Then Allah revealed: So wait for the Day when the sky shall bring forth a kind of smoke (or mist)

plainly visible, enveloping the people. This is a painful ordeal. (They will say) Our Lord remove the torment from us, for we do really believe. How can there be remem-brance for them? While a manifest Messenger has already come to them. Yet they turn away from him and say: 'A man tutored and possessed.' We shall indeed remove the torment for a while (but) truly you will revert (to your old ways). On the Day when We strike with the mighty power, We shall indeed (then) exact Retribution! (Q.44: 10-16).

32. *Anas ibn Malik* said: Eight armed men from the people of Makka descended upon the Messenger of Allah (peace & blessings of Allah be with him) from Mount Tanem with the intention of assassinating the holy Prophet and his companions. They were caught and they surren-dered, and the Apostle of Allah (peace & blessings of Allah be with him) spared their lives. Then it was revealed: 'And Allah is The One Who restrained their hands from you and your hands from them in the valley of Makka, after He granted you victory over them. And Allah sees well all that ye do.' (Q. 48: 24)

33. *Anas ibn Malik* said: When the verse: 'O you who believe! Do not raise your voices above the voice of the Prophet, and do not speak loudly to him as you speak to one another, lest your deeds are ren-

dered fruitless' was revea-led, Thabit ibn Qais sat in his house and said. 'I am in the Fire.' And he kept himself away from the Prophet. The Prophet asked Sa'ad ibn Muaz: 'O Abu Amr, what is the matter with Thabit? He is complaining.' Sa'ad said: 'He is my neighbor and I have not heard any complaint from him.' So Sa'ad visited him and told him what the Messenger of Allah (peace & blessings of Allah be with him) had said. Thabit said: This verse has been revealed and I know that I am the loudest mouth of all with the Prophet (peace & blessings of Allah be with him). Then I am in the Fire.' Sa'ad told the Apostle of Allah about it and he remarked: But he is in Paradise.

34. It is reported from *Hadrat Ayesha* that the Apostle of Allah said: The angels were created from lights, while the jinn were created from smokeless fire and Adam was created of what was described to you.

35. *Ibn Abbas* said explaining the verse: Stir not your tongue to hasten this (to remember the revelation of the Qur'an) that the meaning of this is that the Apostle of Allah was keen to remem-ber all that was being revealed to him and used to move his lips fast at the time of receiving the revelation. Then it was revealed: Stir not your tongue to hasten this (memorizing the revelation) surely it is for us to

set it in your heart and its recitation.' Ibn Abbas added: This meant that Allah promised to bless him with the ability to recite it and to remember the revelation by heart. Allah revealed it: So when WE recite it, follow its recitation. It is for Us to make it manifest. Ibn Abbas said: This meant that revelation be listened to in silence and Allah shall give the ability to recite it and make its meaning clear. Thereafter the holy Prophet used to listen to Gabriel when-ever he appeared and used to recite it after the Archangel left.

36. *Ubayd Allah ibn Uqba* is reported to have related that Ibn Abbas asked him about the last Surah of the Qur'an to be revealed. Ibn Uqba said: I said Yes, 'When comes the Help from Allah, and victory ...celebrate the praises of your Lord, and pray for His forgiveness; for He is Oft-Returning (in Grace and Mercy)-(Q.110: 1). Ibn Abbas said you have told the truth.

Glossary

Ayah (pl. *ayaat*)	sign /a verse of the Qur'an
Abbasids	The dynasty of Caliphs who ruled from 750-1258AD; Descendants of al-Abbas, one of the uncles of Prophet Muhammad
Adat	Customary usage
Alawites	The partisan of Hadrat Ali
A'am	generally applicable; with reference to Quranic ruling.
Ansars	Lit. Helpers; the people of Medina who initially helped Prophet Muhammad to set up abode in Yathrib
Bidah	heresy (any innovated practice) Innovation, connoting impiety
Deen	Religion
Da'eef	weak, unauthentic narration.
Fatwa	authorized legal opinion/religious verdict.
Fiqh	(understanding) Religious Jurisprudence.
Fuqaha	Religious jurists
Fard *Kifaya*	collective obligation.
Faqih	scholar with ability to give religious verdicts.
Fitnah	(pl. fitan) conflicts & strife among Muslims.
Halal	Licit/ Praiseworthy
Haram	Illicit/Blameworthy
Hadith :	Report or narrative of what the Prophet Muhammad said or did. Tradition

Hijrah	lit. to migrate; Migration from the land of unbelief to the land of Islam.
Ijma	Consensus, a unified opinion of scholars regarding certain verse.
Ijtihaad	Exertion or effort ; reasoned decision by a scholar on an issue.
Imam	leader, leader in prayers, knowledge, fiqh, leader of a state.
Isnad	Chain of narrators linking the collection of the narration to the person quoted.
Istihsan	Juristic preference; to decide in favour of something that is considered good by the jurist, against the conclusion arrived through analogy
Istihsab	Presumption of continuity, or presuming continuation of status quo ante
Ilm:	knowledge or learning, esply. Religious knowledge
Iman	Faith, to affirm all that was revealed to the Prophet.
Jihad	Holy war, personal striving against ones lower self or in the way of Allah.
Khalifa	Caliph, Deputy/Successor/Leader of Muslim community
Khilafa:	caliphate, deputyship, office of khalifa
Madarsa:	Religious college
Kaba	a square stone building in the Grand Mosque of Makkah.
Kalam	theology and dogmatics; Kalam begins from the revealed tradition and employs rationalistic methods in order to understand it and resolve contradictions
Kufr	act of disbelief; one who knows the truth but covers it and denies it.
Madhhab	position or opinion of a scholar; School of Islamic jurisprudence.
Masalih	
Mursala	Consideration of public interest, human welfare or utility not explicitly supported by the text

Muhaddith	scholar of the science of Hadith.
Mufti	one appointed or qualified to give a legal opinion or fatwa.
Mujtahid	one qualified to pass judgement using ijtihad.
Mushrik	polytheists, pagans & disbelieves in the oneness of Allah and the prophethood of Muhammad.
Mutwatir	Hadith narrated by a large number of reporters.
Mawqoof	narration from a companion not going back to the prophet.
Mawsoob	connected, a continuous isnad (can be narrated back to the Prophet)
Mutassil	Hadith that has an uninterrupted isnad
Nass	unequivocal, clear injunction or prohibition; an explicit textual meaning
Qadr	power; divine pre-ordainment, pre-Decree that which Allah has ordained for His creation.
Qadariyya	a sect who believed that people have absolute power over their actions and hence free will
Qadi	religious judge
Qiyas	reasoning of analogy (in law)
Sharia	Religious law, Right, Rectitude, code The whole body of rules guiding the life of a Muslim in law, ethics & etiquette
Shaykh	chief or tribe, sufi teacher, religious expert
Shura	consultation
Sunna	custom, religious tradition.
Sunni	largest sect of Muslims proclaiming adherence to the Sunna as defined by four schools of law.
Ulema	learned, religious experts
Umma	people the community (of Islam) ; nation
Ra'y	opinion; personal discretion
Saad adh-dhara'i	blocking of means that might lead to undesired consequences

Sahaba	companions of the Prophet who believed in him until their death.
Saheeh	authentic (Hadith)
Salaf	pious predecessors, the Muslims of the first three generations- companions, successors and followers.
Seerah	(also seerat) biography of the Prophet Muhammad
Shahada	bearing witness; testifying that there is no God but Allah & Muhammad is the last Prophet of Allah; Fundamental belief of all Muslims
Shariah	the orthodox code of law in Islam.
Shia	collective name for various sects claiming love for Ahl al-bayt (holy family of the Prophet).
Shirk	associating partners with Allah directly or indirectly, compromising any aspect of Tauheed.
Shura	consultation; process/ body of consultation
Surah	chapter on the Quran
Sunnah	example, practice, the Prophet's way of life, consisting of his words, actions and silent approvals. The sunnah is contained in various hadeeth.
Tafseer	explanation / commentary of the Quran
Tabi'i	generation after the companions of the Prophet.
Tabi'un	The followers; second generation of early Muslims
Taqleed	Blind following; to follow someone's opinion without evidence.
Taqwa	acting in obedience to Allah
Tauheed	Islamic monotheism; The oneness of Allah. Doctrine of divine unity.
Ulema	(sing. Aalim) Scholar of religious knowledge.
Ummah	community or nation of Islam.
Urf	Non-religious customary law; Common acknowledgement; customary practice.
Usul	Basic principles of any source, used in fiqh

Wahi	the revelation or inspiration of Allah to His Prophets.
Wali	protector, patron, companion; saints orfriends of Allah
Yaqeen	perfect & absolute faith
Zakaat	Financial levy; wealth tax; charity obligatory on all Muslims who have wealth over & above a certain limit over which a year has passd (2.5% of saved wealth)